Lecture Notes in Computer Science　　9333

Commenced Publication in 1973
Founding and Former Series Editors:
Gerhard Goos, Juris Hartmanis, and Jan van Leeuwen

More information about this series at http://www.springer.com/series/7408

Ezio Bartocci · Rupak Majumdar (Eds.)

Runtime Verification

6th International Conference, RV 2015
Vienna, Austria, September 22–25, 2015
Proceedings

 Springer

Editors
Ezio Bartocci
TU Wien
Vienna
Austria

Rupak Majumdar
Max Planck Institute for Software Systems
Kaiserslautern
Germany

ISSN 0302-9743　　　　　　ISSN 1611-3349　(electronic)
Lecture Notes in Computer Science
ISBN 978-3-319-23819-7　　　ISBN 978-3-319-23820-3　(eBook)
DOI 10.1007/978-3-319-23820-3

Library of Congress Control Number: 2015947804

LNCS Sublibrary: SL2 – Programming and Software Engineering

Printed on acid-free paper

Springer International Publishing AG Switzerland is part of Springer Science+Business Media
(www.springer.com)

Preface

This volume contains the proceedings of the 15th International Conference on Runtime Verification (RV 2015), which was held on September 22–25, 2015 at TU Wien, Vienna, Austria.

The RV series is an annual meeting that gathers together scientists from both academia and industry interested in investigating novel lightweight formal methods to monitor, analyze, and guide the execution of programs. The discussion centers around two main aspects. The first is to understand whether the runtime verification techniques can practically complement the traditional methods for proving programs correct before their execution, such as model checking and theorem proving. The second concerns formal methods and how their application can improve traditional ad-hoc monitoring techniques used in performance monitoring, hardware design emulation, etc.

RV started in 2001 as an annual workshop and turned into a conference in 2010. The workshops were organized as satellite events to an established forum, including CAV and ETAPS. The proceedings for RV from 2001 to 2005 were published in the Electronic Notes in Theoretical Computer Science. Since 2006, the RV proceedings have been published in Springer's Lecture Notes in Computer Science. The previous five editions of the RV conference took place in Malta (2010), San Francisco, USA (2011), Instanbul, Turkey (2012), Rennes, France (2013), Toronto, Canada (2014).

RV 2015 received 45 submissions, from which the Program Committee accepted 15 regular papers, 4 short papers, and 2 tool demonstration papers. All papers received at least 4 reviews. The paper selection process involved extensive discussion among the members of the Program Committee and external reviewers through the EasyChair conference manager. The status of the papers had been decided once a consensus had been reached by the committee.

To complement the contributed papers, we also included in the program three invited lectures by P. Godefroid (Microsoft Research, USA), S. Sankaranarayanan (University of Colorado Boulder, USA), and G. Weissenbacher (TU Wien, Austria), and four tutorials presented during the first day.

RV 2015 also hosted two co-located events: the 5th International Challenge on the Rigorous Examination of Reactive Systems (RERS) and the 2nd International Competition on Runtime Verification (CRV).

We are extremely grateful to the members of the Program Committee and their sub-reviewers for their insightful reviews and discussion. The editors are also grateful to the authors of the accepted papers for revising the papers according to the suggestions of the Program Committee and for their responsiveness on providing the camera-ready copies within the deadline.

We would also like to thank Klaus Havelund and all the members of the RV Steering Committee for their advice on organizing and running the conference.

Special thanks also to the Austrian Association of Computer Science, and in particular, Karin Hiebler and Christine Haas, for their support and valuable assistance with the online registration.

The EasyChair conference management system was used in the submission, review, and revision processes, as well as for the assembly of the symposium proceedings. We thank the developers of EasyChair for this invaluable service. Finally, we thank NVIDIA for providing their equipment as the best paper award.

June 2015   Ezio Bartocci
                                                          Rupak Majumdar

Organization

General Chair

Radu Grosu   TU Wien, Austria

Program Chairs

Ezio Bartocci   TU Wien, Austria
Rupak Majumdar   Max Planck Institute, Germany

Tools Track Chair

Dejan Ničković   Austrian Institute of Technology, Austria

Runtime Monitoring Competition Chairs

Yliès Falcone   Université Joseph Fourier, France
Dejan Ničković   Austrian Institute of Technology, Austria
Giles Reger   University of Manchester, UK
Daniel Thoma   University of Lübeck, Germany

Publicity Chair

Dejan Ničković   Austrian Institute of Technology, Austria

Program Committee

Thomas Ball   Microsoft Research, USA
Howard Barringer   The University of Manchester, UK
Ezio Bartocci   TU Wien, Austria
David Basin   ETH Zurich, Switzerland
Andreas Bauer   KUKA Systems, Germany
Saddek Bensalem   CEA-Leti, France
Eric Bodden   Fraunhofer SIT and TU Darmstadt, Germany
Borzoo Bonakdarpour   McMaster University, Canada
Luca Bortolussi   University of Trieste, Italy
Laura Bozzelli   Technical University of Madrid (UPM), Spain
Rohit Chadha   University of Missouri, USA
Satish Chandra   Samsung Electronics, USA
Dino Distefano   Queen Mary, University of London, UK

Alastair Donaldson	Imperial College London, UK
Alexandre Donzé	UC Berkeley, USA
Georgios Fainekos	Arizona State University, USA
Yliès Falcone	Université Joseph Fourier, France
Bernd Finkbeiner	Saarland University, Germany
Milos Gligoric	University of Illinois at Urbana-Champaign, USA
Radu Grosu	TU Wien, Austria
Kim Guldstrand Larsen	Aalborg University, Denmark
Klaus Havelund	NASA/JPL, USA
Aditya Kanade	Indian Institute of Science, India
Panagiotis Katsaros	Aristotle University of Thessaloniki, Greece
Sarfraz Khurshid	The University of Texas at Austin, USA
Marta Kwiatkowska	University of Oxford, UK
Insup Lee	University of Pennsylvania, USA
Axel Legay	IRISA/Inria, Rennes, France
Martin Leucker	University of Lübeck, Germany
Rupak Majumdar	Max Planck Institute, Germany
Oded Maler	VERIMAG, France
Leonardo Mariani	University of Milano Bicocca, Italy
Dejan Ničković	Austrian Institute of Technology, Austria
Joel Ouaknine	University of Oxford, UK
Gordon Pace	University of Malta, Malta
Doron Peled	Bar Ilan University, Israel
Pavithra Prabhakar	IMDEA Software Institute, Spain
Grigore Rosu	University of Illinois at Urbana-Champaign, USA
Abhik Roychoudhury	National University of Singapore, Singapore
Koushik Sen	U.C. Berkeley, USA
Scott. A. Smolka	Stony Brook University, USA
Oleg Sokolsky	University of Pennsylvania, USA
Bernhard Steffen	TU Dortmund, Germany
Scott Stoller	Stony Brook University, USA
Serdar Taşiran	Koç University, Turkey
Emina Torlak	University of Washington, USA
Lenore Zuck	University of Illinois at Chicago, USA

Additional Reviewers

Barbot, Benoit	Donzé, Alexandre
Biondi, Fabrizio	Fahrenberg, Uli
Caravagna, Giulio	Faymonville, Peter
Colombo, Christian	Feng, Lu
Decker, Normann	Ghorbal, Khalil
Defrancisco, Richard	Gligoric, Milos
Deligiannis, Pantazis	Graf, Susanne

Grigore, Radu
Isakovic, Haris
Ivanov, Radoslav
Jovanovic, Aleksandra
Kim, Chang Hwan Peter
Kuester, Jan-Christoph
Kulahcioglu Ozkan, Burcu
Lascu, Andrei
Legunsen, Owolabi
Lluch Lafuente, Alberto
Lukina, Anna
Maubert, Bastien
Mehne, Ben
Mereacre, Alexandru
Mikučionis, Marius
Moore, Brandon
Moy, Matthieu
Naujokat, Stefan
Nenzi, Laura
Neubauer, Johannes

Nouri, Ayoub
Olsen, Petur
Pace, Gordon
Park, Junkil
Phan, Dung
Pinisetty, Srinivas
Poplavko, Peter
Pouget, Kevin
Poulsen, Danny Bøgsted
Ratasich, Denise
Sanchez, Cesar
Sankaranarayanan, Sriram
Stümpel, Annette
Thoma, Daniel
Thomson, Paul
Torfah, Hazem
Vandin, Andrea
Wang, Shaohui
Zalinescu, Eugen

Abstract of Invited Papers

Towards a Verified Artificial Pancreas: Challenges and Solutions for Runtime Verification

Fraser Cameron[1], Georgios Fainekos[2], David M. Maahs[3]
and Sriram Sankaranarayanan[4]

[1] Department of Mechanical Engineering, University of Texas, El Paso
[2] School of Computing, Informatics and Decision Systems Engg.,
Arizona State Univ., Tempe
[3] Barbara Davis Center for Childhood Diabetes, University of Colorado, Denver
[4] Department of Computer Science, University of Colorado, Boulder

Abstract. In this paper, we briefly examine the recent developments in artificial pancreas controllers, that automate the delivery of insulin to patients with type-1 diabetes. We argue the need for offline and online runtime verification for these devices, and discuss challenges that make verification hard. Next, we examine a promising simulation-based falsification approach based on robustness semantics of temporal logics. These ideas are implemented in the tool S-Taliro that automatically searches for violations of metric temporal logic (MTL) requirements for Simulink(tm)/Stateflow(tm) models. We illustrate the use of S-Taliro for finding interesting property violations in a PID-based hybrid closed loop control system.

Twenty Years of Dynamic Software Model Checking

Patrice Godefroid

Microsoft Research
pg@microsoft.com

Abstract. Dynamic software model checking consists of adapting model checking into a form of systematic testing that is applicable to industrial-size software. Over the last two decades, dozens of tools following this paradigm have been developed for checking concurrent and data-driven software. This talk will review twenty years of research on dynamic software model checking. It will highlight some key milestones, applications, and successes. It will also discuss limitations, disappointments, and future work.

Explaining Heisenbugs

Georg Weissenbacher

TU Wien, Austria

Abstract. Heisenbugs are complex software bugs that alter their behaviour when attempts to isolate them are made. The term heisenbug is a pun on the name of physicist Werner Heisenberg and refers to bugs whose analysis is complicated by the probe effect, an unintended alteration of system behaviour caused by an observer.

Heisenbugs are most prevalent in concurrent systems, where the interplay of multiple threads running on multi-core processors leads to intricate effects not anticipated by the developer. Faced with a heisenbug, it is the tedious task of the programmer to reproduce the erroneous behaviour and analyse its cause before the bug can be fixed.

It is exactly in these situations that automated analyses are the most desirable. Model checkers and systematic testing tools, for instance, can automatically reproduce erroneous executions manifesting the bug. The subsequent inspection of the error trace, however, is still a time-consuming process that requires substantial insight.

My group developed two approaches to analyse erroneous executions and explain concurrency bugs, attacking the problem from different angles. In both cases, the goal is to allow the programmer to focus on the essence of the bug rather than the specifics of the failed execution. On the one hand, we use data mining to extract explanations from execution logs by juxtaposing successful runs of the program with failed executions. The resulting explanations highlight potentially problematic data dependencies that frequently occur in failing executions. The second approach relies on static analysis and automated reasoning to obtain a slice of an erroneous execution trace that reflects the core of the problem.

After introducing both approaches, I will discuss their advantages as well as shortcomings, and explain differences regarding soundness and comprehensibility using case studies and empirical results.

G. Weissenbacher — Supported by the Austrian National Research Network S11403-N23 (RiSE) of the Austrian Science Fund (FWF) and by the Vienna Science and Technology Fund (WWTF) through grant VRG11-005.

Contents

Short Papers

Tool Papers

Tutorial Papers

Software Competitions

Invited Paper

Towards a Verified Artificial Pancreas: Challenges and Solutions for Runtime Verification

Fraser Cameron[1], Georgios Fainekos[2], David M. Maahs[3],
and Sriram Sankaranarayanan[4](✉)

[1] Department of Mechanical Engineering, University of Texas, El Paso, USA
[2] School of Computing, Informatics and Decision Systems Engineering,
Arizona State University, Tempe, USA
[3] Barbara Davis Center for Childhood Diabetes,
University of Colorado, Denver, USA
[4] Department of Computer Science, University of Colorado, Boulder, USA
srirams@colorado.edu

Abstract. In this paper, we briefly examine the recent developments in artificial pancreas controllers, that automate the delivery of insulin to patients with type-1 diabetes. We argue the need for offline and online runtime verification for these devices, and discuss challenges that make verification hard. Next, we examine a promising simulation-based falsification approach based on robustness semantics of temporal logics. These ideas are implemented in the tool S-Taliro that automatically searches for violations of metric temporal logic (MTL) requirements for Simulink(tm)/Stateflow(tm) models. We illustrate the use of S-Taliro for finding interesting property violations in a PID-based hybrid closed loop control system.

1 Introduction: Artificial Pancreas

Type-1 Diabetes (T1D) is a chronic condition caused by the inability of the pancreas to secrete insulin, a hormone that is critical to maintaining blood glucose levels inside a tight *euglycemic* range [42,59]. The standard treatment for T1D consists of delivering insulin externally through injections, or more recently, through insulin pumps that deliver short acting artificial insulin analog, subcutaneously. Insulin pumps provide many features, including the accurate delivery of insulin at varying rates over time. However, insulin pumps are controlled manually by the patient, who is ultimately responsible for increasing insulin delivery at meal times (meal bolus), or decreasing/disabling insulin delivery during physical activity [11]. The manual control of insulin delivery poses a heavy burden on the patients themselves, is error-prone and can sometimes lead to dangerous outcomes [57]. Too much insulin causes a dangerous drop in blood

E. Bartocci and R. Majumdar (Eds.): RV 2015, LNCS 9333, pp. 3–17, 2015.
DOI: 10.1007/978-3-319-23820-3_1

glucose levels (hypoglycemia), whereas too little insulin causes the blood glucose levels to remain high (hyperglycemia), resulting in long term damage to organs such as the kidneys, eye and peripheral nerves.

The artificial pancreas (AP) project envisions a series of increasingly sophisticated control systems to automate the delivery of insulin to patients with T1D. At it's core, the AP system combines a continuous glucose monitor (CGM) which senses blood glucose levels periodically, and an insulin pump that delivers insulin in a closed loop managed by a software-based controller. Table 1 shows the original stage wise development for the overall AP concept. A recently revised pathway acknowledges that all stages are currently technologically feasible and classifies insulin delivery beyond stage 3 simply as "insulin-only" control and "multihormonal" control [39]. The first (and simplest) stage simply shuts off the pump when the blood glucose level is sensed below a widely accepted threshold for hypoglycemia. Further improvements add the ability to forecast future trends of the blood glucose and perform predictive pump shutoff, introduce extra insulin when blood glucose levels are high, predict the onset of meals and finally a fully closed loop that is expected to completely eliminate the need for manual control of insulin infusions.

Table 1. Original pathway to the artificial pancreas project with representative papers showing technological feasibility. Source: Juvenile Diabetes Research Foundation (JDRF). See [39] for a recently proposed revised pathway.

ID	Description	Refs.
1	Very Low Glucose Pump Shutoff	[48]
	Pump shutoff during hypoglycemia	
2	Hypoglycemia Minimizer	[10]
	Pump shutoff in advance of predicted future hypoglycemia	
3	Hypo/Hyperglycemia Minimizer	[4,32,50]
	Same as # 2 plus addition of insulin when glucose is above threshold	
4	Hybrid Closed Loop	[33–35]
	Closed loop insulin delivery with manual bolus	
5	Fully Autoamted Closed Loop	[7–9,15,19,38,44]
	#4 with all manual meal boluses eliminated	
6	Multihormone Closed Loop	[25,26]
	Use glucagon and insulin to achieve bidirectional control	

The AP project promises a drastically improved approach to treating T1D by improving glucose control and reducing the burden of care to the patient. However, it's use potentially presents numerous risks to the patient. Too much insulin delivered to the patient can drive their blood glucose levels too low, causing seizures, coma or even death [6]. At the other end, a failure to deliver adequate insulin to cover meals can result in too high blood glucose levels that can lead to near-term complications such as ketacidosis. In order to be successful, the AP controller must tolerate significant sensor noise, and unpredictable events such as meals, physical activity and pump/sensor failures [16,36]. Furthermore, software errors in the controller software can have frightening and unexpected consequences [29].

Since it's inception in 2001, the *Runtime Verification* (RV) community has pioneered numerous techniques in efficient monitoring of temporal requirements of systems both during deployment (online monitoring) and development (offline monitoring). Progress in AP controllers bring about two important classes of challenges to the larger verification community, and specifically to the runtime verification community:

1. AP controllers have large state-spaces, a rich set of behaviors and are subject to large disturbances such as meals, exercise, sensor and infusion set failures, that makes these systems hard to reason with for existing symbolic methods. We examine the use of *simulation-based verification* techniques, particularly for the artificial pancreas controllers.
2. Beyond offline monitoring, it is also necessary to perform online monitoring of deployed artificial pancreas control systems to detect failures, caused due to rare events that may be hard to observe in clinical trials. In fact, the idea of robustness of a trace with respect to a logical specification can also be used to perform online monitoring for detecting potential failures early [21,23].

In this paper, we focus mainly on offline monitoring and illustrate how simulation-based falsification techniques can be employed as a first step towards verified artificial pancreas controllers.

2   Simulation-Based Falsification

In this section, we briefly survey simulation-based falsification approaches. We focus primarily on *robustness-guided falsification*, a promising approach that combines the notion of robustness of temporal logic formulas with stochastic optimization techniques for automatically search for falsifying traces.

2.1   Simulation-Based Falsification

Model-based falsification techniques for cyber-physical systems (CPS) seek behaviors of a system that violate a given property φ of interest. Falsification techniques can be *symbolic*, exploring the system behavior using a constraint solver [5], or *numeric*, using numerical simulations of the model to find property violations. In practice, significant strides in symbolic falsification have been made towards faster constraint solvers that support richer logics [20]. Nevertheless, the state-of-the-art for symbolic model checking techniques are currently restricted to linear models that involve controllers with linear assignments/conditionals and plants with linear dynamics [30]. Symbolic model checkers for nonlinear models and nonlinear controllers are currently a topic of ongoing research [13,14,31]. However, significant algorithmic challenges currently limit the scalability of these approaches. Furthermore, the use of these techniques on nonlinear, software-based control system with nonlinear plant models expressed in popular frameworks such as Simulink(tm)/Stateflow(tm) in Matlab(tm) requires a significant tool building effort.

Therefore, in this exposition, we focus on simulation-based approaches. Broadly, a simulation-based falsification technique performs repeated simulations of the system under various inputs and initial conditions, using results of past simulations to guide the future inputs to the system. Simulation-based falsification techniques offer two main features: (a) They are able to handle the system itself as a *black box*. This is an enormous advantage when the model is specified in a widely-used formalism such as Simulink(tm)/Stateflow(tm). Simulink/Stateflow models have complex semantics that change substantially over successive versions of the Matlab(tm) framework. On the other hand, the absence of detailed system knowledge is a drawback: repeated simulations are well-known to be inadequate for exploring systems with large state-spaces. As a result, simulation-based falsification techniques typically have very weak mathematical guarantees. (b) Simulation is cheap, parallelizable and can be performed quite accurately even for large nonlinear systems that are beyond the reach of many symbolic tools. However, numerical simulation tools are approximate: the simulation trajectories may deviate from the actual system trajectories due to integration and floating-point errors. Many simulation-based approaches have been proposed, especially for falsifying properties of CPS. We restrict our discussion below to two main approaches: (a) Rapid Exploration of Random Trees (RRTs) and (b) Robustness-Guided Falsification.

RRTs explore the behaviors of the system by building a tree whose nodes are system states and edges are trajectories connecting these states [41]. At each step, the tree is grown towards a current target state through a local search technique. Many variants of the basic RRT approach have been explored, some specifically designed for the falsification of temporal logic properties of CPS [18,24,53–55]. Recently, the RRT approach has been increasingly successful on larger benchmarks [24]. However, the performance can be quite variable, depending on the specific RRT scheme used. Furthermore, the techniques are also quite sensitive to the choice of distance metrics. Finally, the practical application of RRTs, specifically to Simulink(tm) /Stateflow(tm) models is currently challenging due to the large costs of setting up a simulation run. This is disadvantageous since the standard RRT approach relies on numerous simulations over a short time period for the local search.

In contrast, robustness-guided approaches are based on two main ingredients: (a) First, the notion of temporal property satisfaction is extended to allow us to have a distance metric to property violation [23,27,56]. Such a metric is referred to as the "trace robustness". Intuitively, a trace with a smaller robustness is therefore "closer" to a violation when compared to a trace that has a larger robustness. (b) In turn, the robustness metric can be used as an objective function to guide the system towards property violations in a systematic manner by seeking trajectories of ever decreasing robustness [1,3,49]. This is usually achieved inside a global optimization technique such as Nelder-Mead, simulated annealing, ant-colony optimization or the cross-entropy method that uses the robustness as an objective function to minimize.

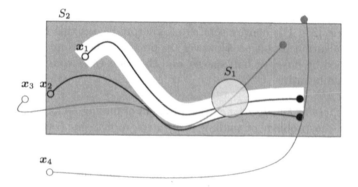

Fig. 1. Trace robustness for temporal property $\varphi : \lozenge S_1 \wedge \square S_2$. Traces x_1, x_2 both satisfy the property: $\rho(x_1, \varphi) > \rho(x_2, \varphi) > 0$. Likewise, x_3, x_4 both violate the property: $\rho(x_4, \varphi) < \rho(x_3, \varphi) < 0$. The robustness cylinder for x_1 is highlighted.

We will now briefly outline the robustness-guided approach for falsifying Metric Temporal Logic (MTL) properties of systems [40], following the work of Fainekos and Pappas [27]. The TaLiRo tool implements the MTL monitoring algorithm inside Matlab(tm). The ideas presented are conceptually similar to those of Donzé and Maler, using the alternative formalism of Signal Temporal Logic (STL) [23]. This is implemented in the Breach tool [22]. As mentioned earlier, the notion of robustness extends the standard Boolean notion of property satisfaction of a trace (i.e., a trace either satisfies a property or it does not) to a real-valued notion. Let $x : \mathbb{R}_{\geq 0} \rightarrow X$ be a trajectory, mapping time $t \geq 0$ to state $x(t) \in X$ and φ be a MTL property.

Definition 1 (Robustness Metric). *The robustness of $x(\cdot)$ w.r.t φ is a real number $\rho(x, \varphi)$ that has the following properties: (a) $\rho(x, \varphi) > 0$ if $x \models \varphi$, and (b) $\rho(x, \varphi) < 0$ if $x \not\models \varphi$. Furthermore, the magnitude $v : |\rho(x, \varphi)|$ denotes the maximum radius of a cylinder around the trace x so that any other trace in the cylinder also has the same outcome for φ as x.*

Example 1. Figure 1 illustrates robustness using the property $\varphi : \Diamond S_1 \wedge \Box S_2$ that requires the trace to stay entirely inside the blue rectangle S_2 while intersecting the red circle S_1. We see that traces $\boldsymbol{x}_1, \boldsymbol{x}_2$ satisfy the property. The robustness cylinder around trace $\boldsymbol{x}_1$ is illustrated in the figure. The cylinder represents all perturbations of $\boldsymbol{x}_1$ that also satisfy the property φ and the robustness $\rho(\boldsymbol{x}_1, \varphi)$ is taken to be the radius of the cylinder. It is evident upon a visual inspection that $\rho(\boldsymbol{x}_1, \varphi) > \rho(\boldsymbol{x}_2, \varphi) > 0$.

Similarly, we see that $\boldsymbol{x}_3, \boldsymbol{x}_4$ violate the property. The robustness cylinder around $\boldsymbol{x}_3$ represents all perturbations of $\boldsymbol{x}_3$ that will also violate φ. The robustness $\rho(\boldsymbol{x}_3, \varphi) < 0$ to denote the violation and $|\rho(\boldsymbol{x}_3, \varphi)|$ is set to the radius of the robustness cylinder. It is easy to see that $\rho(\boldsymbol{x}_4, \varphi) < \rho(\boldsymbol{x}_3, \varphi) < 0$.

In fact, robustness for a given trace and property can be computed efficiently using polynomial time in the size of the formula and the number of sample points in the trace $\boldsymbol{x}$ [28]. For convex sets as atomic predicates this requires solving convex optimization problems. However, in practice, the atomic predicates are often described by boxes or half-spaces, and the robustness computation can be optimized significantly.

From Robustness to Falsifications: The problem of finding a violation translates naturally to the problem of finding a negative robustness trace. In turn, we will consider the following optimization problem that seeks to minimize the robustness metric over all traces of a system: $\rho^* : \text{minimize}_{\boldsymbol{x} \in \text{Traces}} \rho(\boldsymbol{x}, \varphi)$. If the minimum robustness is $\rho^* < 0$, then we conclude that the system violates the property and the trace $\boldsymbol{x}^*$ that corresponds to the violation is obtained. On the other hand, the robustness function can be quite complicated, even for simple systems. As a result, the optimization problem is hard to solve precisely. To this end, numerous heuristic global optimization algorithms such as simulated annealing [1,49], ant-colony optimization [2], genetic algorithms or the cross-entropy method [58] can be applied to this problem. If these techniques discover a negative robustness trace, then a property violation is concluded. Otherwise, the least robust trace often provides valuable information to the designer, as to how close we get towards violating the property.

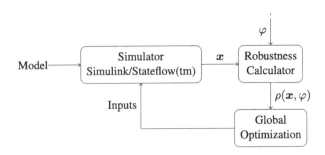

Fig. 2. Illustration of the overall robustness-guided falsification setup.

2.2   S-Taliro Tool

Figure 2 shows a schematic diagram for S-Taliro[1], a robustness guided falsification tool that supports MTL properties [3]. S-Taliro has been implemented inside the Matlab (tm) environment, and can support models described inside Simulink/Stateflow (tm). The tool uses the inbuilt simulator and computes the robustness for a trace. The resulting robustness is used as an objective function by a global optimization engine that seeks to minimize this value. The global optimizer, in turn, decides on future test inputs to the simulator based on the past inputs and the robustness values of the resulting traces. Currently, the tool supports many optimization engines including uniform random exploration, simulated annealing search, ant-colony optimization, cross-entropy method and genetic algorithms. Since no single optimization engine can guarantee finding a global minimum, the typical practice of using the tool consists of using multiple optimization engines, repeatedly and in parallel. If the tool fails to discover a violation, one of the key advantages of robustness metrics is that the least robust trace can provide a relaxed property that can be violated by S-Taliro. S-Taliro is available as an open source tool[2], and is built to be extensible through the addition of new solvers and alternative robustness computation techniques. The latest version uses multiple cores to perform numerous simulations in parallel. It also supports features such as property-directed parameter tuning for models and requirements. These features will be enhanced in future releases of the tool.

3   AP Controller Falsification

We now illustrate the use of S-Taliro on an example PID-based controller design that provides a hybrid closed loop for overnight insulin infusion control. Figure 3 shows the overall diagram of the closed loop system. We note that the controller design here simply serves to illustrate the ideas behind the use of robustness-guided falsification to find potentially harmful scenarios. In particular, the results presented can be improved through systematic and personalized tuning the key controller parameters. We will investigate the overnight use of this control system assuming manual boluses for meals. Such overnight control has the benefit of preventing dangerous seizures due to prolonged hypoglycemia through pump shutoff. Additionally, it helps bring the early morning blood glucose levels inside a tight euglycemic range of $[70, 150]$ mg/dl, leading to desirable longer term outcomes [43].

Controller Design: The controller used in this example is directly inspired by the PID control scheme proposed by Steil et al. [60–62]. A detailed analysis of this control scheme was presented by Palerm [51]. Let $G(t)$ represent the value of the blood glucose at time t. The controller operates through periodic sampling of the glucose sensor readings with a period Δ. The insulin level $u(k)$

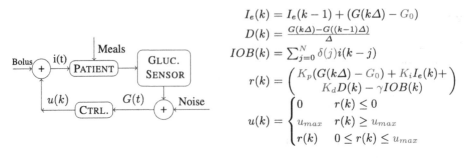

$$I_e(k) = I_e(k-1) + (G(k\Delta) - G_0)$$

$$D(k) = \frac{G(k\Delta) - G((k-1)\Delta)}{\Delta}$$

$$IOB(k) = \sum_{j=0}^{N} \delta(j) i(k-j)$$

$$r(k) = \left(\begin{array}{c} K_p(G(k\Delta) - G_0) + K_i I_e(k) + \\ K_d D(k) - \gamma IOB(k) \end{array} \right)$$

$$u(k) = \begin{cases} 0 & r(k) \leq 0 \\ u_{max} & r(k) \geq u_{max} \\ r(k) & 0 \leq r(k) \leq u_{max} \end{cases}$$

Fig. 3. Closed loop diagram for the hybrid PID control system, and equations defining the controller. The controller gains and other parameters are shown in blue.

at the kth time period $t = k\Delta$ is calculated as shown in Fig. 3. The insulin infusion rate is held constant for the subsequent time period $[k\Delta, (k+1)\Delta)$. The overall insulin rate $i(t)$ is derived as the sum of the controller input and the patient's manual meal bolus. The terms involved are $I_e(k)$, the integrated error at the kth period, $D(k)$ the derivative term and $IOB(k)$, an *insulin-on-board* compensation term. These are calculated as shown in Fig. 3. The parameters for the controller include the target glucose value G_0, taken to be $100\,mg/dl$, the gains K_p, K_i, K_d, γ that are chosen by trial and error starting from initial values based on the total daily insulin requirements of the patient as explained by Weinzimer et al. [62]. Likewise, the cutoff parameters u_{max} that are adjusted by trial and error, starting from the patient's open loop basal rate. The parameters $\delta(j)$ for $j = 0, \ldots, N$ specify the amount of active insulin in the blood at time $t = j\Delta$ corresponding to a unit bolus at time $t = 0$, and is based on available physiological data [61]. Finally, the time period Δ is taken to be $5\,min$ for our simulation. The controller code along with the parameter values will be made available to researchers upon request.

Patient Model: Patient modeling is an important part of the overall *in silico* verification process. To this end, many detailed models of insulin-glucose regulation have been proposed. The monograph by Chee and Fernando provides a detailed, historical account of numerous mathematical models [12]. For this simulation study, we use the Dalla-Man et al. model [17,45,47]. This model is a nonlinear ordinary differential equation (ODE) with 10 state variables. The model and corresponding parameters are available as part of the FDA approved T1DM simulator that can now be used as an alternative to animal testing [46]. The model has been increasingly popular inside a simulation environment for "in-silico" or "virtual" clinical trials [44,52].

Nevertheless, to the best of our knowledge, the typical use of this model is through a finite set of fixed "in-silico clinical protocol", that is simulated for multiple sets of patient parameters [52]. The performance statistics such as total time in the euglycemic range or number of hypoglycemic events are reported for each "virtual" patient defined by values of the model parameters. In this exposition, we illustrate a different approach that uses S-Taliro to search over a *set of possible scenarios* to potentially discover the worst case, as defined by the robustness metric, for a given property.

Verification Protocol: For the purposes of falsifying properties of the proposed controller, we use a *set* of possible scenarios, as specified below. Let $t = 0$ represent 7 pm in the evening. Each usage scenario is as follows:

(a) The patient consumes dinner, and manually infuses an insulin bolus at some time $T_1 \in [0, 60]$ min. The amount of carbohydrates consumed at dinner X_1 can vary between $[50, 150]$ g. The bolus is delivered using an insulin-to-CHO ratio IC_1 that can also vary between $[0, 0.01]$ U/g. Finally, the timing of the bolus relative to the meal time can vary in the range $\delta_1 \in [-15, 15]$ min.
(b) The controller is turned on at some time $T_c \in [40, 60]$ min, each night.
(c) The patient may possibly consume a snack after the controller is turned on. The snack is consumed sometime between $T_2 \in [180, 300]$, and can vary between $X_2 \in [0, 40]$ g of carbohydrates. The insulin-to-CHO ratio IC_2 and relative timing δ_2 fall in the same ranges as for dinner.
(d) The controller is turned off at "wake up time" $T_w = 720$.

Finally, we assume that a sensor error of $d(t) \in [-20, 20]$ mg/dl is possible at each sampling instant. This is the error between the sensor output of the Dalla-Man model and the value input to the controller. To decrease the number of parameters, we simply use the values at $d(100), d(105), \ldots, d(720)$ as parameters input to the simulator. These parameters lie in the range $[-20, 20]$ mg/dl, and are also controlled by the S-Taliro tool while exploring the worst-case.

Table 2. Inputs that are set by S-Taliro to falsify properties for the AP control system.

T_1	$[0, 60]$ mins	Dinner time
X_1	$[50, 150]$ g	Amount of CHO in dinner.
T_2	$[180, 300]$ mins	Snack time.
X_2	$[0, 40]$ g	Amount of CHO in snack
IC_1, IC_2	$[0, 0.01]$ U/gm	Insulin-to-CHO ratio for meal boluses
δ_1, δ_2	$[-15, 15]$ min	timing of insulin relative to meal j
$d(100), d(105), \ldots, d(720)$	$[-20, 20]$ mg/dl	sensor error at each sample time

Table 2 summarizes the inputs that S-Taliro can modify to obtain various behaviors of the model. Including the sensor noise inputs, the search space for S-Taliro has nearly 130 parameters. We employed three solvers: uniform random exploration, simulated annealing and the cross-entropy method.

Hypoglycemia: The first property concerns worst case hypoglycemia (low blood glucose levels) possible for this controller. We wish to check whether the system satisfies the MTL property: ψ_1 : $\square_{[100,700]}$ $(G(t) \geq 70)$, which states that during the time period $t \in [100, 700]$, the blood glucose level should remain above $70 \, mg/dl$ in all scenarios. The time interval $[100, 700]$ is used to allow a run-in period with the controller switched on.

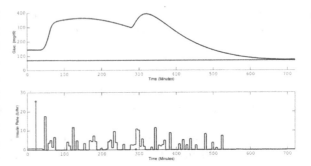

Fig. 4. Least robust trace found by S-Taliro for property ψ_1 : $\square_{[100,700]}(G(t) \geq 70)$. The top plot for shows the blood glucose levels (mg/dl) over time (minutes) while the bottom plots show the insulin infusion (U/hr) over time (mins). The red impulses represent Bolus amounts in U/hr assuming the bolus amount is delivered over 5 minutes.

As a result, property violations before the controller has warmed up will not be considered. We used three parallel process to search using the simulated-annealing, uniform random and cross-entropy method. While, S-Taliro could not violate the property, the least robust scenario (found by the uniform random search) involves $G(t) \sim 75 \, mg/dl$. In other words, the trace approaches *quite close* to violating the property. The search takes nearly 3200 seconds using three parallel Matlab (tm) R2014 instances on a 4 core, 800 MHz 64 bit AMD Phenom(tm) II processor with 8 GB RAM running Linux. Figure 4 shows the resulting output trace obtained from S-Taliro.

Hyperglycemia: The next property concerns whether hyperglycemia (high blood glucose levels) are possible. We wish to check the MTL property ψ_2 : $\square_{[100,700]}(G(t) \leq 350)$, which states that during the time period $t \in [100, 700]$, can the blood glucose level go above $350 \, mg/dl$. S-Taliro finds a violation of this property with the maximum glucose

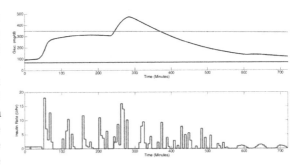

Fig. 5. Least robust trace found by S-Taliro for property ψ_2 : $\square_{[100,700]}(G(t) \leq 350)$.

level of $472 \, mg/dl$. This is found by the cross entropy solver requiring under 5 seconds of total running time. Figure 5 shows the violation trace produced by S-Taliro.

Insulin Infusion below Target: The next property concerns whether the controller can infuse insulin while the blood glucose level is below a target level of 90 mg/dl: ψ_3 : $\square_{[100,700]}(G(t) \leq 90 \Rightarrow u(t) = 0)$. The property states that whenever $G(t) \leq 90$ mg/dl, the controller should not command additional insulin, or in other words $u(t) = 0$ should hold. Infusing insulin when the blood glucose is low, can be quite dangerous, worsening the hypoglycemia. The property is violated by S-Taliro in nearly 90 s. While all three engines discover a violation, the least robust violation is discovered by the cross entropy (CE) solver.

Hyperglycemia at Wakeup: One of the important objectives of nighttime insulin infusion control is to provide a blood glucose level as close to the normal range as possible at wake up time. Recent clinical evidence indicates that starting off with a normal blood glucose level at wake up time can have beneficial longer term outcomes [43]. To this end, we check whether the morning wakeup blood glucose level can exceed 200 mg/dl.

$$\psi_4 : \quad \square_{[600,700]}(G(t) \leq 200).$$

The property states that the blood glucose levels must remain below 200 mg/dl during the time period $t \in [600, 700]$. S-Taliro cannot violate the property. The minimal robustness trace shows a blood glucose level of 180 mg/dl at wakeup time, and is discovered by the uniform random search after 3500 s.

Prolonged Hyperglycemia: We now focus on the possibility of prolonged hyperglycemia that can potentially give rise to ketacidosis: ψ_5 in Fig. 6. The property states that during the time $t \in [200, 600]$ the blood glucose cannot be continuously above 240 mg/dl for more than 180 minutes. S-Taliro easily falsifies this property: the cross-entropy search discovers the least robust trace within 3 s.

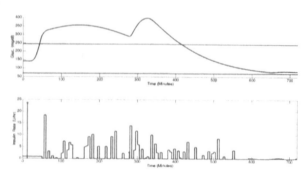

Fig. 6. Least robust trace found by S-Taliro for the prolonged hyperglycemia property ψ_5 : $\neg\lozenge_{[200,600]}\square_{[0,180]}(G(t) \geq 240)$.

Prolonged Hypoglycemia: Finally, we conclude by searching for the possibility of a prolonged hypoglycemia that can potentially lead to seizures [6]: ψ_6 : $\neg\lozenge_{[200,600]}\square_{[0,150]}(G(t) \leq 70)$. The property states that there cannot be a contiguous interval of 150 minutes during which $G(t) \leq 70$ mg/dl. The property cannot be violated by S-Taliro. The least robust trace is discovered by uniform random search in 3550 s shows a scenario where $G(t) \leq 85$ over a 150 min interval.

4   Conclusions

In conclusion, we have outlined the need for verifying artificial pancreas controllers and the challenges faced by current verification technique. We have illustrated the use of simulation-based falsification as a first step towards full formal verification. Ongoing work is addressing important gaps in our verification framework including careful modeling of disturbances such as meals, exercise and various sources of sensor noise. We are also working towards making the tool S-Taliro more user friendly to allow control designers to directly use the tool. To this end, we envision simpler and more visual formalisms for specifying temporal properties [37].

Acknowledgments. This material is based upon work supported by the US National Science Foundation (NSF) under grant numbers CPS-1446900, CNS-1319457, CPS-1446751, and CNS-1319560. All opinions expressed are those of the authors, and not necessarily of the NSF.

References

1. Abbas, H., Fainekos, G., Sankaranarayanan, S., Ivancic, F.: Probabilistic temporal logic falsification of cyber-physical systems. Trans. Embedded Comput. Syst. (TECS) **12**, 95 (2013)
2. Annapureddy, Y.S.R., Fainekos, G.E.: Ant colonies for temporal logic falsification of hybrid systems. In: Proceedings of the 36th Annual Conference of IEEE Industrial Electronics, pp. 91–96 (2010)
3. Annpureddy, Y., Liu, C., Fainekos, G., Sankaranarayanan, S.: S-TaLiRo: a tool for temporal logic falsification for hybrid systems. In: Abdulla, P.A., Leino, K.R.M. (eds.) TACAS 2011. LNCS, vol. 6605, pp. 254–257. Springer, Heidelberg (2011)
4. Atlas, E., Nimri, R., Miller, S., Grunberg, E.A., Phillip, M.: MD-Logic artificial pancreas system: a pilot study in adults with type 1 diabetes. Diabetes Care **33**(5), 1072–1076 (2010)
5. Baier, C., Katoen, J.-P.: Principles of Model Checking. MIT Press, Cambridge (2008)
6. Buckingham, B., Wilson, D.M., Lecher, T., Hanas, R., Kaiserman, K., Cameron, F.: Duration of nocturnal hypoglycemia before seizures. Diabetes Care **31**(11), 2110–2112 (2008)
7. Cameron, F.: Explicitly minimizing clinical risk through closed-loop control of blood glucose in patients with type 1 diabetes mellitus. Ph.D. thesis, Stanford University (2010)
8. Cameron, F., Wayne Bequette, B., Wilson, D.M., Buckingham, B., Lee, H., Niemeyer, G.: Closed-loop artificial pancreas based on risk management. J. Diabetes Sci. Technol. **5**(2), 36879 (2011)
9. Cameron, F., Niemeyer, G., Wayne Bequette, B.: Extended multiple model prediction with application to blood glucose regulation. J. Process Control **22**(8), 1422–1432 (2012)
10. Cameron, F., Wilson, D.M., Buckingham, B.A., Arzumanyan, H., Clinton, P., Peter Chase, H., Lum, J., Maahs, D.M., Calhoun, P.M.: Inpatient studies of a kalman-filter-based predictive pump shutoff algorithm. J. Diabetes Sci. Technol. **6**(5), 1142–1147 (2012)

11. Peter Chase, H., Maahs, D.: Understanding Diabetes (Pink Panther Book), 12th edn. Children's Diabetes Foundation, Denver (2011). Available online through CU Denver Barbara Davis Center for Diabetes
12. Chee, F., Fernando, T.: Closed-Loop Control of Blood Glucose. Springer, Heidelberg (2007)
13. Chen, X., Ábrahám, E., Sankaranarayanan, S.: Taylor model flowpipe construction for non-linear hybrid systems. In: Proceeding of the RTSS 2012, pp. 183–192. IEEE (2012)
14. Chen, X., Ábrahám, E., Sankaranarayanan, S.: Flow*: an analyzer for non-linear hybrid systems. In: Sharygina, N., Veith, H. (eds.) CAV 2013. LNCS, vol. 8044, pp. 258–263. Springer, Heidelberg (2013)
15. Cobelli, C., et al.: First use of model predictive control in outpatient wearable artificial pancreas. Diabetes Care **37**(5), 1212–1215 (2014)
16. Cobelli, C., Dalla Man, C., Sparacino, G., Magni, L., De Nicolao, G., Kovatchev, B.P.: Diabetes: models, signals and control (methodological review). IEEE Rev. Biomed. Eng. **2**, 54–95 (2009)
17. Dall Man, C., Rizza, R.A., Cobelli, C.: Meal simulation model of the glucose-insulin system. IEEE Trans. Biomed. Eng. **1**(10), 1740–1749 (2006)
18. Dang, T., Nahhal, T.: Coverage-guided test generation for continuous and hybrid systems. Formal Methods Syst. Des. **34**(2), 183–213 (2009)
19. Dassau, E., Zisser, H., Harvey, R.A., Percival, M.W., Grosman, B., Bevier, W., Atlas, E., Miller, S., Nimri, R., Jovanovic, L., Doyle, F.J.: Clinical evaluation of a personalized artificial pancreas. Diabetes Care **36**(4), 8019 (2013)
20. de Moura, L., Bjørner, N.S.: Z3: an efficient SMT solver. In: Ramakrishnan, C.R., Rehof, J. (eds.) TACAS 2008. LNCS, vol. 4963, pp. 337–340. Springer, Heidelberg (2008)
21. Dokhanchi, A., Hoxha, B., Fainekos, G.: On-line monitoring for temporal logic robustness. In: Bonakdarpour, B., Smolka, S.A. (eds.) RV 2014. LNCS, vol. 8734, pp. 231–246. Springer, Heidelberg (2014)
22. Donzé, A.: Breach, a toolbox for verification and parameter synthesis of hybrid systems. In: Touili, T., Cook, B., Jackson, P. (eds.) CAV 2010. LNCS, vol. 6174, pp. 167–170. Springer, Heidelberg (2010)
23. Donzé, A., Maler, O.: Robust satisfaction of temporal logic over real-valued signals. In: Chatterjee, K., Henzinger, T.A. (eds.) FORMATS 2010. LNCS, vol. 6246, pp. 92–106. Springer, Heidelberg (2010)
24. Dreossi, T., Dang, T., Donzé, A., Kapinski, J., Jin, X., Deshmukh, J.V.: Efficient guiding strategies for testing of temporal properties of hybrid systems. In: Havelund, K., Holzmann, G., Joshi, R. (eds.) NFM 2015. LNCS, vol. 9058, pp. 127–142. Springer, Heidelberg (2015)
25. El-Khatib, F., Jiang, J., Damiano, E.R.: Adaptive closed-loop control provides blood-glucose regulation using dual subcutaneous insulin and glucagon infusion in diabetic swine. J. Diabetes Sci. Technol. **1**(2), 18192 (2007)
26. El-Khatib, F.H., Russell, S.J., Nathan, D.M., Sutherlin, R.G., Damiano, E.R.: A bihormonal closed-loop artificial pancreas for type 1 diabetes. Sci. Transl. Med. **2**, 27ra27 (2010)
27. Fainekos, G., Pappas, G.J.: Robustness of temporal logic specifications for continuous-time signals. Theor. Comput. Sci. **410**, 4262–4291 (2009)
28. Fainekos, G., Sankaranarayanan, S., Ueda, K., Yazarel, H.: Verification of automotive control applications using s-taliro. In: Proceedings of the American Control Conference (2012)

29. Forlenza, G.P., Sankaranarayanan, S., Maahs, D.M.: Refining the closed loop in the data age: research-to-practice transitions in diabetes technology. Diabetes Technol. Ther. **17**(5), 304–306 (2015)

30. Frehse, G., Le Guernic, C., Donzé, A., Cotton, S., Ray, R., Lebeltel, O., Ripado, R., Girard, A., Dang, T., Maler, O.: SpaceEx: scalable verification of hybrid systems. In: Gopalakrishnan, G., Qadeer, S. (eds.) CAV 2011. LNCS, vol. 6806, pp. 379–395. Springer, Heidelberg (2011)

31. Gao, S., Kong, S., Clarke, E.M.: dReal: an SMT Solver for nonlinear theories over the reals. In: Bonacina, M.P. (ed.) CADE 2013. LNCS, vol. 7898, pp. 208–214. Springer, Heidelberg (2013)

32. Grosman, B., Dassau, E., Zisser, H.C., Jovanovic, L., Doyle, F.J.: Zone model predictive control: a strategy to minimize hyper- and hypoglycemic events. J. Diabetes Sci. Technol. **4**(4), 961–975 (2010)

33. Hovorka, R., Allen, J.M., Elleri, D., Chassin, L.J., Harris, J., Xing, D., Kollman, C., Hovorka, T., Larsen, A.M., Nodale, M., De Palma, A., Wilinska, M., Acerini, C., Dunger, D.: Manual closed-loop delivery in children and adolescents with type 1 diabetes: a phase 2 randomised crossover trial. Lancet **375**, 743–751 (2010)

34. Hovorka, R., Canonico, V., Chassin, L.J., Haueter, U., Massi-Benedetti, M., Frederici, M.O., Pieber, T.R., Shaller, H.C., Schaupp, L., Vering, T., Wilinska, M.E.: Nonlinear model predictive control of glucose concentration in subjects with type 1 diabetes. Physiol. Measur. **25**, 905–920 (2004)

35. Hovorka, R., Shojaee-Moradie, F., Carroll, P.V., Chassin, L.J., Gowrie, I.J., Jackson, N.C., Tudor, R.S., Umpleby, A.M., Hones, R.H.: Partitioning glucose distribution/transport, disposal and endogenous production during IVGTT. Am. J. Physiol. Endocrinol. Metab. **282**, 992–1007 (2002)

36. Hovorka, R.: Continuous glucose monitoring and closed-loop systems. Diabetic Med. **23**(1), 1–12 (2005)

37. Hoxha, B., Bach, H., Abbas, H., Dokhanchi, A., Kobayashi, Y., Fainekos, G.: Towards formal specification visualization for testing and monitoring of cyber-physical systems. In: International Workshop on Design and Implementation of Formal Tools and Systems (2014)

38. Kovatchev, B., Cobelli, C., Renard, E., Anderson, S., Breton, M., Patek, S., Clarke, W., Bruttomesso, D., Maran, A., Costa, S., Avogaro, A., Dalla Man, C., Facchinetti, A., Magni, L., De Nicolao, G., Place, J., Farret, A.: Multinational study of subcutaneous model-predictive closed-loop control in type 1 diabetes mellitus: summary of the results. J. Diabetes Sci. Technol. **4**(6), 137481 (2010)

39. Kowalski, A.: Pathway to artificial pancreas revisited: moving downstream. Diabetes Care **38**, 1036–1043 (2015)

40. Koymans, R.: Specifying real-time properties with metric temporal logic. Real-Time Syst. **2**(4), 255–299 (1990)

41. LaValle, S.M.: Planning Algorithms. Cambridge University Press, New York (2006)

42. Maahs, D., Mayer-Davis, E., Bishop, F., Wang, L., Mangan, M., McMurray, R.G.: Outpatient assessment of determinants of glucose excursions in adolescents with type-1 diabetes. Diabetes Technol. Ther. **14**(8), 658–664 (2012)

43. Maahs, D.M., Peter Chase, H., Westfall, E., Slover, R., Huang, S., Shin, J.J., Kaufman, F.R., Pyle, L., Snell-Bergeon, J.K.: The effects of lowering nighttime and breakfast glucose levels with sensor-augmented pump therapy on hemoglobin a1c levels in type 1 diabetes. Diabetes Technol. Ther. **16**(5), 284–291 (2014)

44. Magni, L., Raimondo, D.M., Bossi, L., Dalla Man, C., De Nicolao, G., Kovatchev, B., Cobelli, C.: Model predictive control of type 1 diabetes: an in silico trial. J. Diabetes Sci. Technol. **1**(6), 804–812 (2007)

45. DallaMan, C., Camilleri, M., Cobelli, C.: A system model of oral glucose absorption: validation on gold standard data. IEEE Trans. Biomed. Eng. **53**(12), 2472–2478 (2006)
46. Dalla Man, C., Micheletto, F., Lv, D., Breton, M., Kovatchev, B., Cobelli, C.: The UVA/PADOVA type 1 diabetes simulator: new features. J. Diabetes Sci. Technol. **8**(1), 26–34 (2014)
47. DallaMan, C., Raimondo, D.M., Rizza, R.A., Cobelli, C.: GIM, simulation software of meal glucose-insulin model. J. Diabetes Sci. Tech. **1**(3), 323–330 (2007)
48. Medtronic Inc. "paradigm" insulin pump with low glucose suspend system (2012). http://www.medtronicdiabetes.ca/en/paradigm_veo_glucose.html
49. Nghiem, T., Sankaranarayanan, S., Fainekos, G.E., Ivančić, F., Gupta, A., Pappas, G.J.: Monte-carlo techniques for falsification of temporal properties of non-linear hybrid systems. In: Hybrid Systems: Computation and Control, pp. 211–220. ACM Press (2010)
50. Nimri, R., Muller, I., Atlas, E., Miller, S., Kordonouri, O., Bratina, N., Tsioli, C., Stefanija, M.A., Danne, T., Battelino, T., Phillip, M.: Night glucose control with md-logic artificial pancreas in home setting: a single blind, randomized crossover trial-interim analysis. Pediatr. Diabetes **15**(2), 91–100 (2014)
51. Palerm, C.C.: Physiologic insulin delivery with insulin feedback: a control systems perspective. Comput. Methods Programs Biomed. **102**(2), 130–137 (2011)
52. Patek, S.D., Bequette, B.W., Breton, M., Buckingham, B.A., Dassau, E., Doyle III, F.J., Lum, J., Magni, L., Zisser, H.: In silico preclinical trials: methodology and engineering guide to closed-loop control in type 1 diabetes mellitus. J Diabetes Sci. Technol. **3**(2), 269–282 (2009)
53. Plaku, E., Kavraki, L.E., Vardi, M.Y.: Falsification of LTL safety properties in hybrid systems. In: Kowalewski, S., Philippou, A. (eds.) TACAS 2009. LNCS, vol. 5505, pp. 368–382. Springer, Heidelberg (2009)
54. Plaku, E., Kavraki, L.E., Vardi, M.Y.: Hybrid systems: from verification to falsification. In: Damm, W., Hermanns, H. (eds.) CAV 2007. LNCS, vol. 4590, pp. 463–476. Springer, Heidelberg (2007)
55. Plaku, E., Kavraki, L.E., Vardi, M.Y.: Falsification of ltl safety properties in hybrid systems. Int. J. Softw. Tools Technol. Transf. **15**(4), 305–320 (2013)
56. Rizk, A., Batt, G., Fages, F., Soliman, S.: On a continuous degree of satisfaction of temporal logic formulae with applications to systems biology. In: Heiner, M., Uhrmacher, A.M. (eds.) CMSB 2008. LNCS (LNBI), vol. 5307, pp. 251–268. Springer, Heidelberg (2008)
57. Sankaranarayanan, S., Fainekos, G.: Simulating insulin infusion pump risks by *In-Silico* modeling of the insulin-glucose regulatory system. In: Gilbert, D., Heiner, M. (eds.) CMSB 2012. LNCS, vol. 7605, pp. 322–341. Springer, Heidelberg (2012)
58. Sankaranarayanan, S., Fainekos, G.E.: Falsification of temporal properties of hybrid systems using the cross-entropy method. In: HSCC, pp. 125–134. ACM (2012)
59. Skyler, J.S. (ed.): Atlas of Diabetes, 4th edn. Springer Science+Business Media, New York (2012)
60. Steil, G.M.: Algorithms for a closed-loop artificial pancreas: the case for proportional-integral-derivative control. J. Diabetes Sci. Technol. **7**, 1621–1631 (2013)
61. Steil, G.M., Panteleon, A.E., Rebrin, K.: Closed-loop insulin delivery - the path to physiological glucose control. Adv. Drug Delivery Rev. **56**(2), 125–144 (2004)
62. Weinzimer, S., Steil, G., Swan, K., Dziura, J., Kurtz, N., Tamborlane, W.: Fully automated closed-loop insulin delivery versus semiautomated hybrid control in pediatric patients with type 1 diabetes using an artificial pancreas. Diabetes Care **31**, 934–939 (2008)

Regular Papers

Qualitative and Quantitative Monitoring of Spatio-Temporal Properties

Laura Nenzi[1]([✉]), Luca Bortolussi[2,3,4], Vincenzo Ciancia[4],
Michele Loreti[1,5], and Mieke Massink[4]

[1] IMT, Lucca, Italy
laura.nenzi@imtlucca.it
[2] MOSI, Saarland University, Saarbrücken, Germany
[3] DMG, University of Trieste, Trieste, Italy
[4] CNR-ISTI, Pisa, Italy
[5] DiSIA, University of Firenze, Florence, Italy

Abstract. We address the specification and verification of spatio-temporal behaviours of complex systems, extending *Signal Spatio-Temporal Logic* (SSTL) with a spatial operator capable of specifying topological properties in a discrete space. The latter is modelled as a weighted graph, and provided with a boolean and a quantitative semantics. Furthermore, we define efficient *monitoring algorithms* for both the boolean and the quantitative semantics. These are implemented in a Java tool available online. We illustrate the expressiveness of SSTL and the effectiveness of the monitoring procedures on the formation of patterns in a Turing reaction-diffusion system.

Keywords: Signal Spatio-Temporal Logic · Boolean semantics · Quantitative semantics · Monitoring algorithms · Weighted graphs · Turing patterns

1 Introduction

There is an increasing interest in the introduction of smart solutions in the world around us. A huge number of computational devices, located in space, is interacting in an open and changing environment, with humans and nature in the loop that form an intrinsic part of the system. Yet, science and technology are still struggling to tame the challenges underlying the design and control of such systems. In this paper, in particular, we focus on the challenge of spatially located systems, for which the spatial and temporal dimensions are strictly correlated and influence each other. This is the case in many Cyber-Physical Systems, like

Work partially funded by the EU-FET project QUANTICOL (nr. 600708), by the German Research Council (DFG) as part of the Cluster of Excellence on Multimodal Computing and Interaction at Saarland University and the IT MIUR project CINA. We thank Diego Latella and Ezio Bartocci for the discussions and EB for sharing the code to generate traces of the example.

E. Bartocci and R. Majumdar (Eds.): RV 2015, LNCS 9333, pp. 21–37, 2015.
DOI: 10.1007/978-3-319-23820-3_2

pacemaker devices controlling the rhythm of heart beat, and for many Collective Adaptive Systems, like the guidance of crowd movement in emergency situations or the improvement of the performance of bike sharing systems in smart cities.

Controlling and designing spatio-temporal behaviours requires proper formal tools to describe such properties, and to monitor and verify whether, and to which extent and how robustly, they are satisfied by a system. Formal methods play a central role, in terms of formal languages to specify spatio-temporal models and properties, and in terms of algorithms for the verification of such properties on such models and on monitored systems. The type of systems that we are considering are very large and complex for which standard model checking procedures (checking whether all event sequences produced by a system satisfy a property) are not feasible. For these kind of systems simulation and testing is a preferred validation method. This is the area of the run-time verification, as reported in [8,15], where an individual simulation trace **x** of a system is checked against a formula, using an automatic verification procedure.

Related work. Logical specification and monitoring of temporal properties is a well-developed area. Here we mention Signal Temporal Logic (STL) [8,15], an extension of Metric Interval Temporal Logic (MITL) [2], describing linear-time properties of real-valued signals. STL has monitoring routines both for its boolean and quantitative semantics, the latter measuring the satisfaction degree of a formula [8,9,15].

Much work has been done also in the area of spatial logic [1], yet focussing more on expressivity and decidability, often in continuous space. Less attention has been placed on more practical aspects, like model checking routines in discrete space. An exception is the work of some of the authors [5], in which the Spatial Logic for Closure Spaces (SLCS) is proposed for a discrete and topological notion of space, based on closure spaces [11]. First applications of that work in the context of smart transportation can be found in [7]. Another spatial logic equipped with practical model checking algorithms, and with learning procedures, is that of [12,13], in which spatial properties are expressed using ideas from image processing, namely quad trees. This allows one to capture very complex spatial structures, but at the price of a complex formulation of spatial properties, which are in practice only learned from some template image.

In this work, we will focus on a notion of discrete space. The reason is that many applications, like bike sharing systems or metapopulation epidemic models [16], are naturally framed in a discrete spatial structure. Moreover, in many circumstances continuous space is abstracted as a grid or as a mesh. This is the case, for instance, in many numerical methods to simulate the spatio-temporal dynamics of Partial Differential Equations (PDE). Hence, this class of models is naturally dealt with by checking properties on such a discretisation.

The combination of spatial and temporal operators is even more challenging [1], and few works exist with a practical perspective. In [4], some of the authors proposed an extension of STL with a *somewhere* spatial modality, which can be arbitrarily nested with temporal operators, proposing a monitoring algorithm for both the boolean and the quantitative semantics. An extension of SLCS with temporal aspects can be found in [6] where the logic has been applied in the context of smart public transportation. In [14], instead, the authors merge the spatial logic of [13] within linear temporal logic, by considering atomic spatial properties. They also provide a qualitative and quantitative semantics, and apply it to smart grids and to the formation of patterns in a reaction diffusion model.

Contributions. In this work, we present an extension of the Signal Spatio-Temporal Logic (SSTL), that combines the works in [4,5]. We extend SSTL with the topological *spatial surround operator*, inspired by the spatial until modality defined in [5].

We provide a qualitative and quantitative semantics for this new operator and we define efficient monitoring algorithms for both of them. The major challenge is to monitor the surround operator for the quantitative semantics, for which we propose a novel fixed point algorithm, discussing its correctness and computational cost. Spatial monitoring requires very different algorithms from those developed for timed modalities, as space is bi-directional, thus it makes sense to observe both *reaching* and *being reached*; classical path-based model checking does not coincide with spatial model checking also because loops in space are not relevant in the definition of *surrounded* operators. The monitoring algorithms have been implemented in Java, and applied and tested on a case study of pattern formation in a Turing reaction-diffusion system modelling a process of morphogenesis [18].

Paper structure[1]. The paper is organised as follows: Sect. 2 introduces some background concepts on STL and on discrete topologies. Section 3 presents the syntax and the semantics of SSTL. Section 4 introduces the monitoring algorithms. Section 5 is devoted to the example of pattern formation, while conclusions are drawn in Sect. 6.

2   Background Material

Weighted undirected graphs. We will consider discrete models of space that can be represented as a finite undirected graph. Edges of the graph are equipped with a positive weight, giving a metric structure to the space, in terms of shortest path distances. The weight will often represent the distance between two nodes. This is the case, for instance, when the graph is a discretization of continuous space. However, the notion of weight is more general, and may be used to encode different kinds of information. As an example, in a model where nodes are locations in the city and edges represent streets, the weight could represent the average travelling time, which can be different between two paths with the same physical length but different levels of congestion or different number of traffic lights.

We represent a weighted undirected graph with a tuple $G = \langle L, E, w \rangle$, where:

---

[1] Due to lack of space all proofs are omitted. The interested reader may refer to [17].

L is the finite set of locations (nodes), L

$E \subseteq L \times L$ is a symmetric relation, namely the set of connections (edges),

$w : E \to \mathbb{R}_{\geq 0}$ is the function that returns the cost/weight of each edge. Furthermore, we denote by E^* the set containing all the pairs of connected locations, i.e. the transitive closure of E. We will also use an overloaded notation and extend w to the domain E^*, so that for arbitrary nodes x, y (not necessarily connected by an edge) we let $w(x, y)$ be the cost of the shortest path between two different locations. Finally, for all $\ell \in L$ and $w_1, w_2 \geq 0$, we let $L^\ell_{w_1, w_2}$ be the set of locations ℓ' such that $w_1 \leq w(\ell, \ell') \leq w_2$.

Closure spaces and the boundary of a set of nodes. In this work, we focus on graphs as an algorithmically tractable representation of space. However, *spatial* logics traditionally use more abstract structures, very often of a topological nature (see [1] for an exhaustive reference). We can frame a generalised notion of topology on graphs within the so called *Čech closure spaces*, a superclass of topological spaces allowing a clear formalisation of the semantics of the spatial surround operator on both topological and graph-like structures (see [5] and the references therein). What is really relevant for this work, because of the restriction to finite (weighted and undirected) graphs, is the notion of *external boundary* of a set of nodes A, i.e. the set of nodes directly connected with an element of A but not part of it.

Definition 1. *Given a subset of locations $A \subseteq L$, we define the boundary of A as:*

$$B(A) = \{\ell \in L \mid \ell \notin A \land \exists \ell' \in A \text{ s.t. } (\ell, \ell') \in E\}.$$

Signal Temporal Logic. *Signal Temporal Logic* (STL) [8,15] is a linear dense time-bounded temporal logic that extends *Metric Interval Temporal Logic* (MITL) [2] with a set of atomic propositions $\mu_1, ..., \mu_m$ that specify properties of real valued traces, therefore mapping real valued traces into boolean values.

Let $\mathbf{x} : \mathbb{T} \to \mathbb{D}$ be a trace that describes an evolution of our system, where $\mathbb{T} \subseteq \mathbb{R}_{\geq 0}$ is the time set and $\mathbb{D} = \mathbb{D}_1 \times \cdots \times \mathbb{D}_n \subseteq \mathbb{R}^n$ is the domain of evaluation; then each $\mu_j : \mathbb{D} \to \mathbb{B}$ is of the form $\mu_j(x_1, ..., x_n) = f_j(x_1, ..., x_n) \geq 0$, where $f_j : \mathbb{D} \to \mathbb{R}$ is a (possibly non-linear) real-valued function and $\mathbb{B} = \{true, false\}$ is the set of boolean values. The projections $x_i : \mathbb{T} \to \mathbb{D}_i$ on the ith coordinate/variable are called the *primary signals* and, for all j, the function $s_j : \mathbb{T} \to \mathbb{R}$ defined by pointwise application of f_j to the image of $\mathbf{x}$, namely $s_j(t) = f_j(x_1(t), ..., x_n(t))$, is called the *secondary signal* [9].

The syntax of STL is given by

$$\varphi := \mu \mid \neg \varphi \mid \varphi_1 \land \varphi_2 \mid \varphi_1 \, U_{[t_1, t_2]} \, \varphi_2,$$

where conjunction and negation are the standard boolean connectives, $[t_1, t_2]$ is a real positive dense intervals with $t_1 \leq t_2$, $U_{[t_1, t_2]}$ is the *bounded until* operator and μ is an atomic proposition. The *eventually* operator $\Diamond_{[t_1, t_2]}$ and the *always* operator $\Box_{[t_1, t_2]}$ can be defined as usual: $\Diamond_{[t_1, t_2]} \varphi \equiv \top \, U_{[t_1, t_2]} \, \varphi$, $\Box_{[t_1, t_2]} \varphi \equiv \neg \Diamond_{[t_1, t_2]} \neg \varphi$.

3   SSTL: Signal Spatio-Temporal Logic

Signal Spatio-Temporal Logic (SSTL) is a spatial extension of Signal Temporal Logic [8,15] with two spatial modalities: the *bounded somewhere* operator $\diamondsuit_{w_1,w_2}$, defined in [4], and the *bounded surround* operator $\mathcal{S}_{w_1,w_2}$, that we will define here, inspired by the work [5]. In the following, we first introduce spatio-temporal signals, and then present the syntax and the boolean and quantitative semantics of SSTL.

Spatio-Temporal Signals. SSTL is interpreted on spatio-temporal, real-valued signals. Space is discrete and described by a weighted graph $G = (L, E, w)$, as in Sect. 2, while the time domain $\mathbb{T}$ will usually be the real-valued interval $[0, T]$, for some $T > 0$. A spatio-temporal trace is a function $\mathbf{x} : \mathbb{T} \times L \to \mathbb{D}$, where $\mathbb{D} \subseteq \mathbb{R}^n$ is domain of evaluation. As for temporal traces, we write $\mathbf{x}(t, \ell) = (x_1(t, \ell), \ldots, x_n(t, \ell)) \in \mathbb{D}$, where each $x_i : \mathbb{T} \times L \to \mathbb{D}_i$, for $i = 1, \ldots, n$, is the projection on the ith coordinate/variable. Spatio-temporal traces can be obtained by simulating a stochastic model or by computing the solution of a deterministic system. In the previous work [4], some of the authors discussed the framework of patch-based population models, which generalise population models and are a natural setting from which both stochastic and deterministic spatio-temporal traces of the considered type emerge. An alternative source of traces are measurements of real systems. For the purpose of this work, it is irrelevant which is the source of traces, as we are interested in their off-line monitoring.

Spatio-temporal traces are then converted into spatio-temporal boolean or quantitative signals. Similarly to the case of STL, each *atomic predicate* μ_j is of the form $\mu_j(x_1, \ldots, x_n) = (f_j(x_1, \ldots, x_n) \geq 0)$, for $f_j : \mathbb{D} \to \mathbb{R}$. Each atomic proposition gives rise to a spatio-temporal signal. In the boolean case, one may define function $s_j : \mathbb{T} \times L \to \mathbb{B}$; given a trace $\mathbf{x}$, this gives rise to the boolean signal $s_j(t, \ell) = \mu_j(\mathbf{x}(t, \ell))$ by point-wise lifting. Similarly, a quantitative signal is obtained as the real-valued function $s_j : \mathbb{T} \times L \to \mathbb{R}$, with $s_j(t, \ell) = f_j(\mathbf{x}(t, \ell))$.

When the space L is finite, as in our case, we can represent a spatio-temporal signal as a finite collection of temporal signals. More specifically, the signal $s(t, \ell)$ can be equivalently represented by the collection $\{s_\ell(t) \mid \ell \in L\}$. We will stick mostly to this second notation in the following, as it simplifies the presentation.

Syntax. The syntax of SSTL is given by

$$\varphi := \mu \mid \neg \varphi \mid \varphi_1 \wedge \varphi_2 \mid \varphi_1 \, \mathcal{U}_{t_1,t_2} \varphi_2 \mid \diamondsuit_{w_1,w_2} \varphi \mid \varphi_1 \, \mathcal{S}_{w_1,w_2} \varphi_2.$$

Atomic predicates, boolean operators, and the until operator $\mathcal{U}_{t_1,t_2}$ are those of STL. The spatial operators are the *somewhere* operator, $\diamondsuit_{w_1,w_2}$, and the *bounded surround* operator $\mathcal{S}_{w_1,w_2}$, where $[w_1, w_2]$ is a closed real interval with $w_1 \leq w_2$. The spatial somewhere operator $\diamondsuit_{w_1,w_2} \varphi$ requires φ to hold in a location reachable from the current one with a total cost greater than or equal to w_1 and lesser than or equal to w_2. The surround formula $\varphi_1 \, \mathcal{S}_{w_1,w_2} \varphi_2$ is true in a location ℓ, for the trace $\mathbf{x}$, when ℓ belongs to a set of locations

A satisfying φ_1, such that its external boundary B^+A (i.e., all the nearest neighbours external to A of locations in A) contains only locations satisfying φ_2. Furthermore, locations in B^+A must be reached from ℓ by a shortest path of cost between w_1 and w_2. Hence, the surround operator expresses the topological notion of being surrounded by a φ_2-region, with additional metric contraints. We can also derive the *everywhere* operator $\boxdot_{w_1,w_2}\varphi := \neg\diamondsuit_{w_1,w_2}\neg\varphi$ requiring φ to hold in all the locations reachable from the current one with a total cost between w_1 and w_2. Several examples of SSTL formulas, that can be used to clarify one's intuition about the operators defined above, are provided in Sect. 5.

Semantics. We now define the boolean and the quantitative semantics for SSTL. The boolean semantics, as customary, returns true/false depending on whether the observed trace satisfies the SSTL specification.

Definition 2 (Boolean semantics). *The boolean satisfaction relation for an SSTL formula φ over a spatio-temporal trace $\mathbf{x}$ is given by:*

$$
\begin{aligned}
&\mathbf{x},t,\ell \models \mu && \Leftrightarrow && \mu(\mathbf{x}(t,\ell)) = 1 \\
&\mathbf{x},t,\ell \models \neg\varphi && \Leftrightarrow && \mathbf{x},t,\ell \not\models \varphi \\
&\mathbf{x},t,\ell \models \varphi_1 \land \varphi_2 && \Leftrightarrow && \mathbf{x},t,\ell \models \varphi_1 \land \mathbf{x},t,\ell \models \varphi_2 \\
&\mathbf{x},t,\ell \models \varphi_1 \mathcal{U}_{t_1,t_2} \varphi_2 && \Leftrightarrow && \exists t' \in t+[t_1,t_2]:\mathbf{x},t',\ell \models \varphi_2 \land \forall t'' \in (t,t'), \mathbf{x},t'',\ell \models \varphi_1 \\
&\mathbf{x},t,\ell \models \boxdot_{w_1,w_2}\varphi && \Leftrightarrow && \forall \ell' \in L^{\ell}_{w_1,w_2}[\ell,\ell'] : E(w_1 \le w(\ell,\ell') \le w_2) \land \mathbf{x},t,\ell' \models \varphi \\
&\mathbf{x},t,\ell \models \varphi_1 \mathcal{S}_{w_1,w_2} \varphi_2 && \Leftrightarrow && \exists A \subseteq L^{\ell}_{0,w_2}:\ell \in A \land \forall \ell' \in A, \mathbf{x},t,\ell' \models \varphi_1 \\
& && && \land B^+A \subseteq L^{\ell}_{w_1,w_2} \land \forall \ell' \in B^+A, \mathbf{x},t,\ell' \models \varphi_2.
\end{aligned}
$$

A trace $\mathbf{x}$ satisfies φ in location ℓ, denoted by $\mathbf{x},\ell \models \varphi$, if and only if $\mathbf{x},0,\ell \models \varphi$.

The quantitative semantics returns a real value that can be interpreted as a measure of the strength with which the specification is satisfied or falsified by an observed trajectory. More specifically, the sign of such a satisfaction score is related to the truth of the formula (positive stands for true), while the absolute value of the score is a measure of the robustness of the satisfaction or dissatisfaction. This definition of quantitative measure is based on [8,9], and it is a reformulation of the robustness degree of [10].

Definition 3 (SSTL Quantitative Semantics). *The quantitative satisfaction function $\rho(\varphi,\mathbf{x},t,\ell)$ for an SSTL formula φ over a spatio-temporal trace $\mathbf{x}$ is given by:*

$$
\begin{aligned}
&\rho(\mu,\mathbf{x},t,\ell) && = && f(\mathbf{x}(t,\ell)) && \text{where } \mu \equiv f \ge 0 \\
&\rho(\neg\varphi,\mathbf{x},t,\ell) && = && -\rho(\varphi,\mathbf{x},t,\ell) \\
&\rho(\varphi_1 \land \varphi_2,\mathbf{x},t,\ell) && = && \min(\rho(\varphi_1,\mathbf{x},t,\ell),\rho(\varphi_2,\mathbf{x},t,\ell)) \\
&\rho(\varphi_1 \mathcal{U}_{t_1,t_2} \varphi_2,\mathbf{x},t,\ell) && = && \sup_{t' \in t+[t_1,t_2]} \min\Big(\rho(\varphi_2,\mathbf{x},t',\ell), \inf_{t'' \in (t,t')} \rho(\varphi_1,\mathbf{x},t'',\ell)\Big) \\
&\rho(\boxdot_{w_1,w_2}\varphi,\mathbf{x},t,\ell) && = && \max_{\ell' \in L^{\ell}_{w_1,w_2}, [\ell,\ell']:E,w_1 \le w(\ell,\ell') \le w_2} \rho(\varphi,\mathbf{x},t,\ell') \\
&\rho(\varphi_1 \mathcal{S}_{w_1,w_2} \varphi_2,\mathbf{x},t,\ell) && = && \max_{A \subseteq L^{\ell}_{0,w_2},\ell \in A, B^+A \subseteq L^{\ell}_{w_1,w_2}} \Big(\min\big(\min_{\ell' \in A} \rho(\varphi_1,\mathbf{x},t,\ell'), \\
& && && \min_{\ell' \in B^+A} \rho(\varphi_2,\mathbf{x},t,\ell') \big),
\end{aligned}
$$

where ρ is the quantitative satisfaction function, returning a real number $\rho(\varphi, \mathbf{x}, t)$ quantifying the degree of satisfaction of the property φ by the trace $\mathbf{x}$ at time t. Moreover, $\rho(\varphi, \mathbf{x}, \ell) = \rho(\varphi, \mathbf{x}, 0, \ell)$.

The definition for the surround operator is essentially obtained from the boolean semantics by replacing conjunctions and universal quantifications with the minimum and disjunctions and existential quantifications with the maximum, as done in [8,9] for STL.

4 Monitoring Algorithms

In this section, we present the monitoring algorithms to check the validity of a formula φ on a trace $\mathbf{x}(t, \ell)$. The monitoring procedure, which is similar to the ones for STL [9,15], works inductively bottom-up on the parse tree of the formula. In the case of the boolean semantics, for each subformula ψ, it constructs a spatio-temporal signal s_ψ s.t. $s_\psi(\ell, t) = 1$ iff the subformula is true in position ℓ at time t. In the case of the quantitative semantics, for each subformula ψ, the signal s_ψ corresponds to the value of the quantitative satisfaction function ρ, for any time t and location ℓ. In this paper, we discuss the algorithms to check the bounded surround operator. The procedures for the boolean and temporal operators are those of STL [8,9,15], while the methods for the somewhere spatial modality have been previously discussed in [4]. The treatment of the bounded surround modality $\psi = \varphi_1 \mathcal{S}_{w_1, w_2} \varphi_2$, instead, deviates substantially from these procedures. In the following, we will present two recursive algorithms to compute the boolean and the quantitative satisfaction, taking inspiration from [5] and assuming the boolean/quantitative signals of φ_1 and φ_2 being known.

4.1 Description of the Algorithms

Preliminary notions on boolean signals. Before describing Algorithm 1, we need to introduce the definition of *minimal interval covering* $\mathcal{I}_{s_1, ..., s_n}$ *consistent with a set of temporal signals* $s_1, ... s_n$, see also [15].

Definition 4. *Given an interval I, and a set of temporal signals $s_1, ... s_n$ with $s_i(I) \in \mathbb{B}$, the **minimal interval covering** $\mathcal{I}_{s_1, ..., s_n}$ of I consistent with the set of signals $s_1, ..., s_n$ is the shortest finite sequence of left-closed right-open intervals $I_1, ..., I_h$ such that $\bigcup_j I_j = I$, $I_i \cap I_j = \emptyset$, $i \neq j$, and for $k \in \{1, ..., n\}$, $s_k(t) = s_k(t')$ for all t, t' belonging to the same interval. The **positive minimal interval covering** of s is $\mathcal{I}_s = \{ I \in \mathcal{I}_s | \forall t \in I \, s(t) = 1 \}$.*

Monitoring the Boolean semantics of the bounded surround. Algorithm 1 presents the procedure to monitor the boolean semantics of a surround formula $\psi = \varphi_1 \mathcal{S}_{w_1, w_2} \varphi_2$ in a location $\hat{\ell}$, returning the boolean signal $s_{\psi, \hat{\ell}}$ of ψ at location $\hat{\ell}$. The algorithm first computes the set of locations $L^{\hat{\ell}}_{0, w_2}$ that are at distance w_2 or less from $\hat{\ell}$, and then, recursively, the boolean signals $s_{\varphi_1, \ell}$ and

---

Algorithm 1. Boolean monitoring for the surround operator

1: **input** $\hat{\ell}, \psi$ φ_1 w_1, w_2 φ_2
2: ℓ $L^{\hat{\ell}}_{0,w_2}$ compute $s_{\varphi_1, \ell}, s_{\varphi_2, \ell}$
3: compute $s_{\psi, \ell}$ {the minimal interval covering consistent with $s_{\varphi_1, \ell}, s_{\varphi_2, \ell}$, ℓ

   $L^{\hat{\ell}}_{0,w_2}$ }
4: **for all** I_i $s_{\psi, \ell}$ **do**
5:    V ℓ $L^{\hat{\ell}}_{0,w_2}$ $s_{\varphi_1, \ell}$ I_i 1
6:    Q ℓ $L^{\hat{\ell}}_{w_1, w_2}$ $s_{\varphi_2, \ell}$ I_i 1
7:    T B Q V
8:    **while** T **do**
9:       T
10:       **for all** ℓ T **do**
11:          N pre ℓ V ℓ V $\ell E \ell$
12:          V V N
13:          T T N Q
14:       **end for**
15:       T T
16:    **end while**
17:    $s_{\psi, \hat{\ell}}$ I_i $\begin{cases} 1 & \text{if } \ell \quad V, \\ 0 & \text{otherwise.} \end{cases}$
18: **end for**
19: merge adjacent positive interval I_i, i.e. I_i s.t. $s_{\psi, \hat{\ell}}$ I_i 1
20: **return** $s_{\psi, \hat{\ell}}$

$s_{\varphi_2, \ell}$, for ℓ $L^{\hat{\ell}}_{0,w_2}$. These signals provide the satisfaction of the sub-formula φ_1 and φ_2 at each point in time, and for each location of interest. Then, a minimal interval covering consistent to all the signals $s_{\varphi_1, \ell}$ and $s_{\varphi_2, \ell}$ is computed, and to each such interval, a core procedure similar to that of [5] is applied. More specifically, we first compute the set of locations T in which both φ_1 and φ_2 are false, and that are in the external boundary of the locations that satisfy φ_1 (V) or φ_2 (Q). The locations in T are "bad" locations, that cannot be part of the external boundary of the set A of φ_1-locations which has to be surrounded only by φ_2-locations. Hence, the main loop of the algorithm removes iteratively from V all those locations that have a neighbour in T (set N, line 13), constructing a new set T containing only those locations in N that do not satisfy φ_2, until a fixed point is reached. As each location can be added to T and be processed only once, the complexity of the algorithm is linear in the number of locations and linear in the size of the interval covering. Correctness can be proven in a similar way as in [5].

Piecewise constant approximation of quantitative signals. The quantitative semantics for STL is defined for arbitrary signals, but algorithms are provided for piecewise linear continuous ones [8,9], considered as the interpolation of continuous functions. In this paper, we deviate from this interpretation, and consider instead a simpler interpolation based on piecewise constant signals. In particular, we discretise time with step $h > 0$, so that our signals in each location ℓ, $s_\ell : [0, T] \to L \subseteq \mathbb{R}$, are represented by the finite set $\{s_\ell(0), s_\ell(h), \ldots, s_\ell(mh)\}$, where $mh = T$. Then the piecewise constant approximation of $s_\ell(t)$ is the signal $\hat{s}_\ell(t) = s_\ell(kh)$ for $t \in [kh, (k+1)h)$. We further assume, without loss of generality[2], that all time bounds appearing in the temporal operators of a SSTL formula are multiples of h.

Under the assumption that secondary signals are Lipschitz continuous[3], and letting K be the maximum of their individual Lipschitz constants, we have that the following properties hold: (a) $s_\ell(kh) = \hat{s}_\ell(kh)$; and (b) $|s_\ell(t) - \hat{s}_\ell(t)| \leq Kh/2$, uniformly in t.

Monitoring the quantitative semantics. We now turn to the monitoring algorithm for the quantitative semantics, assuming the input is a piecewise constant signal, where the time domain has been discretised with step h. Monitoring boolean operators is straightforward, we just need to apply the definition of the quantitative semantics pointwise in the discretisation. Monitoring the somewhere operator $\diamondsuit_{w_1,w_2} \varphi$ is also immediate: once the location $\hat{\ell}$ of interest is fixed, we can just turn it into a disjunction of the signals $s_{\varphi,\ell}$ for each location $\ell \in L^{\hat{\ell}}_{w_1,w_2}$, see [4] for further details. The time bounded until operator, instead, can also be easily computed by replacing the min and max over dense real intervals in its definition by the corresponding min and max over the corresponding finite grid of time points. In this case, however, we can introduce an error due to the discrete approximation of the Lipschitz continuous signal in intermediate points, yet this error accumulates at a rate proportional to Kh, where K is the previously defined Lipschitz constant.

The only non-trivial monitoring algorithm is the one for the spatial surround operator, which will be discussed below. However, as the satisfaction score is computed at each time point of the discretisation and depends on the values of the signals at that time point only, this algorithm introduces no further error w.r.t. the time discretisation. Hence, we can globally bound the error introduced by the time discretisation:

Proposition 1. *Let the primary signal* $\mathbf{x}$ *be Lipschitz continuous, as the functions defining the atomic predicates. Let K be a Lipschitz constant for all secondary signals, and h be the discretisation step. Given a SSTL formula φ, let $u(\varphi)$ counts the number of temporal until operators in φ, and denote by $\rho(\varphi, \mathbf{x})$ its satisfaction score over the trace $\mathbf{x}$ and by $\rho(\varphi, \hat{\mathbf{x}})$ the satisfaction score over the discretised version $\hat{\mathbf{x}}$ of $\mathbf{x}$ with time step h. Then $|\rho(\varphi, \mathbf{x}) - \rho(\varphi, \hat{\mathbf{x}})| \leq u(\varphi) Kh$.*

Monitoring the quantitative semantics of the bounded surround. The quantitative monitoring procedure for the bounded surround operator is shown

---

in Algorithm 2. Similarly to the boolean case, the algorithm for the surround formula $\psi = \varphi_1 \mathcal{S}_{w_1,w_2} \varphi_2$ takes as input a location $\hat{\ell}$ and returns the quantitative signal $s_{\psi,\hat{\ell}}$, or better its piecewise constant approximation with time-step h (an additional input, together with the signal duration T). As a first step, it computes recursively the quantitative satisfaction signals of subformula φ_1 for all locations $\ell \in L^{\hat{\ell}}_{0,w_2}$ and of subformula φ_2 for all locations $\ell \in L^{\hat{\ell}}_{w_1,w_2}$. Furthermore, it sets all the quantitative signals for φ_1 and φ_2 for the other locations to the constant signal equal to minus infinity. The algorithm runs a fixpoint computation for each time instant in the discrete time set $\{0, h, 2h, \ldots, mh\}$. The procedure is based on computing a function τ, with values in the extended reals $\overline{\mathbb{R}}$, which is executed on the whole set of locations L, but for the modified signals equal to $-\infty$ for locations not satisfying the metric bounds for ℓ. The function τ is defined below.

Definition 5. *Given a finite set of locations L and two functions $s_1 : L \to \overline{\mathbb{R}}$, $s_2 : L \to \overline{\mathbb{R}}$. The function $\tau : \mathbb{N} \times L \to \overline{\mathbb{R}}$ is inductively defined as: (1) $\tau(0,\ell) = s_1(\ell)$ (2) $\tau(i+1,\ell) = \min\{\tau(i,\ell), \min_{\ell' E \ell} \max\{\tau(i,\ell'), s_2(\ell)\}\}$.*

The algorithm then computes the function τ iteratively, until a fixed-point is reached.

Theorem 1. *Let be s_1 and s_2 as in Definition 5, and*

$$s(\ell) = \max_{A \subseteq L, \ell \in A} \min\{\min_{\ell \in A} s_1(\ell), \min_{\ell \in B(A)} s_2(\ell)\},$$

then $\lim_i \tau(i,\ell) = s(\ell)$, $\forall \ell \in L$. Moreover, $\exists K > 0$ s. t. $\tau(j,\ell) = s(\ell), \forall j > K$.

The following corollary provides the correctness of the method. It shows that, when τ is computed for the modified signals constructed by the algorithm, it returns effectively the quantitative satisfaction score of the spatial surround.

Corollary 1. *Given an $\hat{\ell} \in L$, let $\psi = \varphi_1 \mathcal{S}_{w_1,w_2} \varphi_2$ and*

$$s_1(\ell) = \begin{cases} \rho(\varphi_1, \mathbf{x}, t, \ell) & \text{if } 0 \le w(\hat{\ell}, \ell) \le w_2 \\ -\infty & \text{otherwise.} \end{cases} \qquad s_2(\ell) = \begin{cases} \rho(\varphi_2, \mathbf{x}, t, \ell) & \text{if } w_1 \le w(\hat{\ell}, \ell) \le w_2 \\ -\infty & \text{otherwise.} \end{cases}$$

Then $\rho(\psi, \mathbf{x}, t, \hat{\ell}) = s(\hat{\ell}) = \max_{A \subseteq L, \hat{\ell} \in A} \min\{\min_{\ell \in A} s_1(\ell), \min_{\ell \in B(A)} s_2(\ell)\}$.

In order to discuss the complexity of the monitoring procedure, we need an upper bound on the number of iterations of the algorithm. This is given by the following

Proposition 2. *Let d_G be the diameter of the graph G and $\tau(\ell)$ the fixed point of $\tau(i,\ell)$, then $\tau(\ell) = \tau(d_G + 1, \ell)$ for all $\ell \in L$.*

It follows that the computational cost for each location is $O(d_G|L|m)$, where m is the number of sampled time-points. The cost for all locations is therefore $O(d_G|L|^2 m)$.

Algorithm 2. Quantitative monitoring for the surround operator

---

1: **inputs:** $\hat{\ell}, \psi \equiv \varphi_1 \; \mathcal{S}_{[w_1,w_2]} \varphi_2 \,, h, T$
2: **for all** $\ell \in L$ **do**
3: **if** $0 \leq w[\hat{\ell}, \ell] \leq w_2$ **then**
4:   compute $s_{\varphi_1, \ell}$
5:    **if** $w[\hat{\ell}, \ell] \geq w_1$ **then** compute $s_{\varphi_2, \ell}$ **else** $s_{\varphi_2, \ell} \equiv \bot$
6:   **else** $s_{\varphi_1, \ell} \equiv \bot, s_{\varphi_2, \ell} \equiv \bot$
7: **end for**
8: **for all** $t \in 0, h, 2h, \ldots, T$ **do**
9: **for all** $\ell \in L$ **do**
10:   $prec \equiv \ell$
11:    $\ell \equiv s_{\varphi_1, \ell} \ t$
12: **end for**
13: **while** $\exists \ell \in L$, s.t. $prec[\ell] \neq \ell$ **do**
14:   $prec \equiv$
15:   **for all** $\ell \in L$ **do**
16:    $\ell \equiv \min(prec[\ell], \min_{\ell \in E \ell} \max(s_{\varphi_2, \ell} \ t, prec[\ell]))$
17:   **end for**
18: **end while**
19: $s_{\psi, \hat{\ell}} \ t \equiv \hat{\ell}$
20: **end for**
21: **return** $s_{\psi, \hat{\ell}}$

4.2 Implementation

To support qualitative and quantitative monitoring of SSTL properties, a Java library has been developed. This library, named jSSTL[4], consists of three main packages: core, util and io. Package core provides the classes used to represent SSTL formulas. These classes mimic the *abstract syntax tree* of formulas. This package also includes the implementations of the monitoring algorithms presented in this section and of those previously introduced in [4].

Monitoring algorithms are implemented following the *visitor pattern*. Hence, monitoring is performed via a visit of a formula that implements a bottom-up evaluation. It is important to remark that the use of this pattern simplifies the integration of possible alternative monitoring algorithms. Each monitoring algorithm is rendered in terms of a class that is parametrised with respect to a *weighted graph* and provides the method check. The former represents the topology of the considered locations, while the latter takes as parameters an SSTL formula and a list of *piecewise constant signals* (one for each location) and returns a list of piecewise constant signals providing monitoring evaluation. The classes used to represent and manage *piecewise constant signals* are provided within package util. The implementation of weighted graphs relies on JGraphT[5]. This is a free Java graph library that provides mathematical graph-theory objects

---

[4] jSSTL is available on-line at https://bitbucket.org/LauraNenzi/jsstl.
[5] http://jgrapht.org.

and algorithms. Package io provides a set of classes that can be used to read graph models and input signals from an input stream and to write monitoring results to an output stream. Specific interfaces are also provided to simplify the integration of new specific input/output data formats.

5   Example: Pattern Formation in a Reaction-Diffusion System

In this section, we show how SSTL can be used to identify the formation of *patterns* in a reaction-diffusion system. From the point of view of formal verification, the formation of patterns is an inherently spatio-temporal phenomenon, in that the relevant aspect is how the spatial organisation of the system changes over time. Alan Turing theorised in [18] that pattern formation is a consequence of the coupling of reaction and diffusion phenomena involving different chemical species, and can be described by a set of PDE reaction-diffusion equations, one for each species.

Our model, similar to [12,14], describes the production of skin pigments that generate spots in animal furs. The reaction-diffusion system is discretised, according to a Finite Difference scheme, as a system of ODEs whose variables are organised in a $K \times K$ rectangular grid. More precisely, we treat the grid as a weighted undirected graph, where each cell $i,j \in L$ $1,...,K$ $1,...,K$ is a location (node), edges connect each pairs of neighbouring nodes along four directions (so that each node as at most 4 adjacent nodes), and the weight of each edge is always equal to the spatial length-scale δ of the system[6]. We consider two species A and B in a $K \times K$ grid, obtaining the system:

$$\begin{aligned} \frac{dx_{i,j}^A}{dt} &= R_1 x_{i,j}^A x_{i,j}^B - x_{i,j}^A + R_2 + D_1 \mu_{i,j}^A - x_{i,j}^A & i \in 1..,K, \; j \in 1,..,K, \\ \frac{dx_{i,j}^B}{dt} &= R_3 x_{i,j}^A x_{i,j}^B - R_4 + D_2 \mu_{i,j}^B - x_{i,j}^B & i \in 1..,K, \; j \in 1,..,K, \end{aligned} \tag{1}$$

where: $x_{i,j}^A$ and $x_{i,j}^B$ are the concentrations of the two species in the cell i,j ; R_i, $i \in 1,...,4$ are the parameters that define the reaction between the two species; D_1 and D_2 are the diffusion constants; $\mu_{i,j}^A$ and $\mu_{i,j}^B$ are the inputs for the i,j cell, that is

$$\mu_{i,j}^n = \frac{1}{\nu_{i,j}} \sum_{\nu \in \nu_{i,j}} x_\nu^n \qquad n \in A,B , \tag{2}$$

where $\nu_{i,j}$ is the set of indices of cells adjacent to i,j . The spatio-temporal trace of the system is the function $\mathbf{x} = x^A, x^B$ $0,T \times L \to \mathbb{R}^{K \times K} \times \mathbb{R}^{K \times K}$ where each x^A and x^B are the projection on the first and second variable, respectively. In Fig. 1, we report the concentration of A for a number of time points, generated by the numerical integration of System 1; at time $t = 20$ and $t = 50$, the shape of the pattern is apparent and remains stable. We can see that some regions (in blue)

---

[6] For simplicity, here we fix $\delta = 1$. Note that using a non-uniform mesh the weights of the edges of the resulting graph will not be uniform.

have a low concentration of A surrounded by regions with a high concentration of A. We consider as spots of our pattern the regions with low concentration of A. The opposite happens for the value of B (high density regions surrounded by low density regions, not shown).

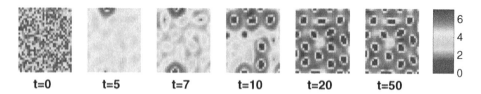

t=0   t=5   t=7   t=10   t=20   t=50

Fig. 1. Value of x^A for the system (1) for $t = 0, 5, 7, 12, 20, 50$ time units with parameters $K = 32, R_1 = 1, R_2 = 12, R_3 = 1, R_4 = 16, D_1 = 5.6$ and $D_2 = 25.5$. The initial condition has been set randomly. The colour map for the concentration is specified in the legend on the right (Color figure online).

The following shows how we can use the surround operator to characterise the behaviour of this system. In order to classify spots, one should identify the sub-regions of the grid that present a high (or low) concentration of a certain species, surrounded by a low (high, respectively) concentration of the same species. Formally, one can e.g., capture the spots of the A species using the spatial formula

$$\varphi_{\text{spot}} = x^A \le h \boxdot_{w_1, w_2} x^A > h . \tag{3}$$

A trace $\mathbf{x}$ satisfies φ_{spot} at time t, in the location (i, j), $(\mathbf{x}, t, (i, j)) \models \varphi_{\text{spot}}$, if and only if there is a subset $L' \subseteq L$, that contains (i, j), such that all elements have a distance less than w_2 from (i, j), and x^A, at time t, is less or equal to h. Furthermore, each element in the boundary of L' has a concentration of A, at time t, greater than h, and its distance from (i, j) is in the interval $[w_1, w_2]$. Note that the use of distance bounds in the surround operator allows one to constrain the size/ diameter of the spot to $[w_1, w_2]$. Recall that we are considering a spatio-temporal system, so this spatial property alone is not enough to describe the formation of a pattern over time; to identify the insurgence time of the pattern and whether it remains stable over time we have to combine the spatial property with temporal operators in this way:

$$\varphi_{\text{pattern}} = \Diamond_{[T_{\text{pattern}}, T_{\text{pattern}} + \delta]} \Box_{[0, T_{\text{end}}]} \varphi_{\text{spot}} ; \tag{4}$$

φ_{pattern} states that eventually at a time between T_{pattern} and $T_{\text{pattern}} + \delta$ the property surround becomes true and remains true for at least T_{end} time units. In Fig. 2(b) we show the validity of the property φ_{pattern} in each cell $(i, j) \in L$, for both the boolean and the quantitative semantics. Recalling that $(\mathbf{x}, \ell) \models \varphi$, if and only if $(\mathbf{x}, 0, \ell) \models \varphi$, for this reason the plots show the satisfaction at time $t = 0$. It is evident how well the procedure is able to identify which locations belong to the spots or not. If we make the distance constraint stricter, by reducing the width of the interval w_1, w_2 , we are able to identify only the "centre" of the spot, as shown in Fig. 2(d). However, in this case we may fail to identify spots that have an irregular shape (i.e., that deviate too much from a circular shape).

Formula φ_{pattern} describes the persistence of a spot in a specific location. To describe a global spatial pattern, i.e. that every location is part of a spot or has a nearby spot, can be expressed in SSTL by the following formula:

$$\varphi_{\text{ST pattern}} \quad 0, w \quad 0, w \quad \varphi_{\text{pattern}}, \tag{5}$$

where   and   are the everywhere and somewhere operators, w is chosen to cover all space, and w measures the maximal distance between spots. Checking this formula in a random location of our space is enough to verify the presence of the pattern; this is enough because the first part of the formula, $0,w$, permits us to reach all the locations of the grid. This is an example of how we can describe global property also with a semantics that verifies properties in the single locations. We verify the property (5) with w 45 and w 15 (the other parameters as in Fig. 2), for a solution of the system (1) obtaining true for the boolean semantics and 0.3 for the quantitative one. The low value of the quantitative semantics is due to the choice of the threshold h.

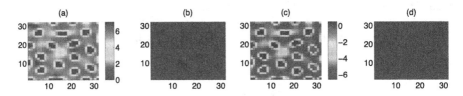

Fig. 2. Validity of formula (4) with h 0.5, T_{pattern} 19, δ 1, T_{end} 30, w_1 1, w_2 6 for (b), (c) and w_2 4 for (d). (a) Concentration of A at time t = 50; (b) (d) Boolean semantics of the property φ_{pattern}; the cells (locations) that satisfy the formula are in red, the others are in blue; (c) Quantitative semantics of the property φ_{pattern}; The value of the robustness is given by a colour map as specified in the legend on the right of the figure (Color figure online).

Changing the diffusion constants D_1 and D_2 affects the shape and size of the spots or disrupts them (Fig. 3(a)). We evaluate formula (5) for model (1) with parameters D 1.5, 23.6 and D 8.5, 40.7 , as in Fig. 2(a), and it results false with a quantitative value equal to -0.05 for both. Formula (4), instead, is still true in some locations. This is due to the irregularity of the spots (where, as Fig. 3(a) left, some spots can have a shape similar to the model in Fig. 2(a)), or due to particular boundary effects on the border of the grid (where fractions of spots still remain, as in Fig. 3(a) right).

A strength of spatio-temporal logics is the possibility to nest the temporal and spatial operators. We illustrate this in the following scenario. We assume as initial conditions of the system (1) its stable state, i.e. the concentrations of A and B at time 50 (see Fig. 2(a)). We introduce a small perturbation, by changing a single value in a specific location in the centre of a spot. The idea is to study the effect of this perturbation, i.e. checking if it will disrupt the system or not. Specifically, we perturb the cell $6, 6$, setting $x^A_{6,6} = 0 \ll 10$. Dynamically, the perturbation is quickly absorbed and the system returns to the previous steady state. Formally, we can consider the following property:

$$\varphi_{\text{pert}} = x^A < h_{\text{pert}} \land \varphi_1 \boxminus_{w_m, w_M} \varphi_2 ; \tag{6}$$

$\mathbf{x}, i, j \vDash \varphi_{\text{pert}}$, i.e. a trace $\mathbf{x}$ satisfies φ_{pert} in the location i, j, if and only if $x^A_{i,j} < 0 < h_{\text{pert}}$ (the location is perturbed) and if there is a subset $L \subseteq L$ that contains i, j such that all its elements have a distance less than w_M from i, j and satisfy $\varphi_1 = \mathcal{F}_{0,T_p} \mathcal{G}_{0,T_d} x^A > h$; φ_1 states that the perturbation of x^A is absorbed within T_p units of time, stabilising back to a value $x^A > h$ for additional T_d time units. Furthermore, within distance w_m, w_M from the original perturbation, where w_M is chosen such that we are within the spot of the non-perturbed system, $\varphi_2 = \mathcal{G}_{0,T} x^A < h$ is satisfied; i.e. no relevant effect is observed, the value of x^A stably remains below h. The meaning of φ_{pert} is that the induced perturbation remains confined inside the original spot. In Fig. 3(b) we report the evaluation of the quantitative semantics for φ_{pert}, zooming in on the 15×15 lower left corner of the original grid. All the locations that are not plotted have been evaluated and do not satisfy the property. As shown in the figure, the only location that satisfies this property is the perturbed one, $6, 6$.

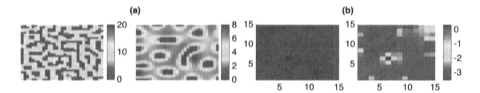

Fig. 3. (a) Snapshots at time $t = 50$ of x^A for the model (1) with $D = 1.5, 23.6$ (on the left) and $D = 8.5, 40.7$ (on the right). (b) Boolean and quantitative semantics for the formula φ_{pert} with $h_{\text{pert}} = 10$, $w_m = 1$, $w_M = 2$, $T_p = 1$, $T_d = 10$, $h = 3$, and $T = 20$.

Model (1) has been coded in Matlab/Octave, and the monitoring has been performed by our Java implementation. As time performance, the verification of property φ_{pattern} took 1.04 s (boolean) and 69.39 s (quantitative) for all locations and 100 time points, while property $\varphi_{\text{ST pattern}}$ took 1.81 s and 70.06 s, and property φ_{pert} took 28, 19 s and 55, 31 s, respectively. The computation of the distance matrix can be done just once because it remains always the same for a given system, this takes about 23 s. All the experiments were run on a Intel Core i5 2.6 GHz CPU, with 8 GB 1600 MHz RAM.

6 Discussion

We extended the Signal Spatio-Temporal Logic [4], a spatio-temporal extension of STL [9], with the spatial surround operator from [5]. In SSTL, spatial and temporal operators can be arbitrarily nested. We provided the logic with a boolean and a quantitative semantics in the style of STL [9], and defined novel monitoring algorithms to evaluate such semantics on spatio-temporal trajectories. The monitoring procedures, implemented in Java, have been applied on a Turing reaction-diffusion system modelling a process of morphogenesis [18] in which spots are formed over time.

This work can be extended in several directions. First, we plan to perform a more thorough investigation of the expressivity of the logic, and to apply it on further case studies. In particular, we remark that SSTL can also be applied to describe properties of stochastic spatio-temporal systems, and the monitoring algorithms can be plugged in seamlessly into statistical model checking routines. Secondly, we plan to extend our logic to more general quasi-discrete metric spatial structures, exploiting the topological notion of closure spaces [5] and extending it to the metric case. Note that the current monitoring algorithms work already for more general spatial structures, like finite directed weighted graphs, but we plan to provide a more precise characterisation of the class of discrete spatial structures on which they can be applied. We will also optimise the implementation to improve performance, and additionally investigate if and how directionality can be expressed in SSTL. Finally, we plan to exploit the quantitative semantics for the robust design of spatio-temporal systems, along the lines of [3].

References

1. Aiello, M., Pratt-Hartmann, I., van Benthem, J. (eds.): Handbook of Spatial Logics. Springer, Netherlands (2007)
2. Alur, R., Feder, T., Henzinger, T.: The benefits of relaxing punctuality. J. ACM **43**(1), 116–146 (1996)
3. Bartocci, E., Bortolussi, L., Nenzi, L., Sanguinetti, G.: System design of stochastic models using robustness of temporal properties. Theor. Comput. Sci. **587**, 3–25 (2015)
4. Bortolussi, L., Nenzi, L.: Specifying and monitoring properties of stochastic spatio-temporal systems in signal temporal logic. In: Proceedings of VALUETOOLS (2014)
5. Ciancia, V., Latella, D., Loreti, M., Massink, M.: Specifying and verifying properties of space. In: Diaz, J., Lanese, I., Sangiorgi, D. (eds.) TCS 2014. LNCS, vol. 8705, pp. 222–235. Springer, Heidelberg (2014)
6. Ciancia, V., Gilmore, S., Grilletti, G., Latella, D., Loreti, M., Massink, M.: Spatio-temporal model-checking of vehicular movement in public transport systems. (Submitted, 2015)
7. Ciancia, V., Gilmore, S., Latella, D., Loreti, M., Massink, M.: Data verification for collective adaptive systems: spatial model-checking of vehicle location data. In: Proceedings of SASOW (2014)
8. Donzé, A., Ferrère, T., Maler, O.: Efficient robust monitoring for STL. In: Sharygina, N., Veith, H. (eds.) CAV 2013. LNCS, vol. 8044, pp. 264–279. Springer, Heidelberg (2013)

9. Donzé, A., Maler, O.: Robust satisfaction of temporal logic over real-valued signals. In: Chatterjee, K., Henzinger, T.A. (eds.) FORMATS 2010. LNCS, vol. 6246, pp. 92–106. Springer, Heidelberg (2010)

10. Fainekos, G.E., Pappas, G.J.: Robustness of temporal logic specifications for continuous-time signals. Theore. Comput. Sci. **410**(42), 4262–4291 (2009)

11. Galton, A.: The mereotopology of discrete space. In: Freksa, C., Mark, D.M. (eds.) COSIT 1999. LNCS, vol. 1661, pp. 251–266. Springer, Heidelberg (1999)

12. Gol, E.A., Bartocci, E., Belta, C.: A formal methods approach to pattern synthesis in reaction diffusion systems. In: Proceedings of CDC (2014)

13. Grosu, R., Bartocci, E., Corradini, F., Entcheva, E., Smolka, S.A., Wasilewska, A.: Learning and detecting emergent behavior in networks of cardiac myocytes. In: Egerstedt, M., Mishra, B. (eds.) HSCC 2008. LNCS, vol. 4981, pp. 229–243. Springer, Heidelberg (2008)

14. Haghighi, I., Jones, A., Kong, J.Z., Bartocci, E., Grosu, R., Belta, C.: SpaTeL: a novel spatial-temporal logic and its applications to networked systems. In: Proceedings of HSCC (2015)

15. Maler, O., Nickovic, D.: Monitoring temporal properties of continuous signals. In: Lakhnech, Y., Yovine, S. (eds.) FORMATS 2004 and FTRTFT 2004. LNCS, vol. 3253, pp. 152–166. Springer, Heidelberg (2004)

16. Mari, L., Bertuzzo, E., Righetto, L., Casagrandi, R., Gatto, M., Rodriguez-Iturbe, I., Rinaldo, A.: Modelling cholera epidemics: the role of waterways, human mobility and sanitation. J. Roy. Soc. Interface **9**(67), 376–388 (2012)

17. Nenzi, L., Bortolussi, L., Ciancia, V., Loreti, M., Massink, M.: Qualitative and quantitative monitoring of spatio-temporal properties. extended version. Technical report 06, QUANTICOL (2015). http://goo.gl/fWx88i

18. Turing, A.M.: The chemical basis of morphogenesis. Philos. Trans. Roy. Soc. Lond. B Biol. Sci. **237**(641), 37–72 (1952)

Runtime Adaptation for Actor Systems

Ian Cassar and Adrian Francalanza[✉]

CS, ICT, University of Malta, Msida, Malta
{icas0005,afra1}@um.edu.mt

Abstract. We study the problem of extending RV techniques in the context of (asynchronous) actor systems, so as to be able to carry out a degree of system *adaptation* at runtime. We propose extensions to specification logics that provide handles for *programming* both monitor synchronisations (with individual actors), as well as the administration of the *resp.* adaptations once the triggering behaviour is observed. Since this added functionality allows the specifier to introduce *erroneous* adaptation procedures, we also develop *static analysis* techniques based on substructural type systems to assist the construction of correct adaptation scripts.

1   Introduction

Runtime Adaptation (RA) [16,17] is a technique prevalent to long-running, highly available software systems, whereby system characteristics (*e.g.,* its structure, locality *etc.*) are altered *dynamically* in response to runtime events (*e.g.,* detected hardware faults or software bugs, changes in system loads), while causing *limited disruption* to the execution of the system. Numerous examples can be found in service-oriented architectures [15,21] (*e.g.,* cloud-services, web-services, *etc.*) for self-configuring, self-optimising and self-healing purposes; the inherent component-based, decoupled organisation of such systems facilitates the implementation of adaptive actions *affecting a subset* of the system while allowing other parts to continue executing normally.

Actor systems [2,9,14] consist of *independently*-executing components called *actors*. Every actor is *uniquely-identifiable*, has its own *local memory*, and can either *spawn* other actors or interacting with them through *asynchronous messaging*.[1] Actors are often used to build service-oriented systems with limited downtime [3,14]. Coding practices such as *fail-fast* design-patterns [9,14] already advocate for a degree of RA for building robust, fault-tolerant systems: through mechanisms such as *process linking* and *supervision trees*, crashed actors are detected by *supervisor* actors, which respond through adaptations such as *restarting* the actors, *replacing* them with limp-home surrogate actors, or *killing* further actors that may potentially be affected by the crash.

In this paper, we study ways how RA for actor systems can be *extended* to respond to runtime events that go beyond actor crashes. For instance, we would

---

[1] Messages are received in a message buffer called a *mailbox*, read only by the owning actor.

E. Bartocci and R. Majumdar (Eds.): RV 2015, LNCS 9333, pp. 38–54, 2015.
DOI: 10.1007/978-3-319-23820-3_3

like to observe *sequences of events* that allow us to take *preemptive* action before a crash happens; alternatively, we would also like to observe *positive* (liveness) events that allow us to adapt the system to execute more *efficiently* (*e.g.*, by switching off unused parts). More generally, we intend to develop a framework for extending actor-system functionality through RA, so as to improve aspects such as resilience and resource management.

We propose to do this by *extending existing* Runtime Verification (RV) tools such as [10–12,25]. The appeal of such an approach is that RV tools *already* provide mechanisms for *specifying* the behaviour to be observed, together with *instrumentation mechanisms* for observing such behaviour. As a proof-of-concept, our study focusses on one of these actor-based RV tools — detectEr[2] [7,12] — and investigates ways how violation detections can be *replaced* by adaptation actions that respond to behaviours detected, while reusing as many elements as possible from the hosting technology.

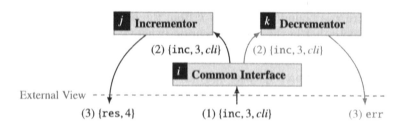

Fig. 1. A server actor implementation offering integer increment and decrement services

Example 1. Figure 1 depicts a server consisting of a front-end *Common Interface* actor with identifier i receiving client requests, a back-end *Incrementor* actor with identifier j, handling integer increment requests, and a back-end *Decrementor* actor k, handing decrement requests. A client sends service requests to actor i of the form $\{tag, arg, ret\}$ where *tag* selects the type of service, *arg* carries the service arguments and *ret* specifies the return address for the result (typically the client actor ID). The interface actor forwards the request to one of its back-end servers (depending on the *tag*) whereas the back-end servers process the requests, sending results (or error messages) to *ret*. The tool detectEr allows us to specify safety properties such as (1), explained below:

$$\varphi \overset{\text{def}}{=} \max Y. [i?\{\text{inc}, x, y\}] \left(\left([j \triangleright y!\{\text{res}, x+1\}] Y \right) \& \left([\_\triangleright y!\text{err}] \text{ff} \right) \right) \quad (1)$$

It is a (recursive, max Y....) property requiring that, from an *external* viewpoint, *every* increment request received by i, action $i\{\text{inc}, x, y\}$, is followed by an answer from j to the address y carrying $x+1$, action $j \triangleright y!\{\text{res}, x+1\}$ (recursing through variable Y). However, increment requests followed by an error message sent from

---

[2] An RV tool for long-running reactive (actor) systems written in Erlang [3].

any actor back to y, action $\_ \triangleright y!\mathtt{err}$, represent a violation, ff. detectEr can synthesise a monitor (a system of actors) corresponding to (1) and instrument it with a system execution [12].

$$\mathsf{max}\ Y.[i?\{\mathtt{inc}, x, y\}]\ (([j \triangleright y!\{\mathtt{res}, x + 1\}]\ Y)\ \&\ ([z \triangleright y!\mathtt{err}]\ \mathsf{restr}(i)\ \mathsf{prg}(z)\ Y))\tag{2}$$

We aim to *extend* properties such as (1) with *adaptation actions* to be taken by the monitor once a violation is detected, as shown in property (2) above. The specifier presumes that the error (which may arise after a number of correct interactions) is caused by the interface actor i (as shown in Fig. 1, where an $\mathtt{inc}$ request is erroneously forwarded to the decrementor actor k) — she may, for instance, have prior knowledge that actor i is a newly-installed, untested component. The monitor thus restarts actor i, adaptation $\mathsf{restr}(i)$, and empties the mailbox of the backend server—which may contain more erroneously forwarded messages—through adaptation $\mathsf{prg}(z)$ (the actor to be purged is determined at runtime, where z is bound to identifier k from the previous action $[z \triangleright y!\mathtt{err}]$). Importantly, note that in the above execution (where k is the actor sending the error message), actor j is *not affected* by any adaptation action taken. ∎

To implement adaptation sequences such as those in Example 1, the *resp.* monitors require adequate synchronisation control over the asynchronous system being monitored. For instance, to mitigate effects of erroneous components as soon as detections are made, the monitor may want to synchronise with the execution of actor i from Fig. 1 each time a client request is received, temporarily suspending its execution until it determines that the request is serviced correctly (at which point it is released again). Moreover, adaptations such as actor restarts and mailbox purging require the *resp.* actors to be *temporarily suspended* for the adaptation implementation to execute correctly.

Adequate synchronisation procedures are generally hard to infer and automate from specification scripts such as (2) of Example 1 (*e.g.,* an early suspension of actor i's execution — before it communicates with one of its backend actors — stalls the entire system) and is exacerbated by findings in prior work [7], concluding that actor synchronisations carry substantial overheads and should thus be kept to a minimum. In our work, we thus extend the specification language to include *explicit* de/synchronisation commands, thereby transferring synchronisation responsibility to the specifier of the adaptation property. This allows for *fine-tuned* synchronisations carrying low overheads, but also permits the specifier to *introduce synchronisation errors* herself (*e.g.,* applying synchronous adaptations to actors that are not yet synchronised).

Therefore, in this paper we also develop a type system that analyses specification scripts with adaptations and de/synchronisation commands and identifies errors prior to deployment. We also prove that the type system is—in some sense—sound, accepting scripts are free from certain monitor runtime errors. Since static analyses typically approximate computation, the type system may reject otherwise valid specification scripts; in such cases, the specifier may use the type system as a tool assisting script development, directing her to the parts that may potentially lead to errors.

In what follows, Sect. 2 presents the logic used by detectEr and Sects. 3 and 4 extend this with synchronisation directives and adaptation mechanisms. Section 5 presents our type system. This is accompanied in Sect. 6 by an extended runtime semantics for monitors carrying dynamic checks corresponding to the type disciplines of Sect. 5; we prove type system soundness *wrt.* this runtime semantics. Section 7 concludes.

2   The Logic

Following [7,12], detectEr (safety) properties are expressed using the logic sHML [1], a syntactic subset of the modal μ-calculus [18]. The syntax is defined in Fig. 2 and assumes two distinct denumerable sets of *term variables*, $x, y, \ldots \in$ VAR (to quantify over values) and *formula variables* $X, Y, \ldots \in$ LVAR (to define recursive logical formulas). It is parametrised by boolean expressions, $b, c \in$ BOOL equipped with a *decidable* evaluation function, $b \Downarrow c$ where $c \in \{\text{true}, \text{false}\}$, and a set of action patterns $e \in$ PAT that may contain term variables. Formulas include truth and falsehood, tt and ff, conjunctions, $\varphi \& \psi$, modal necessities, $[e]\varphi$, maximal fixpoints (for recursive properties), max $X.\varphi$, and conditionals to reason about data, if b then φ else ψ. Free term variables in a subformula φ of a necessity formula, $[e]\varphi$ are *bound* by the variables used in the pattern e; similarly max $X.\varphi$ is a binder for X in φ. We work up-to *alpha*-conversion of formulas.

Syntax

$$\varphi, \psi \in \text{FRM} ::= \text{tt} \mid \text{ff} \mid \varphi \& \psi \mid [e]\varphi \mid X \mid \text{max } X.\ \varphi \mid \text{if } b \text{ then } \varphi \text{ else } \psi$$

Semantics

$$\varphi_1 \& \varphi_2 \equiv \varphi_2 \& \varphi_1 \qquad \varphi_1 \& (\varphi_2 \& \varphi_3) \equiv (\varphi_1 \& \varphi_2) \& \varphi_3 \qquad \text{tt} \& \varphi \equiv \varphi \qquad \text{ff} \& \varphi \equiv \text{ff}$$

$$\text{RIDEM1} \frac{}{\text{ff} \xrightarrow{\alpha} \text{ff}} \qquad\qquad \text{RIDEM2} \frac{}{\text{tt} \xrightarrow{\alpha} \text{tt}}$$

$$\text{RTRU} \frac{b \Downarrow \text{true}}{\text{if } b \text{ then } \varphi \text{ else } \psi \xrightarrow{\tau} \varphi} \qquad \text{RFLS} \frac{b \Downarrow \text{false}}{\text{if } b \text{ then } \varphi \text{ else } \psi \xrightarrow{\tau} \psi} \qquad \text{RSTR} \frac{\varphi \equiv \varphi' \xrightarrow{\gamma} \psi' \equiv \psi}{\varphi \xrightarrow{\gamma} \psi}$$

$$\text{RCN1} \frac{\varphi \xrightarrow{\alpha} \varphi' \quad \psi \xrightarrow{\alpha} \psi'}{\varphi \& \psi \xrightarrow{\alpha} \varphi' \& \psi'} \qquad \text{RCN2} \frac{\varphi \xrightarrow{\tau} \varphi'}{\varphi \& \psi \xrightarrow{\tau} \varphi' \& \psi} \qquad \text{RCN3} \frac{\psi \xrightarrow{\tau} \psi'}{\varphi \& \psi \xrightarrow{\tau} \varphi \& \psi'}$$

$$\text{RMAX} \frac{}{\text{max } X.\ \varphi \xrightarrow{\tau} \varphi[\text{max } X.\ \varphi/X]} \qquad \text{RNc1} \frac{\text{mtch}(e, \alpha) = \sigma}{[e]\varphi \xrightarrow{\alpha} \varphi\sigma} \qquad \text{RNc2} \frac{\text{mtch}(e, \alpha) = \bot}{[e]\varphi \xrightarrow{\alpha} \text{tt}}$$

Fig. 2. The logic and its derivative semantics

A derivative semantics [24] for the *closed and guarded* logic formulas is given as a Labelled Transition System (LTS), defined by the transition rules in Fig. 2. It models the monitoring for violations of the *resp.* (safety) property, and assumes a set of (visible) actions $\alpha, \beta \in$ ACT and a distinguished *silent* action, τ (we let γ range over ACT $\cup \{\tau\}$). Visible actions represent system operations and contain values $v, u \in$ VAL, that range over either actor identifiers, $i, j, h \in$ PID, or generic data such as integers, $d \in$ DATA. The semantics also assumes a partial function $\mathsf{match}(e, \alpha)$ matching action patterns, e, with visible actions, α; when a match is successful, the function returns a substitution from the term variable found in the pattern to the corresponding values of the matched action, $\sigma :: \text{VAR} \rightharpoonup \text{VAL}$. We work up-to structural equivalence of formulas $\varphi \equiv \psi$; see rules in Fig. 2 for commutativity, associativity *etc.*

In Fig. 2, formulas tt and ff are idempotent *wrt.* external transitions and interpreted as final states (verdicts). Conditional formulas silently branch to the *resp.* subformula depending on the evaluation of the boolean expression (RTRU and RFLS) whereas rule RMAX silently unfolds a recursive formula. Necessity formulas, $[e]\varphi$, transition only with a *visible* action, α: if the action matches the pattern, $\mathsf{mtch}(e, \alpha) = \sigma$, it transitions to the necessity subformula where the variables bound by the matched pattern are substituted with the *resp.* matched values obtained from the action, $\varphi\sigma$; otherwise, the necessity formula transitions to tt in case of a mismatch (RNc2) — see [7] for details. The rules for conjunction formulas model the parallel execution of subformulas as described in [12]: subformulas are allowed to perform independent silent transitions (RCN2 and RCN3) but transition together for external actions, depending on their individual transitions (RCN1). Finally, RSTR allows us to abstract over structurally equivalent formulas. We write $\varphi \overset{\gamma}{\Rightarrow} \psi$ in lieu of $\varphi(\overset{\tau}{\longrightarrow})^* \overset{\gamma}{\longrightarrow} (\overset{\tau}{\longrightarrow})^*\psi$. We let $t \in$ ACT* range over *lists* of *visible* actions and write $\varphi \overset{t}{\Rightarrow} \psi$ to denote $\varphi \overset{\alpha_1}{\Longrightarrow} \ldots \overset{\alpha_n}{\Longrightarrow} \psi$ where $t = \alpha_1 \ldots \alpha_n$.

Example 2. Recall property φ from (1) of Example 1. Using the semantics of Fig. 2, we can express an execution leading to a violation detection for the action sequence below as:

$$\varphi \xrightarrow{i?\{\mathrm{inc},5,h\}} \big(\big(\,[j \triangleright h!\{\mathbf{res}, 5+1\}]\,\varphi\big)\ \&\ \big(\,[\_\triangleright h!\mathrm{err}]\,\mathrm{ff}\big)\big)$$

(using rules RMAX and RNc1, where $\mathsf{mtch}(i?\{\mathtt{inc}, x, y\}, i?\{\mathtt{inc}, 5, h\}) = \{x \mapsto 5, y \mapsto h\}$)

$$\xrightarrow{\;j \triangleright h!\{\mathbf{res},6\}\;} \varphi \xrightarrow{i?\{\mathrm{inc},3,h'\}} \big(\big(\,[j \triangleright h'!\{\mathbf{res}, 3+1\}]\,\varphi\big)\ \&\ \big(\,[\_\triangleright h'!\mathrm{err}]\,\mathrm{ff}\big)\big) \xrightarrow{k \triangleright h'!\mathrm{err}} \mathrm{ff} \quad \blacksquare$$

The derivative semantics corresponds to the violation semantics of [12]: actor A with trace t violates φ, assertion $(A, t) \vDash_v \varphi$, iff φ transitions to ff along t and A can generate t.

Theorem 1 (Semantic Correspondence). $(A, t) \vDash_v \varphi$ *iff* $(\varphi \overset{t}{\Rightarrow} \mathrm{ff}$ *and* $A \overset{t}{\Rightarrow})$

3   Designing Runtime Adaptation Mechanisms

(Erlang) actor systems, such as those monitored for by detectEr, provide natural *units of adaptations* in terms of the individual actors themselves. We identify *two* classes of adaptation actions, namely *asynchronous* adaptations, $\mathsf{aA}(w)$, and *synchronous* adaptations, $\mathsf{sA}(w)$: they both take a list of actor references as argument — $w, r \in (\mathrm{PID} \cup \mathrm{VAR})^*$. In particular, whereas asynchronous adaptations may be administered on the *resp.* actors while they are executing, the synchronous ones require the adaptees' execution to be suspended for the adaptation to function correctly. Examples of asynchronous adaptations include actor (*i.e.*, process [3]) killing and actor linking/unlinking; both examples are native (and atomic) commands offered by the host language [3]. We have implemented additional adaptation actions that require a more complex sequence of operations, such as a *purge* action (it empties the messages contained in the actor's mailbox), and a *restart* action (it restarts the actor execution, emptying its mailbox and refreshing its internal state, while preserving its unique identifier); these constitute examples of synchronous adaptations that require the suspension of the *resp.* actor.

Synchronous adaptations require a mechanism for *gradually* suspending the actor executions of interest while a property is being monitored for, so that actors are in the required status when the adaptation is administered. There are many ways how one can program incremental synchronisations between the system and the monitor. We chose to piggyback on the specification scripts presented in Sect. 2 and extend necessity formulas with a synchronisation modality, $[e]^\rho \varphi$, where ρ ranges over either b (blocking), stating that the subject of the action (*i.e.*, an actor) is suspended if the action is matched by pattern e, or a (asynchronous), stating that the action subject is allowed to continue executing asynchronously when the pattern e is matched. We recall that if the necessity formula $[e]\varphi$ mismatches with a trace action, its observation terminates (see RNC2 in Fig. 2); in our case this would also mean that the synchronous adaptation contained in the continuation, φ (for which we have been incrementally blocking actor executions) are never administered. In such cases, we provide a mechanism for *releasing* the actors blocked thus far: necessity formulas are further extended with a list of actor references, r, that denote the (blocked) actors to be released in case the necessity pattern e mismatches, $[e]^\rho_r \varphi$. Since adaptations in a script may be followed by further observations, we also require a similar release mechanism for adaptation actions, $\mathsf{aA}(w)_r$ and $\mathsf{sA}(w)_r$, where the actor list r is unblocked after the adaptation is administered to the actors w.

Remark 1. Although minimally intrusive, the expressivity of our mechanism for incremental synchronisation relies on what system actions can be observed (*i.e.*, the level of abstraction the system is monitored at). For instance, recall the system depicted in Fig. 1. If monitored from an external viewpoint, the communications sent from the interface actor, i, to the backend actors, j and h, are *not* visible (according to [12], they are seen as internal τ-actions). However, for observations required by properties such as (2), we would need to block actor i only *after* it sends a message to either of the backend actors—otherwise the entire system blocks. This requires observing the system at a *lower level of abstraction*, where certain τ-actions are converted into visible ones *e.g.*, the instrumentation used by detectEr allows us to observe internal actions such as function calls or internal messages sent between actors as discussed for Fig. 1. See [7] for more examples of this.

Example 3. The script extensions discussed in this section allow us to augment the adaptation script outlined in (2) from Example 1 as follows:

$$\varphi' \overset{\text{def}}{=} \max Y.[i?\{\texttt{inc},x,y\}]_\epsilon^a$$
$$[\texttt{tau}(i,\_,\{\texttt{inc},x,y\})]_\epsilon^b \left(\begin{array}{l} ([j\triangleright y!\{\texttt{res},x+1\}]_\epsilon^a \ Y) \ \& \\ ([z\triangleright y!\texttt{err}]_i^b \ \texttt{restr}(i)_\epsilon \ \texttt{prg}(z)_{i,z} Y) \end{array} \right)$$
$$(3)$$

After *asynchronously* observing action i ?$\{\texttt{inc},v,h\ \}$ (for some v, h pattern matched to x and y *resp.*), the monitor *synchronously* listens (modality b) for an internal communication action from i to some actor with this data, $\{\texttt{inc},v,h\ \}$, action $[\texttt{tau}(i,\_,\{\texttt{inc},x,y\})]_\epsilon^b$. If this action is observed, the subject of the action, *i.e.*, actor i, is blocked. If the subsequent action observed is an error reply, $z\triangleright h!\texttt{err}$ (from an actor bound to z at runtime), we block actor z (again, note modality b) and start the synchronous adaptation actions, $\texttt{restr}(i)_\epsilon$ and $\texttt{prg}(z)_{i;z}$. Note that the last adaptation action releases the two blocked actors i and z before recursing; similarly the necessity formula for the error reply releases the blocked actor i if the *resp.* action is not matched, $[z\triangleright y!\texttt{err}]_i^b$.   ∎

4   A Formal Model for Runtime Adaptation

Figure 3 describes a semantics for the extended logic with adaptations discussed in Sect. 3. Apart from the extended necessity and the asynchronous/synchronous adaptation formulas, it uses two additional constructs, $\texttt{blk}(r)\ \varphi$ and $\texttt{rel}(r)\ \varphi$; these are not meant to be part of the specification scripts but are used as part of the runtime syntax. Since the extended logic affects the system being monitored through adaptations and synchronisations, the operational semantics is given in terms of *configurations*, $s \triangleright \varphi$. In addition to closed formulas, configurations include the monitored system represented abstractly as a partial map, $s :: \text{PID} \rightharpoonup \{\bullet,\circ\}$, describing whether an actor (through its unique identifier) is currently blocked (suspended), $\bullet$, or executing, $\circ$. We occasionally write $w : \bullet$ to denote the list of mappings $i_1 : \bullet, \ldots, i_n : \bullet$ where $w = i_1, \ldots, i_n$ (similarly for $w : \circ$).

To describe adaptation interactions between the monitor and the system, the LTS semantics of Fig. 3 employs four additional labels, ranged over by the variable μ. These include the asynchronous and synchronous adaptation labels, $\mathbf{a}(w)$ and $\mathbf{s}(w)$, to denote *resp.* that an asynchronous and synchronous action affecting actors w has been executed. They also include a blocking action, $\mathbf{b}(w)$, and an unblocking (release) action, $\mathbf{r}(w)$, affecting the execution of actors with identifiers in the list w.

Extended Logic Syntax with Adaptations and Synchronisations

$$\varphi, \psi \in \text{FRM} ::= \quad \dots \quad | \quad [e]^\rho_w \, \varphi \quad | \quad \text{aA}(r)_w \varphi \quad | \quad \text{sA}(r)_w \varphi \quad | \quad \text{blk}(r) \, \varphi \quad | \quad \text{rel}(r) \, \varphi$$

Monitor Transition Rules

$$\text{RNC1} \, \frac{\text{mtch}(e, \alpha) = \sigma \quad \text{subj}(\alpha) = i}{[e]^b_r \, \varphi \xrightarrow{\alpha} \text{blk}(i) \, (\varphi \sigma)} \qquad \text{RNC2} \, \frac{\text{mtch}(e, \alpha) = \sigma}{[e]^a_r \, \varphi \xrightarrow{\alpha} \varphi \sigma}$$

$$\text{RNC3} \, \frac{\text{mtch}(e, \alpha) = \bot}{[e]^\rho_r \, \varphi \xrightarrow{\alpha} \text{rel}(r) \, \text{tt}} \qquad \text{RADA} \, \frac{}{\text{aA}(w)_r \varphi \xrightarrow{\text{a}(w)} \text{rel}(r) \, \varphi} \qquad \text{RADS} \, \frac{}{\text{sA}(w)_r \varphi \xrightarrow{\text{s}(w)} \text{rel}(r) \, \varphi}$$

$$\text{RREL} \, \frac{}{\text{rel}(r) \, \varphi \xrightarrow{\text{r}(r)} \varphi} \qquad \text{RBLK} \, \frac{}{\text{blk}(r) \, \varphi \xrightarrow{\text{b}(r)} \varphi} \qquad \text{RCN4} \, \frac{\varphi \xrightarrow{\mu} \varphi'}{\varphi \, \& \, \psi \xrightarrow{\mu} \varphi' \, \& \, \psi}$$

System Transition Rules

$$\text{SNEW} \, \frac{}{s \xrightarrow{\tau} s, i : \circ} \qquad \text{SACT} \, \frac{\text{subj}(\alpha) = i \quad \text{ids}(\alpha) \subseteq \text{dom}(s)}{s, i : \circ \xrightarrow{\alpha} s, i : \circ} \qquad \text{SADA} \, \frac{w \subseteq \text{dom}(s)}{s \xrightarrow{\text{a}(w)} s}$$

$$\text{SBLK} \, \frac{}{s, w : \circ \xrightarrow{\text{b}(w)} s, w : \bullet} \qquad \text{SREL} \, \frac{}{s, w : \bullet \xrightarrow{\text{r}(w)} s, w : \circ} \qquad \text{SADS} \, \frac{}{s, w : \bullet \xrightarrow{\text{s}(w)} s, w : \bullet}$$

Instrumentation Transition Rules

$$\text{IADA} \, \frac{\varphi \xrightarrow{\mu} \varphi' \quad s \xrightarrow{\mu} s'}{s \triangleright \varphi \xrightarrow{\tau} s' \triangleright \varphi'} \qquad \text{IACT} \, \frac{\varphi \xrightarrow{\mu} \quad s \xrightarrow{\alpha} s' \quad \varphi \xrightarrow{\alpha} \varphi'}{s \triangleright \varphi \xrightarrow{\alpha} s' \triangleright \varphi'}$$

$$\text{ITRM} \, \frac{\varphi \xrightarrow{\mu} \quad s \xrightarrow{\alpha} s' \quad \varphi \xrightarrow{\alpha}}{s \triangleright \varphi \xrightarrow{\alpha} s' \triangleright \text{tt}} \qquad \text{ISYS} \, \frac{s \xrightarrow{\tau} s'}{s \triangleright \varphi \xrightarrow{\tau} s' \triangleright \varphi} \qquad \text{IMON} \, \frac{\varphi \xrightarrow{\tau} \varphi'}{s \triangleright \varphi \xrightarrow{\tau} s \triangleright \varphi'}$$

Fig. 3. A runtime semantics for instrumented properties with adaptations

The semantics is defined in terms of three LTSs: one for logical formulas (monitors), one for systems, and one for configurations, which is based on the other two LTSs. The LTS semantics for formulas extends the rules in Fig. 2 with the exception of those for the necessity formulas, which are replaced by rules RNC1, RNC2 and RNC3. Whereas RNC2 follows the same format as that of RNC1 from Fig. 2, the rule for *synchronous* necessity formulas, RNC1, transitions into a blocking construct, $\text{blk}(i) \, \varphi$, for the subject of the action, i, in case a pattern match is successful. In case of mismatch, RNC3 transitions the necessity formula to a release construct, $\text{rel}(r) \, \varphi$, with the specified release list of actors, r. Asynchronous and synchronous adaptation formulas transition with the *resp.* labels to a release construct as well (rules RADA and RADS), as do block and release constructs (rules RREL and RBLK). Finally, rule RCN4 allows monitor actions affecting the system, μ, to be carried out under a conjunction formula, independent of the other branch; we elide the obvious symmetric rule RCN5.

The system transition rules allow further actor spawning (sNEW) but restrict actions to those whose subject is currently active, *i.e.*, unblocked $i : \circ$ (sACT). Whereas asynchronous adaptations can be applied to any actor list, irrespective of their status (sADA), synchronous ones require the adaptees to be blocked (sADS). Finally rules sBLK and sREL model the *resp.* actor status transitioning from active to blocked (and viceversa).

The instrumentation rules for configurations describe how system (visible) actions, α, affect the monitors and, dually, how the monitor adaptation and synchronisation actions, μ, affect the system. For instance, if the monitor instigates action μ and the system allows it, they both transition together as a silent move (iADA). Dually, if the system generates action α and the monitor can observe it, they also transition in unison (iACT); if the monitor cannot observe this action (iTRM), it terminates as formula tt. Note that both rules iACT and iTRM require the monitor not to be in a position to perform an adaptation/synchronisation action, *i.e.*, premise $\varphi \xrightarrow{\mu}$; this gives *precedence* to monitor actions over system ones in our instrumentation. Rules iSYS and iMON allow systems and monitors to transition independently *wrt.* τ-actions.

Example 4. Recall the adaptation formula φ' defined in (3) of Example 3. For the system $s = (i : \circ, j : \circ, k : \circ, h : \circ)$ we can model the runtime execution with adaptations:

$$s \rhd \varphi' \xRightarrow{i?\{\text{inc},1,h\}} \cdot \xRightarrow{tau(i,k,\{\text{inc},1,h\})} s \rhd \text{blk}(i) \left(\begin{array}{l} [j \rhd h!\{\text{res},2\}]^{\,a}_{\,\epsilon} \; \varphi' \; \& \\ [z \rhd h!\text{err}]^{\,b}_{\,i} \; \text{restr}(i)_{\,\varepsilon} \; \text{prg}(z)_{i,z} \, \varphi' \end{array} \right) \tag{4}$$

$$\xrightarrow{\tau} \left((j,h,k) : \circ, i : \bullet\right) \rhd \left([j \rhd h!\{\text{res},2\}]^{\,a}_{\,\epsilon} \, \varphi' \; \& \; [z \rhd h!\text{err}]^{\,b}_{\,i} \, \text{restr}(i)_{\,\varepsilon} \text{prg}(z)_{i,z} \varphi' \right) \tag{5}$$

$$\xrightarrow{k \rhd h!\text{err}} \left((j,h,k) : \circ, i : \bullet\right) \rhd \text{blk}(k) \; \text{restr}(i)_{\,\varepsilon} \; \text{prg}(k)_{i,k} \, \varphi' \tag{6}$$

$$\xrightarrow{\tau} \left((j,h) : \circ, i : \bullet, k : \bullet\right) \rhd \text{restr}(i)_{\,\varepsilon} \; \text{prg}(k)_{i,k} \, \varphi' \tag{7}$$

$$\xRightarrow{\tau} \left((j,h) : \circ, i : \bullet, k : \bullet\right) \rhd \text{rel}(i,k) \, \varphi' \xrightarrow{\tau} s \rhd \varphi' \tag{8}$$

In particular, the synchronous pattern-matches in (4) and (6) yield the runtime actor blocking constructs, that are applied (incrementally) in (5) and (7). This allows the synchronous adaptations in (8) to proceed, followed by the unblocking of the *resp.* actors. Erroneous blocking directives result in stuck synchronous adaptations (see sADS). For instance, if we change the first blocking necessity in φ' of (3) to an asynchronous one, $[\mathtt{tau}(i,\_,\{\mathtt{inc},x,y\})]_\varepsilon^a$, it yields the execution below (φ'' is the erroneous formula):

$$s \triangleright \varphi'' \xrightarrow{\ i?\{\mathtt{inc},1,h\}\ } \cdot \xrightarrow{\ \mathtt{tau}(i,k,\{\mathtt{inc},1,h\})\ } \cdot \xrightarrow{\ k \triangleright h!\mathtt{err}\ } \big((i,j,h):\circ, k:\bullet\big) \triangleright \mathtt{restr}(i)_\varepsilon \ \mathtt{prg}(k)_{i,k} \ \varphi''$$

The final configuration is stuck because the synchronous adaptation on i cannot be carried out since i is *not* blocked. A similar situation is reached if a blocked actor is *released prematurely*. For instance, if we erroneously change the release list of the necessity subformula $[j \triangleright y!\{\mathtt{res}, x+1\}]_\varepsilon^a Y$ from ε to i, this releases i upon mismatch, interfering with adaptation actions along the other branch of the conjunction. ∎

   The semantics of Fig. 3 allows us to formalise configurations in an erroneous state, *i.e.*, when a monitor wants to apply synchronous adaptations that the system prohibits.

Definition 1. $\mathtt{error}(s \triangleright \varphi) \stackrel{\text{def}}{=} \varphi \xrightarrow{\ \mathsf{s}(w)\ } \ \ and \ \ s \ \overset{\mathsf{s}(y)}{\not\longrightarrow} \ \ for \ some \ w \in \mathtt{dom}(s)$

5   Static Type Checking

Synchronisation errors in adaptation-scripts, such as those outlined in Example 4 can be hard to detect by the specifier. We therefore develop a type system with the aim of assisting script construction, by filtering out the errors defined in Definition 1. It relies on the type structure defined in Fig. 4 where values are partitioned into either generic data, dat, or actor identifiers; identifiers are further divided into unrestricted, uid, and linear, lid. The type system is substructural [22], using linear types to statically track how the actor identifiers used for adaptations are blocked and released by the parallel branches (*i.e.*, conjunctions) of the *resp.* script. In fact, type checking (internally) uses a sub-category for linear identifier types, lbid, to denote a *blocked* linear identifier. Type checking works on *typed scripts*, where the syntax of Fig. 3 is extended so that the binding variables used in action patterns are annotated by the types dat, uid or lid.

Example 5. The adaptation-script (4) of Example 3 would be annotated as follows:

$$\varphi' \stackrel{\text{def}}{=} \ \max Y.[i?\{\mathtt{inc}, x:\mathtt{dat}, y:\mathtt{uid}\}]_\varepsilon^a \ \begin{pmatrix} ([j \triangleright y!\{\mathtt{res}, x+1\}]_\varepsilon^a \ Y) \ \& \\ [\mathtt{tau}(i,\_,\{\mathtt{inc},x,y\})]_\varepsilon^b \ (([z:\mathtt{lid} \triangleright y!\mathtt{err}]_i^b \ \mathtt{restr}(i)_\varepsilon \ \mathtt{prg}(z)_{i,z} \ Y) \end{pmatrix} \tag{9}$$

In (9) above, pattern variables x, y and z are associated to types dat, uid and lid *resp.* ∎

Our type system for (typed) adaptation-scripts is defined as the least relation satisfying the rules in Fig. 4. Type judgements take the form $\Sigma; \Gamma \vdash \varphi$ where

  − Value environments, $\Gamma \in \textsc{Env}::(\textsc{Pid} \cup \textsc{Var}) \rightharpoonup \textsc{Typ}$, map identifiers or variables to types — we let meta-variable $l \in (\textsc{Pid} \cup \textsc{Var})$ range over identifiers and variables;

– Formula environments, $\Sigma \in \text{LVAR} \rightharpoonup \text{ENV}$, map formula variables to value environments — they are used to analyse recursive formulas (see rules TMAX and TVAR).

We sometimes write $\Gamma \vdash \varphi$ in place of $\emptyset; \Gamma \vdash \varphi$. The rules in Fig. 4 assume standard *environment extensions*, (Γ, Γ'), and use *environment splitting*, $\Gamma_1 + \Gamma_2$, to distribute linearly mappings amongst two environment (see rules sU and sL in Fig. 4 — we elide the symmetric rule sR). Similar to before, we write $w : \mathbf{T}$ to denote the list of mappings $l_1 : \mathbf{T}, \ldots, l_n : \mathbf{T}$ where $w = l_1, \ldots, l_n$. In addition to $\text{subj}(e)$, the typing rules use another auxiliary function on patterns that extracts a map of type bindings, $\text{bnd}(e)$. For instance, from Example 5, we have $\text{bnd}(i?\{\texttt{inc}, x : \texttt{dat}, y : \texttt{uid}\}) = x : \texttt{dat}, y : \texttt{uid}$.

The typing rules for asynchronous and blocking necessities are similar: TNCA extends the environment Γ with the bindings introduced by the pattern e to check that the continuation formula typechecks, $\Sigma; (\Gamma, \text{bnd}(e)) \vdash \varphi$; it also checks that the resultant actor releases (in case of action mismatch) also typecheck, $\Sigma; \Gamma \vdash \text{rel}(r)\, \text{tt}$. Rule TNCB performs similar checks, but the continuation formula typechecking is prefixed by the blocking of the subject of the pattern,

Type Structure and Type Environment Splitting

$\mathbf{T}, \mathbf{U} \in \text{TYP} ::= \texttt{dat}$ *(generic)* | $\texttt{uid}$ *(unrestricted)* | $\texttt{lid}$ *(linear)* | $\texttt{lbid}$ *(blocked)*

$$\text{sE}\frac{}{\emptyset + \emptyset = \emptyset} \qquad \text{sU}\frac{\Gamma_1 + \Gamma_2 = \Gamma_3 \quad \mathbf{T} \in \{\texttt{dat}, \texttt{uid}\}}{(\Gamma_1, l : \mathbf{T}) + (\Gamma_2, l : \mathbf{T}) = (\Gamma_3, l : \mathbf{T})} \qquad \text{sL}\frac{\Gamma_1 + \Gamma_2 = \Gamma_3 \quad \mathbf{T} \in \{\texttt{lid}, \texttt{lbid}\}}{(\Gamma_1, l : \mathbf{T}) + \Gamma_2 = (\Gamma_3, l : \mathbf{T})}$$

Adaptation-Script Typing Rules

$$\text{TNCA}\frac{\Sigma; (\Gamma, \text{bnd}(e)) \vdash \varphi \quad \Sigma; \Gamma \vdash \text{rel}(r)\, \text{tt}}{\Sigma; \Gamma \vdash [e]_r^a\, \varphi} \qquad \text{tFls}\frac{}{\Sigma; \Gamma \vdash \text{ff}} \qquad \text{tTru}\frac{}{\Sigma; \Gamma \vdash \text{tt}}$$

$$\text{TNCB}\frac{\text{subj}(e) = l \quad \Sigma; (\Gamma, \text{bnd}(e)) \vdash \text{blk}(l)\, \varphi \quad \Sigma; \Gamma \vdash \text{rel}(r)\, \text{tt}}{\Sigma; \Gamma \vdash [e]_r^b\, \varphi} \qquad \text{tIf}\frac{\Sigma; \Gamma \vdash \varphi \quad \Sigma; \Gamma \vdash \psi}{\Sigma; \Gamma \vdash \text{if } b \text{ then } \varphi \text{ else } \psi}$$

$$\text{TBLK}\frac{\Gamma = \Gamma', w : \texttt{lid} \quad \Sigma; (\Gamma', w : \texttt{lbid}) \vdash \varphi}{\Sigma; \Gamma \vdash \text{blk}(w)\, \varphi} \qquad \text{TREL}\frac{\Gamma = \Gamma', w : \texttt{lbid} \quad \Sigma; (\Gamma', w : \texttt{lid}) \vdash \varphi}{\Sigma; \Gamma \vdash \text{rel}(w)\, \varphi}$$

$$\text{TADA}\frac{\Gamma = \Gamma', w : \texttt{lid} \quad \Sigma; \Gamma \vdash \text{rel}(r)\, \varphi}{\Sigma; \Gamma \vdash \text{aA}(w)_r\, \varphi} \qquad \text{TADS}\frac{\Gamma = \Gamma', w : \texttt{lbid} \quad \Sigma; \Gamma \vdash \text{rel}(r)\, \varphi}{\Sigma; \Gamma \vdash \text{sA}(w)_r\, \varphi}$$

$$\text{TCN1}\frac{\text{excl}(\varphi, \psi) = \bot \quad \Sigma; \Gamma_1 \vdash \varphi \quad \Sigma; \Gamma_2 \vdash \psi}{\Sigma; (\Gamma_1 + \Gamma_2) \vdash \varphi \,\&\, \psi} \qquad \text{TMAX}\frac{(\Sigma, X \mapsto \Gamma); \Gamma \vdash \varphi}{\Sigma; \Gamma \vdash \text{max } X.\, \varphi}$$

$$\text{TCN2}\frac{\text{excl}(\varphi, \psi) = \langle r_\varphi, r_\psi \rangle \quad \Sigma; \text{eff}(\Gamma, r_\psi) \vdash \varphi \quad \Sigma; \text{eff}(\Gamma, r_\varphi) \vdash \psi}{\Sigma; \Gamma \vdash \varphi \,\&\, \psi} \qquad \text{TVAR}\frac{\Sigma(X) \subseteq \Gamma}{\Sigma; \Gamma \vdash X}$$

Fig. 4. A type system for adaptation sHML scripts

$\Sigma; (\Gamma, \text{bnd}(e)) \vdash \text{blk}(l)\,\varphi$. Typing for actor blocking and releasing changes the respective bindings from lid to lbid (and vice-versa) to typecheck the continuations, rules TBLK and TREL. Typechecking asynchronous adaptations requires the adaptees to be linearly typed, rule TADA, whereas synchronous adaptations require adaptees to be linearly blocked, rule TADS; in both cases, they consider the *resp.* released actors when typechecking the continuations, $\Sigma; \Gamma \vdash \text{rel}(r)\,\varphi$.

We have two rules for typechecking conjunction formulas. Since conjunction subformulas may be executing in parallel (recall rules RCN1, RCN2, RCN3 and RCN4 from Figs. 2 and 3) rule TCN1, typechecks each subformula *wrt.* a split value environment, $\Gamma_1 + \Gamma_2$, as is standard in linear type systems. Unfortunately, this turns out to be too coarse of an analysis and rejects useful adaptation-scripts such as (9) from Example 5.

Example 6. The conjunction formula used in (9) from Example 5 has the form:

$$(\, [j\triangleright y!\{\text{res}, x + 1\}]_\epsilon^a \, Y) \, \& \, (\, [z\,{:}\,\text{lid} \triangleright y!\text{err}]_i^b \, \text{restr}(i)_\epsilon \, \text{prg}(z)_{i,z} \, Y)$$

where the subformulas are necessity formulas with *mutually exclusive* patterns *i.e.*, there is no action satisfying both patterns $j\triangleright y!\{\text{res}, x+1\}$ and $z\,{:}\,\text{lid}\triangleright y!\text{err}$. In such cases, a conjunction formula operates more like an *external choice* construct rather than a parallel composition [20], where only one branch continues monitoring. ∎

In order to refine our analysis, we define an approximating function $\text{excl}(\varphi, \psi)$ that syntactically analyses subformulas to determine whether they are mutually exclusive or not. When this can be determined statically, it means that only one branch will continue, whereas the other will terminate, releasing the actors specified by the *resp.* necessity formulas (recall RNC3 from 3). Accordingly, $\text{excl}(\varphi, \psi)$ denotes that mutual exclusion can be determined by returning a tuple consisting of two release sets, $\langle r_\varphi, r_\psi \rangle$ containing the actors released by the *resp.* subformulas when an action is mismatched. Rule TCN2 then typechecks each subformula *wrt.* the *entire* environment Γ, adjusted to take into consideration the actors release by the other (defunct) branch, *e.g.*, $\Sigma; \text{eff}(\Gamma, r_\psi) \vdash \varphi$. When this cannot be determined, *i.e.*, $\text{excl}(\varphi, \psi) = \bot$, rule TCN1 is used.

The rest of the typing rules are standard. *E.g.*, rule TIF approximates the analysis of the boolean condition and requires typechecking to hold for both branches.

Example 7. We can typecheck (9) *wrt.* $\Gamma = i : \text{lid}, j : \text{uid}$. The typesystem also rejects erroneous scripts discussed earlier. *E.g.*, for any environment, we *cannot* typecheck the erroneous script φ'' from Example 4 — with the necessary type annotations as in (9). Similarly, we *cannot* typecheck the script below (mentioned earlier in Example 4).

$$\varphi''' \stackrel{\text{def}}{=} \max Y. [i?\{\text{inc}, x:\text{dat}, y:\text{uid}\}]_\epsilon^a \begin{pmatrix} (\, [j\triangleright y!\{\text{res}, x + 1\}]_i^a \, Y) \, \& \\ (\, [z:\text{lid} \triangleright y!\text{err}]_i^b \, \text{restr}(i)_\epsilon \, \text{prg}(z)_{i,z} \, Y) \end{pmatrix}$$

φ''' differs from (9) only *wrt.* the necessity subformula $[\not{p}y!\{\mathtt{res}, x+1\}]_i^q\, Y$, which releases i when it mismatches an action. As discussed in Example 4, this results in a premature release of actor i, which interferes with the synchronous adaptation $\mathsf{restr}(i)_\varepsilon$ along the other branch. However, rule TCN2 detects this interference. ■

6   Dynamic Analysis of Typed Scripts

The typed adaptation-scripts of Sect. 5 need to execute *wrt.* the systems described in Sect. 4. Crucially, however, we cannot expect that a monitored system observes the type discipline assumed by the script. This, in turn, may create *type incompatibilities* that need to be detected and handled *at runtime* by the monitor.

Example 8. Recall the typed script (9) from Example 5. There are two classes of type incompatibilities that may arise during runtime monitoring:

- When listening for a pattern, *e.g.*, $i?\{\mathtt{inc}, x : \mathsf{dat}, y : \mathsf{uid}\}$, the system may generate the action $i?\{\mathtt{inc}, 5, 6\}$; matching the two would incorrectly map the identifier variable y (of type uid) to the data value 6; we call this a *type mismatch* incompatibility.
- When listening for pattern $z : \mathsf{lid} \triangleright y!\mathtt{err}$, the system may generate a matching action $i \triangleright h!\mathtt{err}$ mapping variable z to i. Aliasing z with i violates the linearity assumption associated with z, lid, which assumes it to be distinct from any other identifier mentioned in the script [22]; we call this an *aliasing* incompatibility.

A system that is typed *wrt.* the same type environment that (9) is typechecked with (*e.g.*, $\Gamma = i : \mathsf{lid}, j : \mathsf{uid}$ from Example 7) would not generate any of the incompatibilities above. ■

    In the absence of system typing, our monitors need to perform *dynamic type checks* (at runtime) and *abort monitoring* as soon as a type incompatibility is detected: any violations to the type discipline assumed by the script potentially renders unsafe any adaptations specified, and should thus *not* be administered on the system. In order to perform dynamic type checks, the operational semantics of typed scripts is defined *wrt.* the type environment with which they are typechecked — together with the type annotations included for binding (value) variables in the necessity patterns, it captures the (type) assumptions the script makes on the system being monitored.

Example 9. The execution of the typed script (9) would use the type environment $\Gamma = i : \mathsf{lid}, j : \mathsf{uid}$ from Example 5 to determine that an action such as $i?\{\mathtt{inc}, 5, i\}$ cannot be matched with pattern $i?\{\mathtt{inc}, x : \mathsf{dat}, y : \mathsf{uid}\}$, as this would lead to a *type mismatch* between $y : \mathsf{uid}$ and the resulting map to $i : \mathsf{lid}$ (note the mismatching types). Conversely, matching pattern $i?\{\mathtt{inc}, x : \mathsf{dat}, y : \mathsf{uid}\}$ with action $i?\{\mathtt{inc}, 5, h\}$ would not only constitute a *valid match*, but also allow monitoring to *extend* the assumed knowledge of the system from Γ to $\Gamma' = (\Gamma, h : \mathsf{uid})$, where h is associated to the type of the matched pattern variable y. The extended environment Γ' would then allow the monitor to detect a type mismatch between pattern $z : \mathsf{lid} \rhd h!\mathsf{err}$ and action $h \rhd h!\mathsf{err}$. Importantly however, it also allows the monitor to also detect an aliasing violation between the same pattern and action $i \rhd h!\mathsf{err}$ — variable z cannot be mapped to i, since $i \in \mathrm{dom}(\Gamma')$. It would however allow $z : \mathsf{lid} \rhd h!\mathsf{err}$ to be matched to action $k \rhd h!\mathsf{err}$, which would (again) extend the current type environment to $(\Gamma', k : \mathsf{lid})$ using the script type association $z : \mathsf{lid}$. ∎

Although safe, the mechanism discussed in Example 9 turns out to be rather restrictive for recursive properties (using maximal fixpoints). Note that, by alpha-conversion, the variable bindings made by a necessity formula under a fixpoint formula is *different* for every unfolding of that fixpoint formula: *e.g.*, unfolding script (9) twice yields

$$[i?\{\mathsf{inc}, x : \mathsf{dat}, y : \mathsf{uid}\}]^{\,a}_{\,e} \left(\ldots [z : \mathsf{lid} \rhd y!\mathsf{err}]^{\,b}_{\,i} \ldots \left(\begin{array}{c} [i?\{\mathsf{inc}, x' : \mathsf{dat}, y' : \mathsf{uid}\}]^{\,a}_{\,e} \\ (\ldots [z' : \mathsf{lid} \rhd y!\mathsf{err}]^{\,b}_{\,i} \ldots \varphi') \end{array} \right) \right)$$

where the outer bindings x, y, z are distinct from the inner bindings x', y', z'. More importantly, however, the scope of these bindings extends until the *next* fixpoint unfolding, and are *not used again* beyond that point, *e.g.*, x, y, z above are not used beyond the *resp.* adaptations of the first unfolding. Thus, one possible method for allowing a finer dynamic analysis for adaptation-scripts, *esp.* relating to linearity and aliasing violations, is to employ a mechanism that keeps track of which bindings *are still in use*. In the example above, this would allow us to bind k twice — once with z during the first iteration, and another time with z' — safe in the knowledge that by the time the second binding occurs (z'), the first binding (z) is not in use anymore, *i.e.*, there is no aliasing.

To implement this mechanism, our formalisation uses three additional components. First, the operational semantics for adaptation-scripts uses an extra environment, $\Delta \in \mathrm{PID} \rightharpoonup \mathcal{P}(\mathrm{LVAR})$, keeping track of the *recursion variables under which an identifier binding is introduced* by associating that identifier to a set of formula variables, $\kappa \in \mathcal{P}(\mathrm{LVAR})$. Environment Δ keeps track of the linear identifiers that are currently in use. Second, to facilitate updates to environment Δ, the patterns in necessity formulas are *decorated by sets of formula variables*, denoting their *resp.* recursion scope: *e.g.*, formula $\max X.[e]^{\,\rho}_{\,r} \ldots \max Y.[e']^{\,\rho'}_{\,w} \mathsf{ff}$ is decorated[3] as $\max X.[e_{\{X\}}]^{\,\rho}_{\,r} \ldots \max Y.[e'_{\{X,Y\}}]^{\,\rho'}_{\,w} \mathsf{ff}$. Third, the runtime syntax uses an additional construct, $\mathsf{clr}(X)\varphi$, when unfolding a recursive formula: the new runtime construct demarcates the *end of an unfolding* and, upon execution, removes all identifier entries in Δ with X in their *resp.* set of formula variables so as to record that they are not in use anymore.

Figure 5 describes the main transition rules for typed adaptation-scripts, defined over triples $\langle \Gamma, \Delta, \varphi \rangle$. Together with the system and instrumentation rules of Fig. 3 (adapted to triples $\langle \Gamma, \Delta, \varphi \rangle$), they form the complete operational semantics. By contrast to the rule in Fig. 2, RMAX in Fig. 5 unfolds a recursive formula to one prefixed by a clear construct, $\mathsf{clr}(X)\max X.\varphi$. Rule RCLR removes

---

[3] Decoration is easily performed through a linear scan of the script.

$$\text{RMax} \frac{}{\langle \Gamma, \Delta, \max X. \varphi \rangle \xrightarrow{\tau} \langle \Gamma, \Delta, \varphi[(\text{clr}(X)\max X. \varphi)/X] \rangle}$$

$$\text{RClr} \frac{}{\langle \Gamma, \Delta, \text{clr}(X)\varphi \rangle \xrightarrow{\tau} \langle \Gamma, \{i{:}\kappa \mid i{:}\kappa \in \Delta \wedge X \notin \kappa\}, \varphi \rangle}$$

$$\text{RNc1} \frac{\text{mtch}(e, \alpha) = \sigma \quad \text{subj}(\alpha) = i \quad \Gamma' = \text{bnd}(e)\sigma \quad \|\text{lin}(\Gamma')\| = \|\text{lin}(\text{bnd}(e))\| \quad \text{dom}(\Delta) \cap \text{dom}(\Gamma') = \emptyset}{\langle \Gamma, \Delta, [e_\kappa]_w^b \varphi \rangle \xrightarrow{\alpha} \langle (\Gamma, \Gamma'), (\Delta \cup \{i{:}\kappa \mid \Gamma'(i) = \text{lid}\}), \text{blk}(i) \varphi\sigma \rangle}$$

$$\text{RNc2} \frac{\text{mtch}(e, \alpha) = \sigma \quad \Gamma' = \text{bnd}(e)\sigma \quad \|\text{lin}(\Gamma')\| = \|\text{lin}(\text{bnd}(e))\| \quad \text{dom}(\Delta) \cap \text{dom}(\Gamma') = \emptyset}{\langle \Gamma, \Delta, [e_\kappa]_w^a \varphi \rangle \xrightarrow{\alpha} \langle (\Gamma, \Gamma'), (\Delta \cup \{i{:}\kappa \mid \Gamma'(i) = \text{lid}\}), \varphi\sigma \rangle}$$

$$\text{RCn1} \frac{\langle \Gamma, \Delta, \varphi \rangle \xrightarrow{\alpha} \langle \Gamma', \Delta', \varphi' \rangle \quad \langle \Gamma, \Delta, \psi \rangle \xrightarrow{\alpha} \langle \Gamma'', \Delta'', \psi' \rangle \quad \text{dom}(\Delta) = (\text{dom}(\Delta') \cap \text{dom}(\Delta''))}{\langle \Gamma, \Delta, \varphi \& \psi \rangle \xrightarrow{\alpha} \langle (\Gamma', \Gamma''), \Delta' \cup \Delta'', \varphi' \& \psi' \rangle}$$

Fig. 5. Dynamically typed adaptation-script rules (main rules)

all entries in Δ containing X. The new version of RNc1 in Fig. 5 implicitly checks for type mismatch incompatibilities by requiring that the environment extension, (Γ, Γ'), is still a map — conflicting entries $e.g.$, i : uid, i : lid would violate this condition. It also checks that the new bindings, $\text{dom}(\Gamma')$ are distinct from the linear identifiers currently in use, $\text{dom}(\Delta)$, as these constitute aliasing incompatibilities, and that pattern matching does not introduce aliasing for linear variables itself, $i.e.$, $\|\text{lin}(\Gamma')\| = \|\text{lin}(\text{bnd}(e))\|$. Finally, it transitions by updating Δ accordingly. Rule RNc2 is analogous. Rule RCn1 performs similar checks $e.g.$, it ensures that linear aliasing introduced along separate branches do not overlap, $\text{dom}(\Delta) = (\text{dom}(\Delta') \cap \text{dom}(\Delta''))$. If any of the conditions for RNc1, RNc2 and RCn1 are not satisfied, the adaptation-script blocks and is terminated in an instrumented setup using rule ITrm from Fig. 3, $i.e.$, it aborts as soon as type incompatibilities are detected.

Using a straightforward extension of Definition 1, we prove type soundness $wrt.$ the dynamic semantics of typed adaptation-scripts: configurations with typed scripts (and initial Δ) never transition to an erroneous configuration (for any trace t).

Theorem 2 (Type Soudness). *Whenever* $\Gamma \vdash \varphi$ *then, for initial* $\Delta_{init} = \{i{:}\emptyset \mid \Gamma(i) = \text{lid}\}$:

$$s \triangleright \langle \Gamma, \Delta_{init}, \varphi \rangle \xRightarrow{t} s' \triangleright \langle \Gamma', \Delta', \varphi' \rangle \quad implies \quad \neg\text{error}(s' \triangleright \langle \Gamma', \Delta', \varphi' \rangle)$$

7 Conclusion

We have designed language extensions for an RV tool monitoring actor systems, $cf.$ Sect. 3. These extensions weave synchronisation and adaptation directives over behavioural specifications expressed in the tool logic. We then formalised the *resp.* behaviour of these new constructs (Figs. 3 and 5). Through the formalisation, we also identified execution errors that may be introduced by the synchronisation and adaptation directives. Subsequently, we defined a type system for assisting the construction of such adaptation-scripts, Sect. 5, and proved soundness properties for it, Theorem 2. We conjecture that our techniques and methodologies are generic enough to be applied, at least in part, to other RA extensions of existing RV logics and tools.

Related Work: Perhaps the closest work to ours is [26], where an extension to the logic LTL called A-LTL is developed so as to describe properties of self-adaptive systems. In [13] the authors also implement an RV tool that checks for these adaptation properties at runtime. A crucial difference between this work and ours is that in [13,26] systems are assumed to be self-adaptive already; by contrast, we take (normal) systems and *introduce* degrees of adaptation through monitoring. We also spend substantial effort contending with the specific issue of partial monitor synchronisation in the context of inherently asynchronous (actor) systems.

In [4], the authors explore an interplay between static and dynamic type-checking in a message passing setting through monitoring. This framework of synthesising monitors from (session) types is further extended in [8] to carry out degrees of adaptations for security purposes. No type checking is carried out on the synthesised monitors in either of these works. Runtime Adaptation through monitoring are also explored in [19,23] for C programs to attain "failure-oblivious computing" that can adapt to errors such as null-dereferencing through a technique called reverse shepherding. Again, no static analysis is performed on the monitors themselves. Finally, in [5,6], the authors extend Aspect-J with dependent advices, and subsequently perform static analysis on these RV scripts (using typestates) in order to determine optimisations in monitor instrumentations. However, the static analysis does not consider aspects relating to monitor safety.

References

1. Aceto, L., Ingólfsdóttir, A.: Testing hennessy-milner logic with recursion. In: Thomas, W. (ed.) FOSSACS 1999. LNCS, vol. 1578, pp. 41–55. Springer, Heidelberg (1999)
2. Agha, G.: Actors: A Model of Concurrent Computation in Distributed Systems. MIT Press, Cambridge (1986)
3. Armstrong, J.: Programming Erlang: Software for a Concurrent World. Pragmatic Bookshelf (2007). ISBN: 193435600X
4. Bocchi, L., Chen, T.-C., Demangeon, R., Honda, K., Yoshida, N.: Monitoring networks through multiparty session types. In: Beyer, D., Boreale, M. (eds.) FORTE 2013 and FMOODS 2013. LNCS, vol. 7892, pp. 50–65. Springer, Heidelberg (2013)
5. Bodden, E.: Efficient hybrid typestate analysis by determining continuation-equivalent states. ICSE, pp. 5–14. ACM (2010)

6. Bodden, E., Lam, P.: Clara: partially evaluating runtime monitors at compile time. In: Barringer, H., Falcone, Y., Finkbeiner, B., Havelund, K., Lee, I., Pace, G., Roşu, G., Sokolsky, O., Tillmann, N. (eds.) RV 2010. LNCS, vol. 6418, pp. 74–88. Springer, Heidelberg (2010)

7. Cassar, I., Francalanza, A.: On synchronous and asynchronous monitor instrumentation for actor-based systems. FOCLASA **175**, 54–68 (2014)

8. Castellani, I., Dezani-Ciancaglini, M., Pérez, J.A.: Self-adaptation and secure information flow in multiparty structured commun.: a unified perspective. In: BEAT, pp. 9–18 (2014)

9. Cesarini, F., Thompson, S.: ERLANG Programming, 1st edn. O'Reilly (2009). ISBN: 0596518188, 9780596518189

10. Colombo, C., Francalanza, A., Gatt, R.: Elarva: a monitoring tool for erlang. In: Khurshid, S., Sen, K. (eds.) RV 2011. LNCS, vol. 7186, pp. 370–374. Springer, Heidelberg (2012)

11. Falcone, Y., Jaber, M., Nguyen, T.-H., Bozga, M., Bensalem, S.: Runtime verification of component-based systems. In: Barthe, G., Pardo, A., Schneider, G. (eds.) SEFM 2011. LNCS, vol. 7041, pp. 204–220. Springer, Heidelberg (2011)

12. Francalanza, A., Seychell, A.: Synthesising correct concurrent runtime monitors. In: Formal Methods in System Design (FMSD), pp. 1–36 (2014)

13. Goldsby, H.J., Cheng, B.H.C., Zhang, J.: AMOEBA-RT: run-time verification of adaptive software. In: Giese, H. (ed.) MODELS 2008. LNCS, vol. 5002, pp. 212–224. Springer, Heidelberg (2008)

14. Haller, P., Sommers, F.: Actors in Scala. Artima Inc., Walnut Creek (2012)

15. Irmert, F., Fischer, T., Meyer-Wegener, K.: Runtime adaptation in a service-oriented component model. In: SEAMS, pp. 97–104. ACM (2008)

16. Kalareh, M.A.: Evolving Software Systems for Self-Adaptation. Ph.D. thesis, University of Waterloo, Ontario, Canada (2012)

17. Kell, S.: A survey of pract. software adaptation techniques. J. UCS **14**, 2110–2157 (2008)

18. Kozen, D.: Results on the propositional μ-calculus. TCS **27**, 333–354 (1983)

19. Long, F., Sidiroglou-Douskos, S., Rinard, M.: Automatic runtime error repair and containment via recovery shepherding. SIGPLAN Not. **49**, 227–238 (2014)

20. Milner, R.: Communication and Concurrency. Prentice-Hall Inc, Upper Saddle River (1989)

21. Oreizy, P., Medvidovic, N., Taylor, R.N.: Runtime software adaptation: framework, approaches, and styles. In: ICSE Companion, pp. 899–910. ACM (2008)

22. Pierce, B.C. (ed.): Advanced Topics in Types and Prog. Languages. MIT Press, Cambridge (2005)

23. Rinard, M., Cadar, C., Dumitran, D., Roy, D., Leu, T., Beebee, W.: Enhancing availability & security through failure-oblivious computing. In: OSDI, pp. 303–316. USENIX (2004)

24. Roşu, G., Havelund, K.: Rewriting-based techniques for runtime verification. Autom. Softw. Eng. **12**, 151–197 (2005)

25. Sen, K., Vardhan, A., Agha, G., Roşu, G.: Efficient decentralized monitoring of safety in distributed systems. ICSE, pp. 418–427 (2004)

26. Zhang, J., Cheng, B.H.: Using temporal logic to specify adaptive program semantics. JSS **79**, 1361–1369 (2006)

Robust Online Monitoring
of Signal Temporal Logic

Jyotirmoy V. Deshmukh[1]([✉]), Alexandre Donzé[2], Shromona Ghosh[2],
Xiaoqing Jin[1]([✉]), Garvit Juniwal[2], and Sanjit A. Seshia[2]

[1] Toyota Technical Center, Gardena, CA, USA
{jyotirmoy.deshmukh,xiaoqing.jin}@tema.toyota.com
[2] University of California Berkeley, Berkeley, CA, USA
{donze,shromona.ghosh,garvitjuniwal,sseshia}@eecs.berkeley.edu

Abstract. Requirements of cyberphysical systems (CPS) can be rigorously specified using Signal Temporal Logic (STL). STL comes equipped with semantics that are able to quantify how robustly a given signal satisfies an STL property. In a setting where signal values over the entire time horizon of interest are available, efficient algorithms for *offline* computation of the robust satisfaction value have been proposed. Only a few methods exist for the *online* setting, i.e., where only a partial signal trace is available and rest of the signal becomes available in increments (such as in a real system or during numerical simulations). In this paper, we formalize the semantics for robust online monitoring of *partial signals* using the notion of robust satisfaction intervals (RoSIs). We propose an efficient algorithm to compute the RoSI and demonstrate its usage on two real-world case studies from the automotive domain and massively-online CPS education. As online algorithms permit early termination when the satisfaction or violation of a property is found, we show that savings in computationally expensive simulations far outweigh any overheads incurred by the online approach.

1 Introduction

Embedded software designers typically validate designs by inspecting concrete observations of system behavior. For instance, in the model-based development (MBD) paradigm, designers use numerical simulation tools to obtain traces from models of systems. An important problem is to efficiently test whether some logical property φ holds for a given simulation trace. It is increasingly common [2,3,11,14–16,18] to specify such properties using a real-time temporal logic such as Signal Temporal Logic (STL) [9] or Metric Temporal Logic (MTL) [12]. An *offline monitoring* approach involves performing an *a posteriori* analysis on *complete* simulation traces (i.e., traces starting at time 0, and lasting till a user-specified time horizon T). Theoretical and practical results for offline monitoring [7,9,12,20] focus on the efficiency of monitoring as a function of the length of the trace, and the size of the formula representing the property φ.

There are a number of situations where offline monitoring is unsuitable. Consider the case where the monitor is to be deployed in an actual system to detect

© Springer International Publishing Switzerland 2015
E. Bartocci and R. Majumdar (Eds.): RV 2015, LNCS 9333, pp. 55–70, 2015.
DOI: 10.1007/978-3-319-23820-3_4

erroneous behavior. As embedded software is typically resource constrained, offline monitoring is impractical as it requires storing the entire observed trace. In a simulation tool that uses numerical techniques to compute system behaviors, obtaining even one signal trace may require several minutes or even hours. If we wish to monitor a property over the simulation, it is usually sensible to stop the simulation once the satisfaction or violation of the property is detected. Such situations demand an *online monitoring algorithm*, which has markedly different requirements. In particular, a good online monitoring algorithm must: (1) be able to generate intermediate estimates of property satisfaction based on *partial signals*, (2) use minimal amount of data storage, and (3) be able to run fast enough in a real-time setting.

Most works on online monitoring algorithms for logics such as Linear Temporal Logic (LTL) or Metric Temporal Logic (MTL) have focussed on the Boolean satisfaction of properties by partial signals [10,13,21]. Recent work shows that by assigning quantitative semantics to real-time logics such as MTL and STL, problems such as bug-finding, parameter synthesis, and robustness analysis can be solved using powerful off-the-shelf optimization tools [1,6]. The quantitative semantics define a function mapping a property φ and a trace $\mathbf{x}(t)$ to a real number, known as the *robust satisfaction value*. A large positive value suggests that $\mathbf{x}(t)$ easily satisfies φ, a positive value near zero suggests that $\mathbf{x}(t)$ is close to violating φ, and a negative value indicates a violation of φ. While the recursive definitions of quantitative semantics naturally define offline monitoring algorithms to compute robust satisfaction values [7,9,12], there is limited work on an online monitoring algorithm to do the same [5].

The theoretical challenge of online monitoring lies in the definition of a practical quantitative semantics for a temporal logic formula over a partial signal, i.e., a signal trace with incomplete data which may not yet validate or invalidate φ. Past work [10] has identified three views for the satisfaction of a LTL property φ over a partial trace τ: (1) a *weak view* where τ satisfies φ if there is some suffix τ' such that $\tau.\tau'$ satisfies φ, (2) a *strong view* where τ does not satisfy φ if there is some suffix τ' such that $\tau.\tau'$ does not satisfy φ and (3) a *neutral view* when the satisfaction is defined using a truncated semantics of LTL restricted to *finite* paths. In [13], the authors extend the truncated semantics to MTL. In [5], the authors introduce the notion of a *predictor*, which works as an oracle to complete a partial trace and provide an estimated satisfaction value. In general, such a value cannot be formally trusted as long as the data is incomplete.

The layout of the paper is as follows: In Sect. 3, we present *robust interval* semantics for an STL property φ on a partial signal (with data available till time t_i, denoted $\mathbf{x}_{[0,i]}$) that unifies the different semantic views of real-time logics on truncated paths. Informally, we define a function that maps $\mathbf{x}_{[0,i]}$ and φ to the robust satisfaction interval (RoSI) (ℓ, υ), with the interpretation that for any suffix $\mathbf{x}_{[t_{i+1}, t_N]}$, ℓ is the greatest lower bound on the robust satisfaction value of $\mathbf{x}_N$, and υ is the corresponding lowest upper bound. There is a natural correspondence between the RoSI and three-valued semantics: (1) φ is violated according to the weak view iff υ is negative, and is satisfied otherwise; (2) φ is satisfied according to the strong view iff ℓ is positive, and violated otherwise;

and (3) a neutral semantics, e.g., based on some predictor, can be defined when $\ell < 0 < \upsilon$, i.e., when there exist suffixes that can violate or satisfy φ.

In Sect. 4, we present an efficient online algorithm to compute the RoSI for a bounded-time-horizon STL formula by extending the offline algorithm of [7]. In spite of being online, the extension imposes minimal runtime overhead. It works in a fashion similar to incremental Boolean monitoring of STL implemented in the tool AMT [21]. In Sect. 5, we present algorithms that can perform online monitoring of commonly-used unbounded time-horizon formulas using only a bounded amount of memory.

Finally, we present experimental results on two large-scale case studies: (i) industrial-scale Simulink models from the automotive domain in Sect. 6, and (ii) an automatic grading system used in a massive online education initiative on CPS [17]. Since the online algorithm can abort simulation as soon as the satisfaction of the property is determined, we see a consistent 10 %–20 % savings in simulation time (which is typically several hours) in a majority of experiments, with negligible overhead (<1 %). In general, our results indicate that the benefits of our online monitoring algorithm over the offline approach far outweigh any overheads.

2   Background

Interval Arithmetic. We now review interval arithmetic. An interval I is a convex subset of $\mathbb{R}$. A singular interval $[a, a]$ contains exactly one point. Intervals (a, a), $[a, a)$, $(a, a]$, and $\emptyset$ denote empty intervals. We enumerate interval operations below assuming open intervals. Similar operations can be defined for closed, open-closed, and closed-open intervals.

$$
\begin{aligned}
&1. \; -I_1 \;\; = (-b_1, -a_1) \qquad\quad 3. \; I_1 \oplus I_2 \;\;\; = (a_1 + a_2, b_1 + b_2) \\
&2. \; c + I_1 = (c + a_1, c + b_1) \qquad 4. \; \min(I_1, I_2) = (\min(a_1, a_2), \min(b_1, b_2)) \\
&5. \; I_1 \cap I_2 = \begin{cases} \emptyset & \text{if } \min(b_1, b_2) < \max(a_1, a_2) \\ (\max(a_1, a_2), \min(b_1, b_2)) & \text{otherwise.} \end{cases}
\end{aligned}
$$
$$(2.1)$$

Definition 1 (Signal). *A time domain $\mathcal{T}$ is a finite or infinite set of time instants such that $\mathcal{T} \subseteq \mathbb{R}^{\geq 0}$ with $0 \in \mathcal{T}$. A signal $\mathbf{x}$ is a function from $\mathcal{T}$ to $\mathcal{X}$. Given a time domain $\mathcal{T}$, a partial signal is any signal defined on a time domain $\mathcal{T}' \subseteq \mathcal{T}$.*

Note that $\mathcal{X}$ can be any set, but it is usual to assume some subset of $\mathbb{R}^n$. Simulation frameworks typically provide signal values at discrete time instants, usually this is a by-product of using a numerical technique to solve the differential equations in the underlying system. These discrete-time solutions are assumed to be sampled versions of the actual signal, which can be reconstructed using some form of interpolation. In this paper, we assume constant interpolation to reconstruct the signal $\mathbf{x}(t)$, i.e., given a sequence of time-value pairs $(t_0, \mathbf{x}_0), \ldots, (t_n, \mathbf{x}_n)$, for all $t \in [t_0, t_n)$, we define $\mathbf{x}(t) = \mathbf{x}_i$ if $t \in [t_i, t_{i+1})$, and $\mathbf{x}(t_n) = \mathbf{x}_n$. Further, let $\mathcal{T}_n \subseteq \mathcal{T}$ represent the finite subset of time instants at which the signal values are given.

Signal Temporal Logic. We use Signal Temporal Logic (STL) [9] to analyze time-varying behaviors of signals. We now present its syntax and semantics. A *signal predicate* μ is a formula of the form $f(\mathbf{x}) > 0$, where $\mathbf{x}$ is a variable that takes values from $\mathcal{X}$, and f is a function from $\mathcal{X}$ to $\mathbb{R}$. For a given f, let $f_{\inf}$ denote $\inf_{\mathbf{x} \in \mathcal{X}} f(\mathbf{x})$, i.e., the *greatest lower bound* of f over $\mathcal{X}$. Similarly, let $f_{\sup} = \sup_{\mathbf{x} \in \mathcal{X}} f(\mathbf{x})$. The syntax of an STL formula φ is defined in Eq. (2.2). Note that $\Box$ and $\Diamond$ can be defined in terms of the $\mathbf{U}$ operator, but we include them for convenience.

$$\varphi ::= \mu \mid \neg\varphi \mid \varphi \wedge \varphi \mid \Box_{(u,v)}\varphi \mid \Diamond_{(u,v)}\varphi \mid \varphi\mathbf{U}_{(u,v)}\varphi \tag{2.2}$$

Quantitative semantics for timed-temporal logics have been proposed for STL in [9]; we include the definition below. In the usual Boolean sense of satisfaction, a signal $\mathbf{x}$ satisfies φ at a time τ iff the robust satisfaction value $\rho(\varphi, \mathbf{x}, \tau) \geq 0$.

Definition 2 (Robust Satisfaction Value). *We first define a function ρ mapping an STL formula φ, the signal $\mathbf{x}$, and a time $\tau \in \mathcal{T}$ as follows:*

$$
\begin{aligned}
\rho\left(f(\mathbf{x}) > 0, \mathbf{x}, \tau\right) &= f(\mathbf{x}(\tau)) \\
\rho\left(\neg\varphi, \mathbf{x}, \tau\right) &= -\rho(\varphi, \mathbf{x}, \tau) \\
\rho\left(\varphi_1 \wedge \varphi_2, \mathbf{x}, \tau\right) &= \min\left(\rho(\varphi_1, \mathbf{x}, \tau), \rho(\varphi_2, \mathbf{x}, \tau)\right) \\
\rho\left(\Box_I\varphi, \mathbf{x}, \tau\right) &= \inf_{t \in \tau + I} \rho(\varphi, \mathbf{x}, t) \\
\rho\left(\Diamond_I\varphi, \mathbf{x}, \tau\right) &= \sup_{t \in \tau + I} \rho(\varphi, \mathbf{x}, t) \\
\rho\left(\varphi_1 \mathbf{U}_I \varphi_2, \mathbf{x}, \tau\right) &= \sup_{t_2 \in \tau + I} \min\left(\rho(\varphi_2, \mathbf{x}, t_2), \inf_{t_1 \in (\tau, t_2)} \rho(\varphi_1, \mathbf{x}, t_1)\right)
\end{aligned}
\tag{2.3}
$$

The robust satisfaction value of a given signal $\mathbf{x}$ w.r.t. a given formula φ is then defined as $\rho(\varphi, \mathbf{x}, 0)$.

3   Robust Interval Semantics

We assume finite time-horizon T for signals. Further, we assume that the signal is obtained by applying constant interpolation to a sampled signal defined over time-instants $\{t_0, t_1, \ldots, t_N\}$, such that $t_N = T$ and $\forall i : t_i < t_{i+1}$. In the online monitoring context, at any time t_i, only the partial signal over time instants $\{t_0, \ldots, t_i\}$ is available, and the rest of the signal becomes available in discrete time increments. We define new semantics for STL formulas over partial signals using intervals. A *robust satisfaction interval* (RoSI) includes all possible robust satisfaction values corresponding to the suffixes of the partial signal. In this section, we formalize the recursive definitions for RoSI of an STL formula with respect to a partial signal, and next we will discuss an efficient algorithm to compute and maintain these intervals.

Definition 3 (Prefix, Completions). *Let $\{t_0, \ldots, t_i\}$ be a finite set of time instants such that $t_i \leq T$, and let $\mathbf{x}_{[0,i]}$ be a partial signal over the time domain $[t_0, t_i]$. We say that $\mathbf{x}_{[0,i]}$ is a prefix of a signal $\mathbf{x}$ if for all $t \leq t_i$, $\mathbf{x}(t) = \mathbf{x}_{[0,i]}(t)$. The set of completions of a partial signal $\mathbf{x}_{[0,i]}$ (denoted by $\mathcal{C}(\mathbf{x}_{[0,i]})$) is defined as the set $\{\mathbf{x} \mid \mathbf{x}_{[0,i]} \text{ is a prefix of } \mathbf{x}\}$.*

Definition 4 (Robust Satisfaction Interval (RoSI)). *The robust satisfaction interval of an STL formula φ on a partial signal $\mathbf{x}_{[0,i]}$ at a time $\tau \in [t_0, t_i]$ is an interval I s.t.:*

$$\inf(I) = \inf_{\mathbf{x} \in \mathcal{C}(\mathbf{x}_{[0,i]})} \rho(\varphi, \mathbf{x}, \tau) \quad \text{and} \quad \sup(I) = \sup_{\mathbf{x} \in \mathcal{C}(\mathbf{x}_{[0,i]})} \rho(\varphi, \mathbf{x}, \tau)$$

Definition 5. *We define a recursive function $[\rho]$ that maps a given formula φ, a partial signal $\mathbf{x}_{[0,i]}$ and a time $\tau \in \mathcal{T}$ to an interval $[\rho](\varphi, \mathbf{x}_{[0,i]}, \tau)$.*

$$[\rho]\left(f(\mathbf{x}_{[0,i]}) > 0, \mathbf{x}_{[0,i]}, \tau\right) = \begin{cases} [f(\mathbf{x}_{[0,i]}(\tau)), f(\mathbf{x}_{[0,i]}(\tau))] & \tau \in [t_0, t_i] \\ [f_{\inf}, f_{\sup}] & \text{otherwise.} \end{cases}$$

$$[\rho]\left(\neg\varphi, \mathbf{x}_{[0,i]}, \tau\right) = -[\rho](\varphi, \mathbf{x}_{[0,i]}, \tau)$$

$$[\rho]\left(\varphi_1 \wedge \varphi_2, \mathbf{x}_{[0,i]}, \tau\right) = \min([\rho](\varphi_1, \mathbf{x}_{[0,i]}, \tau), [\rho](\varphi_2, \mathbf{x}_{[0,i]}, \tau))$$

$$[\rho]\left(\square_I\varphi, \mathbf{x}_{[0,i]}, \tau\right) = \inf_{t \in \tau + I}\left([\rho](\varphi, \mathbf{x}_{[0,i]}, t)\right)$$

$$[\rho]\left(\Diamond_I\varphi, \mathbf{x}_{[0,i]}, \tau\right) = \sup_{t \in \tau + I}\left([\rho](\varphi, \mathbf{x}_{[0,i]}, t)\right)$$

$$[\rho]\left(\varphi_1 \mathbf{U}_I\varphi_2, \mathbf{x}_{[0,i]}, \tau\right) = \sup_{t_2 \in \tau + I} \min \begin{pmatrix} [\rho](\varphi_2, \mathbf{x}_{[0,i]}, t_2), \\ \inf_{t_1 \in (\tau, t_2)} [\rho](\varphi_1, \mathbf{x}_{[0,i]}, t_1)) \end{pmatrix}$$

$$(3.1)$$

It can be shown that the RoSI of a signal $\mathbf{x}$ w.r.t. an STL formula φ is equal to $[\rho](\varphi, \mathbf{x}, 0)$; we defer the proof to the full version [4].

4 Online Algorithm

Donzé et al. [7] present an offline algorithm for monitoring STL formulas over (piecewise) linearly interpolated signals. A naïve implementation of an online algorithm is as follows: at time t_i, use a modification of the offline monitoring algorithm to recursively compute the robust satisfaction intervals as defined by Definition 5 to the signal $\mathbf{x}_{[0,i]}$. We observe that such a procedure does many repeated computations that can be avoided by maintaining the results of intermediate computations. Furthermore, the naïve procedure requires storing the signal values over the entire time horizon, which makes it memory-intensive. In this section, we present the main technical contribution of this paper: *an online algorithm that is memory-efficient and avoids repeated computations.*

As in the offline monitoring algorithm in [7], an essential ingredient of the online algorithm is Lemire's running maximum filter algorithm [19]. The problem this algorithm addresses is the following: given a sequence of values $a_1, \ldots, a_n$, find the maxima over windows of size w, i.e., for all j, find $\max_{i \in [j, j+w)} a_i$ (similarly, for finding the corresponding minima). We briefly review an extension of Lemire's algorithm over piecewise-constant signals with variable time steps, given as Algorithm 1. The main observation in Lemire's algorithm is that it is sufficient to maintain a descending (resp. ascending) monotonic edge (denoted F in Algorithm 1) to compute the sliding maxima (resp. minima), in order to achieve an optimal procedure (measured in terms of the number of comparisons

Algorithm 1. SlidingMax($(t_0, \mathbf{x}_0), \ldots, (t_N, \mathbf{x}_N), [a, b]$).

Output: Sliding maximum $\mathbf{y}(t)$ over times in $[t_0, t_N]$

```
1  F := {0} // F is the set of times representing the monotonic edge
2  i := 0 ; s, t := t_0 − b
3  while t + a < t_N do
4      if F ≠ ∅ then  t := min(t_min(F) − a, t_{i+1} − b)
5      else  t := t_{i+1} − b
6      if t = t_{i+1} − b then
7          while x_{i+1} ≥ x_max(F) ∧ F ≠ ∅ do
8              F: = F − max(F)
9          F: = F ∪ {i + 1}, i := i + 1
10     else // Slide window to the right
11         if s > t_0 then  y(s) := x_min(F)
12         else  y(t_0) := x_min(F)
13         F: = F − min(F), s := t
```

---

between elements). The descending edge satisfies the property that if $i \in F$, then $t_i \in t + [a, b]$, and for all $t_j > t_i$ in $t + I$, $\mathbf{x}(t_j) < \mathbf{x}(t_i)$. Lines 8 and 9 incrementally update the edge when a new point is encountered that is still within the $t + [a, b]$ window, and lines 11–13 correspond to the case where the window is slid right as a result of updating the t. These lines then providing the sliding maximum over $t + [a, b]$ at the t from which the window was advanced.

We first focus on the fragment of STL where each temporal operator is scoped by a time-interval I, where $\sup(I)$ is finite. The algorithm for online monitoring maintains the syntax tree of the formula φ to be monitored in memory, and augments the tree with some book-keeping information. First, we formalize some notation. For a given formula φ, let $\mathcal{T}_\varphi$ represent the syntax tree of φ, and let root($\mathcal{T}_\varphi$) denote the root of the tree. Each node in the syntax tree (other than a leaf node) corresponds to an STL operator $\neg, \vee, \wedge, \Box_I$ or $\Diamond_I$.[1] We will use $\mathbf{H}_I$ to denote any temporal operator bounded by interval I. For a given node v, let op(v) denote the operator for that node. For any node v in $\mathcal{T}_\varphi$ (except the root node), let parent(v) denote the unique parent of v.

Algorithm 2 is a dynamic programming algorithm operating on the syntax tree of the given STL formula, i.e., computation of the RoSI of a formula combines the RoSIs for its constituent sub-formulas in a bottom-up fashion. As computing the RoSI at a node v requires the RoSIs at the child-nodes, this computation has to be delayed till the RoSIs at the children of v in a certain time-interval are available. We call this time-interval the *time horizon* of v (denoted hor(v)), and define it recursively in Eq. (4.1).

$$\text{hor}(v) = \begin{cases} [0] & \text{if } v = \text{root}(\mathcal{T}_\varphi) \\ I \oplus \text{hor}(\text{parent}(v)) & \text{if } v \neq \text{root}(\mathcal{T}_\varphi) \text{ and op}(\text{parent}(v)) = \mathbf{H}_I \\ \text{hor}(\text{parent}(v)) & \text{otherwise.} \end{cases} \quad (4.1)$$

We illustrate the working of the algorithm using a small example then give a brief sketch of the various steps in the algorithm.

---

[1] We omit the case of $\mathbf{U}_I$ here for lack of space, although the rewriting approach of [7] can be adapted here and is implemented in our tool.

Example 1. For the formula[2] in (4.2), we show $\mathcal{T}_\varphi$ and hor(v) for each v in $\mathcal{T}_\varphi$ in Fig. 1.

$$\varphi \triangleq \Box_{[0,a]} \left(\neg(y > 0) \vee \Diamond_{[b,c]}(x > 0) \right) \tag{4.2}$$

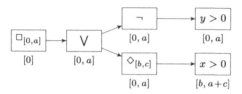

Fig. 1. Syntax tree $\mathcal{T}_\varphi$ for φ (given in (4.2)) with each node v annotated with hor(v)

The algorithm augments each node v of $\mathcal{T}_\varphi$ with a double-ended queue, that we denote worklist[v]. Let ψ be the subformula denoted by the tree rooted at v. For the partial signal $\mathbf{x}_{[0,i]}$, the algorithm maintains in worklist[v], the RoSI $[\rho](\psi, \mathbf{x}_{[0,i]}, t)$ for each $t \in$ hor(v) $\cap [t_0, t_i]$. We denote by worklist[v](t) the entry corresponding to time t in worklist[v]. When a new data-point $\mathbf{x}_{i+1}$ corresponding to the time t_{i+1} is available, the monitoring procedure updates each $[\rho](\psi, \mathbf{x}_{[0,i]}, t)$ in worklist[v] to $[\rho](\psi, \mathbf{x}_{[0,i+1]}, t)$.

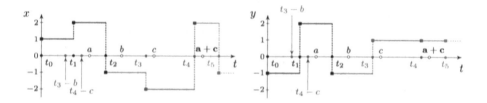

Fig. 2. These plots show the signals $x(t)$ and $y(t)$. Each signal begins at time $t_0 = 0$, and we consider three partial signals: $\mathbf{x}_{[0,3]}$ (black + blue), and $\mathbf{x}_{[0,4]}$ ($\mathbf{x}_{[0,3]}$ + green), and $\mathbf{x}_{[0,5]}$ ($\mathbf{x}_{[0,4]}$ + red) (Color figure online).

In Fig. 3, we give an example of a run of the algorithm. We assume that the algorithm starts in a state where it has processed the partial signal $\mathbf{x}_{[0,2]}$, and show the effect of receiving data at time-points t_3, t_4 and t_5. The figure shows the states of the worklists at each node of $\mathcal{T}_\varphi$ at these times when monitoring the STL formula φ presented in Eq. (4.2). Each row in the table adjacent to a node shows the state of the worklist after the algorithm processes the value at the time indicated in the first column (Fig. 3).

The first row of the table shows the snapshot of the worklists at time t_2. Observe that in the worklists for the subformula $y > 0$, $\neg y > 0$, because $a < b$,

---

[2] We remark that φ is equivalent to $\Box_{[0,a]} \left((y > 0) \implies \Diamond_{[b,c]}(x > 0) \right)$, which is a common formula used to express a timed causal relation between two signals.

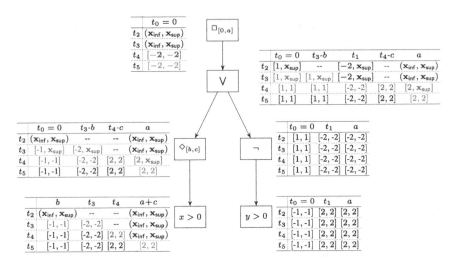

Fig. 3. We show a snapshot of the worklist[v] maintained by the algorithm for four different (incremental) partial traces of the signals $x(t)$ and $y(t)$. Each row indicates the state of worklist[v] at the time indicated in the first column. An entry marked -- indicates that the corresponding element did not exist in worklist[v] at that time. Each colored entry indicates that the entry was affected by availability of a signal fragment of the corresponding color (Color figure online).

the data required to compute the RoSI at t_0, t_1 and the time a, is available, and hence each of the RoSIs is singular. On the other hand, for the subformula $x > 0$, the time horizon is $[b, a + c]$, and no signal value is available at any time in this interval. Thus, at time t_2, all elements of worklist[$v_{x>0}$] are (x_{inf}, x_{sup}) corresponding to the greatest lower bound and lowest upper bound on x.

To compute the values of $\lozenge_{[b,c]}(x > 0)$ at any time t, we take the max. over values from times $t+b$ to $t+c$. As the time horizon for the node corresponding to $\lozenge_{[b,c]}(x > 0)$ is $[0, a]$, t ranges over $[0, a]$. In other words, we wish to perform the sliding max. over the interval $[0 + b, a + c]$, with a window of length $c - b$. We can use Algorithm 1 for this purpose. One caveat is that we need to store separate monotonic edges for the upper and lower bounds of the RoSIs. The algorithm then proceeds upward on the syntax tree, only updating the worklist of a node when there is an update to the worklists of its children.

The second row in each table is the effect of obtaining a new time point (at time t_3) for both signals. Note that this does not affect worklist[$v_{y>0}$] or worklist[$v_{\neg y>0}$], as all RoSIs are already singular, but does update the RoSI values for the node $v_{x>0}$. The algorithm then invokes Algorithm 1 on worklist[$v_{x>0}$] to update worklist[$v_{\lozenge_{[b,c]}(x>0)}$]. Note that in the invocation on the second row (corresponding to time t_3), there is an additional value in the worklist, at time t_3. This leads Algorithm 1 to produce a new value of SlidingMax (worklist[$v_{x>0}$], [b, c]) ($t_3 - b$), which is then inserted in worklist[$v_{\lozenge_{[b,c]}x>0}$]. This leads to additional points appearing in worklists at the ancestors of this node.

Finally, we remark that the run of this algorithm shows that at time t_4, the RoSI for the formula φ is $[-2, -2]$, which yields a negative upper bound, showing

---

Algorithm 2. updateWorkList(v_ψ, t_{i+1}, $\mathbf{x}_{i+1}$)

```
// v_ψ is a node in the syntax tree, (t_{i+1}, x_{i+1}) is a new timepoint
1 switch ψ do
```

2   **case** $f(\mathbf{x}) > 0$
3   **if** $t_{i+1} \in \mathsf{hor}(v_\psi)$ **then**
4             $\mathsf{worklist}[v_\psi](t_{i+1}) := [f(\mathbf{x}_{i+1}), f(\mathbf{x}_{i+1})]$

5   **case** $\neg \varphi$
6   updateWorkList(v_φ, t_{i+1}, $\mathbf{x}_{i+1}$) ;
7          $\mathsf{worklist}[v_\psi] := -\mathsf{worklist}[v_\varphi]$

8   **case** $\varphi_1 \wedge \varphi_2$
9   updateWorkList(v_{φ_1}, t_{i+1}, $\mathbf{x}_{i+1}$) ;
10   updateWorkList(v_{φ_2}, t_{i+1}, $\mathbf{x}_{i+1}$) ;
11         $\mathsf{worklist}[v_\psi] := \min(\mathsf{worklist}[v_{\varphi_1}], \mathsf{worklist}[v_{\varphi_2}])$

12   **case** $\square_I \varphi$
13   updateWorkList(v_φ, t_{i+1}, $\mathbf{x}_{i+1}$) ;
14         $\mathsf{worklist}[v_\psi] := \mathsf{SlidingMax}(\mathsf{worklist}[v_\varphi], I)$

---

that the formula is not satisfied irrespective of the suffixes of x and y. In other words, the satisfaction of φ is known before we have all the data required by $\mathsf{hor}(\varphi)$.

Algorithm 2 is essentially a procedure that recursively visits each node in the syntax tree $\mathcal{T}_\varphi$ of the STL formula φ that we wish to monitor. Line 4 corresponds to the base case of the recursion, i.e. when the algorithm visits a leaf of $\mathcal{T}_\varphi$ or an atomic predicate of the form $f(\mathbf{x}) > 0$. Here, the algorithm inserts the pair $(t_{i+1}, \mathbf{x}_{i+1})$ in $\mathsf{worklist}[v_{f(\mathbf{x})>0}]$ if t_{i+1} lies inside $\mathsf{hor}(v_{f(\mathbf{x})>0})$. In other words, it only tracks a value if it is useful for computing the RoSI of some ancestor node.

For a node corresponding to a Boolean operation, the algorithm first updates the worklists at the children, and then uses them to update the worklist at the node. If the current node represents $\neg \varphi$ (Line 5), the algorithm flips the sign of each entry in $\mathsf{worklist}[v_\varphi]$; this operation is denoted as $-\mathsf{worklist}[v_\varphi]$. Consider the case where the current node v_ψ is a conjunction $\varphi_1 \wedge \varphi_2$. The sequence of upper bounds and the sequence of lower bounds of the entries in $\mathsf{worklist}[v_{\varphi_1}]$ and $\mathsf{worklist}[v_{\varphi_1}]$ can be each thought of as a piecewise-constant signal (likewise for $\mathsf{worklist}[v_{\varphi_2}]$). In Line 11, the algorithm computes a pointwise-minimum over piecewise-constant signals representing the upper and lower bounds of the RoSIs of its arguments. Note that if for $i = 1, 2$, if $\mathsf{worklist}[v_{\varphi_i}]$ has N_i entries, then the pointwise-min would have to be performed at most $N_1 + N_2$ distinct timepoints. Thus, $\mathsf{worklist}[v_{\varphi_1 \wedge \varphi_2}]$ has at most $N_1 + N_2$ entries. A similar phenomenon can be seen in Fig. 3, where computing a max over the worklists of $v_{\lozenge_{[b,c]}(x>0)}$ and $v_{\neg(y>0)}$ leads to an increase in the number of entries in the worklist of the disjunction.

For nodes corresponding to temporal operators, e.g., $\lozenge_I \varphi$, the algorithm first updates $\mathsf{worklist}[v_\varphi]$. It then applies Algorithm 1 to compute the sliding maximum over $\mathsf{worklist}[v_\varphi]$. Note that if $\mathsf{worklist}[v_\varphi]$ contains N entries, so does $\mathsf{worklist}[v_{\lozenge_I \varphi}]$.

A further optimization can be implemented on top of this basic scheme. For a node v corresponding to the subformula $\mathbf{H}_I\varphi$, the first few entries of worklist$[v]$ (say up to time u) could become singular intervals once the required RoSIs for worklist$[v_\varphi]$ are available. The optimization is to only compute SlidingMax over worklist$[v_\varphi]$ starting from $u + \inf(I)$. We omit the pseudo-code for brevity.

5 Monitoring Untimed Formulas

If the STL formula being monitored has untimed (i.e. infinite-horizon) temporal operators, a direct application of Algorithm 2 requires every node in the subtree rooted at the untimed operator to have a time horizon that is unbounded, or in other words, the algorithm would have to keep track of every value over arbitrarily long intervals. For a large class of formulae (shown in Theorem 1), we can perform robust online monitoring using only a constant amount of memory. The question whether an arbitrary STL formula outside of the fragment stated thus far can be monitored using constant memory remains an open problem. We now show how constant memory monitoring can be performed for the first set of formulae. In what follows, we assume that the subformulae φ and ψ are atomic predicates of the form $f(\mathbf{x}) > 0$. Also, as we assume that signals are obtained by constant interpolation over a finite number of time-points, there is only a finite collection of values of $f(\mathbf{x})$ for any atomic predicate. Thus, we replace inf and sup in the definitions of $[\rho]$ by min and max respectively.

First, we introduce some equivalences over intervals a, b, c that we use in the theorem and the proof to follow:

$$\min(\max(a, b), \max(a, c)) = \max(a, \min(b, c)) \tag{5.1}$$

$$\min(a, \max(b, c)) = \max(\min(a, b), \min(a, c)) \tag{5.2}$$

$$\max(\max(a, b), c) = \max(a, b, c) \tag{5.3}$$

$$\min(\max(a, b), a) = a \tag{5.4}$$

Theorem 1. *For each of the following formulae, where φ and ψ are atomic predicates of the form $f(\mathbf{x}) > 0$, we can monitor interval robustness in an online fashion using constant memory: (1) $\Box\varphi$, $\Diamond\varphi$, (2) $\varphi\mathbf{U}\psi$, (3) $\Box(\varphi\vee\Diamond\psi)$, $\Diamond(\varphi\wedge\Box\psi)$, (4) $\Box\Diamond\varphi$, $\Diamond\Box\varphi$, and (5) $\Diamond(\varphi \wedge \Diamond\psi)$, $\Box(\varphi \vee \Box\psi)$.*

Proof. We consider each of the five cases of the theorem in turn. The proof strategy is to show that if a constant memory buffer has been used to monitor up to n samples, then receiving an additional sample does not require the memory to grow. In what follows, we use the following short-hand notation:

$$p_i \equiv [\rho](f(\mathbf{x}) > 0, \mathbf{x}_{[0,n+1]}, t_i) \qquad q_i \equiv [\rho](g(\mathbf{x}) > 0, \mathbf{x}_{[0,n+1]}, t_i) \tag{5.5}$$

Note that if $i \in [0, n]$, then p_i is the same over the partial signal $\mathbf{x}_{[0,n]}$, i.e., $p_i = [\rho](f(\mathbf{x}) > 0, \mathbf{x}_{[0,n]}, t_i)$ (and respectively for q_i). We will use this equivalence in several of the steps in what follows.

(1) $\Box\varphi$, where $\varphi \equiv f(\mathbf{x}) > 0$. Observe the following:

$$[\rho](\varphi, \mathbf{x}_{[0,n+1]}, 0) = \min_{i \in [0,n+1]} p_i = \min\left(\min_{i \in [0,n]} p_i, \; p_{n+1}\right) \tag{5.6}$$

In the final expression above, observe that the first entry does not contain any p_{n+1} terms, i.e., it can be computed using the data points $x_1, \ldots, x_n$ in the partial signal $x_{[0,n]}$ itself. Thus, for all n, if we maintain the one interval representing the min of the first n values of $f(x)$ as a *summary*, then we can compute the interval robustness of $\square(f(x) > 0)$ over $x_{[0,n+1]}$ with the additional data x_{n+1} available at t_{n+1}. Note for the dual formula $\lozenge(f(x) > 0)$, a similar result holds with min substituted by max.

(2) $\varphi \mathbf{U} \psi$, where $\varphi \equiv f(x) > 0$, and $\psi \equiv g(x) > 0$. Observe the following:

$$[\rho](\varphi \mathbf{U} \psi, x_{[0,n+1]}, 0) = \max_{i \in [0,n+1]} \min(q_i, \min_{j \in [0,i]} p_j) \tag{5.7}$$

We can rewrite the RHS of Eq. (5.7) to get:

$$\max\left(\underline{\max_{i \in [0,n]} \min\left(q_i, \min_{j \in [0,i]} p_j\right)}, \ \min\left(\underline{\min_{j \in [0,n]} p_j}, p_{n+1}, q_{n+1}\right) \right) \tag{5.8}$$

Let U_n and M_n respectively denote the first and second underlined terms in the above expression. Note that for any n, U_n and M_n can be computed only using data $x_1, \ldots, x_n$. Consider the recurrences $M_{n+1} = \min(M_n, p_{n+1}, q_{n+1})$ and $U_{n+1} = \max(U_n, M_{n+1})$; we can observe that to compute M_{n+1} and U_{n+1}, we only need M_n, U_n, and x_{n+1}. Furthermore, U_{n+1} is the desired interval robustness value over the partial signal $x_{[0,n+1]}$. Thus storing and iteratively updating the two interval-values U_n and M_n is enough to monitor the given formula.

(3) $\square(\varphi \vee \lozenge \psi)$, where $\varphi \equiv f(x) > 0$, and $\psi \equiv g(x) > 0$. Observe the following:

$$[\rho](\square(\varphi \vee \lozenge \psi), x_{[0,n+1]}, 0) = \min_{i \in [0,n+1]} \max\left(p_i, \max_{j \in [i,n+1]} q_j\right)$$
$$= \min_{i \in [0,n+1]} \max\left(p_i, \max_{j \in [i,n]} q_j, q_{n+1}\right) \tag{5.9}$$

Repeatedly applying the equivalence (5.1) to the outer min in (5.9) we get:

$$\max\left(q_{n+1}, \min_{i \in [0,n+1]} \max\left(p_i, \max_{j \in [i,n]} q_j\right)\right) \tag{5.10}$$

The inner min simplifies to:

$$\max\left(q_{n+1}, \min\left(p_{n+1}, \underline{\min_{i \in [0,n]} \left(\max\left(p_i, \max_{j \in [i,n]} q_j\right)\right)}\right)\right) \tag{5.11}$$

Let T_n denote the underlined term; note that we do not require any data at time t_{n+1} to compute it. Using the recurrence $T_{n+1} = \max(q_{n+1}, \min(p_{n+1}, T_n))$, we can obtain the desired interval robustness value. The memory required is that for storing the one interval value T_n. A similar result can be established for the dual formula $\lozenge(f(x) > 0 \wedge \square(g(x) > 0))$.

(4) $\square \lozenge(\varphi)$, where $\varphi \equiv f(x) > 0$. Observe the following:

$$[\rho](\square \lozenge(\varphi, x_{[0,n+1]}, 0) = \min_{i \in [0,n+1]} \max_{j \in [i,n+1]} p_j \tag{5.12}$$

Rewriting the outer min operator and the inner max more explicitly, we get:

$$\min\left(\underline{\min_{i \in [0,n]} \max\left(\max_{j \in [i,n]} p_j, p_{n+1}\right)}, \ p_{n+1}\right) \tag{5.13}$$

Repeatedly using (5.1) to simplify the above underlined term we get:

$$\min\left(\max\left(p_{n+1}, \min_{i\in[0,n]}\max_{j\in[i,n]} p_j\right), p_{n+1}\right) = p_{n+1}. \tag{5.14}$$

The simplification to p_{n+1}, follows from (5.4). Thus, to monitor $\Box\Diamond(f(\mathbf{x})>0)$, we do not need to store any information, as the interval robustness simply evaluates to that of the predicate $f(\mathbf{x})>0$ at time t_{n+1}. A similar result can be obtained for the dual formula $\Diamond\Box(f(\mathbf{x})>0)$.

(5) $\Diamond(\varphi \wedge \Diamond(\psi))$, where $\varphi \equiv f(\mathbf{x})>0$ $\psi \equiv \Diamond(g(\mathbf{x})>0))$. Observe the following:

$$[\rho](\Diamond(\varphi \wedge \Diamond(\psi)), \mathbf{x}_{[0,n+1]}, 0) = \max_{i\in[0,n+1]}\left(\min\left(p_i, \max_{j\in[i,n+1]} q_j\right)\right) \tag{5.15}$$

We can rewrite the RHS of Eq. (5.15) as the first expression below. Applying the equivalence in (5.2) and (5.3) to the expression on the left, we get the expression on the right.

$$\max\begin{pmatrix}\min\left(p_0, \max\left(q_0, \ldots, q_{n+1}\right)\right)\\ \ldots \\ \min\left(p_n, \max\left(q_n, q_{n+1}\right)\right)\\ \min\left(p_{n+1}, q_{n+1}\right)\end{pmatrix} = \max\begin{pmatrix}\min(p_0, q_0), \ldots, \min(p_0, q_{n+1}),\\ \ldots \\ \min(p_n, q_n), \min(p_n, q_{n+1}),\\ \min(p_{n+1}, q_{n+1})\end{pmatrix} \tag{5.16}$$

Grouping terms containing q_{n+1} together and applying the equivalence in (5.2) we get:

$$\max\begin{pmatrix}\max\begin{pmatrix}\min(p_0, q_0), \min(p_0, q_1), \ldots, \min(p_0, q_n),\\ \min(p_1, q_1), \ldots, \min(p_1, q_n),\\ \ldots \\ \min(p_n, q_n)\end{pmatrix},\\ \min(q_{n+1}, \underline{\max(p_0, p_1, \ldots, p_n)}),\\ \min(p_{n+1}, q_{n+1})\end{pmatrix} \tag{5.17}$$

Observe that the first argument to the outermost max can be computed using only $\mathbf{x}_1, \ldots, \mathbf{x}_n$. Suppose we denote this term T_n. Also note that in the second argument, the inner max (underlined) can be computed using only $\mathbf{x}_1, \ldots, \mathbf{x}_n$. Let us denote this term by M_n. We now have a recurrence relations:

$$M_{n+1} = \max(M_n, p_{n+1}), \tag{5.18}$$

$$T_{n+1} = \max(T_n, \min(q_{n+1}, M_n), \min(q_{n+1}, p_{n+1})), \tag{5.19}$$

where $T_0 = \min(p_0, q_0)$ and $M_0 = p_0$. Thus, the desired interval robustness can be computed using only two values stored in T_n and M_n. The dual result holds for the formula $\Box(\varphi \vee \Box(\psi))$.

Remarks on extending the above result: The result in Theorem 1 can be generalized to allow φ and ψ that are not atomic predicates, under following two conditions:

1. Bounded horizon subformulae condition: For each formula, the subformulae φ and ψ have a bounded time-horizon, i.e., $\mathsf{hor}(\varphi)$ and $\mathsf{hor}(\psi)$ are closed intervals.
2. Smallest step-size condition: Consecutive time-points in the signal are at least Δ seconds apart, for some finite Δ, which is known *a priori*.

We defer the proof of the general case to the full version of the paper [4], but remark that the proof techniques are very similar. Let w denote the least upper bound of the time horizon for all subformulae of a given untimed formula. At any time t_n, additional book-keeping is required to store partial information for time-points in the range $[t_n - w, t_n]$. By the step-size condition there can be at most $\lceil \frac{w}{\Delta} \rceil$ time-points in this range. This is then used to show that constant memory proportional to $\lceil \frac{w}{\Delta} \rceil$ is sufficient to monitor such an untimed formula (with bounded-horizon subformulae).

6   Experimental Results

We implemented Algorithm 2 as a stand-alone tool that can be plugged in loop with any black-box simulator and evaluated it using two practical real-world applications. We considered the following criteria: (1) On an average, what fraction of simulation time can be saved by online monitoring? (2) How much overhead does online monitoring add, and how does it compare to a naïve implementation that at each step recomputes everything using an offline algorithm?

Diesel Engine Model (DEM). The first case study is an industrial-sized Simulink® model of a prototype airpath system in a diesel engine. The closed-loop model consists of a plant model describing the airpath dynamics, and a controller implementing a proprietary control scheme. The model has more than 3000 blocks, with more than 20 lookup tables approximating high-dimensional nonlinear functions. Due to the significant model complexity, the speed of simulation is about 5 times slower, i.e., simulating 1 s of operation takes 5 s in Simulink®. As it is important to simulate this model over a long time-horizon to characterize the airpath behavior over extended periods of time, savings in simulation-time by early detection of requirement violations is very beneficial. We selected two parameterized safety requirements after discussions with the control designers, (shown in Eqs. (6.1) and (6.2)). Due to proprietary concerns, we suppress the actual values of the parameters used in the requirements.

$$\varphi_{overshoot}(\mathbf{p_1}) = \Box_{[a,b]}(\mathbf{x} < c) \tag{6.1}$$

$$\varphi_{transient}(\mathbf{p_2}) = \Box_{[a,b]}(|\mathbf{x}| > c \implies (\Diamond_{[0,d]}|\mathbf{x}| < e)) \tag{6.2}$$

Property $\varphi_{overshoot}$ with parameters $\mathbf{p_1} = (a, b, c)$ specifies that in the interval $[a, b]$, the overshoot on the signal $\mathbf{x}$ should remain below a certain threshold c. Property $\varphi_{transient}$ with parameters $\mathbf{p_2} = (a, b, c, d, e)$ is a specification on the settling time of the signal $\mathbf{x}$. It specifies that in the time interval $[a, b]$ if at some time t, $|\mathbf{x}|$ exceeds c then it settles to a small region ($|\mathbf{x}| < e$) before $t + d$. In Table 1, we consider three different valuations ν_1, ν_2, ν_3 for $\mathbf{p_1}$ in the requirement $\varphi_{overshoot}(\mathbf{p_1})$, and two different valuations ν_4, ν_5 for $\mathbf{p_2}$ in the requirement $\varphi_{transient}(\mathbf{p_2})$.

The main reason for the better performance of the online algorithm is that simulations are time-consuming for this model. The online algorithm can terminate a simulation earlier (either because it detected a violation or obtained a concrete robust satisfaction interval), thus obtaining significant savings. For $\varphi_{overshoot}(\nu_3)$, we choose the parameter values for a and b such that the online

68   J.V. Deshmukh et al.

Table 1. Experimental results on DEM.

Requirement	Num. traces	Early termination	Simulation time (h)	
			Offline	Online
$\varphi_{overshoot}(\nu_1)$	1000	801	33.3803	26.1643
$\varphi_{overshoot}(\nu_2)$	1000	239	33.3805	30.5923
$\varphi_{overshoot}(\nu_3)$	1000	0	33.3808	33.4369
$\varphi_{transient}(\nu_4)$	1000	595	33.3822	27.0405
$\varphi_{transient}(\nu_5)$	1000	417	33.3823	30.6134

Table 2. Evaluation of online monitoring for CPSGrader.

STL test bench	Num. traces	Early termination	Sim. time (mins)		Overhead (s)	
			Offline	Online	Naïve	Algorithm 2
avoid_front	1776	466	296	258	553	9
avoid_left	1778	471	296	246	1347	30
avoid_right	1778	583	296	226	1355	30
hill_climb$_1$	1777	19	395	394	919	11
hill_climb$_2$	1556	176	259	238	423	7
hill_climb$_3$	1556	124	259	248	397	7
filter	1451	78	242	236	336	6
keep_bump	1775	468	296	240	1.2×10^4	268
what_hill	1556	71	259	253	1.9×10^4	1.5×10^3

algorithm has to process the entire signal trace, and is thus unable to terminate earlier. Here we see that the total overhead (in terms of runtime) incurred by the extra book-keeping by Algorithm 2 is negligible (about 0.1 %).

CPSGrader. CPSGrader [8,17] is a publicly-available automatic grading and feedback generation tool for online virtual labs in cyber-physical systems. It employs temporal logic based testers to check for common fault patterns in student solutions for lab assignments. CPSGrader uses the National Instruments Robotics Environment Simulator to generate traces from student solutions and monitors STL properties (each corresponding to a particular faulty behavior) on them. In the published version of CPSGrader [17], this is done in an offline fashion by first running the complete simulation until a pre-defined cut-off and then monitoring the STL properties on offline traces. At a step-size of 5 ms, simulating 6 s. of real-world operation of the system takes 1 s. for the simulator. When students use CPSGrader for active feedback generation and debugging, simulation constitutes the major chunk of the application response time. Online monitoring helps in reducing the response time by avoiding unnecessary simulations, giving the students feedback as soon as faulty behavior is detected.

We evaluated Algorithm 2 on the signals and STL properties used in CPS-Grader [8,17]. These signal traces result from running actual student submissions on a battery of tests such as failure to avoid obstacles in front, failure to re-orient after obstacle avoidance, failure to reach the target region (top of a hill), failure to detect the hill, and failure to use a correct filter in order to climb a hill. For lack of space, we refer the reader to [17] for further details. As an illustrative example, consider keep_bump property in Eq. 6.3:

$$\varphi_{\text{keep\_bump}} = \Diamond_{[0,60]}\Box_{[0,5]} \left(\text{bump\_right}(t) \vee \text{bump\_left}(t) \right) \tag{6.3}$$

The keep_bump formula checks whether when the bump signal is activated (i.e., the robot bumps into an obstacle either from the left or the right), the controller keeps moving forward for some time instead of driving back in order to avoid the obstacle. For each STL property, Table 2 compares the total simulation time needed for both the online and offline approaches, summed over all traces. For the offline approach, a suitable simulation cut-off time of 60 sec. is chosen. At a step-size of 5 ms, each trace is roughly of length 1000. For the online algorithm, simulation terminates before this cut-off if the truth value of the property becomes known, otherwise it terminates at the cut-off. Table 2 also shows the monitoring overhead incurred by a naïve online algorithm that performs complete recomputation at every step against the overhead incurred by Algorithm 2. Table 2 demonstrates that online monitoring ends up saving up to 24 % simulation time (>10 % in a majority of cases). The monitoring overhead of Algorithm 2 is negligible (<1 %) as compared to the simulation time and it is less than the overhead of the naïve online approach consistently by a factor of 40x to 80x.

7   Conclusions and Future Work

We have defined robust interval semantics for Signal Temporal Logic formulas over partial signal traces. The robust satisfaction interval (RoSI) of a partial signal contains the robust satisfaction value of any possible suffix of the given partial signal. We present an online algorithm to compute RoSI for a large class of STL formulas. Generalizations to full STL and considering signal traces defined by piecewise linear interpolation over given discrete-time points are important directions for future work.

Acknowledgments. This work was supported in part by TerraSwarm, one of six centers of STARnet, a Semiconductor Research Corporation program sponsored by MARCO and DARPA, by NSF Expeditions grant CCF-1139138, and by Toyota under the CHESS center at UC Berkeley.

References

1. Annpureddy, Y., Liu, C., Fainekos, G., Sankaranarayanan, S.: S-TALiRo: a tool for temporal logic falsification for hybrid systems. In: Abdulla, P.A., Leino, K.R.M. (eds.) TACAS 2011. LNCS, vol. 6605, pp. 254–257. Springer, Heidelberg (2011)
2. Bartocci, E., Bortolussi, L., Nenzi, L., Sanguinetti, G.: System design of stochastic models using robustness of temporal properties. Theor. Comput. Sci. **587**, 3–25 (2015)

3. Bartocci, E., Bortolussi, L., Sanguinetti, G.: Data-driven statistical learning of temporal logic properties. In: Legay, A., Bozga, M. (eds.) FORMATS 2014. LNCS, vol. 8711, pp. 23–37. Springer, Heidelberg (2014)

4. Deshmukh, J.V., Donzé, A., Ghosh, S., Jin, X., Juniwal, G., Seshia, S.A.: Robust Online Monitoring of Signal Temporal Logic (2015). arXiv pre-print

5. Dokhanchi, A., Hoxha, B., Fainekos, G.: On-line monitoring for temporal logic robustness. In: Bonakdarpour, B., Smolka, S.A. (eds.) RV 2014. LNCS, vol. 8734, pp. 231–246. Springer, Heidelberg (2014)

6. Donzé, A.: Breach, a toolbox for verification and parameter synthesis of hybrid systems. In: Touili, T., Cook, B., Jackson, P. (eds.) CAV 2010. LNCS, vol. 6174, pp. 167–170. Springer, Heidelberg (2010)

7. Donzé, A., Ferrère, T., Maler, O.: Efficient robust monitoring for STL. In: Sharygina, N., Veith, H. (eds.) CAV 2013. LNCS, vol. 8044, pp. 264–279. Springer, Heidelberg (2013)

8. Donzé, A., Juniwal, G., Jensen, J.C., Seshia, S.A.: CPSGrader website. http://www.cpsgrader.org

9. Donzé, A., Maler, O.: Robust satisfaction of temporal logic over real-valued signals. In: Chatterjee, K., Henzinger, T.A. (eds.) FORMATS 2010. LNCS, vol. 6246, pp. 92–106. Springer, Heidelberg (2010)

10. Eisner, C., Fisman, D., Havlicek, J., Lustig, Y., McIsaac, A., Van Campenhout, D.: Reasoning with temporal logic on truncated paths. In: Hunt Jr., W.A., Somenzi, F. (eds.) CAV 2003. LNCS, vol. 2725, pp. 27–39. Springer, Heidelberg (2003)

11. Fainekos, G., Sankaranarayanan, S., Ueda, K., Yazarel, H.: Verification of automotive control applications using S-TaLiRo. In: Proceedings of the American Control Conference (2012)

12. Fainekos, G.E., Pappas, G.J.: Robustness of temporal logic specifications for continuous-time signals. Theor. Comput. Sci. **410**(42), 4262–4291 (2009)

13. Ho, H.-M., Ouaknine, J., Worrell, J.: Online monitoring of metric temporal logic. In: Bonakdarpour, B., Smolka, S.A. (eds.) RV 2014. LNCS, vol. 8734, pp. 178–192. Springer, Heidelberg (2014)

14. Hoxha, B., Abbas, H., Fainekos, G.: Benchmarks for temporal logic requirements for automotive systems. In: Proceedings of Applied Verification for Continuous and Hybrid Systems (2014)

15. Jin, X., Donzé, A., Deshmukh, J.V., Seshia, S.A.: Mining requirements from closed-loop control models. In: Proceedings of Hybrid Systems: Computation and Control, pp. 43–52 (2013)

16. Jones, A., Kong, Z., Belta, C.: Anomaly detection in cyber-physical systems: a formal methods approach. In: Proceedings of IEEE Conference on Decision and Control, pp. 848–853 (2014)

17. Juniwal, G., Donzé, A., Jensen, J.C., Seshia, S.A.: CPSGrader: synthesizing temporal logic testers for auto-grading an embedded systems laboratory. In: Proceedings of Conference on Embedded Software, October 2014

18. Kong, Z., Jones, A., Medina Ayala, A., Aydin Gol, E., Belta, C.: Temporal logic inference for classification and prediction from data. In: Proceedings of Hybrid Systems: Computation and Control, pp. 273–282 (2014)

19. Lemire, D.: Streaming Maximum-Minimum Filter Using no More Than Three Comparisons per Element (2006). arXiv preprint cs/0610046

20. Maler, O., Nickovic, D.: Monitoring temporal properties of continuous signals. In: Lakhnech, Y., Yovine, S. (eds.) FORMATS 2004 and FTRTFT 2004. LNCS, vol. 3253, pp. 152–166. Springer, Heidelberg (2004)

21. Nickovic, D., Maler, O.: AMT: a property-based monitoring tool for analog systems. In: Raskin, J.-F., Thiagarajan, P.S. (eds.) FORMATS 2007. LNCS, vol. 4763, pp. 304–319. Springer, Heidelberg (2007)

On Verifying Hennessy-Milner Logic with Recursion at Runtime

Adrian Francalanza[1][(✉)], Luca Aceto[2], and Anna Ingolfsdottir[2]

[1] CS, ICT, University of Malta, Msida, Malta
adrian.francalanza@um.edu.mt
[2] ICE-TCS, Reykjavik University, Reykjavik, Iceland
{luca,anna}@ru.is

Abstract. We study μHML (a branching-time logic with least and greatest fixpoints) from a runtime verification perspective. We establish which subset of the logic can be verified at runtime and define correct monitor-synthesis algorithms for this subset. We also prove completeness results *wrt.* these logical subsets that show that no other properties apart from those identified can be verified at runtime.

1 Introduction

Runtime Verification (RV) [14,20] is a lightweight verification technique whereby the *execution of a system* is analysed with the aim of inferring correctness *wrt.* some property. Despite its advantages, the technique is generally limited when compared to other verification techniques such as model-checking because certain correctness properties cannot be verified at runtime [10,21]. For instance, *online* RV analyses *partial* executions incrementally (up to the current execution point of the system) which limits its applicability to satisfaction verdicts relating to correctness properties describing complete (*i.e.*, potentially infinite) executions.

There are broadly two approaches to address such a limitation. The first approach is to *restrict* the expressive power of the correctness specifications: typically, one either limits specifications to *descriptions of finite traces* such as regular expressions (RE) [12,15], or else *redefines* the semantics of existing logics (*e.g.*, LTL) so as to reflect the limitations of the runtime setting [5–7,13]. The second approach is to leave the semantics of the specification logic *unchanged*, and study which *subsets* of the logic can be verified at runtime [11,16,17,24].

Both approaches have their merits. The first approach is, in general, more popular and tends to produce specifications that are closely related to the monitors that check for them (*e.g.*, RE and automata in [15,23]), thus facilitating aspects such as monitor correctness. On the other hand, the second approach does not hinder the expressive power of the logic. Instead, it allows a verification framework to determine whether either to check for a property at runtime

The research of L. Aceto and A. Ingolfsdottir was supported by the project 001-ABEL-CM-2013 of the NILS Science and Sustainability Programme and the project Nominal SOS (nr. 141558-051) of the Icelandic Research Fund.

E. Bartocci and R. Majumdar (Eds.): RV 2015, LNCS 9333, pp. 71–86, 2015.
DOI: 10.1007/978-3-319-23820-3_5

(when possible), or else to employ more powerful (and expensive) verification techniques such as model-checking. One can even envisage a hybrid approach, where parts of a property are verified using RV and other parts are checked using other techniques. More importantly, however, the second approach leads to better separation of concerns: since it is *agnostic* of the verification technique used, one can change the method of verification without impinging on the property semantics.

This paper follows this second approach. In particular, it revisits Hennessy-Milner Logic with recursion [3], μHML, a reformulation of the expressive modal μ-calculus [19], used to describe correctness properties of reactive system; subsets of the logic have already been adapted for detectEr [25], an RV tool for runtime-verifying actor-based systems [8,16], whereas constructs from the modal μ-calculus have been used in other RV tools such as Eagle [4]. In this study we consider the logic in its entirety, and investigate the monitorability of the logic wrt. an operational definition of a general class of monitors that employ both acceptance and rejection verdicts [7,14]. In particular, our results extend the class of monitorable μHML properties used in [16] and establish monitorability upper bounds for this logic. We also present new results that relate the utility of multi-verdict monitors wrt. logics defined over programs (as opposed to traces). To the best of our knowledge, this is one of the first bodies of work investigating the limits of RV wrt. a *branching-time* logic that specifies properties about the *execution graph* of a program; other work pertaining to the aforementioned second approach has focussed on *linear-time* logics defined over *execution traces*, and has explored RV's limits along the linear-time dimension, e.g., [11].

In the rest of the paper, Sect. 2 introduces our model for reactive systems and Sect. 3 presents the logic μHML defined over this model. Section 4 formalises our abstract RV operational setup in terms of monitors and our instrumentation relation. In Sect. 5 we argue for a particular correspondence between monitors and μHML properties within this setup. Section 6 identifies monitorability limits for the logic but also establishes a monitorable logical subset that satisfies the correspondence of Sect. 5. Section 7 shows that this subset is maximally expressive, using a result about multi-verdict monitors. Section 8 concludes.

2   The Model

We describe systems abstractly as Labelled Transition Systems (LTSs) [3,19]. An LTS is a triple $\langle \text{PROC}, (\text{ACT} \cup \{\tau\}), \longrightarrow \rangle$ consisting of a set of states, PROC, a set of actions, ACT with distinguished silent action τ (we assume $\mu \in \text{ACT} \cup \{\tau\}$ and $\tau \notin \text{ACT}$), and a transition relation, $\longrightarrow \subseteq (\text{PROC} \times (\text{ACT} \cup \{\tau\}) \times \text{PROC})$. LTS states can be expressed as processes, PROC, from the regular fragment of CCS [22] as defined in Fig. 1. Assuming a set of (visible) actions, $\alpha, \beta \in \text{ACT}$ and a set of (recursion) variables $x, y, z \in \text{VARS}$, processes may be either inactive, prefixed by an action, a mutually-exclusive choice amongst two processes, or recursive; rec $x.p$ acts as a *binder* for x in p and we work up to alpha-conversion of bound variables. All recursive processes are assumed to be guarded.

Syntax

$$p, q, r \in \text{PROC} ::= \text{nil} \quad \text{(inaction)} \quad | \quad \alpha.p \quad \text{(prefixing)} \quad | \quad p + q \quad \text{(choice)}$$
$$| \quad \text{rec}\, x.p \quad \text{(recursion)} \quad | \quad x \quad \text{(rec. variable)}$$

Dynamics

$$\text{ACT} \frac{}{\alpha.p \xrightarrow{\alpha} p} \qquad \text{REC} \frac{}{\text{rec}\, x.p \xrightarrow{\tau} p[\text{rec}\, x.p/x]} \qquad \text{SELL} \frac{p \xrightarrow{\mu} p'}{p + q \xrightarrow{\mu} p'}$$

Fig. 1. A model for describing systems

The dynamic behaviour is then described by the transition rules of Fig. 1, defined over the closed and guarded terms in PROC (we elide the symmetric rule SELR). The suggestive notation $p \xrightarrow{\mu} p'$ denotes $(p, \mu, p') \in \longrightarrow$; we also write $p \xrightarrow{\alpha}$ to denote $\neg(\exists p'.\ p \xrightarrow{\alpha} p')$. For example, $p_1 + p_2 \xrightarrow{\mu} q$ if either $p_1 \xrightarrow{\mu} q$ or $p_2 \xrightarrow{\mu} q$. As usual, we write $p \Longrightarrow p'$ in lieu of $p(\xrightarrow{\tau})^* p'$ and $p \overset{\mu}{\Longrightarrow} p'$ for $p \Longrightarrow \cdot \xrightarrow{\mu} \cdot \Longrightarrow p'$, referring to p' as a μ-derivative of p. We let $t, u \in \text{ACT}^*$ range over sequences of visible actions and write $p \overset{\alpha_1}{\Longrightarrow} \ldots \overset{\alpha_n}{\Longrightarrow} p_n$ as $p \overset{t}{\Longrightarrow} p_n$, where $t = \alpha_1, \ldots, \alpha_n$. See [3, 22] for more details.

Example 1. A (reactive) system that acts as a server that repeatedly accepts *requests* and subsequently *answers* them, with the possibility of terminating through the special *close* request, may be expressed as the following process, p.

$$p = \text{rec}\, x.\big(\text{req.ans}.x + \text{cls.nil}\big)$$

A server that non-deterministically stops offering the close action is denoted by process q, whereas r only offers the close action after the first serviced request.

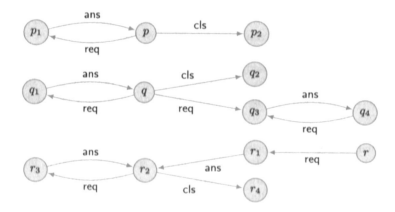

Fig. 2. A depiction of the system in Example 1

Syntax

$$\varphi, \phi \in \mu\text{HML} ::= \text{tt} \quad \text{(truth)} \qquad | \text{ff} \qquad \text{(falsehood)}$$

$$| \quad \varphi \vee \phi \qquad \text{(disjunction)} \qquad | \quad \varphi \wedge \phi \qquad \text{(conjunction)}$$

$$| \quad \langle \alpha \rangle \varphi \qquad \text{(possibility)} \qquad | \quad [\alpha]\varphi \qquad \text{(necessity)}$$

$$| \quad \min X.\varphi \qquad \text{(min. fixpoint)} \qquad | \quad \max X.\varphi \qquad \text{(max. fixpoint)}$$

$$| \quad X \qquad \text{(rec. variable)}$$

Semantics

$$[\![\text{tt}, \rho]\!] \overset{\text{def}}{=} \text{PROC} \qquad\qquad [\![\text{ff}, \rho]\!] \overset{\text{def}}{=} \emptyset$$

$$[\![\varphi_1 \wedge \varphi_2, \rho]\!] \overset{\text{def}}{=} [\![\varphi_1, \rho]\!] \cap [\![\varphi_2, \rho]\!] \qquad [\![\varphi_1 \vee \varphi_2, \rho]\!] \overset{\text{def}}{=} [\![\varphi_1, \rho]\!] \cup [\![\varphi_2, \rho]\!]$$

$$[\![[\alpha]\varphi, \rho]\!] \overset{\text{def}}{=} \left\{ p \mid p \overset{\alpha}{\Rightarrow} q \text{ implies } q \in [\![\varphi, \rho]\!] \right\} \quad [\![\langle \alpha \rangle \varphi, \rho]\!] \overset{\text{def}}{=} \left\{ p \mid p \overset{\alpha}{\Rightarrow} q \text{ and } q \in [\![\varphi, \rho]\!] \right\}$$

$$[\![\min X.\varphi, \rho]\!] \overset{\text{def}}{=} \bigcap \{ S \mid [\![\varphi, \rho[X \mapsto S]]\!] \subseteq S \}$$

$$[\![\max X.\varphi, \rho]\!] \overset{\text{def}}{=} \bigcup \{ S \mid S \subseteq [\![\varphi, \rho[X \mapsto S]]\!] \} \qquad\qquad [\![X, \rho]\!] \overset{\text{def}}{=} \rho(X)$$

Fig. 3. μHML syntax and semantics

$$q = \text{rec } x.(\text{req.ans}.x + \text{cls.nil} + (\text{rec } y.\text{req.ans}.y))$$

$$r = \text{req.ans.rec } x.(\text{req.ans}.x + \text{cls.nil})$$

Pictorially, the resp. LTSs denoted by processes p, q and r are shown in Fig. 2, where the arcs correspond to weak transitions, $\overset{\mu}{\Longrightarrow}$. ∎

3   The Logic

The logic μHML assumes a countable set of logical variables $X, Y \in \text{LVAR}$, and is defined as the set of *closed* formulae generated by the grammar of Fig. 3. Apart from the standard constructs for truth, falsehood, conjunction and disjunction, the logic is equipped with possibility and necessity modal operators, together with recursive formulae expressing least or greatest fixpoints; formulae $\min X.\varphi$ and $\max X.\varphi$ resp. bind free instances of the logical variable X in φ, inducing the usual notions of open/closed formulae and equality up to alpha-conversion.

Formulae are interpreted over the process powerset domain, $S \in \mathcal{P}(\text{PROC})$. The semantic definition of Fig. 3 is given for *both* open and closed formulae and employs an environment from variables to sets of processes, $\rho \in \text{LVAR} \rightharpoonup \mathcal{P}(\text{PROC})$; this permits an inductive definition on the structure of the formula. For instance, in Fig. 3, the semantic meaning of a variable X wrt. an environment ρ is the mapping for that variable in ρ. The semantics of truth, falsehood, conjunction and disjunction are standard (e.g., $\vee$ and $\wedge$ are interpreted as set-theoretic union and intersection). Possibility formulae $\langle \alpha \rangle \varphi$ describe processes with *at least one* α-derivative satisfying φ whereas necessity formulae $[\alpha]\varphi$ describe processes where *all* of their α-derivatives (possibly none) satisfy φ. The powerset domain $\mathcal{P}(\text{PROC})$ is a complete lattice wrt. set-inclusion, $\subseteq$, which guarantees the existence of least and largest solutions for the recursive formulae of the logic; as usual, these can be *resp.* specified as the intersection of all the pre-fixpoint solutions and the union of all post-fixpoint solutions [3]. Note that $\rho[X \mapsto S]$ denotes an environment ρ' where $\rho'(X) = S$ and $\rho'(Y) = \rho(Y)$ for all other $Y \neq X$. Since the interpretation of closed formulae is independent of the environment ρ, we sometimes write $[\![\varphi]\!]$ in lieu of $[\![\varphi, \rho]\!]$. We say that a process p *satisfies* a formula φ whenever $p \in [\![\varphi]\!]$, and violates a formula whenever $p \notin [\![\varphi]\!]$.

Example 2. Formula $\langle \alpha \rangle \mathsf{tt}$ describes processes that *can* perform action α whereas formula $[\alpha]\mathsf{ff}$ describes processes that *cannot* perform action α.

$$\varphi_1 = \min X.(\langle \mathsf{req} \rangle \langle \mathsf{ans} \rangle X \vee [\mathsf{cls}]\mathsf{ff}) \qquad \varphi_2 = \max X.(\langle \mathsf{req} \rangle \langle \mathsf{ans} \rangle X \vee [\mathsf{cls}]\mathsf{ff})$$
$$\varphi_3 = \max X.([\mathsf{req}][\mathsf{ans}]X \wedge \langle \mathsf{cls} \rangle \mathsf{tt}) \qquad \varphi_4 = \max X.([\mathsf{req}][\mathsf{ans}]X \wedge [\mathsf{cls}]\mathsf{ff})$$

Formula φ_1 denotes a *liveness* property describing processes that *eventually* stop offering the action cls after any number of serviced request, (req.ans)*— processes q and r from Example 1 satisfy this property but p does not. Changing the fixpoint into a maximal one, *i.e.,* φ_2, would include p in the property as well. Formulae φ_3 and φ_4 denote *safety* properties: e.g., φ_3, describes (terminating and non-terminating) processes that can *always* perform a cls action after any number of serviced request (p satisfies this property but q and r do not).

$$\varphi_5 = \langle \mathsf{req} \rangle \langle \mathsf{ans} \rangle \max X.(([\mathsf{req}]\mathsf{ff} \vee \langle \mathsf{req} \rangle \langle \mathsf{ans} \rangle X) \wedge [\mathsf{cls}]\mathsf{ff})$$
$$\varphi_6 = \min X.((\langle \mathsf{req} \rangle \langle \mathsf{ans} \rangle \mathsf{tt} \wedge [\mathsf{req}][\mathsf{ans}]X) \vee \langle \mathsf{cls} \rangle \mathsf{tt})$$

Formula φ_5 is satisfied by processes that, after one serviced request, req.ans, exhibit *a* complete[1] transition sequence (req.ans)* that never offers action cls (q from Example 1 satisfies this property whereas p and r do not). Formula φ_6 describes processes that along *all* serviced request sequences, (req.ans)*, eventually reach a stage where they offer action cls (processes p and q satisfy the criteria immediately, whereas r satisfies it for (req.ans)* sequences longer than 1). ∎

4   Monitors and Instrumentation

Monitors may also be viewed as LTSs, through the syntax of Fig. 4; this is similar to that of processes, with the exception that nil is replaced by three *verdict* constructs, yes, no and end, *resp.* denoting acceptance, rejection and termination (*i.e.,* an inconclusive outcome). Monitor behaviour is similar to that of processes for the common constructs; see rules in Fig. 4. The only new transition concerns verdicts, MVER, stating that a verdict may transition with *any* $\alpha \in$ ACT and go back to the same state, modelling the requirement that verdicts are *irrevocable*.

---

[1] A transition sequence is complete if it is either infinite or affords no more actions.

Syntax

$$m, n \in \text{MON} ::= v \quad\mid\ \alpha.m \quad\mid\ m + n \quad\mid\ \text{rec}\, x.m \quad\mid\ x$$
$$v, u \in \text{VERD} ::= \text{end} \quad\mid\ \text{no} \quad\mid\ \text{yes}$$

Dynamics

$$\text{MACT} \frac{}{\alpha.m \xrightarrow{\alpha} m} \qquad\qquad \text{MREC} \frac{}{\text{rec}\, x.m \xrightarrow{\tau} m[\text{rec}\, x.m/x]}$$

$$\text{MSELL} \frac{m \xrightarrow{\mu} m'}{m + n \xrightarrow{\mu} m'} \qquad \text{MSELR} \frac{n \xrightarrow{\mu} n'}{m + n \xrightarrow{\mu} n'} \qquad \text{MVER} \frac{}{v \xrightarrow{\alpha} v}$$

Instrumentation

$$\text{IMON} \frac{p \xrightarrow{\alpha} p' \quad m \xrightarrow{\alpha} m'}{m \triangleleft p \xrightarrow{\alpha} m' \triangleleft p'} \qquad \text{ITER} \frac{p \xrightarrow{\alpha} p' \quad m \xslashed{\xrightarrow{\alpha}} \quad m \xslashed{\xRightarrow{\tau}}}{m \triangleleft p \xrightarrow{\alpha} \text{end} \triangleleft p'}$$

$$\text{IASYP} \frac{p \xrightarrow{\tau} p'}{m \triangleleft p \xrightarrow{\tau} m \triangleleft p'} \qquad \text{IASYM} \frac{m \xrightarrow{\tau} m'}{m \triangleleft p \xrightarrow{\tau} m' \triangleleft p}$$

Fig. 4. Monitors and instrumentation

Figure 4 also describes an instrumentation relation connecting the behaviour of a process p with that of a monitor m: the configuration $m \triangleleft p$ denotes a *monitored system*. In an instrumentation, the process leads the (visible) behaviour of a monitored system (*i.e.*, if the process cannot α-transition, then the monitored system will not either) while the monitor passively follows, transitioning accordingly; this is in contrast with well-studied parallel composition relations of LTSs [18, 22]. Specifically, rule IMON states that if a process can transition with action α and the *resp.* monitor can follow this by transitioning with the same action, then in an instrumented monitored system they transition in lockstep. However, if the monitor cannot follow such a transition, $m \xslashed{\xrightarrow{\alpha}}$, even after any number of internal actions, $m \xslashed{\xRightarrow{\tau}}$, instrumentation forces it to terminate with an inconclusive verdict, end, while the process is allowed to proceed unaffected; see rule ITER. Rules IASYP and IASYM allow monitors and processes to transition independently *wrt.* internal moves.[2]

Proposition 1. $m \triangleleft p \xRightarrow{t} m' \triangleleft p'$ *iff* $p \xRightarrow{t} p'$ *and*

- *either* $m \xRightarrow{t} m'$
- *or* $m' = \text{end}$ *and* $\exists t', \alpha, t'', m''.\ t = t'\alpha t'',\ m'' \xslashed{\xrightarrow{\tau}}$ *and* $m \xRightarrow{t'} m'' \xslashed{\xrightarrow{\alpha}}$.

Remark 1. Since we strive towards a general theory, the syntax in Fig. 4 allows for non-deterministic monitors such as $\alpha.\text{yes} + \alpha.\text{no}$ or $\alpha.\text{nil} + \alpha.\beta.\text{yes}$. There are

---

[2] If a monitor cannot match a process action, but can transition silently, it is allowed to do so, and the matching check is applied again to the τ-derivative monitor.

settings where determinism is unattainable (*e.g.*, distributed monitoring [15]) or desirable (*e.g.*, testers [23]), and others where non-determinism expresses under-specification (*e.g.*, program refinement [1]). Thus, expressing non-determinism allows us to study the cases where it is tolerated or considered erroneous.

Example 3. Monitor m_1 (defined below) monitors for executions of the form (req.ans)*.cls returning the acceptance verdict yes, whereas m_2 dually rejects executions of that form. When composed with process p from Example 1, the monitored system $m_1 \triangleleft p$ may either service requests forever, $m_1 \triangleleft p \overset{\text{req}}{\Longrightarrow} \cdot \xrightarrow{\text{ans}}$ $m_1 \triangleleft p$, or else terminate with a yes verdict, $m_1 \triangleleft p \overset{\text{cls}}{\Longrightarrow}$ yes $\triangleleft$ nil. By contrast, when instrumented over a process capable of the transition $p' \xrightarrow{\text{ans}} p''$, m_1 may terminate its process observation after one transition, *i.e.*, $m_1 \triangleleft p' \overset{\text{ans}}{\Longrightarrow}$ end $\triangleleft p''$.

$$m_1 = \operatorname{rec} x.\big(\text{req.ans}.x + \text{cls.yes}\big) \qquad m_3 = \operatorname{rec} x.\big(\text{req.ans}.x + \text{cls.yes} + \text{req.req}.x\big)$$
$$m_2 = \operatorname{rec} x.\big(\text{req.ans}.x + \text{cls.no}\big) \qquad m_4 = \operatorname{rec} x.\big(\text{req.ans}.x + \text{cls.yes} + \text{cls.no}\big)$$

Monitor m_3 may either behave like m_1 or non-deterministically terminate upon a serviced request, *i.e.*, $m_3 \triangleleft p \overset{\text{req}}{\Longrightarrow}$ req.$m_3 \triangleleft p_1 \xrightarrow{\text{ans}}$ end $\triangleleft p$. Conversely, monitor m_4 non-deterministically returns verdict yes or no upon a cls action, *e.g.*, $m_4 \triangleleft p \overset{\text{cls}}{\Longrightarrow}$ yes $\triangleleft$ nil but also $m_4 \triangleleft p \overset{\text{cls}}{\Longrightarrow}$ no $\triangleleft$ nil.   ∎

5   Correspondence

Our goal is to establish a correspondence between the verdicts reached by monitors over an instrumented system from Sect. 4 and the properties specified using the logic of Sect. 3. In particular, we would like to relate acceptances (yes) and rejections (no) reached by a monitor m when monitoring a process p with satisfactions ($p \in \llbracket \varphi \rrbracket$) and violations ($p \notin \llbracket \varphi \rrbracket$) for that process *wrt.* some μHML formula, φ. This will, in turn, allow us to determine when a monitor m *represents* (in some precise sense) a property φ.

Example 4. Monitor m_1 from Example 3 monitors for *satisfactions* of the property

$$\varphi_7 = \min X.(\langle\text{req}\rangle\langle\text{ans}\rangle X \vee \langle\text{cls}\rangle\text{tt})$$

describing processes that can perform a cls action after a number of serviced requests. Stated otherwise, m_1 produces a yes verdict for a computation of the form (req.ans)*.cls from a process p, attesting that $p \in \llbracket \varphi_7 \rrbracket$. Similarly, m_2 from Example 3 monitors for *violations* of the property φ_4 from Example 2. The same *cannot* be said for m_4 from Example 3 and φ_7 above: for some processes, *e.g.*, p from Example 1, it may produce both verdicts yes and no for witness computations (req.ans)*.cls, which leads to contradictions at a logical level *i.e.*, we cannot have both $p \in \llbracket \varphi_7 \rrbracket$ and $p \notin \llbracket \varphi_7 \rrbracket$. A similar argument applies to m_4 and m_2 from Example 3.   ∎

Remark 2. A monitor may behave non-deterministically in other ways wrt. a process. For instance, m_3 from Example 3 may sometimes flag an acceptance but at other times may not when monitoring p from Example 1, *even when p produces the same trace*: e.g., for $t =$ req.ans.cls we have $m_3 \lhd p \stackrel{t}{\Longrightarrow} \text{yes} \lhd \text{nil}$ but also $m_3 \lhd p \stackrel{t}{\Longrightarrow} \text{end} \lhd \text{nil}$. However, since any other terminal monitor state apart from yes and no (*i.e.*, end and any other non-verdict state) is of no consequence from a logical satisfaction/violation point of view, we abstract from such outcomes.

We investigate conditions that one could require for establishing the correspondence between monitors and formulae. We start with Definition 2 (below): it defines when m is able to *monitor soundly for a property* φ, $\mathbf{smon}(m, \varphi)$, by requiring that acceptances (*resp.* rejections) imply satisfactions (*resp.* violations) for every monitored execution of a process p.

Definition 1 (Acceptance/Rejection). $\mathbf{acc}(p, m) \stackrel{def}{=} \exists t, p'.\ m \lhd p \stackrel{t}{\Longrightarrow} \text{yes} \lhd p'$ and $\mathbf{rej}(p, m) \stackrel{def}{=} \exists t, p'.\ m \lhd p \stackrel{t}{\Longrightarrow} \text{no} \lhd p'$.

Definition 2 (Sound Monitoring).

$$\mathbf{smon}(m, \varphi) \stackrel{def}{=} \forall p.\big(\mathbf{acc}(p, m)\ \text{implies}\ p \in [\![\varphi]\!]\big)\ \text{and}\ \big(\mathbf{rej}(p, m)\ \text{implies}\ p \notin [\![\varphi]\!]\big)$$

Note that, if $\mathbf{smon}(m, \varphi)$ and $\exists p.\mathbf{acc}(p, m)$, by Definition 2 we know $p \in [\![\varphi]\!]$; thus, $\neg(p \notin [\![\varphi]\!])$ and by the contrapositive of Definition 2, we must also have $\neg\mathbf{rej}(p, m)$.

Example 5. From Example 4, we formally have $\mathbf{smon}(m_1, \varphi_7)$, $\mathbf{smon}(m_2, \varphi_2)$ and $\mathbf{smon}(m_3, \varphi_7)$. We can also show that $\neg\mathbf{smon}(m_4, \varphi_7)$ and $\neg\mathbf{smon}(m_4, \varphi_2)$. ∎

Sound monitoring is arguably the least requirement for relating a monitor with a logical property. Further to this, the obvious additional requirement would be to ask for the dual of Definition 2, *i.e.*, *complete monitoring* for m and φ, stating that for all p, $p \in [\![\varphi]\!]$ implies $\mathbf{acc}(p, m)$, and also that $p \notin [\![\varphi]\!]$ implies $\mathbf{rej}(p, m)$. However, such a requirement turns out to be too strong for a large part of the logic presented in Fig. 3.

Example 6. Consider the basic formula $\langle \alpha \rangle \text{tt}$. One could ascertain that the simple monitor $\alpha.\text{yes}$ satisfies the condition that $p \in [\![\varphi]\!]$ implies $\mathbf{acc}(p, m)$ for all p. However, there does not exist a sound monitor that can satisfy $\forall p.p \notin [\![\varphi]\!]$ implies $\mathbf{rej}(p, m)$ for $\langle \alpha \rangle \text{tt}$. Arguing by contradiction, assume that one such monitor m exists. Since nil $\notin [\![\langle \alpha \rangle \text{tt}]\!]$ then we should have $\mathbf{rej}(\text{nil}, m)$. By Definition 1 and Proposition 1, this means $m \Longrightarrow \text{no}$ which, in turn, implies that $\mathbf{rej}(\alpha.\text{nil}, m)$ although, clearly, $\alpha.\text{nil} \in [\![\langle \alpha \rangle \text{tt}]\!]$. This makes m unsound, contradicting our initial assumption.

A similar, albeit dual, argument can be carried out for another core basic formula, $[\alpha]\text{ff}$: although there are sound monitors satisfying the condition $\forall p.p \notin [\![\varphi]\!]$ implies $\mathbf{rej}(p, m)$, there are none that also satisfy the other condition $\forall p.p \in [\![\varphi]\!]$ implies $\mathbf{acc}(p, m)$. ∎

Concretely, requiring complete monitoring would limit correspondence to a trivial subset of the logic, namely **tt** and **ff**. We therefore define the weaker forms of completeness that are stated below.

Definition 3 (Satisfaction/Violation/Partially-Complete Monitoring).

$$\boldsymbol{scmon}(m, \varphi) \stackrel{def}{=} \forall p.p \in [\![\varphi]\!] \text{ implies } \boldsymbol{acc}(p, m) \qquad \textit{(satisfaction complete)}$$
$$\boldsymbol{vcmon}(m, \varphi) \stackrel{def}{=} \forall p.p \notin [\![\varphi]\!] \text{ implies } \boldsymbol{rej}(p, m) \qquad \textit{(violation complete)}$$
$$\boldsymbol{cmon}(m, \varphi) \stackrel{def}{=} \boldsymbol{scmon}(m, \varphi) \text{ or } \boldsymbol{vcmon}(m, \varphi) \qquad \textit{(partially complete)}$$

We can now formalise monitor-formula correspondence: m *monitors* for φ, $\boldsymbol{mon}(m, \varphi)$, if it can do it *soundly*, and in a *partially-complete* manner, i.e., if it is *either* satisfaction complete *or* violation complete.

Definition 4 (Monitoring). $\boldsymbol{mon}(m, \varphi) \stackrel{def}{=} \boldsymbol{smon}(m, \varphi)$ *and* $\boldsymbol{cmon}(m, \varphi)$.

6   Monitorability

Using Definition 4, we can define what it means for a formula to be monitorable.

Definition 5 (Monitorability). *Formula* φ *is* monitorable *iff* $\exists m. \boldsymbol{mon} m, \varphi$. *A language* $\mathcal{L} \subseteq \mu\text{HML}$ *is* monitorable *iff every* $\varphi \in \mathcal{L}$ *is monitorable.*

We immediately note that not all logical formulae are monitorable.

Example 7. Through the witness outlined in Example 6, we can show that formulae $\langle \alpha \rangle$tt and $\langle \beta \rangle$tt are monitorable with a satisfaction complete monitor. However, $\varphi_8 = \langle \alpha \rangle$tt$\wedge \langle \beta \rangle$tt (their conjunction), is *not*. Intuitively, this is so because once a monitor observes one of the actions, it cannot "go back" to check for the other. Formally, we argue towards a contradiction by assuming that $\exists m.\boldsymbol{mon}(m, \varphi_8)$. There are two subcases to consider.

If m is satisfaction complete, then $\boldsymbol{acc}(\alpha.\text{nil} + \beta.\text{nil}, m)$ since $\alpha.\text{nil} + \beta.\text{nil} \in [\![\varphi_8]\!]$. By Proposition 1, m reaches verdict **yes** along one of the traces ϵ, α or β. If the trace is ϵ, then m also accepts nil, which is unsound (since nil $\notin [\![\varphi_8]\!]$) whereas if the trace is α, m must also accept $\alpha.\text{nil}$, which is also unsound ($\alpha.\text{nil} \notin [\![\varphi_8]\!]$); the case for β is analogous.

If m is violation complete then $\boldsymbol{rej}(\beta.\text{nil}, m)$ since $\beta.\text{nil} \notin [\![\varphi_8]\!]$. By Proposition 1, we either have $m \stackrel{\epsilon}{\Longrightarrow}$ no or $m \stackrel{\beta}{\Longrightarrow}$ no and for both cases we can argue that m also rejects process $\alpha.\text{nil} + \beta.\text{nil}$, which is unsound since $\alpha.\text{nil} + \beta.\text{nil} \in [\![\varphi_8]\!]$. ∎

We now identify a syntactic subset of μHML formulae called MHML, with the aim of showing that it is a monitorable subset of the logic. At an intuitive level, it consists of the safe and co-safe syntactic subsets of μHML, sHML and cHML respectively.

Definition 6 (Monitorable Logic). $\psi, \chi \in \text{MHML} \overset{\text{def}}{=} \text{SHML} \cup \text{CHML}$ *where:*

$$\theta, \vartheta \in \text{SHML} ::= \text{tt} \quad | \text{ff} \quad | [\alpha]\theta \quad | \theta \wedge \vartheta \quad | \max X.\theta \quad | X$$
$$\pi, \varpi \in \text{CHML} ::= \text{tt} \quad | \text{ff} \quad | \langle\alpha\rangle\pi \quad | \pi \vee \varpi \quad | \min X.\pi \quad | X$$

To prove monitorability for MHML, we define a monitor synthesis function $(\!|\text{-}|\!)$ generating a monitor for each $\psi \in \text{MHML}$. We then show that $(\!|\psi|\!)$ is the witness monitor required by Definition 5 to demonstrate the monitorability of ψ.

Definition 7 (Monitor Synthesis).

$$(\!|\text{ff}|\!) \overset{\text{def}}{=} no \qquad\qquad (\!|\text{tt}|\!) \overset{\text{def}}{=} yes \qquad\qquad (\!|X|\!) \overset{\text{def}}{=} x$$

$$(\!|[\alpha]\psi|\!) \overset{\text{def}}{=} \begin{cases} \alpha.(\!|\psi|\!) & \text{if } (\!|\psi|\!) \neq yes \\ yes & otherwise \end{cases} \qquad (\!|\langle\alpha\rangle\psi|\!) \overset{\text{def}}{=} \begin{cases} \alpha.(\!|\psi|\!) & \text{if } (\!|\psi|\!) \neq no \\ no & otherwise \end{cases}$$

$$(\!|\psi_1 \wedge \psi_2|\!) \overset{\text{def}}{=} \begin{cases} (\!|\psi_1|\!) & \text{if } (\!|\psi_2|\!) = yes \\ (\!|\psi_2|\!) & \text{if } (\!|\psi_1|\!) = yes \\ (\!|\psi_1|\!) + (\!|\psi_2|\!) & otherwise \end{cases} \quad (\!|\psi_1 \vee \psi_2|\!) \overset{\text{def}}{=} \begin{cases} (\!|\psi_1|\!) & \text{if } (\!|\psi_2|\!) = no \\ (\!|\psi_2|\!) & \text{if } (\!|\psi_1|\!) = no \\ (\!|\psi_1|\!) + (\!|\psi_2|\!) & otherwise \end{cases}$$

$$(\!|\max X.\psi|\!) \overset{\text{def}}{=} \begin{cases} \text{rec } x.(\!|\psi|\!) & \text{if } (\!|\psi|\!) \neq yes \\ yes & otherwise \end{cases} \quad (\!|\min X.\psi|\!) \overset{\text{def}}{=} \begin{cases} \text{rec } x.(\!|\psi|\!) & \text{if } (\!|\psi|\!) \neq no \\ no & otherwise \end{cases}$$

A few comments are in order. We first note that Definition 7 is *compositional*; see e.g., [23] for reasons why this is desirable. It also assumes a bijective mapping between the denumerable sets LVAR and VARS; see synthesis for X, $\max X.\psi$ and $\min X.\psi$, where the logical variable X is converted to the process variable x. Although Definition 7 covers both SHML and CHML, the syntactic constraints of Definition 6 mean that synthesis for a formula ψ uses at most the first row and then either the first column (in the case of SHML) or the second column (in case of CHML). The conditional cases handle logically equivalent formulae, e.g., since $[\![\text{ff}]\!] = [\![\min X.\langle\alpha\rangle\text{ff}]\!]$ we have $(\!|\text{ff}|\!) = (\!|\min X.\langle\alpha\rangle\text{ff}|\!) = no$. In the case of conjunctions and disjunctions, these are essential to be able to generate sound monitors.

Example 8. Consider the CHML formula $\langle\alpha\rangle\text{tt}\vee\text{ff}$ (which is logically equivalent to $\langle\alpha\rangle\text{tt}$). A naive synthesis without the case checks would generate the monitor $\alpha.yes + no$ which is not only redundant, but *unsound* e.g., for $p = \alpha.\text{nil}$ we have both $\mathbf{acc}(p, \alpha.yes + no)$ and $\mathbf{rej}(p, \alpha.yes + no)$. Similar problems would manifest themselves for less obvious cases, e.g., $\langle\alpha\rangle\text{tt}\vee(\min X.\langle\alpha\rangle\text{ff})\vee(\langle\alpha\rangle\min X.\text{ff})$. However, in all of these cases, our monitor synthesis of Definition 7 generates $\alpha.yes$. ∎

Theorem 1 (Monitorability). $\varphi \in \text{MHML}$ *implies* φ *is monitorable.*

Proof. We show that for all $\varphi \in \text{MHML}$, $\mathbf{mon}((\!|\varphi|\!), \varphi)$ holds. □

Theorem 1 provides us with a simple syntactic check to determine whether a formula is monitorable; as shown earlier in Example 7, determining whether a formula is monitorable is in general non-trivial. Moreover, the proof of Theorem 1 (through Definition 7) provides us with an automatic monitor synthesis algorithm that is correct according to Definition 4.

Example 9. Since φ_4 from Example 2 is in MHML, we know it is monitorable. Moreover, we can generate the *correct* monitor $(\!|\varphi_4|\!) = \mathrm{rec}\, x.(\mathsf{req.ans}.x+\mathsf{cls.no}) = m_2$ (from Example 3). Using similar reasoning, φ_7 (Example 4) is also monitorable, and a correct monitor for it is m_1 from Example 3. ∎

7 Expressiveness

The results obtained in Sect. 6 beg the question of whether MHML is the *largest* monitorable subset of μHML. One way to provide an answer to this question would be to show that, in some sense, every monitor corresponds to a formula in MHML according to Definition 4. However, this approach quickly runs into problems since there are monitors, such as yes + no, that make little sense from the point of view of Definition 4. To this end, we prove a general (and perhaps surprising) result.

Theorem 2 (Multi-verdict Monitors and Monitoring). $\forall m \in \text{MON}$

$$(\exists t, u \in \text{ACT}^*.\ m \overset{t}{\Longrightarrow} \mathsf{yes}\ \textit{and}\ m \overset{u}{\Longrightarrow} \mathsf{no})\quad \textit{implies}\quad \not\exists \varphi \in \mu\text{HML}.\ \boldsymbol{mon}(m, \varphi).$$

Proof. By contradiction. Assume that $\exists \varphi.\boldsymbol{mon}(m, \varphi)$. Using t and u, we can construct the obvious process $p = t + u$, where $m \triangleleft p \overset{t}{\Longrightarrow} \mathsf{yes} \triangleleft \mathsf{nil}$ and $m \triangleleft p \overset{u}{\Longrightarrow} \mathsf{no} \triangleleft \mathsf{nil}$. We therefore have $\mathbf{acc}(p, m)$ and $\mathbf{rej}(p, m)$, and by monitor soundness (Definition 2), that $p \in [\![\varphi]\!]$ and $p \notin [\![\varphi]\!]$. This is clearly a contradiction. □

Stated otherwise, Theorem 2 asserts that multi-verdict monitors are necessarily *unsound*, at least wrt. properties defined over processes (as opposed to logics defined over other domains such as traces, e.g., [7,11,14]). This also implies that, in order to answer the aforementioned question, it suffices to focus on *uni-verdict* monitors that flag either acceptances or rejections (but not both). In fact, a closer inspection of the synthesis algorithm of Definition 7 reveals that all the monitors generated using it are, in fact, uni-verdict.

We partition uni-verdict monitors into the obvious classes: *acceptance monitors*, AMON (using verdict yes), and *rejection monitors*, RMON (using no). In what follows, we focus our technical development on one monitor class, in the knowledge that the corresponding development for the other class is analogous.

Definition 8 (Rejection Expressive-Complete). *A subset $\mathcal{L} \subseteq \mu$HML is expressive-complete wrt. rejection monitors iff*

$$\forall m \in \text{RMON}.\ \exists\ \varphi \in \mathcal{L}\ \ \textit{such that}\ \ \boldsymbol{mon}(m, \varphi).$$

We show that the language sHML (Definition 6) is rejection expressive-complete. We do so with the aid of a mapping function from a rejection monitor to a corresponding formula in sHML defined below. Definition 9 is fairly straightforward, thanks to the fact that we only need to contend with a single verdict. Again, it assumes a bijective mapping between the denumerable sets LVAR and VARS (as in the case of Definition 7). The mapping function is defined inductively on the structure of m where we note that (i) no translation is given for the monitor yes (since these are rejection monitors) and (ii) the base case end is mapped to formula tt, which contrasts with the mapping used in Definition 7.

Definition 9 (Rejection Monitors to sHML Formulae).

$$\langle\!\langle no \rangle\!\rangle \stackrel{def}{=} ff \qquad\qquad \langle\!\langle end \rangle\!\rangle \stackrel{def}{=} tt \qquad\qquad \langle\!\langle x \rangle\!\rangle \stackrel{def}{=} X$$

$$\langle\!\langle \alpha.m \rangle\!\rangle \stackrel{def}{=} [\alpha]\langle\!\langle m \rangle\!\rangle \qquad \langle\!\langle m+n \rangle\!\rangle \stackrel{def}{=} \langle\!\langle m \rangle\!\rangle \wedge \langle\!\langle n \rangle\!\rangle \qquad \langle\!\langle rec\, x.m \rangle\!\rangle \stackrel{def}{=} max\, X.\langle\!\langle m \rangle\!\rangle$$

Proposition 2. sHML *is Rejection Expressive-Complete.*

Proof. We show that for all $m \in$ RMON, $\mathbf{mon}(m, \langle\!\langle m \rangle\!\rangle)$ holds.   □

Definition 10 (Acceptance Expressive-Complete). *Language* $\mathcal{L} \subseteq \mu$HML *is* expressive-complete wrt. *acceptance monitors iff* $\forall m \in$ AMON. $\exists\, \varphi \in \mathcal{L}$ *such that* $\mathbf{mon}(m, \varphi)$.

Proposition 3. cHML *is Acceptance Expressive-Complete.*

Equipped with Propositions 2 and 3, it follows that MHML is expressive complete wrt. uni-verdict monitors.

Definition 11 (Expressive-Complete). $\mathcal{L} \subseteq \mu$HML *is expressive-complete* wrt. uni-verdict monitors, iff $\forall m \in$ AMON $\cup$ RMON. $\exists\, \varphi \in \mathcal{L}.\ \mathbf{mon}(m, \varphi)$.

Theorem 3. MHML *is Expressive-Complete.*

Proof. Follows from Propositions 2 and 3   □

We are now in a position to prove the result alluded to at the beginning of this section, namely that MHML is the largest monitorable subset of μHML up to logical equivalence, *i.e.*, Theorem 4. First, however, we define what we understand by language inclusion up to formula semantic equivalence, Definition 12.

Definition 12 (Language Inclusion). *For all* $\mathcal{L}_1, \mathcal{L}_2 \in \mu$HML

$$\mathcal{L}_1 \sqsubseteq \mathcal{L}_2 \stackrel{def}{=} \forall \varphi_1 \in \mathcal{L}_1. \exists \varphi_2 \in \mathcal{L}_2 \text{ such that } [\![\varphi_1]\!] = [\![\varphi_2]\!]$$

We also prove the following important proposition, that gives an upper bound to the expressiveness of languages satisfying monitorability properties.

Proposition 4. *For any* $\mathcal{L} \subseteq \mu$HML:

1. $\big(\forall \varphi \in \mathcal{L}. \exists m \in$ AMON. $\forall p.(\mathbf{acc}(p, m)$ *iff* $p \in [\![\varphi]\!])\big)$ *implies* $\mathcal{L} \sqsubseteq$ cHML.

2. $\big(\forall\varphi \in \mathcal{L}. \exists m \in \mathrm{RMON}. \forall p.(\boldsymbol{rej}(p, m) \text{ iff } p \notin [\![\varphi]\!])\big)$ *implies* $\mathcal{L} \sqsubseteq \mathrm{sHML}$.

Proof. We prove the first clause; the second clause is analogous. Assume $\varphi \in \mathcal{L}$. We need to show that $\exists \pi \in \mathrm{cHML}$ such that $[\![\varphi]\!] = [\![\pi]\!]$. For φ we know that

$$\exists m \in \mathrm{AMON}. \big(\forall p.(\mathbf{acc}(p, m) \text{ iff } p \in [\![\varphi]\!])\big). \tag{1}$$

By Proposition 3, for the monitor m used in (1), we also know

$$\exists \pi \in \mathrm{cHML}. \big(\forall p.(\mathbf{acc}(p, m) \text{ iff } p \in [\![\pi]\!])\big). \tag{2}$$

Assume an arbitrary $p \in [\![\varphi]\!]$. By (1) we obtain $\mathbf{acc}(p, m)$, and by (2) we obtain $p \in [\![\pi]\!]$. Thus $[\![\varphi]\!] \subseteq [\![\pi]\!]$. Dually, we can also reason that $[\![\pi]\!] \subseteq [\![\varphi]\!]$.   □

Theorem 4 (Completeness). $(\mathcal{L} \subseteq \mu\mathrm{HML}$ *is monitorable*$)$ *implies* $\mathcal{L} \sqsubseteq$ MHML.

Proof. Since $\mathcal{L}$ is monitorable, by Definitions 5 and 4 we know:

$$\forall \varphi \in \mathcal{L}. \exists m \text{ such that } \mathbf{smon}(m, \varphi) \text{ and } \mathbf{cmon}(m, \varphi) \tag{3}$$

By Theorem 2, we know that every m used in (3) is uni-verdict. This means that we can partition the formulae in $\mathcal{L}$ into two disjoint sets $\mathcal{L}_{\mathrm{acc}} \uplus \mathcal{L}_{\mathrm{rej}}$ where:

$$\big(\forall \varphi \in \mathcal{L}_{\mathrm{acc}}. \exists m \in \mathrm{AMON}. \forall p.(\mathbf{acc}(p, m) \text{ iff } p \in [\![\varphi]\!])\big) \tag{4}$$

$$\big(\forall \varphi \in \mathcal{L}_{\mathrm{rej}}. \exists m \in \mathrm{RMON}. \forall p.(\mathbf{rej}(p, m) \text{ iff } p \notin [\![\varphi]\!])\big) \tag{5}$$

By (4), (5) and Proposition 4 we obtain $\mathcal{L}_{\mathrm{acc}} \sqsubseteq \mathrm{CHML}$ and $\mathcal{L}_{\mathrm{rej}} \sqsubseteq \mathrm{sHML}$ *resp.*, from which the required result follows.   □

   Theorems 2 and 4 constitute powerful results wrt. the monitorability of our branching-time logic. Completeness, Theorem 4, guarantees that limiting one-self to the syntactic subset MHML does not hinder the *expressive power* of the specifier when formulating monitorable properties. Alternatively, one could also determine whether a formula is monitorable by rewriting it as a logically equiv-alent formula in MHML.[3] This would enable a verification framework to decide whether to check for a μHML property at runtime, or resort to more expressive (but expensive means) otherwise. Whenever the property is monitorable, The-orem 2 guarantees that a uni-verdict monitor is the best monitor that we can synthesise. This is important since multi-verdict monitor constructions, such as those in [7], generally carry *higher overheads* than uni-verdict monitors.

Example 10. By virtue of Theorem 4, we can conclude that properties $\varphi_1, \varphi_2,$ φ_3, φ_5 and φ_6 from Example 2 are all non-monitorable properties according to Definition 5, since no logically equivalent formulae in MHML exist. Arguably, the problem of establishing logical equivalence through syntactic manipulation of

---

[3] The problem of determining whether a (general) formula is logically equivalent to one in MHML is decidable in exponential time — probably EXPTIME complete.

formulae is easier to determine and automate, when compared to direct reasoning about the semantic definitions of monitorability and those of the *resp.* properties; recall that Definition 5 (Monitorability) — through Definition 2 and Definition 3 — universally quantifies over all processes, which generally poses problems for automation.

For instance, in the case of φ_1, we could use Theorem 2 to substantially reduce the search space of our witness monitor to the uni-verdict ones, but this still leaves us with a lot of work to do. Specifically, we can reason that the witness *cannot* be an *acceptance monitor*, since it would need to accept process nil, which implies that it must erroneously also accept the process cls.nil (using reasoning similar to that used in Example 6). It is less straightforward to argue that the witness *cannot* be a *rejection monitor* either. We argue towards a contradiction by assuming that such a monitor exists. Since it is violationspscomplete (Definition 3) it should reject the process req.nil + cls.nil since this process does not satisfy φ_1: by Proposition 1 we know that it can do so along either of the traces ϵ, req or cls. If it rejects it along ϵ, then it also rejects the satisfying process nil; if it rejects along trace req, it also rejects the satisfying process req.ans.nil; finally, if it rejects it along cls, it must also reject the satisfying process req.ans.nil+cls.nil. Thus, the monitor must be unsound, meaning that it cannot be a rejection monitor.   ∎

8   Conclusion

We have investigated monitorability aspects of a branching-time logic called μHML, which impinges on what properties can be verified at runtime. It extends and generalises prior work carried out in the context of reactive systems modelled as LTSs [16]. The concrete contributions of the paper are:

1. An operational definition of monitorability, Definition 4, specified over an instrumentation relation unifying the individual behaviour of processes and monitors, Fig. 4, which is used to define monitorable subsets of μHML, Definition 5.
2. The identification of a subset of μHML, Definition 6, that is shown to be monitorable, Theorem 1, and also maximally expressive, Theorem 4, *wrt.* Definition 5.
3. A result asserting that, *wrt.* Definition 4, uni-verdict monitors suffice for monitoring branching-time properties, Theorem 2.

Future Work: It is worth exploring other definitions of monitorability apart from that of Definition 4, and determining how this affects the monitorable subset of μHML identified in this work. For instance, one could relax the conditions of Definition 4 by only requiring soundness (Definition 2), or require more stringent conditions *wrt.* verdicts and monitor non-determinism; see [16] for a practical motivation of this. Moreover, monitorability is also largely dependent on the underlying instrumentation relation used; there may be other sensible relations apart from the one defined in Fig. 4 that are worth investigating within this setting.

A separate line of research could investigate manipulation techniques that decompose formulae into monitorable components. For instance, reformulating a generic formula φ as the disjunction $\phi \vee \pi$ (recall $\pi \in$ cHML) could allow for a *hybrid* verification approach that distributes the load between the pre-deployment phase and the runtime phase whereby we model-check for the satisfaction of a system wrt. ϕ and, if this fails, runtime verify the system wrt. π.

Related Work: In [23], monitorability is defined for *formulae defined over traces* (e.g., LTL) whenever the formula semantics does not contain *ugly* prefixes; an ugly prefix is a trace from which *no* finite extension will ever lead to a conclusive verdict. Falcone *et al.* [14] revisit this classical definition, extending it to the Safety-Progress property classification, while proposing an alternative definition in terms of the structure of the recognising Streett Automata of the *resp.* property. Although our definition is cast within a different setting (a logic over processes), and has a distinct operational flavour in terms of monitored system executions, it is certainly worthwhile to try to reconcile the different definitions.

The logic μHML has been previously studied from a linear-time perspective in [2,9], in order to find subsets that characterise may/must testing equivalences. Although tests are substantially different from our monitor instrumentations, the logic subsets identified in [2,9] are related to (albeit different from) MHML.

References

1. Abrial, J.R.: Modeling in Event-B: System and Software Engineering. Cambridge University Press, New York (2010)
2. Aceto, L., Ingólfsdóttir, A.: Testing Hennessy-Milner logic with recursion. In: Thomas, W. (ed.) FOSSACS 1999. LNCS, vol. 1578, pp. 41–55. Springer, Heidelberg (1999)
3. Aceto, L., Ingólfsdóttir, A., Larsen, K.G., Srba, J.: Reactive Systems: Modelling, Specification and Verification. Cambridge University Press, New York (2007)
4. Barringer, H., Goldberg, A., Havelund, K., Sen, K.: Rule-based runtime verification. In: Steffen, B., Levi, G. (eds.) VMCAI 2004. LNCS, vol. 2937, pp. 44–57. Springer, Heidelberg (2004)
5. Bauer, A., Leucker, M., Schallhart, C.: The good, the bad, and the ugly, but how ugly is ugly? In: Sokolsky, O., Taşıran, S. (eds.) RV 2007. LNCS, vol. 4839, pp. 126–138. Springer, Heidelberg (2007)
6. Bauer, A., Leucker, M., Schallhart, C.: Comparing LTL semantics for runtime verification. Logic Comput. 20(3), 651–674 (2010)
7. Bauer, A., Leucker, M., Schallhart, C.: Runtime verification for LTL and TLTL. TOSEM 20(4), 14 (2011)
8. Cassar, I., Francalanza, A.: On synchronous and asynchronous monitor instrumentation for actor systems. In: FOCLASA, vol. 175, pp. 54–68 (2014)
9. Cerone, A., Hennessy, M.: Process behaviour: formulae vs. tests. In: EXPRESS. EPTCS, vol. 41, pp. 31–45 (2010)
10. Chang, E., Manna, Z., Pnueli, A.: Characterization of temporal property classes. In: Kuich, W. (ed.) ICALP 1992. LNCS, vol. 623, pp. 474–486. Springer, Heidelberg (1992)

11. Cini, C., Francalanza, A.: An LTL proof system for runtime verification. In: Baier, C., Tinelli, C. (eds.) TACAS 2015. LNCS, vol. 9035, pp. 581–595. Springer, Heidelberg (2015)

12. Colombo, C., Pace, G., Schneider, G.: LARVA – safer monitoring of real-time Java programs (Tool paper). In: SEFM, pp. 33–37 (2009)

13. Eisner, C., Fisman, D., Havlicek, J., Lustig, Y., McIsaac, A., Van Campenhout, D.: Reasoning with temporal logic on truncated paths. In: Hunt Jr., W.A., Somenzi, F. (eds.) CAV 2003. LNCS, vol. 2725, pp. 27–39. Springer, Heidelberg (2003)

14. Falcone, Y., Fernandez, J.-C., Mounier, L.: What can you verify and enforce at runtime? STTT **14**(3), 349–382 (2012)

15. Francalanza, A., Gauci, A., Pace, G.J.: Distributed system contract monitoring. JLAP **82**(5–7), 186–215 (2013)

16. Francalanza, A., Seychell, A.: Synthesising correct concurrent runtime monitors. In: Formal Methods in System Design (FMSD), pp. 1–36 (2014)

17. Geilen, M.: On the construction of monitors for temporal logic properties. In: RV. ENTCS, vol. 55, pp. 181–199 (2001)

18. Hoare, C.A.R.: Communicating Sequential Processes. Prentice-Hall, Upper Saddle River (1985)

19. Kozen, D.: Results on the propositional μ-calculus. TCS **27**, 333–354 (1983)

20. Leucker, M., Schallhart, C.: A brief account of runtime verification. JLAP **78**(5), 293–303 (2009)

21. Manna, Z., Pnueli, A.: Completing the temporal picture. TCS **83**(1), 97–130 (1991)

22. Milner, R.: A Calculus of Communicating Systems. LNCS, vol. 92. Springer, Heidelberg (1982)

23. Pnueli, A., Zaks, A.: PSL model checking and run-time verification via testers. In: Misra, J., Nipkow, T., Sekerinski, E. (eds.) FM 2006. LNCS, vol. 4085, pp. 573–586. Springer, Heidelberg (2006)

24. Sen, K., Roşu, G., Agha, G.: Generating optimal linear temporal logic monitors by coinduction. In: Saraswat, V.A. (ed.) ASIAN 2003. LNCS, vol. 2896, pp. 260–275. Springer, Heidelberg (2003)

25. detectEr Project. http://www.cs.um.edu.mt/svrg/Tools/detectEr/

Assuring the Guardians

Jonathan Laurent[1], Alwyn Goodloe[2(✉)], and Lee Pike[3]

[1] École Normale Supérieure, Paris, France
jonathan.laurent@ens.fr
[2] NASA Langley Research Center, Hampton, VA, USA
a.goodloe@nasa.gov
[3] Galois, Inc., Portland, OR, USA
leepike@galois.com

Abstract. Ultra-critical systems are growing more complex, and future systems are likely to be autonomous and cannot be assured by traditional means. Runtime Verification (RV) can act as the last line of defense to protect the public safety, but only if the RV system itself is trusted. In this paper, we describe a model-checking framework for runtime monitors. This tool is integrated into the Copilot language and framework aimed at RV of ultra-critical hard real-time systems. In addition to describing its implementation, we illustrate its application on a number of examples ranging from very simple to the Boyer-Moore majority vote algorithm.

1 Introduction

Runtime Verification (RV), where monitors detect and respond to property violations at runtime, can help address several of the verification challenges facing ultra-critical systems [20, 24]. As RV matures it will be employed to verify increasingly complex properties such as checking complex stability properties of a control system or ensuring that a critical system is fault-tolerant. As RV is applied to more complex systems, the monitors themselves will become increasingly sophisticated and as prone to error as the system being monitored. Applying formal verification tools to the monitors to ensure they are correct can help safeguard that the last line of defense is actually effective.

The work reported here is part of a larger program aimed at creating a framework for *high assurance RV*. In order to be used in ultra-critical environments, high-assurance RV must:

1. Provide evidence for a safety case that the RV enforces safety guarantees.
2. Support verification that the specification of the monitors is correct.
3. Ensure that monitor code generated implements the specification of the monitor.

These guiding principles inform the continued development of the Copilot language and framework that is intended to be used in RV of ultra-critical systems [18, 22]. Earlier work focused on verifying that the monitor synthesis

E. Bartocci and R. Majumdar (Eds.): RV 2015, LNCS 9333, pp. 87–101, 2015.
DOI: 10.1007/978-3-319-23820-3_6

process is correct (Requirement 3 above) [21]. Here, the focus is on the second requirement for high-assurance RV - making sure the monitor specification is correct. Requirement 1, in the spirit of Rushby's proposal [24] is future work.

Contributions. In this paper we describe the theory and implementation of a k-induction based model-checker [5,25] for Copilot called `copilot-kind`. More precisely, `copilot-kind` is a model-checking *framework* for Copilot, with two existing backends: a lightweight implementation of k-induction using Yices [4] and a backend based on *Kind2*, implementing both k-induction and the IC3 algorithm [26].

After providing a brief introduction to Copilot in Sect. 2 and to Satisfiability Modulo Theories (SMT)-based k-induction in Sect. 3, we introduce `copilot-kind` in Sect. 4. Illustrative examples of `copilot-kind` are provided in Sect. 5, and implementation details are given in Sect. 6. The final two sections discuss related work and concluding remarks, respectively.

Copilot and `copilot-kind` are open-source (BSD3) and in current use at NASA.[1]

2   Copilot

Copilot is a domain specific language (DSL) embedded in the functional programming language Haskell [14] tailored to programming monitors for hard real-time, reactive systems. Given that Copilot is deeply embedded in Haskell, one must have a working knowledge of Haskell to effectively use Copilot. However, the benefit of an embedded DSL in Haskell is that the host-language serves as a type-safe, Turing-complete macro language, allowing arbitrary compile-time computation, while keeping the core DSL small.

Copilot is a *stream* based language where a stream is an infinite ordered sequence of values that must conform to the same type. All transformations of data in Copilot must be propagated through streams. In this respect, Copilot is similar to Lustre [2], but is specialized for RV. Copilot guarantees that specifications compile to constant-time and constant-space implementations to update stream states.

Copilot's Expression Language. In the following, we briefly and informally introduce Copilot's expression language. Copilot streams mimic both the syntax and semantics of Haskell lazy lists with the exception that operators are automatically promoted point-wise to the list level.

Two types of temporal operators are provided in Copilot, one for delaying streams and one for looking into the future of streams:

```
(++) :: [a] → Stream a → Stream a
drop :: Int → Stream a → Stream a
```

---

[1] https://github.com/Copilot-Language.

Here xs ++ s prepends the list xs at the front of the stream s. The expression drop k s skips the first k values of the stream s, returning the remainder of the stream. For example, the Fibonacci sequence modulo 2^{32} can be written in Copilot as follows:

```
fib :: Stream Word32
fib = [1,1] ++ (fib + drop 1 fib)
```

The base types of Copilot over which streams are built include Booleans, signed and unsigned words of 8, 16, 32, and 64 bits, floats, and doubles. Type-safe casts in which overflow cannot occur are permitted.

Sampling. Copilot programs are meant to monitor arbitrary C programs. They do so by periodically *sampling* values in the program under observation. Currently, Copilot can be used to sample variables, arrays, and the return values of side-effect free functions—sampling arbitrary structures is future work. For a Copilot program compiled to C, symbols become in-scope when arbitrary C code is linked with the code generated by the Copilot compiler. Copilot provides the operator extern to introduce an external symbol to sample.

The following stream samples the C variable e0 of type uint8_t to create each new stream index. If e0 takes the values 2, 4, 6, 8, ... the stream ext has the values 1, 3, 7, 13,....

```
ext :: Stream Word8
ext = [1] ++ (ext + extern "e0" )
```

3   Background on SMT-based k-induction

The focus of our investigation has been on applying model checking to prove invariant properties of our monitors. We employ a technique known as k-induction [5,25] for verifying inductive properties of infinite state systems. k-induction has the advantage that it is well suited to SMT based bounded model checking. This section profiles the basic concepts of the k-induction proof technique needed in the remainder of the paper. In practice, we use tools that implement enhancements of the basic procedure such as path compression [3] that help the process scale, but are beyond the focus of the paper.

Consider a state transition system (S, I, T), where S is a set of states, $I \subseteq S$ is the set of initial states and $T \subseteq S \times S$ is a transition relation over S. To show P holds in the transition system one must show that (1) the base case holds—that P holds in all states reachable from an initial state in k steps, and (2) the induction step holds—that if P holds in states $s_0, \ldots, s_{k-1}$ then it holds in state s_k. The k-induction principle is formally expressed in the following two entailments:

$$I(s_0) \wedge T(s_0, s_1) \wedge \cdots \wedge T(s_{k-1}, s_k) \models P(s_k)$$
$$P(s_0) \wedge \cdots \wedge P(s_{k-1}) \wedge T(s_0, s_1) \wedge \cdots \wedge T(s_{k-1}, s_k) \models P(s_k)$$

If one cannot show the property to be true, the property is strengthened by either extending the formula or progressively increasing the length of the reachable states considered.

Property P said to be a k-inductive property with respect to (S, I, T) if there exists some $k \in \mathbb{N}^{0<}$ such that P satisfies the k-induction principle. As k increases, weaker invariants may be proved. If P is a safety property that does not hold, then the first entailment will break for a finite k and a counterexample will be provided. The trick is to find an invariant that is tractable by the SMT solver yet weak enough to satisfy the desired property.

4   Copilot Prover Interface

The `copilot-kind` model-checker is an extensible interface to multiple provers used to verify safety properties of Copilot programs. Currently, two backends for `copilot-kind` have been implemented: the first is a homegrown prover we call "the light prover" built on top of Yices [4] and the second is the Kind2 model checker being developed at the University of Iowa [17].

To begin, we describe how safety properties are specified in Copilot. Using the "synchronous observer" approach [10], properties *about* Copilot programs are specified *within* Copilot itself. In particular, properties are encoded with standard Boolean streams and Copilot streams are sufficient to encode past-time linear temporal logic [12]. We bind a Boolean stream to a property name with the `prop` construct in the specification, where the specification has type `Spec`.

For instance, here is a straightforward specification declaring one property:

```
spec = prop "gt0" (x > 0)
  where
  x = [1] ++ (1 + x)
```

In order to check that property gt0 holds, we use a `prove` function implemented as part of `copilot-kind`. Here, we can discharge the proof-obligation for the program above with the light prover using the command:

<code>prove (lightProver def) (check "gt0") spec</code>

where `lightProver def` stands for the *light prover* with default configuration.

While numeric types are bounded in Copilot, they are abstracted as integers in the prover, so we ignore overflow; see Sect. 6 for details.

Combining Provers. Copilot-Kind allows provers to be combined. Given provers A and B, the `combine` function returns a prover C which launches both

A and B and returns the most *precise* output of the two upon termination. "Precise" in this case means returning the least element in the following partial order: for a given execution, classify prover outputs as valid (V), unknown (U), invalid with countexample (C), and invalid with no counterexample (N); the partial order is the least relation such that

(Merging provers that handle non-termination within a bound is future work.)
In practice, we used the following prover in the examples of Sect. 5:

```
prover = lightProver def {kTimeout = 5} 'combine' kind2Prover def
```

which uses both the light and Kind2 provers, the first being limited to 5 steps of the k-induction.

Proof Schemes. Consider the example :

```
spec = do
  prop "gt0"  (x > 0)
  prop "neq0" (x /= 0)
  where
    x = [1] ++ (1 + x)
```

and suppose we want to prove "neq0". Currently, the two available solvers fail at showing this non-inductive property (if at index i, $x = -k$, then it satisfies the induction hypothesis but fails the induction step for all k). Yet, we can prove the more general inductive lemma "gt0" and deduce our main goal from this. For this, we apply our proof scheme feature as follows:

```
assert "gt0" ➤ check "neq0"
```

A *proof scheme* is a chain of primitive proof operations glued together by the >> operator to combine proofs, and in particular, provide lemmas. The available primitives are:

- check "prop" checks whether or not a given property is true in the current context.
- assume "prop" adds an assumption in the current context.
- assert "prop" is a shortcut for check "prop" >> assume "prop".
- assuming props scheme assumes the list of properties *props*, executes the proof scheme *scheme* in this context, and forgets the assumptions.
- msg "..." displays a string in the standard output.

5   Examples

In this section, we will present several examples of `copilot-kind` applied to verify properties on Copilot monitors.

First, let us reexamine the Copilot program from Sect. 2 that generates the Fibonacci sequence. A fundamental property of this program is that it produces a stream of values that are always positive. We express this as follows:

```
spec = prop "pos" (fib > 0)
  where
    fib :: Stream Word64
    fib = [1, 1] ++ (fib + drop 1 fib)
```

This invariant property is clearly inductive and is easily discharged. Note that, as discussed in Sect. 6, 64-bit words are modelled by integers and eventual overflow problems are ignored here.

The next example uses `copilot-kind` to prove properties relating two different specifications. Consider the following specification:

```
intCounter :: Stream Bool → Stream Word64
intCounter reset = time
  where
    time = if reset then 0
              else [0] ++ if time == 3 then 0 else time + 1
```

that acts as a counter performing modulo arithmetic, but is reset when the `reset` stream value is true. Now consider the specification

```
greyTick :: Stream Bool → Stream Bool
greyTick reset = a && b
  where
    a = (not reset) && ([False] ++ not b)
    b = (not reset) && ([False] ++ a)
```

After a reset, `greyTick`'s output stream forms a cycle of Boolean values with the third item in the cycle having value `true` and the rest being `false`. Thus, the two specifications both have a cyclic structure and with a cycle that begins when the `reset` stream is set to `true`.

```
spec = do
  prop "iResetOk"   (r ⟹ (ic == 0))
  prop "eqCounters" (it == gt)
  where
    ic = intCounter r
    it = ic == 2
    gt = greyTick r
    r  = extern "reset" Nothing
```

Fig. 1. Spec listing.

From the above observations we conjecture that given the same input stream, when `reset` is true, the `intCounter` is 0 and `greyTick` is `true` when `intCounter` is 2. (Extern streams are uninterpreted; see Sect. 6.) We formalize these two properties in our framework as shown in Fig. 1. These predicates are discharged using the proof scheme.

```
scheme :: ProofScheme
scheme = do
  check "iResetOk"
  check "eqCounters"
```

5.1 Boyer-Moore Majority Vote

Earlier research on Copilot has investigated fault-tolerant runtime verification [22]. Fault-tolerant algorithms often include a variant of a majority vote over values (e.g., sensor values, clock values, etc.). The Boyer-Moore Majority Vote Algorithm is a linear-time voting algorithm [13,16]. In this case-study, we verify the algorithm.

The algorithm operates in two passes, first it chooses a candidate and the second pass verifies that the candidate is indeed a majority. The algorithm is subtle and the desire to apply formal verification to our Copilot implementation helped motivate the effort described here.

Two versions of this algorithm were checked with `copilot-kind`. The first algorithm was the one implemented as part of the aforementioned research on fault tolerance and flew on a small unmanned aircraft. This algorithm is a parallel implementation, where at each tick, the algorithm takes n inputs from n distinct streams and is fully executed. The second version of the algorithm is a sequential version, where the inputs are delivered one by one in time and where the result is updated at each clock tick. Both can be checked with the basic k-induction algorithm, but the proofs involved are different.

The Parallel Version. The core of the algorithm is the following:

```
majorityVote :: (Typed a, Eq a) => [Stream a] -> Stream a
majorityVote [] = error "empty list"
majorityVote (x : xs) = aux x 1 xs
  where
  aux p _s [] = p
  aux p s (l : ls) =
    local (if s == 0 then l else p) $ \ p' ->
    local (if s == 0 || l == p then s + 1 else s - 1) $ \ s' ->
    aux p' s' ls
```

Let us denote A as the set of the elements that can be used as inputs for the algorithm. Assume l is a list and $a \in A$, we denote $|l|_a$ as the number of occurrences of a in l. The total length of a list l is simply written $|l|$. The `majorityVote` function takes a list of streams l as its input and returns an output maj such that:

$$\forall a \in A, (a \neq maj) \Longrightarrow (|l|_a \leq |l|/2)$$

Given that quantifiers are handled poorly by SMT solvers and their use is restricted in most model-checking tools, including `copilot-kind`, we use a simple trick to write and check this property. If $P(n)$ is a predicate of an integer n, we have $\forall n . P(n)$ if and only if $\neg P(n)$ is unsatisfiable, where n an unconstrained integer, which can be solved by a SMT solver. The corresponding Copilot specification can be written as:

```
okWith :: (Typed a, Eq a) ⇒
          Stream a → [Stream a] → Stream a → Stream Bool
okWith a l maj = (a /= maj) ⟹ ((2 * count a l) ≤ length l)
  where
     count _e [] = 0
     count e (x : xs) = (if x == e then 1 else 0) + count e xs

spec = prop "OK" (okWith (arbitraryCst "n") ss maj)
  where
     ss = [ arbitrary ("s" ++ show i) | i ← [1..10] ]
     maj = majorityVote
```

The function `arbitrary` is provided by the `copilot-kind` standard library and introduces an arbitrary stream. In the same way, `arbitraryCst` introduces a stream taking an unconstrained but constant value.

Note that we prove the algorithm for a fixed number of N inputs (here $N = 10$). Therefore, no induction is needed for the proof and the invariant of the Boyer-Moore algorithm does not need to be made explicit. However, the size of the problem discharged to the SMT solver grows in proportion to N.

The Serial Version. Now, we discuss an implementation of the algorithm where the inputs are read one by one in a single stream and the result is updated at each clock tick. As the number of inputs of the algorithm is not bounded anymore, a proof by induction is necessary and the invariant of the Boyer-Moore algorithm, being non-trivial, has to be stated explicitly. As stated in Hesselink [13], this invariant is:

$$\forall m \in A, \quad (m \neq p) \Longrightarrow (s + 2|l|_m \leq |l|) \quad \wedge \quad (m = p) \Longrightarrow (2|l|_m \leq s + |l|)$$

where l is the list of processed inputs, p is the intermediary result and s is an internal state of the algorithm. The problem here is that the induction invariant needs universal quantification to be expressed. Unfortunately, this quantifier cannot be removed by a similar trick like the one seen previously. Indeed, when an invariant is of the form $\forall x.P(x, s)$, s denoting the current state of the world, the induction formula we have to prove is:

$$\forall x.P(x, s) \wedge T(s, s') \models \forall x.P(x, s')$$

Sometimes, the stronger entailment

$$P(x, s) \wedge T(s, s') \models P(x, s')$$

holds and the problem becomes tractable for the SMT solver by replacing a universally quantified variable by an unconstrained one. In our current example, it is not the case.

Our solution to the problem of dealing with quantifiers is restricted to the case where A is finite and we replace each formula of the form $\forall x \in A \; P(x)$ by $\bigwedge_{x \in A} P(x)$. This can be done with the help of the forAllCst function provided by the copilot-kind standard library. It is defined as:

```
forAllCst :: (Typed a) ⇒
  [a] → (Stream a → Stream Bool) → Stream Bool
forAllCst l f = conj $ map (f o constant) l
  where conj = foldl (&&) true
```

The code for the serial Boyer-Moore algorithm and its specification is then:

```
allowed :: [Word8]
allowed = [1, 2]

majority :: Stream Word8 → (Stream Word8, Stream Word8, Stream
      Bool)
majority l = (p, s, j)
  where
    p  = [0] ++ if s ≤ 0 then l else p
    s  = [0] ++ if p == l || s ≤ 0 then s + 1 else s - 1
    k  = [0] ++ (1 + k)

    count m = cnt
      where cnt = [0] ++ if l == m then cnt + 1 else cnt

    j = forAllCst allowed $ λ m →
          local (count m) $ λ cnt →
          let j0 = (m /= p) ⟹ ((s + 2 * cnt) ≤ k)
              j1 = (m == p) ⟹ ((2 * cnt) ≤ (s + k))
          in j0 && j1

spec = do
  prop "J" j
  prop "inRange" (existsCst allowed $ λ a → input == a)
  where
    input = externW8 "in" Nothing
    (p, s, j) = majority input

scheme = assuming ["inRange"] $ check "J"
```

We make the hypothesis that all the elements manipulated by the algorithm are in the set `allowed`, which is finite. The SMT proofs are generally exponential with respect to the number of variables, so this approach does not scale well.

6   Implementation

In this section, we shall outline the structure of the implementation of our Copilot verification system. After Copilot type-checking and compilation, a Copilot program is approximated so it can be expressed in a theory handled by most SMT solvers, as described below. Any information of no use for the model checking process is thrown away. The result of this process is encoded in *Cnub* format, which is is structurally close to the Copilot core format, but supports fewer datatypes and operators. Then, it can be translated into one of two available representation formats:

- The IL format: a list of quantifier-free equations over integer sequences, where each sequence roughly corresponds to a stream. This format is similar to the one developed by Hagen [8], but customized for Copilot. The *light prover* works with this format.
- The TransSys format: a modular representation of a *state transition system*. The *Kind2 prover* uses this format, which can be printed into Kind2's native format [17].

6.1   Approximating a Specification

The complexity of the models that are built from Copilot specifications is limited by the power and expressiveness of the SMT solvers in use. For instance, most SMT solvers do not handle real functions like trigonometric functions. Moreover, bounded integer arithmetic is often to be approximated by standard integer arithmetic.

The Cnub format is aimed at approximating a Copilot specification in a format relying on a simple theory including basic integer arithmetic, real arithmetic, and uninterpreted functions. The stream structure is kept from the Copilot core format, but the following differences have to be emphasized:

- In contrast to the great diversity of numeric types available in Copilot, we restrain ourselves to three basic types which are handled by the SMTLIB standard: `Bool`, `Integer`, and `Real`. Problems related to integer overflows and floating point arithmetic are ignored.
- Uninterpreted functions are used to model operators that are not handled. They are abstract as function symbols satisfying the equality:

$$(\forall i.\ x_i = y_i) \implies f(x_1, \cdots, x_n) = f(y_1, \cdots, y_n).$$

in the quantifier-free theory of uninterpreted function symbols, as provided by most SMT solvers.

– Copilot extern variables are modelled by unconstrained streams. Particular precautions have to be taken to model access to external arrays in order to express the constraint that several requests to the same index inside a clock period must yield the same result.

Excepting the first point, the approximations made are sound: they result in a superset of possible behaviors for the RV.

The problem of integer overflows can be tackled by adding automatically to the property being verified some bound-checking conditions for all integer variables. However, this solution can generate a great overhead for the proof engine. Moreover, it treats every program which causes an integer overflow as wrong, although this behaviour could be intended. An intermediate way to go would be to let the developer annotate the program so he can specify which bounds have to be checked automatically or to use the bit vector types of SmtLib, which will be implemented in a future release.

6.2 The Light Prover and the IL Format

Our homegrown prover relies on an intermediate representation format called IL. An IL specification mostly consists of a list of quantifier-free equations over integer sequences. These equations contain a free variable n which is implicitly universally quantified. The IL format is similar to the one used by Hagen [8].

A stream of type a is modeled by a function of type $\mathbb{N} \rightarrow a$. Each stream definition is translated into a list of constraints on such functions. For instance, the stream definition

```
fib = [1, 1] ++ (fib + drop 1 fib)
```

is translated into the IL chunk:

$$f : \mathbb{N} \rightarrow \mathbb{N}$$
$$f(0) = 1$$
$$f(1) = 1$$
$$f(n + 2) = f(n + 1) + f(n).$$

Suppose we want to check the property `fib > 0` which translates into $f(n) > 0$. This can be done in two steps of the k-induction seen in Sect. 3 by taking

$$T[n] \equiv (f(0) = 1 \wedge f(1) = 1 \wedge f(n + 2) = f(n + 1) + f(n))$$

$$P[n] \equiv (f(n) > 0)$$

and checking that both

$$T[0] \wedge T[1] \wedge \neg(P[0] \wedge P[1])$$

and

$$T[n] \wedge T[n + 1] \wedge P[n] \wedge P[n + 1] \wedge \neg P[n + 2]$$

are non-satisfiable, the last one being equivalent to

$$(f(n+2) = f(n+1) + f(n)) \wedge (f(n) > 0) \wedge (f(n+1) > 0) \wedge (f(n+2) \leq 0) \wedge \cdots$$

This simple example illustrates that the construction of SMTLIB requests from an IL specification is straightforward.

6.3   The Kind2 Prover and the TransSys format

Recall that a state transition system is a triple (S, I, T), where S is a set of states, $I \subseteq S$ is the set of initial states, and $T \subseteq S \times S$ is a transition relation over S. Here, a state consists of the values of a finite set of variables, with types belonging to $\{\texttt{Int}, \texttt{Real}, \texttt{Bool}\}$. I is encoded by a logical formula whose free variables correspond to the state variables and that holds for a state q if and only if q is an initial state. Similarly, the transition relation is given by a formula T such that $T[q, q']$ holds if and only if $q \rightarrow q'$.

The TransSys format is a modular encoding of such a state transition system. Related variables are grouped into *nodes*, each node providing a distinct namespace and expressing some constraints between its variables. A significant task of the translation process to TransSys is to flatten the Copilot specification so the value of all streams at time n only depends on the values of all the streams at time $n-1$ which is not the case in the Fibonacci example shown earlier. This is done by a simple program transformation which turns

```
fib = [1, 1] ++ (fib + drop 1 fib)
```

into

```
fib0 = [1] ++ fib1
fib1 = [1] ++ (fib1 + fib0)
```

After this, it is natural to associate a variable to each stream. Here, the variables `fib0` and `fib1` would be grouped into a single node in order to keep some structure in the representation of the transition system.[2] Such a modular transition system is almost ready to be translated into the Kind2 native format. However, we first have to merge each node's pair whose components are mutually dependent as Kind2 requires a topological order on its nodes.

7   Related Work

The research reported here builds on recent research conducted in a number of areas including formal verification, functional programming and DSL design, and RV.

---

[2] Maintaining structure is important for two reasons. First, the model checker can use this structural information to optimize its search; see *structural abstraction* in [8]. Second, structured transition systems are easier to read, debug, and transform.

Copilot has many features common to other RV frameworks aimed at monitoring distributed or real-time systems. There are few other instances of RV frameworks targeted to C code. One exception is RMOR, which generates constant-memory C monitors [11]. RMOR does not address real-time behavior or distributed system RV, though. To our knowledge no other RV framework has integrated monitor verification tools into their systems.

Haskell-based DSLs are of growing popularity and given that they are all embedded into the same programming language, they share many similarities with Copilot. For instance, Kansas Lava [7], which is designed for programming field programmable gate arrays, and Ivory [19], which is designed for writing secure autonomous systems, are both implemented using techniques similar to Copilot.

The ROSETTE extension to the Racket language [6] provides a framework for building DSLs that integrate SMT solvers. Smten [23] is a DSL with embedded SMT solvers that is targeted at writing satisfiability based searches.

As we have already mentioned, Copilot is similar in spirit to other languages with stream-based semantics, notably represented by the Lustre family of languages [15]. Copilot is a simpler language, particularly with respect to Lustre's clock calculus, focused on monitoring (as opposed to developing control systems). The work that is most relevant the research presented in this paper is the application of the Kind model checking tool to verify Lustre programs [9]. Kind and its most recent incarnation [17] is designed to model check Lustre programs and due to the similarities between Copilot and Lustre we targeted the Kind2 prover to be one of our back ends as well. Yet, to the best of our knowledge, the Boyer-Moore majority voting examples given in Sect. 5.1 are more sophisticated than published results using Kind with Lustre.

8   Conclusion

In this paper, we have presented the development of copilot-kind that enhances the Copilot RV framework with an integrated model-checking capability for verifying monitors and illustrated its applicability to verify a range of monitors.

In practice, our tool turned out to be very useful, indeed, even when the property being checked is not inductive or the induction step is too hard, it is very useful to test the first entailment of the k-induction algorithm for small values of k, proving the property cannot be violated in the first k time steps or displaying a counterexample trace. Many subtle bugs can be captured for reasonable values of k.

Yet, k-induction does have limitations. For instance, writing k-inductive specifications can be difficult. Newer advances like the IC3 algorithm, implemented by Kind2, are aimed at proving non-inductive properties by splitting it into concise and relevant inductive lemmas. However, our experiments showed that currently available tools fail at proving very simple properties as soon as basic arithmetic is involved.

The development of `copilot-kind` has reinforced the efficacy of the embedded DSL approach. Being embedded in a higher-order functional language facilitated the creation of a number of features such as our proof scheme capability. We have also found it quite advantageous to be able to write properties in the familiar style of Haskell programs. For instance, in Sect. 5.1, the function `forAllCst` for the serial Boyer-Moore example in that it uses both a `fold` and a `map` operator to model finite conjunctions. Beyond our own purposes, we believe that other embedded DSL developers could use our designs in order to interface their languages with proof engines.

Having successfully applied our tool to rather sophisticated monitors, future extensions are planned. Given that we are focused on cyber-physical systems, the limitations of SMT-based provers go beyond the fact that they become prohibitively slow as the size of their input increases. SMT-solvers do not generally handle quantifiers or special real-valued functions well. A promising way to deal with both these issues would be an extension of the *proof scheme* system where properties involving arbitrary streams are seen as universally quantified lemmas which can be specialized and added to the proof context by an explicit use of a new `apply` directive. An interface to MetiTarski [1] will also allow us to automatically prove some of the mathematical properties of interest, but connecting to an interactive prover may also be necessary.

References

1. Akbarpour, B., Paulson, L.C.: MetiTarski: an automatic theorem prover for real-valued special functions. J. Automat. Reasoning **44**(3), 175–205 (2010)
2. Caspi, P., Pialiud, D., Halbwachs, N., Plaice, J.: LUSTRE: a declarative language for programming synchronous systems. In: 14th Symposium on Principles of Programming Languages, pp. 178–188 (1987)
3. de Moura, L., Rueß, H., Sorea, M.: Bounded model checking and induction: from refutation to verification. In: Hunt Jr., W.A., Somenzi, F. (eds.) CAV 2003. LNCS, vol. 2725, pp. 14–26. Springer, Heidelberg (2003)
4. Dutertre, B.: Yices 2.2. In: Biere, A., Bloem, R. (eds.) CAV 2014. LNCS, vol. 8559, pp. 737–744. Springer, Heidelberg (2014)
5. Eén, N., Sörensson, N.: Temporal induction by incremental SAT solving. Electr. Notes Theor. Comput. Sci. **89**(4), 543–560 (2003)
6. Torlak, E., Bodik, R.: A lightweight symbolic virtual machine for solver-aided host languages. In: Proceedings of the 35th ACM SIGPLAN Conference on Programming Language Design and Implementation, PLDI 2014, pp. 530–541. ACM (2014)
7. Gill, A.: Domain-specific languages and code synthesis using Haskell. Commun. ACM **57**(6), 42–49 (2014)
8. Hagen, G.: Verifying safety properties of Lustre programs: an SMT-based approach. PhD thesis, University of Iowa (2008)
9. Hagen, G., Tinelli, C.: Scaling up the formal verification of lustre programs with SMT-based techniques. In: Proceedings of the 8th International Conference on Formal Methods in Computer-Aided Design (FMCAD 2008). IEEE (2008)
10. Halbwachs, N., Lagnier, F., Raymond, P.: Synchronous observers and the verification of reactive systems. In: Nivat, M., Rattray, C., Rus, T., Scollo, G. (eds.) AMAST 1993. Workshops in Computing, pp. 83–96. Springer, London (1994)

11. Havelund, K.: Runtime verification of C programs. In: Suzuki, K., Higashino, T., Ulrich, A., Hasegawa, T. (eds.) TestCom/FATES 2008. LNCS, vol. 5047, pp. 7–22. Springer, Heidelberg (2008)
12. Havelund, K., Roşu, G.: Efficient monitoring of safety properties. Int. J. Softw. Tools Technol. Transf. **6**(2), 158–173 (2004)
13. Hesselink, W.H.: The Boyer-Moore majority vote algorithm (2005)
14. Jones, S.P. (ed.): Haskell 98 Language and Libraries: The Revised Report. Cambridge University Press, Cambridge (2002). http://haskell.org/
15. Mikáč, J., Caspi, P.: Formal system development with Lustre: Framework and example. Technical Report TR-2005-11, Verimag Technical Report (2005)
16. Moore, S.J., Boyer, R.S.: MJRTY - A Fast Majority Vote Algorithm. Technical Report 1981–32, Institute for Computing Science, University of Texas, February 1981
17. University of Iowa: Kind Research Group. Kind 2: Multi-engine SMT-based Automatic Model Checker. http://kind2-mc.github.io/kind2/
18. Pike, L., Goodloe, A., Morisset, R., Niller, S.: Copilot: a hard real-time runtime monitor. In: Barringer, H., Falcone, Y., Finkbeiner, B., Havelund, K., Lee, I., Pace, G., Roşu, G., Sokolsky, O., Tillmann, N. (eds.) RV 2010. LNCS, vol. 6418, pp. 345–359. Springer, Heidelberg (2010)
19. Pike, L., Hickey, P.C., Bielman, J., Elliott, T., DuBuisson, T., Launchbury, J.: Programming languages for high-assurance autonomous vehicles: extended abstract. In: Programming Languages Meets Program Verification, pp. 1–2. ACM (2014)
20. Pike, L., Niller, S., Wegmann, N.: Runtime verification for ultra-critical systems. In: Khurshid, S., Sen, K. (eds.) RV 2011. LNCS, vol. 7186, pp. 310–324. Springer, Heidelberg (2012)
21. Pike, L., Wegmann, N., Niller, S., Goodloe, A.: Experience report: a do-it-yourself high-assurance compiler. In: Proceedings of the International Conference on Functional Programming (ICFP). ACM, September 2012
22. Pike, L., Wegmann, N., Niller, S., Goodloe, A.: Copilot: monitoring embedded systems. Innovations Syst. Softw. Eng. **9**(4), 235–255 (2013)
23. Uhler, R., Dave, N.: Smten with satisfiability-based search. In: Proceedings of the 2014 ACM International Conference on Object Oriented Programming Systems Languages and Applications, OOPSLA 2014, pp. 157–176. ACM (2014)
24. Rushby, J.: Runtime certification. In: Leucker, M. (ed.) RV 2008. LNCS, vol. 5289, pp. 21–35. Springer, Heidelberg (2008)
25. Sheeran, M., Singh, S., Stålmarck, G.: Checking safety properties using induction and a SAT-solver. In: Johnson, S.D., Hunt Jr., W.A. (eds.) FMCAD 2000. LNCS, vol. 1954, pp. 108–125. Springer, Heidelberg (2000)
26. Somenzi, F., Bradley, A.R.: Ic3: where monolithic and incremental meet. In: Proceedings of the International Conference on Formal Methods in Computer-Aided Design, FMCAD 2011, pp. 3–8. FMCAD Inc. (2011)

A Case Study on Runtime Monitoring
of an Autonomous Research Vehicle (ARV)
System

Aaron Kane[1]([✉]), Omar Chowdhury[2], Anupam Datta[1],
and Philip Koopman[1]

[1] Carnegie Mellon University, Pittsburgh, PA, USA
akane@alumni.cmu.edu, {danupam,koopman}@cmu.edu
[2] Purdue University, West Lafayette, IN, USA
ochowdhu@purdue.edu

Abstract. Runtime monitoring is a versatile technique for detecting property violations in safety-critical (SC) systems. Although instrumentation of the system under monitoring is a common approach for obtaining the events relevant for checking the desired properties, the current trend of using black-box commercial-off-the-shelf components in SC system development makes these systems unamenable to instrumentation. In this paper we develop an online runtime monitoring approach targeting an autonomous research vehicle (ARV) system and recount our experience with it. To avoid instrumentation we passively monitor the target system by generating atomic propositions from the observed network state. We then develop an efficient runtime monitoring algorithm, EgMon, that *eagerly* checks for violations of desired properties written in future-bounded, propositional metric temporal logic. We show the efficacy of EgMon by implementing and empirically evaluating it against logs obtained from the testing of an ARV system. EgMon was able to detect violations of several safety requirements.

1 Introduction

Runtime verification (RV) is a promising alternative to its static counterparts (*e.g.*, model checking [9] and theorem proving [6]) for checking safety and correctness properties of safety-critical embedded systems. In RV, a runtime monitor observes the concrete execution of the system in question and checks for violations of some stipulated properties. When the monitor detects a violation of a property, it notifies a command module which then attempts to recover from the violation. *In this paper, we develop a runtime monitor that monitors an autonomous research vehicle (ARV) and describe our experience with it.*

The ARV is an autonomous heavy truck which is being designed for use in vehicle platoons. It is representative of common modern ground vehicle designs. These systems are generally built by system integrators who utilize commercial-off-the-shelf components developed by multiple vendors, some of which may be provided as black-box systems. These systems are also often hard real-time systems which leads to additional constraints on system monitoring [13]. This type

ⓒ Springer International Publishing Switzerland 2015
E. Bartocci and R. Majumdar (Eds.): RV 2015, LNCS 9333, pp. 102–117, 2015.
DOI: 10.1007/978-3-319-23820-3_7

of system architecture is incompatible with many existing runtime monitoring techniques, which often require program or system instrumentation [4,7,15,19] to obtain the relevant events or system properties (*e.g.*, propositions) necessary to check for violations. Without access to component source code instrumenting systems is more difficult, and even when the source is available there are risks of affecting the timing and correctness of the target system when instrumented.

Obtaining Relevant System State. To avoid instrumentation, we obtain the relevant information for monitoring the ARV system through passive observation of its broadcast buses. Controller area network (CAN) is a standard broadcast bus for ground vehicles which is the primary system bus in the ARV. We can obtain useful amounts of system-state relevant information for monitoring the system safety specification by observing the data within the CAN messages that are broadcasted between system components. Before we can start monitoring the ARV system, we need a component, which we call the StP (in short, *state to proposition map*), that observes messages transmitted on the bus and interprets them into propositions relevant to monitoring which are then fed into the monitor. We want to emphasize that the limits of external observability can cause significant challenges in designing the StP when considering the state available from the system messages and the necessary atomic propositions [17].

Specification Logic. To obtain the relevant safety requirements and invariants for monitoring the ARV system we consulted the safety requirements of the ARV system. Many desired properties for these types of systems are timing related, so using an explicit-time based specification language for expressing these properties is helpful. System requirements of the form "*the system must perform action a within t seconds of event e*" are common, for instance, "*Cruise control shall disengage for 250 ms within 500 ms of the brake pedal being depressed*". For efficient monitoring, we use a fragment of propositional, discrete time, future-bounded metric temporal logic (MTL) [20].

Monitoring Algorithm. We have developed a runtime monitoring algorithm, which we call EgMon, that incrementally takes as input a system state (*i.e.*, a state maps propositions to either true/false) and a MTL formula and eagerly checks the state trace for violations. Some existing monitoring algorithms that support bounded future formulas wait for the full-time of the bound before evaluating the formula (*e.g.*, [2]). EgMon uses a dynamic programming based iterative algorithm that tries to reduce the input formula as soon as possible using history summarizing structures and formula-rewriting (leaving a partially reduced formula when future input is required). This eager nature of the algorithm can detect a violation earlier, leaving the system more time to attempt a graceful recovery. We have also proved the correctness of our algorithm. As the target systems we envision to monitor have strict time restriction, it is possible that the eager checks performed by EgMon are not finished before the next trace state arrives, possibly leaving trace properties unchecked. To overcome this, we have developed a hybrid monitoring algorithm, HMon, that first performs conservative checking like traditional runtime monitoring algorithms for MTL and performs as many eager checks as the remaining time permits.

Empirical Evaluation. We have implemented both EgMon and HMon on an inexpensive embedded platform and empirically evaluated it against logs obtained from the testing of an ARV system using properties derived from its safety requirements. EgMon (resp., HMon) has moderate monitoring overhead and detected several safety violations.

2 Background and Existing Work

In this section we briefly introduce the background concepts and discuss relevant existing work that will put the current work in perspective.

Monitoring Architecture. Goodloe and Pike present a thorough survey of monitoring distributed real-time systems [13]. Notably, they present a set of monitor architecture constraints and propose three abstract monitor architectures in the context of monitoring these types of systems. One of the proposed distributed real-time system monitor architectures is the bus-monitor architecture. This architecture contains an external monitor which receives network messages over an existing system bus, acting as another system component. The monitor can be configured in a silent or receive only mode to ensure it does not perturb the system. This is a simple architecture which requires minor changes to the target system. We utilize this architecture for our monitoring framework.

Controller Area Network. Controller Area Network is a widely used automotive network developed by Bosch in the 1980s [5]. In this work we primarily focus on CAN as it is a common automotive bus which typically conveys enough of the state information so that we can check for interesting safety properties of the system. CAN is an event-based broadcast network with data rates up to 1 Mb/s. Messages on CAN are broadcast with an identifier which is used to denote both the message and the intended recipients. The message identifiers are also used as the message priorities for access control. Although CAN is an event-based bus, it is often used with periodic scheduling schemes so the network usage can be statically analyzed. Hence, our monitoring approach is based on a time-triggered, network sampling model which allows it to monitor time-triggered networks as well. We use EgMon as a passive external bus-monitor which can only check system properties that are observable by passive observation of the messages transmitted through CAN.

Monitoring Algorithm. Our monitoring algorithm is similar to existing dynamic programming and formula-rewriting based algorithms [3,14,15,24,25]. Our main area of novelty is the combination of eager and conservative specification checking used in a practical setting showing the suitability of our bounded future logic for safety monitoring. Our monitoring algorithm is inspired by the algorithms *reduce* [12] and *précis* [8], adjusted for propositional logic and eager checking. The structure of our algorithm is based on *reduce. reduce, précis,* and

EgMon can handle future incompleteness but *reduce* additionally considers incompleteness for missing information which we do not consider. The NASA PathExplorer project has led to both a set of dynamic programming-based monitoring algorithms as well as some formula-rewriting based algorithms [15] for past-time LTL. The formula rewriting algorithms utilize the Maude term rewriting engine to efficiently monitor specifications through formula rewriting [24]. Thati and Roşu [25] describe a dynamic programming and rewriting-based algorithm for monitoring MTL formulas. They perform eager runtime monitoring by formula rewriting which resolves past-time formulas into equivalent formulas without unguarded past-time operators and derive new future-time formulas which separate the current state from future state. While they have a tight encoding of their canonical formulas, they still require more memory than some existing algorithms (formulas grow in size as they are rewritten), including EgMon.

Heffernan et al. present a monitor for automotive systems using ISO 26262 as a guide to identify the monitored properties [16]. They monitor past-time linear temporal logic (LTL) formulas and obtain system state from target system buses (CAN in their example). Our StP component is similar to their "filters" used to translate system state to the atomic propositions used in the policy. Their motivation and goals are similar to ours, but they use system-on-a-chip based monitors which utilize instrumentation to obtain system state, which is not suitable for monitoring black-box commercial-off-the-shelf (COTS) systems. Reinbacher et al. present an embedded past-time MTL monitor in [23] which generates FPGA-based non-invasive monitors. The actual implementation they describe does however presume system memory access to obtain system state (rather than using state from the target network). Pellizzoni et al. describe a monitor for COTS peripherals in [22]. They generate FPGA monitors that passively observe PCI-E buses to verify system properties, but they only check past-time LTL and regular expressions which cannot capture timing properties. Basin et al. compare runtime monitoring algorithms for MTL properties [3]. EgMon works similarly to their point-based monitoring algorithm but EgMon checks future temporal operators more aggressively. Donzé et al. [11] developed a robustness monitor for Signal Temporal Logic which supports continuous signals. Nickovic and Maler [21] developed the AWT tool which monitors analog systems. We only consider discrete events. Dokhanchi et al. [10] developed an online runtime monitoring algorithm for checking the robustness of formulas written in a future-bounded MTL fragment. We consider satisfaction of the formula instead of robustness.

3   Monitoring Algorithm

For checking whether the given ARV system adheres to its specification, we need an algorithm which incrementally checks explicit time specifications (*i.e.*, propositional metric-time temporal logic [20]) over finite, timed system traces. This has led to our algorithm EgMon which is an iterative monitoring algorithm based on formula rewriting and summarizing the relevant history of the trace in *history-structures*. To detect violations early, EgMon eagerly checks whether it can reduce subformulas of the original formula to a truth value by checking the (potentially incomplete) trace history and using formula simplifications (*e.g.*, $a \wedge false \equiv false$). Many of the existing algorithms for evaluating formulas such as $\Diamond_{[l,h]}a \vee b$ (*i.e.*, either b is true or sometimes in the future a is true such that the time difference between the evaluation state and the future state in which a is true, t_d, is within the bound $[l,h]$) wait enough time so that $\Diamond_{[l,h]}a$ can be fully evaluated. EgMon however tries to eagerly evaluate both $\Diamond_{[l,h]}a$ and b immediately and see whether it can reduce the whole formula to a truth value. For another eagerness checking example, let us assume we are checking the property $a\mathcal{U}_{[l,h]}b$ (read, the formula is true at trace position i if there is a trace position j in which b holds such that $j \geq i$ and the time difference between position i and j is in the range $[l,h]$ and for all trace positions k such that $i \leq k < j$ the formula a holds) at trace position i. While monitoring if we can find a trace position $k > i$ for which a is false and no previous b's (*e.g.*, at position $l, i \leq l < k$) are true then we can evaluate the formula to be false without waiting for a trace position in which b is true. We want to emphasize that EgMon optimistically checks for violations and hence we could have a trace in which each formula can only be evaluated at the last possible trace position which causes our algorithm will behave in the exact same way as the non-eager algorithms modulo the extra computation for eager checking.

3.1 Specification Logic

Our safety specification language for the ARV system, which we call $\alpha\mathcal{VSL}$, is a future-bounded, discrete time, propositional metric temporal logic (MTL [20]). The syntax of $\alpha\mathcal{VSL}$ is as follows:

$$\varphi ::= \mathsf{t} \mid \mathsf{p} \mid \neg\varphi \mid \varphi_1 \vee \varphi_2 \mid \varphi_1 \mathcal{S}_\mathbb{I} \varphi_2 \mid \varphi_1 \mathcal{U}_\mathbb{I} \varphi_2 \mid \ominus_\mathbb{I} \varphi \mid \bigcirc_\mathbb{I} \varphi$$

Syntax. $\alpha\mathcal{VSL}$ has logical true (*i.e.*, t), propositions p, logical connectives (*i.e.*, $\neg, \vee$), past temporal operators *since* and *yesterday* ($\mathcal{S}, \ominus$), and future temporal operators *until* and *next* ($\mathcal{U}, \bigcirc$). Other temporal operators (*i.e.*, $\Diamond, \boxminus, \Diamond, \Box$) can be easily derived from the ones above. There is a bound $\mathbb{I}$ of form $[l,h]$ ($l \leq h$ and $l, h \in \mathbb{N} \cup \infty$) associated with each temporal operator. Note that the bound $[l,h]$ associated with the future temporal operators must be finite. Specification propositions p come from a finite set of propositions provided in the system trace by the StP. These propositions are derived from the observable system state and represent specific system properties, for instance, proposition speedLT40mph could describe whether the vehicle speed is less than 40 mph. We use φ, ϕ, α, and β (possibly with subscripts) to denote valid $\alpha\mathcal{VSL}$ formulas.

Semantics. $\alpha\mathcal{VSL}$ formulas are interpreted over time-stamped *traces*. A trace σ is a sequence of states, each of which maps all propositions in StP, to either t or f. We denote the ith position of the trace with σ_i where $i \in \mathbb{N}$. Moreover, each σ_i has an associated time stamp denoted by τ_i where $\tau_i \in \mathbb{N}$. We denote the sequence of time stamps with τ. For all $i, j \in \mathbb{N}$ such that $i < j$, we require

$\tau_i < \tau_j$. For a given trace σ and time stamp sequence τ, we write $\sigma, \tau, i \models \varphi$ to denote that the formula φ is true with respect to the ith position of σ and τ. The semantics of $a\mathcal{VSL}$ future bounded MTL is standard, see for instance, [2]. Each property φ has an implicit unbounded $\square$ future operator ($\square\varphi$ signifies that φ is true in all future trace positions including the current trace position) at the top-level which is handled by checking whether φ is true in each trace position.

$$\texttt{tempSub}(\varphi) = \begin{cases} \emptyset & \text{if } \varphi \equiv p \\ \{\alpha\} \cup \{\beta\} \cup \texttt{tempSub}(\alpha) \cup \texttt{tempSub}(\beta) & \text{if } \varphi \equiv \alpha\mathcal{U}_\mathbb{I}\beta | \alpha\mathcal{S}_\mathbb{I}\beta \\ \texttt{tempSub}(\alpha) \cup \texttt{tempSub}(\beta) & \text{if } \varphi \equiv \alpha \vee \beta \\ \texttt{tempSub}(\alpha) & \text{if } \varphi \equiv \neg\alpha \end{cases}$$

We now introduce the readers with some auxiliary notions which will be necessary to understand our algorithm EgMon. We first define "*residual formulas*" or, just "*residues*". Given a formula φ, we call another formula ϕ as φ's residual, if we obtain ϕ after evaluating φ with respect to the current information of the trace. Note that a formula residue might not be a truth value if the formula could not conclusively be reduced given the current trace state (e.g., if future state is required to determine the truth value). A residue r_φ^j is a tagged pair $\langle j, \phi \rangle_\varphi$ where j is a position in the trace in which we intend to evaluate φ (the original formula) and ϕ is the current residual formula. We use these residues to efficiently hold trace history for evaluating temporal formulas. The next notion we introduce is of "*wait delay*". It is a function Δ^w that takes as input a formula φ and $\Delta^w(\varphi)$ returns an upper bound on the time one has to wait before they can evaluate φ with certainty. For past- and present-time formulas ϕ, $\Delta^w(\phi) = 0$. Future time formulas have a delay based on the interval of the future operator (e.g., $\Delta^w(\lozenge_{[0,3]}p) = 3$). The length of a formula φ, denoted $|\varphi|$, returns the total number of subformulas of φ.

3.2   EgMon Algorithm

Our runtime monitoring algorithm EgMon takes as input an $a\mathcal{VSL}$ formula φ and monitors a growing trace, building history structures and reporting the specification violations as soon as they are detected. We summarize the relevant algorithm functions below:

EgMon(φ) is the top-level function.
reduce($\sigma_i, \tau_i, \mathbb{S}_\varphi^i, \langle i, \varphi \rangle_\varphi$) reduces the given residue based on the current state (σ_i, τ_i) and the history $\mathbb{S}_\varphi^i$.
tempSub(φ) identifies the subformulas which require a history structure to evaluate the formula φ.
incrS($\mathbb{S}_\varphi^{i-1}, \mathbb{S}_\varphi^i, \sigma_i, \tau_i, i$) updates the history structure $\mathbb{S}_\varphi^{i-1}$ to step i given the current trace and history state.

Top-Level Monitoring Algorithm. The top-level monitoring algorithm EgMon is a sampling-based periodic monitor which uses history structures to store trace state for evaluating temporal subformulas. *History structures* are lists of residues along with past-time markers for evaluating infinite past-time formulas. The algorithm checks the given formula φ periodically at every trace sample step. When the formula cannot be decided at a given step (*e.g.*, it requires future state to evaluate), the remaining formula residue is saved in a history structure for evaluation in future steps when the state will be available. The history structure for formula ϕ at trace step i is denoted S_ϕ^i. We use $\mathbb{S}_\varphi^i$ to denote the set of history structures for all temporal subformula of φ, *i.e.*, $\mathbb{S}_\varphi^i = \bigcup_{\phi \in \text{tempSub}(\varphi)} S_\phi^i$.

The high level algorithm EgMon is shown in Fig. 1. First, all the necessary history structures S_ϕ are identified using $\text{tempSub}(\varphi)$ and initialized. Once these structures are identified, the monitoring loop begins. In each step, all the history structures are updated with the new trace step. This is done in increasing formula size since larger formula can depend on the history of smaller formula (which may be their subformula). Each structure is updated using $\text{incrS}(S_\phi^{i-1}, \mathbb{S}_\phi^i, \sigma_i, \tau_i, i)$ which adds a residue for the current trace step to the structure and reduces all the contained residues with the new step state. Then, the same procedure is performed for the top level formula that is being monitored – the formula's structure is updated with $\text{incrS}(S_\varphi^{i-1}, \mathbb{S}_\varphi^i, \sigma_i, \tau_i, i)$. Once updated, this structure contains the evaluation of the top-level formula. The algorithm reports any identified formula violations (*i.e.*, any f residues) before continuing to the next trace step. We note that due to the recursive nature of the monitoring algorithm, the top-level formula is treated exactly the same as any temporal subformula would be (which follows from the fact that the top-level formula contains an implicit *always* $\square$). The history structure updates for the top-level formula are separated in the algorithm description for clarity only. The only difference between the top-level formula and other temporal subformula is that violations are reported for the top-level formula.

Reducing Residues. EgMon works primarily by reducing formula residues down to truth values. Residues are reduced by the $\text{reduce}(\sigma_i, \tau_i, \mathbb{S}_\varphi^i, \langle j, \phi \rangle_\varphi)$ function, which uses the current state (σ_i, τ_i) and the stored history in $\mathbb{S}_\varphi^i$ to

1: For all recognized formulas $\phi \in \text{tempSub}(\varphi)$: $S_\phi^{-1} \leftarrow \emptyset$
2: $i \leftarrow 0$
3: **loop**
4:     Obtain next trace step (σ_i, τ_i)
5:     **for** every $\phi \in \text{tempSub}(\varphi)$ in increasing size **do**
6:         $S_\phi^i \leftarrow \text{incrS}(S_\phi^{i-1}, \mathbb{S}_\phi^i, \sigma_i, \tau_i, i)$
7:     **end for**
8:     $S_\varphi^i \leftarrow \text{incrS}(S_\varphi^{i-1}, \mathbb{S}_\varphi^i, \sigma_i, \tau_i, i)$
9:     **for** all $\langle j, \text{f} \rangle \in S_\varphi^i$ **do**
10:         Report violation on σ at position j
11:     **end for**
12:     $i \leftarrow i + 1$
13: **end loop**

Fig. 1. EgMon Algorithm

rewrite the formula ϕ to a reduced form, either a truth value or a new formula which will evaluate to the same truth value as the original. For past or present-time formulas, reduce() is able to return a truth value residue since all the necessary information to decide the formula is available in the history and current state. In a given state, if the input formula $\varphi \equiv p$, reduce returns true only if p is true in the state and returns false otherwise. For input formula of form $\varphi \equiv \varphi_1 \vee \varphi_2$, reduce is recursively called for φ_1 and φ_2, respectively, and the formula $\varphi_1 \vee \varphi_2$ is reduced to $\varphi_a \vee \varphi_b$ (simplified if necessary) where φ_a and φ_b are reduced form of φ_1 and φ_2, respectively. Negation is handled similarly. Future-time policies may be fully-reducible if enough state information is available. If a future-time formula cannot be reduced to a truth value, it is returned as a reduced (potentially unchanged) residue. For residues whose formula is an *until* formula $\alpha \mathcal{U}_{[l,h]} \beta$, the history structures S_α^i and S_β^i are used to reduce the formula. If the formula can be evaluated conclusively then the truth value is returned, otherwise the residue is returned unchanged. The reduction algorithm for *until* temporal formula is shown below. Reducing *since* formulas is essentially the same except with reversed minimum/maximums and past time bounds.

reduce$(\sigma_i, \tau_i, i, S^i_{\alpha \mathcal{U}_{[l,h]} \beta}, \langle j, \alpha \mathcal{U}_{[l,h]} \beta \rangle) ::=$

let $a_a \leftarrow min(\{k | \tau_j \leq \tau_k \leq \tau_j + h \wedge \langle k, \bot \rangle \in S_\alpha^i \}, i)$

$a_u \leftarrow max(\{k | \tau_k \in [\tau_j, \tau_j + h] \wedge \forall k' \in [j, k-1].(\langle k', \alpha' \rangle \in S_\alpha^i \wedge \alpha' \equiv \top \}, i)$

$b_a \leftarrow min(\{k | \tau_j + l \leq \tau_k \leq \tau_j + h \wedge \langle k, \beta' \rangle \in S_\beta^i \wedge \beta' \neq \bot \})$

$b_t \leftarrow min(\{k | \tau_j + l \leq \tau_k \leq \tau_j + h \wedge \langle k, \top \rangle \in S_\beta^i \})$

$b_n \leftarrow \top$ if $(\tau_i - \tau_j \geq \Delta^w(\psi)) \wedge \forall k.(\tau_j + l \leq \tau_k \leq \tau_j + h).\langle k, \bot \rangle \in S_\beta^i$

if $b_t \neq \emptyset \wedge a_u \geq b_t$ **return**$\langle j, \top \rangle$

else if $(b_a \neq \emptyset \wedge a_a < b_a)$ or $b_n = \top$ **return**$\langle j, \bot \rangle$

else   **return**$\langle j, \alpha \mathcal{U}_{[l,h]} \beta \rangle$

The reduce function for *until* formulas uses marker values to evaluate the semantics of *until*. reduce calculates five marker values: a_a is the earliest step within the time interval where α is known false. a_u is the latest step within the interval that $\alpha \mathcal{U}_{[l,h]} \beta$ would be true if β were true at that step. b_a is the earliest step within the interval at which β is not conclusively false, and b_t is the earliest step within the interval at which β is conclusively true. b_n holds whether the current step i is later than the wait delay and all β values within the interval are false. With these marker variables, reduce can directly check the semantics of *until*, and either return the correct value or the unchanged residue if the semantics are not conclusive with the current history. Reducing *since* formulas works in the same way (using the same marker values) adjusted to past time intervals and utilizing the unbounded past time history values.

Incrementing History Structures. To evaluate past and future-time policies, we must correctly store trace history which can be looked up during a residue reduction. We store the trace history of a formula ϕ in a history structure S_ϕ. This history structure contains a list of residues for the number of steps required to evaluate the top-level formula. History structures are incre-

mented by the function $\texttt{incrS}(S_\phi^{i-1}, \mathbb{S}_\phi^i, \sigma_i, \tau_i, i) = (\bigcup_{r \in S_\phi^{i-1}} \texttt{reduce}(\sigma_i, \tau_i, S_\phi^i, r)) \cup$
$\texttt{reduce}(\sigma_i, \tau_i, S_\phi^i, \langle i, \phi \rangle)$. This function takes the previous step's history structure S_ϕ^{i-1} and the current state σ_i and performs two actions: (1) Adds a residue for the current step i to S_ϕ^i and (2) Reduces all residues contained in S_ϕ^{i-1} using σ_i.

3.3 Algorithm Properties

There are two important properties of `EgMon` which need to be shown. First, *correctness* states that the algorithm's results are correct. That is, that if `EgMon` reports a property violation, the trace really did violate the property. Second, *promptness* requires that the algorithm provide a decision for the given property in a timely fashion. Promptness precisely requires that the algorithm decides satisfaction of the given property at trace position i as soon as there is another trace position j available such that $j \geq i$ and $\tau_j - \tau_i \geq \Delta^w(\varphi)$. The following theorem states that `EgMon` is correct and prompt. It requires the history structures $\mathbb{S}_\varphi^i$ to be consistent at i analogous to the trace σ, τ, that is, the history structures contain correct history of σ till step i.

Theorem 1 (Correctness and Promptness of `EgMon`). *For all $i \in \mathbb{N}$, all formula φ, all time stamp sequences τ and all traces σ it is the case that (1) if $\langle j, f \rangle \in S_\varphi^i$ then $\sigma, \tau, j \nvDash \varphi$ and if $\langle j, t \rangle \in S_\varphi^i$ then $\sigma, \tau, j \vDash \varphi$ (Correctness) and (2) if $\tau_i - \tau_j \geq \Delta^w(\varphi)$ then if $\sigma, \tau, j \nvDash \varphi$ then $\langle j, f \rangle \in S_\varphi^i$ and if $\sigma, \tau, j \vDash \varphi$ then $\langle j, t \rangle \in S_\varphi^i$ (Promptness).*

Proof. By induction on the formula φ and time step i. See [18]

We now discuss the runtime complexity of `EgMon` while checking satisfaction of a property φ. For any evaluation position of the trace σ, let us assume we have maximum L positions in σ for which φ has not yet been reduced to a boolean value. Note that the maximum number of positions in that are not yet reduced must be $\frac{\Delta^w(\varphi)}{P}$ where P is the monitor's period. Additionally, for each temporal subformula $\phi_1 \mathcal{U} \phi_2$ of φ, we build history structures that keep track of segments of positions in σ for which ϕ_1 is true. Let us assume we have a maximum of M such segments that are relevant for φ evaluation. Hence, the complexity of `EgMon` is $\mathcal{O}(LM|\varphi|)$.

4 Monitor Implementation and Evaluation

To evaluate the feasibility of our monitoring algorithm for safety-critical real-time systems we have built a real-time CAN monitor on an ARM Cortex-M4 development board. This allowed us to explore the necessary optimizations and features required to perform real-time checking of realistic safety policies.

Challenges. Software for safety-critical embedded systems typically contains more strict design and programming model constraints than less critical software.

Two important and common constraints for these systems are avoiding recursion and dynamic memory allocation. As $\alpha\mathcal{VSL}$ is future bounded, we avoid dynamic allocation in our EgMon implementation by statically allocating space for the maximum number of entries for our history structures and other temporary data structures. Although EgMon is defined recursively, we implement EgMon using a traditional iterative traversal of the specification formulas instead.

Discussion. Passive monitoring of running systems requires attention to timing issues with regards to system state sampling. The monitor possesses a copy of the target system state which is updated when a new CAN message is observed. The monitor periodically takes a snapshot of this constantly updated state and uses that snapshot as the trace state which is monitored. Thus, the actual monitored state (*i.e.*, the trace) is a discrete sampling of the monitor's constantly updated system state. The monitor's period must be fast enough that any changes in system state which are relevant to the specification are seen in the sampled trace. To ensure this, the monitor's period should be twice as fast as the shortest CAN message period. If the monitor's period is not fast enough, multiple CAN messages announcing the same system value may end up in the same trace state causing those values to not be seen in the trace. For example, if the monitor is sampling at $2\,ms$, and three messages announcing the value of property X are received at times $0\,ms$, $1\,ms$, and $1.5\,ms$, only the value announced at $1.5\,ms$ will be seen in the trace. To avoid this, the monitor would need to run faster than the messages inter-arrival rate (at least $0.5\,ms$ in this case).

Along with requiring the monitor to sample its trace state fast enough to see all the relevant state changes, the specification time bounds must be a multiple of the monitoring period. This ensures that each time step in the formula is evaluated on the updated information. A simple way of understanding this is to use monitor steps as the temporal bounds instead of explicit time bounds. For example, if the monitor is running at $2\,\mathrm{ms}$ intervals, we can use $\Box_{[0,50]}p$ as an equivalent to $\Box_{[0,100ms]}p$. If a bound is not a multiple of the monitor's interval, then formulas with different bounds can look indistinguishable, *e.g.*, $\Box_{[0,5ms]}p$ is equivalent to $\Box_{[1ms,4ms]}p$ for a $2\,ms$ monitor. To summarize, using a monitoring period at least twice as fast as the shortest CAN message period (*i.e.*, shortest time between a CAN message retransmission) and only using temporal bound values that are multiples of this period provides intuitive monitoring results.

Hybrid Algorithm (HMon). The eager monitoring algorithm attempts to evaluate specification rules as soon as possible which requires checking properties which may not be fully reducible given the current trace. Continuously attempting to check partially reduced residues which need future information to evaluate requires extra computation. In some cases, the worst-case execution time to eagerly check a property (or set of properties) over a trace may be longer than the monitor's period. In this case the eager algorithm cannot guarantee prompt monitoring since some residues will be left unchecked. This is unacceptable for safety-critical system monitoring, as without a promptness guarantee the results cannot be fully trusted. To enable the benefits of eager checking while avoiding the risks of losing real-time correctness, we can use a hybrid approach (called

HMon) which first performs non-eager (conservative) checking and then uses any spare time left in the monitoring period to perform as much eager checking as possible. HMon preserves the monitor's promptness guarantee (all violations will be detected within their delay Δ^w) even if the EgMon cannot finish eager checking the specification. HMon preserves promptness while providing a chance to eagerly detect specification violations. HMon is functionally equivalent to EgMon when it finishes execution before the monitoring period whereas HMon is equivalent to the conservative algorithm when there is no spare execution time to perform eager checks.

Figure 2 shows the violation detection latency for HMon while checking the property (CruiseActive $\wedge$ brakePressed) $\rightarrow \Box_{[250ms,1s]}(\neg$CruiseActive) over a synthetic trace using different monitoring periods. With a $1\,ms$ monitoring period HMon is able to eagerly detect every violation early. For $8.2\,us$ monitoring period, HMon is able to detect some violations early, but it does not detect all of them right away. For $1us$ monitoring period, HMon only evaluates conservatively due to lack of left-over time, identifying the violations at the promptness limit of $1s$.

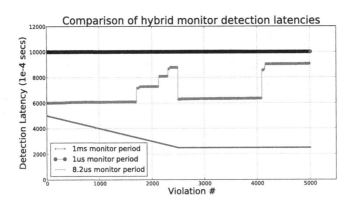

Fig. 2. Detection latencies with different hybrid monitor periods

We have also implemented HMon in our embedded board. HMon updates the history structures (shared between the conservative and eager checking) and performs a conservative check once every monitoring period. Eager checking is then performed until the next monitor period interrupts it.

4.1   Case Study

This section reports our case study performing real-time monitoring of a CAN network for realistic safety properties. For this case study we have obtained CAN network logs from a series of robustness tests on the ARV which we have replayed on a test CAN bus. This setup helps us show the feasibility of performing external bus monitoring on this class of system with a realistic safety specification.

The logs contain both normal system operation as well as some operation under network-based robustness testing. During robustness testing, the testing framework can intercept targeted network messages on the bus and inject its own testing values. A PC was connected to a PCAN-USB Pro [1] device which provides a USB interface to two CAN connections. One CAN channel was used to replay the logs, while the other was used as a bus logger for analysis purposes.

Requirements documentation for this system was available, so we were able to build a monitoring specification based on actual system requirements. The specification evaluated in the embedded monitor on the test logs are shown in Table 1. This specification was derived from the system requirements based on the observable system state available in the testing logs. We note that the safety specification is simple and does not fully exercise the monitor's constraints. Since this specification is small, does not have long duration future-time formulas, and the monitor period is relatively slow ($25\,ms$) HMon and EgMon function equivalently for the case study – EgMon can always finish within the monitoring period in the worst case. We use the HMon for the study since it acts the same as EgMon when there is excess monitoring time. Using HMon allows us to avoid worrying about the execution time and has little downside.

Table 1. Case study monitoring specification

Rule #	Informal Rule MTL
0	A feature heartbeat will be sent within every 500ms HeartbeatOn → $\Diamond_{[0,500ms]}$ HeartBeat
1	The interface component heartbeat counter is correct HeartbeatOn → HeartbeatCounterOk
2	The vehicle shall not transition from manual mode to autonomous mode ¬(($\ominus_{[0,25ms]}$IntManualState) ∧ IntAutoStat)
3	The vehicle controller shall not command a transition from manual mode to autonomous mode ¬(($\ominus_{[0,25ms]}$VehManualModeCmd) ∧ VehAutoModeCmd)
4	The vehicle shall not transition from system off mode to autonomous mode ¬(($\ominus_{[0,25ms]}$IntSDState) ∧ IntAutoStat)
5	The vehicle controller shall not command a transition from system off mode to autonomous mode ¬(($\ominus_{[0,25ms]}$VehSDModeCmd) ∧ VehAutoModeCmd)

Table 1 shows the monitored specification. HeartBeatOn is a guard used to avoid false-positive violations during system startup. The system's heartbeat message contains a single heartbeat status bit which we checked directly in Rule #0 to ensure the component is still running (essentially a watchdog message). The heartbeat message also has a rolling counter field. We use the StP to ensure that this counter is incrementing correctly and output this check as the HeartbeakOk proposition which is monitored in Rule #1. We also checked for illegal state transitions. Rules #2 through #5 check both for illegal transition commands from the vehicle controller and actual illegal state transitions in the interface component.

4.2   Monitoring Results

Monitoring the test logs with the above specification resulted in identifying two real violations as well as some false positive violation detections caused by the testing infrastructure. Three different types of heartbeat violations were identified after inspecting the monitor results, with one being a false positive. We also identified infrastructure-caused false-positive violations of the transition rules.

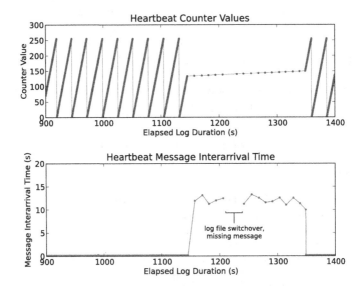

Fig. 3. Heartbeat counter values over time

Specification violations. The first violation is a late heartbeat message. In one of the robustness testing logs the heartbeat message was not sent on time, which is clearly a heartbeat violation. Figure 3 shows the heartbeat counter values and the inter-arrival time of the heartbeat messages over time for this violation. We can see here that the heartbeat counter did in fact increment in a valid way, just too slowly. The second violation is on-time heartbeat status message but the heartbeat status field is 0. We do not know from the available documentation whether a bad status in an on-time message with a good counter is valid or not. So without more information we cannot tell whether these violations are false positives or not. This is worthy of further investigation.

False-positive violations. The last type of heartbeat violation is a bad counter. A good rolling counter should increment by one every message up to its maximum (255 in this case) before wrapping back to zero. Every consecutive heartbeat

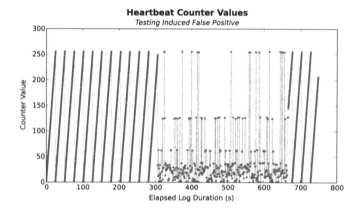

Fig. 4. Bad heartbeat counter values

status message must have an incremented heartbeat counter or a violation will be triggered. Figure 4 shows the counter value history for one of the traces with a heartbeat violation caused by a bad counter value. Further inspection of this violation showed that the bad counter values were sent by the testing framework rather than the actual system. In this case, the network traffic the monitor is seeing is not real system state instead are observing messages that are being injected by the testing framework. This is a false positive violation since the violating state is not actual system state.

The monitor also reported violations of the legal transition rules, but these, similar to the heartbeat counter violation, also turned out to be false positives triggered by message injections by the robustness testing harness. Since the monitor checks network state, if we perform testing that directly affects the values seen on the network (such as injection/interception of network messages) we may detect violations which are created by the testing framework rather than the system. Information about the test configurations can be used to filter out these types of false positives which arise from test-controlled state. This type of filtering can be automated if the test information can be input to the monitor, either directly on the network (e.g., adding a message value to injected messages) or through a side-channel (i.e., building a testing-aware monitor).

5   Conclusion and Future Work

We have developed a runtime monitoring approach for an ARV system. Instead of instrumentation, we passively monitor the system, generating the system trace from the observed network state. We have developed an efficient runtime monitoring algorithm, EgMon, that eagerly checks for violations of properties written in future-bounded propositional MTL. We have shown the efficiency of EgMon by implementing it and evaluating it against logs obtained from system testing of the ARV. EgMon was able to detect violations of several safety requirements in real-time. We want to further explore runtime monitors executing in multi-core environment to provide increased monitoring power as well as further formalizing the StP (in a domain specific language). Currently, we do not investigate the energy consumption of the runtime monitors. It could be possible that the extra checks required for eager checking might not feasible due to energy consumption restrictions in which case one has to investigate energy-efficient alternatives.

References

1. Pcan-usb pro: Peak system. http://www.peak-system.com/PCAN-USB-Pro.200. 0.html?&L=1
2. Basin, D., Klaedtke, F., Mller, S., Pfitzmann, B.: Runtime monitoring of metric first-order temporal properties. FSTTCS **8**, 49–60 (2008)
3. Basin, D., Klaedtke, F., Zălinescu, E.: Algorithms for monitoring real-time properties. In: Khurshid, S., Sen, K. (eds.) RV 2011. LNCS, vol. 7186, pp. 260–275. Springer, Heidelberg (2012)
4. Bonakdarpour, B., Fischmeister, S.: Runtime monitoring of time-sensitive systems. In: Khurshid, S., Sen, K. (eds.) RV 2011. LNCS, vol. 7186, pp. 19–33. Springer, Heidelberg (2012)
5. Bosch, R.: CAN specification version 2.0, September 1991
6. Chang, C.L., Lee, R.C.T.: Symbolic Logic and Mechanical Theorem Proving, 1st edn. Academic Press Inc., Orlando (1997)
7. Chen, F., Rosu, G.: Towards monitoring-oriented programming: a paradigm combining specification and implementation. Electron. Notes Theoret. Comput. Sci. **89**(2), 108–127 (2003)
8. Chowdhury, O., Jia, L., Garg, D., Datta, A.: Temporal mode-checking for runtime monitoring of privacy policies. In: Biere, A., Bloem, R. (eds.) CAV 2014. LNCS, vol. 8559, pp. 131–149. Springer, Heidelberg (2014)
9. Clarke, E.M., Wing, J.M.: Formal methods: state of the art and future directions. ACM Comput. Surv. **28**, 626–643 (1996)
10. Dokhanchi, A., Hoxha, B., Fainekos, G.: On-line monitoring for temporal logic robustness. In: Bonakdarpour, B., Smolka, S.A. (eds.) RV 2014. LNCS, vol. 8734, pp. 231–246. Springer, Heidelberg (2014)
11. Donzé, A., Ferrère, T., Maler, O.: Efficient robust monitoring for STL. In: Sharygina, N., Veith, H. (eds.) CAV 2013. LNCS, vol. 8044, pp. 264–279. Springer, Heidelberg (2013)
12. Garg, D., Jia, L., Datta, A.: Policy auditing over incomplete logs: theory, implementation and applications. In: Proceedings of the 18th ACM Conference on Computer and Communications Security, pp. 151–162. ACM (2011)
13. Goodloe, A., Pike, L.: Monitoring distributed real-time systems: a survey and future directions (NASA/CR-2010-216724), July 2010
14. Havelund, K., Roşu, G.: Synthesizing monitors for safety properties. In: Katoen, J.-P., Stevens, P. (eds.) TACAS 2002. LNCS, vol. 2280, pp. 342–356. Springer, Heidelberg (2002)
15. Havelund, K., Rosu, G.: Efficient monitoring of safety properties. Int. J. Softw. Tools Technol. Transf. **6**(2), 158–173 (2004)
16. Heffernan, D., MacNamee, C., Fogarty, P.: Runtime verification monitoring for automotive embedded systems using the iso 26262 functional safety standard as a guide for the definition of the monitored properties. Software, IET **8**(5), 193–203 (2014)

17. Kane, A., Fuhrman, T., Koopman, P.: Monitor based oracles for cyber-physical system testing: practical experience report. In: Dependable Systems and Networks (DSN), pp. 148–155 (2014)
18. Kane, A., Chowdhury, O., Koopman, P., Datta, A.: A case study on runtime monitoring of an autonomous research vehicle (arv) system. Technical report, CMU (2015)
19. Kim, M., Viswanathan, M., Kannan, S., Lee, I., Sokolsky, O.: Java-mac: a run-time assurance approach for java programs. Formal Methods Syst. Des. **24**(2), 129–155 (2004)
20. Koymans, R.: Specifying real-time properties with metric temporal logic. Real-Time Syst. **2**, 255–299 (1990)
21. Nickovic, D., Maler, O.: Amt: a property-based monitoring tool for analog systems. In: Formal Modeling and Analysis of Timed Systems (2007)
22. Pellizzoni, R., Meredith, P., Caccamo, M., Rosu, G.: Hardware runtime monitoring for dependable COTS-based real-time embedded systems. In: 2008 Real-Time Systems Symposium, pp. 481–491, November 2008
23. Reinbacher, T., Függer, M., Brauer, J.: Runtime verification of embedded real-time systems. Formal Methods Syst. Des. **44**(3), 203–239 (2014)
24. Rosu, G., Havelund, K.: Rewriting-based techniques for runtime verification. Autom. Softw. Eng. **12**(2), 151–197 (2005)
25. Thati, P., Roşu, G.: Monitoring algorithms for metric temporal logic specifications. Electron. Notes Theor. Comput. Sci. **113**, 145–162 (2005)

Monitoring Electronic Exams

Ali Kassem[1]($\boxtimes$), Yliès Falcone[2], and Pascal Lafourcade[3]

[1] Univ. Grenoble Alpes, VERIMAG, F-38000 Grenoble, France
`Ali.Kassem@imag.fr`
[2] Univ. Grenoble Alpes, Inria, LIG, F-38000 Grenoble, France
`Ylies.Falcone@imag.fr`
[3] Clermont Univ., Univ. d'Auvergne, LIMOS, Clermont-Ferrand, France
`Pascal.Lafourcade@udamail.fr`

Abstract. Universities and other educational organizations are adopting computer-based assessment tools (herein called *e-exams*) to reach larger and ubiquitous audiences. While this makes examination tests more accessible, it exposes them to unprecedented threats not only from candidates but also from authorities, which organize exams and deliver marks. Thus, e-exams must be checked to detect potential irregularities. In this paper, we propose several monitors, expressed as Quantified Event Automata (QEA), to monitor the main properties of e-exams. Then, we implement the monitors using MarQ, a recent Java tool designed to support QEAs. Finally, we apply our monitors to logged data from real e-exams conducted by *Université Joseph Fourier* at pharmacy faculty, as a part of *Epreuves Classantes Nationales informatisées*, a pioneering project which aims to realize all french medicine exams electronically by 2016. Our monitors found discrepancies between the specification and the implementation.

1 Introduction

Electronic exams, also known as *e-exams*, are computer-based systems employed to assess the skills, or the knowledge of candidates. Running e-exams promises to be easier than running traditional pencil-and-paper exams, and cheaper on the long term. E-exams are deployed easily, and they are flexible in where and when exams can be set; their test sessions are open to a very large public of candidates and, if the implementation allows automatic marking, their results are immediately available.

We do not want to argue about the actual benefits of e-exams in promoting and supporting education, but as a matter of facts, their use has considerably raised (and will likely continue to raise). Nowadays, several universities, such as MIT, Stanford, and Berkeley, just to cite a few, have began to offer university courses remotely using the Massive Open Online Course platforms (*e.g.,* Coursera[1] and edX[2]) which offer e-exams. Even in a less ambitious and

---

[1] www.coursera.org.
[2] www.edx.org.

© Springer International Publishing Switzerland 2015
E. Bartocci and R. Majumdar (Eds.): RV 2015, LNCS 9333, pp. 118–135, 2015.
DOI: 10.1007/978-3-319-23820-3_8

more traditional setting, universities start adopting e-exams to replace traditional exams, especially in the case of multiple-choice questions and short open answers. For example, pharmacy exams at *Université Joseph Fourier* (UJF) have been organized electronically using tablet computers since 2014 [1]. Since several french medicine exams are multiple-choice tests, the French government plans to realize all medicine exams electronically by 2016.[3] Other institutions, such as ETS[4], CISCO[5], and Microsoft[6], have for long already adopted their own platforms to run, generally in qualified centers, electronic tests required to obtain their program certificates.

This migration towards information technology is changing considerably the proceeding of exams, but the approach in coping with their security still focuses only on preventing candidates from cheating with invigilated tests. Wherever it is not possible to have human invigilators, a software running on the student computer is used, *e.g.,* ProctorU[7]. However, such measures are insufficient, as the trustworthiness and the reliability of exams are today threatened not only by candidates. Indeed, threats and errors may come from the use of information technology, as well as, from bribed examiners and dishonest exam authorities which are willing to tamper with exams as recent scandals have shown. For example, in the Atlanta scandal, school authorities colluded in changing student marks to improve their institution's rankings and get more public funds [2]. The BBC revealed another scandal where ETS was shown to be vulnerable to a fraud perpetrated by official invigilators in collusion with the candidates who were there to get their visas: the invigilators dictated the correct answers during the test [3].

To address these problems, e-exams must be checked for the presence/absence of irregularities and provide evidence about the fairness and the correctness of their grading procedures. Assumptions on the honesty of authorities are not justifiable anymore. Verification should be welcomed by authorities since verifying e-exams provides transparency and then public trust. E-exams offer the possibility to have extensive data logs, which can provide grounds for the verification and checking process, however, the requirements to be satisfied by e-exams have to be clearly defined and formalized before.

Contributions. To the best of our knowledge, this paper proposes the first formalization of e-exams properties, using Quantified Event Automata (QEAs) [4,5], and their off-line runtime verification on actual logs. Our contributions are as follows. First, we define an event-based model of e-exams that is suitable for monitoring purposes. Moreover, we formalize eight fundamental properties as QEAs: no unregistered candidate try to participate in the exam by submitting an answer; answers are accepted only from registered candidates; all

---

[3] The project is called *Épreuves Classantes Nationales informatisées*, see www.side-sante.org.

[4] www.etsglobal.org.

[5] www.cisco.com.

[6] www.microsoft.com/learning/en-us/default.aspx.

[7] www.proctoru.com.

accepted answers are submitted by candidates, and for each question at most one answer is accepted per candidate; all candidates answer the questions in the required order; answers are accepted only during the examination time; another variant of the latter that offers flexibility in the beginning and the duration of the exam; all answers are marked correctly; and the correct mark is assigned to each candidate. Our formalization also allows us for some properties to detect the cause of the potential failures and the party responsible for them. Note, formalizing the above properties entailed to add features to QEAs. Then, we implement the monitors using MarQ[8] [6], a Java tool designed to support QEA specification language. Finally, we perform off-line monitoring, based on the available data logs, for an e-exam organized by UJF; and reveal both students that violate the requirements, and discrepancies between the specification and the implementation.

Outline. In Sect. 2, we define the events and a protocol for e-exams. We specify the properties and propose the corresponding monitors in Sect. 3. Then, in Sect. 4, we analyze two actual e-exams organized by UJF. We discuss related work in Sect. 5. Finally, we conclude in Sect. 6. An extended version of this paper is available as [7].

2   An Event-Based Model of E-exams

We define an *e-exam execution* (or *e-exam run*) by a finite sequence of events, called *trace*. Such event-based modelling of e-exam runs is appropriate for monitoring actual events of the system. In this section, we specify the parties and the phases involved in e-exams. Then, we define the events related to an e-exam run. Note, the e-exam model introduced in this section refines the one proposed in [8].

2.1   Overview of an E-exam Protocol

An exam involves at least two roles: the *candidate* and the *exam authority*. An exam authority can have several sub-roles: the *registrar* registers candidates; the *question committee* prepares the questions; the *invigilator* supervises the exam, collects the answers, and dispatches them for marking; the *examiner* corrects the answers and marks them; the *notification committee* delivers the marking. Generally, exams run in four phases: (1) *Registration*, when the exam is set up and candidates enrol; (2) *Examination*, when candidates answer the questions, submit them to the authority, and have them officially accepted; (3) *Marking*, when the answers are marked; (4) *Notification*, when the grades are notified to the candidates. Usually, each phase ends before the next one begins.

2.2   Events Involved in an E-exam

Events flag important steps in the execution of the exam. We consider *parametric events* of the form $e(p_1, \ldots, p_n)$, where e is the event name, and $p_1, \ldots, p_n$ is

---

[8] www.github.com/selig/qea.

the list of symbolic parameters that take some data values at runtime. We define the following events that are assumed to be recorded during the exam or built from data logs.

- Event $register(i)$ is emitted when candidate i registers to the exam.
- Event $get(i, q)$ is emitted when candidate i gets question q.
- Event $change(i, q, a)$ is emitted when candidate i changes on his computer the answer field of question q to a.
- Event $submit(i, q, a)$ is emitted when candidate i submits answer a to question q.
- Event $accept(i, q, a)$ is emitted when the exam authority receives and accepts answer a to question q from candidate i.
- Event $corrAns(q, a)$ is emitted when the authority specifies a as a correct answer to question q. Note that more than one answer can be correct for a given question.
- Event $marked(i, q, a, b)$ is emitted when the answer a from candidate i to question q is scored with b. In our properties we assume that the score b ranges over $\{0, 1\}$ (1 for correct answer and 0 for wrong answer), however other scores can be considered.
- Event $assign(i, m)$ is emitted when mark m is assigned to candidate i. We assume that the mark of a candidate is the sum of all the scores assigned to his answers. However, more complex functions can be considered (e.g., weighted scores).
- Event $begin(i)$ is emitted when candidate i begins the examination phase.
- Event $end(i)$ is emitted when candidate i ends the examination phase. The candidate terminates the exam himself, e.g., after answering all questions before the end of the exam duration.

In general, all events are time stamped, however we parameterize them with time only when it is relevant for the considered property. Moreover, we may omit some parameters from the events when they are not relevant to the property. For instance, we may use $submit(i)$ when candidate i submits an answer regardless of his answer. We also use $marked(q, a, b)$ instead of $marked(i, q, a, b)$ to capture anonymous marking.

3   Properties of E-exams

In this section, we define eight properties that aim at ensuring e-exams correctness. They mainly ensure that only registered candidates can take the exam, all accepted answers are submitted by the candidates, all answers are accepted during the exam duration, and all marks are correctly computed and assigned to the corresponding candidates. Note that in case of failure, two of the properties report all the individuals that violate the requirement of the property. This notion of reporting can be applied to all other properties (see [7]).

Each property represents a different e-exam requirement and can be monitored independently. An *exam run* may satisfy one property and fail on another one, which narrows the possible source of potential failures and allows us to deliver a detailed report about the satisfied and unsatisfied properties.

Quantified Event Automata (QEAs). We express properties as QEAs [4,5]. We present QEAs at an abstract level using intuitive terminology and refer to [4] for a formal presentation. A QEA consists of a list of quantified variables together with an *event automaton*. An event automaton is a finite-state machine with transitions labeled by parametric events, where parameters are instantiated with data-values at runtime. Transitions may also include guards and assignments to variables. Note, not all variables need to be quantified. Unquantified variables are left free, and they can be manipulated through assignments and updated during the processing of the trace. Moreover, new free variables can be introduced while processing the trace. We extend the initial definition of QEAs in [4] by (i) allowing variable declaration and initialization before reading the trace, and (ii) introducing the notion of global variable shared among all event automaton instances. Note, we use global variables in our case study presented in Sect. 4.2 and in the extended version of this paper. Global variables are mainly needed in QEAs to keep track and report data at the end of monitoring. Such QEAs may also require some manipulation of the quantified variables which is not currently supported by MarQ. Thus, we could not implement them and hence omitted them from the paper. The shaded states are final (accepting) states, while white states are failure states. Square states are closed to failure, *i.e.*, if no transition can be taken, then there is a transition to an implicit failure state. Circular states are closed to self (skip) states, *i.e.*, if no transition can be taken, then there is an implicit self-looping transition. We use the notation $\frac{[guard]}{assignment}$ to write guards and assignments on transitions: $:\hat{=}$ for variable declaration then assignment, $:=$ for assignment, and $=$ for equality test. A QEA formally defines a language (*i.e.*, a set of traces) over instantiated parametric events.

Correct Exam run. An exam run satisfies a property if the resulting trace is accepted by the corresponding QEA. A *correct exam run* satisfies all the properties. We assume that an input trace contains events related to a single exam run. To reason about traces with events from more than one exam run, the events have to be parameterized with an exam run identifier, which has to be added to the list of quantified variables.

Candidate Registration. The first property is *Candidate Registration*, which states that only already registered candidates can submit answers to the exam. An exam run satisfies *Candidate Registration* if, for every candidate i, event $submit(i)$ is preceded by event $register(i)$. A violation of *Candidate Registration* does not reveal a weakness in the exam system (as long as the answers submitted from unregistered candidates are not accepted by the authority). However, it allows us to detect if a candidate tries to fake the system, which is helpful to be aware of *spoofing* attacks.

Definition 1. (Candidate Registration). *Property* Candidate Registration *is defined by the QEA depicted in Fig. 1 with alphabet* $\Sigma_{CR} = \{register(i), submit(i)\}$.

The input alphabet Σ_{CR} for *Candidate Registration* contains only the events $register(i)$ and $submit(i)$, so any other event in the trace is ignored. The QEA for

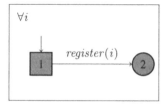

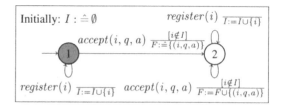

Fig. 1. QEA for *Candidate Registration*

Fig. 2. QEA for *Candidate Eligibility*

Candidate Registration has two accepting states, and one quantified variable i. Note, the empty trace is accepted by the QEA. State (1) is a square state, so an event *submit*(i) that is not preceded by event *register*(i) leads to a failure. An event *register*(i) in state (1) leads to state (2) which is a skipping (circular) state, so after event *register*(i) any sequence of events is accepted. The quantification $\forall i$ means that the property must hold for all values that i takes in the trace, *i.e.*, the values obtained when matching the symbolic events in the specification with concrete events in the trace. For instance, let us consider the following trace: *register*(i_1).*submit*(i_2).*submit*(i_1).*register*(i_2). To decide whether it is accepted or not, the trace is sliced based on the values that can match i, resulting in the two slices: $i \mapsto i_1$: *register*(i_1).*submit*(i_1), and $i \mapsto i_2$: *submit*(i_2).*register*(i_2).

Then, each slice is checked against the event automata instantiated with the appropriate values for i. The slice associated to i_1 is accepted as it reaches the final state (2), while the slice associated to i_2 does not reach a final state since event *submit*(i_2) leads from state (1) to an implicit failure state. Therefore, the whole trace is not accepted by the QEA. Note, we omit parameters q and a from event *submit*(i, q, a) since only the fact that a candidate i submits an answer is significant for the property, regardless of the question he is answering, and the answer he submitted.

Candidate Eligibility. Property *Candidate Eligibility* states that no answer is accepted from an unregistered candidate. *Candidate Eligibility* can be modeled by a QEA similar to that of *Candidate Registration* depicted in Fig. 1, except that event *submit*(i, q, a) has to be replaced by *accept*(i, q, a) in the related alphabet. However, we formalize *Candidate Eligibility* in a way that, in addition to checking the main requirement, it reports all the candidates that violate the requirement, *i.e.*, those that are unregistered but some answers are accepted from them. Note, *Candidate Registration* can also modeled similarly by replacing *accept*(i, q, a) with *submit*(i, q, a).

Definition 2. (Candidate Eligibility). *Property* Candidate Eligibility *is defined by the QEA depicted in Fig. 2 with alphabet* $\Sigma_{CE} = \{register(i), accept(i, q, a)\}$.

The QEA of *Candidate Eligibility* has three free variables I, F, and i, and no quantified variables. Instead of being instantiated for each candidate i, the

QEA of *Candidate Eligibility* collects all the registered candidates in set I, so that any occurrence of event $accept(i, q, a)$ at state (1) with $i \notin I$ fires a transition to the failure state (2). Such a transition results in the failure of the property since all transitions from state (2) are self-looping transitions. Set F is used to collect all the unregistered candidates that submitted an answer. Note, variable I is pre-declared and initialized to $\emptyset$. Trace $register(i_1).accept(i_2, q_0, a_2).accept(i_1, q_0, a_1).register(i_2)$ is not accepted by *Candidate Eligibility*, and results in $F = \{(i_2, q_0, a_2)\}$. Note, reporting the candidates that violates the requirements requires to monitor until the end of the trace.

Answer Authentication. Property *Answer Authentication* states that all accepted answers are submitted by candidates. Moreover, for every question, exactly one answer is accepted from each candidate that submitted at least one answer to that question.

Definition 3. (Answer Authentication). *Property* Answer Authentication *is defined by the QEA depicted in Fig. 3 with alphabet* $\Sigma_{AA} = \{submit(i, q, a), accept(i, q, a)\}$.

The QEA of *Answer Authentication* fails if an unsubmitted answer is accepted. A candidate can submit more than one answer to the same question, but exactly one answer has to be accepted. Note, any answer among the submitted answers can be accepted. However, the QEA can be updated to allow only the acceptance of the last submitted answers by replacing set A with a variable, which acts as a placeholder for the last submitted answer. If no answer is accepted after at least one answer has been submitted, the QEA ends in the failure state (2), while acceptance of an answer leads to the accepting state (3). A candidate can submit after having accepted an answer from him to that question. However, if more than one answer is accepted, an implicit transition from state (3) to a failure state is fired. Trace $submit(i_1, q_0, a_1).submit(i_1, q_0, a_2).accept(i_1, q_0, a_2)$ – where candidate i_1 submits two answers a_1 and a_2 to question q_0, then only a_2 is accepted – is accepted by *Answer Authentication*. While the traces $accept(i_1, q, a)$, where an unsubmitted answer is accepted from i_1, and $submit(i_1, q, a_1). submit(i_1, q, a_2).accept(i_1, q, a_1).accept(i_1, q, a_2)$, where two answers to the same question are accepted from same candidate, are not accepted.

Answer Authentication can be further split into three different properties which allow us to precisely know whether, for a certain question, an unsubmitted answer is accepted, no answer is accepted from a candidate that submitted

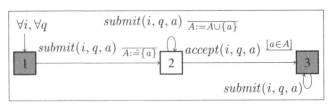

Fig. 3. QEA for *Answer Authentication*

an answer, or more than one answer is accepted from the same candidate. For instance, updating the QEA depicted in Fig. 3 by getting rid of state (3), converting state (2) into an accepting state, and adding a self loop transition on state (2) labeled by $accept(i, q, a)$ $^{[a \in A]}$ results in a QEA that fails only when an unsubmitted answer is accepted (see [7] for more details).

Question Ordering. The previous properties formalize the main requirements that are usually needed concerning answer submission and acceptance. However, additional requirements might be needed. For example, candidates may be required to answer questions in a certain order: a candidate should not get a question before validating his answer to the previous question. This is ensured by *Question Ordering*.

Definition 4. (Question Ordering). *Let $q_1, \ldots, q_n$ be n questions such that the order $ord(q_k)$ of q_k is k. Property* Question Ordering *is defined by the QEA depicted in Fig. 4 with alphabet $\Sigma_{QO} = \{get(i, q), accept(i, q)\}$.*

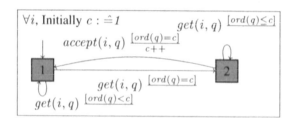

Fig. 4. QEA for *Question Ordering*

The QEA of *Question Ordering* fails if a candidate gets (or an answer is accepted from him for) a higher order question before his answer to the current question is accepted. Note, *Question Ordering* also allows only one accepted answer per question. Otherwise, there is no meaning for the order as the candidate can resubmit answers latter when he gets all the questions.

Exam availability. An e-exam must allow candidates to take the exam only during the examination phase. *Exam Availability* states that questions are obtained, and answers are submitted and accepted only during the examination time.

Definition 5. (Exam Availability). *Let t_0 be the starting instant, and t_f be the ending instant of the exam. Property* Exam Availability *is defined by the QEA depicted in Fig. 5 with alphabet $\Sigma_{EA} = \{get(i, t), change(i, t), submit(i, t), accept(i, t)\}$.*

The QEA of *Exam Availability* checks that all the events in Σ_{EA} are emitted between t_0 and t_f. It also collects all the candidates that violates the requirements in a set F. Note, any other event can be added to Σ_{EA} if required.

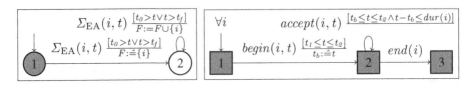

Fig. 5. QEA for *Exam Availability*

Fig. 6. QEA for *Exam Availability with Flexibility*

Exam availability with flexibility. Some exams offer flexibility to the candidates, so that a candidate is free to choose the beginning time within a certain specified period. To capture that, we define *Exam Availability with Flexibility* which states that no answer can be accepted from a candidate before he begins the exam, after he terminates the exam, after the end of his exam duration, or after the end of the specified period. The beginning time of the exam may differ from one candidate to another, but in any case it has to be within a certain specified period. The exam duration may also differ between candidates. For example, an extended duration may be offered to certain candidates with disabilities.

Definition 6. (Exam Availability With Flexibility). *Let t_1 and t_2 respectively be the starting and the ending time instants of the allowed period, and let $dur(i)$ be the exam duration for candidate i. Property* Exam Availability with Flexibility *is defined by the QEA depicted in Fig. 6 with alphabet* $\Sigma_{EA} = \{begin(i,t), end(i), accept(i,t)\}$.

Exam Availability with Flexibility also requires that, for each candidate i, there is only one event $begin(i,t)$ per exam. Hence, it fails if event $begin(i)$ is emitted more than once. A candidate can begin his exam at any time t_b such that $t_1 \leq t_b \leq t_2$. Note, no answer can be accepted from a candidate after then ending time t_2 of the period, if the duration of the candidate is not finished yet. Assume that $t_1 = 0$, $t_2 = 1,000$, $dur(i_1) = 90$, and $dur(i_2) = 60$. Then, trace $begin(i_1, 0).accept(i_1, 24).begin(i_2, 26).accept$ $(i_2, 62).accept(i_1, 90)$ is accepted. While, trace $accept(i_1, 5).begin\ (i_1, 20)$ and trace $begin(i_1, 0).accept(i_1, 91)$ are not accepted since in the first one an answer is accepted from candidate i_1 before he begins the exam, and in the second one an answer is accepted after the exam duration expires.

Event *submit* is not included in Σ_{EA}, thus an answer submission outside the exam time is not considered as an irregularity if the answer is not accepted by the authority. However, again other events (*e.g.*, *get* and *submit*) can be considered. In such a case, the QEA in

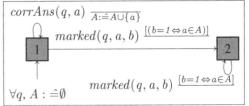

Fig. 7. QEA for *Marking Correctness*

Fig. 6 has to be edited by looping over state (2) with any added event.

Marking correctness. The last two properties state that each candidate should get the correct mark, the one computed correctly from his answers. *Marking Correctness* states that all answers are marked correctly. In the QEA of *Marking Correctness*, the correct answers for the considered question are collected in a set A (self loop over state (1)).

Definition 7. (Marking Correctness). *Property* Marking Correctness *is defined by the QEA depicted in Fig. 7 with alphabet* $\Sigma_{MC} = \{corrAns(q, a),$ *marked*$\}(q, a, b)\}.$

In state (1), once an answer to the considered question is marked correctly, a transition to state (3) is fired, otherwise if an answer is marked in a wrong way a transition to an implicit failure state occurs. In state (3), the property fails either if an answer is marked in a wrong way, or if an event $corrAns(q, a)$ is encountered as this means that certain answers are marked before all the correct answers are set.

Mark integrity. Property *Mark Integrity* states that all accepted answers are marked, and that exactly one mark is assigned to each candidate, the one attributed to his answers. *Mark Integrity* together with *Marking Correctness*, guarantee that each candidate participated in the exam gets the correct mark corresponding to his answers. The QEA of *Mark Integrity* collects, for each candidate, the submitted answers in a set A.

Definition 8. (Mark Integrity). *Property* Mark Integrity *is defined by the QEA depicted in Fig. 8 with alphabet* $\Sigma_{MI} = \{accept(i, q, a), marked(q, a, b),$ *assign*$(i, m)\}.$

   For each accepted answer, the QEA accumulates the corresponding score b in the sum s. If the accepted answers are not marked, the property fails (failure state (2)). If the candidate is not assigned a mark or assigned a wrong mark the property fails (failure state (3)). Once the the correct mark is assigned to the candidate, if another mark is assigned or any other answer is accepted from him, the property fails (square state (4)).

4   Case Study: UJF E-exam

In June 2014, the pharmacy faculty at UJF organized a first e-exam, as a part of *Epreuves Classantes Nationales informatisées* project which aims to realize all medicine exams electronically by 2016. The project is lead by UJF and the e-exam software is developed by the company THEIA[9] specialized in e-formation platforms. This software is currently used by 39 french universities. Since then, 1,047 e-exams have been organized and 147,686 students have used the e-exam software.

---

[9] www.theia.fr.

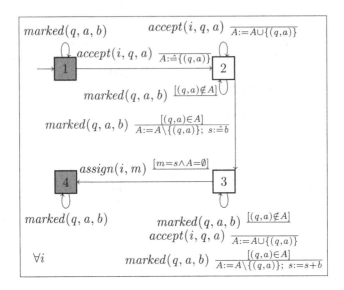

Fig. 8. QEA for *Mark Integrity*

We validate our framework by verifying two real e-exams passed with this system. All the logs received from the e-exam organizer are anonymized; nevertheless we were not authorized to disclose them. We use MarQ[10] [6] (Monitoring At Runtime with QEA) to model the QEAs and perform the verification. We provide a description for this system that we call *UJF e-exam*[11], then we present the results of our analysis.

4.1   Exam Description

Registration. The candidates have to register two weeks before the examination time. Each candidate receives a username/password to authenticate at the examination.

Examination. The exam takes place in a supervised room. Each student handled a previously-calibrated tablet to pass the exam. The internet access is controlled: only IP addresses within an certain range are allowed to access the exam server. A candidate starts by logging in using his username/password. Then, he chooses one of the available exams by entering the exam code, which is provided at the examination time by the invigilator supervising the room. Once the correct code is entered, the exam starts and the first question is displayed. The pedagogical exam conditions mention that the candidates have to answer the

---

[10] https://github.com/selig/qea.

[11] We have also designed an event-based behavioral model of the e-exam phases that is not reported in this paper for space reasons. The description was obtained and validated through discussions with the engineers at THEIA.

questions in a fixed order and cannot get to the next question before answering the current one. A candidate can change the answer as many times as he wants before validating, but once he validates, then he cannot go back and change any of the previously validated answers. Note, all candidates have to answer the same questions in the same order. A question might be a one-choice question, multiple-choice question, open short-text question, or script-concordance question.

Marking. After the end of the examination phase, the grading process starts. For each question, all the answers provided by the candidates are collected. Then, each answer is evaluated anonymously by an examiner to 0 if it is wrong, $0 < s < 1$ if it is partially correct, or 1 if it is correct. An example of a partially-correct answer is when a candidate provides only one of the two correct answers for a multiple-choice question. The professor specifies the correct answer(s) and the scores to attribute to correct and partially-correct answers, as well, as the potential penalty. After evaluating all the provided answers for all questions, the total mark for each candidate is calculated as the summation of all the scores attributed to his answers.

Notification. The marks are notified to the candidates. A candidate can consult his submission, obtain the correct answer and his score for each question.

4.2   Analysis

We analyzed two exams: Exam 1 involves 233 candidates and contains 42 questions for a duration of 1h35. Exam 2 involves 90 candidates, contains 36 questions for a duration of 5h20. The resulting traces for these exams are respectively of size 1.85 MB and 215 KB and contain 40,875 and 4,641 events. The result of our analysis together with the time required for MarQ to analyze the whole trace on a standard PC (AMD A10-5745M–Quad-Core 2.1 GHz, 8 GB RAM), are summed up in Table 1. ($\checkmark$) means satisfied, ($\times$) means not satisfied, and [1] indicates the number of violations. Only four of the eight general properties presented in Sect. 3 were compatible with UJF E-exam. We considered five additional and specific properties for the *UJF e-exam*.

   Property *Candidate Registration* was satisfied, that is, no unregistered candidate submits an answer. *Candidate Eligibility* is also satisfied. We note that, in MarQ tool the *Candidate Eligibility* monitor stops monitoring as soon as a transition to state (2) is made since there is no path to success from state (2). Thus, only the first candidate that violates the property is reported. In order to report all such candidates, we had to add an artificial transition from state (2) to an accepting state that could never be taken. Then, monitoring after reaching state (2) remains possible. Moreover, the current implementation of MarQ does not support sets of tuples. Consequently, we could only collect the identities i in a set F instead of the tuples (i, q, a).

   Answer Authentication was violated only in Exam 1. We reported the violation to the e-exam's developers. The violation actually revealed a discrepancy between the initial specification and the current features of the e-exam software:

a candidate can submit the *same answer* several times and this answer remains accepted. Consequently, an event *accept* can appear twice but only with the same answer. To confirm that the failure of *Answer Authentication* is only due to the acceptance of a same answer twice, we updated property *Answer Authentication* and its QEA presented in Fig. 3 by storing the accepted answer in a variable a_v, and adding a self loop transition on state (3) labeled by $accept(i, q, a) \xrightarrow{[a=a_v]}$. We refer to this new weaker property as *Answer Authentication**, which differs from *Answer Authentication* by allowing the acceptance of the same answer again; but it still forbids the acceptance of a different answer. We found out that *Answer Authentication** is satisfied, which confirms the claim about the possibility of accepting the same answer twice. After diagnosing the source of failure, we defined property *Answer Authentication Reporting* presented in Fig. 9, which fails if more than one answer (identical or not) is accepted from the same candidate to the same question. At the same time, it collects all such candidates in a set F. *Answer Authentication Reporting* is defined by the QEA depicted in Fig. 9 with the input alphabet $\Sigma_{AAR} = \{accept(i, q, a)\}$. The analysis of *Answer Authentication Reporting* shows that, for Exam 1, there is only one candidate such that more than one answer are accepted from him to the same question. The multiple answers that are accepted for the same question are supposed to be equal since *Answer Authentication** is satisfied. Note that MarQ currently does not support global variables, so for *Answer Authentication Reporting*, a set is required for each question. Note for Exam 1, *Answer Authentication* required less monitoring time than *Answer Authentication** and *Answer Authentication Reporting* as the monitor for *Answer Authentication* stops monitoring as soon as it finds a violation.

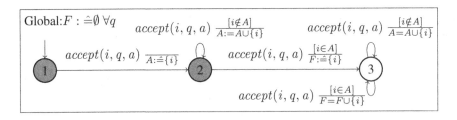

Fig. 9. QEA for *Answer Authentication Reporting*

Furthermore, *UJF exam* has a requirement stating that after acceptance the writing field is "blocked" and the candidate cannot change it anymore. Actually, in *UJF exam* when a candidate writes a potential answer in the writing field the server stores it directly, and once the candidate validates the question the last stored answer is accepted. As *Answer Authentication* shows, several answers can still be accepted after the first acceptance, then the ability of changing the answer in the writing field could result in an acceptance of a different answer. For this purpose, we defined property *Answer Editing* that states that a candidate cannot change the answer after acceptance. *Answer Editing* is defined by the QEA depicted in Fig. 10 with the input alphabet $\Sigma_{\mathrm{AE}} = \{change(i, q), accept(i, q, a)\}$.

Note, we allowed the acceptance of the same answer to
avoid the bug found by *Answer
Authentication*. Our analysis
showed that *Answer Editing*
was violated in Exam 2: at
least one student was able to
change the content of the writing field after having his answer
accepted.

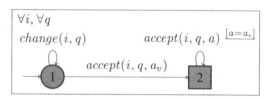

Fig. 10. QEA for *Answer Editing*

Concerning *Question Ordering* the developers did not log anything related to the event $get(i, q)$. However, we defined *Question Ordering** which fails if a candidate changes the writing field of a future question before an answer for the current question is accepted. *Question Ordering** is defined by the QEA depicted in Fig. 11 with the input alphabet $\Sigma_{\mathrm{QO'}} = \{change(i, q), accept(i, q)\}$. The idea is that if a candidate changes the answer field of a question, he must have received the question previously. Moreover, we allow submitting the same answer twice, and also changing the previous accepted answers to avoid the two bugs previously found. Note, *UJF exam* requires the candidate to validate the question even if he left it blank, thus we also allow acceptance for the current question before changing its field (self loop above state (2)). The analysis showed that *Question Ordering** was violated in both exams.

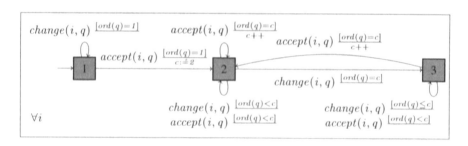

Fig. 11. QEA for *Question Ordering**

Alternatives to *Answer Editing* and *Question Ordering* can be defined to report all the candidates who violate the requirement (see [7]). However, it cannot be implemented using MarQ as it requires the ability either to manipulate the quantified variables or to build sets of pairs which are both currently not supported by MarQ. However, the tool still outputs the first candidate who violates the property.

Note, the manual check of *Question Ordering** showed that some candidates were able to skip certain questions (after writing an answer) without validating them, and then validating the following questions.

As we found a violation for *Question Ordering**, we defined *Acceptance Order* that checks, for each candidate, whether all the accepted answers are accepted in order, *i.e.,* there should be no answer accepted for a question that is followed by an accepted answer for a lower order question. *Acceptance Order* is defined by the QEA depicted in Fig. 12 with the input alphabet $\Sigma_{AO} = \{accept(i, q, a)\}$.

Exam Availability is also violated in Exam 2. A candidate was able to change and submit an answer, which is accepted, after the end of the exam duration. We could not analyze *Exam Availability with Flexibility*, since it is not supported by the exam. We also did not consider *Marking Correctness*, and *Mark Integrity* properties since the developers did not log anything concerning

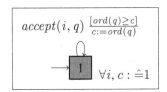

Fig. 12. QEA for *Acceptance Order*

the marking and the notification phase is done by each university and we were not able to get the logs related to this phase. This shows that universities only look for cheating candidates, and do not look for internal problems or insider attacks. We expect the developers of the e-exam software to include logging features for every phase. Note, we implemented all properties in MarQ and validated them on toy traces as we expect to obtain the actual traces of the marking phase in the near future.

Table 1. Results of the off-line monitoring of two e-exams.

Property	Exam 1		Exam 2	
	Result	Time (ms)	Result	Time (ms)
Candidate Registration	✓	538	✓	230
Candidate Eligibility	✓	517	✓	214
Answer Authentication	✗	310	✓	275
*Answer Authentication**	✓	742	✓	223
Answer Authentication Reporting	✗[1]	654	✓	265
Answer Editing	✓	641	✗	218
*Question Ordering**	✗	757	✗	389
Acceptance Order	✓	697	✓	294
Exam Availability	✓	518	✗[1]	237

5   Related Work and Discussion

To the best of our knowledge, this is the first paper to address the runtime verification of e-exams. However, a formal framework for checking verifiability properties of e-exams based on abstract tests has been proposed by Dreier *et al.* in [8]. Note, the proposed tests in [8] need to be instantiated for each exam depending on its specifications. The authors of [8] have validated their framework by (i) modeling two exams in the applied π-calculus [9], and then (ii) analyzing them using ProVerif [10]. More precisely, they proposed a set of individual and universal properties that allow to verify the correctness of e-exams. The individual properties allow the candidate to check himself whether he received the correct mark that corresponds to his answers. While the universal properties allow an outsider auditor to check whether only registered candidates participate in the exam, all accepted answers are marked correctly, and all marks are assigned to the corresponding candidates. The universal properties that we proposed revisit the properties defined in [8]. However, as mentioned before, this paper is concerned with the monitoring of actual exam executions rather than operating on the abstract models of the exam specification. Furthermore, in general, formal verification techniques such as the one in [8] suffer from the so-called state explosion that may limit the size of systems that can be verified. Moreover, as formal methods operate on models, they introduce an additional question concerning the correctness of the abstraction. In contrast, as runtime verification operates only on the actual event traces, it is less dependent on the size of the system and, at the same time, does not require as much abstraction. Our properties can be monitored only by observing the events of trace from an exam run.

System verification is also addressed in some other related domains $e.g.$, in auctions [11], and voting [12,13]. Back to e-exams, Dreier et $al.$ also propose a formal framework, based on π-calculus, to analyze other security properties such as authentication and privacy [14]. These complementary approaches study security and not verification, however both aspects are important to develop such sensitive systems.

All the mentioned related approaches only allow symbolic abstract analysis of the protocols specifications, mainly looking for potential flaws in the used cryptographic primitives. What is more, these approaches support neither on-line nor off-line analysis of the actual logs obtained from system executions.

On the other hand, off-line runtime verification of user-provided specifications over logs has been addressed in the context of several tools in the runtime verification community [15]: Breach for Signal Temporal Logic. RiTHM and StePr for (variants of) Linear Temporal Logic, LogFire for rule-based systems, and Java-MOP for various specification formalisms provided as plugins. MarQ [6] is a tool for monitoring Quantified Event Automata [4,5]. Our choice of using QEA stems from two reasons. First, QEAs is one of the most expressive specification formalism to express monitors. The second reason stems from our interviews of the engineers who were collaborating with us and responsible for the development of the e-exam software at UJF. To validate our formalization of the protocol and the desired properties for e-exams, we presented the existing alternative specification languages. QEAs turned out to be the specification language that was most accepted and understood by the engineers. Moreover, MarQ came top in the 1st international competition on Runtime Verification (2014)[12], showing that MarQ is one of the most efficient existing monitoring tools for both off-line and

---

[12] http://rv2014.imag.fr/monitoring-competition/results.

on-line monitoring. Note, off-line runtime verification was successfully applied to other case studies, *e.g.*, for monitoring financial transactions with LARVA [16], and monitoring IT logs with MonPoly [17].

6   Conclusions and Future Work

We define an event-based model for e-exams, and formalize several essential properties as Quantified Event Automata, enriched with global variables and pre-initialization. Our model handles e-exams that offer flexible independent beginning time and/or different exam duration for the candidates. We validate the properties by analyzing real logs from e-exams at UJF. We perform off-line verification of certain exam runs using the MarQ tool. We find several discrepancies between the specification and the implementation. Analyzing logs of real e-exams requires only a few seconds on a regular computer. Due to the lack of logs about the marking and notification phases, we were not able to analyze all properties. The *UJF E-exam* case study clearly demonstrates that the developers do not think to log these two phases where there is less interaction with the candidates. However, we believe that monitoring the marking phase is essential since a successful attempt from a bribed examiner or a cheating student can be very effective.

Several avenues for future work are opened by this paper. First, we intend to analyze more existing e-exams: from other universities and the marking phase of the pharmacy exams at UJF. We encourage universities and educational institutions to incorporate logging features in their e-exam software. Moreover, we plan to perform on-line verification during live e-exams, and to study to what extent runtime enforcement (cf [18] for an overview) can be applied during a live e-exam run. Finally, we plan to study more expressive and quantitative properties that can detect possible collusion between students through similar answer patterns.

Acknowledgment. The authors would like to thank François Géronimi from THEIA, Daniel Pagonis from TIMC-IMAG, and Olivier Palombi from LJK for providing us with a description of e-exam software system, for sharing with us the logs of some real french e-exams, and for validating and discussing the properties presented in this paper. The authors also thank Giles Reger for providing us with help on using MarQ. The authors also would like to thank the "Digital trust" Chair from the University of Auvergne Foundation for the support provided to conduct this research. This work has been partly done in the context of the ICT COST Action IC1402 Runtime Verification beyond Monitoring (ARVI).

References

1. Le Figaro: Etudiants: les examens sur tablettes numériques appellés à se multiplier. Press release (2015). http://goo.gl/ahxQJD
2. Copeland, L.: School cheating scandal shakes up atlanta. USA TODAY (2013). http://goo.gl/wGr40s

3. Watson, R.: Student visa system fraud exposed in BBC investigation (2014). http://www.bbc.com/news/uk-26024375

4. Barringer, H., Falcone, Y., Havelund, K., Reger, G., Rydeheard, D.: Quantified event automata: towards expressive and efficient runtime monitors. In: Giannakopoulou, D., Méry, D. (eds.) FM 2012. LNCS, vol. 7436, pp. 68–84. Springer, Heidelberg (2012)

5. Reger, G.: Automata based monitoring and mining of execution traces. Ph.D. thesis, University of Manchester (2014)

6. Reger, G., Cruz, H.C., Rydeheard, D.E.: MarQ: monitoring at runtime with QEA. In: Baier, C., Tinelli, C. (eds.) ETAPS 2015. LNCS, vol. 9035, pp. 596–610. Springer, Heidelberg (2015)

7. Kassem, A., Falcone, Y., Lafourcade, P.: Monitoring electronic exams. Technical report TR-2015-4, Verimag, Laboratoire d'Informatique de Grenoble Research Report (2015)

8. Dreier, J., Giustolisi, R., Kassem, A., Lafourcade, P., Lenzini, G.: A framework for analyzing verifiability in traditional and electronic exams. In: Lopez, J., Wu, Y. (eds.) ISPEC 2015. LNCS, vol. 9065, pp. 514–529. Springer, Heidelberg (2015)

9. Abadi, M., Fournet, C.: Mobile values, new names, and secure communication. In: POPL 2001. ACM, New York (2001)

10. Blanchet, B.: An efficient cryptographic protocol verifier based on prolog rules. In: CSFW, Cape Breton, Canada, pp. 82–96. IEEE Computer Society (2001)

11. Dreier, J., Jonker, H., Lafourcade, P.: Defining verifiability in e-auction protocols. In: 8th ACM Symposium on Information, Computer and Communications Security, ASIA CCS 2013, pp. 547–552, Hangzhou, China (2013)

12. Kremer, S., Ryan, M., Smyth, B.: Election verifiability in electronic voting protocols. In: Gritzalis, D., Preneel, B., Theoharidou, M. (eds.) ESORICS 2010. LNCS, vol. 6345, pp. 389–404. Springer, Heidelberg (2010)

13. Backes, M., Hritcu, C., Maffei, M.: Automated verification of remote electronic voting protocols in the applied pi-calculus. In: CSF, pp. 195–209 (2008)

14. Dreier, J., Giustolisi, R., Kassem, A., Lafourcade, P., Lenzini, G., Ryan, P.Y.A.: Formal analysis of electronic exams. In: SECRYPT 2014 - Proceedings of the 11th International Conference on Security and Cryptography, pp. 101–112, Vienna, Austria (2014)

15. Bartocci, E., Bonakdarpour, B., Falcone, Y.: First international competition on software for runtime verification. In: [19], pp. 1–9

16. Colombo, C., Pace, G.J.: Fast-forward runtime monitoring — an industrial case study. In: Qadeer, S., Tasiran, S. (eds.) RV 2012. LNCS, vol. 7687, pp. 214–228. Springer, Heidelberg (2013)

17. Basin, D.A., Caronni, G., Ereth, S., Harvan, M., Klaedtke, F., Mantel, H.: Scalable offline monitoring. In: [19], pp. 31–47

18. Falcone, Y.: You should better enforce than verify. In: Barringer, H., Falcone, Y., Finkbeiner, B., Havelund, K., Lee, I., Pace, G., Roşu, G., Sokolsky, O., Tillmann, N. (eds.) RV 2010. LNCS, vol. 6418, pp. 89–105. Springer, Heidelberg (2010)

19. Bonakdarpour, B., Smolka, S.A. (eds.): RV 2014. LNCS, vol. 8734. Springer, Heidelberg (2014)

Monitoring Real Android Malware

Jan-Christoph Küster[1,2]($\boxtimes$) and Andreas Bauer[3]

[1] NICTA, Canberra, Australia
[2] Australian National University, Canberra, Australia
jan-christoph.kuester@nicta.com.au
[3] TU München, Munich, Germany

Abstract. In the most comprehensive study on Android attacks so far (undertaken by the Android Malware Genome Project), the behaviour of more than 1,200 malwares was analysed and categorised into common, recurring groups of attacks. Based on this work (and the corresponding actual malware files), we present an approach for specifying and identifying these (and similar) attacks using runtime verification.

While formally, our approach is based on a first-order logic abstraction of malware behaviour, it practically relies on our Android event interception tool, MonitorMe, which lets us capture almost any system event that can be triggered by apps on a user's Android device.

This paper details on MonitorMe, our formal specification of malware behaviour and practical experiments, undertaken with various different Android devices and versions on a wide range of actual malware incarnations from the above study. In a nutshell, we were able to detect real malwares from 46 out of 49 different malware families, which strengthen the idea that runtime verification may, indeed, be a good choice for mobile security in the future.

1 Introduction

The landmark work undertaken by the Android Malware Genome Project (AMGP, [15]) is the first that comprehensively collected and systematically analysed more than 1,200 Android malware samples. Despite the high total amount of unique samples, their study reveals that those can be divided into only 49 families and described by even fewer recurring attack patterns, which fall into the following categories: information stealing, financial charges, privilege escalation and malicious payload activation.

Inspired by those patterns, we formalise in this paper common malicious behaviour in our own specification language (published prior in [2]) to dynamically identify real malware on a user's Android device; that is, by checking its runtime footprint against our specifications. As our approach has access to the actual executed behaviour of apps, it can complement static analysis techniques, whose malware detection often faces difficulties in face of code obfuscation (cf. [11]). Dynamic analysis techniques on the other hand, which are often used on an emulator in order to detect malware, face difficulties with samples that

NICTA is funded by the Australian Government as represented by the Department of Broadband, Communications and the Digital Economy and the Australian Research Council through the ICT Centre of Excellence program.

E. Bartocci and R. Majumdar (Eds.): RV 2015, LNCS 9333, pp. 136–152, 2015.
DOI: 10.1007/978-3-319-23820-3_9

employ recent emulator-detection techniques (cf. [13]). Naturally, this is not a problem either when working directly on the device.

We were able to detect suspicious behaviour of 46 out of 49 malware families from the AMGP, while generating 28 % positive alerts when monitoring a representative set of 61 benign apps with our specifications.

For conducting our experiments we have developed a standalone monitoring app, called MonitorMe. Compared to other approaches, which are usually either *app- or platform-centric* (see discussion in Sect. 5), its major advantage is that it combines the strengths of both "worlds", i.e., while it is easy to install on a user's off-the-shelf device, it is also capable of gathering all system events necessary for our analysis, without requiring the modification of either the Android platform or apps themselves (cf. [1,4,6,14]). Hence, for a future, stable version of our prototype, we have the average phone user in mind, assuming that specifications are centrally created by security experts and that the app receives regular updates to them over the internet. Currently, MonitorMe runs on various devices of the Google Nexus family (tested for Nexus S, 7 and 5), and is portable to older and very recent Android versions (2.3.6, 4.3 and 5.0.1). However, we require devices to be rooted to load a Linux kernel module. This may seem restrictive, but one should keep in mind that it has become common practice by now and does not disrupt the user experience by reinstalling the system on the device at hand.

Outline. In the next section, we give a technical overview of MonitorMe. Our specification language and its use for monitoring malware is introduced in Sect. 3, followed by experiments (Sect. 4.1) demonstrating that our policies help identify most AMGP-families. The experiments further demonstrate (Sect. 4.2) that only few false positives for benign apps are generated and that performance- and portability-wise our approach does, indeed, lend itself to be executed on almost arbitrary end-user Android devices.

2 Event Interception with MonitorMe

To enable our modular way of malware detection on a user's device, we have developed a monitoring app,[1] which has two main components (depicted in Fig. 1): a framework for collecting system events on the Android platform (grey area, named *DroidTracer*[2]), and an analysis component (on top of DroidTracer), which receives those events in chronological order and incrementally "feeds" them into monitors

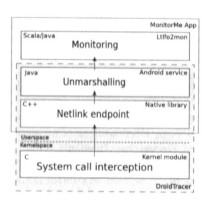

Fig. 1. Architecture of MonitorMe.

---

[1] http://kuester.multics.org/MonitorMe/.
[2] http://kuester.multics.org/DroidTracer/.

generated by Ltlfo2mon.[3] We create a monitor for each of our policies that specifies a certain malware behaviour and run a copy of them per app under inspection. Ltlfo2mon is written in Scala, but is compatible to run as part of an Android app in Java. In short, the monitoring algorithm creates an automaton for each LTL-like subformula in a policy. These are then spawned with concrete values based on observed system events at runtime (for details of the algorithm see [2]). It is worth pointing out that DroidTracer works without polling for events, i.e., a Java callback method is triggered whenever a new system event occurs. Furthermore, DroidTracer is implemented as a *standalone library* so that it can be integrated in third-party apps for other analyses.

DroidTracer. In the following we explain the inner workings of DroidTracer (three sub-components marked as white inside the grey area); that is, the novel way on how we intercept interactions between apps and the Android platform without requiring platform or app modifications. As there is no public API for this task, not even on a rooted device, nor any complete documentation about Android's internal communication mechanism, our approach is mainly based on insights gained from reverse engineering.

System Call Interception. We exploit the fact of Android's security design that the control flow of all apps' actions that require permission, such as requesting sensitive information (GPS coordinates, device id, etc.) or connecting with the outside world (via SMS, internet, etc.), *must* eventually pass one of the system calls in the Linux kernel; for example, to be delegated to a more privileged system process that handles the request. In other words, intercepting the control flow at a central point in kernel space does not allow apps to bypass our approach. Furthermore, system calls are unlikely to change so that hooking into them is fairly robust against implementation details on different Android versions.

Hence, our idea is to use kprobes[4] (the kernel's internal debugging mechanism) to intercept system calls in a non-intrusive way. More specifically, we built a custom kernel module (bottom sub-component in Fig. 1), which contains handler methods that get invoked by small bits of trampoline code (so called probes). We add those with kprobes dynamically to the following system calls:

- sys_open(const char __user *filename, ...), opens files with filename for read/write.
- sys_connect(int sockfd, const struct sockaddr *addr, ...), where addr contains the IPv4 or IPv6 address of an established internet connection.
- do_execve(char *filename, char __user *__user *argv, ...), where filename is a program or shell script being executed with the arguments argv.
- ioctl(...), is used to control kernel drivers, such as Android's Binder driver.

From the function arguments of ioctl we cannot directly retrieve relevant information (unlike for the other system calls shown above, which provide to us IP

---

[3] https://github.com/jckuester/ltlfo2mon.
[4] https://www.kernel.org/doc/Documentation/kprobes.txt.

addresses, opened files, or executed program names). The reason is that information is compactly *encoded* (for efficiency reasons), when sent through ioctl by Android's own *inter process communication* (IPC) mechanism, called Binder.[5] As Binder handles the majority of interesting interactions between apps and the Android platform, its decoding is crucial for our analysis. Hence, for a deeper understanding of Binder's control flow, we look at the following Java code snippet of a method call that an app developer might write to send an SMS.

```
SmsManager sms = SmsManager.getDefault();
sms.sendTextMessage("12345", null,"Hello!", null, null);
```

Figure 2 illustrates the control flow of the Binder communication when this code is executed. All Java code of an app is compiled into a single Dalvik executable classes.dex (upper left box), which runs on its own Dalvik VM. The called method sendTextMessage() is part of the Android API (lower left box), which is linked into every app as a JAR file. But instead of implementing the functionality of sending an SMS itself, it rather hides away the technical details of a *remote procedure call* (RPC); that is, a call of a Java method that lives in another Dalvik VM (right box). What further happens is that SmsManager calls the method sendText() of the class Proxy, which has been automatically generated for the ISms interface. The Proxy then uses the class Parcel to *marshall* the method arguments of sendText() into a byte stream, which is sent (together with other method call details) via the Binder driver to the matching Stub of ISms (lower right box). There, the arguments are *unmarshalled* and the final implementation of sendText() in the SMS service is executed. As the SMS service is running on a Dalvik VM privileged to talk to the radio hardware, it can send the SMS.

Unmarshalling. The main challenge in reconstructing method calls was to reverse engineer how Binder encodes them to send them through the kernel, such that the task of unmarshalling for our analysis can be automated. Like for the code snippet of sending an SMS, we aim at reconstructing every method call in its original human readable format (including its Java method arguments and types). In what follows, we describe how we achieved it and what the implementation of this feature looks like on a technical level. All we can intercept in the kernel is the following C structure, which wraps the information copied by Binder driver from the sender into the address space of the receiving process.

```
struct binder_transaction_data {
 unsigned int code;         // value 5 for our SMS example
 uid_t sender_euid;         // UID of the app initiating the request
 const void *buffer;        // Fig.4 shows its content for our example
};
```

A comprehensive technical report contains more details on the implementation [10] and shows how we intercept binder_transaction_data during a certain stage of the Binder driver communication, which follows a strict protocol. The integer

---

[5] http://developer.android.com/reference/android/os/Binder.html.

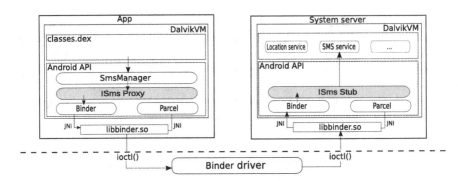

Fig. 2. An app (left) requesting the Android platform (right) to send an SMS.

sender_euid provides us with the UID to unambiguously identify the sender app of a request. However, the method name the integer code translates to, and which arguments are encoded in the byte stream of buffer, is not transmitted, mainly for efficiency reasons. We have a closer look at some code of the Stub and Proxy (shown in Fig. 3), which are *automatically* generated for the interface ISms, to better understand why there is no need for Binder to send this information.

```
01: public void sendText(String destAddr, ...,    01: private ... String DESCRIPTOR =
02:                       String text, ...) ...    02:   "com.android.internal.telephony.ISms";
03: {                                              03: ...
04:   android.os.Parcel _data =                    04: switch (code) { ...
05:                   android.os.Parcel.obtain();  05:   case TRANSACTION_sendText: {
06:   ...                                          06:     data.enforceInterface(DESCRIPTOR);
07:   _data.writeInterfaceToken(DESCRIPTOR);       07:     ...
08:   _data.writeString(destAddr);                 08:     _arg0 = data.readString();
09:   ...                                          09:     ...
10:   _data.writeString(text);                     10:     _arg2 = data.readString(); ...
11:   ...                                          11:     this.sendText(_arg0,..., _arg2,...);
12:   mRemote.transact(Stub.TRANSACTION_sendText,  12: }}
13:                    _data, ...);                13: ...
14:   ...                                          14: static final int TRANSACTION_sendText =
15: }                                              15:   (IBinder.FIRST_CALL_TRANSACTION + 4);
```

Fig. 3. Auto-generated Proxy (left) and Stub class (right) for the ISms interface.

When the Proxy makes the actual RPC for sendText() via Binder (left, line 12), it includes the integer TRANSACTION_sendText defined in its corresponding Stub (right, lines 14–15). We discovered that this is the value of code we find in binder_transaction_data. The second argument _data is an instance of the class Parcel and relates on a lower level to the buffer we intercept. More specifically, the Proxy takes a Parcel object (reused from a pool for efficiency) and then writes the DESCRIPTOR (left, line 7), which is the name of the interface ISms (right, lines 1–2), followed by the method arguments into it (left, lines 8–10). We can observe that this is done in the *order* of the arguments appearing in the method signature. Furthermore, dedicated write methods are used provided by Parcel, such as writeString(). When the Stub receives the call, it executes the TRANSACTION_sendText part of a switch construct (right, line 5), which reconstructs the arguments from the byte stream of the Parcel object; that is, using the equivalent read methods in the exact same order as the write methods have been used. Based on those key observations, we designed the following (three-step) algorithm to automate unmarshalling for arbitrary method calls with DroidTracer (top sub-component in Fig. 1):

1. **Unmarshall interface name (e.g., ISms)**
   (a) Take a Parcel object and fill it with the byte stream buffer. This is possible, as the class Parcel is public and provides an according method.
   (b) Read the DESCRIPTOR from the Parcel object via readString(), as it is always the first argument in buffer (see Fig. 4).
2. **Unmarshall method name (e.g., sendText)**
   (a) Use Java reflection to find the variable name with prefix TRANSACTION_ and code assigned to in the Stub of the unmarshalled interface name. This works, as every app, and so MonitorMe, has access to the JAR of the Android API.
3. **Unmarshall method arguments (e.g., "12345", null, "Hello!", null, null)**
   (a) Determine the order and types of method arguments by accessing the signature of the unmarshalled method name via reflection.
   (b) Apply Parcel's read methods according to the type and order of arguments appearing in the method signature. This works for Java primitives, but we also reverse engineered how complex objects are composed into Java primitives.

It is worth pointing out that our unmarshalling algorithm does not rely on low-level Binder implementations, which might vary for different Android versions, as we are able to use the exact Java read methods of the class Parcel that are also used by the Android framework itself on a specific device.

Netlink Endpoint. As event interception takes place solely inside the kernel space and unmarshalling relies on access to the Android API, we need a mechanism that allows us to pass data from inside the kernel module up to DroidTracer in user space. Moreover, we need to send data also in the other direction so that the user can control the kernel module for even the most basic tasks, for example, to switch event interception on and off. Android has no built-in way to serve as a solution, but we were able to use netlink[6] (a socket based mechanism of the Linux kernel) to bidirectionally communicate with user space. As only the kernel but not the Android API offers netlink support, we had to build a *custom* endpoint for our app (middle sub-component in Fig. 1), using the *Netlink Protocol Library Suite* (libnl[7]). Note that netlink implements a callback principle so that rather than polling the kernel module for new occurring system events, DroidTracer can push them all the way to our analysis component.

---

[6] http://www.linuxfoundation.org/collaborate/workgroups/networking/generic_netlink_howto.
[7] http://www.carisma.slowglass.com/~tgr/libnl/.

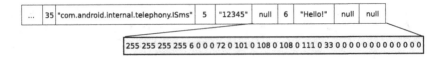

Fig. 4. The buffer sent via Binder containing the arguments of sendTextMessage().

3   Specifying Malware Behaviour

Whenever an app causes a system event on the Android platform that we can intercept with DroidTracer, we capture it as an *action*. We represent actions in our internal, logical model by ground terms $p(c_1, \ldots, c_n)$, where p is a predicate symbol and c_i is a constant. Typically, p denotes the method and interface name of an intercepted method call, and c_i (if any) its ith unmarshalled method argument. That is, we write $sendText@ISms($ "12345", $null$, "Hello!", $null, null)$ for a ground term representing the sending of an SMS, given as an example in Sect. 2, where we conventionally delimit method and interface name by the @-symbol. Let us refer to finite sets of actions as *worlds*. An app's behaviour, observed over time, is therefore a finite trace of worlds. Note that in the case of our analysis, worlds contain only one action and are ordered by the position at which the corresponding system event has been sent from our kernel module via netlink. That is, there is no predefined delay between worlds as the trace is only extended by one world whenever a new system event occurs. Table 1 shows a selection of events collected for a sample of the malware family Walkinwat. Distinct malware samples (i.e., with different hash values) are usually grouped under the same family name if they share the same behaviour and manner in which they spread. Each row contains a system event, where the ID indicates its position in the trace and the remaining columns show the outcome of the three steps in our unmarshalling algorithm (see Sect. 2). For all other system calls, our algorithm returns "syscall" as the interface name, and beyond that the actual syscall function name and its intercepted arguments in the kernel. For example, look at the third row, which means an internet connection has been established via the system call sys_connect to URL wringe.ispgateway.de. An action at position $i \in \mathbb{N}$ in some trace means that at time i this action holds (or, from a practical point of view for the 397th world in Table 1 that Walkinwat has requested the Android framework to send an SMS to number "451-518-646" with text "Hey, just ...").

We specify undesired malware behaviour in terms of formulae (or policies) in a first-order linear temporal logic, called LTL^{FO}. From a formal point of view, we merely used safety formulae and our tool to detect finite counterexamples. For brevity, we recall here only the key concepts of LTL^{FO} by explaining an example policy, whereas the full syntax and semantics as well as our monitoring algorithm can be found in [2]. LTL^{FO} is an extension of propositional future LTL with quantifiers that are restricted to reason over those actions that appear in a trace, and not arbitrary elements from a (possibly infinite) domain (i.e., we can't

Table 1. Trace of system events for malware Walkinwat collected by DroidTracer.

ID	Interface	Method	Arguments
334	IPhoneSubInfo	getDeviceId	
386	IContentProvider	QUERY	content://contacts/phones, null, null, null, display_name ASC
392	syscall	sys_connect	wringe.ispgateway.de
397	ISms	sendText	451-518-646, null, "Hey,just downlaoded a pirated App off the Internet, Walk and Text for Android. Im stupid and cheap,it costed only 1 buck.Don't steal like I did!", null, null
407	IActivityManager	getIntentSender	1, com.incorporateapps.walktext, null, null, 0, Intent { act=SMS_SENT }, null, 0
408	IActivityManager	getIntentSender	1, com.incorporateapps.walktext, null, null, 0, Intent { act=SMS_DELIVERED }, null, 0
414	ISurfaceComposer	N/A, code: 10	
578	IActivityManager	startActivity	null, Intent { act=android.intent.action.VIEW dat=market://details?id= com.incorporateapps.walktext }, null, N/A, N/A, N/A, N/A, N/A, N/A, N/A

express "for all numbers x of SMS messages that an app has not sent"). Let us consider the example that apps must not send SMS messages to numbers not in a user's contact book. Assuming there exists a predicate $sendText@ISms$, which is true (i.e., appears in the trace), whenever an app sends an SMS message to phone number $dest$, we could formalise said behaviour in terms of of a policy $G\forall(dest,\_) : sendText@ISms. inContactBook(dest)$, shown as φ_{18} in Table 2. Note how in this formula the meaning of $dest$ is given implicitly by the first argument of $sendText@ISms$ and must match the definition of $inContactBook$ in each world. We use the "$\_$"-symbol simply as placeholder for one or more remaining program variablesthat are not used in the formula. Also note that we call $sendText@ISms$ an uninterpreted predicate as it is interpreted indirectly via its occurrence in the trace, whereas $inContactBook$ never appears in the trace, even if true. $inContactBook$ can be thought of as interpreted via a program that queries a user's contact database, whose contents may change over time. An interpreted predicate can also be rigid; that is, its truth value never changes for the same arguments. For example, look at $regex(uri, ".* calls.*")$ in policy ψ_6 in Table 3, which is true if uri (an identifier for Android's content providers), matches the regular expression "$.* calls.*$". This way, we check whether the database that stores the call history on a phone is accessed.

As we can't anticipate when or if an app stops, a policy φ normally specifies behaviour in terms of an *infinite* trace. But the monitor we build to check φ will only see a prefix (observed system events so far), denoted u, and therefore return $\bot$ if u is a *bad* prefix, and ? otherwise. This means that a monitor for φ_{18}, when it processes the 397th event, will return $\bot$ and terminate, as the number "451-518-646" is not in the contact book. Furthermore, there exists a third case, that the monitor returns $\top$ if u is a good prefix, but as we only monitor safety formulae, this case is not relevant for our study. Our monitoring semantics is akin to the 3-valued finite-trace semantics for LTL introduced in [3].

Based on the patterns from four different categories identified by the AMGP [15], we have formally specified various key characteristics of malware behaviour in LTL^{FO}. The results are the policies listed in Table 2. For readability, we write $\varphi_{i\in[a,b]}$, grouping policies of the same pattern together, where ψ_i, ψ' or ψ'' are

Table 2. Key characteristics of Android malware behaviour specified in LTL^{FO}.

Information stealing			
$\varphi_{i \in [1,14]}$	$\mathsf{G}\neg\psi_i$	$[\varphi_{i \in [1,14]}]$	$\mathsf{G}(\psi_i \rightarrow \neg\mathsf{F}\psi')$
$[[\varphi_{i \in [1,14]}]]$	$\mathsf{G}(\psi_i \wedge \neg\psi' \rightarrow (\neg\psi'\mathsf{W}(N/A@ISurfaceComposer \wedge \neg\psi')))$	$[[\varphi_{i \in [1,4]}]]'$	$\mathsf{G}(\psi_i \rightarrow \neg\mathsf{F}\psi'')$
Privilege escalation			
φ_{15}	$\mathsf{G}\neg\exists(args) : do\_execv@syscall.\ regex(args,\ ".*su|pm\ (un)?install|am\ start.*")$		
Launching malicious payloads			
$\varphi_{i \in [16,17]}$	$\mathsf{G}\neg\psi_i$ $[\varphi_{17}]$ $\mathsf{G}(\psi_{17} \rightarrow \neg\mathsf{F}\psi')$	$[[\varphi_{17}]]$	$\mathsf{G}(\psi_{17} \rightarrow \neg\mathsf{F}\psi'')$
Financial charges			
φ_{18}	$\mathsf{G}\forall(dest,\_) : sendText@ISms.\ inContactBook(dest)$		
φ_{19}	$\mathsf{G}(\psi_{17} \rightarrow \neg\mathsf{F}\exists(w,x,y,z,abort) : finishReceiver@IActivityManager.\ regex(abort, "true"))$		

auxiliary formulae listed in Table 3. We surround a policy φ_i with n square brackets (calling it the nth refinement of φ_i), if its bad prefixes are a strict subset of the bad prefixes of φ_i surrounded with $n-1$ square brackets. For example a bad prefix of $[\varphi_1]$, the first refinement of φ_1, has to contain after accessing the device id as well an event of establishing a connection to the internet, describing from a practical point of view a more severe malware behaviour for the user.

Information Stealing. The AMGP discovered that malware is often actively harvesting various sensitive information on infected devices. Thus, our policies $\varphi_{i \in [1,11]}$ specify that an app should neither request any permission secured sensitive data, such as the device or subscriber id, SIM serial or telephone number, or device software version, nor query any of the content providers that contain the call history, contact list, phone numbers, browser bookmarks, carrier settings or SMS messages. Policy φ_{12} covers the harvesting of installed app or package names on a device, and φ_{13} the reading of system logs via the Android logging system, called logcat. Note that before Android 4.1, an app could read other apps' logcat logs, which might contain sensitive messages. Policy φ_{14} specifies that neither the coarse grain location based on cell towers nor the more precise GPS location should be accessed. The policies $[\varphi_{i \in [1,14]}]$ refine the policies above towards the more suspicious behaviour that an app should not, after requesting the sensitive information, eventually connect to the internet, send an SMS or exchange data with another app. Even though a detected bad prefix for those polices does not guarantee that information has been leaked, the usage of above sinks bears at least its potential. However, the data could have been encrypted or in other ways obscured, which makes it hard to prove leakage in general based on the trace we collect. Furthermore, $[[\varphi_{i \in [1,14]}]]$ expresses the absence of any screen rendering (via *N/A@ISurfaceComposer*) in between information request and potential leakage. This excludes the case that the sending of data was caused by some user interaction with the app, but rather by some app's malicious background service. Note that we represent with "N/A" methods which we could not unmarshall. Also note that we used the well-known specification patterns [5] to specify our policies, where the first and second refinements are based on

Table 3. Auxiliary formulae for Table 2.

ψ_1	getDeviceId@IPhoneSubInfo	ψ_6	$\exists(uri,\_) : \text{QUERY@IContentProvider. } regex(uri, \text{".*calls.*"})$
ψ_2	getSubscriberId@IPhoneSubInfo	ψ_7	$\exists(uri,\_) : \text{QUERY@IContentProvider. } regex(uri, \text{".*contacts.*"})$
ψ_3	getIccSerialNumber@IPhoneSubInfo	ψ_8	$\exists(uri,\_) : \text{QUERY@IContentProvider. } regex(uri, \text{".*phones.*"})$
ψ_4	getLine1Number@IPhoneSubInfo	ψ_9	$\exists(uri,\_) : \text{QUERY@IContentProvider. } regex(uri, \text{".*bookmarks.*"})$
ψ_5	getDeviceSvn@IPhoneSubInfo	ψ_{10}	$\exists(uri,\_) : \text{QUERY@IContentProvider. } regex(uri, \text{".*preferapn.*"})$
c_{16}	".*BOOT_COMPLETED.*"	ψ_{11}	$\exists(uri,\_) : \text{QUERY@IContentProvider. } regex(uri, \text{".*sms.*"})$
c_{17}	".*SMS_RECEIVED.*"	ψ_{13}	$\exists(args) : \text{do\_execv@syscall. } regex(args, \text{".*logcat.*"})$

ψ_{12} $(\exists(\_) : \text{getInstalledPackages@IPackageManager. } true)\vee$

$(\exists(\_) : \text{getInstalledApplications@IPackageManager. } true)$

ψ_{14} $(\exists(\_) : \text{notifyCellLocation@ITelephonyRegistry. } true)\vee$

$(\exists x : \text{getLastLocation@ILocationManager. } regex(x, \text{".*gps.*"}))$

$\psi_{i\in[16,17]}$ $\exists(intent, txt, \_) : \text{system\#scheduleReceiver@IApplicationThread. } (regex(intent, c_i) \wedge regex(txt, \text{".*<pkg>.*"}))$

ψ' $(\exists(\_) : \text{sys\_connect@syscall. } true) \vee (\exists(\_) : \text{sendText@ISms. } true)\vee$

$(\exists(x, intent, \_) : \text{startActivity@IActivityManager. } regex(intent, \text{"action.SEND"})$

ψ'' $(\exists(dest, x, msg, \_) : \text{sendText@ISms. } regex(msg, \text{".*<sensitiveInfo>.*"}))\vee$

$(\exists(x, intent, \_) : \text{startActivity@IActivityManager. } regex(intent, \text{".*<sensitiveInfo>.*"})$

the "absence after", and "exists between" patterns, respectively. $[[\varphi_{i\in[1,4]}]]'$ are further refinements as they only trigger if we find the device id, etc. cleartext (represented by the placeholder "<sensitiveInfo>") in the trace.

Privilege Escalation. The attack of exploiting bugs or design flaws in software to gain elevated access to resources that are normally protected from an application, is called privilege escalation. From the samples in [15], 36.7 % exploit a version-specific known software vulnerability of either the Linux kernel or some open-source libraries running on the Android platform, such as WebKit or SQLite, to gain root access (e.g., to replace real banking apps with a fake one, for phishing attacks). Therefore, policy φ_{15} lets us detect when an app opens a root shell, secretly starts, installs or removes other packages via the *activity manager* (am) or *the package manager* (pm). Monitoring of this behaviour is possible, because the do_execv() system call is exclusively used for the execution of any binary, shell command or script on the underlying Linux OS.

Launching Malicious Payloads. Apps' background services, which don't have any UI, can't only be actively started when clicking on an app's launch icon, but also by registering for Android system-wide events (called broadcasts). The AMGP discovered that 29 of the 49 malware families contain a malicious service that is launched after the system was booted, or for 21 families when an SMS was received (i.e., they registered for the BOOT_COMPLETED or SMS_RECEIVED broadcast, respectively). Therefore, we consider it as suspicious if services are activated by the broadcasts mentioned above; which we specify in form of $\varphi_{i\in[16,17]}$, where we replace "<pkg>" for each app specifically with its package name. Note that, to monitor this behaviour, we need to intercept system events of the Android system (UID 1000) as it starts the services that have registered for a certain broadcast (via *scheduleReceiver@IApplicationThread*). We prefix those predicates with "system#"; that is, to distinguish them from an app's events in a trace. Since malware, after registering for SMS_RECEIVED, gets access to the sender and content of an incoming SMS, we check with the refinements $[\varphi_{17}]$ and $[[\varphi_{17}]]$ for information stealing. This means, similar as specified by the refinements of $\varphi_{i\in[1,14]}$, the internet should not be accessed, and so on, after the broadcast was received.

Financial Charges. The AMGP discovered apps, such as the first Android malware FakePlayer, that secretly call or register for premium services via an SMS. As this behaviour can result in high financial charges for the user, Google labels the permissions that allow to call or send an SMS with "services that cost you money". Instead of defining policies that check outgoing messages against a fixed list of potential premium numbers, φ_{18} more generically specifies that an SMS should not be sent to a number not in the user's contact book. Since Android 4.2, Google added a similar security check, where a notification is provided to the user if an app attempts to send messages to short codes as those could be premium numbers. Note that we could have specified that apps should not make phone calls to numbers not in the phone book as well, but as we have not observed this behaviour during our experiments, we neglect the policy for it.

Before Android 4.4, apps could block incoming SMS messages, which was used by malware to suppress received confirmations from premium services or mobile banking *transaction authentication numbers* (TANs). The latter were then forwarded to a malicious user. Thus, policy φ_{19} checks if apps *abort* a broadcast after receiving SMS_RECEIVED, in which case the SMS would not be delivered further to appear in the usual messaging app on a device.

4   Identifying Malware Behaviour

We installed MonitorMe, provided with the polices introduced in Sect. 3, on our test device Nexus S running Android 2.3.6. We then monitored separately one malware sample for each of the AMGP-families. That is, we first installed its *application package* (APK), and before starting it (i.e., clicking on its launch icon if it had any), test using and finally uninstalling it, we tried to activate potential background services by sending the broadcast BOOT_COMPLETE via the *Android Debug Bridge* (adb) and an SMS to our phone. Even though MonitorMe performed *online* monitoring, which means that monitors processed events incrementally when they occurred, we also persisted the trace for each malware in an SQLite database on the phone;[8] both, for repeatability of our own experiments, and to provide them to other researchers.

4.1   Experiments' Results

Table 4 summarises for which malware families (49 in total) and policies MonitorMe detected bad prefixes during our experiments. The second column indicates, whether a malware or one of its services crashed during our experiments; e.g., due to incompatibility with the Android version on our test device. Thus, we might have missed observing some critical behaviour. The third column tells us if a malware had no launch icon, which is usually intended to stay hidden and spy on the user. SMSReplicator, for example, is used by parents to secretly

---

[8] Traces are available at http://kuester.multics.org/DroidTracer/malware/traces.

forward all SMS messages received on their childrens' phones. As we monitored in general all UIDs above 10000,[9] apps without an icon could not bypass our analysis unnoticed. The fourth column shows the number of system events we have recorded for each malware. Between the double lines are the individual monitor results, where the single lines separate results from the four categories introduced in Table 2. The cell containing $[[\varphi_{18}]]_{397}$ in the row for Walkinwat denotes that the monitor for $[[\varphi_{18}]]$ found a bad prefix for the Walkinwat sample after 397 worlds. As this implies that the same prefix is also a bad one for lower refinements of φ_{18}, we neglect showing this information. The last column shows the number of bad prefixes found in total per malware. In summary, for 46 (93.9 %) out of 49 families, we detected suspicious behaviour. This is under the assumption that we consider bad prefixes for φ_{16} alone as *not* critical. Note that our results take into account that, according to [15], we would have observed additional malicious behaviours guarded by φ_{15}, φ_{18} and φ_{19} (indicated by an ↯ in Table 4). The reason for φ_{15} is that the nine marked families targeted Android versions below 2.3.6. Thus, their exploits were not attempted in the first place or unsuccessful. We missed bad prefixes for φ_{18} as malware often waited to receive instructions from a remote server, which wasn't active anymore. The servers are needed for malware to send an SMS, as they provide premium numbers dynamically. Regarding φ_{19}, we could rarely observe the blocking of incoming SMS messages as most malware was designed to only suppress the received confirmation from specific premium numbers. Out of 46 detected families, 34 can be associated with potential information stealing, as they use the internet or other sinks after accessing sensitive information. For NickySpy and SMSReplicator we discovered that the device id was leaked *cleartext* via an SMS, and an SMS received was forwarded to a malicious user, respectively. To discuss limits of our malware detection, which are by no means unique to our approach, consider the FakeNetflix family. It uses a phishing attack for which is no observable behaviour in the trace; that is, it shows a fake login screen to the user and then sends the entered credentials to a malicious server.

False Positives. Finally, we checked if our policies are suitable to distinguish malware from benign apps. Therefore, we ran MonitorMe on a Nexus 5 with Android 5.0.1 that had more than 60 apps from common app categories installed: social (Facebook, Twitter, LinkedIn, etc.), communication (Whatsapp, etc.), transportation (Uber, etc.), travel &local (Yelp, TripAdvisor, etc.), and games (Cut the rope, etc.) to name a few. We discovered suspicious behaviour for 17 (28 %) out of 61 apps, using the same assumption as above that φ_{16} alone is not critical. The false positive rate seems high at first glance, but a closer look reveals that some benign apps bear unwanted behaviour for the user so that a warning of MonitorMe seems reasonable. For example, eleven apps surprisingly requested the device or subscriber id, which is explicitly not recommended by the Google developer guidelines.[10] Under those apps were a soccer news and Yoga app, which in our opinion both do not require this data for its functionality, but rather

---

[9] UIDs below 10000 are reserved for system apps with higher privileges.
[10] http://developer.android.com/training/articles/security-tips.html#UserData.

Table 4. Monitor results for malware of the Android Malware Genome Project.

Malware family	Crash	Hide	Worlds	Monitor results for $\varphi_1 - \varphi_{19}$	Total $\perp$
ADRD			983		3
AnserverBot			2201		7
Asroot			192		3
BaseBridge	✓		754		5
BeanBot			2030		2
Bgserv	✓		2248		1
CoinPirate			895		7
CruseWin			120		2
DogWars			550		
DroidCoupon			841		1
DroidDeluxe			1167		3
DroidDream			480		5
DroidDreamLight			536		1
DroidKungFu1			892		4
DroidKungFu2			2012		1
DroidKungFu3			370		2
DroidKungFu4			974		6
DroidKungFuSapp	✓		1392		5
DroidKungFuUpdate			506		6
Endofday			594		1
FakeNetflix	✓		731		5
FakePlayer	✓	✓	16		1
GamblerSMS			564		4
Geinimi			659		1
GGTracker			508		4
GingerMaster			627		3
GoldDream			1517		4
Gone60			555		3
GPSSMSSpy	✓		23		1
HippoSMS			888		2
Jifake			584		4
jSMSHider	✓		1283		3
KMin			850		3
LoveTrap	✓		1791		2
NickyBot			619		1
NickySpy			441		4
Pjapps			1808		3
Plankton			561		2
RogueLemon			2077		1
RogueSPPush			1653		4
SMSReplicator	✓		316		5
SndApps	✓	✓	559		7
Spitmo			771		1
Tapsnake			355		1
Walkinwat			848		2
YZHC			631		
zHash			865		
Zitmo	✓		2027		
Zsone			553		
Total $\perp$					

collect sensitive data from the user. Another app was the private taxi app Uber, which has been criticised in the past due to collecting personal data without the user's permission.[11] Only five apps started after boot, such as dropbox, which we consider as necessary regarding its purpose, and only two apps after an SMS was received, which were a secure SMS app and Twitter.

4.2   Performance and Portability

We evaluated (1) the performance of DroidTracer and MonitorMe, i.e., the bare system event interception including unmarshalling as well as when running our

---

[11] http://thehackernews.com/2014/11/ubers-android-app-is-literally-malware_28. html.

Table 5. Execution of Android method calls (each up to 10,000 times) with and without DroidTracer. The margin of error is given for the 95 % confidence interval.

Interface	Method	Android (in ms)	Kprobes (in ms)	DroidTracer (in ms)	Kprobes Overhead	DroidTracer Overhead
IPhoneSubInfo	getDeviceId	5309 ± 15	5517 ± 18	5811 ± 11	3.92%	9.46%
IPhoneSubInfo	getIccSerialNumber	5346 ± 16	5524 ± 16	5817 ± 7		8.81%
LocationManager	getLastKnownLocation	3516 ± 13	3562 ± 13	4126 ± 5		17.35%
ISms	sendText	9166 ± 13	9396 ± 13	10216 ± 10	2.51%	11.46%
IPackageManager	getInstalledApplications	15730 ± 204	15514 ± 202	15422 ± 172		
IConnectivityManager	getAllNetworkInfo	5769 ± 53	5841 ± 60	5671 ± 7		
syscall	sys_open	15360 ± 72	15531 ± 67	15455 ± 38		

monitors on top. Moreover, we (2) demonstrate that our automated approach to unmarshalling is portable to different Android devices and versions.

Performance. We wrote seven test apps, where each was designed to generate 100 runs of up to 10,000 system events named by the interface and method names in Table 5. When MonitorMe is being executed with the policies in Sect. 3 and monitors our test apps individually, the *highest* performance overhead is 38.6 % for the system event $sendText@ISms$. This was determined on a Nexus 7 (quad-core CPU, 1 GB RAM) with Android 4.3. Note that the overhead involves the monitor for φ_{18} checking the contact book each time an SMS was sent.

Furthermore, as the results of these test runs are specific only to our implementation of runtime verification, we also need to measure the performance overhead of DroidTracer when no further analysis is undertaken. Table 5, shows the execution time when intercepting the method calls of the above seven system events in three different modes of operation: (1) without DroidTracer enabled to get a reference execution time for the unmodified system, (2) with only the event interception part of our kernel module enabled, and (3) with unmarshalling and netlink communication added. During the experiments, we ran all four cores of the Nexus 7 on a fixed frequency rate, which allowed us to reduce the margin of error dramatically. Note that we left cells empty, where overhead could not significantly be determined wrt. the t-test. As the results show, the actual performance overhead of using just our kernel module with kprobes is only 2.51–3.92 %, whereas the complete performance overhead of DroidTracer is 8.81–17.35 %. What is noteworthy is that getDeviceId() and getIccSerialNumber() have significant lower overhead than getLastKnownLocation() and sendText(), as both former method signatures have no arguments that require unmarshalling. The call getLastKnownLocation() has the highest overhead, probably because its arguments contain several complex objects, for example, one of type LocationRequest, which unmarshalling involves additional reflection calls. As sendText() contains only Java primitives as arguments, its unmarshalling overhead is slightly lower.

Portability. We ran DroidTracer on three different devices and Android versions, including 5.0.1, which is, at the time of writing, the most recent one. Table 6

Table 6. Unmarshable parts of observed system events.

Device	Android version	Events Unique	Interfaces Unique	Methods			Events with arguments		
				Unique	Unmarsh.	Succ. rate	Total	Unmarsh. (Totally / Partially)	Succ. rate
Nexus S	2.3.6	102,545	58	804	368	45.77%	54,596	43,318 / 47,923	79.34% / 87.78%
Nexus 7	4.3	107,977	89	378	236	62.43%	70,746	67,866 / 69,474	95.93% / 98.20%
Nexus 5	5.0.1	449,429	108	474	326	68.78%	264,058	227,708 / 255,263	86.23% / 96.67%

demonstrates the success of unmarshalling events we have intercepted. While we could unmarshall the interface name of all method calls, we could unmarshall 45.77 %-68.78 % of unique method names; that is, we were able discover for an integer code its according method name in the Android API via reflection. The number of unmarshalled method names seem low, but missing ones are mainly specific to Android internals, for example to render the screen. As such, they have no Stub or Proxy in the Android API, but only in some native C library. This is not accessible to the developer and therefore usually contain no relevant events for our analysis. If method calls had arguments, we could unmarshall for 79.34 %-95.93 % all and for 87.78 %-98.20 % at least some arguments. Note that if we failed to unmarshall one argument of a call, we also failed for all the remaining of that call, as Parcel's read methods have to be applied in the correct order.

5   Conclusions and Related Work

To the best of our knowledge, our work is the first runtime verification approach to comprehensively monitor the collected malwares by the AMGP. Arguably, detection rates are promising and help substantiate the claim that methods developed in the area of runtime verification are, in fact, suitable not only for safety-critical systems, but also when security is critical. Indeed, at the time of writing, the samples of the AMGP are ca. three years old, which in the rapid development of new attacks seems like a long time. However, the database has grown over a number of years and the underlying patterns emerged as a result of that. While there are always innovative, hard to detect malwares, it is not unreasonable to expect the bulk of new malwares to also fall into the existing categories, identified by the AMGP, and therefore detectable by our approach. Validation of this hypothesis, however, must be subject to further work.

Besides MonitorMe, one corner stone of our approach is the ability to specify policies over traces that contain parameters. Other runtime verification works that haven't been applied to Android, but also allow monitoring parametric traces are, for example, Hallé and Villemaire's [7], who use a logic with quantification identical to ours, but without arbitrary computable predicates. Furthermore, JavaMOP [9] is by now a quasi-standard when dealing with parametric-traces, although it is not based on first-order logic, but on "trace-slicing".

Most monitoring approaches for Android can be divided into two categories. *App-centric* ones (cf. [1,12,14]) intercept events inside the apps by rewriting and repackaging them, so that neither root access nor modifying the Android platform is necessary. As a consequence, they are portable to most phones and Android versions, and are easy to install even for non-experts. Examples are AppGuard [1] and Aurasium [14], which is even able to enforce security polices for apps' native code as it rewrites Android's own libc.so that is natively linked into every app. However, the ease in portability comes at the expense of inherent vulnerabilities, namely that security controls run inside the apps under scrutiny and thus could be bypassed; e.g., by dynamically loading code after rewriting. Also, as apps have to be actively selected for rewriting, hidden malware, such as the ones without launch icon that we came across in Sect. 4.1, might be overlooked.

Platform-centric approaches (cf. [4,6,8]) usually tie deep into the source code of the Android platform and are therefore less portable. TaintDroid [6], a pioneering platform-centric tool for taint flow analysis, requires modifications from the Linux kernel all the way up to the Dalvik VM. Although it is being actively ported, users have to be sufficiently experienced to not only compile their own version of Android, including the TaintDroid changes, but also to make it work on a hardware of their choice. Our approach is, conceptually, a combination of the advantages of app- and platform-centric monitoring; that is, MonitorMe can be loaded even into a currently running Android system, yet is able to trace app (even preinstalled Google apps that can't be rewritten) and Android system interactions all the way down to the OS kernel level.

References

1. Backes, M., Gerling, S., Hammer, C., Maffei, M., von Styp-Rekowsky, P.: App-Guard – enforcing user requirements on Android apps. In: Piterman, N., Smolka, S.A. (eds.) TACAS 2013 (ETAPS 2013). LNCS, vol. 7795, pp. 543–548. Springer, Heidelberg (2013)
2. Bauer, A., Küster, J.-C., Vegliach, G.: The ins and outs of first-order runtime verification. To appear in: Formal Methods in System Design (FMSD) (2015)
3. Bauer, A., Leucker, M., Schallhart, C.: Runtime verification for LTL and TLTL. ACM Trans. Softw. Eng. Methodol. **20**(4), 14 (2011)
4. Bugiel, S., Davi, L., Dmitrienko, A., Fischer, T., Sadeghi, A.-R., Shastry, B.: Towards taming privilege-escalation attacks on Android. In: NDSS (2012)
5. Dwyer, M.B., Avrunin, G.S., Corbett, J.C.: Patterns in property specifications for finite-state verification. In: ICSE, pp. 411–420. IEEE (1999)
6. Enck, W., Gilbert, P., Chun, B.-G., Cox, L.P., Jung, J., McDaniel, P., Sheth, A.N.: TaintDroid: an information-flow tracking system for realtime privacy monitoring on smartphones. In: OSDI. USENIX (2010)
7. Halle, S., Villemaire, R.: Runtime monitoring of message-based workflows with data. In: EDOC, pp. 63–72. IEEE (2008)
8. Hornyack, P., Han, S., Jung, J., Schechter, S., Wetherall, D.: These aren't the droids you're looking for: retrofitting Android to protect data from imperious applications. In: CCS, pp. 639–652. ACM (2011)
9. Jin, D., Meredith, P.O., Lee, C., Rosu, G.: JavaMOP: efficient parametric runtime monitoring framework. In: ICSE, pp. 1427–1430. IEEE (2012)

10. Küster, J.-C., Bauer, A.: Platform-centric Android monitoring–modular and efficient. Comp. Research Repository (CoRR) arXiv:1406.2041. ACM, June 2014
11. Moser, A., Kruegel, C., Kirda, E.: Limits of static analysis for malware detection. In: ACSAC, pp. 421–430. IEEE (2007)
12. Rasthofer, S., Arzt, S., Lovat, E., Bodden, E.: DroidForce: Enforcing complex, data-centric, system-wide policies in Android. In: ARES, pp. 40–49. IEEE (2014)
13. Vidas, T., Christin, N.: Evading Android runtime analysis via sandbox detection. In: ASIACCS, pp. 447–458. ACM (2014)
14. Xu, R., Saïdi, H., Anderson, R.: Aurasium: practical policy enforcement for Android applications. In: USENIX Security Symposium, pp. 27–27. USENIX (2012)
15. Zhou, Y., Jiang, X.: Dissecting Android malware: characterization and evolution. In: S&P, pp. 95–109. IEEE (2012)

Time-Triggered Runtime Verification
of Component-Based Multi-core Systems

Samaneh Navabpour[1], Borzoo Bonakdarpour[2]([⊠]), and Sebastian Fischmeister[3]

[1] TD Bank, Toronto, Canada
navabs2@td.com
[2] Department of Computing and Software, McMaster University, Hamilton, Canada
borzoo@mcmaster.ca
[3] University of Waterloo, Waterloo, Canada
sfischeme@uwaterloo.ca

Abstract. In this paper, we characterize and solve the problem of augmenting a component-based system with time-triggered runtime verification (TTRV), where different components are expected to run on different computing cores with minimum monitoring overhead at run time. We present an optimization technique that calculates (1) the mapping of components to computing cores, and (2) the monitoring frequency, such that TTRV's runtime overhead is minimized. Although dealing with runtime overhead of concurrent systems is a challenging problem due to their inherent complex nature, our experiments show that our optimization technique is robust and reduces the monitoring overhead by 34%, as compared to various near-optimal monitoring patterns of the components at run time.

1 Introduction

Embedded systems are engineering artifacts that involve computations subject to physical world constraints [12]. These systems interact with the physical world as well as execute on physical platforms. Since embedded systems are normally deployed in safety/mission-critical systems, assurance about their *correctness* is significantly vital. In addition, as embedded applications are increasingly being deployed on multi-core platforms, due to their inherent complex nature, the need for guaranteeing their correctness is further amplified. Consequently, it is essential to augment such systems with *runtime verification* technology, where a monitor inspects the system's correctness at run time.

The conventional monitoring approach in runtime verification has been *event-triggered*, where the occurrence of an event of interest triggers the monitor to evaluate properties. This technique leads to unpredictable monitoring overhead and potentially bursts of monitoring invocations at run time, which may cause undesirable behavior and, hence, catastrophic consequences in real-time embedded systems. To tackle this problem, the notion of *time-triggered* runtime verification (TTRV) is introduced [5], where the monitor runs in parallel with the program and reads the program state at fixed time intervals (called the *polling*

© Springer International Publishing Switzerland 2015
E. Bartocci and R. Majumdar (Eds.): RV 2015, LNCS 9333, pp. 153–168, 2015.
DOI: 10.1007/978-3-319-23820-3_10

period) to evaluate a set of logical properties. Although a time-triggered monitor exhibits bounded overhead and predictable monitoring invocations, the approach in [5] falls short in handling multi-core applications when several computing components execute concurrently.

In this paper, we focus on extending the notion of TTRV to the context of component-based multi-core embedded systems. The main challenge in this context is to identify the polling period of the monitors and a mapping from components and monitors to a set of computing cores, such that the cumulative monitoring overhead is minimized. To further describe this problem consider a system with four components C_1, C_2, C_3, and C_4 that are executed only once. The system runs on two interconnected and identical computing cores P_1 and P_2, where each core hosts one time-triggered monitor. Each monitor has a fixed polling period and monitors all the components running on its host computing core. Table 1 shows the results of an experiment (see Subsection 4.3 for the settings) which measures the monitoring overhead (in milliseconds) imposed by a time-triggered monitor onto a component for different polling periods.

Table 1. Example of monitoring overhead [ms].

	Polling Period [CPU cycles]								
	10	20	30	40	50	60	70	80	90
C_1	81	136	140	140	145	142	140	138	137
C_2	120	70	84	91	94	92	63	74	79
C_3	120	70	88	95	99	91	61	76	77
C_4	120	83	86	93	91	80	77	78	76

To demonstrate the importance of the mapping of components to computing cores, we randomly map the components in two ways:

- $\{C_1, C_2, C_3\}$ runs on P_1 and $\{C_4\}$ runs on P_2, and
- $\{C_2, C_3, C_4\}$ runs on P_1 and $\{C_1\}$ runs on P_2.

In the first mapping, on P_1, the polling period of 20 cycles and on P_2, the polling period of 90 cycles achieve the optimal cumulative monitoring overhead (i.e., overall overhead on P_1 and P_2) which is 352 ms. In the second mapping, on P_1, the polling period of 70 cycles and on P_2, the polling period of 20 cycles achieve the optimal overall monitoring overhead which is 337 ms. Hence, the second mapping imposes 20 % less monitoring overhead. This simple experiment indicates that the mapping of components to the computing cores affects the monitoring overhead and since embedded systems are usually resource constrained, it is highly desirable to find the mapping which results in the *least* monitoring overhead throughout the system run.

With this motivation, in this paper, we propose an approach for optimizing the monitoring overhead of TTRV in component-based multi-core embedded systems. That is, given a set of components, computing cores, and a set of allowed polling periods, the goal is to identify (1) the mapping of components to computing cores, and (2) the polling period of each monitor, such that the monitoring overhead of TTRV is minimized. To achieve this goal, first, we formalize the notion of monitoring overhead associated with terminating and non-terminating components. This notion incorporates different sources of runtime monitoring overhead such as monitor invocation, event buffering, and execution of instrumentation instructions. Since the optimization problem is known to be intractable even for single component uni-core systems [5], we introduce a mapping from our problem to Integer Linear Programming (ILP). In order to incorporate the runtime characteristics of each component in our ILP model, we employ symbolic execution techniques [14].

Our approach is fully implemented within a tool chain and we report the results of rigorous experiments using the SNU [1] benchmark suite. Experimental results show that on average, our approach can reduce the monitoring overhead of TTRV by 34 % as compared to various near-optimal monitoring patterns of the components at run time.

Organization. The rest of the paper is organized as follows. Section 2 presents the background concepts. Section 3 formally states our optimization problem. Section 4 presents the tool chain and the experimental results. Section 5 discusses related work. Finally, in Sect. 6, we make our concluding remarks.

2 Preliminaries

2.1 Software Components

We adapt the general view of [18], where a software component is a binary unit of independent production, acquisition, and deployment that interacts with other components to form a system. Our view of a software component is in terms of a *control-flow graph*.

Definition 1. *The* control-flow graph *of a component C is a weighted directed simple graph $CFG_C = \langle V, v^0, A, w \rangle$, where:*

- V: *is a set of* vertices, *each representing a basic block of C. Each basic block consists of a sequence of instructions in C.*
- v^0: *is the* initial vertex *with indegree 0, which represents the initial basic block of C.*
- A: *is a set of arcs of the form (u, v), where $u, v \in V$. An arc (u, v) exists in A, if and only if the execution of basic block u can immediately lead to the execution of basic block v.*
- w: *is a function $w : A \to \mathbb{N}$, which defines a weight for each arc in A. The weight of an arc is the* best-case execution time *(BCET) of the source basic block.*   □

Two components interact with each other using conventional methods such as shared variables, message passing, etc. For example, consider the two components in Fig. 1(a) and (c) which interact with each other via the shared variable alert. Component1 reads a temperature sensor every 5 time units and when the temperature exceeds 100 Celsius, it will set alert to 1. Component2 reads a pressure sensor every 10 time units and when the pressure exceeds 20 Pascals while alert is equal to 1, it will start checking the pressure every 3 time units. In this example, we assume that the BCET of each instruction in both components is 1 time unit. As a result, Fig. 1(b) and (d) show the CFG of Component1 and Component2, respectively. Each vertex is annotated with the corresponding line numbers in the code. Note that since we focus on BCET of instructions, we consider the least delay (3 time units) for the wait instruction (line 5) in Component2.

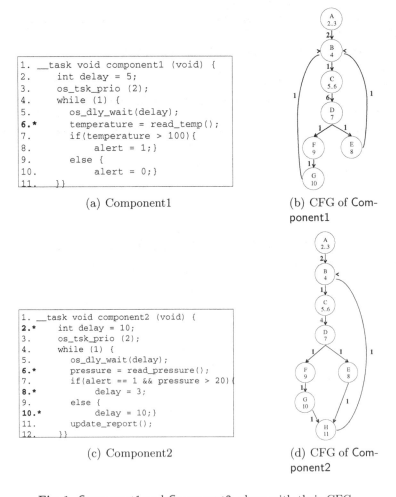

```
1.  __task void component1 (void) {
2.      int delay = 5;
3.      os_tsk_prio (2);
4.      while (1) {
5.          os_dly_wait(delay);
6.*         temperature = read_temp();
7.          if(temperature > 100){
8.              alert = 1;}
9.          else {
10.             alert = 0;}
11.     }}
```

(a) Component1

(b) CFG of Component1

```
1.  __task void component2 (void) {
2.*     int delay = 10;
3.      os_tsk_prio (2);
4.      while (1) {
5.          os_dly_wait(delay);
6.*         pressure = read_pressure();
7.          if(alert == 1 && pressure > 20){
8.*             delay = 3;
9.          else {
10.*            delay = 10;}
11.         update_report();
12.     }}
```

(c) Component2

(d) CFG of Component2

Fig. 1. Component1 and Component2, along with their CFGs.

2.2   Time-Triggered Runtime Verification (TTRV)

The main challenge in implementing TTRV is to compute the *longest* polling period (LPP), such that the monitor polls (i.e., observes) all the changes in the value of the *variables of interest*. The following recaps the procedure to calculate LPP [5].

Let C be a component and Π be a logical property, where C is expected to satisfy Π. Let $\mathcal{V}_\Pi$ be the set of variables whose values can change the valuation of Π (i.e., variables of interest) and CFG_C be the control-flow graph of C. We use control-flow analysis to estimate the time intervals between consecutive state changes of C with respect to the variables in $\mathcal{V}_\Pi$. In order to calculate LPP, we modify CFG_C in two steps.

Step 1 (Identifying critical vertices). We modify CFG_C, such that each *critical instruction* (i.e., an instruction that updates the value of a variable in $\mathcal{V}_\Pi$) resides in one and only one vertex by itself. We refer to such a vertex as a *critical vertex*. For example, if $\mathcal{V}_\Pi = \{\mathsf{pressure}, \mathsf{delay}\}$ in Component2, then the critical instructions are at lines 2, 6, 8, and 10. Figure 2(a) shows the transformed CFG of Component2. We call this graph a *critical CFG*.

Step 2 (Calculating LPP). The polling period of the monitor must be such that the monitor does not overlook any state changes that could occur in C at run time. Such a polling period is defined as follows.

Definition 2. *Let $CCFG = \langle V, v^0, A, w \rangle$ be a critical control-flow graph and $V_c \subseteq V$ be the set of critical vertices. The longest polling period (LPP) for $CCFG$ is the minimum-length shortest path between two vertices in V_c.*   □

For example, LPP of Component2 is 2 time units.

To reduce the overhead of time-triggered monitoring by increasing LPP, in [5], the authors propose employing *auxiliary memory* to build a *history* of state changes between consecutive monitoring polls. More specifically, let v be a critical vertex in a critical CFG, where the critical instruction I updates the value of a variable x. The following graph transformation results in a new critical CFG with a larger LPP: it (1) removes v, (2) merges the incoming and outgoing arcs of v, and (3) adds an instruction $I' : x' \leftarrow x$ after instruction I in the component's source code, where x' is an auxiliary memory location. For example, the graph in Fig. 2(b) is the result of applying this transformation to vertices E and G of Component2 (see Fig. 2(a)), where vertices E and G are removed, and two new arcs (D, H) and (F, H) with weights of $1 + 1 = 2$ are added. The new graph has $LPP = 6$ due to the length of the path between A_1 and C_2.

3   Optimal Monitoring of Component-Based Systems

3.1   System Architecture

We follow an abstract view towards the underlying architecture of the system which is independent of the hardware, operating system, network protocol, etc.

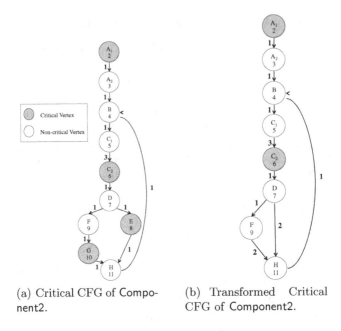

(a) Critical CFG of Component2.

(b) Transformed Critical CFG of Component2.

Fig. 2. Critical CFG.

That is, a component-based system runs on a set of interconnected and potentially heterogeneous computing cores. However, we make the following assumptions:

- A component is either nonterminating or is invoked infinitely often throughout the system run.
- Given a set $\mathcal{C} = \{C_1 \cdots C_n\}$ of components and a set $\mathcal{P} = \{P_1 \cdots P_m\}$ of computing cores, where $m \leq n$, a function $\mathcal{F} : \mathcal{P} \rightarrow 2^{\mathcal{C}}$ maps each core in $\mathcal{P}$ to a unique subset of components of $\mathcal{C}$. Moreover, for any two distinct cores $P_1, P_2 \in \mathcal{P}$, we have $\mathcal{F}(P_1) \cap \mathcal{F}(P_2) = \{\}$. This function remains unchanged throughout the system execution.
- We assume a fully preemptive scheduler.
- The components can be invoked *aperiodically*.
- When a timing property involving a set of components requires verification, this set of components must run on the same core, so the property is soundly verified.
- We assume time-triggered monitors $\mathcal{M} = \{M_1 \cdots M_m\}$, where monitor M_i is deployed on core P_i, for all $i \in \{1 \cdots m\}$. Each monitor observes and verifies *all* the components in $\mathcal{F}(P_i)$.
- No two components share a *variable of interest*; i.e., shared variables cannot be monitored.

3.2   Underlying Objective

Definition 3. *An* execution path *of a component C with $CFG_C = \langle V, v^0, A, w \rangle$ is a sequence of the form $\gamma = \langle (v_0, \omega_0, v_1), (v_1, \omega_1, v_2), \ldots \rangle$, where:*

- *$v_0 = v^0$.*
- *For all $i \geq 0$, $v_i \in V$.*
- *For all (v_i, ω_i, v_{i+1}), where $i \geq 0$, there exists an arc (v_i, v_{i+1}) in A.*
- *For all $i \geq 0$, $\omega_i = w(v_i)$.*
- *If C is a terminating component, then $\gamma = \langle (v_0, \omega_0, v_1), \ldots, (v_{n-1}, \omega_{n-1}, v_n) \rangle$ is finite and v_n is a vertex in V with outdegree of zero.* □

When it is clear from the context, we abbreviate an execution path $\gamma = \langle (v_0, \omega_0, v_1), (v_1, \omega_1, v_2), \ldots \rangle$ by the sequence of its vertices $\gamma = \langle v_0, v_1, v_2, \ldots \rangle$. Moreover, for an infinite execution path γ, we represent the finite sub-execution path $\langle v_0, v_1, v_2, \ldots, v_n \rangle$ with γ^n, where $n \geq 0$.

For a finite path γ^n, monitored with a polling period δ, we identify the following types of *time-related* overheads:

- $\mathcal{O}_c^\delta(\gamma^n)$ denotes the cumulative time spent for invoking the monitor throughout γ^n.
- $\mathcal{O}_r^\delta(\gamma^n)$ denotes the cumulative time spent for executing the monitoring code throughout γ^n (i.e., reading variables of interest and auxiliary memory).
- $\mathcal{O}_i^\delta(\gamma^n)$ denotes the cumulative time spent for executing the instrumentation instructions in γ^n. Recall that (from Subsect. 2.2) instrumentation is used to increase LPP of a component.

Hence, the *time-related* monitoring overhead for γ^n is

$$\mathcal{O}_T^\delta(\gamma^n) = \mathcal{O}_c^\delta(\gamma^n) + \mathcal{O}_r^\delta(\gamma^n) + \mathcal{O}_i^\delta(\gamma^n)$$

Moreover, we identify the *memory-related* overhead, denoted by $\mathcal{O}_M^\delta(\gamma^n)$, which represents the auxiliary memory required to increase LPP (see Subsect. 2.2). To this end, we consider both the time-related and memory-related overheads to represent the overhead associated with time-triggered monitoring. Thus, we present *monitoring overhead* as the pair $\mathcal{O}^\delta(\gamma^n) = \langle \mathcal{O}_T^\delta(\gamma^n), \mathcal{O}_M^\delta(\gamma^n) \rangle$.

Observe that the polling period δ of a monitor considerably affects $\mathcal{O}^\delta(\gamma^n)$. That is, increasing δ results in decreasing the monitor invocations (i.e., $\mathcal{O}_c^\delta(\gamma^n)$), and increasing instrumentation instructions and the memory consumption (i.e., $\mathcal{O}_i^\delta(\gamma^n)$ and $\mathcal{O}_M^\delta(\gamma^n)$). For instance, in Component2, consider execution path $\gamma_1 = \langle A, (B, C, D, E, H)^\omega \rangle$, where ω denotes the infinite execution of a sequence of basic blocks. Assuming that an instrumentation instruction takes 2 CPU cycles, for $\delta = 2$, where vertices E and G are instrumented, we have $\mathcal{O}_i^\delta(\gamma_1^n) = \frac{2n}{5}$. Note that for each polling period δ, there is one and only one set of associated overheads and, hence, a unique $\mathcal{O}^\delta(\gamma^n)$.

Clearly, for a finite path γ^n and two polling periods δ_1 and δ_2, the time-related overhead incurred by δ_1 is better than the time-related overhead incurred by δ_2

iff $\mathcal{O}_T^{\delta_1}(\gamma^n) < \mathcal{O}_T^{\delta_2}(\gamma^n)$. Accordingly, for an infinite path γ, the overhead incurred by δ_1 is better than the overhead incurred by δ_2 iff

$$\lim_{n \to \infty} \frac{\mathcal{O}_T^{\delta_1}(\gamma^n)}{\mathcal{O}_T^{\delta_2}(\gamma^n)} < 1 \tag{1}$$

For instance, for execution path γ_1 and $\delta_1 = 2$, the monitor is invoked $\frac{8n}{5 \times 2}$ times where 8 is the BCET of $\langle B, C, D, E, H \rangle$. Assuming that the monitoring code and monitor invocation each takes 5 CPU cycles, $\mathcal{O}_c^{\delta_1}(\gamma_1^n) = \mathcal{O}_r^{\delta_1}(\gamma_1^n) = 5 \times \frac{8n}{5 \times 2}$. For $\delta_2 = 6$, where once again vertices E and G are instrumented, $\mathcal{O}_c^{\delta_2}(\gamma_1^n) = \mathcal{O}_r^{\delta_2}(\gamma_1^n) = 5 \times \frac{8n}{5 \times 6}$, and $\mathcal{O}_i^{\delta_2}(\gamma_1^n) = \frac{2n}{5}$. As a result, δ_2 imposes less time-related overhead since:

$$\lim_{n \to \infty} \frac{\mathcal{O}_T^{\delta_2}(\gamma_1^n) = 2(5 \times \frac{8n}{5 \times 6}) + \frac{2n}{5}}{\mathcal{O}_T^{\delta_1}(\gamma_1^n) = 2(5 \times \frac{8n}{5 \times 2}) + \frac{2n}{5}} < 1$$

Our goal is to minimize the monitoring overhead associated with a component. Thus, for a finite set of possible polling periods PP, and a component C with set of execution paths Γ, we want to find the polling period $\Delta \in PP$ such that:

$$\forall \delta \in PP : \lim_{n \to \infty} \frac{\mathcal{O}_T^{\Delta}(C) = \sum_{\gamma \in \Gamma} \mathcal{O}_T^{\Delta}(\gamma^n)}{\mathcal{O}_T^{\delta}(C) = \sum_{\gamma \in \Gamma} \mathcal{O}_T^{\delta}(\gamma^n)} \leq 1 \tag{2}$$

As discussed, the internal structure of a component determines the polling period Δ. Moreover, the features of the computing cores define the possible polling periods in PP which in practice is always finite.

In the general case, where a monitor M inspects a set of components $\mathcal{C}$, our underlying objective is to minimize the time-related overhead over all components. In other words, our objective is to identify Δ such that:

$$\forall \delta \in PP : \lim_{n \to \infty} \frac{\mathcal{O}_T^{\Delta}(M) = \sum_{C \in \mathcal{C}} \mathcal{O}_T^{\Delta}(C)}{\mathcal{O}_T^{\delta}(M) = \sum_{C \in \mathcal{C}} \mathcal{O}_T^{\delta}(C)} \leq 1 \tag{3}$$

One can develop the corresponding equations identical to Eqs. 1–3 for the memory-related overhead, and, hence, generalize these equations for the monitoring overhead.

3.3   Optimization Problem

In a system with multiple components that run on multiple computing cores, to minimize the *overall* monitoring overhead, in addition to calculating Δ (see Eq. 3), one has to also identify an efficient mapping from components to cores. Thus, our optimization problem is as follows:

Problem statement.   Given a set of components $\mathcal{C}$, a set of computing cores $\mathcal{P}$, where $|\mathcal{C}| \geq |\mathcal{P}|$, and a set of polling periods PP, identify function $\mathcal{F} : \mathcal{P} \to 2^{\mathcal{C}}$ and polling period Δ_P for each $\mathcal{F}(P)$, where $P \in \mathcal{P}$, such that

– the following is minimized:

$$\sum \{\mathcal{O}^{\Delta_P}(M_P) \mid P \in \mathcal{P}\}$$

– $\Delta_P \in PP$ (i.e., the polling period of monitor M_P for components in $\mathcal{F}(P)$) satisfies Eq. 3 with respect to the monitoring overhead,
– for any two computing cores $P_1, P_2 \in \mathcal{P}$, we have $\mathcal{F}(P_1) \cap \mathcal{F}(P_2) = \{\}$.

In [5], the authors show that optimizing the memory-related overhead and the polling period even for one component is NP-complete. Thus, the NP-hardness of our optimization problem immediately follows. To tackle this obstacle, we propose a mapping from our optimization problem to integer linear programming (ILP). For reasons of space, this mapping is described in detail in http://www.cas.mcmaster.ca/borzoo/Publications/15/RV/rv15.pdf.

4   Implementation and Experimental Results

4.1   Implementation

Fig. 3 presents the modules of our tool chain that implements our solution for solving the optimization problem described in Subsect. 3.3.

opt_instrument. This module uses the techniques from [5] to optimally instrument the source code of the set of components $\mathcal{C}$ for each polling period in PP. It takes as input the source code of each component in $\mathcal{C}$, a set of Linear Temporal Logic (LTL) properties, and the set PP of possible polling periods. *Globalizer* extracts the set of variables of interest from the LTL properties and prepares the components in $\mathcal{C}$ for monitoring. *CFG Builder* extracts the CFG of each component in $\mathcal{C}$ and *Critical Instruction Identifier* finds the set of critical instructions

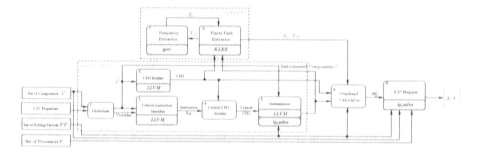

Fig. 3. Tool chain.

of each component in $\mathcal{C}$. *Critical CFG Builder* uses the set of critical instructions and the set of CFGs to create the set of critical CFGs. *Instrumentor* uses the set of critical CFGs to optimally instrument the components in $\mathcal{C}$ for each polling period in PP by leveraging the ILP solver lp_solve and LLVM [15].

get_paths. This module extracts the set of finite execution paths of each instrumented component in $\mathcal{C}'$. *Finite Path Extractor (FPE)* leverages the symbolic execution tool KLEE [6]. FPE initially *adjusts* the terminating components in $\mathcal{C}'$ and runs KLEE to extract the set of execution paths Γ_{γ^n} of the components in $\mathcal{C}'$. Since the components in $\mathcal{C}'$ are non-terminating, we set an upper bound on the analysis time of KLEE. If all the paths in Γ_{γ^n} achieve path and CFG coverage, FPE sends Γ_{γ^n} to *Frequency Extractor*, otherwise, FPE increases the analysis time and restarts KLEE. When CFG coverage is not satisfied, FPE checks whether the uncovered CFG is dead code. If so, FPE flags CFG coverage as unnecessary. Note that for an execution path, by increasing the analysis time of KLEE, we can potentially increase the length of the path. *Frequency Extractor* uses gcov to extract the execution frequency of each instruction of an execution path in Γ_{γ^n}. If the paths in Γ_{γ^n} do not satisfy frequency coverage, FPE increases the analysis time of KLEE. When the paths in Γ_{γ^n} satisfy all three coverages, FPE reports Γ_{γ^n} and the set of execution frequencies f_γ.

Overhead Calculator. This module estimates overheads using the characteristics of the computing cores and the overhead associated with each instrumentation instruction, memory read and write, running the monitoring code, etc.

ILP Mapper. This module solves the optimization problem and returns the polling period of each monitor (i.e., Δ) and the mapping of components to computing cores (i.e., function $\mathcal{F}$). It uses lp_solve to solve the ILP model for all the possible combinations of polling periods in PP.

4.2   Experimental Settings

We use two interconnected MCB1700 boards, Core1 and Core2, both running the RTX operating system. The time-triggered monitor on each board is a task with read access to all the variables of interest. At each poll the monitor writes the variables of interest and the auxiliary memory to an SD card for the verification engine to retrieve. The auxiliary memory on each board is 1600 bytes. We consider the following factors: (1) the mapping function $\mathcal{F}$, (2) the polling period of each monitor, and (3) the probability distribution for executing the components. For evaluation, we run each experiment for one hour and measure the following metrics in 1-minute intervals (i.e., each experiment provides 60 data points): (1) the number of polls, (2) $\mathcal{O}_c^\delta$, $\mathcal{O}_i^\delta$, $\mathcal{O}_r^\delta$, and $\mathcal{O}_M^\delta$.

Our case study leverages the SNU benchmark suite [1] to create a component-based embedded system. Each program is a component that is invoked infinitely often according to a normal distribution. Moreover, the set of possible polling periods is $PP = \{5 \cdots 30\}$.

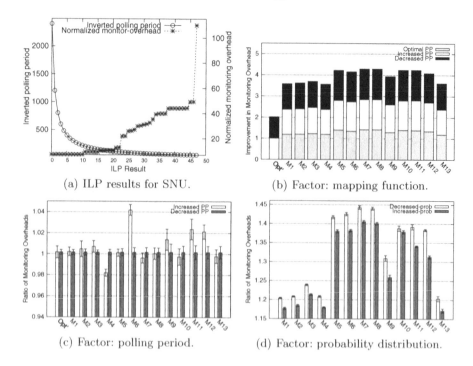

(a) ILP results for SNU.

(b) Factor: mapping function.

(c) Factor: polling period.

(d) Factor: probability distribution.

Fig. 4. Experimental results.

4.3   Analysis of Experiments

We ran the ILP model for each possible combination of polling periods used by the monitors running on the two boards. Figure 4(a) shows the ILP results (i.e., the optimal normalized monitoring overhead for each combination of polling periods). Since the normalized monitoring overhead is a complex number, in Fig. 4(a), normalized monitor-overhead is the distance of the optimal normalized monitoring overhead to the origin of a complex plane. Inverted polling period, in Fig. 4(a), presents $\frac{1}{\sum_{m \in \mathcal{M}} s_m \times factor}$, where $\mathcal{M} = \{\mathsf{Core1}, \mathsf{Core2}\}$, s_m is the polling period of the monitor on each core, and *factor* presents the impact that a monitor invocation along with monitoring code execution has on the monitoring overhead in comparison to an instrumentation. *factor* has a value of 100 in our experiments. Figure 4(a) shows that the settings from point 20 is the solution to the optimization problem. Row *Opt* in Table 2 presents the solution. Metric $\mathcal{F}$ is the mapping of components to cores and Δ is the optimal polling period.

Impact of Mapping Function. We now evaluate the effectiveness of the mapping function of *Opt*. To this end, we change function $\mathcal{F}$ and recalculate Δ for each monitor using Eq. 3. We create 13 different mappings, denoted by $M_{\mathcal{F}}$. Three mappings from $M_{\mathcal{F}}$ that have the closest monitoring overhead to *Opt* are shown in Table 2 (for reasons of space). Table 3 shows the experimental results

Table 2. Settings for SNU programs.

Setting	Metric	Core1	Core2
Opt	Δ	21 cycles	23 cycles
	$\mathcal{F}$	bs, jfd, ludcmp, sqrt, matmul, minver, qsort, insertsort, select	crc, fibcall, fft, fir, lms, qurt
M_1	Δ	16 cycles	23 cycles
	$\mathcal{F}$	bs, crc, fft, fibcall, jfd, fir	minver, lms, ludcmp, matmul, qsort, select, sqrt
M_2	Δ	16 cycles	23 cycles
	$\mathcal{F}$	bs, fft, lms, ludcmp, minver	crc, fibcall, fir, jfd, matmul, qurt, qsort, select, sqrt
M_3	Δ	16 cycles	23 cycles
	$\mathcal{F}$	bs, crc, fibcall, jfd, matmul, ludcmp	fft, fir, lms, minver, qurt, qsort, select, sqrt

Table 3. Monitoring overhead of SNU programs.

Setting	Poll	$\mathcal{O}_c^\Delta$ [ms]	$\mathcal{O}_i^\Delta$ [ms]	$\mathcal{O}_r^\Delta$ [ms]	$\mathcal{O}_T^\Delta$ [ms]	$\mathcal{O}_M^\Delta$ [byte]	$\mathcal{O}_T^\Delta$%	$\mathcal{O}_M^\Delta$%	$\sigma_{\mathcal{O}_T^\Delta}$	$\sigma_{\mathcal{O}_M^\Delta}$	$\mathcal{O}^\Delta$ [ms]	$\sigma_{\mathcal{O}^\Delta}$
Opt	250,617.98	1,700.69	6.26	2,607.79	4,314.75	925.33	7.02	57.83	4.75	24.73	4,412.84	12.30
M_1	361,275.83	2,443.04	5.82	2,727.42	5,176.29	827.2	8.62	51.7	4.48	28.67	5,242.58	10.81
M_2	360,929.61	2,441.17	7.74	2,744.72	5,193.64	984	8.65	61.5	4.68	27.29	5,279.62	13.28
M_3	368,088.71	2,493.52	9.07	2,828.90	5,331.50	1,004.26	8.88	62.73	5.13	31.83	5,425.21	12.84

for the mappings in Table 2. All the values are averages over 60 data points. *Polls* is the number of monitoring polls, $\mathcal{O}_T^\Delta$% is the percentage of the execution time consumed by the time-related overhead $\mathcal{O}_T^\Delta$, $\mathcal{O}_M^\Delta$% is the percentage of the consumed auxiliary memory $\mathcal{O}_M^\Delta$, $\mathcal{O}^\Delta$ is the absolute value of the monitoring overhead (i.e., the distance to the origin of a complex plane), and $\sigma_{\mathcal{O}_T^\Delta}$, $\sigma_{\mathcal{O}_M^\Delta}$, and $\sigma_{\mathcal{O}^\Delta}$ are the standard deviations of $\mathcal{O}_T^\Delta$, $\mathcal{O}_M^\Delta$, and $\mathcal{O}^\Delta$, respectively.

Table 3 shows that on average *Opt* imposes 20.46 % less monitoring overhead in comparison to M_1–M_3. *Opt* imposes 11.86 % more memory-related overhead $\mathcal{O}_M^\Delta$ in comparison to M_2. On the other hand, M_2 imposes 19.98 % more time-related overhead $\mathcal{O}_T^\Delta$. Although, M_2 imposes less $\mathcal{O}_M^\Delta$, the impact of $\mathcal{O}_T^\Delta$ is stronger on $\mathcal{O}^\Delta$ (i.e., *factor* is 100 in our experiments). This observation matches with the observations in [5]. The larger $\mathcal{O}_T^\Delta$ of M_1–M_3 is caused by the larger number of polls which is the outcome of the smaller polling period on Core1. Moreover, the experiments on all the mappings in $M_\mathcal{F}$ show that on average *Opt* imposes 31.1 % less monitoring overhead. *Optimal-PP*, in Fig. 4(b), shows the ratio of the monitoring overhead associated with each mapping in $M_\mathcal{F}$ to the monitoring overhead associated with *Opt*. In addition, the results showed that our optimization approach has an error factor of 0.07. In other words, in one out of 13 mappings, our approach did not accurately reflect the monitoring overhead. The significance test on all these experiments show that the results are statistically significant with a p-value of less than 1^{-100}, hence, our approach can successfully find the mapping that results in the minimum monitoring overhead.

Impact of Polling Period. We change the polling period of the monitor on each core for every mapping in $M_{\mathcal{F}}$. We once increase and once decrease the polling period of each monitor by 2 CPU cycles. Figure 4(b) shows the ratio of the monitoring overhead associated with each mapping in $M_{\mathcal{F}}$ to the monitoring overhead associated with Opt with respect to the changed polling periods. On average Opt imposes 32.81 % less monitoring overhead in comparison to the monitoring overhead associated with the mappings in $M_{\mathcal{F}}$. Moreover, in Fig. 4(c), for each mapping M, *increased/decreased-PP* presents the ratio of the monitoring overhead associated with mapping M when using the increased/decreased polling periods to the monitoring overhead of mapping M when using the optimal polling period Δ. The error bars reflect the standard deviation. The results show that by employing Δ, the mappings in $M_{\mathcal{F}}$ impose 1.39 % less monitoring overhead. The error factor of this set of experiments is 0.19; i.e., in 5 out of 26 experiments, our approach did not correctly calculate Δ.

Robustness Analysis. To calculate the normalize monitoring overhead, we assumed that the execution paths of each component and the set of components are executed based on a normal distribution. We change the probability distribution as follows to evaluate the robustness of our optimization approach:

1. We increase the probability distribution of the execution path(s) and component(s) with the highest normalized monitoring overhead, by 10 units. In Fig. 4(d), *increased-prob* shows the ratio of the monitoring overhead associated with each mapping in $M_{\mathcal{F}}$ to the monitoring overhead associated with Opt with respect to the new probability distribution. The error bars reflect the standard deviation. Figure 4(d) shows that with moderate increases in the probability distribution, our approach is still effective since on average Opt imposes 33.14 % less monitoring overhead. By also changing the polling period as in Subsect. 4.3, on average Opt imposes 34.1 % less overhead. The experiments show an error factor of 0.38, meaning that in 15 out of 39 experiments, our approach did not either correctly reflect the monitoring overhead or calculate the optimal polling period.
2. Likewise, we decrease the probability distribution of the execution path(s) and component(s). Figure 4(d) shows that with moderate decreases in the probability distribution, our approach is still effective since on average Opt imposes 27.27 % less monitoring overhead. By also changing the polling period as in Subsect. 4.3, on average Opt imposes 29.2 % less overhead. The experiments show an error factor of 0.25, meaning that in 10 out of 39 experiments, our approach did not either correctly reflect the monitoring overhead or calculate the optimal polling period.

Note that the above error factors are expected, since our overhead calculations are based on normal distribution. Having said that, these experiments shows that changing the probability distribution does not significantly undermine the robustness of our approach. Thus, the insight is when the probability distribution of the components are approximately known, it is advisable to use the knowledge when calculating the normalized monitoring overheads. In addition, in all the aforementioned experiments, the significance test show that the results are statistically significant with a p-value of less than 1^{-100}.

5   Related Work

Most runtime verification frameworks [7,11,13] use event-triggered monitoring. These frameworks are not suitable for time-sensitive systems. Time-triggered monitoring [5] ensures periodic monitoring with sound program state reconstruction. To reduce the overhead, the approach in [4,5,17] uses auxiliary memory to increase the polling period. The technique in [16] uses symbolic execution to adjust the monitor's polling period at run time according to the execution path. Reference [2] discards instrumentation with respect to the system's execution path in event-based monitoring. References [3,8] discards/adds monitoring instrumentation with respect to the properties being monitored.

To our knowledge, our approach is the first that handles time-triggered monitoring for component-based multi-core systems. Reference [10] uses the BIP modelling language to formally model and introduce runtime verification into software components. Reference [19] uses a software monitor that observes the system's input, output and partial internal states to check a set of assumption-guarantee rules and suffers from high computation runtime overhead. In [9], the authors design a monitor over the Eclipse modelling framework where its monitoring coverage changes at run time to keep the monitoring overhead bounded.

6   Conclusion

In this paper, we presented an effective optimization approach to minimize the monitoring overhead associated with time-triggered runtime verification (TTRV) of component-based multi-core embedded systems. In TTRV, a monitor runs in parallel with the components under inspection and polls the component's state periodically to evaluate a set of properties. The overhead imposed by TTRV is mainly affected by (1) the mapping of the components to computing cores, and (2) the polling period of the time-triggered monitors. Our proposed approach leverages control-flow analysis and symbolic execution to characterize the monitoring overhead associated with monitoring each component at run time. Then, it transforms the optimization problem (for finding the mapping of components to cores that incurs minimum overhead) to an integer linear program. We evaluated our approach using the SNU benchmark. Experimental results show that our approach finds the optimal solution with a success rate of 80 %. On average, our approach can reduce the monitoring overhead by 34 %, as compared to various near-optimal monitoring patterns of the components at run time.

In addition, our technique shows resilience towards changes in the probability distribution of invoking the components.

As for future work, we plan to further reduce the monitoring overhead by adjusting the polling period of the monitors at run time using symbolic execution techniques. Another interesting extension is to consider TTRV for distributed applications.

Acknowledgment. This work was partially sponsored by Canada NSERC Discovery Grant 418396-2012 and NSERC Strategic Grants 430575-2012 and 463324-2014.

References

1. SNU Real-Time Benchmarks. http://www.cprover.org/goto-cc/examples/snu.html
2. Artho, C., Drusinksy, D., Goldberg, A., Havelund, K., Lowry, M., Păsăreanu, C.S., Roşu, G., Visser, W.: Experiments with test case generation and runtime analysis. In: Börger, E., Gargantini, A., Riccobene, E. (eds.) ASM 2003. LNCS, vol. 2589, pp. 87–107. Springer, Heidelberg (2003)
3. Bodden, E., Hendren, L., Lam, P., Lhoták, O., Naeem, N.A.: Collaborative runtime verification with tracematches. In: Sokolsky, O., Taşiran, S. (eds.) RV 2007. LNCS, vol. 4839, pp. 22–37. Springer, Heidelberg (2007)
4. Bonakdarpour, B., Navabpour, S., Fischmeister, S.: Sampling-based runtime verification. In: Formal Methods (FM), pp. 88–102 (2011)
5. Bonakdarpour, B., Navabpour, S., Fischmeister, S.: Time-triggered runtime verification. Formal Methods Syst. Design (FMSD) **43**(1), 29–60 (2013)
6. Cadar, C., Dunbar, D., Engler, D.: Klee: unassisted and automatic generation of high-coverage tests for complex systems programs. In: Proceedings of the 8th USENIX Conference on Operating Systems Design and Implementation, OSDI 2008, pp. 209–224 (2008)
7. Chen, F., Roşu, G.: Java-MOP: a monitoring oriented programming environment for Java. In: Halbwachs, N., Zuck, L.D. (eds.) TACAS 2005. LNCS, vol. 3440, pp. 546–550. Springer, Heidelberg (2005)
8. Dwyer, M.B., Kinneer, A., Elbaum, S.: Adaptive online program analysis. In Proceedings of the 29th International Conference on Software Engineering, ICSE 2007, pp. 220–229 (2007)
9. Ehlers, J., Hasselbring, W.: A self-adaptive monitoring framework for component-based software systems. In: Crnkovic, I., Gruhn, V., Book, M. (eds.) ECSA 2011. LNCS, vol. 6903, pp. 278–286. Springer, Heidelberg (2011)
10. Falcone, Y., Jaber, M., Nguyen, T.-H., Bozga, M., Bensalem, S.: Runtime verification of component-based systems. In: Barthe, G., Pardo, A., Schneider, G. (eds.) SEFM 2011. LNCS, vol. 7041, pp. 204–220. Springer, Heidelberg (2011)
11. Havelund, K., Roşu, G.: An overview of the runtime verification tool java pathexplorer. Form. Methods Syst. Des. **24**(2), 189–215 (2004)
12. Henzinger, T.A., Sifakis, J.: The embedded systems design challenge. In: Formal Methods (FM), pp. 1–15 (2006)
13. Kim, M., Viswanathan, M., Kannan, S., Lee, I., Sokolsky, O.: Java-mac: A run-time assurance approach for java programs. Form. Methods Syst. Des. **24**(2), 129–155 (2004)

14. King, J.C.: Symbolic execution and program testing. Comm. ACM **19**(7), 385–394 (1976)
15. Lattner, C., Adve, V.: LLVM: a compilation framework for lifelong program analysis and transformation. In: International Symposium on Code Generation and Optimization: Feedback Directed and Runtime Optimization, p. 75 (2004)
16. Navabpour, S., Bonakdarpour, B., Fischmeister, S.: Path-aware time-triggered runtime verification. In: Third International Conference on Runtime Verification (RV), pp. 199–213 (2012)
17. Navabpour, S., Wu, C.W., Bonakdarpour, B., Fischmeister, S.: Efficient techniques for near-optimal instrumentation in time-triggered runtime verification. In: Runtime Verification (RV), pp. 208–222 (2011)
18. Szyperski, C.: Component Software: Beyond Object-Oriented Programming, 2nd edn. Addison-Wesley Longman Publishing Co., Inc. (2002)
19. Zulkernine, M., Seviora, R.: Towards automatic monitoring of component-based software systems. J. Syst. Softw. **74**(1), 15–24 (2005)

Monitoring for a Decidable Fragment of MTL-∫

André de Matos Pedro[1]([⊠]), David Pereira[1], Luís Miguel Pinho[1],
and Jorge Sousa Pinto[2]

[1] CISTER/INESC TEC, ISEP, Polytechnic Institute of Porto, Porto, Portugal
{anmap,dmrpe}@isep.ipp.pt
[2] HASLab/INESC TEC & Universidade do Minho, Braga, Portugal

Abstract. Temporal logics targeting real-time systems are traditionally undecidable. Based on a restricted fragment of MTL-∫, we propose a new approach for the runtime verification of hard real-time systems. The novelty of our technique is that it is based on incremental evaluation, allowing us to effectively treat duration properties (which play a crucial role in real-time systems). We describe the two levels of operation of our approach: offline simplification by quantifier removal techniques; and online evaluation of a three-valued interpretation for formulas of our fragment. Our experiments show the applicability of this mechanism as well as the validity of the provided complexity results.

1 Introduction

Temporal logics are widely used formalisms in the field of specification and verification of reactive systems [17], since they provide a natural and abstract technique for the analysis of safety and liveness properties. Linear Temporal Logic (LTL) describes properties concerning the temporal order of the input model, and is well studied in terms of expressiveness, decidability and complexity. *Timed temporal logics* are extensions of temporal logics with quantitative constraints to handle temporal logic specifications [2]. Metric Temporal Logic (MTL) [10,15] is an undecidable real-time extension of LTL, describing the temporal order constrained by quantitative intervals on the temporal operators.

These formalisms have been used for formal verification, either by deductive or by algorithmic methods [9]. However, real-time logics are notably less well-behaved than traditional temporal logics. In particular, the model checking problem for MTL is known to be undecidable [15]. Decidable real-time formalisms that can be used as alternatives are currently the focus of much attention.

A diversity of MTL fragments reveal that the undecidable results of MTL are due to the excessive precision of the timing constraints (i.e., *punctuality* [1]), the presence of unbounded temporal operators (*unboundedness*), the presence of *unsafe formulas*, and the excessive richness of the *semantic model* [15]. Metric Interval Temporal Logic (MITL) is a fragment that avoids punctuality by constraining any interval on the temporal operators to be non-singular; Bounded MTL (BMTL) is another fragment that, instead of avoiding punctual intervals,

© Springer International Publishing Switzerland 2015
E. Bartocci and R. Majumdar (Eds.): RV 2015, LNCS 9333, pp. 169–184, 2015.
DOI: 10.1007/978-3-319-23820-3_11

bounds intervals that are infinitely large. Both are decidable fragments. Syntactic restrictions on temporal logic operators of MTL may also result in decidable fragments. Ouaknine and Worrell [14] describe a fragment of MTL named Safety MTL (SMTL), that does not allow expressing invariant formulas, and Bouyer et al. [5] have introduced the term *flatness* for MTL.

In addition to being undecidable, the previous logics also fail to capture the notion of *duration*. This notion, however, is of paramount importance when specifying and developing real-time systems, mainly because the fundamental results about the reliability of this class of systems are related to ensuring that the execution time of the involved components does not miss some predetermined deadline. Lakhnech and Hooman [11] came up with *Metric temporal logic with durations* (MTL-$\int$) and Chaochen and colleagues [8] with Duration Calculus, which provide expressive power to specify and reason about durations within *real intervals*. By applying syntactic and semantic restrictions it is possible to derive decidable fragments for duration properties.

The motivation for this work is that of providing an expressive formal language that fits the timing requirements of real-time systems, from the point of view of *runtime verification* (RV). RV is concerned with the problem of generating monitors from formal specifications, and adding these monitors into the target code as a safety-net that is able to detect abnormal behaviors and, possibly, respond to them via the release of counter-measures. As such, RV methods can be applied to systems where the source code is not available due to intellectual property, or in those cases where we have access to the code but the complexity of the system's requirements is too high to be addressed via any of the known static verification approaches.

The major contribution of this paper is a new mechanism for runtime verification of hard real-time systems regarding duration properties, based on a decidable fragment of MTL-$\int$ and a three-valued abstraction of this fragment. The fragment allows for expressing quantified formulae, and is adequate for quantifier elimination: we give an algorithm for the simplification of formulas containing quantifiers and free logic variables. Intuitively, we abstract our fragment into *first order logic of real numbers* (FOL$_R$) to obtain quantifier-free formulas.

One particular application scenario for RV is in scheduling theory of hard real-time systems. Rigorous calculation of the *worst case execution time* (WCET) is commonly difficult, and the known approximation methods based on statistical abstractions degrade the dependability of the systems, since the available schedulability theory tends to assume the WCET. Application of monitors in this case will make the system more reliable. We will show through an application example (based on *resource models*, which are mechanisms that ensure time isolation for execution units) the interest of allowing formal specifications to express existential quantification over durations, for real applications.

The paper is organized as follows: in Sect. 2 we introduce suitable restrictions over MTL-$\int$; Sect. 3 describes the three-valued semantics of restricted MTL-$\int$, and Sect. 4 describes an algorithm for inequality abstraction. In Sect. 5 we then introduce an evaluation algorithm for the restricted MTL-$\int$ with three-valued semantics. Section 6 describes our experimental work and finally Sect. 7 discusses related work and concludes the paper.

2   Specification Language RMTL-∫

MTL-∫ is more expressive than DC [11], but is undecidable since the relation over terms or the term function may themselves be undecidable. Let us begin by briefly reviewing MTL-∫.

Definition 1. *Let $\mathcal{P}$ be a set of propositions and $\mathcal{V}$ a set of logic variables. The syntax of MTL-∫ terms η and formulas φ is defined inductively as follows:*

$$\eta ::= \alpha \mid x \mid f(\eta_1, \dots, \eta_n) \mid \int^\eta \varphi$$

$$\varphi ::= p \mid R(\eta_1, \dots, \eta_n) \mid \varphi_1 \vee \varphi_2 \mid \neg\varphi \mid \varphi_1 \, U_{\sim\gamma} \, \varphi_2 \mid \varphi_1 \, S_{\sim\gamma} \, \varphi_2 \mid \exists x \, \varphi$$

where $\alpha \in \mathbb{R}$, $x \in \mathcal{V}$ is a logic variable, f a function symbol of arity n, $\int^\eta \varphi$ is the duration of the formula φ in an interval, $p \in \mathcal{P}$ is an atomic proposition, U and S are temporal operators with $\sim \in \{<, =\}$, $\gamma \in \mathbb{R}_{\geq 0}$, and the meaning of $R(\eta_1, \dots, \eta_n), \varphi_1 \vee \varphi_2, \neg\varphi, \exists x \, \varphi$ is defined as usual.

We will use the following abbreviations: $\varphi \wedge \psi$ for $\neg(\neg\varphi \vee \neg\psi)$, $\varphi \rightarrow \psi$ for $\neg\varphi \vee \psi$, tt for $\varphi \vee \neg\varphi$, ff for $\varphi \wedge \neg\varphi$, $\Diamond_{\sim\gamma} \varphi$ for tt $U_{\sim\gamma} \varphi$, and $\Box_{\sim\gamma} \varphi$ for $\neg(\text{tt } U_{\sim\gamma} \neg\varphi)$.

An observation function σ of length $\delta \in \mathbb{R}_{\geq 0} \cup \{\infty\}$ over $\mathcal{P}$ is a function from $\mathcal{P}$ into the set of functions from interval $[0, \delta)$ into $\{\text{tt}, \text{ff}\}$. The length of σ is denoted by $\#\sigma$. A *logical environment* is any function $\upsilon : \mathcal{V} \rightarrow \mathbb{R}_{\geq 0}$. For any such υ, $x \in \mathcal{V}$ and $r \in \mathbb{R}$, we will denote by $\upsilon[x \mapsto r]$ the logical environment that maps x to r and every other variable y to $\upsilon(y)$. The following auxiliary definition will be used in the interpretation of the duration of a formula.

Definition 2 (MTL-∫ Semantics). *The truth value of a formula φ will be defined relative to a model (σ, υ, t) consisting of an observation σ, a logical environment υ, and a time instant $t \in \mathbb{R}_{\geq 0}$. We will write $(\sigma, \upsilon, t) \models \varphi$ when φ is interpreted as true in the model (σ, υ, t). Terms and formulas will be interpreted in a mutual recursive way. First of all, for each formula φ, observation σ and logical environment υ, the auxiliary indicator function $1_{\varphi(\sigma, \upsilon)} : \mathbb{R}_{\geq 0} \rightarrow \mathbb{R}_{\geq 0}$ is defined as follows, making use of the satisfaction relation:*

$$1_{\varphi(\sigma, \upsilon)}(t) = \begin{cases} 1 & \text{if } (\sigma, \upsilon, t) \models \varphi, \\ 0 & \text{otherwise.} \end{cases}$$

The value $\mathcal{T}[\![\eta]\!](\sigma, \upsilon)\, t$ of a term η relative to a model can then be defined. A Riemann integral [7] of $1_{\varphi(\sigma, \upsilon)}$ is used for the case of a duration $\int^\eta \varphi$:

$$\mathcal{T}[\![\alpha]\!](\sigma, \upsilon)\, t = \alpha$$

$$\mathcal{T}[\![x]\!](\sigma, \upsilon)\, t = \upsilon(x)$$

$$\mathcal{T}[\![f(\eta_1, \dots, \eta_n)]\!] = f(\mathcal{T}[\![\eta_1]\!](\sigma, \upsilon)\, t, \dots, \mathcal{T}[\![\eta_n]\!](\sigma, \upsilon)\, t)$$

$$\mathcal{T}\left[\!\left[\int^\eta \varphi\right]\!\right] = \begin{cases} \int_t^{t + \mathcal{T}[\![\eta]\!](\sigma, \upsilon)\, t} 1_{\varphi(\sigma, \upsilon)}(t_*)\, dt_* & \text{if } (*) \\ 0 & \text{otherwise} \end{cases}$$

where $(*)$ *means that* $1_{\varphi(\sigma,v)}$ *satisfies the Dirichlet condition [11, p.7] and the sub-term* $\mathscr{T}[\![\eta]\!](\sigma,v)\,t$ *is non-negative, otherwise the function is non Riemann integrable. The satisfaction relation in turn is defined as:*

$$(\sigma,v,t) \models p \qquad\qquad \textit{iff}\quad \sigma(p)(t) = \mathsf{tt} \textit{ and } t < \#\sigma$$

$$(\sigma,v,t) \models R(\eta_1,\dots,\eta_n) \quad \textit{iff}\quad R(\mathscr{T}[\![\eta_1]\!](\sigma,v)\,t,\dots,\mathscr{T}[\![\eta_n]\!](\sigma,v)\,t)$$

$$(\sigma,v,t) \models \varphi_1 \vee \varphi_2 \qquad \textit{iff}\quad (\sigma,v,t) \models \varphi_1 \textit{ or } (\sigma,v,t) \models \varphi_2$$

$$(\sigma,v,t) \models \neg\varphi \qquad\qquad \textit{iff}\quad (\sigma,v,t) \not\models \varphi$$

$$(\sigma,v,t) \models \varphi_1\,U_{\sim\gamma}\,\varphi_2 \quad \textit{iff}\quad \textit{there exists } t' \textit{ such that } t < t' \sim t+\gamma,\ (\sigma,v,t') \models \varphi_2,$$
$$\textit{and for all } t'',\ t < t'' < t',\ (\sigma,v,t'') \models \varphi_1$$

$$(\sigma,v,t) \models \varphi_1\,S_{\sim\gamma}\,\varphi_2 \quad \textit{iff}\quad \textit{there exists } t' \textit{ such that } t-\gamma \sim t' < t,\ (\sigma,v,t') \models \varphi_2,$$
$$\textit{and for all } t'',\ t' < t'' < t,\ (\sigma,v,t'') \models \varphi_1$$

$$(\sigma,v,t) \models \exists x\,\varphi \qquad\qquad \textit{iff}\quad \textit{there exists an } r \in \mathbb{R} \textit{ such that } (\sigma, v[x \mapsto r], t) \models \varphi$$

Note that the semantics of the until operator is strict and non-matching [4].

To overcome the undecidability results of MTL-$\int$, we apply restrictions over MTL-$\int$. *Restricted metric temporal logic with durations* (RMTL-$\int$) is a syntactically and semantically restricted fragment of MTL-$\int$; the syntactic restrictions over MTL-$\int$ include the use of *bounded formulas*, of a single relation $<$ over the real numbers, the restriction of the n-ary function terms to use one of the $+$ or $\times$ operators, and a restriction of α constants to the set or rationals $\mathbb{Q}$. Tarski's theorem [19] states that the first-order theory of reals with $+$, $\times$, and $<$ allows for quantifiers to be eliminated. Algorithmic quantifier elimination leads to decidability, assuming that the truth values of sentences involving only constants can be computed. We will denote by Φ the set of RMTL-$\int$ formulas.

The semantic restrictions on the other hand include the conversion of the *continuous* semantics of MTL-$\int$ into an *interval-based* semantics, where models are timed state sequences and formulas are evaluated in a given logical environment at a time $t \in \mathbb{R}_{\geq 0}$. A timed state sequence κ is an infinite sequence of the form $(p_0, [i_0, i'_0[), (p_1, [i_1, i'_1[) \dots$, where $p_j \in \mathcal{P}$, $i'_j = i_{j+1}$ and $i_j, i'_j \in \mathbb{R}_{\geq 0}$ such that $i_j < i'_j$ and $j \geq 0$. Let $\kappa(t)$ be defined as $\{p_j\}$ if there exists a tuple $(p_j, [i_j, i'_j[)$ such that $t \in [i_j, i'_j[$, and as $\emptyset$ otherwise. Note that there exists at most one such tuple. The replacement rule for propositions is $(\kappa, v, t) \models p$ iff $p \in \kappa(t)$, and σ is globally replaced by κ. In particular the indicator function $1_{\varphi(\kappa,v)}$ is defined as 1 if $(\sigma, v, t) \models \varphi$, and 0 otherwise. An important property of our restriction is that RMTL-$\int$ satisfies by construction the Dirichlet conditions implying the Riemann property:

Lemma 1. *For any formula φ in RMTL-$\int$, timed state sequence κ, and logical environment v, the indicator function $1_{\varphi(\kappa,v)}$ is Riemann integrable.*

Example 1 (Application of Durations). Let us now consider an example using the duration term where the evolution of a real-time system formed by tasks depends entirely on the occurrence of events, the evaluation of the propositions is performed over these events, and all of its tasks have an associated fixed set of events. Let ϕ_m be a formula that specifies the periodic release of a renewal event for a timed resource in the system, and let ψ_m be a formula specifying every event triggered by tasks belonging to that resource. To monitor utilization and the release of timed resources, we employ the formula,

$$\Box_{<\infty} \phi_m \rightarrow \int^t \psi_m \leq \beta,$$

where t is the budget renewal period, and β is the allowed budget (i.e., the execution time of tasks belonging to the timed resource). However, the incremental evaluation as t evolves is inconsistent in the two-valued setting since we could have a false verdict at $t = 0$ and a true verdict at $t = 10$ (different from the solution that will be presented in the next section).

3   Three-Valued Abstraction of RMTL-∫

The three-valued logic abstraction of RMTL-∫, which we will call *three-valued restricted metric temporal logic with durations* (RMTL-$\int_3$), is syntactically defined as before, but contains two new terms. These terms allow variables to be maximized and minimized in certain intervals, subject to a constraint given as a formula. The terms must be introduced here due to the situation in which no minimum or maximum exists (the formula is not satisfied in the interval), since we need to define an infeasible value instead of assigning a real number to these terms. The language of terms of RMTL-$\int_3$ is defined as follows:

$$\eta ::= \alpha \mid x \mid \min_{x \in I} \varphi \mid \max_{x \in I} \varphi \mid \eta_1 \circ \eta_2 \mid \int^\eta \varphi$$

where $x \in I \min \varphi$ and $x \in I \max \varphi$, with $I = [I_{min}, I_{max}]$ and $I_{min}, I_{max} \in \mathbb{R}$, and $\circ \in \{+, \times\}$. All other formulas and terms are as in RMTL-∫. We will denote by Φ^3 the set of RMTL-$\int_3$ formulas, and by Γ the set of RMTL-$\int_3$ terms.

Definition 3 (RMTL-$\int_3$ Semantics). *The truth value of a formula φ will again be defined relative to a model (κ, υ, t) consisting of a timed state sequence κ, a logical environment υ, and a time instant $t \in \mathbb{R}_{\geq 0}$. The auxiliary indicator function $1_{\varphi(\kappa,\upsilon)} : \mathbb{R}_{\geq 0} \to \{0, 1\} \cup \{-1\}$ is defined as follows:*

$$1_{\varphi(\kappa,\upsilon)}(t) = \begin{cases} 1 & \text{if } [\![\varphi]\!](\kappa, \upsilon, t) = \text{tt}, \\ 0 & \text{if } [\![\varphi]\!](\kappa, \upsilon, t) = \text{ff}, \\ -1 & \text{if } [\![\varphi]\!](\kappa, \upsilon, t) = \bot \end{cases}$$

The interpretation of the term η will be given by $\mathscr{T}[\![\eta]\!](\sigma, \upsilon) t \in \mathbb{R} \cup \{\bot_\mathbb{R}\}$, as defined by the following rules. Whenever $\mathscr{T}[\![\eta]\!](\sigma, \upsilon) t = \bot_\mathbb{R}$, this means that the term η is infeasible.

Rigid Terms:

$\mathscr{T}[\![\eta_1]\!](\sigma, \upsilon) t$ *is defined as α if $\eta_1 = \alpha$, and as $\upsilon(x)$ if $\eta_1 = x$*

Minimum and Maximum Terms:

- If $\eta_1 = \min_{x \in I} \varphi$ (resp. $\max_{x \in I} \varphi$), then $\mathscr{T}[\![\eta_1]\!](\sigma, v)\, t =$ is defined as:

$$\begin{cases} \mathfrak{I} = m\{r \mid r \in I \text{ and } (\kappa, v[x \mapsto r], t) \models_3 \varphi\} & \text{if } \mathfrak{I} \neq \emptyset \\ \bot_R & \text{otherwise} \end{cases}$$

where m is one of the operators $\min$ or $\max$ as appropriate.

Duration Term:

- If $\eta_1 = \int^{\eta_2} \phi$, then $\mathscr{T}[\![\eta_1]\!](\sigma, v)\, t$ is defined as:

$$\begin{cases} \int_t^{t + \mathscr{T}[\![\eta_2]\!](\sigma, v)\, t} 1_{\phi(\kappa, v)}(t')\, dt' & \text{if } \begin{array}{l} \mathscr{T}[\![\eta_2]\!](\sigma, v)\, t \geq 0 \text{ and for all } t'', \\ t'' \in [t, t + \mathscr{T}[\![\eta_2]\!](\sigma, v)\, t], 1_{\phi(\kappa, v)}(t'') \in \{0, 1\} \end{array} \\ \bot_R & \text{otherwise} \end{cases}$$

Turning to the interpretation of formulas, we define $[\![\varphi]\!]_{(\kappa, v, t)}$ to be one of the three values in $\{\mathsf{tt}, \mathsf{ff}, \bot\}$, according to the following rules.

Basic Formulae:

- If $\phi = p$, then $[\![\phi]\!]_{(\kappa, v, t)}$ is tt if $p \in \kappa(t)$, ff if $p \notin \kappa(t)$ and $\kappa(t) \neq \emptyset$, and $\bot$ if $\kappa(t) = \emptyset$.

Relation Operator:

- If $\phi = \eta_1 < \eta_2$, then $[\![\phi]\!]_{(\kappa, v, t)}$ is defined as:

$$\begin{cases} \mathsf{tt} & \text{if } \mathscr{T}[\![\eta_1]\!](\sigma, v)\, t < \mathscr{T}[\![\eta_2]\!](\sigma, v)\, t, \text{ and} \\ & \quad \mathscr{T}[\![\eta_1]\!](\sigma, v)\, t, \mathscr{T}[\![\eta_2]\!](\sigma, v)\, t \in \mathbb{R} \\ \mathsf{ff} & \text{if } \mathscr{T}[\![\eta_1]\!](\sigma, v)\, t \geq \mathscr{T}[\![\eta_2]\!](\sigma, v)\, t, \text{ and} \\ & \quad \mathscr{T}[\![\eta_1]\!](\sigma, v)\, t, \mathscr{T}[\![\eta_2]\!](\sigma, v)\, t \in \mathbb{R} \\ \bot & \text{otherwise} \end{cases}$$

Boolean Operators:

- If $\phi = \neg\varphi$, then $[\![\phi]\!]_{(\kappa, v, t)}$ is tt if $[\![\varphi]\!]_{(\kappa, v, t)} = \mathsf{ff}$, ff if $[\![\varphi]\!]_{(\kappa, v, t)} = \mathsf{tt}$, and $\bot$ otherwise.
- If $\phi = \varphi_1 \vee \varphi_2$, then $[\![\phi]\!]_{(\kappa, v, t)}$ is tt if $[\![\varphi_1]\!]_{(\kappa, v, t)} = \mathsf{tt} \vee [\![\varphi_2]\!]_{(\kappa, v, t)} = \mathsf{tt}$, ff if $[\![\varphi_1]\!]_{(\kappa, v, t)} = \mathsf{ff} \wedge [\![\varphi_2]\!]_{(\kappa, v, t)} = \mathsf{ff}$, and $\bot$ otherwise.

Temporal Operators:

- If $\phi = \varphi_1 U_{\sim\gamma} \varphi_2$, then $[\![\phi]\!]_{(\kappa, v, t)}$ is defined as:

$$\begin{cases} \mathsf{tt} & \text{if } \exists t', t < t' \sim t + \gamma \text{ such that } [\![\varphi_2]\!]_{(\kappa, v, t')} = \mathsf{tt}, \text{ and} \\ & \quad \forall t'', t < t'' < t', [\![\varphi_1]\!]_{(\kappa, v, t'')} = \mathsf{tt} \\ \mathsf{ff} & \text{if } \forall t', t < t' \sim t + \gamma \text{ such that} \\ & \quad [\![\varphi_1]\!]_{(\kappa, v, t')} = \mathsf{ff} \rightarrow \exists t'', t < t'' < t', [\![\varphi_1]\!]_{(\kappa, v, t'')} = \mathsf{ff} \\ \bot & \text{otherwise} \end{cases}$$

- If $\phi = \varphi_1 \, S_{\sim \gamma} \, \varphi_2$, then $[\![\phi]\!]_{(\kappa,\upsilon,t)}$ is defined as:

$$
\begin{cases}
\text{tt} & \text{if } \exists t', \, t - \gamma \sim t' < t \text{ such that } [\![\varphi_2]\!]_{(\kappa,\upsilon,t')} = \text{tt}, \text{ and} \\
& \quad \forall t'', \, t' < t'' < t, [\![\varphi_1]\!]_{(\kappa,\upsilon,t'')} = \text{tt} \\
\text{ff} & \text{if } \forall t', \, t - \gamma \sim t' < t \text{ such that} \\
& \quad [\![\varphi_1]\!]_{(\kappa,\upsilon,t')} = \text{ff} \rightarrow \exists t'', \, t' < t'' < t, [\![\varphi_1]\!]_{(\kappa,\upsilon,t'')} = \text{ff} \\
\bot & \text{otherwise}
\end{cases}
$$

Existential Operator:

- If $\phi = \exists x \; \varphi$, then $[\![\phi]\!]_{(\kappa,\upsilon,t)}$ is defined as:

$$
\begin{cases}
\text{tt} & \text{if there exists a value } r \in \mathbb{R} \text{ such that } [\![\varphi]\!]_{(\kappa,\upsilon[x \mapsto r],t)} = \text{tt} \\
\text{ff} & \text{if for all } r \in \mathbb{R} \text{ such that } [\![\varphi]\!]_{(\kappa,\upsilon[x \mapsto r],t)} = \text{ff} \\
\bot & \text{otherwise}
\end{cases}
$$

We will write $(\kappa, \upsilon, t) \models_3 \varphi$ when $[\![\varphi]\!]_{(\kappa,\upsilon,t)} = \text{tt}$, and $(\kappa, \upsilon, t) \not\models_3 \varphi$ when $[\![\varphi]\!]_{(\kappa,\upsilon,t)} = \text{ff}$. In what follows we will often write $x \in I$ as an abbreviated form for $I_{min} < x \wedge x < I_{max}$, and $\eta_1 = \eta_2$ for $\neg(\eta_1 < \eta_2) \wedge \neg(\eta_1 > \eta_2)$.

Preservation of RMTL-$\int$ Semantics. An immediate motivation for the choice of defining a three-valued semantics for our logic fragment comes from the nature of runtime verification, which evaluates timed sequences where it is not possible to determine a definitive true or false value without analyzing the complete trace. For instance, considering a prefix $\varkappa_p$ of a timed sequence $\varkappa$, we have that the evaluation of the same formula in the models $(\varkappa, \upsilon, t)$ and $(\varkappa_p, \upsilon, t)$ produces different truth values. Classic semantics cannot provide a common truth value to make consistent incremental evaluations of the model, which is an important feature for RV.

The semantic preservation of both truth and falsity for the three-valued logic is defined using the following two relations: a partial relation $\prec$ on $\{\text{tt}, \text{ff}, \bot\}$ defined by $\bot \prec \text{tt}$, $\bot \prec \text{ff}$, $\bot \prec \bot$, $\text{tt} \prec \text{tt}$, and $\text{ff} \prec \text{ff}$; and a partial relation $\lhd : \mathbb{R} \times \mathbb{R} \cup \{\bot_{\mathbb{R}}\}$ defined by $0 \lhd \bot_{\mathbb{R}}$, and $n \lhd m$, for all $n, m \in \mathbb{R}$, which gives a distinct treatment to duration terms that evaluate to 0 in the standard semantics.

Definition 4. *Let (κ, υ, t) be a model. The three-valued semantics is said to preserve the two-valued semantics iff the following rules hold:*

1. *For basic formulas containing the relation operator, for all terms $\eta_1 \in$ RMTL-$\int$ and $\eta_2 \in$ RMTL-$\int_3$ excluding minimum and maximum terms, $\mathcal{T}[\![\eta_1]\!](\sigma, \upsilon) \, t \, \lhd \, \mathcal{T}[\![\eta_2]\!](\sigma, \upsilon) \, t$ holds and it implies that $0 \lhd \bot_{\mathbb{R}}$ if η_1 has the form $\int^{\eta_3} \phi$ and $\mathcal{T}[\![\eta_3]\!](\sigma, \upsilon) \, t < 0$; and $0 \lhd 0$ otherwise.*
2. *For each basic formula ϕ containing Boolean, temporal, and existential operators, $[(\kappa, \upsilon, t) \models_3 \gamma] \prec [(\kappa, \upsilon, t) \models \gamma]$ holds.*

We will now formulate two auxiliary results required to prove the semantic preservation of RMTL-$\int$ in RMTL-$\int_3$. From a close examination of the minimum and maximum term semantics, we have that these terms are indeed quantified formulas, interpreted as a minimum or a maximum value that satisfies the quantification, or as $\bot_{\mathbb{R}}$ when this minimum or maximum is nonexistent. First of all we observe that the following axioms [19, p. 205] extend to our present setting:

A 1. $\eta_1 \circ \min_{x \in I} \phi \sim \eta_2$ *implies that there exists an x such that $\eta_1 \circ x \sim \eta_2$, $x \in I$, and ϕ implies that for all y, $y < x$ and $\neg\phi$.*

A 2. $\eta_1 \circ \max_{x \in I} \phi \sim \eta_2$ *implies that there exists an x such that $\eta_1 \circ x \sim \eta_2$, $x \in I$, and ϕ implies that for all y, $y > x$ and $\neg\phi$.*

Theorem 1. *Let (κ, υ, t) be a model, ϕ^3 a formula in RMTL-$\int_3$, and $f_t : \Phi^3 \to \Phi$ a mapping of formulas. Then $[(\kappa, \upsilon, t) \models_3 \phi^3] \prec [(\kappa, \upsilon, t) \models f_t(\phi^3)]$.*

4   Inequality Abstraction Using a Theory of Reals

A close examination of the semantics of RMTL-$\int_3$ reveals that the timed state sequence κ and the logic environment υ are not directly related as parameters for evaluating the truth value of formulas. This property allows us to define a mechanism for introducing isolation by splitting formulas and/or abstract them into inequality conditions. Conditions are discarded prior to execution, and the resulting formula is then suitable for runtime monitoring.

The axiom system for the arithmetic of real numbers provided by Tarski [19] can be used as an abstraction of inequalities in RMTL-$\int_3$. Several properties provided by this well-known fragment will be used to facilitate the removal of quantifiers, when properties expressed as quantified formulas are monitored at execution time. From the Tarski–Seidenberg theorem [19] we have that for any formula in FOL$_{\mathbb{R}}$ ($\mathbb{R}, <, +, \times$) there is an equivalent one not containing any existential quantifiers. Thus there exists a decision procedure for quantifier elimination over FOL$_{\mathbb{R}}$. One of the most efficient algorithms, with complexity 2-EXPTIME, is *cylindrical algebraic decomposition* (CAD), later proposed by Collins [3,6]. To use it we require a set of axioms for isolation of temporal operators and duration terms, and a mechanism to abstract formulas with free variables.

Let us now describe the constraint required for an RMTL-$\int_3$ formula to be interpreted as a formula of FOL$_{\mathbb{R}}$.

Definition 5 (Inequality Abstraction Constraint). *Let ϕ_3 be a formula in RMTL-$\int_3$. ϕ_3 is a formula in FOL$_{\mathbb{R}}$ if it is free of duration terms, minimum/maximum terms, temporal operators, and propositions.*

Let $\phi_<^i$ be a formula in FOL$_{\mathbb{R}}$; ϕ_i a formula in RMTL-$\int_3$ without quantifiers and free variables; op_i one of the operators $\wedge$ or $\vee$, and $i \in \mathbb{N}$ an index for operators/formulas. Axioms A3 and A4 below describe how formulas $\phi_<^i$ can be isolated outside the scope of the temporal operator. Axiom A5 replaces a formula containing a duration constrained in an interval by a duration term constrained by a logic variable. Axiom A6 isolates inequalities inside duration terms.

A 3. $\left(\left(\phi_<^1 \, op_1 \, \phi_1\right) \, U \, \left(\phi_<^2 \, op_2 \, \phi_2\right)\right) \rightarrow \left(\phi_<^2 \, op_2 \, \left(\neg(\phi_<^2) \rightarrow \left(\left(\phi_<^1 \, op_1 \, \phi_1\right) \, U \, \phi_2\right)\right)\right)$

A 4. $\left(\left(\phi_< \, op_1 \, \phi_1\right) \, U \, \phi_2\right) \rightarrow \left(\left(\phi_< \rightarrow true \, U \, \phi_2\right) op_1 \, \phi_1 \, U \, \phi_2\right)$

A 5. $\int^{\eta_x} \phi_1 \circ \eta_1 \sim \eta_2 \rightarrow \exists x \left(x = \eta_x \wedge \neg(x < 0) \wedge \int^x \phi_1 \circ \eta_1 \sim \eta_2\right)$

A 6. $\int^\eta \phi \vee \psi = \int^\eta \phi + \int^\eta \psi - \int^\eta \phi \wedge \psi$

These axioms can be used to provide isolation of formulas only for certain patterns, due to the changing nature of temporal operators and the duration terms over the model parameter t. To abstract any formula in RMTL-$\int_3$ into a formula in FOL$_\mathbb{R}$ compliant with Definition 5, we require an algorithm for generating weaker inequality conditions. Algorithm 1 can be used to replace duration terms with new free variables constrained by the nature of those terms, and propositions with fixed valued logic variables (e.g., $p = 1$ means that the proposition P is true in a certain interval). It begins by testing if a formula contains free logic variables and existential quantifiers. If the formula can be simplified we proceed, otherwise we return the input formula ϕ_3 (Line 2). Next, the duration terms are recursively replaced by new fresh variables in υ, minimum and maximum terms are transformed into quantified inequalities, and weaker inequality conditions are generated (Line 3). The function Reduce_MinMax_Terms applies min/max term substitutions as provided by Axioms A1, A2, and A5; and the auxiliary function Map_RMTLD3_into_FOLR abstracts formulas in RMTL-$\int_3$ into FOL$_\mathbb{R}$ formulas. It begins by replacing duration terms with new free variables (Line 7), and for each replaced term the same function is recursively applied (Line 12). The function Gen_Weaker_Inequality_Conditions generates the inequality conditions for temporal operators and duration terms using axioms A3, A4, A5, and A6. Let us now see an illustration of its functionality.

Require: a formula ϕ_3 in RMTL-$\int_3$
Ensure : a simplified formula ϕ_s with pre-calculated inequality conditions without min/max terms

```
1  Function Simplification_of_RMTLD3_Inequalities (φ₃) is
   begin
2      If Is_Variable_Free(Reduce_MinMax_Terms(φ₃)) then return φ₃;
3      map, φ< ← Map_RMTLD3_into_FOLR (Reduce_MinMax_Terms(φ₃));
4      φsimplified ← CAD(φ<);
5      return Reduce_Inequality_Conditions_into_RMTLD3(φsimplified, map);
   end

6  Function Map_RMTLD3_into_FOLR (φ) is
   begin
7      Smap, φr ← Replace_Duration_Terms(φ);
8      φsmp ← true; Sumap ← ∅;
9      for fmap ∈ Smap do
       begin
10         φf, ηf ← get φ and η from fmap = ∫ⁿ φ;
11         φη ← Gen_Weaker_Inequality_Conditions(φr, fmap);
12         m, φ<s ← Map_RMTLD3_into_FOLR (φf);
13         φsmp ← φsmp ∧ (φη ∧ φ<s)
14         Sumap ← Sumap ∪ m;
       end
15     return Smap ∪ Sumap, (φr ∧ φsmp)
   end
```

Algorithm 1. Simplification of RMTL-$\int_3$ Inequalities

Example 2. Consider the duration term $0 < \int^{10} P \vee \phi_<$. The result of applying the function `Replace_Duration_Terms` to this term is $0 < x$. Applying axiom A6 over the formula, and knowing the sub-formula $\phi_f := P \vee \phi_<$ and the sub-term $\eta_f := 10$, results in $x = b + c - a$ and then $0 + \int^{10} P \wedge \phi_< < \int^{10} P + \int^{10} \phi_<$. Now we are able to generate the weaker conditions. They are $(\phi_< \rightarrow (c = 10 \wedge a = b))$ and $(\neg \phi_< \rightarrow c = 0 \wedge a = 0 \wedge ((p = 0 \rightarrow b = 0) \wedge (p = 1 \rightarrow 0 < b)))$ with $a, b, c \in [0, 10[$ and $p \in \{0, 1\}$.

After this step we have the inequality conditions ready to be simplified using the CAD technique (Line 4). The formula that was decomposed can then be reduced or recursively replaced with the terms initially found in the original formula (Line 5). Note that the function `Gen_Weaker_Inequality_Conditions` is not formally described; we assume the existence of mechanisms for application of the axioms and for calculating the weaker inequality conditions.

Example 3. Let us now see a practical application of the algorithm for a simple formula. Consider the formula $x < \int^{x+1} (P \wedge x < 10)$, with P a proposition whose truth value depends on the model parameter t. Since the logic variable x is used at the level of the relation operator of the formula and in the duration term, finding a valuation of x that satisfies the formula is not trivial; we can use our algorithm that generates inequality conditions and reduce the latter conditions into an RMTL-$\int_3$ formula. We begin by replacing $\int^{x+1} (P \wedge x < 10)$ by y and constraining it by the formula $\phi_s := x < y \wedge 0 \le y \le x + 1$; replacing proposition P by $p = 1$ we get: $\phi_s := \phi_s \wedge (x < 10) \rightarrow \left(p = 0 \rightarrow \left(x < \int^{x+1} P \le x + 1 \right) \right) \wedge \neg (x < 10) \rightarrow$ ff. After simplification of ϕ_s using CAD we have $y = 0 \wedge (z = 0 \vee (0 < z \le x + 1 \wedge p = 1))) \vee (0 < y \le x + 1 \wedge 0 < z \le x + 1 \wedge p = 1)$ if $x \in [-1, 0[$; and $(x < y \le x + 1 \wedge x < z \le x + 1 \wedge p = 1)$ if $x \in [0, 10[$. After applying the function `Reduce_Inequality_Conditions_into_RMTLD3`, the free logic variables are recursively substituted following the structure of the formula, with the exception of x that remains unchanged. In the case that x is substituted by a duration term then we have a decision procedure to compute the truth value of the term based on the outcome of the procedure; if x has not been replaced by a duration term and x is not quantified then we need to quantify it explicitly, otherwise the formula cannot be evaluated. Note that $\forall x \, \phi_s \leftrightarrow$ ff and $\exists x \, \phi_s \leftrightarrow$ tt.

5   Computation of RMTL-$\int_3$ Formulae

Given the definition of RMTL-$\int_3$, we can derive an evaluation algorithm for monitor synthesis. In what follows we will present the algorithm and study the time complexity of the computation with respect to both trace and formula size.

We begin with a set of preliminary definitions. The set of timed sequences is denoted by **K**, the duration of the timed state sequence $\kappa \in \mathbf{K}$ is denoted by $d^{(\kappa)}$, and the set of logic environments is denoted by Υ. Let $\mathbf{B}_4$ be the set $\{tt_4, ff_4, \bot_4\} \cup \{\mathfrak{r}\}$ where $\mathfrak{r}$ is a new symbol that will be used only for purposes of formulae evaluation, and **D** the set $\mathbb{R}_{\ge 0} \cup \{\bot_R\}$. The function $sub_\mathbf{K} : (\mathbf{K} \times$

$\Upsilon \times \mathbb{R}_{\geq 0}) \to \mathbb{R}_{\geq 0} \to \mathbf{K}$ defines a timed sub-sequence constrained by the interval $]t, t + \gamma]$, where t and γ are real numbers to be used as parameters in $sub_{\mathbf{K}}$. The function $map^{\mathbf{B}_4} : \mathbb{B}_3 \to \mathbf{B}_4$ maps tt to tt$_4$, ff to ff$_4$ and $\bot$ to $\bot_4$; $map^{\mathbb{B}_3} :$ $\mathbb{B} \times \mathbf{B}_4 \to \mathbb{B}_3$ maps (tt, r) to $\bot$; (ff, r), (ff, ff$_4$), and (tt, ff$_4$) to ff; and (ff, tt$_4$) and (tt, tt$_4$) to tt. We will employ a left $fold$ function defined in the usual way.

From close examination of the operators, the corresponding Compute$_{(\neg)}$ and Compute$_{(\vee)}$ evaluation functions have time complexity constant in the number of timed sequence symbols, and linear in the size of the formula. Let us consider the functions Compute$_{(\eta)} :: (\mathbf{K} \times \Upsilon) \to \mathbb{R} \to \Gamma \to \mathbf{D}$ and Compute$_{\varphi} :: (\mathbf{K} \times \Upsilon \times \mathbb{R}_{\geq 0}) \to \Phi^3 \to \mathbb{B}_3$ for the evaluation of $U_<$ and $<$, and the term $\int$.

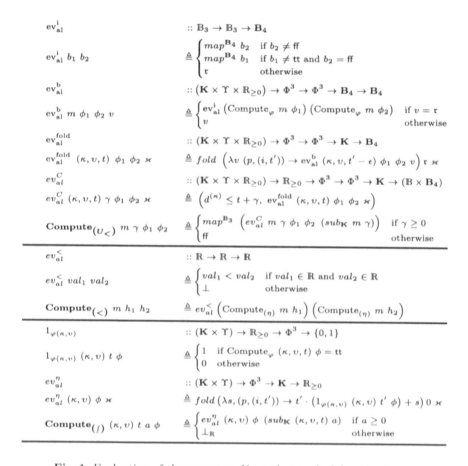

Fig. 1. Evaluation of the operators $U_<$ and $<$, and of duration terms

Operator $U_<$. Given formulas ϕ_1, ϕ_2 and $\gamma \in \mathbb{R}_{\geq 0}$, the formula $\phi_1 U_{<\gamma} \phi_2$ is evaluated in a model (κ, υ, t) by the function Compute$_{(U_<)} :$ $(\mathbf{K} \times \Upsilon \times \mathbb{R}_{\geq 0}) \to \mathbb{R}_{\geq 0} \to \Phi^3 \to \Phi^3 \to \mathbb{B}_3$, defined in Fig. 1. We report here only on the computation function $\text{Compute}_{(U_<)}$; the remaining functions would be $\text{Compute}_{(U_=)}$ for punctual until, $\text{Compute}_{(S_<)}$ for the non-punctual dual operator, and $\text{Compute}_{(S_=)}$ for the punctual dual operator. These operators have at most two new branches. Given an input κ with size n_κ, and m a measure of the number of temporal operators in φ, we obtain from the structure of the computation the lower bound of time complexity $2(n_\kappa)^2 \cdot m(\varphi) - 4(n_\kappa)^2 + n_\kappa \cdot m(\varphi) - 2(n_\kappa)$.

Operator $<$. Given two terms $\eta_1, \eta_2 \in \Gamma$, the formula $\eta_1 < \eta_2$ is evaluated relative to a model (κ, υ, t) by the function $\text{Compute}_{(<)} : (\mathbf{K} \times \Upsilon \times \mathbb{R}_{\geq 0}) \rightarrow \Gamma \rightarrow \Gamma \rightarrow \mathbb{B}_3$, also shown in Fig. 1. The time complexity of this computation is constant, since any formula containing only the relation operator $<$ cannot have the size of the formula greater than one or consume any input symbols.

Term $\int$. The evaluation of a duration term $\int^a \phi$ in the model (κ, υ, t) is performed by the function $\text{Compute}_{(\int)} : (\mathbf{K} \times \Upsilon) \rightarrow \mathbb{R}_{\geq 0} \rightarrow \mathbb{R} \rightarrow \Phi^3 \rightarrow \mathbf{D}$, again defined in Fig. 1. It has linear time complexity in the size of the timed sequence, and constant time complexity in the formula size. $+$ and $\times$ terms are directly mapped into their respective computational operations. The complexity of those operations is directly related to the number of terms. Given a formula φ and a measure m_η describing the number of operators $+$ and $\times$ occurring in a formula φ, we have a linear lower bound of time complexity in $m_\eta(\varphi)$.

Function $\text{Compute}_{(\eta)}$ (κ, υ) t $h :: (\mathbf{K} \times \Upsilon) \rightarrow \mathbb{R} \rightarrow \Gamma \rightarrow \mathbf{D}$ **is**

    case h **of**

α	:	$eval_\alpha\ \alpha$
$h_1 + h_2$	:	$\left(\text{Compute}_{(\eta)}\ m\ h_1\right) + \left(\text{Compute}_{(\eta)}\ m\ h_2\right)$
$h_1 \times h_2$	:	$\left(\text{Compute}_{(\eta)}\ m\ h_1\right) \times \left(\text{Compute}_{(\eta)}\ m\ h_2\right)$
$\int^{h_1} \phi$	:	$\text{Compute}_{(\int)}\ (\kappa, \upsilon)\ t\ \left(\text{Compute}_{(\eta)}\ (\kappa, \upsilon)\ t\ h_1\right)\ \phi$

    end

end

Function Compute_φ m $\phi :: (\mathbf{K} \times \Upsilon \times \mathbb{R}_{\geq 0}) \rightarrow \Phi^3 \rightarrow \mathbb{B}_3$ **is**

    case ϕ **of**

p	:	$eval_p\ m\ p$	– base case
$\neg\phi$	:	$\text{Compute}_{(\neg)}\ m\ \phi$	– Boolean operators
$\phi_1 \vee \phi_2$	:	$\text{Compute}_{(\vee)}\ m\ \phi_1\ \phi_2$	
$\phi_1\ U_{<\gamma}\ \phi_2$	:	$\text{Compute}_{(U_<)}\ m\ \gamma\ \phi_1\ \phi_2$	– temporal operators
$\phi_1\ S_{<\gamma}\ \phi_2$	:	$\text{Compute}_{(S_<)}\ m\ \gamma\ \phi_1\ \phi_2$	
$\eta_1 < \eta_2$	:	$\text{Compute}_{(<)}\ m\ \eta_1\ \eta_2$	– relational operator

    end

end

Algorithm 2. Computation of RMTL-$\int_3$ formulas (Compute_φ)

Time Complexity of the Evaluation Algorithm. We are now in a position to present the recursive top-level evaluation Algorithm 2 excluding *punctual* temporal operators, using the previous definitions for auxiliary computations. Let m be a measure for $\vee$, $<$, temporal operators, and non-rigid terms. Given the complexity of these formulas and term operators, and knowing that all temporal operators have the same complexity as the until operator, we have by semantic definition that any combination of formulas has higher complexity. As such, the complexity of Algorithm 2 is polynomial in the input size of the formula and the timed state sequence, as given by the lower bound identified above.

6   Experiments

Our approach uses an offline algorithm for formula simplification, and an online evaluation procedure that can be directly applied for the synthesis of runtime monitors. We will now show an example of application of Algorithm 1 for monitoring the budget of a set of *resource model* (RMs); then we will present the empirical validation of the complexity results for Algorithm 2.

RMs are mechanisms to ensure time isolation between tasks. In the case of periodic RMs [18], they are defined by a replenishment period and a budget supply. The budget supply is available as time passes, and is replenished at each period by the resource model. Elastic periodic RMs are resource models containing *elastic coefficients* (similar to spring coefficients in physics), describing how a task can be compressed when the system is overloaded, allowing RV of imprecise computation. Naturally, the coefficients need to be constrained (linearly or non-linearly) before execution. Intuitively, the idea is to check the coefficients according to the polynomial constraints using our static phase, and provide the simplified formulas for the further runtime evaluation phase.

Let us now extend Example 1 for multiple RMs, considering without loss of generality the case of two RMs. We will use indexed formulas ϕ_{m_i}, ψ_{m_i} with $0 \leq i < 2$, and let α_i, α_{ai} be pre-defined constants. For measuring their budgets we could use the following invariant:

$$\bigwedge_{i=0}^{n-1} \phi_{m_i} \wedge \Box_{<\infty^*} \left(\left(\bigwedge_{i=0}^{n-1} \phi_{m_i} \right) \rightarrow \left(0 \leq \sum_{i=0}^{n-1} c_i \times \int^{\alpha_i} \psi_{m_i} < \alpha_b \wedge r_m \wedge \Diamond_{=\pi} \bigwedge_{i=0}^{n-1} \phi_{m_i} \right) \right),$$

where c_i are coefficients that have different weights for each RM, compliant with the restrictions r_m constrained in the interval $[0, \alpha_b[, \alpha_b \in \mathbb{R}_{\geq 0}$, and $\bigwedge_{i=0}^{n-1} \phi_{m_i}$ corresponds to the periodic release of the RMs with period π. A more detailed description can be found in [12]. The problem is then to find values for c_1, c_2 satisfying the constraints $r_1 := \frac{1}{250}(245 - 444x + 200c_1{}^2) = c_2$, $r_2 := 1 - c_1 = c_2$, or $r_3 := 1 - c_1{}^2 = c_2$, as shown in Fig. 2, based on two duration observations over ψ_{m_i} formulas.

We will use Algorithm 1 for discarding possible inconsistencies, and decompose the formulas into subformulas that are free of quantifiers. Let us simplify the previously defined invariant for two resource models where the coefficient c_0 is existentially quantified and constrained by r_2. After some transformations on the formula we obtain

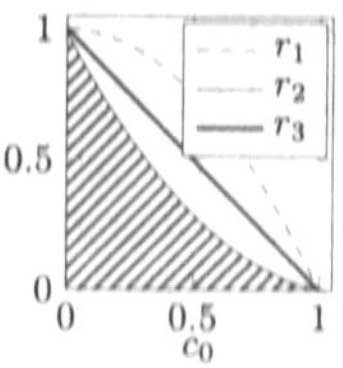

Fig. 2. Inequality constraints

$$\phi^1_{\nleqslant} := \phi_{m_0} \wedge \phi_{m_1} \wedge \neg (\text{tt}\, U_{<\infty^*} ((\phi_{m_0} \wedge \phi_{m_1} \wedge \neg \Diamond_{=\pi} (\phi_{m_0} \wedge \phi_{m_1})) \vee (\phi_{m_0} \wedge \phi_{m_1} \wedge \neg \phi^1_{<}))),$$

such that $\phi^1_{<} := \exists c_0\, 0 \leq c_0 \times a + c_1 \times b < \alpha_b \wedge 1 - c_0 = c_1 \wedge c_0 \geq 0 \wedge c_1 \geq 0$ holds. Duration terms have been replaced by the logic variables a and b. Since Axioms

A3 and A4 cannot be used here for isolation purposes, we have to substitute the inequality formula by a constant Θ. We will then have an isolated formula, and apply CAD to determine if $\phi^1_<$ is satisfied. If it is, then we directly replace Θ by tt, otherwise we have the bounds that satisfy $\phi^1_<$. For this case, we obtain $(a = 0 \wedge b \geq 10 \wedge 0 \leq c_1 < \frac{10}{b}) \vee (a = 0 \wedge 0 \leq b < 10 \wedge 0 \leq c_1 \leq 1) \vee (a \geq 10 \wedge \frac{a-10}{a-b} < c_1 \leq 1 \wedge 0 \leq b < 10) \vee (b \geq 10 \wedge 0 < a \wedge a < 10 \wedge 0 \leq c_1 < \frac{a-10}{a-b}) \vee (0 < a < 10 \wedge 0 \leq b < 10 \wedge 0 \leq c_1 \leq 1)$. This is applied recursively for all the terms that have been substituted by fresh logic variables. In this particular case there are no subsequent iterations. After these steps the simplified bounds are ready to be evaluated by the online method.

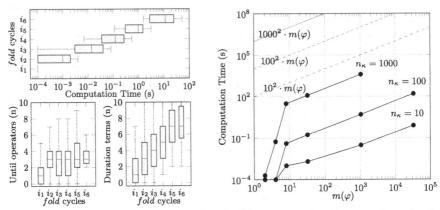

(a) computation time vs. execution cycles of fold functions, $m(\varphi) = 2^5 - 1$ and $n_\kappa = 1000$

(b) computation time vs. formula size constructed with nested Until operators

Fig. 3. Experimental validation of the complexity results

Let us now discuss the complexity of Algorithm 2 and establish an empirical comparison with the lower bounds presented previously. We observe that the generation of nested durations is more critical on average than the nesting of temporal operators. This result matches the semantics of both terms and formulas, since the duration terms can integrate any indicative function provided for any trace, unlike the until operator that requires a successful trace to maximize its search. Consider Fig. 3a, where the boxes i_1 to i_6 are respectively the intervals $]10^j, 10^{j+1}]$ for all $j \in [1, 7[$. They represent the number of cycles performed by folding functions. The results confirm that as the number of until operators stabilizes and the number of duration operators increases, the computation time also increases at a higher rate due to the presence of durations. This occurs for *generated* uniform formulas and traces; deep nesting of until operators and nested durations is unlikely to occur in hand-written specifications (it has not been clearly confirmed whether they are useful for real-life applications). The experiments confirm the theoretical complexity bounds obtained earlier (Fig. 3b). We have performed the experiments on an Intel Core i3-3110M at 2.40 GHz CPU, and 8 GB RAM running Fedora 21 X86'64; the source code is available from the first author's web page.

7 Discussion and Future Work

We have developed a new approach for the RV of hard real-time systems, where duration properties play an important role, and incremental evaluation is required. The closest approaches to ours are that of Nickovic and colleagues [13], who provide synthesis algorithms for MTL specifications, and the work of Pike and colleagues [16], who have developed a framework based on a formal stream language, together with a synthesis mechanism that generates monitors. However, none of these previous approaches is sufficiently expressive to allow reasoning about duration properties, which is the novelty of our work.

The first level of operation of our approach consists of offline analysis for the simplification of formulas by means of quantifier removal techniques; the second is an online evaluation algorithm for RV purposes. We restrict syntactically and semantically the two-valued MTL-$\int$ logic, with a three-valued interpretation. Incremental evaluation allows our technique to handle millions of samples, with formulas containing hundreds of operators. It remains to be seen whether extensions of LTL that are strictly more expressive than MTL, such as TPTL [4] could be used as an alternative for dealing with durations.

Acknowledgments. This work was partially supported by National Funds through FCT/MEC (Portuguese Foundation for Science and Technology), co-financed by ERDF (European Regional Development Fund) under the PT2020 Partnership, within project UID/CEC/04234/2013 (CISTER); by FCT/MEC and the EU ARTEMIS JU within project ARTEMIS/0001/2013 - JU grant nr. 621429 (EMC2).

References

1. Alur, R., Feder, T., Henzinger, T.A.: The benefits of relaxing punctuality. J. ACM **43**(1), 116–146 (1996)
2. Alur, R., Henzinger, T.A.: Logics and models of real time: a survey. In: Huizing, C., de Bakker, J.W., Rozenberg, G., de Roever, W.-P. (eds.) REX 1991. LNCS, vol. 600, pp. 74–106. Springer, Heidelberg (1992)
3. Basu, S., Pollack, R., Roy, M.F.: Algorithms in Real Algebraic Geometry. Algorithms and Computation in Mathematics. Springer, Heidelberg (2006)
4. Bouyer, P., Chevalier, F., Markey, N.: On the expressiveness of TPTL and MTL. Inf. Comput. **208**(2), 97–116 (2010)
5. Bouyer, P., Markey, N., Ouaknine, J., Worrell, J.B.: On expressiveness and complexity in real-time model checking. In: Aceto, L., Damgård, I., Goldberg, L.A., Halldórsson, M.M., Ingólfsdóttir, A., Walukiewicz, I. (eds.) ICALP 2008, Part II. LNCS, vol. 5126, pp. 124–135. Springer, Heidelberg (2008)
6. Collins, G.E.: Quantifier elimination for real closed fields by cylindrical algebraic decomposition: a synopsis. SIGSAM Bull. **10**(1), 10–12 (1976)

7. Gordon, R.A.: The Integrals of Lebesgue. Denjoy, Perron, and Henstock. Graduate studies in mathematics. American Mathematical Society, Providence (1994)
8. Hansen, M.R., Van Hung, D.: A theory of duration calculus with application. In: George, C.W., Liu, Z., Woodcock, J. (eds.) Domaine Modeling. LNCS, vol. 4710, pp. 119–176. Springer, Heidelberg (2007)
9. Huth, M., Ryan, M.: Logic in Computer Science: Modelling and Reasoning About Systems. Cambridge University Press, New York (2004)
10. Koymans, R.: Specifying real-time properties with metric temporal logic. Real-Time Syst. $2(4)$, 255–299 (1990)
11. Lakhneche, Y., Hooman, J.: Metric temporal logic with durations. Theor. Comput. Sci. $138(1)$, 169–199 (1995)
12. Pedro, A.M., Pereira, D., Pinho, L.M., Pinto, J.S.: Logic-based schedulability analysis for compositional hard real-time embedded systems. SIGBED Rev. $12(1)$, 56–64 (2015)
13. Ničković, D., Piterman, N.: From MTL to deterministic timed automata. In: Chatterjee, K., Henzinger, T.A. (eds.) FORMATS 2010. LNCS, vol. 6246, pp. 152–167. Springer, Heidelberg (2010)
14. Ouaknine, J., Worrell, J.B.: Safety metric temporal logic is fully decidable. In: Hermanns, H., Palsberg, J. (eds.) TACAS 2006. LNCS, vol. 3920, pp. 411–425. Springer, Heidelberg (2006)
15. Ouaknine, J., Worrell, J.B.: Some recent results in metric temporal logic. In: Cassez, F., Jard, C. (eds.) FORMATS 2008. LNCS, vol. 5215, pp. 1–13. Springer, Heidelberg (2008)
16. Pike, L., Goodloe, A., Morisset, R., Niller, S.: Copilot: a hard real-time runtime monitor. In: Barringer, H., Falcone, Y., Finkbeiner, B., Havelund, K., Lee, I., Pace, G., Roşu, G., Sokolsky, O., Tillmann, N. (eds.) RV 2010. LNCS, vol. 6418, pp. 345–359. Springer, Heidelberg (2010)
17. Pnueli, A.: The temporal logic of programs. SFCS 1977, pp. 46–57. IEEE Computer Society, Washington (1977)
18. Shin, I., Lee, I.: Periodic resource model for compositional real-time guarantees. RTSS 2003, pp. 2-13. IEEE Computer Society, Washington (2003)
19. Tarski, A.: Introduction to Logic and to the Methodology of Deductive Sciences. Dover Books on Mathematics Series. Dover Publications, New York (1995)

Runtime Verification Through Forward Chaining

Alan Perotti[1]([⊠]), Guido Boella[1], and Artur d'Avila Garcez[2]

[1] University of Turin, Turin, Italy
{perotti,boella}@di.unito.it
[2] City University London, London, England
a.garcez@city.ac.uk

Abstract. In this paper we present a novel rule-based approach for Runtime Verification of FLTL properties over finite but expanding traces. Our system exploits Horn clauses in implication form and relies on a forward chaining-based monitoring algorithm. This approach avoids the branching structure and exponential complexity typical of tableaux-based formulations, creating monitors with a single state and a fixed number of rules. This allows for a fast and scalable tool for Runtime Verification: we present the technical details together with a working implementation.

1 Introduction

We are designing a framework for combining runtime verification and learning in neural networks to improve the verification of compliance of systems based on business processes [15]. By adapting formal specifications of such systems to include tolerable soft-violations occurring in real-practice to optimise the systems, we want to obtain a more realistic representation of compliance. Adaptation is the recent trend in Process Mining [18]: the goal is to discover, monitor and improve real processes (i.e., not assumed processes) by extracting knowledge from event logs readily available in todays (information) systems. Within this wider framework, this paper focuses on the introduction of a novel monitoring system, RuleRunner, built as a set of Horn clauses in implication form and exploiting forward chaining to perform runtime verification tasks. A RuleRunner system can be encoded in a recurrent neural network exploiting results from the Neural-Symbolic Integration [5] area, but this is outside the scope of this paper.

This paper is structured as follows: Sect. 2 introduces background and related work, while Sect. 3 provides a technical introduction of our rule system. Section 4 provides experimental results and Sect. 5 ends the paper with final considerations and directions for future work.

This research was supported by the ITxLaw project funded by Compagnia di San Paolo.

© Springer International Publishing Switzerland 2015
E. Bartocci and R. Majumdar (Eds.): RV 2015, LNCS 9333, pp. 185–200, 2015.
DOI: 10.1007/978-3-319-23820-3_12

2   Background and Related Work

2.1   Horn Clauses and Chaining

A Horn clause [9] is a clause which contains at most one positive literal. The general format of such a clause is thus as follows: $\neg\alpha_1 \vee .. \vee \neg\alpha_n \vee \beta$. This may be rewritten as an implication: $(\alpha_1 \wedge .. \wedge \alpha_n) \rightarrow \beta$, where β is called *head* and $(\alpha_1 \wedge .. \wedge \alpha_n)$ is called *body*. The two formulations are equivalent, and usually the former is called *disjunctive form* and the latter *implication form*. Horn clauses are used for knowledge representation and automatic reasoning; in particular, inference with Horn clauses can be done through backward or forward chaining. Backward chaining algorithms are goal-driven approaches that work their way from a given goal or query; it is implemented in logic programming (e.g. in Prolog) by SLD resolution [19]. Forward chaining is a data-driven approach that starts with the available data and uses inference rules to extract more data until a goal is reached; it is a popular implementation strategy for production rule systems [11].

2.2   Runtime Verification

Runtime Verification (RV) relates an observed system with a formal property ϕ specifying some desired behaviour. An RV module, or monitor, is defined as a device that reads a trace and yields a certain verdict [12]. A trace is a sequence of cells, which in turn are sets of observations occurring in a given discrete span of time. Runtime verification may work on finite (terminated), finite but continuously expanding, or on prefixes of infinite traces. While LTL is a standard semantic for infinite traces [17], there are many semantics for finite traces: FLTL [13], RVLTL [2], LTL3 [3], LTL± [7] just to name some. Since LTL semantics is based on infinite behaviours, the issue is to close the gap between properties specifying infinite behaviours and finite traces. In particular, FLTL differs from LTL as it offers two *next* operators ($X, \bar{X}$ in [2], X, W in this paper), called respectively *strong* and *weak* next. Intuitively, the strong (and standard) X operator is used to express with $X\phi$ that a next state must exist and that this next state has to satisfy property ϕ. In contrast, the weak W operator in $W\phi$ says that if there is a next state, then this next state has to satisfy the property ϕ. More formally, let $u = a_0 .. a_{n-1}$ denote a finite trace of length n. The truth value of an FLTL formula ψ (either $X\phi$ or $W\phi$) w.r.t. u at position $i < n$, denoted by $[u, i \vDash \psi]$, is an element of $\mathbb{B}$ and is defined as follows:

$$[u, i \vDash X\phi] = \begin{cases} [u, i+1 \vDash \phi], & \text{if } i+1 < n \\ \bot, & \text{otherwise} \end{cases} \qquad [u, i \vDash W\phi] = \begin{cases} [u, i+1 \vDash \phi], & \text{if } i+1 < n \\ \top, & \text{otherwise} \end{cases}$$

While RVLTL and LTL3 have been proven to hold interesting properties w.r.t. FLTL (see [2]), we selected FLTL as we think it captures a more intuitive semantics when dealing with finite traces. Suppose to monitor $\phi = \Box a$ over a trace t, where a is observed in all cells: we have that $[t \vDash \phi]$ equals, respectively,

$\top$ in FLTL, ? in LTL3, and T^p in RVLTL. If t is seen as a prefix of a longer trace $t\sigma$, then LTL3 and RVLTL provide valuable information about how ϕ could be evaluated over σ. But if t is a conclusive, self-contained trace (e.g. a daily set of transactions), then the FLTL semantics captures the intuitive positive answer to the query *does a always hold in this trace?*

Several RV systems have been developed, and they can be clustered in three main approaches, based respectively on rewriting, automata and rules [12]. Within rule based approaches, RuleR [1] uses an original approach. It copes with the temporal dimension by introducing rules which may reactivate themselves in later stages of the reasoning, and RuleRunner is inspired by this powerful idea. However, RuleR rules may contain disjunctions in the head and therefore do not correspond to Horn clauses. Furthermore, RuleR creates alternative *observations expectations*, and therefore the application of forward-chaining inference mechanisms on a RuleR system creates a branching, Kripke-like *possible world structure* [10]. We focus on FLTL and encode each formula in a system of rules that correspond to Horn clauses and therefore allow to apply forward-chaining inference algorithms. The next section will describe the difference in the two approaches in more detail.

3   The RuleRunner Rule System

RuleRunner is a rule-based online monitor observing finite but expanding traces and returning an FLTL verdict. RuleRunner accepts formulae ϕ generated by the grammar:

$$\phi ::= true \mid a \mid !a \mid \phi \vee \phi \mid \phi \wedge \phi \mid \phi U \phi \mid X\phi \mid W\phi \mid \Diamond\phi \mid \Box\phi$$

a is treated as an atom and corresponds to a single observation in the trace. We assume, without loss of generality, that temporal formulae are in negation normal form (NNF), e.g., negation operators pushed inwards to propositional literals and cancellations applied. W is the weak next operator. *END* is a special character that is added to the last cell of a trace to mark the end of the input stream.

Given an FLTL formula ϕ and a trace t, Algorithm 1 provides an abstract description of the creation and runtime behaviour of a RuleRunner system monitoring ϕ over t. At first, a monitor encoding ϕ is computed. Second, the monitor enters the verification loop, composed by observing a new cell of the trace and computing the truth value of the property in the given cell. If the property is irrevocably satisfied or falsified in the current cell, RuleRunner outputs a binary verdict. If this is not the case (because the ϕ refers to cells ahead in the trace), the system shifts to the following cell and enters another monitoring iteration. The FLTL semantics guarantees that, if the trace ends, the verdict in the last cell of the trace is binary. RuleRunner is a runtime monitor, as it analyses one cell at a time and never needs to store past cells in memory nor peek into future ones.

Algorithm 1. RuleRunner monitoring (abstract)

1: **function** RR-MONITORING(ϕ,trace t)
2:     Build a monitor RR_ϕ encoding ϕ
3:     **while** new cells exist in t **do**
4:         Observe the current cell
5:         Compute truth values of ϕ in the current cell of t ▷ Evaluation rules
6:         **if** ϕ is verified or falsified **then**
7:             **return** SUCCESS or FAILURE respectively
8:         **end if**
9:         Set up the monitor for the next cell in t ▷ Reactivation rules
10:     **end while**
11: **end function**

3.1   Building the Rule System

Definition. A RuleRunner system is a tuple $\langle R_E, R_R, S \rangle$, where R_E (*evaluation rules*) and R_R (*reactivation rules*) are rule sets, and S (for *state*) is a set of active rules, observations and truth evaluations.

Throughout this paper we mostly use the terms *State* and *rule*, as they are used in the Runtime Verification area. However, our rules correspond to Horn clauses in implication form, and what we call *State* corresponds to a *knowledge base*.

Given a finite set of observations O and an FLTL formula ϕ over (a subset of) O, a state S is a set of observations ($o \in O$), rule names ($R[\psi]$) and truth evaluations ($[\psi]V$); $V \in \{T, F, ?\}$ is a truth value. A rule name $R[\psi]$ in S means that the logical formula ψ is under scrutiny, while a truth evaluation $[\psi]V$ means that the logical formula ψ currently has the truth value V. The third truth value, $?$ (*undecided*), means that it is impossible to give a binary verdict in the current cell.

Evaluation rules follow the pattern $R[\phi], [\psi^1]V, \ldots, [\psi^n]V, \to [\phi]V$ and their role is to compute the truth value of a formula ϕ under verification, given the truth values of its direct subformulae ψ^i (line 5 in Algorithm 1). For instance, $R[\Diamond\psi], [\psi]T \to [\Diamond\psi]T$ reads as *if $\Diamond\psi$ is being monitored and ψ holds, then $\Diamond\psi$ is true*.

Reactivation rules follow the pattern $[\phi]? \to R[\phi], R[\psi^1], \ldots, R[\psi^n]$ and the meaning is that if one formula is evaluated to undecided, that formula (together with its subformulae) is scheduled to be monitored again in the next cell of the trace (line 9 in Algorithm 1). For instance, $[\Diamond\psi]? \to R[\Diamond\psi], R[\psi]$ means that *if $\Diamond\psi$ was not irrevocably verified nor falsified in the current cell of the trace, both ψ and $\Diamond\psi$ will be monitored again in the next cell*.

Evaluation rules are Horn clauses in implication form. Reactivation rules usually have several positive conjuncts in the head, and therefore a reactivation rule $A \to \beta_1, ..\beta_n$ (where $A = \alpha_1, .., \alpha_m$) can be rewritten as n separate Horn clauses $A \to \beta_1, .., A \to \beta_n$. Having different rules with the same head is something to handle with care in case of backward chaining, as many inferential engines implement a depth-first search and therefore the order of these rules impacts on the result. This is not the case when applying forward chaining, as for all rules, if all the premises of the implication are known, then its conclusion is added to the set of known facts.

A RuleRunner feature is that rules never involve disjunctions. In RuleR, for instance, the simple formula $\Diamond a$ is mapped to the rule $R_{\Diamond a} : \longrightarrow a \mid R_{\Diamond a}$ and its meaning, intuitively, is that, if $\Diamond a$ has to be verified, either a is observed (thus satisfying the property) or the whole formula will be checked again (in the next cell of the trace). The same formula corresponds to the following set of rules in RuleRunner:

$$R[\Diamond a], [a]T \rightarrow [\Diamond a]T \qquad\qquad R[\Diamond a], [a]?, END \rightarrow [\Diamond a]F$$

$$R[\Diamond a], [a]? \rightarrow [\Diamond a]? \qquad\qquad [\Diamond a]? \rightarrow R[a], R[\Diamond a]$$

$$R[\Diamond a], [a]F \rightarrow [\Diamond a]?$$

The disjunction in the head of the RuleR rule corresponds to the additional constraints in the body of the RuleRunner rules. Therefore, where RuleR generates a set of alternative hypotheses and later matches them with actual observations, RuleRunner maintains a detailed state of exact information. This is achieved by means of evaluation tables: three-valued truth tables (as introduced by Lukasiewitz [14]) annotated with *qualifiers*. Each evaluation rule for ϕ corresponds to a single cell of the evaluation table for the main operator of ϕ; a *qualifier* is a subscript letter providing additional information to ? truth values. Table 1 gives the example for disjunction. Qualifiers $(B, L, R$ in this case) are used to store and propagate detailed information about the verification status of formulae.

Table 1. Truth table (left) and evaluation tables (right) for $\vee$

$\vee$	T	?	F
T	T	T	T
?	T	?	?
F	T	?	F

$\vee_B$	T	?	F
T	T	T	T
?	T	$?_B$	$?_L$
F	T	$?_R$	F

$\vee_L$	
T	T
?	$?_L$
F	F

$\vee_R$	
T	T
?	$?_R$
F	F

For instance, if ϕ is undecided and ψ is false when monitoring $\phi \vee \psi$ (highlighted cell in Table 1), $?_L$ means that the disjunction is undecided, but that its future verification state will depend on the truth value of the Left disjunct. Note, in fact, how $\vee_L$ is a unary operator. An example for this is monitoring $\Diamond b \vee a$ against a cell including only c: a is false, $\Diamond b$ is undecided (as b may be observed in the future), and the whole disjunction will be verified/falsified in the following cells depending on $\Diamond b$ only.

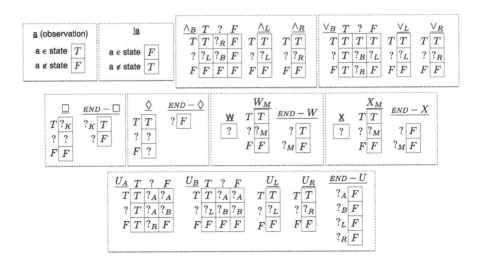

Fig. 1. Evaluation tables

The complete set of evaluation tables is reported in Fig. 1, while the generation of evaluation and reactivation rules is summarised in Algorithm 2. The algorithm parses ϕ in a tree and visits the parsing tree in post-order. The system is built incrementally, starting from the system(s) returned by the recursive call(s). If ϕ is an observation (or its negation), an initial system is created, including two evaluation rules (as the observation may or may not occur), no reactivation rules and the single $R[\phi]$ as initial state. If ϕ is a conjunction or disjunction, the two systems of the subformulae are merged, and the conjunction/disjunction evaluation rules, reactivation rule and initial activation are added. The computations are the same if the main operator is U, but the reactivation rule will have to reactivate the monitoring of the two subformulae; in particular, U_A denotes the standard *until* operator, while U_B is the particular case where the ψ failed and the *until* operator cannot be trivially satisfied anymore. Formulae with X or W as main operator go through two phases: first, the formula is evaluated to undecided, as the truth value can't be computed until the next cell is accessed.

Special evaluation rules force the truth value to false (for X) or true (for W) if no next cell exists. Then, at the next iteration, the reactivation rule triggers the subformula: this means that if $X\phi$ is monitored in cell i, ϕ is monitored in cell $i + 1$. ϕ is then monitored independently, and the $X\phi$ (or $W\phi$) rule enters a 'monitoring state' (suffix M in the table), simply mirroring ϕ truth value and self-reactivating. The evaluation of $\Box\phi$ is false (undecided) when ϕ is false (undecided); it is also undecided when ϕ holds (as $\Box\phi$ can never be true before the end of the trace), but the K suffix indicates when, at the end of the trace, an undecided $\Box$ can be evaluated to true. Finally, $\Diamond\phi$ constantly reactivates itself and its subformula ϕ, unless ϕ is verified at runtime (causing $\Diamond\phi$ to hold), the trace ends ($\Diamond\phi$ fails).

Algorithm 2. Generation of rules

```
 1: function INITIALISE(φ)
 2:     op ← main operator
                                          ▷ Apply recursively to subformula(e)
 3:     if op ∈ {□, ◊, X, W} then
 4:         ⟨R_E^1, R_R^1, S^1⟩ ← Initialise(ψ^1)
 5:         R_E ← R_E^1;
 6:         R_R ← R_R^1;
 7:     else if op ∈ {∨, ∧, U} then
 8:         ⟨R_E^1, R_R^1, S^1⟩ ← Initialise(ψ^1)
 9:         ⟨R_E^2, R_R^2, S^2⟩ ← Initialise(ψ^2)
10:         R_E ← R_E^1 ∪ R_E^2; R_R ← R_R^1 ∪ R_R^2;
11:     else
12:         R_E ← ∅; R_R ← ∅;
13:     end if
                              ▷ Compute and add evaluation rules for main operator
14:     Cells ←op's-evaluation-tables
15:     for all cell ∈ Cells do
16:         Convert cell to single rule r_e, substituting formula names
17:         R_E ← R_E ∪ r_e
18:     end for
19:     if φ-is-main-formula then
20:         R_E ← R_E ∪ ([φ]T → SUCCESS)
21:         R_E ← R_E ∪ ([φ]F → FAILURE)
22:         R_E ← R_E ∪ ([φ]? → REPEAT)
23:     end if
                                       ▷ Compute initial state for this subsystem
24:     if op = a then S ← R[a]
25:     else if op =!a then S ← R[!a]
26:     else if op ∈ {∨, ∧} then S ← S^1 ∪ S^2 ∪ R[φ]B
27:     else if op = U then S ← S^1 ∪ S^2 ∪ R[φ]A
28:     else if op ∈ {□, ◊} then S ← S^1 ∪ R[φ]
29:     else if op ∈ {X, W} then S ← R[φ]
30:     end if
                          ▷ Compute and add reactivation rules for main operator
31:     if op ∈ {∨, ∧} then R_R ← R_R ∪ ([φ]?Z → R[φ]?Z), for Z ∈ L, R, B
32:     else if op = U then R_R ← R_R ∪ ([φ]?Z → R[φ]?Z, S^1, S^2), for Z ∈ A, B, L, R
33:     else if op ∈ {□, ◊} then R_R ← R_R ∪ ([φ]? → R[φ], S^1)
34:     else if op ∈ {X, W} then R_R ← R_R ∪ ([φ]? → R[φ]M, S^1)∪([φ]?M → R[φ]M)
35:     end if
                                                       ▷ Return computed system
36:     return ⟨R_E, R_R, S⟩
37: end function
```

RuleRunner generates several rules for each operator, but this number is constant, as it corresponds to the size of evaluation tables plus special rules (like the SUCCESS one). The number of rules corresponding to $\phi \vee \psi$, for instance, does not depend in any way on the nature of ϕ or ψ, as only the final truth evaluation of the two subformulae is taken into account. The preprocessing phase creates the parse tree of the property to encode and adds a constant number of rules for each node (subformula), and therefore the size of the rule set is linear w.r.t. the structure of the encoded formula ϕ. The obtained rule set does not change at runtime nor when monitoring new traces.

3.2   Verification Through Forward Chaining

A RuleRunner rule system RR_ϕ encodes a FLTL formula ϕ in a set of rules. RR_ϕ can be used to check whether a given trace t verifies or falsifies ϕ. Given a set of Horn clauses in rule form R and a set of atoms A, let the $FC(\cdot)$ (Forward Chaining) function be:

$$FC(R, A) = \{\beta \mid (A_i \to \beta) \in R \ \wedge \ A_i \subseteq A\}$$

Algorithm 3 describes how RuleRunner exploits forward chaining to perform a runtime verification task. At the beginning, the rule system RR_ϕ is created. The monitoring loop iterates until $SUCCESS/FAILURE$ is computed, and the FLTL semantics guarantees this happen in the last cell, if reached. At the beginning of each iteration (corresponding to the monitoring of a cell), the initial state S contains a set of rule names corresponding to the subformulae to be checked in that cell. The observations of that cell are then added to the state of the system, and the state is incrementally expanded by means of forward chaining using the evaluation rules (line 7). This corresponds to computing the truth values of all subformulae of ϕ in a bottom-up way, from simple atoms to ϕ itself. If the monitoring did not compute a final verdict ($SUCCESS/FAILURE$), the state for the next cell is computed with a single application of $FC(\cdot)$ using the reactivation rules (line 12). Note that in this case the state is not expanded, as only the output of the forward chaining is stored ($S' \leftarrow S \cap FC(S, R_E)$ vs $S \leftarrow FC(S, R_R)$). This is used to *flush* all the previous truth evaluation, which are to be computed from scratch in the new cell.

During the runtime verification, for each cell, the $FC(\cdot)$ function is applied to the initial observations until the transitive closure of all evaluation rules is computed. The number of applications depends linearly on the encoded formula ϕ: at each iteration the truth values of new subformulae are added, proceeding bottom-up from atoms to ϕ. For instance, if $\phi = a \vee \Diamond b$, the first iteration would compute the truth values for a and b, the second would add to the state the truth evaluation for $\Diamond b$, and finally the third one would compute the truth value of ϕ in the current cell. Therefore, for each cell the number of iterations of $FC(\cdot)$ is linear w.r.t. the structure of ϕ. Each application of $FC(\cdot)$ depends on the number of rules and is again linear w.r.t. the structure of ϕ, as stated in the previous subsection. This would suggest a quadratic complexity. However, in our implementation, (for each cell of the trace) the system goes through all rules exactly once. This is obtained by the post-order visit of the parsing tree, as shown in Algorithm 2, assuring pre-emption for rules evaluating simpler formulae. Therefore, the complexity of the system is inherently linear. This is not

Algorithm 3. Runtime Verification using RR_ϕ

```
 1: function NN-MONITOR(φ,trace t)
 2:     Create RR_φ = ⟨R_R, R_E, S⟩ encoding φ (Algorithm 2)
 3:     while new observations exist in t do
 4:         S' ← S ∩ obs
 5:         while S ≠ S' do
 6:             S = S'
 7:             S' ← S ∩ FC(S, R_E)
 8:         end while
 9:         if S contains SUCCESS (resp.FAILURE) then
10:             return return SUCCESS (resp.FAILURE)
11:         end if
12:         S ← FC(S, R_R)
13:     end while
14: end function
```

in contrast with known exponential lower bounds for the temporal logic validity problem, as RuleRunner deals with the satisfiability of a property on a trace, thus tackling a different problem from the validity one (this distinction is also mentioned in [6]).

As an example, consider the formula $\phi = a \vee \Diamond b$ and the trace $t = [c - a - b, d - b, END]$ (dashes separate cells and commas separate observations in the same cell). Intuitively, ϕ means *either a now or b sometimes in the future*. If monitoring ϕ over t, a fails straight from the beginning, while b is sought until the third cell, when it is observed. Thus the monitoring yields a success even before the end of the trace.

In RuleRunner, for first, the formula ϕ is parsed into a tree, with $\vee$ as root and a, b as leaves. Then, starting from the leaves, evaluation and reactivation rules for each node are added to the (initially empty) rule system. In our example, (part of) the rule system obtained from ϕ, namely $RR_{(a \vee \Diamond b)}$, and its behaviour over t are the following:

EVALUATION RULES

- $R[a]$, a is not observed $\rightarrow [a]F$
- $R[b]$, b is observed $\rightarrow [b]T$
- $R[b]$, b is not observed $\rightarrow [b]F$
- $R[\Diamond b]$, $[b]T \rightarrow [\Diamond b]T$
- $R[\Diamond b]$, $[b]F \rightarrow [\Diamond b]?$
- $R[a \vee \Diamond b]B$, $[a]F$, $[\Diamond b]? \rightarrow [a \vee \Diamond b]?R$
- $R[a \vee \Diamond b]R$, $[\Diamond b]T \rightarrow [a \vee \Diamond b]T$
- $R[a \vee \Diamond b]R$, $[\Diamond b]? \rightarrow [a \vee \Diamond b]?R$
- $[a \vee \Diamond b]T \rightarrow SUCCESS$

REACTIVATION RULES

- $[\Diamond b]? \rightarrow R[b], R[\Diamond b]$
- $[a \vee \Diamond b]?R \rightarrow R[a \vee \Diamond b]R$

INITIAL STATE

- $R[a], R[b], R[\Diamond b], R[a \vee \Diamond b]B$

EVOLUTION OVER $[c - a - b, d - b, END]$

state	$R[a], R[b], R[\Diamond b], R[a \vee \Diamond b]B$
+ obs	$R[a], R[b], R[\Diamond b], R[a \vee \Diamond b]B, c$
eval	$[a]F, [b]F, [\Diamond b]?, [a \vee \Diamond b]?R$
react	$R[b], R[\Diamond b], R[a \vee \Diamond b]R$
state	$R[b], R[\Diamond b], R[a \vee \Diamond b]R$
+ obs	$R[b], R[\Diamond b], R[a \vee \Diamond b]R, a$
eval	$[b]F, [\Diamond b]?, [a \vee \Diamond b]?R$
react	$R[b], R[\Diamond b], R[a \vee \Diamond b]R$
state	$R[b], R[\Diamond b], R[a \vee \Diamond b]R$
+ obs	$R[b], R[\Diamond b], R[a \vee \Diamond b]R, b, d$
eval	$[b]T, [\Diamond b]T, [a \vee \Diamond b]T, SUCCESS$
STOP	PROPERTY SATISFIED

The behaviour of the runtime monitor is the following:

- At the beginning, the system monitors $a, b, \Diamond b$ and $a \vee \Diamond b$ (initial state $= R[a], R[b], R[\Diamond b], R[a \vee \Diamond b]B$). The $-B$ in $R[a \vee \Diamond b]B$ means that both disjuncts are being monitored.
- In the first cell, c is observed and added to the state S. Using the evaluation rules, new truth values are computed: a is false, b is false, $\Diamond b$ is undecided. The global formula is undecided, but since the trace continues the monitoring goes on. The $-R$ in $R[a \vee \Diamond b]R$ means that only the right disjunct is monitored: the system dropped a, since it could only be satisfied in the first cell.
- In the second cell, a is observed but ignored (the rules for its monitoring are not activated); since b is false again, $\Diamond b$ and $a \vee \Diamond b$ are still undecided.
- In the third cell, d is ignored but observing b satisfies, in cascade, b, $\Diamond b$ and $a \vee \Diamond b$. The monitoring stops, signalling a success. The rest of the trace is ignored.

3.3 Semantics

RuleRunner implements the FLTL [13] semantics; however, there are two main differences in the approach. Firstly, FLTL is based on rewriting judgements, and it has no constraints over the accessed cells, while RuleRunner is forced to complete the evaluation on a cell before accessing the next one. Secondly, FLTL proceeds top-down, decomposing the property and then verifying the observations; RuleRunner propagates truth values bottom up, from observations to the property. In order to show the correspondence between the two formalisms, we introduce the map function:

$$map : \text{Property} \rightarrow \text{FLTL judgement}$$

The map function translates the state of a RuleRunner system into a FLTL judgement, analysing the state of the RuleRunner system monitoring ϕ. Since $\Box$ and $\Diamond$ are derivate operators and they don't belong to FLTL specifications, we omit them from the discussion in this section.

```
function MAP(φ, State,index)
    if SUCCESS ∈ State then return ⊤
    else if FAILURE ∈ State then return
        ⊥
    else if [φ]T ∈ State then return ⊤
    else if [φ]F ∈ State then return ⊥
    else if [φ]?S ∈ State then aux ← S
    else find R[φ]S ∈ State; aux ← S
    end if
    if φ = a then
        return [u, index ⊨ a]_F
    else if φ = !a then
        return [u, index ⊨ ¬a]_F
    else if φ = ψ¹..ψ² and aux = L then
        return map(ψ¹)
    else if φ = ψ¹..ψ² and aux = R then
```

```
        return map(ψ²)
    else if φ = ψ¹ ∨ ψ² and aux = B then
        return map(ψ¹) ⊔ map(ψ²)
    else if φ = ψ¹ ∧ ψ² and aux = B then
        return map(ψ¹) ⊓ map(ψ²)
    else if φ = ψ¹Uψ² and aux = A then
        return  map(ψ²) ⊔ (map(ψ¹) ⊓
            (map(X(ψ¹Uψ²))))
    else if φ = ψ¹Uψ² and aux = B then
        return map(ψ²)⊓(map(X(ψ¹Uψ²)))
        next
    else if φ = Xψ and aux ≠ M then
        return [u, index ⊨ Xψ]_F
    else if φ = Wψ and aux ≠ M then
        return [u, index ⊨ X̄ψ]_F
```

```
else if (φ = Xψ or φ = Wψ) and aux =              end if
    M then                                     end function
    return map(ψ)
```

Theorem. *For any well-formed FLTL formula ϕ over a set of observations, and for every finite trace u, for every intermediate state s_i in RuleRunner's evolution over u there exist a valid rewriting r_j of $[u, 0 \models \phi]_F$ such that $map(\phi) = r_j$. In other words, RuleRunner's state can always be mapped onto an FLTL judgement over ϕ.*

Proof. The proof proceeds by induction on ϕ:

- $\phi = \mathbf{a}$

  If the formula is a simple observation, then the initial state is $R[a]$, and $map(R[a]) = [u, 0 \models a]_F$. Adding observation to the state does not change the resulting FLTL judgement. If a is observed, RuleRunner will add $[a]T$ to the state, and this will be mapped to $\top$. If a is not observed, RuleRunner will add $[a]F$ to the state, and this will be mapped to $\bot$. So for this simple case, the evolution of RuleRunner's state corresponds either to the rewriting $[u, 0 \models a]_F = \top$ (if a is observed) or to the rewriting $[u, 0 \models a]_F = \bot$ (if a is not observed).

- $\phi = !\mathbf{a}$

  This case is analogous tho the previous one, with opposite verdicts.

- $\phi = \psi^1 \vee \psi^2$

  By inductive hypothesis, a RuleRunner system monitoring ψ^1 always corresponds to a rewriting of $[u, i \models \psi^1]$. The same holds for ψ^2. Let $\langle R_R^i, R_E^i, S^i \rangle$ be RuleRunner system monitoring the subformula ψ^1, with $i \in \{1, 2\}$. A RuleRunner system encoding ϕ includes R^1 and R^2 rules and specific rules for $\psi^1 \vee \psi^2$ given the truth values of ψ^1 and ψ^2. The initial state is therefore $R[\psi^1 \vee \psi^2] \cup S^1 \cup S^2$, and this is mapped to $map(S^1) \sqcup map(S^2)$. By inductive hypothesis, this is a valid FLTL judgement. In each iteration, as long as the truth value of $\psi^1 \vee \psi^2$ is not computed, the state is mapped on $map(S^1) \sqcup map(S^2)$. When the propagation of truth values reaches $\psi^1 \vee \psi^2$, the assigned truth value mirrors the evaluation table for the disjunction. If either ψ^1 or ψ^2 is true, then ϕ is true, and $map(\phi) = \top$. This corresponds to the valid rewriting $map(S^1) \sqcup map(S^2) = \top$, given that we are considering the case in which there is a true ψ^i: $[\psi^i]T$ belongs to the state and $map(\psi^i) = \top$. The false-false case is analogous. In the $?_B$ case, the mapping is preserved, and this is justified by the fact that both ψ^1 and ψ^2 are undecided in the current cell, therefore $map(\psi^i) \neq \top, \bot$, therefore $map(\psi^1) \sqcup map(\psi^2)$ could not be simplified. In the $?_L$ case, we have that $[\psi^2]F$, therefore $map(\psi^2) = \bot$. The FLTL rewriting is $map(\psi^1) \sqcup map(\psi^2) = map(\psi^1)$, and this is a valid rewriting since $map(\psi^1) \sqcup map(\psi^2) = map(\psi^1) \sqcup \bot = map(\psi^1)$. The $?_R$ case is symmetrical.

- $\phi = \psi^1 \wedge \psi^2$

  Same as above, with the evaluation table for conjunction on the RuleRunner side and the $\sqcap$ operator on the FLTL judgement side.

- $\phi = \mathbf{X}\psi$

  A RuleRunner system encoding $X\phi$ has initial state $R[X\phi]$, which is mapped on $[u, 0 \models X\psi]_F$. Then, if the current cell is the last one, $R[X\phi]$ evaluates to $[X\phi]F$, and the corresponding FLTL judgement is $\bot$. If another cell exists, $R[X\phi]$ evaluates to $[X\phi]$? (with the same mapping). When the reactivation rules are triggered, $[X\phi]$? is substituted by $R[X\psi]M, R[\psi]$. Over this state, $map(X\psi) = map(\psi)$, and the index is incremented since reactivation rules were fired. Therefore, the FLTL rewriting is $[u, i \models X\psi] = [u, i + 1 \models \psi]$, and this is a valid rewriting.

- $\phi = \mathbf{W}\psi$

  This case is like the previous, but if the current cell is the last then $R[W\psi]$ evolves to $[W\psi]T$; the mapping is rewritten from $[u, i \models W\psi]$ to $\top$, and this is a valid rewriting if there is no next cell.

- $\phi = \psi^1 \mathbf{U}\psi^2$

  The initial RuleRunner system includes rules for ψ^1, ψ^2 and for the U operator. As long as $R[\psi^1 U\psi^2]A$ is not evalued, $map(\psi^1 U\psi^2) = map(\psi^2) \sqcup (map(\psi^1) \sqcap (map(X(\psi^1 U\psi^2))))$, that is, the standard one-step unfolding of the 'until' operator as defined in FLTL. When a truth value for the global property is computed, there are several possibilities. The first one is that ψ^2 is true and $\psi^1 U\psi^2$ is immediately satisfied. RuleRunner adds $[\psi^1 U\psi^2]T$ to the state and $map(\phi) = \top$; this corresponds to the rewriting $map(\psi^2) \sqcup (map(\psi^1) \sqcap (map(X(\psi^1 U\psi^2)))) = \top \sqcup (map(\psi^1) \sqcap (map(X(\psi^1 U\psi^2)))) = \top$, which is a valid rewriting. The case for $[\psi^1]F$ and $[\psi^2]F$ is analogous. The $?_A$ case means that the evaluation for the until is undecided in the current trace, and is mapped on the standard one-step unfolding of the until operator in FLTL. The $?_B$ case implicitly encode the information that 'the until cannot be trivially satisfied anymore', and henceforth the FLTL mapping is $map(\psi^1) \sqcap (map(X(\psi^1 U\psi^2)))$. The cases for $?_L$ and $?_R$ have the exact meaning they had in the disjunction and conjunction cases. For instance, if $[\psi^1]F$ and $[\psi^2]?$, RuleRunner adds $[\psi^1 U\psi^2]?R$ to the state, and for the obtained state $map(\phi) = map(\psi^2)$. The sequence of FLTL rewriting is $map(\psi^2) \sqcup (map(\psi^1) \sqcap (map(X(\psi^1 U\psi^2)))) = map(\psi^2) \sqcup (\bot \sqcap (map(X(\psi^1 U\psi^2)))) = map(\psi^2) \sqcup \bot = map(\psi^2)$.

Corollary. *RuleRunner yields a FLTL verdict.*

Proof. RuleRunner is always in a state that can be mapped on a valid FLTL judgement; therefore, when a binary truth evaluation for the encoded formula is given, this is mapped on the correct binary evaluation in FLTL. But since for such trivial case the *map* function corresponds to an identity, the RuleRunner evaluation is a valid FLTL judgement. The fact that RuleRunner yields a binary verdict is guaranteed provided that the analysed trace is finite, thanks to end-of-trace rules.

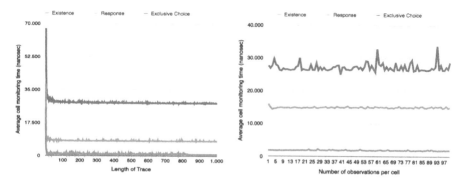

Fig. 2. Average monitoring time vs trace properties)

4   Experiments

In this paper we have described how to build RuleRunner monitors from FLTL formulae. The process is deterministic and the resulting monitor is guaranteed to compute the correct FLTL verdict. We autonomously implemented all the components described in this paper - an online tool is available at www.di.unito.it/~perotti/RuleRunner.jnlp. All experiments reported in this section were run on a 2014 MacBook Pro with a 2.6 GHz dual-core Intel Core i5 processor, 16 GB RAM and SSD SATA disk.

- We tested the impact of the trace length on the monitoring performance:
  - We took into account three Declare [16] patterns: *existence* ($\Diamond a$), *response* ($\Box(a \Rightarrow \Diamond b) \equiv \Box(!a \vee \Diamond b)$) and *exclusive choice* ($((\Diamond a \vee \Diamond b)\wedge!(\Diamond a \wedge \Diamond b) \equiv (\Diamond a \vee \Diamond b) \wedge (\Box!a \vee \Box!b))$).
  - We generated traces where a never occurs: this guarantees that the monitoring process always reaches the end of the trace.
  - We generated traces with an increasing number of cells, from 1 to 1000.
  - We measured the time required by RuleRunner to monitor each formula/trace combination.

  Figure 2(left) shows the average time required to monitor a single cell of a trace. The steep drop at the beginning of all curves is an overhead cost (input/output, etc.) being quickly averaged down by the increasing number of cells. Besides this initial effect, the graph shows how the average time required to monitor a cell is constant wrt. the length of the analysed trace: this behaviour is caused by the fact that RuleRunner keeps a single state rather than relying on a branching structure.

  With a similar setup, we tested the impact of the size of the observational alphabet, with analogous results (Fig. 2(right)).

- We performed tests aimed at evaluating the actual ratio between the complexity of a FLTL formula and the size of the resulting RuleRunner monitor:

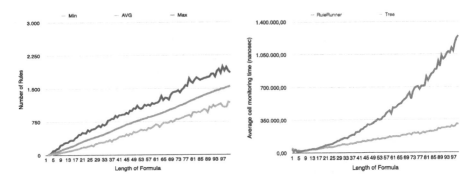

Fig. 3. Monitor size and monitoring time vs formula complexity

1. We took into account formulae ϕ with length spanning from 1 (observations) to 100.
2. For each length, we generated 1000 random FLTL formulae.
3. For each formula, we generated the RuleRunner monitor.
4. For each monitor, we measured the total number of generated rules.
5. For each set of same-length 1000 rules, we computed the minimum, maximum and average size of the resulting monitors.

The results (Fig. 3, left) show how, in fact, the number of rules in a RuleRunner monitor for ϕ is linear wrt. the size of ϕ.

- We analysed the impact of increasingly large monitors on the cell-averaged monitoring time:

1. We took into account formulae ϕ with length spanning from 1 (observations) to 100.
2. For each length, we generated 100 random FLTL formulae.
3. For each formula, we generated a random trace over a fixed-size observational alphabet (including 50 elements).
4. For each formula/trace combination, we ran the monitoring algorithm, measured the performance time, and divided it by the index of the cell that has been reached in the trace. This is necessary, since the monitoring could terminate anywhere in the cell: the measured time alone is not informative enough.

In order to try and optimise the performances, we designed and coded another RuleRunner implementation, strictly based on the concept of parsing trees. Instead of having a single rule list, we scattered the (identical) list of rules over the nodes of the parsing trees, with the goal of fully localising the monitoring process and the storage of the monitoring state. This version (simply called *tree-based*) implements the metaphor of *monitoring as truth-values propagation along the parsing tree of ϕ* which we used throughout the paper. We stress that this implementation uses the same set of rules, as generated by Algorithm 2, and follows the monitoring process of Algorithm 3: the main difference is that it does it on a more distributed data structure. The performance and comparison of the two implementations are visualised in Fig. 3(right).

5   Conclusions and Future Work

In this paper we present RuleRunner, a rule-based runtime verification system that exploits Horn clauses in implication form and forward chaining to perform a monitoring task. RuleRunner is a module in a wider framework that includes the encoding of the rule system in a neural network, the exploitation of GPUs to improve monitoring performances (as computation in neural networks boils down to matrix-based operations) and the adoption of machine learning algorithms to adapt the encoded property to the observed trace. Our final goal is the development of a system for scalable and parallel monitoring and capable to provide a description of patterns that falsified the prescribed temporal property. The applications of this frameworks spans from multi-agent systems (where a system designer may want to use an agent's unscripted solution to a problem as a benchmark for all other agents [8]) to security (where a security manager may want to correct some false positives when monitoring security properties [4]).

Concerning RuleRunner, a future direction of work is to create rule systems for other finite-trace semantics. For instance, we conjecture that removing all rules with END would be a valid starting point for the development of a rule system for LTL3; the rule systems for FLTL and LTL3 will then be used to build a rule system for RVLTL. A second direction of future work will be to modify RuleRunner in such a way to use external forward chaining tools for the monitoring (as we use our own inference engine), such as the Constraint Handling Rules extension included in several Prolog implementations.

References

1. Barringer, H., Rydeheard, D.E., Havelund, K.: Rule systems for run-time monitoring: from eagle to ruler. J. Logic Comput. **20**, 675–706 (2010)
2. Bauer, A., Leucker, M., Schallhart, C.: The good, the bad, and the ugly, but how ugly is ugly? In: Sokolsky, O., Taşıran, S. (eds.) RV 2007. LNCS, vol. 4839, pp. 126–138. Springer, Heidelberg (2007)
3. Bauer, A., Leucker, M., Schallhart, C.: Monitoring of real-time properties. In: Arun-Kumar, S., Garg, N. (eds.) FSTTCS 2006. LNCS, vol. 4337, pp. 260–272. Springer, Heidelberg (2006)
4. Breitgand, D., Goldstein, M., Shehory, E.H.: Efficient control of false negative and false positive errors with separate adaptive thresholds. IEEE Trans. Netw. Serv. Manage. **8**, 128–140 (2011)
5. d'Avila Garcez, A.S., Zaverucha, G.: The connectionist inductive learning and logic programming system. Appl. Intell. **11**, 59–77 (1999)
6. Drusinsky, A.: The temporal rover and the ATG rover. In: Havelund, K., Penix, J., Visser, W. (eds.) SPIN 2000. LNCS, vol. 1885, pp. 323–330. Springer, Heidelberg (2000)
7. Eisner, C., Fisman, D., Havlicek, J., Lustig, Y., McIsaac, A., Van Campenhout, D.: Reasoning with temporal logic on truncated paths. In: Hunt Jr., W.A., Somenzi, F. (eds.) CAV 2003. LNCS, vol. 2725, pp. 27–39. Springer, Heidelberg (2003)
8. Hollander, C.D., Annie, S.W.: The current state of normative agent-based systems. J. Artif. Soc. Soc. Simul. **14**, 47–62 (2011)

9. Horn, A.: On sentences which are true of direct unions of algebras. J. Symb. Log. **16**, 14–21 (1951)
10. Kripke, S.A.: Semantical considerations on modal logic. Acta Philosophica Fennica **16**, 83–94 (1963)
11. Lassez, J.-L., Maher, M.J.: The denotational semantics of horn clauses as aproduction system. In: Proceedings of the Association for the Advancement of Artificial Intelligence 1983, pp. 229–231 (1983)
12. Leucker, M., Schallhart, C.: A brief account of runtime verification. J. Logic Algebraic Program. **78**, 293–303 (2009)
13. Lichtenstein, O., Pnueli, A., Zuck, L.: The glory of the past. In: Parikh, R. (ed.) Logics of Programs. Lecture Notes in Computer Science, vol. 193, pp. 196–218. Springer, Heidelberg (1985)
14. Lukasiewicz, J.: O logice trjwartosciowej (On Three-Valued Logic) (1920)
15. Perotti, A., d'Avila Garcez, A.S., Boella, G.: Neural networks for runtime verification. In: 2014 International Joint Conference on Neural Networks, IJCNN 2014, Beijing, China, July 6–11, 2014, pp. 2637–2644. IEEE (2014)
16. Pesic, M., Schonenberg, H., van der Aalst, W.M.P.: Declare: full support for loosely-structured processes. In: 11th IEEE International Enterprise Distributed Object Computing Conference, EDOC 2007, pp. 287–287 (2007)
17. Pnueli, A.: The temporal logic of programs. In: Proceedings of the Annual Symposium on Foundations of Computer Science 1977, pp. 46–57 (1977)
18. van der Aalst, W., et al.: Process mining Manifesto. In: Daniel, F., Barkaoui, K., Dustdar, S. (eds.) BPM Workshops 2011, Part I. LNBIP, vol. 99, pp. 169–194. Springer, Heidelberg (2012)
19. Van Emden, M.H., Kowalski, R.A.: The semantics of predicate logic as a programming language. J. ACM **23**, 733–742 (1976)

Collision Avoidance for Mobile Robots with Limited Sensing and Limited Information About the Environment

Dung Phan[1], Junxing Yang[1], Denise Ratasich[2], Radu Grosu[2],
Scott A. Smolka[1], and Scott D. Stoller[1(✉)]

[1] Department of Computer Science, Stony Brook University, Stony Brook, NY, USA
stoller@cs.stonybrook.edu
[2] Department of Computer Science, Vienna University of Technology,
Vienna, Austria

Abstract. This paper addresses the problem of safely navigating a mobile robot with limited sensing capability and limited information about stationary obstacles. We consider two sensing limitations: blind spots between sensors and limited sensing range. We identify a set of constraints on the sensors' readings whose satisfaction at time t guarantees collision-freedom during the time interval $[t, t + \Delta t]$. Here, Δt is a parameter whose value is bounded by a function of the maximum velocity of the robot and the range of the sensors. The constraints are obtained under assumptions about minimum internal angle and minimum edge length of polyhedral obstacles. We apply these constraints in the switching logic of the Simplex architecture to obtain a controller that ensures collision-freedom. Experiments we have conducted are consistent with these claims. To the best of our knowledge, our study is the first to provide runtime assurance that an autonomous mobile robot with limited sensing can navigate without collisions with only limited information about obstacles.

1 Introduction

Autonomous mobile robots are becoming increasingly popular. They are used in homes, warehouses, hospitals and even on the roads. In most applications, collision avoidance is a vital safety requirement. Ideally, the robots would have $360°$ field-of-view. One approach to achieve this is to closely place a sufficient number of sensors (e.g., infrared, laser, or ultrasound) on the robot. The biggest problem with this approach is interference between sensors. It is difficult to install the sensors close enough to achieve $360°$ sensing while at the same time avoiding interference.[1] In addition, the use of numerous sensors increases cost, power

---

[1] Cameras, i.e., sensing based on computer vision, do not interfere with each other but are less common as a basis for navigation due to other disadvantages: cameras depend on good lighting; accurate ranging from stereoscopic vision is impossible on small robots, is generally less accurate than and requires significantly more computational power than ranging from lasers, ultrasound, IR, etc..

© Springer International Publishing Switzerland 2015
E. Bartocci and R. Majumdar (Eds.): RV 2015, LNCS 9333, pp. 201–215, 2015.
DOI: 10.1007/978-3-319-23820-3_13

consumption, weight, and size of the robot. Another option is to use sensors that have wide angle of observation, such as the Hokuyo URG-04LX laser range finder with 240° range. This approach, however, adds thousands of dollars to the cost. Due to these difficulties, 360° sensing capability is often not a practical option. Consequently, many well-known cost-effective mobile robots, such as E-puck, Khepera III, Quickbot and AmigoBot, lack this capability. These robots have a small number of narrow-angle infrared or ultrasound sensors that do not provide 360° field-of-view. The resulting blind spots between sensors make the robot vulnerable to collision with undetected obstacles that are narrow enough to fit in the blind spots.

One approach to prevent such collisions is for the robot to repeatedly stop or slow down (depending on the sensor range), rotate back and forth to sweep its sensors across the original blind spots, and then continue (this assumes the robot can rotate without moving too much). This approach, however, is inefficient: it significantly slows the robot and wastes power. A similar approach is to mount the sensors so that they can rotate relative to the robot. Unfortunately, this approach adds hardware and software complexity, increases power usage, and limits the maximum safe speed of the robot (depending on the rotation speed of the sensors).

In this paper, we present a runtime approach, based on the Simplex architecture [8,9], to ensure collision-freedom for robots with limited field-of-view and limited sensing range in environments where obstacles are polyhedral and satisfy reasonable assumptions about minimum internal angle and minimum edge length. One example of such an environment is an automated warehouse, where some information is known about the shapes and sizes of shelving racks, pallets, etc. Our work is also applicable to robots designed with 360° sensing capability that temporarily acquire blind spots due to one or more sensor failures. Our approach does not suffer from the above disadvantages, and requires only some weak assumptions about the shape of the obstacles. Our approach guarantees collision-freedom if the obstacles are stationary. If the environment contains moving obstacles, and a bound on their velocity is known, our approach can easily be extended to also ensure *passive safety*, which means that no collisions can happen while the robot is moving.

Many navigation algorithms have been proposed for autonomous mobile robots. Few of these algorithms, however, have been verified to ensure the safety of the robot. One consequence of this state of affairs is that supposedly superior but uncertified navigation algorithms are not deployed in safety-critical applications. The Simplex architecture allows these uncertified algorithms, which in Simplex terms are called *advanced controllers* (ACs), to be used along side a pre-certified controller, called the *baseline controller* (BC). The BC will take control of the robot if something goes wrong with the AC. The key component of the Simplex architecture that makes this happen is the *decision module*, which uses *switching logic* to determine when to switch from the AC to the BC.

In this paper, we present a Simplex-based approach that offers runtime assurance that a mobile robot with limited sensing capability can safely navigate an unknown environment with stationary obstacles. By "safely navigate" we mean without colliding with an obstacle. We consider two sensing limitations: blind spots between sensors, and limited sensing range. We identify a set of constraints on the sensors' readings whose satisfaction at time t guarantees collision-freedom during the time interval $[t, t + \Delta t]$. Here, Δt is a parameter whose value is bounded by a function of the maximum velocity of the robot and the range of the sensors. The constraints are obtained under assumptions about minimum internal angle and minimum edge length of polyhedral obstacles, and form the basis for the switching logic. The simulation results we have obtained are consistent with our runtime-assurance claims.

Another distinguishing feature of our work is the manner in which the switching condition is computed, using extensive geometric reasoning. Existing approaches to computation of switching condition are based on Lyapunov stability theory (e.g., [8,9]) or, more recently, state-space exploration (e.g., [2]). These existing approaches cannot be applied to the problem at hand, because of the incomplete knowledge of the shapes and locations of the obstacles in the robot's environment. To the best of our knowledge, our study is the first to provide runtime assurance that a mobile robot with limited sensing can navigate in such an environment without colliding with obstacles.

The paper is organized as follows. Section 2 considers related work on provable collision avoidance. Section 3 provides background on the Simplex architecture. Section 4 contains a detailed derivation of the switching condition. Section 5 discusses our implementation and experimental results. Section 6 offers our concluding remarks and directions for future work.

2   Related Work

Prior work [1,3–5] has focused on establishing collision-freedom for specific navigation algorithms. In contrast, we employ the Simplex architecture to ensure the safety of the robot in the presence of any navigation algorithm, however faulty it may be. We consider each of these approaches in turn.

Theorem-proving techniques are used in [4] to establish two safety properties of the Dynamic Window algorithm for collision avoidance: passive safety and passive friendly safety, both of which apply to stationary and moving obstacles. Infinite sensor detection range is assumed. Our approach, in contrast, accounts for the limited detection range of sensors.

In [3], the authors present the PassAvoid navigation algorithm, which avoids "braking-inevitable collision states" to achieve passive safety. In [7], a biologically inspired navigation algorithm for a unicycle-like robot moving in a dynamic environment is presented. Both algorithms assume 360° sensing capability. We do not make this assumption, and instead rely on certain weak assumptions about the shapes of obstacles.

In [1], the authors propose an algorithm that constrains the velocity of a mobile robot moving on a known trajectory such that it stops before colliding with moving obstacles. They assume 360° field-of-view and a pre-planned trajectory that guides the robot through an environment with known static obstacles. We do not make any of these assumptions.

A method is presented in [5] for computing a smooth, collision-free path from a piecewise linear collision-free trajectory produced by sampling-based planners. They assume the given sampling-based trajectory is collision-free and use cubic B-splines to generate a smooth trajectory that guarantees collision-freedom. We do not make any assumptions about robot trajectories.

3   The Simplex Architecture

The Simplex architecture [8,9] was developed to allow sophisticated control software to be used in safety-critical systems. This sophisticated software, called an *advanced controller*, is designed to achieve high performance according to specified metrics (e.g., maneuverability, fuel economy, mission completion time). As a result, it might be so complex that it is difficult to achieve the desired level of safety assurance in all possible scenarios. Its complexity might also prevent it from achieving required certifications (e.g., RTCA DO-178C for flightworthiness). The Simplex architecture allows such advanced controllers to be used safely, by pairing them with a simpler *baseline controller* for which the desired level of safety assurance can be achieved, and with a *decision module* that determines which controller is in control of the plant.

While the system is under the control of the advanced controller, the decision module monitors the system state and periodically checks whether the system is in imminent danger of violating a given safety requirement. If so, the decision module switches control of the system from the advanced controller to the baseline controller. The period with which the decision module makes the switching decision is called the *decision period* and denoted Δt. The condition on the system state that it evaluates to determine whether to switch to the baseline controller is called the *switching condition*. The switching condition depends on the safety requirements, the system dynamics, and the decision period. A state is *correct* if it satisfies the given safety requirements. A state is *recoverable* if, starting from that state, the baseline controller can ensure that the system remains correct; i.e., remains in correct states.

The correctness requirement for the switching condition is: If the switching condition is false (i.e., "don't switch"), then the system is guaranteed to remain in recoverable states for the next Δt time units, regardless of the control inputs to the plant produced by the advanced controller during that interval. The quantification over all possible control inputs to the plant is needed because we make no assumptions about the advanced controller's behavior. If the baseline controller and switching condition are correct, then correctness of the system is ensured, regardless of the advanced controller's behavior.

4   Switching Logic

Our approach uses the Simplex architecture with a baseline controller that immediately stops the robot. To simplify the derivation of the switching condition slightly, we make the following assumptions: (1) the execution time of the decision module is negligible; (2) the switching latency is negligible (i.e., the baseline controller can take over immediately); (3) the robot can instantly come to a full stop from any velocity; (4) the robot's shape is a single point, as in [4]. None of these assumptions is essential. Our derivation can easily be extended to eliminate them.

Since we assume instantaneous stop, the decision module only needs to ensure that no collisions can occur within Δt time units. Since we make no assumptions about the advanced controller's behavior, and do not assume any limits on how rapidly the robot can turn or accelerate, the robot may immediately move in any direction at its maximum speed, denoted v_{max}. The speed v_{max} and the decision period Δt define the robot's *safety disk*, a circular disk with radius $R = v_{max}\Delta t$ centered at the robot. The choice of the decision period Δt is constrained by the requirement that $R < R_s$, where R_s is the maximum detection range of the sensors. To ensure collision-freedom for time Δt, there must not be any obstacles within the safety disk.

The robot is equipped with N distance sensors with angle of detection β_s and maximum range R_s, as shown in Fig. 1. For simplicity, we assume the sensors are evenly spaced; it is easy to analyze other spacings in a similar way. The angle (in radians) of the gap between the fields-of-view of adjacent sensors is $\beta_g = (2\pi - N\beta_s)/N$. We assume N and β_s are such that $\beta_g > 0$; in other words, the robot has blind spots.

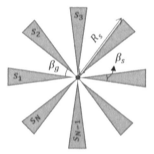

Fig. 1. The robot has N evenly spaced sensors $s_1, s_2, ..., s_N$ with angle of detection β_s and maximum range R_s. The angle of the gap between two adjacent sensors is β_g.

When an obstacle intersects a sensor's cone of observation at multiple distances, depending on the exact nature of the sensor, it may report the closest distance to the obstacle, the farthest distance, or something in between. Our derivation of the switching condition is based on the worst-case (from the perspective of collision avoidance) assumption about sensor behavior, namely, that the sensor reports the farther distance to the obstacle.

4.1   Notation

Let $E_{AB}^\alpha = \{P \mid \angle APB = \alpha\}$ be the α-*equiangular arcs* of AB, i.e., the locus of points that see the line segment AB under angle α. Geometrically, E_{AB}^α forms two circular arcs that pass through A and B, shown as the red boundary of the blue shape in Fig. 2. Let S_{AB}^α be the set of points that lie within the area enclosed by α-equiangular arcs of AB including the boundary. It is easy to show that $S_{AB}^\alpha = \{C \mid \angle ACB \geq \alpha\}$, which means S_{AB}^α is the locus of all possible vertices with angle at least α such that one edge passes through A and the other edge passes through B.

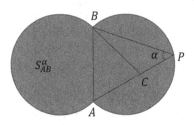

Fig. 2. Illustration of S_{AB}^α. The α-equiangular arcs of AB is the boundary.

Let O be the position of the robot. Let S_{safe} be the set of points that lie within the safety disk, i.e., $S_{safe} = \{P \mid OP \leq R\}$. Let $S_{obstacle}$ be the set of points that belong to the obstacle. S_{safe} and $S_{obstacle}$ are illustrated in Fig. 3. By definition of the safety disk, a collision is possible within Δt time units iff $S_{obstacle} \cap S_{safe} \neq \emptyset$.

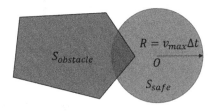

Fig. 3. Illustration of S_{safe} and $S_{obstacle}$. A collision may happen within Δt time units iff $S_{obstacle} \cap S_{safe} \neq \emptyset$

Let $S_{safe}^{ii'}$ be the set of points in the safety disk and in or between the cones of observation of sensors s_i and $s_{i'}$, shown as the orange region in Fig. 4.

4.2   Collision-Freedom Constraints

We derive the constraints that guarantee collision-freedom for Δt time units under the following assumptions about obstacles: (1) obstacles are polyhedra;

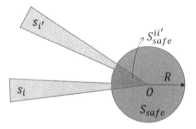

Fig. 4. Illustration of $S_{safe}^{ii'}$, the set of points in the safety disk and in or between the cones of observation of sensors s_i and $s_{i'}$.

(2) there is a known lower bound α on the internal angles between edges and $\alpha > \beta$, where β is the angle of the wedge $S_{safe}^{ii'}$ (i.e., $\beta = \beta_g + 2\beta_s$); (3) there is a known lower bound l_{min} on the edge lengths and $l_{min} \geq L$, where L is defined below; (4) the separation between obstacles is such that whenever two adjacent sensors detect an obstacle, they are detecting the same obstacle. Intuitively, the lower bound on internal angles ensures that vertices of obstacles are wide enough so that they will be detected by the robot's sensors despite blind spots.

Suppose sensor s_i detects an obstacle at B_i, $i = 1..N$. We define A_i as the point in the cone of observation of s_i such that $OA_i = l_{min}$, if s_i does not detect any obstacle and $OA_i = \min\{OB_i, l_{min}\}$, otherwise. Consider a sensor $s_{i'}$, where $i' = (i \mod N) + 1$, that is adjacent to s_i. The definition of A_i implies there is at most one obstacle vertex inside triangle $OA_iA_{i'}$. The assumptions about α and l_{min} are designed such that $S_{A_iA_{i'}}^{\alpha} \cap S_{safe}^{ii'} = \emptyset$ if $OA_i = OA_{i'} = l_{min}$. We prove the constraints $S_{A_iA_{i'}}^{\alpha} \cap S_{safe}^{ii'} = \emptyset$ for $i = 1..N$, where $i' = (i \mod N) + 1$, imply $S_{obstacle} \cap S_{safe} = \emptyset$ and hence guarantee collision-freedom for Δt time units. The proof is in the extended version of this paper, available at http://www.fsl.cs.stonybrook.edu/~dphan/rv2015-extended.pdf.

Figure 5 shows what the constraints look like geometrically. Intuitively, each constraint guarantees collision-freedom in one wedge of the safety disk. These wedges overlap and cover the safety disk.

Figure 6 shows the lower bound L on l_{min}. Let O_{arc} be the center of the α-equiangular arc of $A_{iL}A_{i'L}$ as shown in Fig. 6. L can be derived from the following equations.

$$A_{iL}A_{i'L} = \sqrt{2 \cdot L^2 - 2 \cdot L^2 \cdot \cos\beta} \tag{1}$$

$$R_{arc} = (A_{iL}A_{i'L}/2)/\sin\alpha \tag{2}$$

$$OO_{arc} = R_{arc} + R \tag{3}$$

The assumption $l_{min} \geq L$ ensures that if adjacent sensors s_i and $s_{i'}$ both detect an obstacle at distances greater than l_{min}, then no obstacle point appears within the wedge $S_{safe}^{ii'}$. We prove this in the extended version of this paper (case 1c in Appendix A).

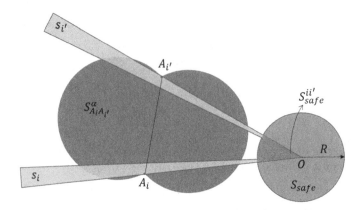

Fig. 5. Geometric meaning of the constraint $S^\alpha_{A_i A_{i'}} \cap S^{ii'}_{safe} = \emptyset$, where s_i and $s_{i'}$ are a pair of adjacent sensors.

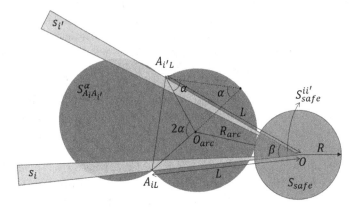

Fig. 6. Lower bound L on l_{min} such that the α-equiangular arcs of $A_{iL} A_{i'L}$ touch the safety disk.

The assumption $\alpha > \beta$ is needed because if $\alpha \leq \beta$, then $\angle A_i O A_{i'} = \beta \geq \alpha$, i.e., $O \in S^\alpha_{A_i A_{i'}}$ for any pair $A_i, A_{i'}$. That means $S^\alpha_{A_i A_{i'}}$ always intersects the safety disk and we cannot guarantee the safety of the robot.

In principle, the constraints $S^\alpha_{A_i A_{i'}} \cap S^{ii'}_{safe} = \emptyset$ for $i = 1..N$, where $i' = (i \mod N) + 1$, can be used as the switching condition for the switching logic in the Simplex architecture. However, checking these constraints exactly is computationally expensive. In the following sections, we derive computationally cheaper but more conservative switching conditions. We derive these switching conditions for two cases: case 1: a sensor s detects an obstacle within distance l_{min} and the adjacent sensors do not; case 2: two adjacent sensors s and s' detect an obstacle within distance l_{min}. Denote these switching conditions by $\phi_1(s)$ and $\phi_2(s, s')$, respectively. The overall switching condition is the disjunction of these two cases, i.e., $(\exists s.\ \phi_1(s)) \vee (\exists s, s'.\ \phi_2(s, s'))$.

We do not need a switching condition for the case when two adjacent sensors detect an obstacle at distances greater than l_{min} because of the assumptions $l_{min} \geq L$ and $\alpha > \beta$ discussed above, which allow us to treat detections at distances above l_{min} as detections at l_{min}.

4.3 Case 1: A Sensor Detects an Obstacle Within l_{min}; Adjacent Sensors Do Not

We use the following property to derive the switching condition in this case. Let OX, OY be two readings by sensor s_i such that $OX < OY$. Let OZ be the reading of sensor $s_{i'}$ that is adjacent to s_i.

Property 1. $\left| S^\alpha_{XZ} \cap S^{ii'}_{safe} \right| = 1 \Rightarrow S^\alpha_{YZ} \cap S^{ii'}_{safe} = \emptyset$

Proof. By contradiction. Suppose $\left| S^\alpha_{XZ} \cap S^{ii'}_{safe} \right| = 1$ and $S^\alpha_{YZ} \cap S^{ii'}_{safe} \neq \emptyset$. Let $C \in S^\alpha_{XZ} \cap S^{ii'}_{safe}$ as shown in Fig. 7 (C is the point where S^α_{XZ} touches $S^{ii'}_{safe}$). Since C lies on the boundary of S^α_{XZ}, we have $\angle XCZ = \alpha$. Let $D \in S^\alpha_{YZ} \cap S^{ii'}_{safe}$. Because OY is strictly greater than OX, the geometry implies $\angle XDZ > \angle YDZ \geq \alpha$. This means $D \in S^\alpha_{XZ}$ and $D \neq C$, therefore $\left| S^\alpha_{XZ} \cap S^{ii'}_{safe} \right| > 1$, a contradiction.

Suppose sensor s_1 detects an obstacle at point A_1, where $OA_1 = d_1$, and adjacent sensors do not detect any obstacle within distance l_{min}, as shown in Fig. 8. In this case, we assume the adjacent sensor s_2 detects an obstacle at

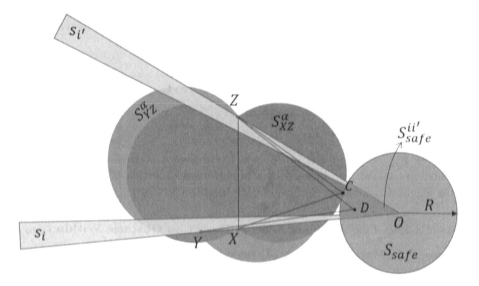

Fig. 7. Illustration of Property 1. S^α_{XZ} touches $S^{ii'}_{safe}$ at C. $S^\alpha_{YZ} \cap S^{ii'}_{safe} = \emptyset$

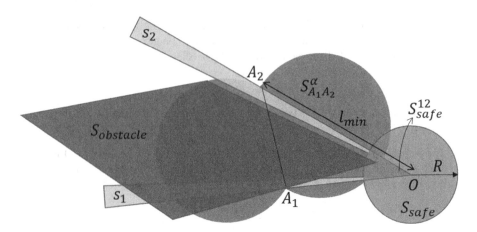

Fig. 8. Illustration of case 1. Sensor s_1 detects an obstacle at distance $OA_1 < l_{min}$. Adjacent sensor s_2 does not detect any obstacle within distance l_{min} so we assume $OA_2 = l_{min}$.

distance $OA_2 = l_{min}$, as described in Sect. 4.2. The switching condition $\phi_1(s_1)$ in this case is of the form $d_1 \leq d_{1switch}$, for the threshold $d_{1switch}$ defined below.

If we can find a point A_T such that $\left| S^\alpha_{A_T A_2} \cap S_{safe} \right| = 1$ (i.e., $S^\alpha_{A_T A_2}$ touches S_{safe}), then by Property 1, we can let $d_{1switch} = OA_T$. This switching condition is more conservative than the constraint $S^\alpha_{A_1 A_2} \cap S^{12}_{safe} = \emptyset$ because there are some cases when $S^\alpha_{A_T A_2}$ touches S_{safe} at a point outside the wedge S^{12}_{safe}. The benefit is that the switching threshold $d_{1switch} = OA_T$ can be computed statically, resulting in a very simple switching condition.

Similar to the computation of lower bound L on l_{min} described in Sect. 4.2, the point A_T must satisfy the following equations, where O_{arc} is the center of the α-equiangular arc of $A_T A_2$ as shown in Fig. 9.

$$A_T A_2 = \sqrt{OA_T^2 + l_{min}^2 - 2 \cdot OA_T \cdot l_{min} \cdot \cos\beta} \tag{4}$$

$$R_{arc} = (A_T A_2 / 2) / \sin\alpha \tag{5}$$

$$OO_{arc} = R_{arc} + R \tag{6}$$

Given l_{min}, α, β and R, all of which are known statically, the switching threshold OA_T can be obtained by straightforward solution of these equations using algebraic geometry. We use Matlab to automate this.

4.4   Case 2: Two Adjacent Sensors Detect an Obstacle Within l_{min}

Suppose s_1 detects an obstacle at A_1 where $OA_1 \leq l_{min}$, and an adjacent sensor s_2 detects an obstacle at A_2 where $OA_2 \leq l_{min}$, as depicted in Fig. 10.

Checking the constraint $S^\alpha_{A_1 A_2} \cap S^{12}_{safe} = \emptyset$ exactly requires a complex algorithm. To obtain a computationally cheaper switching condition, we instead

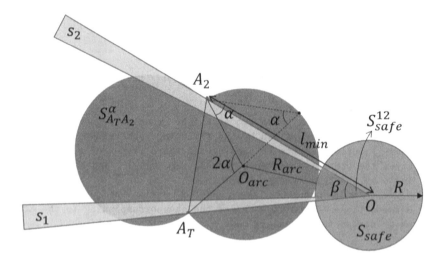

Fig. 9. Illustration of switching threshold OA_T calculation.

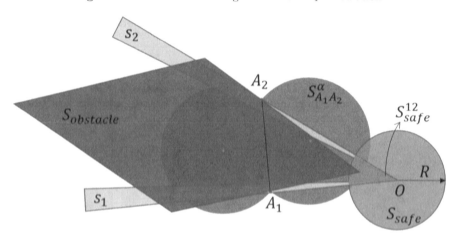

Fig. 10. Sensors s_1 and s_2 detect an obstacle at distance $OA_1 \leq l_{min}$ and $OA_2 \leq l_{min}$, respectively (Color figure online).

check the more conservative constraint $S^\alpha_{A_1 A_2} \cap S_{safe} = \emptyset$. Algorithm 1 computes the switching condition $\phi_2(s_1, s_2)$ by checking whether $S^\alpha_{A_1 A_2} \cap S_{safe} \neq \emptyset$. This algorithm performs only a short sequence of inexpensive geometric calculations. The geometric reasoning underlying Algorithm 1 is similar to the derivation of the lower bound L on l_{min} described in Sect. 4.2.

5   Implementation and Experimental Results

We implemented the Simplex architecture with the baseline controller and switching conditions described in Sect. 4 in the Matlab simulator for the

Input: OA_1, OA_2, α, $\angle A_1OA_2$, R

```
// Distance between points A₁ and A₂
```
$A_1A_2 = \sqrt{OA_2^2 + OA_2^2 - 2 \cdot OA_1 \cdot OA_2 \cdot \cos \angle A_1OA_2};$
```
// Radius of the α-equiangular arcs for A₁A₂, i.e., points C such
   that ∠A₁CA₂ = α
```
$R_{arc} = (A_1A_2/2)/\sin \alpha;$
```
// Find the centers of those two arcs (the green dots in Fig. 10).
   Their position is defined by the following geometric constraints,
   whose solution amounts to finding the third vertex of a triangle,
   given the other two vertices (namely, A₁ and A₂) and the internal
   angle at the third vertex ∠A₁OA₂.
```
$O_{arc,1}, O_{arc,2}$ = the points O_{arc} satisfying $O_{arc}A_1 = O_{arc}A_2 \wedge \angle A_1 O_{arc} A_2 = 2\alpha;$
```
// Between those two points, choose the one corresponding to the arc
   that intersects the safety disk.
```
$O_{arc} = \alpha \le \pi/2 \, ? \, \min\{OO_{arc,1}, OO_{arc,2}\} : \max\{OO_{arc,1}, OO_{arc,2}\};$
```
// Test whether the arc intersects the safety disc by comparing the
   distance between their centers with the sum of their radii.
```
return $OO_{arc} \le R_{arc} + R$

Algorithm 1. Switching condition when adjacent sensors detect an obstacle within distance l_{min}

Quickbot ground robot [6]. The robot has sensor architecture as in Fig. 1 with the following parameters: (1) number of sensors $N = 8$; (2) angle of detection of

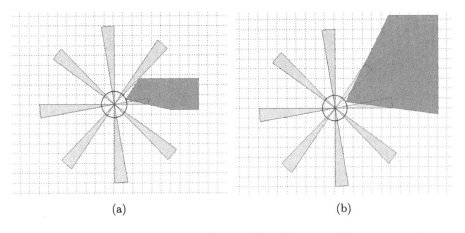

(a)   (b)

Fig. 11. Snapshots from simulations showing the robot correctly stops to ensure no obstacles in the safety disk. The circle around the robot represents the safety disk. The red region represents the obstacle. The blue wedges represent the robot's cones of observation. (a) Snapshot from scenario for case 1: a sensor detects an obstacle within l_{min}; adjacent sensors do not. (b) Snapshot from scenario for case 2: two adjacent sensors detect an obstacle within l_{min} (Color figure online).

the sensors $\beta_s = 10°$; (3) maximum range of the sensors $R_s = 80\,\text{cm}$; (4) maximum velocity $v_{max} = 28\,\text{cm/s}$, and decision period $\Delta t = 0.5\,\text{s}$. The radius of the safety disk is $R = v_{max}\Delta t = 14\,\text{cm}$.

We tested the switching condition in the following two scenarios; snapshots from simulations of these scenarios appear in Fig. 11. Both scenarios involve an obstacle with lower bound on internal angles $\alpha = 70°$. For the scenario in Fig. 11(a), we place the obstacle such that when the robot approaches the obstacle and the vertex with angle α is about to enter the safety disk, only one sensor detects an edge with l_{min} and the other edge barely misses the cone of observation of an adjacent sensor. This is the worst-case scenario for case 1 in Sect. 4.3. For the scenario in Fig. 11(b), we place the obstacle such that when the robot approaches the obstacle and the vertex with angle α is about to enter the safety disk, the vertex is in the gap of two adjacent sensors and both sensors detect an edge of the obstacle within l_{min}. This is the worst-case scenario for case 2 in Sect. 4.4.

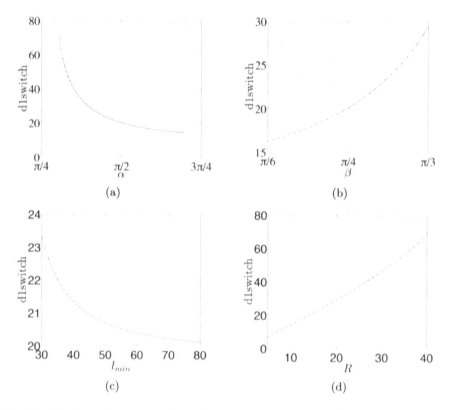

Fig. 12. Graphs of $d_{1switch}$ as a function of various parameters. (a) $d_{1switch}$ as a function of α, with $\beta = \pi/4$, $l_{min} = 80$ and $R = 14$. (b) $d_{1switch}$ as a function of β, with $\alpha = \pi/2$, $l_{min} = 80$ and $R = 14$. (c) $d_{1switch}$ as a function of l_{min}, with $\alpha = \pi/2$, $\beta = \pi/4$, and $R = 14$. (d) $d_{1switch}$ as a function of R, with $\alpha = \pi/2$, $\beta = \pi/4$, and $l_{min} = 80$.

The snapshots in Fig. 11 show the moment when the switching condition becomes true and the robot stops. One observation is that, in both scenarios, the switching condition is *correct*: the obstacle does not enter the safety disk. Of course, this is expected. A more interesting observation is that, in both scenarios, the switching condition is *tight* (not unnecessarily conservative): the robot does not stop until the obstacle is about to enter the safety disk. The actual simulations leading to these snapshots can be viewed at https://www.youtube.com/watch?v=bK-YnGgwjwU.

Figure 12 shows how the switching threshold $d_{1switch}$ in case 1 depends on various parameters. Figure 12(a) shows how $d_{1switch}$ decreases as α increases. It is clear from the worst-case scenario of case 1 that when an obstacle with a sharper corner, i.e., a smaller α, touches the safety disk, the sensor detects its edge at a greater distance than one with a flatter corner, and this necessitates a larger $d_{1switch}$. Figure 12(b) shows how $d_{1switch}$ increases as β increases. Intuitively, a larger β means a larger gap between the cones of observation of two adjacent sensors, so the edge of the obstacle is detected at a larger distance when the vertex is at the boundary of the safety disk. Figure 12(c) shows how $d_{1switch}$ decreases as l_{min} increases. This can be seen from the worst-case scenario: the edge of the obstacle that is not detected within l_{min} will make a smaller angle with the edge of the cone if l_{min} is larger, so the other edge is detected at a smaller distance. Figure 12(d) shows how $d_{1switch}$ increases as R increases (note: it doesn't matter whether the increase in R is due to an increase in v_{max} or Δt). This directly reflects the fact that a robot with a larger safety disk needs to stop farther from obstacles.

6   Conclusions

In this paper, we have shown how it is possible to use the Simplex architecture, equipped with a sophisticated geometric-based switching condition, to ensure at runtime that mobile robots with limited field-of-view and limited sensing range navigate without collisions with only limited information about obstacles.

Future work includes extending our approach to take into account the size and shape of the robot, its braking power (instead of assuming immediate stop), and the minimum detection distance of the sensors. We will also consider more powerful baseline controllers. We also plan to develop algorithms that allow the robot to learn about its environment, enabling it to replace worst-case assumptions with more detailed information about obstacles it has encountered, allowing tighter switching conditions. The geometric analysis that we developed to derive and verify the switching condition can also be used as a basis for the design of collision-avoidance logic in navigation algorithms for mobile robots.

Acknowledgments. This material is based upon work supported in part by AFOSR Grant FA9550-14-1-0261, NSF Grants IIS-1447549, CCF-0926190, CNS-1421893, CNS-1446832, CCF-1414078, ONR Grant N00014-15-1-2208, and Artemis EMC2 Grant 3887039.

References

1. Alami, R., Krishna, K.M., Siméon, T.: Provably safe motions strategies for mobile robots in dynamic domains. In: Laugier, C., Chatila, R. (eds.) Autonomous Navigation in Dynamic Environments. STAR, vol. 35, pp. 85–106. Springer, Heidelberg (2007)
2. Bak, S., Manamcheri, K., Mitra, S., Caccamo, M.: Sandboxing controllers for cyber-physical systems. In: Proceedings of the 2011 IEEE/ACM International Conference on Cyber-Physical Systems, ICCPS, pp. 3–12. IEEE Computer Society (2011)
3. Bouraine, S., Fraichard, T., Salhi, H.: Provably safe navigation for mobile robots with limited field-of-views in dynamic environments. Auton. Robots **32**(3), 267–283 (2012). https://hal.inria.fr/hal-00733913
4. Mitsch, S., Ghorbal, K., Platzer, A.: On provably safe obstacle avoidance for autonomous robotic ground vehicles. In: Newman, P., Fox, D., Hsu, D. (eds.) Robotics: Science and Systems (2013)
5. Pan, J., Zhang, L., Manocha, D.: Collision-free and smooth trajectory computation in cluttered environments. Int. J. Rob. Res. **31**(10), 1155–1175 (2012). http://dx.doi.org/10.1177/0278364912453186
6. QuickBot MOOC v2 (2014). http://o-botics.org/robots/quickbot/mooc/v2/
7. Savkin, A.V., Wang, C.: A reactive algorithm for safe navigation of a wheeled mobile robot among moving obstacles. In: Proceedings of the 2012 IEEE International Conference on Control Applications (CCA), pp. 1567–1571. IEEE (2012)
8. Seto, D., Krogh, B., Sha, L., Chutinan, A.: The Simplex architecture for safe online control system upgrades. In: Proceedings of the 1998 American Control Conference, vol. 6, pp. 3504–3508 (1998)
9. Sha, L.: Using simplicity to control complexity. IEEE Softw. **18**(4), 20–28 (2001)

From First-order Temporal Logic
to Parametric Trace Slicing

Giles Reger[(⊠)] and David Rydeheard

University of Manchester, Manchester, UK
giles.reger@manchester.ac.uk

Abstract. Parametric runtime verification is the process of verifying properties of execution traces of (data carrying) events produced by a running system. This paper considers the relationship between two widely-used specification approaches to parametric runtime verification: *trace slicing* and *first-order temporal logic*. This work is a first step in understanding this relationship. We introduce a technique of identifying *syntactic fragments* of temporal logics that admit notions of *sliceability*. We show how to translate formulas in such fragments into automata with a slicing-based semantics. In exploring this relationship, the paper aims to allow monitoring techniques to be shared between the two approaches and initiate a wider effort to unify specification languages for runtime verification.

1 Introduction

Runtime verification [12] is the process of checking properties of execution traces produced by running a computational system. An execution trace is a finite sequence of *events* generated by the computation. In many applications, events carry *data values* – the so-called parametric, or first-order, case of runtime verification. To formalise runtime verification, we need to provide (a) a specification language for describing properties of execution traces, and (b) a mechanism for checking these formally-defined properties during execution, i.e. a mechanism for generating monitors from specifications. Many different formalisms have been proposed (see Sect. 7). In fact, almost every runtime verification approach introduces its own specification language. One aim of this work is to develop techniques for relating approaches to runtime verification as a first step to bringing some order to this variety of formalisms.

One approach to runtime verification [3,15] is to use automata both to specify trace properties and to act as monitors of execution traces. In the first-order case, the semantics of automata can be defined in terms of so-called *trace slicing* [9], whereby traces are projected according to the values carried by events, and properties are evaluated on these projections. This has been shown to be highly efficient [1]. An alternative approach is to use temporal logic to specify properties of traces. Mechanisms for constructing monitors from first-order temporal logic specifications have been proposed (see, for example, [5,7,10,14,20]). This paper considers the relationship between these two approaches.

© Springer International Publishing Switzerland 2015
E. Bartocci and R. Majumdar (Eds.): RV 2015, LNCS 9333, pp. 216–232, 2015.
DOI: 10.1007/978-3-319-23820-3_14

In general, properties expressed in a first-order temporal logic do not respect trace slicing. We examine the reasons for this and then introduce a technique for exploring the relationship between trace slicing and temporal logic. To do so, we introduce a first-order linear temporal logic with a finite trace semantics. The key step is then to identify *syntactic fragments* of this logic and the corresponding notions of 'sliceability'. We give one example of such a syntactic fragment and prove that it admits a notion of sliceability. We then show how we may construct monitoring automata from formulas in the fragment. To what extent do such syntactic fragments provide specification languages for runtime verification? As we discuss, currently the expressivity of formalisms *for runtime verification* is not easy to assess as we do not have adequate data on specifications likely to occur in runtime verification activities.

There are two main motivations behind this work. Firstly, giving a translation from first-order temporal logic into slicing-based formalisms allows specifications written in the former language to be monitored using techniques based on the latter. Secondly, the wide range of specification languages for (parametric) runtime verification often makes comparison and re-usability of specifications difficult. This work therefore is a contribution to unifying specification languages for runtime verification. More precisely, it is a *necessary first step* in the authors' wider goal of finding a correspondence between the full expressiveness of the slicing-based formalism QEA and temporal logics.

The contributions of this paper are as follows:

- Based on a first-order linear temporal logic (Sect. 2) and slicing (Sect. 3), we describe restrictions that slicing places on the structure of formulas, and introduce a syntactic fragment that satisfies these restrictions (Sect. 4)
- To make the correspondence practically useful we provide a translation from formulas in the fragment to a slicing-based formalism (Sect. 5)

The paper finishes with related work (Sect. 7) and conclusions (Sect. 8).

2   A First-order Linear Temporal Logic

We begin by presenting a first-order discrete linear-time temporal logic, FO-LTL$_f$, with a finite-trace semantics, where traces are finite sequences of events (see [8] for a discussion). As we are focussing on the correspondence with slicing, we do not consider general first-order functions and predicates; we plan to consider these in future work.

Let Σ be a finite set of names of events, *Var* be a finite set of variable names and *Val* be a finite set of value symbols (constants) disjoint from *Var*. An *event* $e(z_1, \ldots, z_n)$ is an element of the set $\Sigma \times (Var \cup Val)^*$. An event is *ground* if all of its parameters are values. We write events as $\mathbf{a}, \mathbf{b} \ldots$ A (ground) *trace* is a finite sequence of (ground) events. We write the empty trace as ϵ. Given a trace τ we write the length of a trace as $|\tau|$ and the i-th element as τ_i where the first element is at index 0.

The syntax of FO-LTL$_f$ is defined as the following formulas:

$$\phi = \mathit{true} \mid \mathbf{a} \mid \forall x : \phi \mid \neg\phi \mid \phi \vee \phi \mid \phi\, \mathcal{U}^\circ\, \phi$$

We use standard identities, defining $\mathit{false} = \neg\mathit{true}$, $\phi_1 \wedge \phi_2 = \neg(\neg\phi_1 \vee \neg\phi_2)$, $\exists x : \phi = \neg\forall x : \neg\phi$ and $\phi_1 \rightarrow \phi_2 = \neg\phi_1 \vee \phi_2$. The logic incorporates a single temporal modality $\mathcal{U}^\circ$ which can be read as *next until*. This is sufficient for defining in FO-LTL$_f$ the temporal modalities that we would expect to see in a discrete linear-time temporal logic: the 'next' modality $\bigcirc\phi = \mathit{false}\, \mathcal{U}^\circ\, \phi$; 'until' $\phi_1\, \mathcal{U}\, \phi_2 = \phi_2 \vee (\phi_1 \wedge (\phi_1\, \mathcal{U}^\circ\, \phi_2))$; 'eventually' $\Diamond\phi = \mathit{true}\, \mathcal{U}\, \phi$; and 'always' $\Box\phi = \phi\, \mathcal{U}\, \mathit{false}$.

A *valuation* is a map (i.e. a partial function with finite domain) from variables to values. For valuations θ_1 and θ_2 let $\theta_1 \dagger \theta_2$ be the valuation where θ_2 *overrides* or *extends* values for variables in θ_1. Valuations can be applied to events and to formulas to replace variables with values. A *domain* is a map from variables to sets of values. Let $\mathtt{events}(\phi)$ be the set of events occurring in ϕ.

A formula ϕ is a *sentence* if it has no free variables. We define the semantics of FO-LTL$_f$ in terms of a models relation $\models$ on sentences:

Definition 1 (Semantics). *We define the semantics of* FO-LTL$_f$ *with respect to a quadruple* $(\mathcal{D}, \tau, v, i)$ *where* $\mathcal{D}$ *is the domains of variables,* τ *is a trace,* v *is a valuation and* i *an index of the trace. The relation* $\models$ *is defined as follows:*

$$\mathcal{D}, \tau, v, i \models \mathit{true}$$
$$\mathcal{D}, \tau, v, i \models \mathbf{a} \qquad \mathit{if}\ \tau_i = v(\mathbf{a})$$
$$\mathcal{D}, \tau, v, i \models \neg\phi \qquad \mathit{if}\ \mathcal{D}, \tau, v, i \not\models \phi$$
$$\mathcal{D}, \tau, v, i \models \phi_1 \vee \phi_2 \quad \mathit{if}\ \mathcal{D}, \tau, v, i \models \phi_1\ \mathit{or}\ \mathcal{D}, \tau, v, i \models \phi_2$$
$$\mathcal{D}, \tau, v, i \models \phi_1\, \mathcal{U}^\circ\, \phi_2 \quad \mathit{if\ there\ exists\ a}\ j > i\ \mathit{such\ that\ either}\ \mathcal{D}, \tau, v, j \models \phi_2\ \mathit{or}$$
$$j = |\tau|\ \mathit{and}\ \phi_2 = \mathit{false}$$
$$\mathit{and\ for\ every}\ k\ \mathit{where}\ i < k < j\ \mathit{we\ have}\ \mathcal{D}, \tau, v, k \models \phi_1$$
$$\mathcal{D}, \tau, v, i \models \forall x : \phi \quad \mathit{if\ for\ every}\ d \in \mathcal{D}(x)\ \mathit{we\ have}\ \mathcal{D}, \tau, v \dagger [x \mapsto d], i \models \phi$$

Linear temporal logics are usually defined on *infinite* traces. However, in runtime verification, we evaluate formulas on *finite* traces. We therefore consider how temporal properties should behave at the end of a trace. A common approach (see [18]) is to assume that *next* and *eventually* evaluate to *false* beyond the end of a finite trace and *always* evaluates to true. This captures the intuition that these modalities represent obligations for something desired to happen in the unfinished trace whereas the *always* modality captures an obligation for something undesired not to happen. We capture this idea with a special treatment of $\phi_1\, \mathcal{U}^\circ\, \phi_2$, where ϕ_2 is *false*. In this case, we allow the obligation to hold after the end of the trace. This gives the above trace semantics for the temporal modality $\mathcal{U}^\circ$.

We write $\tau \models \phi$ if a trace τ satisfies a property ϕ, defined as follows

$$\tau \models \phi \quad \mathit{iff} \quad \mathtt{dom}(\tau, \phi), \tau, [], 0 \models \phi$$

where the domain function dom is defined as:

$$\mathtt{dom}(\tau, \phi)(x) = \{d_i \mid e(\ldots, d_i, \ldots) \in \tau \wedge e(\ldots, x_i, \ldots) \in \mathtt{events}(\phi) \wedge x_i = x\}$$

Prefix Semantics. An alternative way of viewing finite traces is as *prefixes* of infinite traces, leading to a multi-valued semantics based on whether the trace could be extended to an accepting infinite trace [8]. We do not consider this view here but note that QEA [3] has this notion of multi-valued verdicts based on possible extensions. We will explore this correspondence further in future work.

3   Parametric Trace Slicing

Parametric trace slicing [9] is a technique that transforms a monitoring problem involving quantification *over finite domains* into a propositional one. The idea is to take each valuation of the quantified variables and consider the specification *grounded* with that valuation for the trace *projected* with respect to the valuation. Ground events can then be considered as propositional symbols in the specification and in the projected traces. The benefit of this approach is that projection can lead to efficient indexing techniques.

Introductory Example. We illustrate the notion of trace slicing using an example of calls and returns of (non-recursive) methods. A required property is that whenever a method m_2 is called inside a method m_1, the method m_2 should return before m_1. This gives rise to a set of abstract events: $\mathtt{call}(m_1), \mathtt{return}(m_1), \mathtt{call}(m_2), \mathtt{return}(m_2)$. The property should hold *for all* values for m_1 and m_2 and is therefore a *quantified* property. To understand how trace slicing works consider the following trace:

$$\mathtt{call}(A).\mathtt{call}(B).\mathtt{call}(C).\mathtt{return}(C).\mathtt{return}(B).\mathtt{call}(C).\mathtt{return}(C).\mathtt{return}(A)$$

There are three values that m_1 and m_2 can take, A, B or C, and the trace is *sliced* with respect to each valuation of m_1 and m_2. The following table gives the trace slices for the non-equal values for m_1 and m_2, omitting symmetric cases.

m_1	m_2	slice
A	B	$\mathtt{call}(A).\mathtt{call}(B).\mathtt{return}(B).\mathtt{return}(A)$
A	C	$\mathtt{call}(A).\mathtt{call}(C).\mathtt{return}(C).\mathtt{call}(C).\mathtt{return}(C).\mathtt{return}(A)$
B	C	$\mathtt{call}(B).\mathtt{call}(C).\mathtt{return}(C).\mathtt{return}(B).\mathtt{call}(C).\mathtt{return}(C)$

Each slice can be checked against a quantifier-free property for a given m_1 and m_2. The above property is captured in the automaton below which processes the trace by replacing m_1 and m_2 appropriately for each slice.

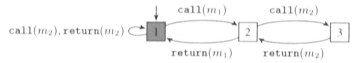

3.1 Defining Slicing

We define a variant of slicing as in [17], which is based on [9]. Let $\mathcal{A}(X)$ be an *event alphabet* (i.e. a set of events) where events use exactly those variables in the set X. A **quantifier-free property** $\mathcal{P}(X)$ over alphabet $\mathcal{A}(X)$ defines a language $\mathcal{L}(\mathcal{P}(X))$ over $\mathcal{A}(X)$. This can be grounded by giving values for X. Given a valuation θ with domain X let the grounded language $\mathcal{L}(\theta, \mathcal{P}(X))$ be given by θ applied to each event in each trace of $\mathcal{L}(\mathcal{P}(X))$. For example we may have $\mathsf{a}(x).\mathsf{b}(y) \in \mathcal{L}(\mathcal{P}(\{x, y\}))$ and therefore $\mathsf{a}(1).\mathsf{b}(2) \in \mathcal{L}([x \mapsto 1, y \mapsto 2], \mathcal{P}(\{x, y\}))$. Slicing can then be defined in terms of the ground events from the trace that match events in the event alphabet:

Definition 2 (Slicing). *Given a trace τ and valuation θ let $\tau \downarrow_\theta$ be the θ-slice of τ*

$$\epsilon \downarrow_\theta \quad = \epsilon$$
$$\tau.e(\overline{v}) \downarrow_\theta = \begin{cases} (\tau \downarrow_\theta).e(\overline{v}) & \text{if } \exists e(\overline{z}) \in \mathcal{A}(X) : \theta(e(\overline{z})) = e(\overline{v}) \\ (\tau \downarrow_\theta) & \text{otherwise} \end{cases}$$

A **quantified property** $\langle \Lambda(X), \mathcal{P}(X) \rangle$ consists of a list of quantifications (quantifiers and variables) and a quantifier-free property over a shared set of variables X. Some systems [15] only consider universal quantification and in this case acceptance is defined as the acceptance by $\mathcal{P}(X)$ of **all** θ-trace slices for all possible valuations θ. However, it is straightforward to introduce existential quantification also [3]. In this case the notion of acceptance captures the boolean combination of the quantifier-free acceptance for possible valuations.

Definition 3 (Acceptance). *The trace τ is accepted for quantification list $\Lambda(X)$ and propositional property $\mathcal{P}(X)$ if $\tau \models_{[]}^{\mathcal{P}(X)} \Lambda(X)$, defined as*

$$\tau \models_\theta^{\mathcal{P}(X)} \forall x : \Lambda \quad \text{if for every } d \in \mathbf{dom}(x) \text{ we have } \tau \models_{\theta \dagger [x \mapsto d]}^{\mathcal{P}(X)} \Lambda$$
$$\tau \models_\theta^{\mathcal{P}(X)} \exists x : \Lambda \quad \text{if for some } d \in \mathbf{dom}(x) \text{ we have } \tau \models_{\theta \dagger [x \mapsto d]}^{\mathcal{P}(X)} \Lambda$$
$$\tau \models_\theta^{\mathcal{P}(X)} \epsilon \quad \quad \text{if } \tau \downarrow_\theta \in \mathcal{L}(\theta, \mathcal{P}(X))$$

3.2 Choices for the Quantifier-Free Language

The JAVAMOP system [15] is based on parametric trace slicing and introduces multiple languages for the quantifier-free part, including finite state automata and linear temporal logic. Quantified Event Automata (QEA) [3,16] use a form of extended finite state machine that allows unquantified variables to capture changing values in the trace. Later (Sect. 8) we discuss how this can be used to extend the fragment of FO-LTL$_f$ defined next. Note that QEA has a very efficient monitoring tool MARQ [17]. Here we use a simplified form of QEA that uses finite state automata as the quantifier-free formalism.

4   Temporal Logic and Trace Slicing

In this section, we introduce a syntactic fragment of FO-LTL$_f$ (see Sect. 2), and show how it relates to trace slicing. We begin by introducing the notion of *slicing invariance* and then discuss restrictions on FO-LTL$_f$ formulas that respect this invariance. Finally, we describe a syntactic fragment that satisfies these restrictions.

4.1   Sliceability

A formula in FO-LTL$_f$ is *sliceable* if its truth value for a valuation of its free variables is the same over a trace and the corresponding trace slice:

Definition 4. *A formula ψ with free variables X is* sliceable *if for valuation θ over X and trace τ*

$$\tau, \theta \models \psi \quad \Leftrightarrow \quad \tau \downarrow_\theta, \theta \models \psi.$$

We can phrase sliceability in terms of invariance with respect to *non-relevant events* i.e. the evaluation is stable under the deletion and addition of those events that are removed during slicing. The events relevant to a formula ψ, for valuation θ, are defined as relevant$(\psi, \theta) = \{\theta(\mathbf{a}) \mid \mathbf{a} \in \text{events}(\psi)\}$. Thus, a trace slice includes exactly those events relevant to the valuation. A formula is *slicing invariant* if adding/removing non-relevant events to/from a trace has no effect on whether the trace satisfies the formula:

Definition 5 (Slicing invariance). *Given a formula ψ with free variables X and valuation θ over X, let $\mathcal{L}(\psi, \theta) = \{\tau \mid \tau, \theta \models \psi\}$ be the set of traces that satisfy ψ. Let the* non-relevance-closure *of $\mathcal{L}(\psi, \theta)$ be inductively defined as the smallest set satisfying*

$$
\begin{aligned}
\tau &\in \mathcal{L}^C(\psi, \theta) \quad \text{if } \tau \in \mathcal{L}(\psi, \theta) \\
\tau_1.\tau_2.\tau_3 &\in \mathcal{L}^C(\psi, \theta) \quad \text{if } \forall \mathbf{a} \in \tau_2 : \mathbf{a} \notin \text{relevant}(\psi, \theta) \text{ and } \tau_1.\tau_3 \in \mathcal{L}^C(\psi, \theta) \\
\tau_1.\tau_3 &\in \mathcal{L}^C(\psi, \theta) \quad \text{if } \exists \tau_1.\tau_2.\tau_3 \in \mathcal{L}^C(\psi, \theta) : \forall \mathbf{a} \in \tau_2 : \mathbf{a} \notin \text{relevant}(\psi, \theta)
\end{aligned}
$$

The formula ψ is slicing invariant *if $\mathcal{L}(\psi, \theta) = \mathcal{L}^C(\psi, \theta)$.*

Note that if we treat ground events as propositional symbols, as is common in slicing approaches, this invariance corresponds to removing/adding symbols from/to the trace that do not occur in the formula ψ.

We show that the notions of being sliceable and being slicing invariant are the same.

Lemma 1. *The* sliceable *and* slicing invariant *formulas coincide. For slicing invariant formula ψ over X, valuation θ over X and trace τ,*

$$\tau \in \mathcal{L}(\psi, \theta) \Leftrightarrow \tau \downarrow_\theta \in \mathcal{L}(\psi, \theta)$$

Proof. Firstly we note that as ψ is slicing invariant $\mathcal{L}(\psi, \theta) = \mathcal{L}^C(\psi, \theta)$ as per Definition 5. The proof proceeds by induction on the length of τ. For the base case where $\tau = \epsilon$ we have $\tau = \tau \downarrow_\theta$ and the property holds trivially. In general, note that if τ and $\tau \downarrow_\theta$ have the same length then τ contains only relevant events and $\tau = \tau \downarrow_\theta$. Therefore, we assume $\tau = \tau_1.\mathbf{a}.\tau_2$ for some non-relevant event $\mathbf{a}$.

In the $\Rightarrow$ direction assume $\tau \in \mathcal{L}(\psi, \theta)$. As $\mathbf{a}$ is non-relevant and by the second rule in Definition 5 we have $\tau_1.\tau_3 \in \mathcal{L}(\psi, \theta)$. As $\tau_1.\tau_3$ is shorter than τ we can apply the induction hypothesis to conclude $(\tau_1.\tau_3) \downarrow_\theta \in \mathcal{L}(\psi, \theta)$. By definition $\tau \downarrow_\theta = (\tau_1 \downarrow_\theta) . (\tau_3 \downarrow_\theta) = (\tau_1.\tau_3 \downarrow_\theta)$ and the property holds. In the $\Leftarrow$ direction assume $\tau \downarrow_\theta \in \mathcal{L}(\psi, \theta)$. By definition $\tau \downarrow_\theta = \tau_1 \downarrow_\theta .\tau_3 \downarrow_\theta$ as $\mathbf{a}$ is non-relevant. As $\tau_1 \downarrow_\theta .\tau_3 \downarrow_\theta$ is shorted than τ we can apply the induction hypothesis to conclude that $\tau_1.\tau_3 \in \mathcal{L}(\psi, \theta)$. Therefore, by the third rule in Definition 5, we have $\tau_1.\mathbf{a}.\tau_3 \in \mathcal{L}(\psi, \theta)$.

Next, we discuss restrictions that this invariance imposes on formulas. This will motivate a syntactic fragment that allows only sliceable formulas to be written.

4.2   Restrictions on the Structure of Formulas

Not all FO-LTL$_f$ formulas are sliceable. We discuss restrictions that the notion of slicing invariance places on FO-LTL$_f$ formulas. We use Fig. 1 to illustrate these restrictions. It gives an example trace where shaded states are not relevant to a formula ψ over $\{x\}$ and to the valuation $[x = b]$.

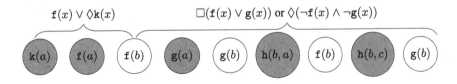

Fig. 1. Illustrating sliceable restrictions

Top-level Quantification: Consider the following formula with *embedded quantifiers* $\exists x : \Box(\mathbf{f}(x) \rightarrow \exists y : \Diamond \mathbf{h}(x, y))$. It is not possible to rewrite this so that the $\exists y$ appears at the top level. Our example trace satisfies the property, but we cannot use slicing to capture this[1]. In the definition of slicing in Sect. 3 *all* variables must be used for slicing. To check this property for $x = b$ it would be necessary to include every $\mathbf{h}(b, y)$ event for an arbitrary number of ys, requiring an arbitrary number of quantifications. Therefore, we consider only FO-LTL$_f$ formulas that have quantification at the top level.

---

[1] Here we refer to the notion of slicing in Sect. 3. A more general notion of slicing involves free variables [3], which could be used for y. It is future work to consider this generalisation.

Starting at the Start: Consider the formula $\mathbf{f}(x) \vee \Diamond\mathbf{k}(x)$ as in Fig. 1. The trace does not satisfy this formula for $x = b$. The first event is not $\mathbf{f}(b)$ and there is no $\mathbf{k}(b)$. However, in the slicing approach, the first event for the $[x = b]$-slice is $\mathbf{f}(b)$ and this would be accepted. The formula $\neg\mathbf{f}(x) \vee \Diamond\mathbf{k}(x)$ would have similar (symmetrical) discrepancy. This means that we cannot allow events (in positive or negative form) at the top level of a sliceable formula. Furthermore, we cannot allow $\mathcal{U}^\circ$ formulas at the top level, as it is not possible to tell whether it should be evaluated from the first or second event in a trace slice, as illustrated by the formula $\neg\mathbf{f}(x) \, \mathcal{U}^\circ \, \mathbf{g}(x)$ for the trace $\mathbf{g}(a).\mathbf{g}(a).\mathbf{f}(b).\mathbf{g}(b)$.

Never Saying Next: Consider the formula $\square(\mathbf{f}(x) \rightarrow \bigcirc\mathbf{g}(x))$ on the trace in Fig. 1. For $x = b$ we have $\mathbf{g}(a)$ after a $\mathbf{f}(b)$; however, in the $[x = b]$-slice this is removed. This shows that evaluation differs after slicing. Formulas must therefore be *next-free*. This *next-freeness* extends to the left side of $\mathcal{U}$ and $\mathcal{U}^\circ$ formulas in general. Consider the formula $\square(\mathbf{f}(x) \vee \mathbf{g}(x)) = (\mathbf{f}(x) \vee \mathbf{g}(x)) \, \mathcal{U} \, false$ as in Fig. 1. The trace does not satisfy the formula; however, for the $[x = b]$-slice it would as the non-relevant events violating $\mathbf{f}(x) \vee \mathbf{g}(x)$ are removed. This shows that the left side of any $\mathcal{U}$ or $\mathcal{U}^\circ$ formula must evaluate to *true* for non-relevant events.

Never Saying Never: Consider the formula $\Diamond(\neg\mathbf{f}(x) \wedge \neg\mathbf{g}(x)) = true \, \mathcal{U} \, (\neg\mathbf{f}(x) \wedge \neg\mathbf{g}(x))$ as in Fig. 1. Here the obligation $(\neg\mathbf{f}(x) \wedge \neg\mathbf{g}(x))$ is never satisfied in the $[x = b]$-slice but it is in the full trace. This shows that the right side of an $\mathcal{U}$ or $\mathcal{U}^\circ$ formula must evaluate to *false* for non-relevant events.

Symmetry: Note that there is a symmetry between the restrictions on the left and right of $\mathcal{U}$ and $\mathcal{U}^\circ$ formulas. This is due to the following identity $\psi_2 \, \mathcal{U} \, \psi_3 = \neg(\neg\psi_3 \, \mathcal{U} \, \neg\psi_2)$ which can turn a restriction on the left to one on the right.

4.3   A Syntactic Fragment

We introduce a syntactic fragment $\mathcal{F}$ of FO-LTL$_f$ that incorporates the restrictions discussed above. The fragment consists of formulas $Q_1 x_1 : \ldots Q_n x_n : \psi_T$ for zero or more quantifications $Q_i x_i$, with $Q_i = \forall$ or $\exists$, and quantifier-free ψ_T inductively defined as:

$$\psi_T = \psi_L \, \mathcal{U} \, \psi_R \mid \psi_T \vee \psi_T \mid \psi_T \wedge \psi_T$$
$$\psi_L = true \mid \psi_L \vee \psi_U \mid \psi_L \wedge \psi_L \mid \neg\mathbf{a}$$
$$\psi_R = false \mid \psi_R \wedge \psi_U \mid \psi_R \vee \psi_R \mid \mathbf{a}$$
$$\psi_U = \psi_L \, \mathcal{U}^\circ \, \psi_R \mid \psi_L \, \mathcal{U} \, \psi_R \mid \psi_U \vee \psi_U \mid \psi_U \wedge \psi_U$$

where $\mathbf{a}$ is an event. This syntax captures the restrictions discussed above: the restricted form of ψ_T captures the restrictions on 'start', and the restrictions on the left and right of $\mathcal{U}$ and $\mathcal{U}^\circ$ formulas are captured by the restricted forms of ψ_L and ψ_R respectively.

Not all identities in FO-LTL$_f$ can be expressed in the fragment $\mathcal{F}$. For example, the definition of the next modality $\bigcirc\phi = false \, \mathcal{U}^\circ \, \phi$ is not in $\mathcal{F}$, as *false* cannot occur by itself on the left side of a $\mathcal{U}^\circ$ formula. The identity $\Diamond\psi_R = true\ \mathcal{U}\ \psi_R$ however, for quantifier-free ψ_R, is expressed in $\mathcal{F}$, but $\Box\phi = \phi\ \mathcal{U}\ false$ is not in general in $\mathcal{F}$ because of the restrictions placed on the left side of $\mathcal{U}^\circ$. However, $\Box(\mathbf{a} \to \psi_R)$ is expressible in $\mathcal{F}$ as $\neg\mathbf{a}\vee\psi_R$ is an allowed left formula for $\mathcal{U}$.

We show that formulas in $\mathcal{F}$ are *sliceable*. Lemma 2 first shows that the structure of formulas in $\mathcal{F}$ allows non-relevant events to be added and removed from a trace.

Lemma 2. *For any formula* $\psi \in \mathcal{F}$ *with free variables* X, *traces* τ_1 *and* τ_2, *valuations* θ *over* X, *events* $\mathbf{a} \notin$ relevant(ψ,θ) *and indices* i *and* j:

> **Case 1.** *If* ψ *is in* ψ_L, ψ_R *or* ψ_U *and* $(\tau_1.\mathbf{a}.\tau_2)_i \in$ relevant(ψ,θ) *then* $\tau_1.\mathbf{a}.\tau_2,\theta,i \models \psi \Leftrightarrow \tau_1.\tau_2,\theta,j \models \psi$ *where* $j = i$ *if* $i < |\tau_1|$ *or* $j = i - 1$ *otherwise.*
> **Case 2.** *If* ψ *is in* ψ_L *then* $\tau_1.\mathbf{a}.\tau_2,\theta,|\tau_1| \models \psi$ *i.e.* ψ *holds at* $\mathbf{a}$.
> **Case 3.** *If* ψ *is in* ψ_R *then* $\tau_1.\mathbf{a}.\tau_2,\theta,|\tau_1| \not\models \psi$ *i.e.* ψ *does not hold at* $\mathbf{a}$.
> **Case 4.** *If* ψ *is in* ψ_T *then* $\tau_1.\mathbf{a}.\tau_2,\theta,0 \models \psi \Leftrightarrow \tau_1.\tau_2,\theta,0 \models \psi$.

Proof. By simultaneous structural induction on ψ, under the assumption that the properties hold for appropriate subformulas.

Case 1. If $i \neq |\tau_1|$ then $(\tau_1.\mathbf{a}.\tau_2)_i = (\tau_1.\tau_2)_j$ and $i = |\tau_1|$ is not allowed as the event at $(\tau_1.\mathbf{a}.\tau_2)_i$ must be relevant. The base cases *true*, *false*, $\mathbf{a}$ and $\neg\mathbf{a}$ hold trivially. The conjunctive and disjunctive cases follow from the induction hypothesis. The interesting cases are $\mathcal{U}$ and $\mathcal{U}^\circ$, we consider $\mathcal{U}$ and then describe the extension to $\mathcal{U}^\circ$.

For the $\Rightarrow$ direction assume $\tau_1.\mathbf{a}.\tau_2,\theta,i \models \psi_L\ \mathcal{U}\ \psi_R$ and therefore there must exist a $k \geq i$ such that $\tau_1.\mathbf{a}.\tau_2,\theta,k \models \psi_R$. By the induction hypothesis $\tau_1.\tau_2,\theta,l \models \psi_R$ where l depends on the location of $\mathbf{a}$, note that the induction hypothesis can be used as by case 3, the event at k is relevant. By the assumption, ψ_L holds at all points $m \geq i$ and $m < l$ in $\tau_1.\mathbf{a}.\tau_2$ and so by the induction hypothesis and case 2 (when the point is not relevant) it holds in all such points in $\tau_1.\tau_2$. Therefore, $\tau_1.\tau_2,\theta,j \models \psi_L\ \mathcal{U}\ \psi_R$.

The $\Leftarrow$ direction is similar. Again, we can assume that $\tau_1.\tau_2,\theta,k \models \psi_R$ for some $k \geq i$ and therefore, by the induction hypothesis, $\tau_1.\mathbf{a}.\tau_2,\theta,l \models \psi_R$. Also we argue by the assumption, the induction hypothesis and case 2 that ψ_L holds for all points i to l, including the new $|\tau_1|$ if included in the range. Therefore, $\tau_1.\mathbf{a}.\tau_2,\theta,i \models \psi_L\ \mathcal{U}\ \psi_R$.

For the $\mathcal{U}^\circ$ case the proof is similar but we reason about ψ_R being satisfied at a point k *strictly greater* than i. This relies on τ_i being relevant as this prevents $i = |\tau_1|$, which is necessary for the $\Rightarrow$ direction. If $i = |\tau_1|$ and $k = |\tau_1| + 1$ then due to the semantics of $\mathcal{U}^\circ$ we can no longer argue that $\tau_1.\tau_2,\theta,l \models \psi_R$ implies that $\tau_1.\tau_2,\theta,j \models \psi_L\ \mathcal{U}^\circ\ \psi_R$ as we would have $l = j$.

Case 2. If $\psi = true$ then this holds trivially. If $\psi = \neg\mathbf{b}$ then this will be satisfied by all non-relevant $\mathbf{a}$. Both the conjunctive and disjunctive cases follows from the inductive hypothesis as in the $\wedge$ case both parts are in ψ_L and in the $\vee$ case at least one is.

Case 3. If $\psi = \mathit{false}$ then this holds trivially. For $\psi = \mathbf{b}$, $\mathbf{b} \neq \mathbf{a}$ as $\mathbf{a}$ is not relevant. Again the conjunctive and disjunctive cases follow from the inductive hypothesis.

Case 4. The conjunctive and disjunctive cases follow from the inductive hypothesis. The $\mathcal{U}$ case is the same as the argument above for case 1 where $i = 0$ and the condition that τ_i is relevant can be dropped as this is not used.

Finally, any formula that can be expressed in $\mathcal{F}$ is sliceable:

Theorem 1. *All formulas in $\mathcal{F}$ are sliceable.*

Proof (Sketch). Any $\psi \in \mathcal{F}$ is slicing invariant. This follows from Lemma 2 by induction on the length of τ using Definition 5 (similar to the proof of Lemma 1).

5   From Temporal Logic to Automata

In this section, we introduce a translation from formulas in $\mathcal{F}$ to the slicing-based formalism QEA. This is based on the notion of *progression* and a normal form that ensures a finite number of syntactically different formulas resulting from progression.

$$\frac{\bar{x} = \bar{y}}{\mathbf{e}(\bar{y}) \xrightarrow{\mathbf{e}(\bar{v})} true} \qquad \frac{\bar{x} \neq \bar{y}}{\mathbf{e}(\bar{y}) \xrightarrow{\mathbf{e}(\bar{v})} false} \qquad \frac{\psi \xrightarrow{\mathbf{e}(\bar{v})} \psi'}{\neg\psi \xrightarrow{\mathbf{e}(\bar{v})} \neg\psi'} \qquad \frac{\psi_1 \xrightarrow{\mathbf{e}(\bar{v})} \psi_1' \quad \psi_2 \xrightarrow{\mathbf{e}(\bar{v})} \psi_2'}{\psi_1 \wedge \psi_2 \xrightarrow{\mathbf{e}(\bar{v})} \psi_1' \wedge \psi_2'}$$

$$\frac{\psi_1 \xrightarrow{\mathbf{e}(\bar{v})} \psi_1' \quad \psi_2 \xrightarrow{\mathbf{e}(\bar{v})} \psi_2'}{\psi_1 \vee \psi 2 \xrightarrow{\mathbf{e}(\bar{v})} \psi_1' \vee \psi_2'} \qquad \frac{}{\psi_1 \, \mathcal{U}^\circ \, \psi_2 \xrightarrow{\mathbf{e}(\bar{v})} \psi_2 \vee (\psi_1 \wedge (\psi_1 \, \mathcal{U}^\circ \, \psi_2))}$$

$$\begin{aligned}
\mathbf{accept}(\mathit{true}) &= \mathit{true} & \mathbf{accept}(\neg\psi) &= \mathbf{not\ accept}(\psi) \\
\mathbf{accept}(\mathbf{a}) &= \mathit{false} & \mathbf{accept}(\psi_1 \, \mathcal{U}^\circ \, \psi_2) &= \\
\mathbf{accept}(\psi_1 \wedge \psi_2) &= \mathbf{accept}(\psi_1) \text{ and } \mathbf{accept}(\psi_2) & \quad \mathit{true} &\quad \text{if } \psi_2 = \mathit{false} \\
\mathbf{accept}(\psi_1 \vee \psi_2) &= \mathbf{accept}(\psi_1) \text{ or } \mathbf{accept}(\psi_2) & \quad \mathit{false} &\quad \text{otherwise}
\end{aligned}$$

Fig. 2. The progression and acceptance rules.

5.1   Progression

Figure 2 gives the progression and acceptance rules for FO-LTL$_f$ formulas. The progression rules show how formulas are rewritten, note that these convert formulas in $\mathcal{F}$ to formulas not necessarily in $\mathcal{F}$. The acceptance rules capture whether a formula is currently accepting. Firstly, we note that progression preserves the semantics of FO-LTL$_f$:

Lemma 3. *For every* FO-LTL$_f$ *formula* ψ, *valuation* θ *and trace* τ *we have*

$$\tau, \theta, 0 \models \psi \qquad \Leftrightarrow \qquad \tau, \theta, |\tau| \models \psi' \text{ for } \psi \xrightarrow{\tau \downarrow_0} \psi'$$

Proof (Sketch). By induction on the structures of τ then ψ, noting that the progression rules follow $\models$ (in Definition 1). For a similar proof, see Lemmas 3 and 4 in [6].

Secondly, the acceptance rules capture the desired behaviour i.e. what the verdict would be if the trace terminated at this point. Note that the rule for $\mathcal{U}^\circ$ reflects the notion of outstanding obligations alongside the finite-trace interpretation of $\Box$:

Lemma 4. *For every $\psi \in \mathcal{F}$ and valuation θ*

$$\epsilon, \theta, 0 \models \psi \Leftrightarrow \tau, \theta, |\tau| \models \psi \Leftrightarrow \texttt{accept}(\theta(\psi))$$

Proof (Sketch). By induction on the structure of ψ, we show that $\texttt{accept}$ respects the semantics $\models$.

5.2   A Normal Form

We give a normal form that gives an upper bound for the number of progression steps to syntactically different formulas. This approach was inspired by [18] and a similar result has recently been established in [19].

The normal form is given by the following rewrite rules.

$$
\begin{array}{llll}
true \wedge \psi \;\rightarrow\; \psi & \neg\neg\psi & \rightarrow \psi & \\
\psi \wedge true \;\rightarrow\; \psi & \psi_1 \wedge \psi_2 & \rightarrow \psi_1 & \text{if } \psi_1 = \psi_2 \\
\neg true \vee \psi \rightarrow \psi & \psi_1 \vee \psi_2 & \rightarrow \psi_1 & \text{if } \psi_1 = \psi_2 \\
\psi \vee \neg true \rightarrow \psi & \left(\bigvee_i \psi_i\right) \wedge \left(\bigwedge_j \psi_j\right) & \rightarrow \bigvee_i \left(\psi_i \wedge \left(\bigwedge_j \psi_j\right)\right) &
\end{array}
$$

A formula is in normal form if none of these rewrite rules can be applied to any of its subformulas. We write $\texttt{nf}(\psi)$ for the normal form of ψ. If $\psi \in \mathcal{F}$ then $\texttt{nf}(\psi)$ is a disjunction of conjunctions where each conjunct is either an event or a *temporal formula* i.e. a $\mathcal{U}^\circ$ formula. We first show:

Lemma 5. *For $\psi \in \mathcal{F}$, let $\mathcal{T}$ be the temporal subformulas of ψ, every formula ψ' such that $\psi \xrightarrow{\tau} \psi'$ for any trace τ, has temporal subformulas $\mathcal{T}' \subseteq \mathcal{T}$.*

Proof. The only progression rule dealing with temporal formulas is the $\mathcal{U}^\circ$ rule. This copies the temporal formula. Therefore, no new temporal formulas are created.

Next we show that there can be no infinite progression sequences without repeating formulas syntactically equivalent up to normal form.

Lemma 6. *Any formula $\psi \in \mathcal{F}$ has a finite number of formulas ψ' such that $\psi \xrightarrow{\tau} \psi'$ for any trace τ.*

Proof. Let $\mathcal{P}(\psi)$ be the set of formulas in normal form that can be built from boolean combinations of events in ψ and formulas in $\mathcal{T}$, the temporal subformulas of ψ. The set $\mathcal{P}(\psi)$ is finite as there are a finite number of events and $\mathcal{T}$ is finite. From Lemma 5, ψ', we have $\psi' \in \mathcal{P}(\psi)$ and therefore there are a finite number of such ψ'.

Furthermore, $\mathcal{P}(\psi)$ is bounded by $2^{|\psi|}$ (see the result in [19]), giving an upper bound on such a sequence.

5.3 Progression-Based Translation

We now introduce a translation based on progression. We begin by introducing a translation from quantifier-free formulas to state machines.

Definition 6 (Quantifier-free translation). *Given a quantifier-free formula* $\psi \in \mathcal{F}$, *let* $\mathtt{translate}(\psi) = \langle Q, q_0, \mathcal{A}, \delta, F \rangle$ *be the automaton such that*

$$
\begin{aligned}
\mathcal{A} &= \mathtt{events}(\psi) & Q &= \{q_0\} \cup \{\mathtt{nf}(\psi') \mid \exists \tau : \psi \xrightarrow{\tau} \psi'\} \\
q_0 &= \mathtt{nf}(\psi) & \delta(\psi', \mathtt{a}) &= \mathtt{nf}(\psi'') \text{ where } \psi' \in Q, \mathtt{a} \in \mathcal{A} \text{ and } \psi' \xrightarrow{\mathtt{a}} \psi'' \\
& & F &= \{\psi' \in Q \mid \mathtt{accept}(\psi')\}
\end{aligned}
$$

It is important that the constructed state machine is finite, so that this translation step terminates. This follows from Lemma 6, as there are only a finite number of syntactically distinct ψ' such that $\psi \xrightarrow{\tau} \psi'$. This also puts an upper bound of $2^{|\psi|}$ on the number of states of the automata.

There exists a simple procedure for building this state machine that begins with a set of states S containing the initial formula/state and the set of events $\mathcal{A}$ and considers all possible progressions from states in S for events in $\mathcal{A}$, producing a new set of reachable states S'. This is then repeated for $S' \backslash S$.

This automata translation captures the progression semantics directly:

Lemma 7. *For every quantifier-free formula* ψ *and trace* τ

$$
\psi \xrightarrow{\tau} \psi' \qquad \Leftrightarrow \qquad \delta(\psi, \tau) = \psi'
$$

where δ *is the transition relation of* $\mathtt{translate}(\psi)$

Proof (Sketch). By induction on the structure of τ. Note that δ is defined directly in terms of progression.

We then define the full translation from quantified temporal formulas in $\mathcal{F}$ to QEA.

Definition 7 (Translation). *Let* $\mathtt{translate}(\phi) = \langle \Lambda(X), \mathcal{E} \rangle$ *such that for* $\phi = Q_1 x_1 : \ldots Q_n x_n : \psi$, $\Lambda(X) = Q_1 x_1 : \ldots Q_n x_n$ *and* $\mathcal{E} = \mathtt{translate}(\psi)$.

5.4 An Example of the Translation

Let us consider the translation of the standard HasNext temporal formula that will be described in Sect. 6. In the following, we use $\mathbf{h} = \mathtt{hasNext}(i)$ and $\mathbf{n} = \mathtt{next}(i)$. The formula for the property is given as follows where we rewrite $\mathcal{U}$, $\square$ and $\rightarrow$.

$$
\psi = (\mathbf{h} \vee (\mathbf{n} \wedge (\neg \mathbf{n} \, \mathcal{U}^\circ \, \mathbf{h}))) \wedge (\neg \mathbf{n} \vee (\neg \mathbf{n} \, \mathcal{U}^\circ \, \mathbf{h})) \wedge ((\neg \mathbf{n} \vee (\neg \mathbf{n} \, \mathcal{U}^\circ \, \mathbf{h})) \, \mathcal{U}^\circ \, \mathit{false})
$$

The following shows the *normal form* of rewriting each subformula of ψ with respect to the events $\mathbf{h}$ and $\mathbf{n}$.

$$\phi_1 = n \quad \xrightarrow{h} \quad false$$
$$\xrightarrow{n} \quad true$$
$$\phi_2 = h \quad \xrightarrow{h} \quad true$$
$$\xrightarrow{n} \quad false$$
$$\phi_3 = \neg\phi_1 \, \mathcal{U}^\circ \phi_2 \xrightarrow{h,n} \phi_4$$

$$\phi_4 = \phi_2 \vee (\neg\phi_1 \wedge \phi_3) \xrightarrow{h} true$$
$$\xrightarrow{n} false$$
$$\phi_5 = \neg\phi_1 \vee \phi_3 \qquad \xrightarrow{h} true$$
$$\xrightarrow{n} \phi_4$$
$$\phi_6 = \phi_5 \, \mathcal{U}^\circ false \qquad \xrightarrow{h,n} \phi_5 \wedge \phi_6$$
$$\psi = \phi_4 \wedge \phi_6 \qquad \xrightarrow{h} \phi_5 \wedge \phi_6$$
$$\xrightarrow{n} false$$

From this we can observe three states: ψ, *false* and $\phi_5 \wedge \phi_6$. Observe that $\phi_5 \wedge \phi_6 \xrightarrow{n} (\phi_4 \wedge \phi_5 \wedge \phi_6) = \psi$. The final states are given by `accept` where `accept`(*false*) = *false* and `accept`(ψ) and `accept`($\phi_5 \wedge \phi_6$) are *true* due to their top level $\mathcal{U}^\circ$ operators. This gives the following automaton.

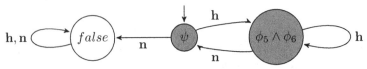

5.5   Correctness of Translation

We show that the translated QEA is trace-equivalent to the original formula. We first establish the unquantified case.

Lemma 8. *For any unquantified $\psi \in \mathcal{F}$ with free variables X, trace τ, and valuation θ over X*

$$\tau, \theta \models \psi \quad \Leftrightarrow \quad \tau \downarrow_\theta \in \mathcal{L}(\texttt{translate}(\psi))$$

Proof. As $\psi \in \mathcal{F}$ is sliceable (by Theorem 1) this can be rewritten as

$$\tau \downarrow_\theta, \theta \models \psi \quad \Leftrightarrow \quad \tau \downarrow_\theta \in \mathcal{L}(\texttt{translate}(\psi)) \tag{1}$$

By definition $\mathcal{L}(\texttt{translate}(\psi)) = \{\tau \mid \delta(\psi, \tau) = \psi' \text{ and } \texttt{accepts}(\psi')\}$. Therefore, by Lemmas 7 and 4 the right side of (1) can be rewritten

$$\psi \xrightarrow{\tau\downarrow_\theta} \psi' \text{ and } \tau \downarrow_\theta, \theta, |\tau \downarrow_\theta | \models \psi' \tag{2}$$

and by Lemma 3, (2) can be rewritten as $\tau \downarrow_\theta, \theta \models \psi$, showing the equivalence holds.

This can be used to show the correctness in the quantified case.

Theorem 2. *For every trace τ and a formula $\phi \in \mathcal{F}$*

$$\tau \models \phi \quad \Leftrightarrow \quad \tau \models_{[]}^{\mathcal{P}(X)} \Lambda(X)$$

where $\texttt{translate}(\phi) = \langle \Lambda(X), \mathcal{P}(X) \rangle$.

Proof (Sketch). By structural induction on the quantification structure of ϕ and Lemma 8.

6 The Fragment $\mathcal{F}$ as a Trace Specification Language

Are syntactic fragments of FO-LTL$_f$ that respect a notion of sliceability expressive enough to be considered as practically useful trace specification languages? We consider how we may answer this question for the syntactic fragment $\mathcal{F}$. However, assessing the (practically useful) expressiveness of a specification language for runtime verification is currently not easy and there are no accepted methods, or accepted corpora of cases or specification patterns likely to occur in real runtime verification applications.

Common Patterns. In 1999 Dwyer et al. conducted a survey of common finite-state properties used for *model-checking* in industry and academia [11]. We consider whether some of the more common properties are expressible in $\mathcal{F}$.

A common pattern is that of *response* written $\Box(P \rightarrow \Diamond Q)$. This can be rewritten to $(\neg P \vee (true \, \mathcal{U} \, Q)) \, \mathcal{U} \, false$, which is a formula expressed in the fragment. Another pattern in the collection is an *absence* property stating that P does not occur before R. We show how this can be rewritten into a formula expressed in the fragment.

$$(\Diamond R \rightarrow \neg P \, \mathcal{U} \, R) = (\neg(true \, \mathcal{U} \, R) \vee (\neg P \, \mathcal{U} \, R)) = (\neg R \, \mathcal{U} \, false) \vee (\neg P \, \mathcal{U} \, R)$$

A more complex absence property that may appear to be outside of the fragment at first is that P does not occur between Q and R, written as $\Box((Q \wedge \bigcirc \Diamond R) \rightarrow (\neg P \wedge \bigcirc(\neg P \, \mathcal{U} \, R)))$. This can be written using the identities such as $\bigcirc \Diamond R = true \, \mathcal{U}^\circ R$ to be $(\neg Q \vee (\neg R \, \mathcal{U}^\circ false) \vee (\neg P \wedge (\neg P \, \mathcal{U}^\circ R))) \, \mathcal{U} \, false$.

A set of patterns from this study that cannot be expressed in $\mathcal{F}$ are the general *universality* patterns $\Box P$. However, specific cases of these may be expressible.

This is but a small sample, and only for common model-checking properties, but the technique is clear.

Specifications in the Literature. There are specifications commonly occurring as examples in RV literature that belong to the fragment $\mathcal{F}$, we give some of these here.

HasNext. For every iterator i the first event is hasNext(i) and whenever a next(i) event occurs there is not another next(i) event until there has been a hasNext(i) event. This can be captured by the following formula in $\mathcal{F}$.

$$\forall i : (\neg \mathtt{next}(i) \, \mathcal{U} \, \mathtt{hasNext}(i)) \wedge \Box(\mathtt{next}(i) \rightarrow (\neg \mathtt{next}(i) \, \mathcal{U}^\circ \, \mathtt{hasNext}(i)))$$

UnsafeMapIter. For every map m, collection c and iterator i, whenever c is created from m and i is created from c, after m is updated i should not be used.

$$\forall m : \forall c : \forall i : \Box(\mathtt{create}(m, c) \rightarrow \Box(\mathtt{iterator}(c, i) \rightarrow \Box(\mathtt{update}(m) \rightarrow \Box \neg \mathtt{use}(i))))$$

CallNesting. The call-nesting property given to motivate the slicing approach earlier can also be specified in $\mathcal{F}$ as follows.

$$\forall m_1 : \forall m_2 : (\neg \texttt{return}(m_1) \ \mathcal{U} \ \texttt{call}(m_1)) \wedge (\neg \texttt{return}(m_2) \ \mathcal{U} \ \texttt{call}(m_2)) \wedge$$
$$\Box(\texttt{call}(m_1) \rightarrow (\neg \texttt{call}(m_1) \ \mathcal{U} \ \texttt{return}(m_1))) \wedge \Box(\texttt{call}(m_1) \rightarrow$$
$$(\texttt{call}(m_2) \rightarrow ((\neg \texttt{return}(m_2) \wedge \neg \texttt{call}(m_2)) \ \mathcal{U} \ \texttt{return}(m_2))) \ \mathcal{U} \ \texttt{return}(m_1))$$

Note how the formula requires many parts to capture the different paths through the previously defined automaton. This demonstrates the differing usability of the two approaches. This study could be extended by considering the slicing-based specifications for the Java JDK given in [13]. We expect all slicing-based specifications from work with JAVAMOP that use a regular propositional language to be expressible in $\mathcal{F}$.

7   Related Work

This work aims to connect approaches based on parametric trace slicing with those based on first-order temporal logic. We give an overview of related work in each area. We have not considered the rule-based system approach [4], where some work has linked the expressiveness of rule systems with (propositional) temporal logic [4].

Slicing. Arguably, the first system to use trace-slicing was tracematches [2], but the paper did not use this terminology, and the suffix-based matching meant that the authors did not need to solve the main technical difficulty in slicing i.e. dealing with partial bindings. The JAVAMOP system [15] has made the slicing approach popular with its highly efficient implementation. The QEA formalism [3,16] and associated MARQ tool [17] were inspired by JAVAMOP. The notion of slicing presented here is compatible with that used in JAVAMOP. Note that the combination of slicing and propositional LTL used in JAVAMOP does not correspond to a first-order temporal logic. For example, the JAVAMOP property $\Lambda x.\Box(\texttt{f}(x) \rightarrow \bigcirc \texttt{g}(x))$ does not have the standard first-order temporal logic interpretation as discussed in Sect. 4.

First-order Temporal Logics in RV. Most approaches that add first-order reasoning to LTL for runtime verification use similar concepts, with the main difference typically being the *domain of quantification*. An early work extending LTL by parameters by Stolz and Bodden [20] makes bindings locally in a PROLOG-style. Bauer et al. [7] have proposed a variant of first-order LTL where quantification is restricted to the values known at a single point in time. Decker et al. [10] introduce the notion of *temporal data logic*, an extension of temporal logic with first-order theories. Monpoly [5] constructs monitors for a safety-fragment of metric first-order temporal logic where temporal operators are augmented with intervals. Yoshi et al. [14] introduce a parallel monitoring approach for first-order LTL extended with second-order numerical constraints. In principle it would be possible to consider restricting all of these logics syntactically so that they could be sliceable. However, in some cases the syntactic fragment may not be useful.

8 Conclusion

The aim of this work is to explore the relationship between first-order temporal logic and parametric trace slicing. We have introduced a technique based on identifying syntactic fragments of temporal logics which respect trace slicing, and defined one such fragment of FO-LTL$_f$. From this fragment, we have shown how we may construct automata with a slicing interpretation i.e. QEA.

The notion of trace slicing, and hence sliceability, used in this work is more restrictive than that used in [3] as it requires all variables to participate in slicing. We briefly discuss possible future work that could lead to different fragments, perhaps of more expressive temporal logics:

Embedded Quantification. There are cases when embedded quantification can be necessary in specification e.g. $\forall x \,:\, \forall t_1 \,:\, \Box(\mathbf{start}(x,t_1) \,\rightarrow\, \exists t_2 \,:\, \mathbf{stop}(x,t_2))$. Here the existential quantification of t_2 cannot be lifted outside of the scope of $\Box$. However, embedded quantification is supported in QEA using *free variables*.

Predicates and Functions. First-order logics usually include predicates and functions. A simple extension would allow predicates on quantified values of the form $\forall x \,:\, p(x) \,\rightarrow\, \psi$ and $\exists x \,:\, p(x) \wedge \psi$. The translation to the slicing setting would be straightforward as QEA support global guards of this form. A more general incorporation of predicates and functions would be supported by the guard and assignments on transitions in the QEA formalism; this would be most appropriate alongside embedded quantification. Predicates and functions require interpretation. These interpretations could be supplied on a built-in or ad-hoc basis or taken from a formal theory, as is done in [10].

Translation from QEA **to Temporal Logic.** Even the restricted form of QEA used in this paper are more expressive than the temporal logic, as it inherits the star-freeness of standard LTL. For example, the language 'there are an even number of a(x) events' cannot be expressed in the logic, but can be expressed as a QEA. Therefore, to translate QEA to temporal logic a more expressive temporal logic is required.

Whilst the fragment $\mathcal{F}$ introduced here does not cover all specifications that might be written in a slicing framework, we have considered how we may assess its practical expressiveness and provided a technique for translating formulas in $\mathcal{F}$ to QEA.

We believe the goal of this work, seeking methods for unifying existing specification languages, is of considerable importance in runtime verification in allowing us to improve the comparability and interoperability of tools.

References

1. CSRV 2014. http://rv2014.imag.fr/monitoring-competition
2. Allan, C., Avgustinov, P., Christensen, A.S., Hendren, L., Kuzins, S., Lhoták, O., de Moor, O., Sereni, D., Sittampalam, G., Tibble, J.: Adding trace matching with free variables to AspectJ. SIGPLAN Not. **40**, 345–364 (2005)

3. Barringer, H., Falcone, Y., Havelund, K., Reger, G., Rydeheard, D.: Quantified event automata: towards expressive and efficient runtime monitors. In: Giannakopoulou, D., Méry, D. (eds.) FM 2012. LNCS, vol. 7436, pp. 68–84. Springer, Heidelberg (2012)
4. Barringer, H., Rydeheard, D., Havelund, K.: Rule systems for run-time monitoring: from EAGLE to RuleR. J. Logic Comput. **20**(3), 675–706 (2010)
5. Basin, D., Harvan, M., Klaedtke, F., Zălinescu, E.: MONPOLY: monitoring usage-control policies. In: Khurshid, S., Sen, K. (eds.) RV 2011. LNCS, vol. 7186, pp. 360–364. Springer, Heidelberg (2012)
6. Bauer, A., Falcone, Y.: Decentralised LTL monitoring. CoRR, abs/1111.5133 (2011)
7. Bauer, A., Küster, J.-C., Vegliach, G.: The ins and outs of first-order runtime verification. Formal Methods in Syst. Des., **46**, 1–31 (2015)
8. Bauer, A., Leucker, M., Schallhart, C.: Comparing LTL semantics for runtime verification. J. Log. Comput. **20**(3), 651–674 (2010)
9. Chen, F., Roşu, G.: Parametric trace slicing and monitoring. In: Kowalewski, S., Philippou, A. (eds.) TACAS 2009. LNCS, vol. 5505, pp. 246–261. Springer, Heidelberg (2009)
10. Decker, N., Leucker, M., Thoma, D.: Monitoring modulo theories. In: Ábrahám, E., Havelund, K. (eds.) TACAS 2014 (ETAPS). LNCS, vol. 8413, pp. 341–356. Springer, Heidelberg (2014)
11. Dwyer, M.B., Avrunin, G.S., Corbett, J.C.: Patterns in property specifications for finite-state verification. In: Proceedings of the 21st International Conference on Software Engineering, ICSE 1999, pp. 411–420. ACM (1999)
12. Falcone, Y., Havelund, K., Reger, G.: A tutorial on runtime verification. In: Summer School Marktoberdorf 2012 - Engineering Dependable Software Systems. IOS Press, Amsterdam (2013)
13. Lee, C., Jin, D., Meredith, P.O., Roşu, G.: Towards categorizing and formalizing the JDK API. Technical report. Department of Computer Science, University of Illinois at Urbana-Champaign (2012). http://hdl.handle.net/2142/30006
14. Medhat, R., Joshi, Y., Bonakdarpour, B., Fischmeister, S.: Parallelized runtime verification of first-order LTL specifications. Technical report, University of Waterloo (2014)
15. Meredith, P., Jin, D., Griffith, D., Chen, F., Roşu, G.: An overview of the MOP runtime verification framework. J. Softw. Tools Technol. Transfer **14**(3), 249–289 (2011)
16. Reger, G.: Automata based monitoring and mining of execution traces. Ph.D. thesis, University of Manchester (2014)
17. Reger, G., Cruz, H.C., Rydeheard, D.: MARQ: monitoring at runtime with QEA. In: Proceedings of the 21st International Conference on Tools and Algorithms for the Construction and Analysis of Systems (TACAS 2015) (2015)
18. Roşu, G., Havelund, K.: Rewriting-based techniques for runtime verification. Autom. Softw. Eng. **12**(2), 151–197 (2005)
19. Shen, Y., Li, J., Wang, Z., Su, T., Fang, B., Pu, G., Liu, W.: Runtime verification by convergent formula progression. In: APSEC 2014 (2014)
20. Stolz, V., Bodden, E.: Temporal assertions using AspectJ. In: Proceedings of the 5th International Workshop on Runtime Verification (RV 2005). ENTCS, vol. 144(4), pp. 109–124. Elsevier (2006)

R2U2: Monitoring and Diagnosis of Security Threats for Unmanned Aerial Systems

Johann Schumann[1]([✉]), Patrick Moosbrugger[1]([✉]), and Kristin Y. Rozier[2]([✉])

[1] SGT, Inc., NASA Ames, Moffett Field, CA, USA
Johann.M.Schumann@nasa.gov, Patrick.Moosbrugger@technikum-wien.at
[2] University of Cincinnati, Cincinnati, OH, USA
Kristin.Y.Rozier@uc.edu

Abstract. We present R2U2, a novel framework for runtime monitoring of security properties and diagnosing of security threats on-board Unmanned Aerial Systems (UAS). R2U2, implemented in FPGA hardware, is a real-time, REALIZABLE, RESPONSIVE, UNOBTRUSIVE Unit for security threat detection. R2U2 is designed to continuously monitor inputs from the GPS and the ground control station, sensor readings, actuator outputs, and flight software status. By simultaneously monitoring and performing statistical reasoning, attack patterns and post-attack discrepancies in the UAS behavior can be detected. R2U2 uses runtime observer pairs for linear and metric temporal logics for property monitoring and Bayesian networks for diagnosis of security threats. We discuss the design and implementation that now enables R2U2 to handle security threats and present simulation results of several attack scenarios on the NASA DragonEye UAS.

1 Introduction

Unmanned Aerial Systems (UAS) are starting to permeate many areas in everyday life. From toy quadcopters, to industrial aircraft for delivery, crop dusting, public safety, and military operations, UAS of vastly different weight, size, and complexity are used. Although the hardware technology has significantly advanced in the past years, there are still considerable issues to be solved before UAS can be used safely. Perhaps the biggest concern is the integration of UAS into the national airspace (NAS), where they have to seamlessly blend into the crowded skies and obey Air Traffic Control commands without endangering other aircraft or lives and property on the ground [5].

A related topic, which has been vastly neglected so far, is security [24]. All sensors and software set up to ensure UAS safety are useless if a malicious attack can cause the UAS to crash, be abducted, or cause severe damage or loss of life. Often, live video feeds from military UAS are not encrypted, so people on the ground, with only minimal and off-the-shelf components, could see the same images as the remote UAS operator [29]. In 2011, Iran allegedly abducted a CIA

This work was supported in part by NASA ARMD 2014 I3AMT Seedling Phase I, NNX12AK33A and the Austrian Josef Ressel Center (VECS).

drone by jamming its command link and spoofing its GPS. Instead of returning to the CIA base, the UAS was directed to land on Iranian territory [6]. Even large research UAS worth millions of dollars are controlled via unencrypted RF connections; most UAS communicate over a large number of possible channels [9], relying on the assumption that "one would have to know the frequencies"[1] to send and receive data.

There are multiple reasons for these gaping security holes: most UAS flight computers are extremely weak with respect to computing power. Thus, on-board encryption is not possible, especially for larger data volumes as produced, for example, by on-board cameras [12]. Another reason is that a lot of UAS technology stems from the Hobby RC area, where security is of low concern. Finally, security aspects have only played a minor role in FAA regulation to date [7].

On a UAS, there are multiple attack surfaces: the communication link, sensor jamming or spoofing, exploitation of software-related issues, and physical attacks like catching a UAS in a net. In this paper, we focus on the detection of communication, sensor, and software-related security threats, but do not elaborate on attack prevention or possible mitigation strategies. Though design-time verification and validation activities can secure a number of attack surfaces, an actual attack will, most likely, happen while the UAS is in the air. We therefore propose the use of dynamic monitoring, threat detection, and security diagnosis.

In order to minimize impact on the flight software and the usually weak flight computer, R2U2 is implemented using FPGA hardware. This no-overhead implementation is designed to uphold the FAA requirements of REALIZABILITY and UNOBTRUSIVENESS. To our knowledge, there are only two previous embedded hardware monitoring frameworks capable of analyzing formal properties: P2V [15] and BusMOP [19,23]. However, P2V is a PSL to Verilog compiler that violates our UNOBTRUSIVENESS requirement by instrumenting software. Like R2U2, BusMOP can monitor COTS peripherals, achieving zero runtime overhead via a bus-interface and an implementation on a reconfigurable FPGA. However, BusMOP violates our REALIZABILITY requirement by reporting only property failures and handling only past-time logics whereas we require early-as-possible reporting of future-time temporal properties passing and intermediate status updates. BusMOP also violates UNOBTRUSIVENESS by executing arbitrary user-supplied code on the occurrence of any property violation.

Previously, we developed our on-board monitoring and diagnosis framework R2U2 for system health management of hardware-only components and developed implementations to detect hardware failures [8,25,27]. We defined and proved correct our FPGA temporal logic observer encodings [25] and our Bayesian network (BN) encodings [8], which comprise R2U2's underlying health model. We also envisioned a compositional building-block framework for integration with other diagnosis technologies that also analyzed software components [27]; in this paper, we follow up on that idea by providing the first implementation of R2U2 that includes software components.

Here, we extend R2U2 to enable the dynamic monitoring of the flight software, the communication stream, and sensor values for indications of a malicious

---

[1] Conversation with an Ikhana/Global Hawk pilot, NASA, 2011.

attack on the autopilot and, even more importantly, to be able to quickly and reliably detect post-attack behavior of the UAS. The temporal and probabilistic health models and their FPGA implementations are suited for fast detection and diagnosis of attacks and post-attack behavior. The separate FPGA implementation of a security extension to R2U2 described in this paper is highly resilient to attacks, being an isolated hardware entity and programmed using VHDL. Javaid et al. [10] also analyze cybersecurity threats for UAS. They simulated the effects of attacks that usually ended in a crash, focusing on identifying different existing attack surfaces and vulnerabilities rather than focusing on runtime detection or post-attack analysis. TeStID [2], ORCHIDS [21], and MONID [20] are intrusion detection systems that use temporal logic to specify attack patterns. These security monitoring frameworks are targeted at IT systems and infrastructure. Our contributions include:

- extending R2U2 from monitoring of safety properties of hardware [8,25] to integrating hardware and software bus traffic monitoring for security threats thus enabling on-board, real-time detection of attack scenarios and post-attack behavior;
- detection of *attack patterns* rather than component failures;
- ensuring monitoring and reasoning are isolated from in-flight attacks; our FPGA implementation provides a platform for secure and independent monitoring and diagnosis that is not re-programmable in-flight by attackers;
- demonstrating R2U2 via case studies on a real NASA DragonEye UAS; and
- implementing a novel extension of R2U2 that we release to enable others to reproduce and build upon our work:
  http://temporallogic.org/research/RV15.html.

The rest of this paper is structured as follows. Section 2 provides background information on our UAS platform, the open-source flight software, and the R2U2 framework. Section 3 is devoted to our approach of using temporal logic observers and BN diagnostic reasoning for detection of security threats and post-attack UAS behavior. In Sect. 4, we will illustrate our approach with several small case studies on attacks through the ground control station (GCS), attempts to hijack a UAS through an attacker GCS, and GPS spoofing. Finally, Sect. 5 discusses future work and concludes.

2   Background

For this paper, we consider a simple and small UAS platform, the NASA DragonEye (Fig. 1A). With a wingspan of 1.1 m it is small, but shares many commonalities with larger and more complex UAS. Figure 1B shows a high-level, generic UAS architecture: the UAS is controlled by an on-board flight computer running the flight software (FSW). It receives measurements from various sensors, like barometric pressure and airspeed, GPS, compass readings, and readings from the inertial measurement unit (IMU). Based upon this information and a flight plan, the FSW calculates the necessary adjustments of the actuators: elevator, rudder, ailerons, throttle. A ground control station (GCS) computer transmits

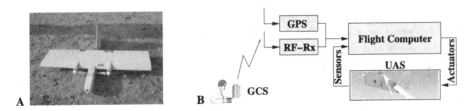

Fig. 1. A: Photo of NASA DragonEye. B: High level system architecture of a small UAS.

commands and flight plans to the UAS, and receives and displays UAS telemetry information. For fully autonomous missions, there is no link between the UAS and the GCS.

Our example system uses the open-source FSW "APM:Plane" [3], which does not contain any security features like command or data encryption for the GCS-UAS link per default. We nevertheless selected this FSW because it very closely resembles the architecture of both similarly small and larger, more complex UAS. This architecture allows us to easily carry out white-box experiments and to study the relationship between attacks and post-attack behavior. Results of our studies can be carried over to highly secure and resilient flight software.

2.1   R2U2

Developed to continuously monitor system and safety properties of a UAS in flight, our real-time R2U2 (REALIZABLE, RESPONSIVE, and UNOBTRUSIVE Unit) has been implemented on an FPGA (Field Programmable Gate Array). Hierarchical and modular models within this framework are defined using Metric Temporal Logic (MTL) and mission-time Linear Temporal Logic (LTL) [25] for expressing temporal properties and Bayesian Networks (BN) for probabilistic and diagnostic reasoning. In the following, we give a high-level overview of the R2U2 framework and its FPGA implementation. For details on temporal reasoning, its implementation, and semantics the reader is referred to [25]; [8] describes details on the FPGA implementation of Bayesian networks. Also [28] provides details on R2U2 modeling and system health management.

Temporal Logic Observers. LTL and MTL formulas consist of propositional variables, the logic operators $\wedge$, $\vee$, $\neg$, or $\rightarrow$, and temporal operators to express temporal relationships between events. For LTL formulas p, q, we have $\Box p$ (ALWAYS p), $\Diamond p$ (EVENTUALLY p), $\mathcal{X}p$ (NEXTTIME p), $p\mathcal{U}q$ (p UNTIL q), and $p\mathcal{R}q$ (p RELEASES q) with their usual semantics [25]. For MTL, each of the temporal operators are accompanied by upper and lower time bounds that express the time period during which the operator must hold. Specifically, MTL includes the operators $\Box_{[i,j]} \, p$, $\Diamond_{[i,j]} \, p$, $p \, \mathcal{U}_{[i,j]} \, q$, and $p \, \mathcal{R}_{[i,j]} \, q$ where the temporal operator applies over the interval between time i and time j, inclusive, and time steps refer to ticks of the system clock. For mission-bounded LTL operators these time bounds are implied to be the start and end of the UAS mission.

Bayesian Networks for Health Models. In many situations, temporal logic monitoring might find several violations of security and safety properties. For example, a certain system state might have been caused by an attack or by a bad sensor; we can use the combination of property violations to determine which one. In order to be able to disambiguate the root causes, the R2U2 framework uses Bayesian Networks (BN) for diagnostic reasoning. BNs are directed acyclic graphs, where each node represents a statistical variable. BNs are well-established in the area of diagnostics and health management (e.g., [18, 22]). Conditional dependencies between the different statistical variables are represented by directed edges; local conditional probabilities are stored in the Conditional Probability Table (CPT) of each node [8, 26, 28]. R2U2 evaluates posterior probabilities, which reflect the most likely root causes at each time step.

2.2 FPGA Implementation

R2U2 is implemented in FPGA hardware (Fig. 2). Signals from the flight computer and communication buses are filtered and discretized in the signal processing (SP) unit to obtain streams of propositional variables. The runtime verification (RV) and runtime reasoning (RR) units comprise the proper health management hardware: the RV unit monitors MTL/LTL properties using pairs of synchronous and asynchronous observers defined in [25]. After the temporal logic formulas have been evaluated, the results are transferred to the RR subsystem, where the compiled Bayesian network is evaluated to yield the posterior marginals of the health model.

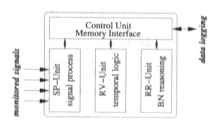

Fig. 2. Principled R2U2 implementation

3   Our Approach to Threat-Detection

For our approach, we consider the "system" UAS (as depicted in Fig. 1B) as a complex feedback system. Commands, GPS readings, and measurements of the sensors are processed by the FSW on the flight computer to calculate new values for the actuators, and to update its internal status. In this paper, we assume that all malicious attacks are attempted via communication during flight.[2] Furthermore, all communications to the UAS are received via a wireless link from the ground control station, or GPS satellites, or transmitters only. Spoofing of the compass sensor, for example, via a strong magnetic field is outside the scope of R2U2.

With our R2U2 framework, we continuously monitor inputs from ground control and GPS and can identify many attack mechanisms and surfaces. Typical examples include denial-of-service, sending of illegal or dangerous commands, or jamming of the GPS receiver. Because, in most cases, information about the communication does not suffice to reliably identify an attack scenario, additional supporting information is necessary. This will be obtained from the analysis of post-attack behavior of the UAS. Any successful attack on the UAS will result in some unusual and undesired behavior of the UAS.

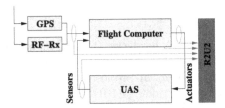

Fig. 3. High-level architecture of R2U2

Monitoring the system inputs and analyzing the post-attack behavior are not independent from each other so we have to model their interactions within our R2U2 framework. Typically, a certain input pattern followed by a specific behavior characterizes an attack. For example, a strong oscillation in the aircraft movement that was triggered by an unusual GCS command indicates an attack (or an irresponsible pilot). Similarly, transients in GPS signals followed by subtle position movements could be telltales of a GPS spoofing attack. Figure 3 shows how our R2U2 framework monitors the various inputs going into the UAS system (GCS and GPS), as well as sensor/actuator signals and status of the flight software for post-attack analysis. We next consider modeling for attacks and post-attack behavior, loosely following [14].

3.1   Attack Monitoring

As all attacks are initiated through the GCS or GPS inputs, we monitor the following attack surfaces. Because of zero-day attack mechanisms, this list will always be incomplete [4]. Note that the occurrence of such a situation does

---

[2] In this paper, we do not model attack scenarios via compromised flight software.

not mean that an actual attack is happening; other reasons like unusual flight conditions, transmission errors, or faulty hard- or software might be the reason.

Ill-formatted and illegal commands should not be processed by the FSW. Such commands could result from transmission errors or might be part of an attack. If such commands are received repeatedly a denial-of-service attack might be happening.

Dangerous commands are properly formatted but might cause severe problems or even a crash depending on the UAS mode. For example, a "reset-FSW" command sent to the UAS while in the air, will, most certainly, lead to a crash of the UAS because all communication and system parameters are lost. Thus, in all likelihood, receiving this command indicates a malicious attack. Other dangerous commands are, for example, the setting of a gain in the control loops during flight. However, there are situations where such a command is perfectly legal and necessary.

Nonsensical or repeated navigation commands could point to a malicious attack. Although new navigation waypoints can be sent to a UAS during flight to update its mission, repeated sending of waypoints with identical coordinates, or weird/erroneous coordinates might indicate an attack.

Transients in GPS signals might be signs of GPS spoofing or jamming. Because the quality of UAS navigation strongly depends on the quality of the received GPS signals, sudden transients in the number of available satellites, or signal strength and noise ratios (Jamming-to-Noise Sensing [9]) might indicate a GPS-based attack.

It should be noted that these patterns do not provide enough evidence to reliably identify an attack. Only in correspondence with a matching post-attack behavior are we able to separate malicious attacks from unusual, but legal command sequences. We therefore also monitor UAS behavior.

3.2   System Behavior Monitoring

Our R2U2 models for monitoring post-attack behavior obtain their information from the UAS sensors, actuators, and the flight computer. In our current setting, we do not monitor those electrical signals directly, but obtain their values from the FSW. This simplification, however, prevents our current implementation from detecting a crash of the flight software initiated by a malicious attack. With our R2U2 framework we are able to monitor the following UAS behaviors, which might (or might not be) the result of a malicious attack.

Oscillations of the aircraft around any of its axes hampers the aircraft's performance and can lead to disintegration of the plane and a subsequent crash. Pilot-induced oscillations (PIO) in commercial aircraft have caused severe accidents and loss of life. In a UAS such oscillations can be caused by issuing appropriate command sequences or by setting gains of the control loops to bad values. Oscillations of higher frequencies can cause damage due to vibration or can render on-board cameras inoperative.

Deviation from flight path: In the nominal case, a UAS flies from one way-point to the next via a direct path. Sudden deviations from such a straight path could indicate some unplanned or possibly unwelcome maneuver. The same observation holds for sudden climbs or descents of the UAS.

Sensor Readings: Sudden changes of sensor readings or consistent drift in the same direction might also be part of a post-attack behavior. Here again, such behavior might have been caused by, for example, a failing sensor.

Unusual software behavior like memory leaks, increased number of real-time failures, or illegal numerical values can possibly point to an on-going malicious attack. In the case of software, such a behavior might be a post-attack behavior or the manifestation of the attack mechanism itself. Therefore, security models involving software health are the most complex ones.

3.3   R2U2 Models

We capture the specific patterns for each of the attack and behavior observers with temporal logic and Bayesian networks. We also use these mechanisms to specify the temporal, causal, and probabilistic relationships between them. As a high-level explanation, an attack is detected if a behavioral pattern B is observed some time after a triggering attack A has been monitored. Temporal constraints ensure that these events are actually correlated. So, for example, we can express that an oscillation of the UAS ($osc = true$) occurs between 100–200 time steps after the control loop parameters have been altered ($param\_change = true$). Any trace satisfying the following formula could indicate an attack.

$$\Box(param\_change \wedge \Diamond_{[100,200]} osc)$$

3.4   Modeling Variants and Patterns

The combination of signal processing, filtering, past-time and future-time MTL, and Bayesian reasoning provides a highly expressive medium for formulating security properties. Further generality can be achieved by grouping related indicators. For example, we can define groups of dangerous commands, unusual repeated commands, or events:

dangerous_cmds $= cmd\_reset \vee cmd\_calibrate\_sensor \vee cmd\_disarm \vee \dots$
unusual_cmds_airborne $= cmd\_get\_params \vee set\_params \vee get\_waypoints \vee \dots$
unusual_cmds_periodic $= cmd\_nav\_to \vee cmd\_mode\_change \vee invalid\_packet\_rcvd$

This enables us to directly use these preprocessed groups in temporal formulas and feed them into a BN, thereby supporting simple reuse of common patterns and assisting more comprehensive security models. The following example demonstrates how we use such patterns to specify that there shall be no dangerous commands between takeoff and landing.

$$\Box[(CMD == \text{takeoff}) \rightarrow ((\neg \textbf{dangerous\_cmds}) \; \mathcal{U} \; landing\_complete)]$$

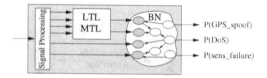

Fig. 4. Threat detection with R2U2 model.

3.5 Bayesian Networks for Security Diagnosis

Most models of attack monitoring and post-attack behavior are capable of indicating that there might have been an attack, but cannot reliably detect one as such, because the observed patterns could have been caused by a sensor failure, for example. However, we can use the BN reasoning engine of R2U2 to perform better probabilistic diagnosis. For details of Bayesian R2U2 models see [28]. The results of all the temporal observers are provided as inputs to the observable nodes (shaded in Fig. 4) of the BN. The internal structure of the BN then determines how likely a specific attack or failure scenario is. Prior information helps to disambiguate the diagnosis. For example, a sudden change in measured altitude could be attributed to a failing barometric altimeter, a failing laser altimeter, a failing GPS receiver, or a GPS spoofing attack. In order to determine the most likely root cause, additional information about recently received commands, or the signal strength of the GPS receiver can be used. So, transients in GPS signal strength with otherwise healthy sensors (i.e., measured barometric and laser altitude coincide) make an attack more likely. On the other hand, strongly diverging readings from the on-board altitude sensors make a sensor failure more likely. With prior information added to the BN, we can, for example, express that the laser altimeter is much more likely to fail than the barometric altimeter or the GPS sensor. Also, GPS transients might be more likely in areas with an overall low signal strength. Since a BN is capable of expressing, in a statistically correct way, the interrelationships of a multitude of different signals and outputs of temporal observers, R2U2 can provide best-possible attack diagnosis results as sketched in Fig. 4.

4   Experiments and Results

Our experiments can be run either in a software-in-the-loop (SITL) simulation or directly on the UAS; most of the experiments in this paper were executed on our Ironbird processor-in-the-loop setup, which consists of the original UAS flight computer hardware components in a laboratory environment. In all configurations, the produced data traces were forwarded via a UART transmission to the R2U2 framework running on an Adapteva Parallella Board [1]. R2U2 is implemented on this credit-card sized, low-cost platform where the actual monitoring is performed inside the Xilinx[3] zynq xc7z010 FPGA. Our R2U2 implementation

---

[3] http://www.xilinx.com.

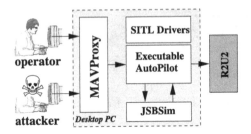

Fig. 5. R2U2 SITL test setup

(Fig. 2) uses 40 % of the FPGA's slice registers and 64 % of its slice look-up tables (LUTs). These numbers are independent of the size and structure of the LTL and MTL formulas. The implementation in this paper used 128 input signals through the UART to the FPGA, though this number could be extended for other implementations. The R2U2 framework is running with a maximum frequency 85.164 MHz. An Ubuntu Linux installation on the Parallella board is used for the interface configuration, signal preprocessing, and evaluation of arithmetic circuits. In our SITL simulation (Fig. 5), the UAS flight behaviors is simulated by the open source JSBSim [11] flight dynamics model. All hardware components are emulated by SITL low-level drivers, which enables us to inject the desired behaviors without the risk of damaging the aircraft during a real test flight. The operator's GCS is connected to the UAS via an open source MAVLink proxy [17]. We also connect a second GCS to the proxy in order to simulate the attackers injected MAVLink packets.

4.1 Dangerous MAV Commands

In addition to commands controlling the actual flight, the MAVLink protocol [16] allows the user to remotely set up and configure the aircraft. In particular, parameters that control the feedback loops inside the FSW can be defined, as they need to be carefully adjusted to match the flight dynamics of the given aircraft. Such commands, which substantially alter the behavior of the UAS can, when given during flight, cause dangerous behavior of the UAS or a potential crash. In 2000, a pilot of a Predator UAS inadvertently sent a command "Program AV EEPROM" while the UAS was in the air. This caused all FSW parameters and information about communication frequencies to be erased on the UAS. Communication to the UAS could not be reestablished and the UAS crashed causing a total loss $3.7 M [31]. If parameters for the FSW control loops are set to extreme values during flight, the aircraft can experience oscillations that could lead to disintegration of the UAS and a subsequent crash. Therefore, such commands might be welcome targets for a malicious attack.

In this experiment, we set up our R2U2 to capture and report such dangerous behaviors. Our security model consists of two parts: (a) detection that a potentially dangerous MAV command has been issued, and (b) that a dangerous behavior (in our case, oscillation around the pitch axis) occurs.

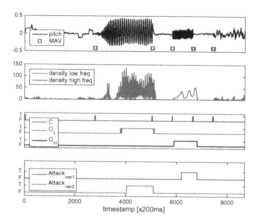

Fig. 6. UAS behavior after malicious setting of gain parameters (Color figure online)

Each of the parts seen individually does not give an indication of an attack: MAV commands to change parameters are perfectly legal in most circumstances. On the other hand, oscillations can be caused by turbulence, aircraft design, or the pilot (pilot-induced-oscillations). Only the right temporal combination of both pieces of information allows us to deduce that a malicious attack has occurred: after receiving the "set parameter" command, a substantial and persistent oscillation must follow soon thereafter. In our model we use the specification $\Box(C \wedge \Diamond_{[0,1200]}(\Box_{[0,300]}O))$ where O is the occurrence of oscillations and C is the event of receiving a "set parameter" command. We require that the oscillation persists for at least 300 time steps and is separated from the command by not more than 1200 time steps. The event C can be directly extracted from the stream of received MAV commands; oscillations can be detected with the help of a Fast Fourier Transform (FFT) on the pitch, roll, or yaw angular values. Figure 6 shows how such an attack occurs. The top panel shows the UAS pitch as well as the points in time when a "set-parameter" command has been received (blue boxes). Caused by a malicious command (setting pitch gain extremely high) issued at around $t = 2800$, a strong low-frequency up-down oscillation appears in the pitch axis. That excessive gain is turned off at around $t = 5100$ and the oscillation subsides. Shortly afterwards, at $t = 5900$, a malicious setting of a damping coefficient causes smaller oscillations but at a higher frequency. This oscillation ramps up much quicker and ends with resetting that parameter. In the second panel, two elements of the power spectrum obtained by an FFT transform of the pitch signals are shown. The signals, which have been subjected to a low-pass filter clearly indicate the occurrence of a low (red) and high (blue) frequency oscillation. The third panel shows the actual Boolean inputs for R2U2: "set-parameter received" C, "Low-frequency-oscillation" O_L, and "high-frequency-oscillation" O_H. The bottom panel shows valuations of formulas $\Box(C \wedge \Diamond_{[0,1200]}(\Box_{[0,300]}O_L))$ and $\Box(C \wedge \Diamond_{[0,500]}(\Box_{[0,200]}O_H))$ as produced by the R2U2 monitor. On the latter property the maximal lead time of the malicious attack has been set to only 500 time steps to reduce the number of false alarms, because the high-frequency oscillation ramps up almost immediately. We estimate that 10 person-hours were spent writing, debugging, and revising the two temporal logic properties used for this experiment and approximately 30 h were spent on experimental setup and simulation.

4.2 DoS Hijack Attack

Attackers continuously find new ways to break into and compromise a system. Therefore, it is challenging to account for every possible attack scenario, since there can always be an unforeseen loophole. The following experiment shows how our R2U2 framework can detect an intrusion without the need for an explicit security model for each specific scenario. Here, we will look at possible indicators that can be grouped into patterns as described earlier.

In our simulation we initiate a sophisticated attack to hijack the UAS by first trying to establish a link from the attacker's GCS to the UAS. Because the attacker has to cope with issues like an incorrect channel, a different version of the protocol, or link encryption, a large number of bad command packets will be received within a short time frame. The top panel of Fig. 7 shows such a typical situation (black). The R2U2 security model could use, for example, the following formula for detection given the rate of received bad command packages R_b per time step:

$$F_1 \equiv \Box_{[0,10]}(R_b = 0 \vee (R_b \geq 1 \; \mathcal{U}_{[0,10]} R_b = 0))$$

The formula F_1 means that no more than one bad command is received within each time interval of length 10 time steps.

Next, an attacker could try to gather information about the UAS, e.g., by requesting aircraft parameters or trying to download the waypoints using the MAVLink protocol. This activity is shown in Fig. 7 as blue spikes between time step 1000 and 1300. For our model, we use the input command groups defined earlier. With C_u as the event of receiving an unusual command, we state that no unusual command should be received after takeoff until the UAS has landed.

$$F_2 \equiv \Box((CMD == \text{takeoff}) \rightarrow (\neg C_u) \; \mathcal{U} \; \text{landing\_complete})$$

Finally, an attacker may flood the communication link in a way similar to a Denial of Service (DoS) attack by sending continuous requests C_{nav} to navigate to the attacker's coordinates, combined with requests $C_{homeloc}$ to set the home location of the UAS to the same coordinates. This phase of the attacks results in a continuously high number of navigation commands starting around $t = 1400$ as shown in the bottom panel of Fig. 7. For attack detection, we specify formulas, either explicitly detecting an unusual period of navigational commands (F_3), or detecting a group of previously-defined unusual periodic commands (F_4). F_3 states that there shall be no continuous navigation requests for more than 30 time steps: $\Box_{[0,30]}C_{nav}$. Finally, F_4 states that there shall be no continuous unusual periodic events for more than 60 time steps: $\Box_{[0,60]}C_u$. The formulas F_1, F_2, F_3, and F_4 are not reliable indicators of an ongoing attack if viewed individually.

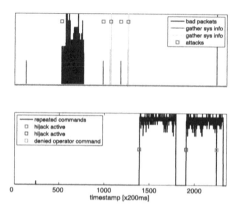

Fig. 7. UAS DoS hijack results (Color figure online)

Only by considering the overall pattern can we calculate a high probability for an ongoing attack. In order to accomplish this, we feed the results of these formulas into a Bayesian network for probabilistic reasoning. We estimate that 6 person-hours were spent writing, debugging, and revising the four temporal logic properties used for this experiment and approximately 15 h were spent on experimental setup and simulation.

Even if the attack was detected by a UAS operator, all attempts to change the UAS to its original course would immediately be overwritten by the attacker's high-rate navigation commands. Due to the altered home coordinates, any attempt of the UAS to return to the launch site would fail as well. Rather it would fly to the target location desired by the attacker. Furthermore, the simulation of this scenario showed that besides crashing the UAS intentionally, there was no simple way for the UAS operator to prevent this kind of hijacking. In particular, for autonomous missions, where the UAS is flying outside the operator's communication range, it is essential that the UAS is capable of detecting such an attack autonomously.

In order to protect a UAS from attacks against command link jamming, a UAS is sometimes deliberately put into a complete autonomous mode, where it does not accept any further external commands [9]. Ironically, what was intended to be a security measure could inhibit the operator's attempts to recover a UAS during such an attack. However, R2U2 enables the UAS to detect an ongoing attack autonomously in order to enable adequate countermeasures.

4.3 GPS Spoofing

GPS plays a central role in the control of autonomous UAS. Typically, a flight plan for a UAS is defined as a list of waypoints, each giving a target specified by its longitude, latitude, and altitude. The FSW in the UAS then calculates a trajectory to reach the next waypoint in sequence. In order to accomplish this, the UAS needs to know its own position, which it obtains with the help of a GPS receiver.

Due to limited accuracy, only GPS longitude and latitude are used for navigation; the UAS's current altitude is obtained using, e.g., the barometric altimeter.

For the control of UAS attitude, the UAS is equipped with inertial sensors. Accelerometers measure current acceleration along each of the aircraft axes; gyros measure the angular velocity for each axis. Integration of these sensor values yields relative positions and velocities. These data streams are produced at a very fast rate and are independent from the outside interference but very noisy. Thus, the inertial sensors alone cannot be used for waypoint navigation. Therefore, the FSW uses an Extended Kalman Filter (EKF) to mix the inertial signals with the GPS position measurements. If the inertial measurements deviate too much from the GPS position, the filter is reset to the current GPS coordinates.

Several methods for attacking the GPS-based navigation of a UAS are known, including GPS jamming and GPS spoofing. In a jamming attack, the signals sent from the GPS satellites are drowned out by a powerful RF transmitter sending white noise. The UAS then cannot receive any useful GPS signals anymore and its navigation must rely on compass and dead reckoning. Such an attack can cause a UAS to miss its target or to crash. A more sophisticated attack involves GPS spoofing. In such a scenario, an attacker gradually overpowers actual GPS signals with counterfeit signals that have been altered to cause the UAS to incorrectly estimate its current position. That way, the UAS can be directed into a different flight path.

This type of attack became widely known when Iran allegedly used GPS spoofing to hijack a CIA drone and forced it to land on an Iranian airfield rather than its base [6,30]. Subsequently, researchers from the University of Texas at Austin successfully demonstrated how an $80M yacht at sea,[4] as well as a small UAS can be directed to follow a certain pattern due to GPS spoofing [13]. Because civil GPS signals are not encrypted it is always possible to launch a GPS spoofing attack. For such an attack, only a computer and a commercially available GPS transmitter is necessary. We can employ our R2U2 framework to detect realistic GPS spoofing attacks like the common attack scenarios described in [13]; whereas that paper discusses attack detection in theory we demonstrate it via hardware-in-the-loop simulation on-board our IronBird UAS. Here we focus on attack detection; techniques to avoid or mitigate GPS spoofing are beyond the scope of this paper.

Our developed R2U2 model monitors the quality of the GPS signal and the inertial navigation information. For our experimental evaluation, we defined a UAS mission that flies, at a fixed altitude, toward the next waypoint south-southwest of the current UAS location. When spoofing occurs, the attacker modifies the GPS signal in such a way that it tricks the UAS into believing it is still flying a direct route as expected. In reality, however, the UAS is actually veering off to reach a target point defined by the attacker. Figure 8 shows the relevant signals during this mission. Here, we focus on the latitude as observed by the UAS. The top panel shows the point of the spoofing attack and the trace for the temporal development of the UAS latitude as observed by the UAS (black) and the actual

---

[4] http://www.ae.utexas.edu/news/features/humphreys-research-group.

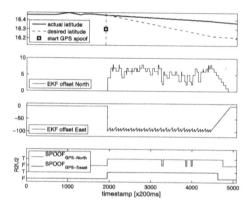

Fig. 8. Set of traces that indicate GPS spoofing (Color figure online)

UAS position (blue). A severe and increasing discrepancy can be observed as the effect of the attack. As the actual position (ground truth) is not available to the on-board FSW, R2U2 reasons about relationships with alternate signals that convey similar information. The inertial navigation unit produces an error or offset signal that reflects the deviation between the current position observed by GPS and the inertial sensors. The next two panels of Fig. 8 shows that these offset signals can become substantially large during the actual spoofing period, when the GPS locations are gradually moved to the attacker's target. The bottom panel shows the spoofing detection output stream from R2U2. We estimate that 10 person-hours were spent on model development and approximately 45 h were spent on experimental setup and simulation.

Again, these signals are not individually absolute indicators that an attack has happened. Flying in areas with weak GPS coverage, for example, in a mountainous or urban environment, could produce similar signals. Therefore, in our R2U2 models, we aim to take into account other observation patterns and use a Bayesian network for probabilistic reasoning. Information supporting the hypothesis of an attack could include prior loss of satellite locks, transients in GPS signals, or other types of attacks. In the case of the captured CIA drone, an Iranian engineer claimed to have jammed the drone's communications link in order to force the drone into an autopilot mode and then initiated the GPS spoofing attack [30].

5 Conclusion

We have extended our REALIZABLE, RESPONSIVE, UNOBTRUSIVE Unit (R2U2) to enable real-time monitoring and diagnosis of security threats. This includes the ability to reason about complex and subtle threats utilizing indicators from both the UAS system and its software. Our embedded implementation on-board a standard, flight-certifiable FPGA meets stated FAA requirements and efficiently recognizes both individual attack indicators and attack patterns, adding a new level of security checks not available in any previous work. Case studies on-board a real NASA DragonEye UAS provide a promising proof-of-concept of this new architecture.

The myriad directions now open for future work include considering software instrumentation to enable more FSW-related compromises and doing hardware-in-the-loop simulation experiments to detect these. We plan to extend this technology to other, more complex UAS and beyond, to other types of aircraft and spacecraft with different configurations and capabilities. A major bottleneck of the current R2U2 is the manual labor required to develop and test every temporal logic formula and BN; we are currently considering methods for making this a semi-automated process to better enable future extensions.

References

1. Adapteva: The Parallella Board. https://www.parallella.org/board
2. Ahmed, A., Lisitsa, A., Dixon, C.: TeStID: a high performance temporal intrusion detection system. In: Proceedings of the ICIMP 2013, pp. 20–26 (2013)
3. APM:Plane, Open Source Fixed-Wing Aircraft UAV. http://plane.ardupilot.com
4. Bilge, L., Dumitras, T.: Before we knew it: an empirical study of zero-day attacks in the real world. In: Proceedings of the CCS 2012, pp. 833–844 (2012)
5. Bushnell, D., Denney, E., Enomoto, F., Pai, G., Schumann, J.: Preliminary recommendations for the collection, storage, and analysis of UAS safety data. Technical report NASA/TM-2013-216624, NASA Ames Research Center (2013)
6. Eulich, W.: Did Iran just down a US drone by 'spoofing'? Christian Science Monitor (2012). http://www.csmonitor.com/World/Security-Watch/terrorism-security/2012/1204/Did-Iran-just-down-a-US-drone-by-spoofing-video
7. GAO: Air Traffic Control: FAA Needs a More Comprehensive Approach to Address Cybersecurity As Agency Transitions to NextGen. Technical report GAO-15-370, United States Government Accountability Office (2015). http://www.gao.gov/assets/670/669627.pdf
8. Geist, J., Rozier, K.Y., Schumann, J.: Runtime observer pairs and Bayesian network reasoners on-board FPGAs: flight-certifiable system health management for embedded systems. In: Proceedings of the RV 2014, pp. 215–230 (2014)
9. Humphreys, T.: Statement on the Vulnerability of Civil Unmanned Aerial Vehicles and Other Systems to Civil GPS Spoofing. University of Texas at Austin (2012)
10. Javaid, A.Y., Sun, W., Devabhaktuni, V.K., Alam, M.: Cyber security threat analysis and modeling of an unmanned aerial vehicle system. In: Proceedings of the HST 2012, pp. 585–590. IEEE (2012)
11. JSBSim: Open Source Flight Dynamics Model. http://jsbsim.sourceforge.net
12. Karimi, N.: Iran Drone Capture Claim: State TV Airs Images Allegedly Extracted From U.S. Aircraft (video). The World Post (2013). http://www.huffingtonpost.com/2013/02/07/iran-drone-capture-claim_n_2636745.html
13. Kerns, A.J., Shepard, D.P., Bhatti, J.A., Humphreys, T.E.: Unmanned aircraft capture and control via GPS spoofing. J. Field Robot. 31(4), 617–636 (2014)
14. Kim, A., Wampler, B., Goppert, J., Hwang, I., Aldridge, H.: Cyber attack vulnerabilities analysis for unmanned aerial vehicles. Infotech@Aerospace (2012)
15. Lu, H., Forin, A.: The Design and Implementation of P2V, An Architecture for Zero-Overhead Online Verification of Software Programs. MSR-TR-2007-99, Microsoft Research (2007). http://research.microsoft.com/apps/pubs/default.aspx?id=70470

16. MAVLink: Micro Air Vehicle Protocol. https://github.com/mavlink
17. MAVProxy: A UAV Ground Station Software Package for MAVLink Based Systems. http://tridge.github.io/MAVProxy
18. Mengshoel, O.J., Chavira, M., Cascio, K., Poll, S., Darwiche, A., Uckun, S.: Probabilistic model-based diagnosis: an electrical power system case study. IEEE Trans. Syst. Man Cybern. Part A: Syst. Hum. **40**(5), 874–885 (2010)
19. Meredith, P.O., Jin, D., Griffith, D., Chen, F., Roşu, G.: An overview of the MOP runtime verification framework. Int. J. Softw. Tools Technol. Transfer **14**(3), 249–289 (2012)
20. Naldurg, P., Sen, K., Thati, P.: A temporal logic based framework for intrusion detection. In: de Frutos-Escrig, D., Núñez, M. (eds.) FORTE 2004. LNCS, vol. 3235, pp. 359–376. Springer, Heidelberg (2004)
21. Olivain, J., Goubault-Larrecq, J.: The ORCHIDS intrusion detection tool. In: Etessami, K., Rajamani, S.K. (eds.) CAV 2005. LNCS, vol. 3576, pp. 286–290. Springer, Heidelberg (2005)
22. Pearl, J.: A constraint propagation approach to probabilistic reasoning. In: Proceedings of the UAI, pp. 31–42. AUAI Press (1985)
23. Pellizzoni, R., Meredith, P., Caccamo, M., Rosu, G.: Hardware runtime monitoring for dependable COTS-based real-time embedded systems. In: RTSS, pp. 481–491 (2008)
24. Perry, S.: Subcommittee hearing: unmanned aerial system threats: exploring security implications and mitigation technologies. Committee on Homeland Security (2015). http://homeland.house.gov/hearing/subcommittee-hearing-unmanned-aerial-system-threats-exploring-security-implications-and
25. Reinbacher, T., Rozier, K.Y., Schumann, J.: Temporal-logic based runtime observer pairs for system health management of real-time systems. In: Ábrahám, E., Havelund, K. (eds.) TACAS 2014 (ETAPS). LNCS, vol. 8413, pp. 357–372. Springer, Heidelberg (2014)
26. Schumann, J., Mbaya, T., Mengshoel, O.J., Pipatsrisawat, K., Srivastava, A., Choi, A., Darwiche, A.: Software health management with Bayesian networks. Innovations Syst. Softw. Eng. **9**(2), 1–22 (2013)
27. Schumann, J., Rozier, K.Y., Reinbacher, T., Mengshoel, O.J., Mbaya, T., Ippolito, C.: Towards real-time, on-board, hardware-supported sensor and software health management for unmanned aerial systems. In: Proceedings of the PHM 2013, pp. 381–401 (2013)
28. Schumann, J., Rozier, K.Y., Reinbacher, T., Mengshoel, O.J., Mbaya, T., Ippolito, C.: Towards real-time, on-board, hardware-supported sensor and software health management for unmanned aerial systems. Int. J. Prognostics Health Manage. **6**(1), 1–27 (2015)
29. Shachtman, N., Axe, D.: Most U.S. drones openly broadcast secret video feeds. Wired (2012). http://www.wired.com/2012/10/hack-proof-drone/
30. Shepard, D.P., Bhatti, J.A., Humphreys, T.E.: Drone hack. GPS World **23**(8), 30–33 (2012)
31. USAF: Aircraft Accident Investigation: Rq-11, s/n 96-3023. AIB Class A Aerospace Mishaps (2000). http://usaf.aib.law.af.mil/ExecSum2000/RQ-1L_Nellis_14Sep00.pdf

A Hybrid Approach to Causality Analysis

Shaohui Wang[1]([✉]), Yoann Geoffroy[2], Gregor Gössler[2],
Oleg Sokolsky[1], and Insup Lee[1]

[1] Department of Computer and Information Science,
University of Pennsylvania, Philadelphia, USA
shaohui@seas.upenn.edu, {sokolsky,lee}@cis.upenn.edu
[2] INRIA Grenoble – Rhône-Alpes and Univ. Grenoble Alpes, Grenoble, France
{yoann.geoffroy,gregor.goessler}@inria.fr

Abstract. In component-based safety-critical systems, when a system safety property is violated, it is necessary to analyze which components are the cause. Given a system execution trace that exhibits component faults leading to a property violation, our causality analysis formalizes a notion of counterfactual reasoning ("what would the system behavior be if a component had been correct?") and algorithmically derives such alternative system behaviors, without re-executing the system itself. In this paper, we show that we can improve precision of the analysis if (1) we can emulate execution of components instead of relying on their contracts, and (2) take into consideration input/output dependencies between components to avoid blaming components for faults induced by other components. We demonstrate the utility of the extended analysis with a case study for a closed-loop patient-controlled analgesia system.

1 Introduction

A key idea in systems engineering is that complex systems are built by assembling components. Component-based systems are desirable because they allow independent development of system components by different suppliers, as well as their incremental construction and modification. The down side of component-based development is that no single entity – neither the integrator, nor component suppliers – have a complete understanding of component behaviors and possible interactions between them. This incomplete knowledge, in turn, requires us to resort to black-box analysis methods, when only the input-output behavior of a component is specified.

In this work, we are interested in the forensic analysis of a component-based system following the discovered violation of system safety properties. Diagnosis of the root cause is crucial for the subsequent recovery and follow-up prevention measures. Such diagnosis requires recording of system executions leading to the failure, as well as methods for the efficient analysis of the recorded data.

Research is supported in part by grants NSF CNS-1035715, IIS-1231547, ACI-1239324, and INRIA associate team Causalysis.

E. Bartocci and R. Majumdar (Eds.): RV 2015, LNCS 9333, pp. 250–265, 2015.
DOI: 10.1007/978-3-319-23820-3_16

There has been a great amount of research following the seminal work of [5,16] in the study of fault diagnosis. In our previous work in [8,9,18], we took a step further and considered the problem of causality analysis for component-based systems. We formalized counterfactual reasoning ("what would the system execution be should a component have behaved correctly?") as a basis for the analysis. Our analysis provided a plausible explanation to how the component faults had contributed to the system property violation.

Specifically, we proposed a general causality analysis framework in [8,18], and identified four major steps in causality analysis. First, the set $\mathcal{F}$ of all faulty components with respect to their corresponding component properties are identified. Second, the set of possible counterfactual behaviors for a suspected subset $\mathcal{S} \subseteq \mathcal{F}$ is constructed. Third, based on our formalization of causality, it is determined whether the suspected subset $\mathcal{S}$ is the culprit. Lastly, minimal culprits are determined based on the results from the third step. The causality analysis we proposed in [18] assumes that the only information available to the analysis are the system definition (system property, component properties, and system topology) and a single system execution trace on which the system property is violated. It was assumed that we cannot re-run the system with some of the component faults removed, risking another failure if the true culprit was not corrected. This assumption limits precision of the analysis, as little additional information can be obtained from the system itself.

We show in this paper that we can improve the analysis without relaxing this assumption for the whole system, if some components of the system—which we refer to as *separable components*—can be run in isolation from the rest of the system to assist in counterfactual trace generation. The use of separable components during analysis phase provides a hybrid way to construct counterfactual traces that combines component traces generated statically, based on the system definition and the observed trace, and dynamic traces of separable components, containing actual outputs of the component on inputs generated during the analysis.

Another piece of under-utilized information in determining causes is the relation in between component property violations, i.e., horizontal causes [9]. For instance, when components A and B together are determined to be a cause for system property violation, by investigating and concluding that component A's fault is the cause of that of component B's, we can exclude B from blame.

To evaluate these extensions, we applied the proposed causality analysis to a patient controlled analgesia (PCA) infusion pump case study from the medical device domain. A post-surgery patient can request pain relief medication by pressing a button on the PCA pump. A pump controller monitors patient state using readings from a pulse-oximeter. To avoid potential overdose, the controller issues tickets to the pump that can limit its ability to respond to repeated patient requests. Errors in computing, delivering, and processing tickets can lead to an overdose, and the faulty component needs to be determined. Results from the case study show that our proposed causality analysis can provide a more fine-grained analysis than our previous approach.

The contribution of this paper is a new algorithm for counterfactual reasoning that incorporates the two extensions to our existing approach, namely the use of separable components and horizontal causality. Evaluation of the new approach shows that the analysis becomes more intuitive and precise. To the best of our knowledge, the proposed approach is also the first to have incorporated both static and run-time analysis for causality analysis. On the application side, we have demonstrated the applicability of the approach to a case study in the safety-critical systems domain.

2   The PCA Example

Patient controlled analgesia (PCA) infusion pumps are used for post-surgical pain treatment in an intensive care unit (ICU). A potential hazard for the patient is overdosing. When continuously in infusion, the patient vital signs, e.g. blood oxygen saturation level (SpO2), would gradually decrease. It is considered a critical condition for the patient when SpO2 drops below 70 %. To prevent overdosing, smart PCA pumps are usually equipped with a controller which reads measurements of patient vital signs and issues to PCA pumps *tickets*, i.e., maximum duration allowed for infusion given the patient vital sign readings. Figure 1 shows a simplified schematic view of the scenario, adapted from a system modeled out of a real component-based system in the clinical setting, presented in [1].

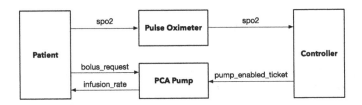

Fig. 1. Schematic view of PCA case study

System and Components. The PCA system consists of four components: the Patient, the pulse-oximeter (PO), the controller (Ctrl), and the PCA pump. The system level safety property is that Patient SpO2 never drops below 70 %.

The Patient component is simulated based on given patient physiological reactions when infusion is and is not in progress. The differential equations describing the dynamics are given in [1]. For the purpose of this case study, it suf-

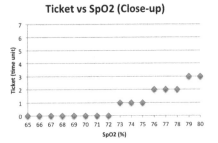

Fig. 2. Ticket vs SpO2

fices to know that patient SpO2 value would gradually decrease (resp., increase) while infusion is in progress (resp., stopped).

Table 1. Example faulty trace for PCA case study

Snapshot	Patient.SpO2	PO.SpO2	Controller.Ticket	Patient.BR	PCA.IR
0.	71	75	3	true	400
1.	70	72	0	false	400
2	69				

PO measures the Patient SpO2 and transmits the measurements to Ctrl.

Ctrl reads the patient SpO2, computes the ticket, and outputs the calculated ticket. The ticket-SpO2 relation given in [1] is pre-calculated and shown in Fig. 2 with values for SpO2 in the range 65 %–80 %.

The PCA component takes patient bolus request and the ticket as input. When there is a patient bolus request, the PCA delivers (a) no drug if ticket is 0; (b) one time unit of infusion if ticket is 1; and (c) two consecutive time units of infusion if ticket is greater than 1.

Traces. An execution of the PCA system with manually injected faults is recorded as a system trace, i.e., a sequence of snapshots of variable values of components' input and output. We use a tabular form to represent a trace illustrated in Table 1.

Example of Causality Analysis Problem. On the trace in Table 1, in Snapshot 0, PO is faulty in measuring the value of the patient SpO2 in that the measured value (75 %) is larger than the actual value (71 %). Ctrl takes the wrong value as input, and makes a faulty computation as well (by outputting the ticket value 3 instead of the expected 1 as shown in Fig. 2). The PCA receives a patient bolus request and reads the ticket value to be 3, so it initiates infusion for two time units consecutively until in Snapshot 2 where the patient SpO2 drops below the critical value 70 %—a patient adverse event represented as a system level property violation occurs.

The causality analysis problem aims to study, in component-based systems where multiple components have committed faults in a given system execution so that system level property violation occurs, which subsets of component faults are the culprits for the system level property violation.

3   Definition of the Causality Analysis Problem

Preliminaries. A *type* T is a set of values. A *typed variable* $x : T$ is a variable with values in T. We only consider finite types in this work. A *snapshot* s_X for a set $X = \{x_1, \ldots, x_m\}$ of typed variables $x_1 : T_1, \ldots, x_m : T_m$ is an assignment of each variable x_i to its value $s_X(x_i)$ in T_i, for $1 \le i \le m$. A *trace* $Tr = s_0, s_1, \ldots$ for a set X of typed variables is a sequence of snapshots, where every snapshot s_i is for X. The snapshot at location i on a trace Tr is denoted $Tr[i]$. The suffix of Tr starting at location i is denoted $Tr[i...]$. A segment of Tr starting from location i and ending at location j (inclusive) is denoted $Tr[i..j]$.

For convenience, we denote by $|Tr[i..j]|$ the length of $Tr[i..j]$, i.e., the number of snapshots on $Tr[i..j]$. A set $\mathbf{TR}$ of traces is called *prefix-closed* if $\forall Tr \in \mathbf{TR}.\forall l < |Tr|.Tr[0..l] \in \mathbf{TR}$. We denote $\mathbf{T}_X$ the set of all possible traces over a set X.[1] The *projection* $\pi_Y(s)$ of a snapshot s for X on to a subset $Y \subseteq X$ is a snapshot for domain Y such that $\forall y \in Y.(\pi_Y(s))(y) = s(y)$. The *projection* $\pi_Y(Tr)$ of a trace $Tr = s_0, s_1, \ldots$ on to a subset $Y \subseteq X$ is a trace for Y, defined as $\pi_Y(Tr) = \pi_Y(s_0), \pi_Y(s_1), \ldots$. We write $\pi_v(\cdot)$ for $\pi_{\{v\}}(\cdot)$.

3.1   System Definition

Definition 1 (Component signature). *A component signature is a tuple* $C = \langle I, O, \mathbf{P}_C \rangle$, *where* I *and* O *are disjoint, and*

- $I = \{i_1 : T_1^i, \ldots, i_m : T_m^i\}$ *is a set of typed variables called the* input,
- $O = \{o_1 : T_1^o, \ldots, o_n : T_n^o\}$ *is a set of typed variables called the* output, *and*
- $\mathbf{P}_C \subseteq \mathbf{T}_{I \cup O}$ *is a prefix-closed set of traces called the* component property.

A component signature describes all knowledge of the component available to causality analysis. The component property can be characterized by formal languages such as regular expressions, first-order logic, temporal logics, etc. Here we take a model-theoretic view and identify the property and the set of traces that satisfy the property.

Definition 2 (Channel and connection). *A channel* $c = (x, y)$ *is a pair of typed variables* $(x : T_x, y : T_y)$ *such that* $T_x \subseteq T_y$. *A connection* θ *is a set of channels.*

We make the following assumptions on component composition: (a) Fan-in connections are not allowed, i.e., it is required that $\forall (x_1, y_1), (x_2, y_2) \in \theta.y_1 = y_2 \rightarrow x_1 = x_2$. (b) Variable name clashes are resolved by associating them with the component names, as is common in component-oriented languages. (c) Channels are reliable. A value passed into a channel will be successfully received by the connected component.

Definition 3 (Composition of components). *Let* $\mathcal{A} = \{C_1, \ldots, C_J\}$ *be a set of* J *components with disjoint sets of variables, where* $C_j = \langle I_j, O_j, \mathbf{P}_j \rangle$ *for* $1 \leq j \leq J$. *Let* θ *be a connection where* $\forall (x, y) \in \theta.\exists j, k \in \{1, \ldots, J\}.x \in O_j \wedge y \in I_k$. *The composition of components* $C_1, \ldots, C_J$, *denoted* $C_1 \| \ldots \| C_J$, *is defined as a component* $A = \langle I, O, \mathbf{P} \rangle$, *where*

- $I = \left(\bigcup_{j=1}^J I_j\right) \setminus \{y \mid \exists x.(x, y) \in \theta\}$ *and* $O = \bigcup_{j=1}^J O_j$, *and*
- $\mathbf{P} = \{Tr = s_0 s_1 \ldots s_\ell \in \mathbf{T}_{I \cup O} \mid \forall 1 \leq j \leq J.\pi_j(Tr) \in \mathbf{P}_j \wedge \forall (x, y) \in \theta \; \forall k \in [0, \ell].s_k(x) = s_k(y)\}$.

---

[1] Throughout the paper we use bold font to represent a set of traces (e.g., $\mathbf{TR}$, $\mathbf{T}_X$) or a property (e.g., $\mathbf{P}$) and calligraphic font to represent a set of components (e.g., $\mathcal{A}$ in Definition 3).

Definition 4 (System). *A system $Sys = \langle \mathcal{A}, \theta, \mathbf{P} \rangle$ is a tuple where Sys is composed of components in $\mathcal{A} = \{C_1, \ldots, C_J\}$ by connection θ, and $\mathbf{P}$ is a prefix-closed superset of $\mathbf{P}_{C_1 \| \ldots \| C_J}$ called the (safety) property for system Sys.*

The system property $\mathbf{P}$ may contain more behaviors than $\mathbf{P}_{C_1 \| \ldots \| C_J}$. This means the composition of $C_1, \ldots, C_J$ is essentially a *refinement* of the system property. This is also an equivalent assumption as in [8, 18] which stipulates that when a system property violation occurs, there must be at least one component property violation among $C_1, \ldots, C_J$.

Definition 5 (System trace). *A system trace Tr for $Sys = \langle \mathcal{A}, \theta, \mathbf{P} \rangle$ composed of components $\mathcal{C} = \{C_1, \ldots, C_J\}$ is a trace where each snapshot is for the set of all components' input and output, $\bigcup_{j=1}^{J} (I_j \cup O_j)$.*

We assume in this work that a violation of a property $\mathbf{P}$ on a trace Tr can be detected and that the minimal prefix of Tr that violates $\mathbf{P}$ can be determined, i.e., if $Tr \notin \mathbf{P}$, then $i_{Tr,\mathbf{P}} = \min\{i \mid Tr[0..i] \notin \mathbf{P}\}$ is well defined. Our formalization of component and system property violation naturally aligns respectively with the definitions of fault and failure: a component property violation is a manifestation of a fault, whereas a system property violation is a failure.

Definition 6 (Faults and failures). *Given a system Sys and a system trace Tr for Sys, a component fault (system failure, resp.) on Tr is a violation of the component (system, resp.) property.*

3.2 Causality Definitions

We state the causality analysis for component-based faulty tolerant systems as follows. Given

- a system definition $Sys = \langle \mathcal{A}, \theta, \mathbf{P} \rangle$,
- a trace Tr for Sys on which the system property is violated, and
- a causality definition CD,

determine the minimal subsets of faulty components that are causes for the system property violation, with respect to a given causality definition CD.

Reasoning for causality is based on counterfactuals. For instance, to establish that event e_1 is a necessary cause of event e_2, we consider whether the event e_2 would happen if event e_1 does not occur in any alternative system execution.

Here, an alternative system execution when certain system events are changed is called a *counterfactual trace*, whereas the observed system execution is called the *actual trace*. The key to reasoning about causality is to construct the set of all possible counterfactual traces.

In an abstract level, the set of counterfactual traces can be viewed as a function on Tr, Sys, and S. We use the notation $\sigma(Tr, Sys, S)$ to represent the reconstructed sets of traces. Note that on those traces, the property violations for components in S are corrected. For simplicity we only consider necessary causality in this paper, but we note that the formalism can be used to express other notions of causality, such as sufficient causality.

In addition, we can distinguish vertical and horizontal causality. Vertical causality refers to the causal relationship between component faults and system failures, whereas horizontal causality refers to the causal relationship between component faults.

Definition 7 (Necessary vertical cause). *Given a system definition Sys and a trace Tr for Sys, let $\mathcal{F} = \{C \in Sys \mid \pi_C(Tr) \notin \mathbf{P}_C\}$ be the set of faulty components on trace Tr and $\mathcal{S} \subseteq \mathcal{F}$ be a non-empty suspected subset of faulty components. The component property violation in $\mathcal{S}$ is a necessary vertical cause for system property violation on trace Tr if and only if $\forall Tr' \in \sigma(Tr, Sys, \mathcal{S}).Tr' \in \mathbf{P}$.*

Definition 8 (Necessary horizontal cause). *Let $\mathcal{F}$ and $\mathcal{S}$ be as in Definition 7, and let $C \in \mathcal{F} \backslash \mathcal{S}$ be another faulty component. The component property violation in $\mathcal{S}$ is a necessary horizontal cause for the property violation of component C on trace Tr if and only if $\forall Tr' \in \sigma(Tr, Sys, \mathcal{S}).\pi_C(Tr') \in \mathbf{P}_C$.*

4   Approach

In this work, we propose two extensions to our existing causality analysis framework in [18,19], illustrated in Fig. 3, one using *separable components* and the other using *horizontal causality*. The four steps involved in a causality analysis are briefly discussed below, whereas using separable components and horizontal causality intervene in Step 2 (*Trace Reconstruction*) and Step 4 (*Culprit Minimization*), respectively.

Step 1. *Offline Analysis & Powerset Construction.* We first determine the set $\mathcal{F}$ as in Definition 7, and construct the powerset $2^\mathcal{F}$ of $\mathcal{F}$.

Step 2. *Trace Reconstruction.* For each subset $\mathcal{S} \in 2^\mathcal{F} \setminus \emptyset$, called a *suspect*, we construct $\sigma(Tr, Sys, \mathcal{S})$.

Step 3. *Causality Analysis & Collecting Causes.* Based on $\sigma(Tr, Sys, \mathcal{S})$ we check whether $\mathcal{S}$ is a cause according to the causality definition CD. If yes, $\mathcal{S}$ is a *culprit* and is collected for the subsequent culprit minimization; otherwise $\mathcal{S}$ is not a cause for the violation of system property $\mathbf{P}$.

Step 4. *Culprit Minimization.* The last step of causality analysis is to check the minimality of each collected culprit. Non-minimal culprits are exempted from blame.

4.1   Separable Components

Determining component behavior, i.e., the set $\sigma(Tr, Sys, \mathcal{S})$ in Step 2 of the causality analysis framework, poses a challenge in previous approaches when a component is faulty but not suspected. Unlike suspected components, which have

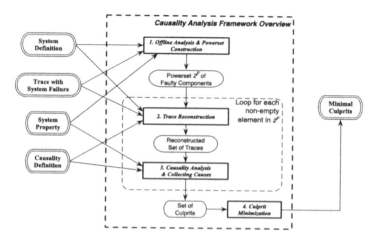

Fig. 3. Casusality analysis framework overview

their outputs corrected according to their contracts, unsuspected components are not supposed to be corrected. When an input of an unsuspected component has changed as a result of correcting outputs of a suspected component, we need to determine, which outputs, possibly faulty, we should use in trace reconstruction. In [18, 19], we assumed that this output was the same as observed on the given system trace. This assumption was due to the unavailable information of how a faulty should behave in such a scenario, where the component's behavior has to be assumed to obtain the output. This assumption may lead to an imprecise analysis if the actual component follows a different behavior model when it is faulty.

A more realistic treatment is to re-execute the components that are available to the analyzer so that the actual output of a component given a changed input can be produced by the component itself whether it being faulty or not. We call such components *separable* since they can be separated from the original system and re-executed in a controlled experiment setting.

Example 1. For the running example, in the trace reconstruction for the case of {PO}, when PO outputs a correct value 71 corresponding to the input 71 from Patient, Ctrl has a changed input 71 other than 75 on the observed trace. With Ctrl being a separable component, it is possible to experimentally feed the new input to Ctrl so as to observe its output. Note that Ctrl is also a faulty component (that we are not suspecting when analyzing {PO}), it may or may not produce the expected value in Fig. 2. If the output ticket value from Ctrl is 0 (resp., 1), then the patient gets no infusion (resp., infusion for 1 time unit). In either case, the patient SpO2 correspondingly does not drop below the 70 threshold, therefore there is no system property violation, so {PO} is a necessary cause. On the other hand, if the output ticket value from Ctrl is 2 or above, then the PCA would continue the infusion for 2 time units, so there is still system property violation. In this case {PO} is not a necessary cause.   □

Being able to re-execute separable components increases analysis precision. The output obtained by assuming the faulty, unsuspected components to always produce the same output as on the observed trace in [18] is essentially one case included in the analysis with separable components. For the example, in the analysis in [18] Ctrl would produce a ticket output 3 as observed, which is on of the cases when the Ctrl output is 2 or above in the analysis in Example 1. With separable components, a more detailed causality analysis result is obtained.

We now provide a formal definition of separable components, of the *re-execute* function, and a property on them. A separable component is simply a trace generator that takes a sequence of input and produces a corresponding output sequence. We require that the behavior of the separable component is deterministic with respect to the sequence of input and the internal states, even when faulty.

Definition 9 (Separable component). *Let* $C = \langle I, O, \mathbf{P}_C \rangle$ *be a component.* C *is separable if* $\forall Tr, Tr' \in \mathbf{T}_{I \cup O}.(\pi_I(Tr) = \pi_I(Tr') \implies Tr = Tr'$.

This definition ensures that the outputs of the component are deterministic and only depend on the inputs fed to it.

Definition 10 (Re-execute function, re-execute(C, Tr)). *Let* $C = \langle I, O, \mathbf{P}_C \rangle$ *be a component and* Tr *be a trace. re-execute(C, Tr) is the trace given by* C *if* $\pi_I(Tr)$ *is fed to* C *as input.*

Property 1. *Let* $C = \langle I, O, \mathbf{P}_C \rangle$ *be a separable component and* Tr *and* Tr' *be two traces, then* $\pi_I(Tr) = \pi_I(Tr') \implies$ *re-execute$(C, Tr) =$ re-execute(C, Tr').*

This property is a direct consequence of the two previous definitions. It means that if we execute the separable component with the same input, it will always produce the same trace as output.

Trace Reconstruction with Separable Components. We use the construction of *cone of influence*, adapted from [8], to over-approximate the impact of the faulty components on the rest of the system. Informally, when a value has changed in a snapshot on a system trace, then the ones in the cone of influence must be updated accordingly to reflect the impact of this change. A trace Tr' is deemed as a counterfactual for a trace Tr if they share the same prefix outside of the cone of influence.

Definition 11 (Cone of influence with separable components, $\mathbf{K}(Tr, \mathcal{S}, \mathcal{R})$). *Given a system* $Sys = \langle \mathcal{A}, \theta, \mathbf{P} \rangle$, *with* $\mathcal{A} = \{C_1, ..., C_J\}$ *and* $C_j = \langle I_j, O_j, \mathbf{P}_j \rangle$ *for* $1 \leq j \leq J$, *a system trace* Tr, *a set* $\mathcal{S} \subseteq \{1, ..., J\}$ *of suspected component indices, and a set* $\mathcal{R} \subseteq \{1, ..., J\}$ *of separable component indices. Let* $A = \langle I, O, \mathbf{P} \rangle$ *be the composition of the components in* $\mathcal{A}$. *The* cone of influence $\mathbf{K} = \mathbf{K}(Tr, \mathcal{S}, \mathcal{R}) = (\ell_v)_{v \in I \cup O}$ *is a vector of maximal indexes which satisfies the following properties:*

$$\forall v \in \left(\bigcup_{i \in \{1,...,J\}} I_i\right) \cup O: \ell_v \leqslant |Tr| \ and$$

$$(1) \ (v \in O \wedge C(v) \in \mathcal{S}) \implies l_v \leqslant fv_{C(v)}(Tr)$$
$$(2) \ \exists v' \in O.(v',v) \in \theta \implies l_v = l_{v'}$$
$$(3) \ \Big(v \in O \wedge \big(C(v) \in \mathcal{R} \ \vee \ fd(v,Tr) \leqslant fv_{C(v)}(Tr)\big)\Big)$$
$$\implies \ell_v \leqslant min(fv_{C(v)}(Tr), fd(v,Tr))$$

with $C(v) = i$ such that $v \in I_i \cup O_i$, $fv_i(Tr) = min(\{\ell \in \{0,...,|Tr|-1 \ | \ \pi_i(Tr[0..\ell]) \notin \mathbf{P}_{C(v)}\} \cup \{|Tr|\})$, $l_{min}(i) = min\{\ell_v \ | \ v \in I_i\}$, and
$fd(v,Tr) = min(\{\ell \in \{l_{min}(v)-1,...,|Tr|\} \ | \ \exists Tr' \in \mathbf{P}_{C(v)}.\forall v' \in I_{C(v)}.$
$$\pi_{v'}(Tr[0..\ell_{v'}-1]) = \pi_{v'}(Tr'[0..\ell_{v'}-1]) \wedge$$
$$\pi_v(Tr[0..l_{min}(v)-1]) = \pi_v(Tr'[0..l_{min}(v)-1]) \wedge$$
$$\pi_v(Tr[\ell+1]) \neq \pi_v(Tr'[\ell+1])\})$$

$C(v)$ is the component to which variable v belongs. $fv_i(Tr)$ is the index of the first violation of $\mathbf{P}_i$ in Tr. $l_{min}(i)$ is the minimal l_v for the inputs v of component C_i. The first constraint means that an output variable from a suspected component must be in the cone if the component is faulty. The second constraint propagates the entry of outputs in the cone to the inputs on which they are linked. The third constraint means that an output v of a non-faulty, or separable, component i receiving inputs from a component in the cone must enter the cone at the latest when component i becomes faulty or at $fd(v,Tr)$. $fd(v,Tr)$ is the first index on which v can differ from its observed value when the component producing v is fed its observed input up to the cone, followed by arbitrary values.

Definition 12 (Counterfactuals). *Let Sys be a system definition, Tr be a system trace, $\mathcal{R} \subseteq \{1,...,J\}$ be the set of separable components indices, and $\mathbf{K} = \mathbf{K}(Tr, \mathcal{S}, \mathcal{R})$ be the cone of influence. Let $A = \langle I, O, \mathbf{P}\rangle$ be the composition of the components in $\mathcal{A}$. We define the counterfactuals of trace Tr given cone $\mathbf{K}$ and separable components $\mathcal{R}$ to be*

$$\sigma(Tr, \mathbf{K}, \mathcal{R}) = \{Tr' \in \mathbf{T} \ | \ \forall v \in I \cup O.\pi_v(Tr')[0..\ell_v-1] = \pi_v(Tr[0..\ell_v-1]) \wedge$$
$$\forall i \in \{1,...,J\}.\big[(i \in \mathcal{S} \vee i \notin \mathcal{R}) \wedge \pi_i(Tr') \in \mathbf{P}_i \vee (i \notin \mathcal{S} \wedge i \in \mathcal{R}) \wedge \pi_i(Tr') \in$$
$$RX(i)\big]\},$$

where $RX(C_i) = \{Tr \in \mathbf{T}_{I_i \cup O_i} \ | \ \exists Tr' \in \mathbf{T}_{I_i}.Tr = re\text{-}execute(C_i, Tr')\}$.

The notion of counterfactuals represents the reconstructed set of possible system traces when the faulty suffixes of the suspected components' observed traces are replaced with correct ones, and the effects of such faults are reconstructed by the separable components. The first condition in the definition of $\sigma(Tr, \mathbf{K}, \mathcal{R})$ states that the counterfactual must begin with the observed *unaffected* prefixes $\pi_v(Tr[0..\ell_v-1])$ before the cone is entered. The second condition states that if a component is not separable, it will be prolonged using its property; for separable components, we re-execute them to build the new trace.

In practice, Tr' is constructed incrementally, without explicitly computing $RX(C_i)$, provided that all components have a finite specification. In that case,

Input:
- observed trace Tr,
- set $\mathcal{F}$ of faulty components,
- set $\mathcal{S} \subseteq \mathcal{F}$ of suspected components,
- set $\mathcal{R}$ of separable components, and
- system definition $Sys = \langle \mathcal{A}, \theta, \mathbf{P} \rangle$.

Output:
- a prefix Tr' of a system trace on which either $Tr' \models \mathbf{P}$ or $Tr' \not\models \mathbf{P}$.

Algorithm for Trace Reconstruction:
(1) Compute the cone of influence $\mathbf{K} = \mathbf{K}(Tr, \mathcal{S}, \mathcal{R})$.
(2) Feed maximal unaffected prefixes $pr_v = \pi_v(Tr[0..\ell_v - 1])$ (Definition 12) of input variables to components. Keep pr_i on output trace Tr'.
(3) Starting from Snapshot 0 on Tr', for each missing value in Snapshot k, (a) identify component C_i responsible for producing the value, (b) read input values for C_i in Snapshot k, (c) obtain component C_i's output, depending on conditions in Definition 12, and (d) add the output to Snapshot k of Tr'.
(4) Repeat the above step until either $Tr' \not\models \mathbf{P}$, or an application-specific length of trace is reached. Return Tr' as the reconstructed trace.

Fig. 4. Trace reconstruction algorithm

the cone and the counterfactuals are computed by the algorithm in Fig. 4. The trace reconstruction depends on the causality definition being used, where we illustrate necessary vertical cause here. In the general case, the algorithm takes the causality definition as an input, based on which different trace reconstruction procedures are selected.

The use of separable components is a hybrid approach in trace reconstruction. For the system behavior that comes before the violations of the suspected components or that is generated by non-faulty components, we want to keep the reconstructed trace as similar as the observed trace, so static information (observed trace Tr and system definition Sys) that is already available at the time of the analysis is used. For the alternative system behavior that depends on dynamic component output, separable components are used to generate run-time output to be used in trace reconstruction.

4.2 Culprit Minimization with Horizontal Causality

A second extension to our existing approach is to replace the use of set containment checking in [18] with the use of horizontal causality, in order to exclude non-minimal subsets of causes from blame. The approach in [18] starts from a viewpoint that always aims to blame the minimal number of components and removes a culprit from blame if one of its proper subsets is also a culprit. While this treatment may have provided one approach to reduce the number of components in a culprit, it is counter-intuitive. Dependency in between component interactions is completely overlooked with this treatment.

With the use of horizontal causality, relationships in between components can be utilized to improve the precision of causality analysis. In details, if the analysis determines that a non-singleton subset S of faulty components is a culprit, then the horizontal causalities between the component property violations are investigated. Let $I = \{i_{Tr_C, \mathbf{P}_C} \mid C \in S\}$ be the set of indices for component violations in S on trace Tr. Then for each $i, j \in I$ such that $i < j$, the horizontal causality between the subset $S_i = \{C_l \in S \mid l = i\}$ and each component C_r in $S_j = \{C_l \in C \mid l = j\}$ is investigated. If the property violations in S_i is a horizontal cause for the property violation in C_r, then C_r is removed from S.

Example 2. For the running example, when the analysis determined that the set $\{PO, Ctrl\}$ is a culprit, the analysis in [18] used simple set minimization to exclude $\{PO, Ctrl\}$ from blame, since the singleton set $\{Ctrl\}$ is a cause as well. With horizontal causality: In the case of $\{PO, Ctrl\}$ being a cause and the fault in PO occurs before the fault in Ctrl, we remove the blame on Ctrl only if the fault in PO causes the fault in Ctrl. In this example, should PO output a correct value 71, the expected output from Ctrl should be 0 time unit. In the approach in [18], Ctrl outputs 3 as on the observed trace, i.e., the property violation in Ctrl does not disappear, so the fault in PO is not a horizontal cause for the fault in Ctrl. Therefore, it is not proper to simply remove $\{PO, Ctrl\}$ from blame. Both $\{Ctrl\}$ and $\{PO, Ctrl\}$ should be taken as blame, as they represent different scenarios that the system property violation can be prevented. □

We note that the two extensions we introduced in this work are orthogonal, and can be applied to our existing approach individually. However, the analysis results, as summarized in Table 2, do not achieve the same precision as when both extensions are incorporated, as shown in Example 3 below.

Example 3. Continuing the running example where $\{PO, Ctrl\}$ is determined to be a necessary vertical cause, if separable component Ctrl is used for causality analysis, then the Ctrl output, given the changed input 71, is not necessarily 3 as on the observed trace. If the Ctrl output is 1 or greater, then the property violation in $\{PO\}$ is not a horizontal cause for the property violation in $\{Ctrl\}$, thus the blame on $\{PO, Ctrl\}$ is not excluded. On the other hand, if Ctrl's output is 0, the horizontal causality between property violations in between $\{PO\}$ and $\{Ctrl\}$ is established. The blame on $\{PO, Ctrl\}$ is reduced to $\{PO\}$, even if $\{PO\}$ itself is not determined as a necessary vertical cause in the first place. □

5   Implementing Causality Analyzer

In this section, we present some key implementation details for the proposed causality analysis. We implemented trace recording, reconstruction, and causality analysis modules based on the publicly available medical device coordination framework (MDCF) [12]. MDCF is a message exchange platform for medical devices operating in a cooperative fashion. The framework implements message publish/subscribe model as specified in the ICE standard [2].

Table 2. Comparison of Causality Analysis Results with Extensions

Analysis in [18, 19]	Analysis in [18, 19] with Horizontal Causality
— {Ctrl} and {PO, Ctrl} are necessary causes — Blame only {Ctrl} — No blame on {PO, Ctrl} due to set minimization	— {Ctrl} and {PO, Ctrl} are necessary causes — No horizontal causality of property violations between {PO} and {Ctrl} — Blame {Ctrl} and {PO, Ctrl}
Analysis in [18, 19] with Separable Components	**Analysis in [18, 19] with both Horizontal Causality and Separable Components**
— {Ctrl} and {PO, Ctrl} are necessary causes — {PO} is a necessary cause when Ctrl outputs 0 or 1 (given input 71) during trace reconstruction — Blame {Ctrl} and {PO} when Ctrl output is 0 or 1; otherwise blame {Ctrl} only — In neither case is {PO, Ctrl} blamed due to set minimization	— {Ctrl} and {PO, Ctrl} are necessary causes — {PO} is a necessary cause when Ctrl outputs 0 or 1 (given input 71) during trace reconstruction — {Ctrl} is blamed — {PO, Ctrl} is blamed only when Ctrl output ≥ 2 — {PO} is blamed if Ctrl output is 0 or 1. When Ctrl output is 1, {PO} is the vertical cause and blamed. When Ctrl output is 0, there may be two explanations: (a) {PO} is the vertical cause, or (b) {PO, Ctrl} is a vertical cause, and {PO} is the horizontal cause for Ctrl, so {PO} is blamed, not {PO, Ctrl}

Trace Recording. The PCA example for our case study is component-based. Each component registers itself as a message publisher to send messages to others and as a subscriber to receive messages from others. We also implemented a network-wide data logger for MDCF. The data logger declares itself as a subscriber to all relevant messages exchanged via message bus. When a message originates from a medical device, it is time-stamped, serialized, and sent to MDCF. MDCF will push the message to the data logger (as well as other subscribers to the message) so that the data logger is able to capture the message together with its time-stamp of creation. The recorded traces are then normalized to the formalism presented in Sect. 3.1 based on the case study's setting that the components are are stepped by a timer of 500 ms.

Implementing Separable Components. In our case study, a component can be viewed as a trace generator in that it takes a sequence of input and produces a sequence of output. A component in MDCF is then naturally separable in that the component can be incorporated in the trace reconstruction module in a controlled fashion.

In details, for components with no internal states, the component implementation is simply executed each time an output is needed. For a separable component C with internal states, the trace reconstruction starts with the initial internal states of C and replays the recorded snapshots on the observed trace Tr back to C, up to the boundary of cone of influence. Afterwards, input to C may have changed as other faulty suspected components may generate new output that is fed to C. The separable component C then reads the input and produces an output. In this way, the internal states of C are implicitly kept within C's implementation, without being explicitly monitored.

Causality Analyzer. The implementation of the causality analyzer follows the functional blocks shown in Fig. 3. Notice that for the analysis of horizontal causality in Step 4 of the causality analysis framework, no additional trace reconstruction is required if we cache the reconstructed traces. For instance, when having determined {PO, Ctrl} as a culprit, we then need to investigate whether the property violation in PO is a cause of the property violation in Ctrl. This requires the reconstruction of the trace when PO alone is suspected. This has already been done, when investigating {PO} for vertical causality.

Result. We have instructed the causality analyzer to output useful human-readable information with regard to the analysis process. A sample run of the analysis outputs (a) set of faulty components, (b) for each suspect, whether it is a culprit, (c) if a suspect is a non-singleton culprit, whether there are horizontal causal relations between its components, and (d) a list of the minimal culprits. The expected analysis result as discussed in Sect. 4 for the running example is summarized in the bottom right cell of Table 2. Note that the result does not invalidate our previous analysis presented in [18, 19] as the criteria of determining minimal culprits are different. Also, with separable components, our proposed analysis is equipped with a more realistic trace reconstruction technique that produces more accurate counterfactual traces, thus we obtain culprits that match our intuition better for this case study.

Scalability. By our problem definition it is inevitable to investigate each non-empty subset of faulty components and determine if it is a culprit. Thus the overall complexity of our approach is exponential in the number of faulty components. However, we note that in practice, the number of faulty components is usually small and tractable. Also, as has been shown in [18, 19] that state-of-the-art SAT/SMT solvers (e.g., Z3 [6]) can be used to efficiently solve a causality analysis problem instance, our approach could benefit from leveraging SAT/SMT solvers with proper encoding.

6 Related Work

Analysis for causes has long been a human intellectual inquisition. Recent philosophical inquisition on causality based on counterfactuals starts from Hume, and is extensively studied in [15]. Halpern and Pearl [10] were among the first to provide a formalism to reason about causality. [10] defines causality for structural equation models (constraints on variables) and does not study component-based or real-time systems, which typically exhibit much more complex behaviors.

Works following Halpern and Pearl's definitions include [3, 13, 14], all requiring a cause to be both necessary and sufficient. The work in [3] illustrated how causality can be used for providing an explanation of system property violation. The work in [13, 14] is based on the assumption that a plethora of system traces can be obtained for analysis so that is possible to categorize the available traces by trace characteristics so that each category can be regarded as a failure mode in the failure mode and effects analysis (FMEA). The work in [3, 13, 14] all model traces as a sequence of observed events, and the occurrence or absence of events are potential causes to the violation of properties, which are modeled as temporal logic properties. These approaches neglect the underlying system components that generate the events as well as the interactions between components. Similarly, work based on using distance metrics [4,17] to measure the similarity between actual and counterfactual traces shares the same limitation.

The work in [11] and our previous work in [18] share similar ideas if program statements are viewed as black-box components. Encoding the program and error trace into a MAX-SAT problem instance can yield a set of program statements so that correcting the identified statements can eliminate the program error. On a larger scale, the delta-debugging technique proposed in [20] can also be viewed as an application of counterfactual reasoning: debugging is by experimentally correcting statements of a program until a set of statements are found to eliminate compiler panic should the identified statements are corrected.

Our line of work [7–9,18,19] starts with preliminary definitions of causalities for component-based systems [9,18] and extends to real-time settings for system definitions with logical constraints [19], synchronous systems [8], and timed automata [7]. A salient difference of our work from existing ones is that, although we assume components are black-boxes, we take expected component behaviors specified in component properties as guidelines for trace reconstruction. This directs us to a set of counterfactual traces that are more relevant to the observed one. We in this work further employs separable components, which first appeared in combinational circuits diagnosis [5] where internal states of components are not considered.

7   Conclusion

We presented an extension of trace reconstruction algorithm for causality analysis. Using a case study from the medical domain, we show that the extension improves precision of the analysis and matches our intuition about the analysis results. The key to the improvement is the ability to re-execute some of the system components separately from the rest of the system. We further show that analysis can be improved by considering horizontal causality; that is, taking input-output dependencies between components into consideration in order to avoid induced faults. Our future work will concentrate on extending causality analysis to cover weaker component contracts that may make some of the faults unobservable.

References

1. Arney, D., Pajic, M., Goldman, J.M., Lee, I., Mangharam, R., Sokolsky, O.: Toward patient safety in closed-loop medical device systems. In: ICCPS 2010, pp. 139–148. ACM, New York, NY, USA (2010)
2. ASTM International. F2761-2009. Medical Devices and Medical Systems – Essential Safety Requirements for Equipment Comprising the Patient-Centric Integrated Clinical Environment (ICE), Part 1, 2009

3. Beer, I., Ben-David, S., Chockler, H., Orni, A., Trefler, R.: Explaining counterexamples using causality. In: Bouajjani, A., Maler, O. (eds.) CAV 2009. LNCS, vol. 5643, pp. 94–108. Springer, Heidelberg (2009)
4. Chaki, S., Groce, A., Strichman, O.: Explaining abstract counterexamples. SIG-SOFT Softw. Eng. Notes **29**(6), 73–82 (2004)
5. de Kleer, J., Williams, B.C.: Diagnosing multiple faults. Artif. Intell. **32**(1), 97–130 (1987)
6. de Moura, L., Bjørner, N.S.: Z3: an efficient SMT solver. In: Ramakrishnan, C.R., Rehof, J. (eds.) TACAS 2008. LNCS, vol. 4963, pp. 337–340. Springer, Heidelberg (2008)
7. Gössler, G., Aştefănoaei, L.: Blaming in component-based real-time systems. In: Proceedings of the 14th International Conference on Embedded Software (2014)
8. Gössler, G., Le Métayer, D.: A general trace-based framework of logical causality. In: Fiadeiro, J.L., Liu, Z., Xue, J. (eds.) FACS 2013. LNCS, vol. 8348, pp. 157–173. Springer, Heidelberg (2014)
9. Gössler, G., Le Métayer, D., Raclet, J.-B.: Causality analysis in contract violation. In: Barringer, H., Falcone, Y., Finkbeiner, B., Havelund, K., Lee, I., Pace, G., Roşu, G., Sokolsky, O., Tillmann, N. (eds.) RV 2010. LNCS, vol. 6418, pp. 270–284. Springer, Heidelberg (2010)
10. Halpern, Y.P., Pearl, J.: Causes and explanations: a structural-model approach. Part I: causes. Br. J. Philos. Sci. **56**(4), 743–887 (2005)
11. Jose, M., Majumdar, R.: Cause clue clauses: error localization using maximum satisfiability. SIGPLAN Not. **46**(6), 437–446 (2011)
12. King, A., Procter, S., Andresen, D., Hatcliff, J., Warren, S., Spees, W., Jetley, R.P., Jones, P.L., Weininger, S.: An open test bed for medical device integration and coordination. In: ICSE Companion, pp. 141–151. IEEE (2009)
13. Kuntz, M., Leitner-Fischer, F., Leue, S.: From probabilistic counterexamples via causality to fault trees. In: Flammini, F., Bologna, S., Vittorini, V. (eds.) SAFE-COMP 2011. LNCS, vol. 6894, pp. 71–84. Springer, Heidelberg (2011)
14. Leitner-Fischer, F., Leue, S.: On the synergy of probabilistic causality computation and causality checking. In: Bartocci, E., Ramakrishnan, C.R. (eds.) SPIN 2013. LNCS, vol. 7976, pp. 246–263. Springer, Heidelberg (2013)
15. Lewis, D.: Counterfactuals, 2nd edn. Wiley-Blackwell, New York (2001)
16. Reiter, R.: A theory of diagnosis from first principles. Artif. Intell. **32**(1), 57–95 (1987)
17. Renieris, M., Reiss, S.P.: Fault localization with nearest neighbor queries. In: ASE 2003, pp. 30–39 (2003)
18. Wang, S., Ayoub, A., Ivanov, R., Sokolsky, O., Lee, I.: Contract-based blame assignment by trace analysis. In: HiCoNS 2013, pp. 117–125 (2013)
19. Wang, S., Ayoub, A., Kim, B.G., Gössler, G., Sokolsky, O., Lee, I.: A causality analysis framework for component-based real-time systems. In: Legay, A., Bensalem, S. (eds.) RV 2013. LNCS, vol. 8174, pp. 285–303. Springer, Heidelberg (2013)
20. Zeller, A.: Isolating cause-effect chains from computer programs. In: ACM International Symposium on Foundations of Software Engineering, pp. 1–10 (2002)

Short Papers

Statistical Model Checking of Distributed Adaptive Real-Time Software

David Kyle, Jeffery Hansen, and Sagar Chaki(✉)

Software Engineering Institute, Carnegie Mellon University, Pittsburgh, USA
{dskyle,jhansen,chaki}@sei.cmu.edu

Abstract. The problem of estimating quantitative properties of distributed cyber-physical software that coordinate and adapt to uncertain environments is addressed. A domain-specific language, called DMPL, is developed to both describe such a system and a target property. Statistical model checking (SMC) is used to estimate the probability with which the property holds on the system. A distributed SMC tool is developed and described. Virtual machines are used to implement a realistic execution environment, and to isolate simulations from one another. Experimental results on a coordinated multi-robot example are presented.

1 Introduction

A Distributed Adaptive Real-Time (DART) system consists of a set of physically disjoint nodes that communicate and coordinate to achieve a set of objectives, and increase the likelihood of achieving these objectives (i.e., success) under an uncertain environment via self-adaptation. Given a stochastic system $\mathcal{M}$, an event Φ in its execution, and an error bound RE, statistical model checking (SMC) [10] is a systematic use of Monte-Carlo simulations to estimate the probability of Φ with an error of no more than RE. In this paper, we present and evaluate an approach for statistical model checking of DART systems (DARTs).

We make three contributions. First, we develop a language called the DART Modeling and Programming Language (DMPL). A DMPL program $\mathcal{P}$ is a triple $(\mathcal{M}, \Phi, T)$, where $\mathcal{M}$ is the DART system, and T (a time limit) and Φ (a predicate over executions of $\mathcal{M}$) express the target property. Our goal is to estimate the probability **p** that Φ holds on a random execution of $\mathcal{M}$ of duration T. Second, we develop a compiler, DMPLC, that given a DMPL program $\mathcal{P}$, generates: (i) a log generator $LogG$; a run of $LogG$ produces one log for each node of $\mathcal{M}$; and (ii) a log analyzer $LogA$ that combines all the logs from one execution of $LogG$, and produces the value of Φ at time T. Finally, we implement a distributed SMC tool, SMCD, that uses $LogG$ and $LogA$ to estimate **p** with a target precision.

We evaluated our approach on a DART example with mobile robots, where success involves avoiding collisions, while maximizing speed, and minimizing exposure to environmental hazards. For our experiments, we use the ZSRM [7] scheduler, the V-REP [9] physics engine, and the MADARA [5] middleware. Our approach easily handles this example system with 5 nodes, each running 3

© Springer International Publishing Switzerland 2015
E. Bartocci and R. Majumdar (Eds.): RV 2015, LNCS 9333, pp. 269–274, 2015.
DOI: 10.1007/978-3-319-23820-3_17

threads, and should scale to much larger systems. We also demonstrated running on clusters with 5 VMs. Further details are provided in Sect. 4.

Related Work. SMC has been applied to various types of "models": stochastic hybrid automata [3], real-time systems [4], and Simulink models of cyber-physical systems [2]. Our work bridges the gap between what is analyzed and what will be executed. In addition, unlike current distributed SMC tools, SMCD handles dynamic addition and removal of simulators. Younes [11] showed that naive parallelization of SMC is incorrect due to a bias caused by differences in execution time, and that [11] this bias is eliminated by performing simulations in "rounds". Bulychev, et. al. [1] proposed two optimizations to round-based parallelization – batching and buffering. Since we simulate the actual system for time T, the time to perform a simulation is relatively large, and the simulation times for "true" and "false" results are close. Hence, we do not believe that batching or buffering will be helpful for us, but we do apply the basic round-based approach to avoid bias. SMC performance can also be improved via techniques orthogonal to ours, e.g., importance splitting [6], and importance sampling [8].

2   The DMPL Language

A DMPL program $\mathcal{P}$ is a triple $(\mathcal{M}, \Phi, T)$. The system $\mathcal{M}$ is a triple (V, F, T), where V is a set of shared variables; F is a set of procedures (functions); T is a set of threads. DMPL defines $\mathcal{M}$ and Φ, through a mostly C-like syntax; however:

- DMPL does not support pointers, to avoid variable aliasing complications.
- DMPL functions in F can be declared **pure**. These functions cannot modify V; DMPLC will reject code that violates this.
- DMPL defines threads statically, like functions, but with the **thread** keyword. DMPL automatically spawns these threads. DMPL threads are inherently periodic; each thread's code runs within an implied infinite loop.
- DMPL variables, comprising V, may be defined as **local** or **global**. Threads on a given node share **local** variables, while threads across all nodes share **global** variables. DMPL uses a "read-execute-write" computation model. Threads operate on cached copies of these variables, read atomically at the start of each period, and write atomically back at the end. Additionally, each node publishes its own version of **global** variables, which other nodes cannot "overwrite". Nodes, however, can "read" others' versions.
- DMPL supports defining a Φ as part of its source, using **expect** clauses. These clauses specify a Boolean expression, over values in V and returned from **pure** functions, whose truth SMC will evaluate.
- DMPL can call arbitrary **extern** C++ functions; however, these functions cannot directly access V. They may be labeled **pure**, indicating that they are safe to call from **expect** clauses, i.e., they do not affect runtime behavior, only gather information about it. DMPLC does not enforce this contract.

DMPLC creates *LogG* and *LogA* from a DMPL program. *LogG* includes an observer thread which periodically logs (with a timestamp) all variables in V

```
 1 pure double coverage()
 2 {
 3   double cover = 0.0, dist, lat, lng, xd, yd;
 4   lat = GET_LAT();
 5   lng = GET_LNG();
 6   forall_other(nid) {
 7     xd = GET_LAT()@nid-lat;
 8     yd = GET_LNG()@nid-lng;
 9     dist = LL2M * sqrt(xd*xd + yd*yd);
10     if(dist == 0.0) continue;
11     cover = cover+asin(RAD/dist)/M_PI;
12   }
13   return cover;
14 }
15
16 @AtLeast(0.5) expect(coverage() > 0.9);
```

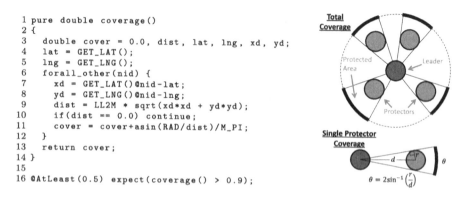

Fig. 1. A DMPL property for coverage, with geometric justification.

appearing in `expect` clauses. The read-execute-write model ensures consistent state observation. Functions declared `pure` are executed in either *LogG* or *LogA* as needed. *LogA* uses the timestamps to cross-reference the logs and evaluate each `expect` clause. Figure 1 shows an example DMPL program for a scenario used later in Experiment 1. The `@AtLeast(0.5)` annotation in the `expect` clause means that the specified coverage property should hold true at least 50 % of the time for a mission run to be successful. DMPL also supports an `@AtEnd` annotation; such `expect` clauses must hold true at the end of a mission run.

3   Statistical Model Checking (SMC)

The goal of SMC is to estimate the probability that the property Φ holds in the system $\mathcal{M}$. We model this as an indicator function $I_{\mathcal{M}\models\Phi} : x \rightarrow \{0,1\}$ where $x \sim f$ (i.e., x is a random input vector distributed by f). We can then state the SMC problem as determining the probability $\mathbf{p} = E[I_{\mathcal{M}\models\Phi}(x)] = \int I_{\mathcal{M}\models\Phi}(x)f(x)dx$ which can be estimated as: $\hat{\mathbf{p}} = \sum_{i=1}^{N} I_{\mathcal{M}\models\Phi}(x_i)$, where x_i is the i-th of N trials. The precision of $\hat{\mathbf{p}}$ is quantified by its "relative error" $RE(\hat{\mathbf{p}}) = \frac{\sqrt{Var(\hat{\mathbf{p}})}}{E[\hat{\mathbf{p}}]}$ where $Var(\hat{\mathbf{p}})$ is the variance of the estimator. It is known [2] that: $RE(\hat{\mathbf{p}}) = \sqrt{\frac{1-\mathbf{p}}{\mathbf{p}N}} \approx \frac{1}{\sqrt{\mathbf{p}N}}$ and $N = \frac{1-\mathbf{p}}{\mathbf{p}RE^2(\hat{\mathbf{p}})} \approx \frac{1}{\mathbf{p}RE^2(\hat{\mathbf{p}})}$.

Our SMC tool SMCD consists of one or more collectors and an aggregator. Each collector is deployed on a VM, where it: (i) awaits a signal from the aggregator; and (ii) runs a simulation η, computes the result $\eta \models \Phi$, and transmits it back to the aggregator. The aggregator manages the SMC in rounds to avoid execution time bias [11]. At the beginning of each round, the aggregator sends a message to each collector to begin a simulation. After all collectors have reported their result, the current probability and relative error is calculated. If the calculated relative error is less than the target relative error RE, the algorithm terminates. If not, a new round of simulations is started.

Since our simulations execute the actual system code, each may take significant time. Moreover, we know that many simulations (N) are needed if **p** and RE are small. Thus, to analyze systems of realistic complexity, SMCD collectors might be deployed on large clusters of machines with varying availability. Hence, the aggregator is designed so that collectors may join and drop at any time. If a collector joins during a round, it is held in reserve until the next round but not used during the current round. If a collector disconnects during a round, an "abort" message is send to the other collectors, and the results of that round are discarded. Thus, we avoid any potential bias in the probability estimation.

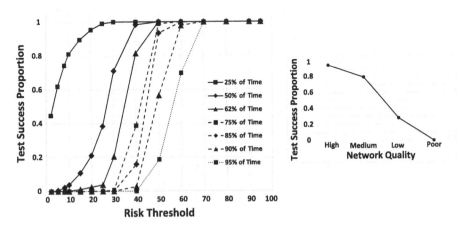

Fig. 2. Graphs of results from experiments 1(left) and 2 (right).

4   Experiments

Our scenario (c.f. Fig. 1 for DMPL code fragment) involves a reconnaissance mission with five flying robots (i.e., nodes) on a 2-dimensional grid. One node (leader) has mission-critical sensors, while the others (protectors) provide physical defense from attackers (so we want to maximize coverage). The leader must follow a specific flight path, and reach a particular location by time T while maintaining a minimum level of protection for mission success. Nodes execute a (presumed correct) collision-avoidance protocol, which slows down the the fleet, due to additional coordination. Each grid cell has a random hazard level with known probability distribution. The system has two formations: (i) tight – the protectors are closer to the leader, and (ii) loose – protectors are further apart. The tight formation provides better coverage to the leader but is about twice as slow. The leader executes a self-adaption algorithm for formation selection, based on upcoming hazards and remaining mission time, to increase likelihood of mission completion. Further details are not germane to this paper. However, our tools and the complete example is available at http://www.andrew.cmu.edu/~schaki/misc/smc-dart.tgz.

Experiment 1: Quality of Formation. First, we analyzed the quality of formation-keeping by the protectors. At any time instant, let us define the leader's risk ($\mathcal{R}$) as the product of the hazard at its location and its exposure (one minus its coverage, computed via the method shown in Fig. 1). We selected 14 $\mathcal{R}$ values: $\{2, 5, 8, 10, 15, 20, 25, 30, 40, 50, 60, 70, 80, 90, 95\}$, and 7 @AtLeast values: $\{.25, .50, .62, .75, .85, .90, .95\}$. For each $\mathcal{R}$ value ρ and @AtLeast value al, we defined an expect clause to express mission success only if the leader's risk remains below ρ for at least al fraction of the time. This yielded 98 properties, whose probabilities were computed using SMCD. We ran 603 simulations, on 5 VMs in parallel, using $T = 115s$. This achieved $RE = 0.1$ for most of the properties. A few properties had $RE > 0.1$, and would require techniques to handle rare events [6,8]. Our results are summarized in Fig. 2. Each curve corresponds to a different @AtLeast value. As expected, the probability increases with the risk threshold, but falls with increasing @AtLeast value.

Experiment 2: Resilience to Network Disruption. Next, we instrumented our simulation to randomly drop messages between the nodes. This slows down the fleet due to increased coordination time for collision avoidance. We defined four network categories based on drop rate ranges: high (0% to 20%), medium (20% to 40%), low (40% to 60%), and poor (60% to 80%). Using an @AtEnd expect clause we defined the following property: at the end of the mission, the leader must be at the target location. We then computed the probability of this property for each network category. For each experiment for a category, we randomly selected a drop rate from that category's range, uniformly distributed. To achieve $RE = 0.1$, we needed 35 experiments for "high", 43 experiments for "medium", and 264 for "low". Figure 2 shows the results. As expected, the probability drops with decreasing network quality. For the "poor" network, we stopped after 43 experiments, since we saw no successes. Techniques to handle rare events in SMC [6,8] are needed for this case as well[1].

References

1. Bulychev, P., David, A., Larsen, K.G., Legay, A., Mikučionis, M., Poulsen, D.B.: Checking and distributing statistical model checking. In: Goodloe, A.E., Person, S. (eds.) NFM 2012. LNCS, vol. 7226, pp. 449–463. Springer, Heidelberg (2012)
2. Clarke, E.M., Zuliani, P.: Statistical model checking for cyber-physical systems. In: Bultan, T., Hsiung, P.-A. (eds.) ATVA 2011. LNCS, vol. 6996, pp. 1–12. Springer, Heidelberg (2011)
3. David, A., Du, D., Larsen, K.G., Legay, A., Mikučionis, M.: Optimizing control strategy using statistical model checking. In: Brat, G., Rungta, N., Venet, A. (eds.) NFM 2013. LNCS, vol. 7871, pp. 352–367. Springer, Heidelberg (2013)
4. David, A., Larsen, K.G., Legay, A., Mikučionis, M., Wang, Z.: Time for statistical model checking of real-time systems. In: Gopalakrishnan, G., Qadeer, S. (eds.) CAV 2011. LNCS, vol. 6806, pp. 349–355. Springer, Heidelberg (2011)

---

[1] This material is based upon work funded and supported by the Department of Defense under Contract No. FA8721-05-C-0003 with Carnegie Mellon University for the operation of the Software Engineering Institute, a federally funded research and development center. This material has been approved for public release and unlimited distribution. DM-0002365.

5. Edmondson, J., Gokhale, A.: Design of a scalable reasoning engine for distributed, real-time and embedded systems. In: Xiong, H., Lee, W.B. (eds.) KSEM 2011. LNCS, vol. 7091, pp. 221–232. Springer, Heidelberg (2011)

6. Jegourel, C., Legay, A., Sedwards, S.: Importance splitting for statistical model checking rare properties. In: Sharygina, N., Veith, H. (eds.) CAV 2013. LNCS, vol. 8044, pp. 576–591. Springer, Heidelberg (2013)

7. de Niz, D., Lakshmanan, K., Rajkumar, R.: On the scheduling of mixed-criticality real-time task sets. In: Proceedings of RTSS (2009)

8. Srinivasan, R.: Importance Sampling: Applications in Communications and Detection. Springer, Heidelberg (2002)

9. V-REP website. http://www.coppeliarobotics.com

10. Younes, H.L.S.: Verification and Planning for Stochastic Processes with Asynchronous Events. Ph.D. thesis, Carnegie Mellon University (2005)

11. Younes, H.L.S.: Ymer: a statistical model checker. In: Etessami, K., Rajamani, S.K. (eds.) CAV 2005. LNCS, vol. 3576, pp. 429–433. Springer, Heidelberg (2005)

Probabilistic Model Checking at Runtime for the Provisioning of Cloud Resources

Athanasios Naskos, Emmanouela Stachtiari, Panagiotis Katsaros[✉],
and Anastasios Gounaris

Aristotle University of Thessaloniki, Thessaloniki, Greece
{anaskos,emmastac,katsaros,gounaria}@csd.auth.gr

Abstract. We elaborate on the ingredients of a model-driven approach for the dynamic provisioning of cloud resources in an autonomic manner. Our solution has been experimentally evaluated using a NoSQL database cluster running on a cloud infrastructure. In contrast to other techniques, which work on a best-effort basis, we can provide probabilistic guarantees for the provision of sufficient resources. Our approach is based on the probabilistic model checking of Markov Decision Processes (MDPs) at runtime. We present: (i) the specification of an appropriate MDP model for the provisioning of cloud resources, (ii) the generation of a parametric model with system-specific parameters, (iii) the dynamic instantiation of MDPs at runtime based on logged and current measurements and (iv) their verification using the PRISM model checker for the provisioning/deprovisioning of cloud resources to meet the set goals (This research has been co-financed by the European Union (European Social Fund - ESF) and Greek national funds through the Operational Program "Education and Lifelong Learning of the National Strategic Reference Framework (NSRF) - Research Funding Program: Thales. Investing in knowledge society through the European Social Fund.").

1 Introduction

A practical model-driven approach is presented for the provisioning of resources to a cloud application, such as a web-enabled NoSQL database on a cluster of virtual machines (VMs). The load of service requests submitted by end-users evolves over time. Each request has to be served within a fixed period of time determined by a threshold on acceptable response latency. To achieve this goal, we rely on horizontal scaling *elasticity actions*, i.e., new VMs may be added on the fly to cope with load increases and VMs can be released when the load decreases. The main challenge is to develop a decision making policy that avoids both resource under-provisioning, which leads to violations of the latency threshold, and over-provisioning, which leads to low infrastructure utilization and unnecessary economic cost.

Existing decision making policies such as the one implemented in Amazon's EC2 manager mainly work on a best-effort basis and there is no way to provide guarantees for their performance in diverse workload scenarios. Some other

© Springer International Publishing Switzerland 2015
E. Bartocci and R. Majumdar (Eds.): RV 2015, LNCS 9333, pp. 275–280, 2015.
DOI: 10.1007/978-3-319-23820-3_18

model-driven proposals [6] combine Markov Decision Process (MDP) models with reinforcement learning-based policies.

Our decision making solution is based on the probabilistic model checking of dynamically instantiated MDPs by using the PRISM tool [1] at runtime. A decision step is activated periodically, e.g., every 30 s or every few minutes. Each decision (or elasticity) step is split into the following three phases:

1. Appropriate MDP models are dynamically instantiated, which reflect the predicted system utility and the possibility of latency threshold violations. These models are constructed based on the monitored incoming load and past log measurements of response latency, for similar incoming load values.
2. MDPs are verified online using PRISM, in order to find the optimal elasticity decisions for the solved model instances.
3. The selected elasticity action to be applied is chosen from the set of possible actions {*add, remove, no_op*} that respectively correspond to adding new VMs, releasing existing VMs and leaving the cluster unchanged. If any of the first two actions are decided, then the run of the next elasticity step is suspended until the system stabilizes.

In [5], we have experimentally evaluated and compared the described approach with the mentioned alternatives. The presented results are based on traces from a real NoSQL database cluster under constantly evolving external load and they are particularly promising: we can support decision policies that improve upon the state-of-the-art in significantly decreasing under-provisioning, while avoiding over-provisioning. Here, we focus on our MDP modeling approach for the first elasticity phase, whereas details for the two other phases are provided in [5].

In Sect. 2, we elaborate on our approach for the specification of an appropriate MDP model. Section 3 discusses the generation of a parametric model with system-specific parameters, the dynamic instantiation of MDPs, and their verification at runtime. Finally, we conclude with a critical review on the practicality and the prospects of the proposed solution.

2 An MDP for the Control of Cloud Resource Provisioning

An MDP allows to capture both the non-deterministic and the probabilistic aspects of the modeled system and it is formally defined as follows:

Definition 1. *[2] An MDP is a tuple $\mathcal{M} = (S, s_0, Act, \mathbf{P}, L)$, where S is a finite set of states with s_0 the initial state, Act a finite set of actions and $L : S \to 2^{AP}$ maps states to a subset of a given set of atomic propositions AP. The transition probability matrix $\mathbf{P}$ is a function $\mathbf{P} : S \times Act \times S \to [0, 1]$. For all states $s \in S$ and actions $\alpha \in Act$, we require that $\sum_{s' \in S} \mathbf{P}(s, \alpha, s') \in \{0, 1\}$. We also require that for each $s \in S$ there is at least one $\alpha \in Act$ with $\sum_{s' \in S} \mathbf{P}(s, \alpha, s') = 1$.*

With $Act(s) = \{\alpha \mid \sum_{s' \in S} \mathbf{P}(s, \alpha, s') = 1\}$ we specify the set of enabled actions in a state. Figure 1 introduces a simplified representation of our MDP state space and the enabled actions in each of the shown states. Every state s_i corresponds to the number of VMs that compose the application cluster (e.g. the NoSQL cluster used in [5]) with i representing the cluster's size at some time instant.

This illustration of the state space is separated in time sections $(t, t+1, t+2, ...)$ with each one corresponding to a distinct decision step of the cloud provisioning policy. We can thus take into account the evolution of the conditions with time, which is

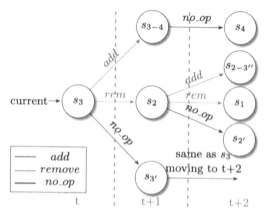

Fig. 1. MDP model overview.

particularly important when a decision policy is coupled with external load prediction[1]. After *remove* and *add* VM actions, the decision maker may be idle for a pre-specified time period (e.g. one decision step) to allow the system to stabilize. In Fig. 1, s_{3-4} at $t+1$ and all other states identified with s_{i-j} represent *transient* states, i.e. unstable system states due to a recent change in the number of active VMs. Thus, based on the enabled actions at t, we have three states at $t+1$ including two *stable* states s_2 and s_3' - if the number of VMs is not changed - and one transient state. States s_3 and s_3' represent a configuration with 3 VMs, however as the environment evolves, these two states can behave differently to the incoming load (e.g. they may receive different incoming load and may be characterized by different response latency). Also, as we observe, after the s_3' state, the same pattern is repeated with different time sections and state naming conventions, with s_3' now being the current state.

The model's representation in Fig. 1 is further elaborated in Fig. 2 to account for the possible variability in the application's performance for a given external load and cluster size. In Fig. 2, s_i can be any possible stable state of the previous model view, where each s_i is in fact represented by n states (shown as $s_i b_m$, $1 \leq m \leq n$). In [5], the most effective decision policies, for a given number of VMs, employ one state representing the possibility of not

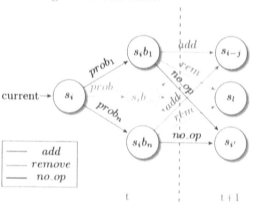

Fig. 2. Detailed MDP model states.

[1] An ARIMA-based predictor of future load can be used in decision policies as suggested by [5].

meeting the latency threshold and other states representing the possibility to meet it. Transition probabilities are based on the prediction of the future incoming load and the collected logs (cf. Sect. 3).

Definition 2. *[2] A reward structure for an MDP with state space S and action set Act is a partial function $\mathbf{r} : S \times Act \rightharpoonup \mathbb{R}_{\geq 0}$ assigning a reward to each state and enabled action.*

In our MDPs, a reward is assigned in states based on measurements of the system's latency and throughput, and a user-defined utility function.

3   MDP Model Instantiation and Verification at Runtime

The described model representation is encoded into a parametric MDP in PRISM's input language. The model is automatically generated using scripts based on: (i) system-specific parameters such as the minimum/maximum allowed number of VMs, the allowed numbers of simultaneous VM additions/removals in a single decision step, the lookahead prediction steps, the duration of the transient states, the number of states representing each cluster size, and (ii) system measurements such as the response latency. Our PRISM model's structure is accessible in [3]. Every model is defined as the parallel composition of three PRISM modules:

1. The *decision* module, where the actual elasticity is modeled (add, remove and no_op actions between model states).
2. The *transient* module, which stores measurements for stable states from which an add action is applied, thus reaching a transient state. These measurements are used to compute the rewards for the transient states.
3. The *cluster* module, where a possible state representation as in Fig. 2 is chosen; here the name "cluster" stems from the log measurements clustering in different groups (states) for the same external load and VM cluster size, as explained below and detailed in [5].

Appropriate PRISM formulas are also used to: (i) find the current system measurements, (ii) define the utility function for reward computation and (iii) control the computation of rewards for specific model transitions.

Dynamic MDP Instantiation. In each decision step, current and logged measurements are gathered through periodic monitoring (e.g., every 30 s). Measurements are then fed after preprocessing into the parametric model to create a new MDP model instance. For the experiments in [5], all model parameters are derived from clustering log measurements for similar past conditions, where similarity is decided based on the external load, the number of VMs and the response latency. This extends the approach in [6], in order to capture the inherent uncertainty in the application's environment. Log measurements are grouped in each step for a specific number of active VMs by their incoming load λ, and they are then fed into a k-means clusterer, which returns k center points. The k centers are mapped to probabilities, proportional to the size of their clusters. Finally, the state representation of Fig. 2 is used during the MDP model instantiation, with the computed center points (states) and their respective probabilities.

Model Verification and Decision Making. The elastic decision is based on the maximum expected reward after a specified number of steps. This property is expressed in Probabilistic Computation Tree Logic (PCTL) as follows: $R\{$"$cumulative\_reward$"$\}max =? [F (stop)]$. The model checking result is the expected maximum cumulative reward and the set of adversaries which yield this reward, i.e. functions $\delta : S \rightarrow Act$ that resolve nondeterminism in the MDP by choosing which action to take in each state.

From the obtained adversaries, we choose the first action of the adversary with the least maximum expected probability for a system measurement threshold violation. The used PCTL properties for this purpose have the form: $Pmax =? [F (stop) \& (meas > meas\_threshold) \& (first\_action = X)]$, where $meas$ is a specific system measurement and X denotes every possible initial action of the processed adversaries. This result represents the preferred elasticity decision.

4   Conclusions and Future Work

We introduced a parametric MDP model for the control of cloud resource provisioning. This model is the key-component of various elasticity decision policies that have been experimentally evaluated [5] using traces from a real NoSQL database cluster under constantly evolving external load. To the best of our knowledge, this is the first initiative towards integrating model checking in cloud elasticity management and the results in [5] show that our model-driven policies outperform compared to existing alternatives in that they can decrease under-provisioning, while at the same time avoiding over-provisioning.

Latest results show that the presented model checking approach at runtime can be also beneficial for the management of trade-offs between the need to meet performance requirements, while respecting critical constraints in cloud security. To this end, we have evaluated the effectiveness of a new security-aware elasticity policy on scaling NoSQL databases in a cloud environment [4].

References

1. Kwiatkowska, M., Norman, G., Parker, D.: PRISM 4.0: verification of probabilistic real-time systems. In: Gopalakrishnan, G., Qadeer, S. (eds.) CAV 2011. LNCS, vol. 6806, pp. 585–591. Springer, Heidelberg (2011)
2. Kwiatkowska, M., Parker, D.: Automated verification and strategy synthesis for probabilistic systems. In: Van Hung, D., Ogawa, M. (eds.) ATVA 2013. LNCS, vol. 8172, pp. 5–22. Springer, Heidelberg (2013)
3. Naskos, A.: Probabilistic model checking at runtime for the provisioning of cloud resources - appendix (2015). http://anaskos.webpages.auth.gr/wp-content/uploads/2015/06/parametricMDPmodel.pdf

4. Naskos, A., Gounaris, A., Mouratidis, H., Katsaros, P.: Security-aware elasticity for nosql databases. In: MEDI (2015)
5. Naskos, A., Stachtiari, E., Gounaris, A., Katsaros, P., Tsoumakos, D., Konstantinou, I., Sioutas, S.: Dependable horizontal scaling based on probabilistic model checking. In: CCGrid. IEEE (2015)
6. Tsoumakos, D., Konstantinou, I., Boumpouka, C., Sioutas, S., Koziris, N.: Automated, elastic resource provisioning for nosql clusters using tiramola. In: CCGrid, pp. 34–41 (2013)

Runtime Verification for Hybrid Analysis Tools

Luan Viet Nguyen[1]([✉]), Christian Schilling[2], Sergiy Bogomolov[3],
and Taylor T. Johnson[1]

[1] University of Texas at Arlington, Arlington, TX, USA
luanvnguyen@mavs.uta.edu, taylor.johnson@gmail.com
[2] Albert-Ludwigs-Universität Freiburg, Freiburg, Germany
schillic@informatik.uni-freiburg.de
[3] IST Austria, Klosterneuburg, Austria
bogom@informatik.uni-freiburg.de

Abstract. In this paper, we present the first steps toward a runtime verification framework for monitoring hybrid and cyber-physical systems (CPS) development tools based on randomized differential testing. The development tools include hybrid systems reachability analysis tools, model-based development environments like Simulink/Stateflow (SLSF), etc. First, hybrid automaton models are randomly generated. Next, these hybrid automaton models are translated to a number of different tools (currently, SpaceEx, dReach, Flow*, HyCreate, and the MathWorks' Simulink/Stateflow) using the HyST source transformation and translation tool. Then, the hybrid automaton models are executed in the different tools and their outputs are parsed. The final step is the differential comparison: the outputs of the different tools are compared. If the results do not agree (in the sense that an analysis or verification result from one tool does not match that of another tool, ignoring time-outs, etc.), a candidate bug is flagged and the model is saved for future analysis by the user. The process then repeats and the monitoring continues until the user terminates the process. We present preliminary results that have been useful in identifying a few bugs in the analysis methods of different development tools, and in an earlier version of HyST.

1 Introduction

Runtime verification is an approach to ensure the correctness and reliability of a system during its execution. It can check and analyze executions of a system under scrutiny that violate or satisfy a given correctness property by using a decision procedure called a monitor. A monitor can also be considered as a device that can read finite traces and output a truth value derived from a truth domain [3]. Runtime verification can be used broadly for many purposes such as debugging, testing, verification, validation, fault protection, and online system repair. In this paper, we describe a preliminary work toward a randomized differential testing framework [5] that may be used as a runtime monitor for various components (from parsers to analysis algorithms) in hybrid and CPS analysis tools such as SpaceEx, dReach, Flow*, HyCreate and the

© Springer International Publishing Switzerland 2015
E. Bartocci and R. Majumdar (Eds.): RV 2015, LNCS 9333, pp. 281–286, 2015.
DOI: 10.1007/978-3-319-23820-3_19

Mathworks' Simulink/Stateflow (SLSF). A test subject is the hybrid automaton randomly generated in the input format for SpaceEx using a prototype tool called HyRG [4][1], which is then translated to other formats including dReach, Flow*, HyCreate and SLSF using the HyST model transformation tool [1]. Our contributions include (a) the first steps toward a randomized differential testing framework to monitor CPS development and verification tools, and (b) identifying some bugs in existing tools, including a semantic difference between SpaceEx and SLSF that we did not know about and some soundness bugs in the verification tools that have been corrected by the tool authors [1].

2   Monitoring with Randomized Differential Testing

We first describe how the hybrid systems are randomly generated in HyRG so they have diverse continuous and discrete behaviors. We then analyze these examples with different hybrid systems development and verification tools, and then compare their outputs to identify possible bugs in the tools. Figure 1 shows the overview of our framework for randomized differential testing to monitor hybrid systems development tools. First, a hybrid automaton A_R is randomly generated by HyRG, then A_R is translated using HyST to equivalent automata in different tools' formats, denoted A_S, A_F, A_D, A_H, A_M, and A_O. Next, the automata can be analyzed using the different tools, such as SpaceEx, Flow*, dReach, and HyCreate, or simulated in SLSF. Then we compare all analysis results by using a function reachCheck shown in Fig. 2.

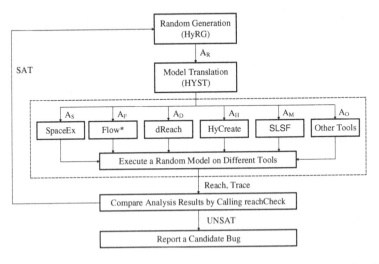

Fig. 1. Overview of monitoring framework for hybrid systems analysis tools with randomized differential testing.

---

[1] The tool and examples are available online: http://www.verivital.com/hyrg/.

```
1   function reachCheck(Reach, Trace, β)
      foreach set of reachable states Rᵢ in Reach
3       foreach set of reachable states Rⱼ in Reach
          if i ≠ j and ∀t ∈ [0, β] Rᵢ(t) ∧ Rⱼ(t) is UNSAT then return UNSAT
5       foreach execution trace Tₖ in Trace
          if ∀t ∈ [0, β] Tₖ(t) ∧ Rᵢ(t) is UNSAT then return UNSAT
7     return SAT
```

Fig. 2. reachCheck checks whether the set of reachable states and traces computed by different tools overlap (have non-empty intersection) at every time instant.

The reachCheck function has three inputs: Reach, Trace, and β, where β is the reachability analysis and simulation time bound. Reach is a list of sets of time-bounded reachable states computed by different tools (e.g., the output of SpaceEx, Flow*, etc.). Each set of reachable states, $\mathcal{R}(t)$, is the set of states that may be visited by following the model's trajectories and transitions, for any time $t \in [0, \beta]$. That is, for a given time t, $\mathcal{R}(t)$ is the set of states reachable at time t (sometimes referred to as a time-slice). The input Trace is a set of all simulation traces produced by SLSF up to a maximum simulation time β.

The reachCheck function can check whether the reachable states or simulation traces computed by different tools at each time have non-empty intersections. Although all of the reachable states and simulation traces are described in different formats such as support functions, Satisfiability Modulo Theories (SMT) formulas, convex sets, etc., there still exists an equivalence among them. For example, reachable sets computed by SpaceEx's LGG algorithm are a representation of convex sets (support functions), but these could be compared to the Taylor models of Flow*. If the reachable sets computed by different tools have a non-empty intersection (pairwise over all the tools), then reachCheck will return SAT, and the monitoring continues by generating a different random model. Otherwise, there is possibly a bug in the HyST translation or the verification tools. For the simulation traces, if some portions of a trace are not contained in any of the reachable states, reachCheck will return UNSAT and there is again possibly a bug in HyST, the verification tools, or SLSF. Obviously all these tools have numerous parameters, so numerical issues, accuracies, etc. must be taken into account by the user to determine whether a candidate bug is real.

Next, we define the structure of a hybrid automaton [2] and then summarize the random generation framework.

Definition 1. *A hybrid automaton* $\mathcal{H}$ *is a tuple,* $\mathcal{H} \triangleq \langle \text{Loc, Var, Flow, Inv, Trans,} \text{Init} \rangle$, *consisting of following components: (a)* Loc: *a finite set of discrete locations.* *(b)* Var: *a finite set of* n *continuous, real-valued variables, where* $\forall x \in$ Var, $v(x) \in \mathcal{R}$ *and* $v(x)$ *is a valuation—a function mapping* x *to a point in its type—here,* $\mathcal{R}$; *and* $Q \triangleq$ Loc $\times \mathcal{R}^n$ *is the state space. (c)* Inv: *a finite set of invariants for each discrete location,* $\forall l \in$ Loc, Inv$(l) \subseteq \mathcal{R}^n$. *(d)* Flow: *a finite set of derivatives for each continuous variable* $x \in$ Var, *and* Flow$(l, x) \subseteq \mathcal{R}^n$ *that describes the continuous dynamics in each location* $l \in$ Loc. *(e)* Trans: *a finite set of transitions between locations; each transition is a tuple* $\tau = \langle \text{src, dst, Grd, Rst} \rangle$, *which can be taken from source location* src *to destination location* dst *when a guard condition*

Grd *is satisfied, and a state is updated by an update map* Rst. *(f)* Init: *an initial condition,* Init $\subseteq \mathcal{Q}$.

We denote a hybrid automaton that has been randomly generated by A_R. We randomly generate each syntactic component of the automaton A_R. Rather than picking only random matrices and vectors for the affine functions used in flows, guards, invariants, assignments, etc., we instead partition these affine functions into classes. While we assume affine functions making up the automaton, the general method may be extended to nonlinear functions. We highlight that *all* structural components of the automaton are selected randomly (i.e., the transitions and continuous dynamics), and are not simply parameters. For brevity,

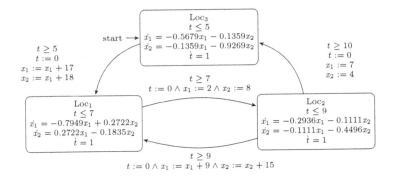

Fig. 3. An example hybrid automaton A_R with time-dependent switching that was randomly generated using HyRG.

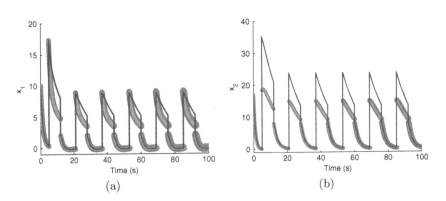

Fig. 4. SLSF simulation (blue), reachable states computed by Flow* (green), SpaceEx's STC algorithm (red), and SpaceEx's LGG algorithm (gray) for A_R showing x_1 and x_2 versus time, respectively. The SLSF simulation traces and the reachable states computed by Flow*, SpaceEx's LGG and STC algorithms do not line up (i.e., have an empty intersection) at some points in time (so reachCheck returns UNSAT) due to a semantic difference (Color figure online).

we do not describe in detail the random generation of all structural components here, but refer to our other preliminary results [4].

3   Preliminary Experimental Results

We evaluate our preliminary[2] monitoring framework in several scenarios to compare differences among several hybrid systems verification tools including SpaceEx, dReach, and Flow*, as well as SLSF simulation. Consider a randomly generated hybrid automaton A_R shown in Fig. 3. The initial state of A_R is Loc_3, and the randomly generated initial values of its variables are respectively $x_1 = 10$, $x_2 = 17$, and $t = 0$. Note that A_R is nondeterministic. The results of simulations and reachability analysis on A_R are shown in Fig. 4. The reachable states restricted to x_1 and x_2 computed by Flow* as well as the STC and LGG algorithms in SpaceEx do not contain a simulation trace for a supposedly equivalent SLSF model created using HyST when A_R takes a transition. In this case, the reachCheck function in Fig. 2 will return UNSAT. This happens because of semantic differences in resets among Flow*, SpaceEx, and SLSF. In SLSF, the variables x_1 and x_2 are updated sequentially, so that x_1 will first be updated to a new value, and then x_2 will be updated using the new (already updated) value of x_1. However, these variables are updated concurrently in Flow* and SpaceEx [2], so x_2 will be updated by using the previous value of x_1. Based on this, we fixed this translation error in HyST.

4   Conclusion and Future Work

In this paper, we describe our preliminary results toward building a randomized differential testing framework to monitor hybrid and CPS development tools like SLSF and verification tools like SpaceEx, dReach, Flow*, etc. Our preliminary results include identifying semantic mismatches between tools automatically that have been integrated into subsequent versions of HyST. Additionally, we have found a couple bugs in some of the verification tools that have been corrected by the tool authors. Based on our promising preliminary results, we plan to fully automate every step of the framework in the future.

Acknowledgments. This material is based on research sponsored by Air Force Research Laboratory under agreement number FA8750-15-1-0105. The U.S. Government is authorized to reproduce and distribute reprints for Governmental purposes notwithstanding any copyright notation thereon. The views and conclusions contained herein are those of the authors and should not be interpreted as necessarily representing the official policies or endorsements, either expressed or implied, of Air Force Research Laboratory or the U.S. Government. This work was also partly supported by

---

[2] Some of the steps are currently manual, particularly the parsing of reachable states and comparison thereof, but the generation with HyRG and translation with HyST is fully automatic.

the German Research Foundation (DFG) as part of the Transregional Collaborative Research Center Automatic Verification and Analysis of Complex Systems (SFB/TR 14 AVACS, http://www.avacs.org/), by the European Research Council (ERC) under grant 267989 (QUAREM) and by the Austrian Science Fund (FWF) under grants S11402-N23 (RiSE) and Z211-N23 (Wittgenstein Award).

References

1. Bak, S., Bogomolov, S., Johnson, T.T.: HyST: a source transformation and translation tool for hybrid automaton models. In: Proceedings of the 18th International Conference on Hybrid Systems: Computation and Control (HSCC). ACM (2015)
2. Frehse, G., et al.: SpaceEx: scalable verification of hybrid systems. In: Gopalakrishnan, G., Qadeer, S. (eds.) CAV 2011. LNCS, vol. 6806, pp. 379–395. Springer, Heidelberg (2011)
3. Leucker, M., Schallhart, C.: A brief account of runtime verification. J. Logic Algebraic Program. **78**(5), 293–303 (2009)
4. Nguyen, L.V., Schilling, C., Bogomolov, S., Johnson, T.T.: Poster: Hyrg: a random generation tool for affine hybrid automata. In: 18th International Conference on Hybrid Systems: Computation and Control (HSCC 2015) (2015)
5. Yang, X., Chen, Y., Eide, E., Regehr, J.: Finding and understanding bugs in c compilers. In: Proceedings of the 32nd ACM SIGPLAN Conference on Programming Language Design and Implementation, PLDI 2011, pp. 283–294. ACM, New York (2011)

Suggesting Edits to Explain Failing Traces

Giles Reger[(✉)]

University of Manchester, Manchester, UK
reger@cs.man.ac.uk

Abstract. Runtime verification involves checking whether an execution trace produced by a running system satisfies a specification. However, a simple 'yes' or 'no' answer may not be sufficient; often we need to understand why a violation occurs. This paper considers how computing the edit-distance between a trace and a specification can explain violations by suggesting correcting edits to the trace. By including information about the code location producing events in the trace, this method can highlight sources of bugs and suggest potential fixes.

1 Introduction

Runtime verification [4] is the process of checking whether an execution trace τ produced by a running system satisfies a specification φ. This means checking $\tau \in \mathcal{L}(\varphi)$ where $\mathcal{L}(\varphi)$ is the *language* of the specification. This paper considers traces as finite sequences of propositional symbols and specifications as finite state automata but the ideas could be transferable to both the parametric case, and cases where the specification can be translated to automata i.e. LTL. In the case of automata the check $\tau \in \mathcal{L}(\varphi)$ is well understood; however, if the answer is 'no' it does not reflect how close the trace is nor give any information about *why* the trace violations the specification.

The aim of this paper is to highlight and encourage the use of the *edit-distance* between a trace and the specification to *measure* the degree to which the trace satisfies the specification. If the trace is failing this approach can also suggest *edits* to the trace that could explain the violation and how to fix it. To motivate this approach consider the following trace of *open* and *close* events extracted from different parts of a system.

$$\underbrace{open.close.open.}_{\text{A.java}} \underbrace{open.close.}_{\text{B.java}} \underbrace{open.close.open.}_{\text{A.java}} \underbrace{open.close}_{\text{C.java}}$$

This violates the specification captured by the regular expression[1] $(open.close)^*$. There are different ways we can *edit* this trace to make it satisfy the specification.

---

[1] For conciseness we will use regular expressions to represent the corresponding automaton.

© Springer International Publishing Switzerland 2015
E. Bartocci and R. Majumdar (Eds.): RV 2015, LNCS 9333, pp. 287–293, 2015.
DOI: 10.1007/978-3-319-23820-3_20

For example,

$$open.close.\underline{open}.open.close.open.close.\underline{open}.open.close$$
$$open.close.open.\underline{open}.close.open.close.\underline{open}.open.close$$
$$open.close.open. \overset{close}{\downarrow} .open.close.open.close.open. \overset{close}{\downarrow} .open.close$$

$$\cdots$$

Producing these edits can suggest ways in which the original system could be modified. Furthermore, if we can label the trace with the source of events we can use this information to suggest which sets of edits might be the most sensible. In this case we should prefer *consistently* editing the file A.java as it would involve the smallest change.

Some Related Work. Distance metrics have been considered before in the area of fault localization. For example, in [8] the distance is measured between a faulty run and a large set of correct runs to select a correct run similar to the faulty run, which is used to report suspicious parts of a program. Other similar approaches exist.

The ideas in this paper are similar to those presented in [3] in the context of using an FSA inferred from correct program runs to detect anomalous behaviours. A failing trace is used to *edit* the inferred FSA to give an interpretation of the failure.

In runtime verification it is common to simply report the event on which the first error occurred. Approaches for parametric runtime monitoring (i.e. JAVA-MOP [5], MARQ [7]) can report on errors per set of parameters. Approaches that *restart* a monitor on failure effectively edit the trace but not necessarily in the most appropriate way.

Structure. Section 2 describes an existing method for computing the edit-distance between a trace and the language of an automaton. Section 3 introduces a method for suggesting sensible edits. Section 4 describes an experiment and Sect. 5 concludes.

2   Computing the Edit Distance

This section gives a brief overview of an existing method for computing the edit distance between a trace and an automaton's language. This was previously described in [6], which uses the approach in [2]. The general idea is to model the trace, automaton and edit operations as weighted transducers and compute their composition. Paths through the composed transducer to a final state represent different ways the trace can be edited to fit the automaton's language and the shortest path gives the edit distance.

Edit Distance. The edit (or Levenshtein) distance between two traces is the minimal number of *edits* required to transform one trace into the other. This distance, using the standard edit operations of addition, removal and replacement, is defined as follows:

Definition 1 (Levenshtein Distance). *The Levenshtein distance between traces τ_1 and τ_2 is* distance(τ_1, τ_2), *defined as*

$$
\text{distance}(\tau_1, \epsilon) = |\tau_1| \qquad \text{distance}(a\tau_1, b\tau_2) = \min \begin{cases} \text{distance}(\tau_1, b\tau_2) + 1 \\ \text{distance}(a\tau_1, \tau_2) + 1 \\ \text{distance}(\tau_1, \tau_2) + 1 & \text{if } a \neq b \\ \text{distance}(\tau_1, \tau_2) & \text{if } a = b \end{cases}
$$

$$\text{distance}(\epsilon, \tau_2) = |\tau_2|$$

i.e. we repeatedly choose the edit (removing a, adding b, replacing a by b) or non-edit that leads to the fewest edits overall. The edit distance between a trace τ and an automaton φ is the smallest distance between τ and a trace in the language of φ:

$$\text{distance}(\tau, \varphi) = \min(\{\text{distance}(\tau, \tau') \mid \tau' \in \mathcal{L}(\varphi)\})$$

Weighted Transducers. A weighted transducer (see [2]) has transitions labeled with input and output symbols and a weight (for this work this is 0 or 1). Input and output symbols can be ϵ i.e. can be taken without consuming or producing a symbol.

The composition $T \circ X$ of two transducers T and X considers all possible sequencing between strings of T and strings of X i.e. if $a/b.a/c$ is a string of T and $b/d.c/a$ is a string of X then $a/d.a/a$ is a string of $T \circ X$. Here we consider a three-way composition i.e. $T \circ X \circ P$. We compute this as a single operation for efficiency reasons - if we computed $T \circ X$ and then $(T \circ X) \circ P$ it is likely that $(T \circ X)$ would contain many superfluous transitions. An algorithm for doing this is presented in [1].

Computing the Edit Distance Using Weighted Transducers. This section briefly describes how to construct the three weighted transducers representing the trace, the edits and the automaton and how their composition is used to find the edit distance.

Traces are translated into weighted transducers by turning each event into a 0-weighted transition between states with ϵ self-looping transitions with the last state being final. The trace $a.a.b.c.b$ would become the following weighted transducer:

An automaton is translated into a weighted transducer by (a) making each transition 0-weighted using the event as input and output, and (b) adding a

0-weight self-looping ϵ transition to each state. The automaton for the regular expression $(ab^*c)^*$ would be:

The edit transducer has a single state with looping transitions for each of the edit operations it can perform - given below for alphabet $\{a, b, c\}$. Note how ϵ is used to model deletions and additions and all edit operations have a weight of 1.

The edit distance is computed using the composition $T \circ X \circ P$ where T, X and P are weighted transducers for the trace, edits and automaton respectively. Every path through this composition represents a way in which the trace T can be rewritten to a path of P using the edits in X. The edit-distance is given by the shortest path. Furthermore, a path describes *how* the trace can be edited. See [6] for an example.

Performance and Online Monitoring. In [1] it is shown that the three-way composition $T \circ X \circ P$ can be computed in time $O(|X||T|)$. This special method prevents a large intermediate result from dominating the computation. In [2] it is shown that the edit-distance between a string and automaton can be found in linear-space.

This approach assumes that the whole trace is available, which is reasonable for log file analysis but not for an online application of runtime monitoring. It may be possible to lazily compute the composition $T \circ X \circ P$ and perform the shortest path search in tandem online. This would involve keeping track of the states reachable in the composition and pruning this set (perhaps heuristically) to ensure it does not become unmanageable. Note that the composition represents a rewriting of the trace such that edits typically take the composition a finite number of steps away from the trace before returning to it. Further investigation is required.

It is clear that we cannot use any online approach that requires the trace to be stored as the space requirements would be impractical. As the composition itself is quadratic in the size of the trace this should also not be stored. Methods for compacting the trace online could be explored - this is briefly suggested in Sect. 4.

3   Suggesting Sensible Edits

The previous section described a technique that gives a set of minimal edit sequences that 'correct' a failing trace. This section explores how to produce *sensible* edits where:

1. Edits are consistently applied
2. Repeating the same edit is preferred to multiple separate edits

Here there is a notion of an *edit* as something more than altering the trace. To capture this we *label* the trace with the source of each event i.e. the source file and line number. In this work we only consider *consistent* labelled traces were each label is associated with a single event i.e. the source of events is deterministic Now a removal of event a at label l_1 is distinct from the removal of a at label l_2.

The composition construction in the previous section can be lifted to *labelled events* by ignoring the labels. The labels will be used to define a notion of a *sensible* edit path. An *edit path* is a finite sequence of edit records $(((a_1, l), a_2, w)$ starting (ending) in an initial (accepting) state of the composition where $\langle a_1, l \rangle$ is a labelled event from the trace and a_2 is an (edited) event from the automaton (possibly ϵ). The *path cost* of an edit path can be defined such that there is no cost to repeat an edit:

Definition 2 (Path Cost). *The cost of an edit path τ is given as $\mathsf{cost}(\tau, \{\})$ defined as*

$$\mathsf{cost}(\epsilon, S) = 0$$

$$\mathsf{cost}((((a_1, l_1), a_2, w).\tau, S) = \mathsf{cost}(\tau, S + (a_1/a_2, l_1)) + \begin{matrix} w & \text{if } (a_1/a_2, l_1) \notin S \\ 0 & \text{if } (a_1/a_2, l_1) \in S \end{matrix}$$

A *sensible* edit path is one that preserves *consistency* and has a minimal path cost.

Finding Sensible Edit Paths. Firstly, it is possible to put an upper bound on minimal edit path cost using a modified version of Djkistra's algorithm; this is only an upper bound as the edit path cost is dependent on the whole path not just the state reached. To identify sensible edit paths we perform the following non-deterministic heuristic search of the composition structure. The search maintains a set S of previously performed edits that is used to ensure consistency. The search is based around the idea that for a successful trace there will be a 0-weighted path through the composition and every failure can be seen as a blockage of this path. When a blockage is met we perform a local search to find the continuation of the trace. The steps taken by the search are:

1. Follow the 0-weighted path until there are no 0-weight transitions. If a transition matching an edit in S is found it must be taken to preserve consistency even if this diverges from the 0-weighted path.
2. Choose a (short) path p to the closest state with a 0-weight transition. The path p must be consistent with S and all edits in p should be added to S.
3. Repeat steps 1 and 2 until the final state is reached

Practically we perform the search in a breadth-first manner, keeping track of all possible choices. These can be pruned either by a *max* value given either by the approximated minimal edit path cost computed as described above or some other heuristic.

Paths found by this search are consistent by construction. Finding all paths of minimal path cost depends on how the path is chosen in step 2. An edit path of minimal path cost may be missed if a smaller set of edits are chosen too early, forcing a larger set to be used later. Note that if the search completes it will find a path of minimal path cost.

Performance. The complexity of this approach is exponential in the number of choices made. However, every choice restricts further choices as consistency must be preserved i.e. a path p cannot make a different edit at a label where an edit has already been made. Nevertheless, it is vital that paths are trimmed. We use the strategy of searching with $max = 0$ first (for the case where there are no failures) and increasing this by 1 until a path is found. Further heuristics for pruning paths should be investigated.

Online Monitoring. As discussed in the previous section, unless the composition can be created and searched lazily this approach will not be applicable to online monitoring. In [6] an approach that edited the trace as it was produced was explored. This was found to be very expensive as many different edit variations had to be tracked. Further work could apply the notion of *sensible path* to filter these edits.

4   A Scalability Experiment

The techniques presented here have been implemented in Scala and are available at https://github.com/selig/RVsuggestEdit. We use the *resource usage* property (ab^*c) to explore the scalability of the approach presented here. As a test trace we use the example trace given in Sect. 1 with use events inserted in-between the open and close events making the trace 100 events long. Let $t(m)$ be the test trace followed by m good events and let $t(m, n)$ be n repetitions of $t(m)$. We vary m and n to produce larger traces; the same edit paths are identified in each case. The results are as follows:

m	n	len	errs	Time (s)	m	n	len	errs	Time (s)	m	n	len	errs	Time (s)
0	1	100	4	0.005	900	1	1k	4	0.4	2.4k	1	2.5k	4	2.3
0	3	300	12	0.038	900	5	3k	12	3.3	2.4k	3	7.5k	12	20.4
0	6	600	24	0.144	900	10	6k	24	13.1	2.4k	6	15k	24	82.2

This demonstrates that this approach has the ability to scale but could certainly benefit from improvements. Two possible extensions would be (a) collapsing repeated sections of the trace, represented by larger weights in T; and (b) collapsing prefixes in the search to tame the exponential branching at each error. This experiment tentatively argues for the viability of the approach but further work with real software systems is needed to support the claim that this is a useful method for understanding failing traces.

5 Conclusion and Related Work

This paper has discussed a method for *measuring* the extent of failure in a trace and *suggesting* possible changes to the trace that could 'fix' it. The approach uses traces labelled with the points that generate events to suggest *sensible* edits. This was inspired by our earlier work using edit-distance in pattern-based specification mining [6].

The final point to be addressed is whether these edit paths are useful in explaining failing traces as the title of this short paper suggests. The motivation here is that by connecting the edit paths to program points via labels (and ensuring the edits are sensible) the edit paths correspond to edits to the program such as the deletion, insertion or replacement of a method call. Describing failures in this way is certainly not a new notion in the area of fault localisation.

Irrespective of their use for explaining failing traces, the author would suggest that using distance metrics is a reasonable direction for detecting *multiple errors* in a trace; an activity not often studied in the runtime verification community.

This is a preliminary investigation into this approach and much can be done to extend the ideas and make them more applicable to runtime verification problems.

References

1. Allauzen, C., Mohri, M.: 3-way composition of weighted finite-state transducers. In: Ibarra, O.H., Ravikumar, B. (eds.) CIAA 2008. LNCS, vol. 5148, pp. 262–273. Springer, Heidelberg (2008)
2. Allauzen, C., Mohri, M.: Linear-space computation of the edit-distance between a string and a finite automaton (2009). CoRR, abs/0904.4686
3. Babenko, A., Mariani, L., Pastore, F.: Ava: automated interpretation of dynamically detected anomalies. In: Proceedings of the Eighteenth International Symposium on Software Testing and Analysis, ISSTA 2009, pp. 237–248. ACM (2009)
4. Falcone, Y., Havelund, K., Reger, G.: A tutorial on runtime verification. In: Summer School Marktoberdorf 2012 - Engineering Dependable Software Systems, to appear. IOS Press (2013)
5. Meredith, P., Jin, D., Griffith, D., Chen, F., Roşu, G.: An overview of the mop runtime verification framework. J. Softw. Tools Technol. Transf. **14**(3), 249–289 (2011)
6. Reger, G., Barringer, H., Rydeheard, D.: Automata-based pattern mining from imperfect traces. In: The 2nd International Conference on Software Mining (2013)
7. Reger, G., Cruz, H.C., Rydeheard, D.: MarQ: monitoring at runtime with QEA. In: Baier, C., Tinelli, C. (eds.) ETAPS 2015. LNCS, vol. 9035, pp. 596–610. Springer, Heidelberg (2015)
8. Renieris, M., Reiss, S.P.: Fault localization with nearest neighbor queries. In: 18th IEEE International Conference on Automated Software Engineering (ASE 2003), pp. 30–9, 6–10 October 2003, Montreal, Canada (2003)

Tool Papers

StaRVOOrS: A Tool for Combined Static and Runtime Verification of Java

Jesús Mauricio Chimento[1], Wolfgang Ahrendt[1]([✉]), Gordon J. Pace[2], and Gerardo Schneider[3]

[1] Chalmers University of Technology, Gothenburg, Sweden
{chimento,ahrendt}@chalmers.se
[2] University of Malta, Msida, Malta
gordon.pace@um.edu.mt
[3] University of Gothenburg, Gothenburg, Sweden
gerardo@cse.gu.se

Abstract. We present the tool StaRVOOrS (Static and Runtime Verification of Object-Oriented Software), which combines static and runtime verification (RV) of Java programs. The tool automates a framework which uses partial results extracted from static verification to optimise the runtime monitoring process. StaRVOOrs combines the deductive theorem prover KeY and the RV tool LARVA, and uses properties written using the ppDATE specification language which combines the control-flow property language DATE used in LARVA with Hoare triples assigned to states. We demonstrate the effectiveness of the tool by applying it to the electronic purse application Mondex.

1 Introduction

In this paper we present StaRVOOrS, a tool for the specification and verification of data- and control-oriented properties combining static and runtime verification techniques. A detailed motivation for the combination along these two dimensions (data- vs. control-oriented, and static vs. dynamic verification) has been reported in [3,4] and will not be repeated here. For this paper, we only emphasise that this combination allows us to get a richer specification language able to express both data- and control-oriented properties, proving some properties once and for all statically, letting others to be checked at runtime.

The tool is a fully automated implementation of the theoretical results presented in [3,4]. Given a property specification and the original program, our tool chain produces a statically optimised monitor and the weaved program to be monitored. This includes the automated triggering of numerous verification attempts of the underlying static verification tool, the analyses of resulting partial proofs, and the monitor generation.[1]

Supported by the Swedish Research Council under the *StaRVOOrS* project (*Unified Static and Runtime Verification of Object-Oriented Software*), no. 2012-4499.

[1] The implementation of StaRVOOrS, its user manual, and a video showing how to use StaRVOOrS, are available from [2].

E. Bartocci and R. Majumdar (Eds.): RV 2015, LNCS 9333, pp. 297–305, 2015.
DOI: 10.1007/978-3-319-23820-3_21

2   The StaRVOOrS Framework

The STARVOORS framework (STAtic and Runtime Verification of Object-ORiented Software) was originally proposed in [4] and its theoretical foundations further developed in [3]. Object oriented software provides an abstract manner in which we replicate properties for every instance of a class, but many of the features in the framework that we discuss in this paper are not specific to object oriented software. The workflow of StaRVOOS is shown in Fig. 1, and is explained in detail in [3]. Here we give a brief overview of the deductive verifier KeY [5], the runtime monitoring tool LARVA [6], and the specification language ppDATE.

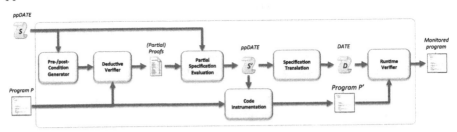

Fig. 1. High-level description of the STARVOORS framework workflow

The Static Verifier KeY. KeY is a deductive verification system for data-centric *functional correctness* properties of Java programs [5]. It features (static) verification of Java source code annotated with specifications written in the *Java Modelling Language* (JML) [7]. JML allows for the specification of pre/post-conditions of methods, and loop invariants. KeY translates the different parts of the specification to proof obligations in Java *dynamic logic* (DL). At the core of KeY is a theorem prover for Java DL, a modal logic for reasoning about programs. KeY uses a *sequent calculus* following the *symbolic execution* paradigm.

The Runtime Verifier LARVA. LARVA (*Logical Automata for Runtime Verification and Analysis*) [6] is an automata-based runtime verification tool for Java programs. LARVA automatically generates a runtime monitor from a property written in a formal language, which in the case of LARVA is an extension of timed automata called *DATEs* (*Dynamic Automata with Timers and Events*). At their simplest level *DATEs* are finite state automata whose transitions are triggered by system events and timers. Further details and the formalisation of *DATEs* can be found in [6]. Given a system to be monitored (a Java program) and a set of properties written in terms of *DATEs*, LARVA generates monitoring code together with AspectJ code to link the system with the monitors.

***ppDATE*: A Specification Language for Data- and Control-Oriented Properties.** STARVOORS uses *ppDATEs* as its property input language, which enables the combination of data- and control-based properties in a single formalism. ppDates are a composition of the control-flow language *DATE*, and of data-oriented specifications in the form of Hoare triples with *pre-/post*-conditions.

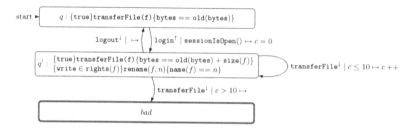

Fig. 2. A *ppDATE* limiting file transfers

Consider the *ppDATE* shown in Fig. 2. The structure of the automaton, less the information given in the states, provides the control-flow aspect of the property in the form of a *DATE*, in which transitions are tagged with triples: $e \mid c \mapsto a$ — indicating that (i) they are triggered when event e occurs and condition c holds; (ii) and apart from changing the state of the property, action a is executed. For instance, the reflexive transition on the middle state is tagged: $\texttt{transferFile}^{\downarrow} \mid c \leq 10 \mapsto c++$, means that if the automaton is in the middle state when the system enters the function named `transferFile` and counter variable c does not exceed 10, then the counter is incremented by 1. Some states are identified as *bad states*, denoted using a double-outline in the figure, and used to indicate that if and when reached, the system has violated the property in question. The property represented in Fig. 2 can thus be understood to ensure that no more than 10 file transfers take place in a single login session.

In *ppDATEs* the data-oriented features of the specification appear in the states. A state may have a number of Hoare triples assigned to it. Intuitively, if Hoare triple $\{\pi\}\texttt{f}\{\pi'\}$ appears in state q, the property ensures that: if the system enters code block `f` while the monitor lies in state q and precondition π holds, upon reaching the corresponding exit from `f`, postcondition π' should hold. Pre-/post-conditions in Hoare triples are expressed using JML boolean expression syntax [7], which is designed to be easily usable by Java programmers. For instance, the Hoare triple appearing in the top state of the property given in Fig. 2, ensures that any attempted file transfer when in the top state (when logged out), should not change the byte-transfer count. Similarly, while logged in (in the middle state of the property) (i) the number of bytes transferred increases when a file transfer is done while logged in; and (ii) renaming a file does indeed change the filename as expected if the user has the sufficient rights.

To ensure efficient execution of monitors, *ppDATEs* are assumed to be deterministic by giving an ordering in which transitions are executed.

3 The StaRVOOrS Tool Implementation

STARVOORS takes three arguments: (i) The Java files to be verified (the path to the main folder), (ii) A description of the *ppDATE* as a script (a file with extension `.ppd`), and (iii) The path of the output folder. The output of the tool is the runtime monitor (this file is placed in the output folder together with an instrumented version of the Java files).

To describe our implementation, we use as working example a *login scenario*, where users attempt to login into a system. The set of logged *users* is implemented as a `HashTable` object, whose class represents an open addressing hash table with linear probing as collision resolution. The method `add`, which is used to add objects into the hash table, first tries to put the corresponding object at the position of the computed hash code. However, if that index is occupied then `add` searches upwards (modulo the array length) for the nearest following index which is free. Within the hash table object, users are stored into a fixed array `h`, meaning that the set has a capacity limited by the length of `h`. In order to have an easy way of checking whether or not the capacity of `h` is reached, a field `size` keeps track of the number of stored objects and a field `capacity` represent the total amount of objects that can be added into the hash table.

In a nutshell, the tool works following these steps: (1) A property is written using our script language for *ppDATEs*; (2) Hoare triples are extracted from the specification of the property, are translated into JML contracts to be added to the Java files; (3) KeY attempts to verify all JML contracts, generating (partial) proofs, the analysis of which results in an XML file, (4) The *ppDATE* is refined based on the XML file; (5) Declarative pre/post-conditions are operationalised; (6) The code is instrumented with auxiliary information for the runtime verifier; (7) The *ppDATE* specification is encoded into *DATEs*; (8) The LARVA compiler generates a runtime monitor. We will now describe some of the above steps in more detail by describing them using our running example.

3.1   *ppDATE* Property: Adding a User

For simplicity we do not present the full specification for the login example but rather focus on the operation of adding a user to the hash table. Figure 3 depicts the *ppDATE* specification. The property is written as the following script.

```
EVENTS {
  add_entry(Object o,int key) = {HashTable users.add(o, key)}
}
PROPERTY add {
```

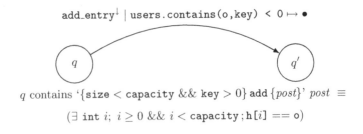

$$\text{add\_entry}^{\downarrow} \mid \text{users.contains(o,key)} < 0 \longmapsto \bullet$$

q contains '{`size` < `capacity` && `key` > 0} add {*post*}' *post* $\equiv$

$(\exists \text{ int } i; \; i \geq 0 \; \&\& \; i < \texttt{capacity} \,; \texttt{h[}i\texttt{]} \; == \; \texttt{o})$

Fig. 3. *ppDATE* specification for adding a user.

```
STATES {  NORMAL{q2;}  STARTING{q1 (add_ok);}  }
 TRANSITIONS { q1 -> q2 [add_entry\users.contains(o, key) < 0] }
}
CINVARIANTS {
 HashTable {h.length == capacity}
 HashTable {h != null}
 HashTable {size >= 0 && size <= capacity}
 HashTable {capacity >= 1}
}
CONTRACTS {
 CONTRACT add_ok {
   PRE {size < capacity && key > 0 }
   METHOD {HashTable.add}
   POST {(\exists int i; i>= 0 && i < capacity; h[i] == o)}
   ASSIGNABLE {size, h[*]}}
}
```

Invariants (section `CINVARIANTS`) are described by `class_name {invariant}`. Section `CONTRACTS` lists named Hoare triples (`CONTRACT`). The predicate in the post-condition follows JML-like syntax and pragmatics. The second semicolon is semantically an 'and', but conveys a certain pragmatics. It separates the 'range predicate' (`i >= 0 && i < capacity`) from the desired property of integers in that 'range', (`h[i] = o`). The constraint `add_ok` specifies that, if there is room for an object o in the hash table and the received key is positive, then after adding that object into the hash table it is found in one of the entries of the array h. Finally, the `PROPERTY` section represents the entire automata, which in this tiny example has only two states, q1 and q2, the second being initial (`STARTING`). The syntax q1 (add_ok) assigns the Hoare triple add_ok to q1.

3.2   Proof Construction and Partial Proof Analysis

The first step in our work-flow is to annotate the Java sources with JML contracts extracted from the Hoare triples specified in the *ppDATE*. We automatically generate such JML annotations and insert them just before the corresponding method declaration. Once the JML annotations are in place, the tool performs static verification, checking whether, or to which extent, the various JML contracts (each corresponding to a Hoare triple in *ppDATE*) can be statically verified. KeY is used to generate proof obligations in Java DL for each contract, and attempts to prove them automatically. Although we could have allowed for user interaction (using KeY's elaborate support for interactive theorem proving), we chose to use KeY in auto-mode, as StARVOORS targets users untrained in theorem proving.

For each Hoare triple KeY's verification attempt will result in either a full proof, where all goals are closed, or a partial proof, where some goals are open while others are closed. Partial proofs are analysed by our tool, and results are collected in an XML file. Most importantly, this file contains, for each Hoare triple specifying a method, say m, additional assumptions on the state in which

m is called, telling whether or not this Hoare triple needs to be checked at runtime for executions of m.

3.3   *ppDATE* Transformation: Hoare Triple Refinement

Our tool uses the output of our previous step for refining, in the *ppDATE*, all Hoare triples based on what was proved/unproved. Hoare triples whose JML translation was fully verified by KeY are deleted entirely. On the other hand, each Hoare triple not fully proved by KeY is refined. The new precondition is a conjunction (&&) of the old precondition and a disjunction of new preconditions corresponding to open proof branches.

In our example, the precondition of add_ok will be strengthened with the condition for the one goal not closed by KeY, !(h[hash_function(key)] == null). The Hoare triple will thus be refined as follows:

```
CONTRACT add_ok {
  PRE {size < capacity && key > 0
      && !(h[hash_function(key)] == null)}
  METHOD {HashTable.add}
  POST {(\exists int i; i>= 0 && i < capacity; h[i] == o)}
  ASSIGNABLE {size, h[*]}  }
```

Once all Hoare triples in the original *ppDATE* are refined this way, reflecting the results from static verification, the tool will translate the resulting *ppDATE* into the pure *DATE* formalism, to be processed by LARVA further on.

3.4   Translation to *DATE* and Monitor Generation with Larva

Once the refinement is performed, the tool syntactically analyses the specification for declarative assertions in pre/post-conditions which may need to be *operationalised* i.e. transformed into algorithmic procedures. This includes, for instance, transforming existential and universal quantification into loops. The next step in the work-flow is to instrument the source code by adding identifiers to each method definition and additional code to get fresh identifiers. These identifiers will be used to distinguish between different calls to the method.

After these modifications, the statically refined (see Sect. 3.3) *ppDATE* specification is translated into the pure *DATE* formalism, enabling monitor generation by LARVA. The control part of the *ppDATE* is already in automaton form, and can be interpreted directly as a *DATE*, but we still have to encode the Hoare triples into *DATE*. We refer to [3] for details of this translation.

The final step is the generation of the monitor by the LARVA compiler, taking as input the *DATE* obtained in the previous step. The compiler not only generates the monitor but also generates aspects, and weaves the code with the Java programs subject to verification. See [6] for further explanation on LARVA.

4   Case Study: Mondex

Mondex is an electronic purse application for smart cards products [1]. We consider a variant of the original presentation, strongly inspired by the JML formalisation given in [8]. One of the main differences with respect to the original presentation is that we consider a Java implementation working on a desktop instead of the Java Card one for smart cards. The full specification and code of this case study can be found from [2].

Mondex essentially provides a financial transaction system supporting transferring of funds between accounts, or 'purses'. Whenever a transaction between two purses is to take place, (i) the source and destination purses should (independently) register with the central fund transferring manager; (ii) then a request to deduct funds from the source purse may arrive, followed by (iii) a request to add the funds to the destination purse; and (iv) finally, there should be an acknowledgement that the transfer took place, before the transaction ends.

Besides specifying the protocol, one has to specify the behaviour of the involved methods, which obviously changes together with the status of the protocol. For instance, transfer of funds from a purse to another should succeed once both purses have been registered, but should fail if attempted before registration or if an attempt is made to perform the transfer multiple times. This behaviour is encoded by different Hoare triples assigned to different S states.

The control-oriented properties ensure that the message exchange goes as expected. In contrast, the pre/post-conditions (in total, there are 26 Hoare triples in the states of the $ppDATE$) ensure the well-behaviour of the individual steps.

We feed StaRVOOrS with the above $ppDATE$ and the source code of Mondex. Our tool automatically produces a runtime monitor which is then run in parallel with the application. Initially, the $ppDATE$ automaton consisted of only one automaton with 10 states and 25 transitions. Except for two Hoare triples related to the initialisation and termination of a transaction which were fully proven by KeY, all the other 24 triples are only partially verified by KeY. The automated analysis of these proofs leads to a refined $ppDATE$ as explained in Sect. 3.3. Besides, it is necessary to deal with the operationalisation of the JML operator \old . This is done by adding a fresh variable at the automaton level, saving the value of the variable annotated with \old before the method (associated to its Hoare triple) is executed. Then, when analysing the postcondition, if the value of the variable has changed, it can be compared with its previous value store in the automaton level variable. The obtained $DATE$ (following the procedure explained in Sect. 3.4) consists on 25 automata, one automaton to control the main property and 24 replicated automata to control postconditions, with 106 states and 196 transitions in total. Also, due to the operationalisation of \old , it were added four new variables at automata level in the main automaton.

The whole process to generate the monitor for Mondex took our tool 2 min 30 sec on PC Pentium Core i7, where most time is used in KeYs static analysis of the Hoare triples (2 min 15 sec). Our original implementation of Mondex weighted 23.5 kB. After, running the tool, the total weight of all the new generated files related to the implementation of the monitor is 177.8 kB.

We have compared the execution times of: (a) the unmonitored implementation, (b) the monitored implementation using the original specification S and translating it unoptimised into a DATE, and (c) the monitored implementation using the specification S', obtained from S via application of STARVOORS. The concrete performance numbers of this experiment are the same as the ones reported in [3, sect. 5]. To summarise the results, the addition of a monitor (case (b)) causes an overhead on the execution time w.r.t. the unmonitored version (a), between 15 and 1000 times. However, this overhead is dramatically reduced by using our approach (case (c)), only doubling the execution time (again w.r.t. (a)). The saving comes from only triggering post-condition checks in states satisfying pre-conditions from open branches in KeY proofs.

5   Conclusions

A key feature of our work is that everything is done fully automatic: STARVOORS is a push-button technology taking as input a specification and a Java program and given as output a partially verified program running in parallel with a runtime monitor. Our current experiments are encouraging as we drastically improve the time complexity of the runtime verifier LARVA. Both the efficiency gain for monitoring and the confidence gain can only increase along with future improvements in the static verifier used. For instance, if ongoing work on loop invariant generation in KeY leads to closing some more branches in typical proofs, this will have an immediate effect that is proportional to the frequency of executing those loop at runtime. For related work on the combination of static verification and static verification, we refer the reader to [3].

Acknowledgements. We would like to thank C. Colombo and M. Henschel for their support concerning implementation issues about LARVA and KeY respectively.

References

1. MasterCard International Inc., Mondex. www.mondexusa.com/
2. StaRVOOrS. www.cse.chalmers.se/chimento/starvoors
3. Ahrendt, W., Chimento, J.M., Pace, G.J., Schneider, G.: A specification language for static and runtime verification of data and control properties. In: Bjørner, N., de Boer, F. (eds.) FM 2015. LNCS, vol. 9109, pp. 108–125. Springer, Heidelberg (2015)
4. Ahrendt, W., Pace, G.J., Schneider, G.: A unified approach for static and runtime verification: framework and applications. In: Margaria, T., Steffen, B. (eds.) ISoLA 2012, Part I. LNCS, vol. 7609, pp. 312–326. Springer, Heidelberg (2012)
5. Beckert, B., Hähnle, R., Schmitt, P.H. (eds.): Verification of Object-Oriented Software: The KeY Approach. LNCS (LNAI), vol. 4334. Springer, Heidelberg (2007)

6. Colombo, C., Pace, G.J., Schneider, G.: LARVA - a tool for runtime monitoring of Java programs. In: SEFM 2009, pp. 33–37. IEEE Computer Society (2009)
7. Leavens, G.T., Poll, E., Clifton, C., Cheon, Y., Ruby, C., Cok, D., Müller, P., Kiniry, J., Chalin, P.: JML Reference Manual. Draft 1. 200 (2007)
8. Tonin, I.: Verifying the Mondex case study. The KeY approach. Technical Report 2007–4. Universität Karlsruhe (2007)

TiPEX: A Tool Chain for Timed Property Enforcement During eXecution

Srinivas Pinisetty[1], Yliès Falcone[2(✉)], Thierry Jéron[3], and Hervé Marchand[3]

[1] Aalto University, Espoo, Finland
srinivas.pinisetty@aalto.fi
[2] Univ. Grenoble Alpes, Inria, LIG, 38000 Grenoble, France
Ylies.Falcone@imag.fr
[3] Inria Rennes - Bretagne Atlantique, Rennes, France
{thierry.jeron,herve.marchand}@inria.fr

Abstract. The TiPEX tool implements the enforcement monitoring algorithms for timed properties proposed in [1]. Enforcement monitors are generated from timed automata specifying timed properties. Such monitors correct input sequences by adding extra delays between events. Moreover, TiPEX also provides modules to generate timed automata from patterns, compose them, and check the class of properties they belong to in order to optimize the monitors. This paper also presents the performance evaluation of TiPEX within some experimental setup.

1 Enforcement of Timed Properties

Runtime enforcement extends runtime verification [2] and refers to the theories, techniques, and tools aiming at ensuring the conformance of the executions of systems under scrutiny w.r.t. some desired property. As shown in Fig. 1, an enforcement monitor (EM) modifies an (untrustworthy) input sequence of events into an output sequence that complies with a property. To be as general as possible, we consider that the enforcement monitor is placed between an event emitter and an event receiver, which can be considered to be e.g., a program or the environment. In [1], we introduced runtime enforcement for timed properties modeled as timed automata. An extensive comparison between runtime enforcement of timed properties and related work is provided in [1].

Fig. 1. Usage of an enforcement monitor at runtime.

1.1 (Deterministic) Timed Automata

A lot of ongoing research efforts are related to the verification of real-time systems by means of e.g., model-checking, testing, and runtime monitoring. Central

E. Bartocci and R. Majumdar (Eds.): RV 2015, LNCS 9333, pp. 306–320, 2015.
DOI: 10.1007/978-3-319-23820-3_22

to these techniques is the use of timed automata (TAs) [3] as a formalism to model requirements or systems. One of the most successful tools for the verification of real-time systems is UPPAAL [4,5]. UPPAAL is based on the theory of TAs and comes with a somewhat standard syntax format for the definition of TAs.

In this paper, we consider timed properties as languages that can be defined by deterministic TAs. We introduce TAs [3] via the example in Fig. 2.

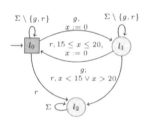

Fig. 2. A TA.

The set of locations is $\{l_0, l_1, l_2\}$, l_0 is initial (incoming edge), and accepting (blue square). The alphabet of actions is $\Sigma = \{r, g\}$. A finite set of real-valued clocks is used to model time ($\{x\}$). A transition between locations (e.g., l_1 to l_0) consists of (i) an action (e.g., r), (ii) a guard specifying a clock constraint (e.g., $15 \leq x \leq 20$), and (iii) a reset of some clocks (e.g., $x := 0$). This TA defines the requirement *"Resource grants (g) and releases (r) should alternate, starting with a grant, and every grant should be released within 15 to 20 time units (t.u.)"*. Upon the first g, the TA moves from l_0 to l_1, and resets x. From l_1, if r is received and $15 \leq x \leq 20$, then the TA moves to l_0 and resets x, otherwise it moves to l_2 (where it is stuck). The semantics of a TA can be defined by timed words recognized by the TA, i.e., sequences of timed events (pairs of actions and delays) reaching accepting locations.

1.2 General Principles of Timed Enforcement

Enforcement monitors proposed in [1] have the ability of *delaying events* to produce a correct output sequence. At an abstract level, an EM for a property φ can be seen as a function from timed words to timed words. An EM operates online and should thus satisfy some *physical-(time) constraints*: i) new events can only be appended to the tail of output words, and ii) any event should be input before being output. An EM should be *sound*: it should only output events that contribute to an output word in φ, and otherwise produce an empty output. An EM should be *transparent*: it should keep the order between events. Finally, an EM should be *optimal*: it should release events as soon as possible.

To ease their design, implementation, and correctness proofs, EMs are described at different levels of abstraction in [1]. An *enforcement algorithm* further concretises the description of an EM as an algorithmic implementation of an enforcement monitor. One of TiPEX's modules implements the enforcement algorithms in Python (see Sect. 2).

Runtime Enforcement on an Example. We provide some intuition on the expected behavior of EMs via an example (see [1] for formal details): enforcing the property defined by the TA in Fig. 2. Let us consider the input sequence $\sigma = (3, g) \cdot (10, r) \cdot (3, g) \cdot (5, g)$, where the delay of each event indicates the time elapsed since the previous event or system initialization: g is received at $t = 3$, r

at $t = 13$, etc. Upon receiving the first g, the EM cannot output it because the event alone does not satisfy the requirement (and the EM does not know yet the next events). Upon receiving action r, then it can output action g followed by r, as it can choose appropriate delays for both actions while satisfying timing constraints. Hence, the output delay associated with g is 13 t.u. However, the EM cannot choose the same (input) delay for r, because the property would not be satisfied. Consequently, the EM chooses a delay of 15 t.u., which is i) the minimal delay satisfying the constraint, and ii) is greater than the corresponding delay in the input sequence. When the EM receives the second g at $t = 16$, it releases it as output. Since the next action observed at $t = 21$ is not r, it becomes impossible for the EM to output a correct sequence. Hence, after $t = 21$, the output remains $(13, g) \cdot (15, r)$.

Contributions and Outline. This paper provides an implementation and test harness of enforcement algorithms. The major improvements (over the initial implementation [1]) provided in this paper are as follows:

- We implemented synthesis of EM for any regular property (while the implementation in [1] supports only safety and co-safety properties) and provide complimentary details on the implementation of EM.[1]
- We implemented a test harness that generates and composes TA.
- We experiment optimized version of EM synthesis for safety and co-safety properties and show performance improvements through experiments.

The paper is organised as follows: Sect. 2 presents the architecture and functionalities of TiPEX, Sect. 3 discusses the evaluation results; and Sect. 4 draws conclusions.

2   Overview and Architecture of TIPEX

TiPEX is a tool of 1,200 LLOC in Python and consists of three modules (see Fig. 3). Module Enforcement *Monitor from Timed Automata* (EMTA) consists in an implementation of the enforcement algorithms described in [1]. Module *Enforcement Monitor Evaluation* (EME) is a test harness for the performance of enforcement monitors, with functionalities such as a trace generator. Module *Timed Automata Generator* (TAG) provides functionalities such as generating and composing TAs (which can be also used in other contexts than enforcement monitoring). Module TAG provides a TA (defining the requirement) to module EMTA, and information such as the class to which the timed automaton belongs. The functionalities of this module are used offline (i.e., prior to monitoring). TAG manipulates TAs described in UPPAAL [5] model written in XML. TAG and EMTA make use of the UPPAAL pyuppaal and DBM libraries, respectively.[2]

---

[1] Regular properties are the ones that can be defined by TA. Safety (resp. co-safety) properties are the prefix-closed (resp. extension-closed) languages. See [1] for more details.

[2] The UPPAAL libraries are provided by Aalborg Univ. at http://people.cs.aau.dk/~adavid/python/.

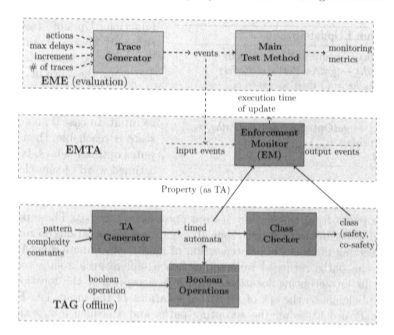

Fig. 3. Overview of TIPEX tool.

2.1   Module EMTA

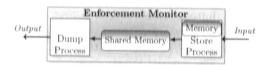

Fig. 4. Implementing an EM.

Module EMTA is the core functionality. It implements enforcement monitors by two concurrently running processes called as *store* and *dump*, communicating via shared memory as shown in Fig. 4. The shared memory contains the corrected sequence that can be released as output. The memory is realized as a queue, shared by the processes *store* and *dump*, where process *store* adds events with corrected delays. Process *dump* reads events stored in the shared memory and releases them as output after the required amount of time. Process *store* also makes use of another internal memory (not shared with any other process), to store the events that cannot be yet corrected (to satisfy the property).

EMTA takes as input a TA and one trace. The most important part of module EMTA is the *store* process which computes optimal output delays for input events by exploring the TA. This computation relies on function Update. The *dump* process of monitors are algorithmically simple and lightweight from a computational point of view.

Algorithm 1 Update(σ_{mc}, q)

   $allPaths \leftarrow$ computeReach(σ_{mc}, q)
   $accPaths \leftarrow$ getAccPaths($allPaths$)
   if $accpaths = \{\}$ **then**
      return($\mathtt{ff}, \sigma_{mc}$)
   else
      $\sigma'_{mc} \leftarrow$ getOptimalWord($accPaths, \sigma_{mc}$)
      return($\mathtt{tt}, \sigma'_{mc}$)
   end if

Function Update (see Algorithm 1) checks if an accepting state is reachable in the TA from the current state q, upon a delayed version of the sequence of events σ_{mc} provided as input. In case if an accepting state is reachable, then it computes optimal delays. It returns a timed word of same length as σ_{mc} and a Boolean indicating the result of this reachability analysis. Function computeReach computes all the reachable paths from the current state q upon events in σ_{mc}. These paths are computed using forward analysis, zone abstraction, and operations on zones such as the resetting of clocks and intersection of guards [4]. Function getAccPaths takes all the paths returned by computeReach and returns a subset of them that end in an accepting location. A path is accepting if the location in its last state belongs to the set of accepting locations of the input TA. Function getOptimalWord takes all the accepting paths and a sequence σ_{mc} and computes optimal delays for events in σ_{mc}. This function first computes an optimal delay for each event, for all accepting paths. Finally, it picks a path among the set of accepting paths whose sum of delays is minimal, and returns it as the result. If the set of accepting paths is empty, then function Update returns $\mathtt{ff}$ and σ_{mc}. Otherwise, it returns $\mathtt{tt}$ and the optimal word computed using getOptimalWord.

We now briefly describe the implementation of process *store*. It first parses an input model and performs the necessary initialization. As seen in Sect. 1, an EM may not output events immediately after they are received. Consequently, process *store* also uses an internal memory (σ_{mc}) to store events. Each event (t, a) of the trace in order is appended to the internal memory, and function Update is invoked, with the current state information and the events in the internal memory ($\sigma_{mc} \cdot (t, a)$). If function Update returns $\mathtt{ff}$, then the monitor waits for the next event. If function Update returns $\mathtt{tt}$ and σ'_{mc}, σ'_{mc} is added to the shared memory (since it contributes to a correct sequence and can be released as output). Before continuing with the next event, the process *store* updates the current state information, and internal memory.

2.2 Module EME

Module EME is a test harness of 150 LLOC to: i) validate through experiments the architecture and feasibility of enforcement monitoring, and ii) measure and analyze the performance of function Update of process *store*. The architecture of module EME is depicted in Fig. 3.

Module *Trace Generator* takes as input the alphabet of actions, the range of possible delays between actions, the desired number of traces, and the increment in length per trace. For example, if the increment in length per trace is 100, then the first trace is of length 100 and the second trace of length 200 and so on. For each event, module Trace Generator picks an action (from the set of possible actions), and a random delay (from the set of possible delays) using methods from the Python random module.

Module *Main Test Method* uses module *Trace Generator* to obtain a set of input traces to test module EM. It sends each sequence to the EM, and keeps track of the result returned by the EM for each trace. Module EM takes as input a property (defined as a TA) and one trace, and returns the total execution time of function Update to process the given input trace. In process *store*, the execution time of Update is measured. Process *store* keeps track of the total time of Update, by adding the time measured after each event to the total time, which is returned as a result of invoking process *store*.

2.3   Module TAG

Motivations. TAG facilitates the translation of informal requirements into formal models by automating the process of generating TAs. Using TAG, one can generate several (meaningful) TAs of some pattern, with varying complexity which can be used as input models for testing EMs. Note, TiPEX can be also used with manually-generated TAs.

Consider the requirement *"There cannot be more than 100 requests in every 10 t.u."*. The TA defining this requirement has more than 100 locations and associated transitions, and manually modeling it (for example using a graphical editor) is tedious and time consuming. Using TAG, the corresponding TA can be obtained almost instantly, just by providing some pattern, time constraint, and actions. TAG also implements the algorithms for the composition of TAs using Boolean operations (defined in [1,3]).

Figure 3 presents the architecture of TAG. Note that the modules inside TAG are loosely coupled: each module can be used independently, and can be easily extended. In the following, we detail each sub-module.

Generating Basic Timed Automata. Module *TA Generator* generates TAs based on some parameters: the *pattern* specifying the form of the TA among those defined in [6]; some *complexity constant* specifying the number of transitions and locations, the maximal constant in guards, and some action alphabets.

Supported Patterns. Currently, the tool supports generation of automata for the requirements of the following forms (see [6]):

- *Absence:* In every consecutive time interval of *TIME_CONSTRAINT_CONSTANT* t.u., there are no more than *COMPLEXITY_CONSTANT* actions from *ACTION_SET1*.
- *Precedence with a delay:* A sequence of *COMPLEXITY_CONSTANT* actions from *ACTION_SET1* enable actions belonging to *ACTION_SET2* after a delay of at least *TIME_CONSTRAINT_CONSTANT* t.u.

– *Timed bounded existence:* There should be *COMPLEXITY_CONSTANT* consecutive actions belonging to *ACTION_SET1* which should be immediately followed by an action from *ACTION_SET2* within *TIME_CONSTRAINT_CONSTANT* time units.

Composing Timed Automata. Module *Boolean Operations* builds a TA by composing two input TAs using Boolean operations (see Fig. 3). All boolean operations are supported. In particular, operations *Union* and *Intersection* are performed by building the synchronous product of the two input TAs, where, in the resulting automaton, each location is a pair, and the guards are the conjunctions of the guards in the input TA. For operation *Union*, accepting locations are the pairs where at least one location is accepting in the input TAs, and for *Intersection* operation, both the locations in the corresponding input TAs are accepting. See [3] for formal details.

Identifying the Class of a Timed Automaton. Module *Class Checker* takes as input a TA and determines the class of the property it defines:[3] *safety* (resp. *co-safety*) if the constraints of a safety (resp. co-safety) TA are satisfied, and "*other*" otherwise. With the class information, one can use simplified enforcement algorithms (see Sect. 3).

3   Performance Evaluation

We focus on the performance evaluation of function Update, the most computationall intensive step as discussed in Sect. 2.1. Experiments were conducted on an Intel Core i7-2720QM at 2.20 GHz CPU, with 4 GB RAM, and running on Ubuntu 12.04 LTS. The reported numbers are mean values over 10 runs and are represented in seconds. To compute the average values, 10 runs turned out to be sufficient because, for all metrics, with 95 % confidence, the measurement error was less than 1 %.

The considered properties follow different patterns [6], and belong to different classes. They are recognized by one-clock TA since this is a current limitation of our implementation. We however expect the trends exposed in the following to be similar when the complexity of automata grows.

– Property φ_s is a safety property expressing that "*There should be a delay of at least 5 t.u. between any two request actions*".
– Property φ_{cs} is a co-safety property expressing that "*A request should be immediately followed by a grant, and there should be a delay of at least 6 t.u between them*".

---

[3] A TA defining a safety (resp. a co-safety) property is said to be a safety (resp. a co-safety) TA. In a safety (resp. co-safety) TA, transitions are not allowed from non-accepting (resp. accepting) to accepting (resp. non-accepting) locations. For formal details, see [1].

– Property φ_{re} is a regular property, but neither a safety nor a co-safety property, and expresses that *"Resource grant and release should alternate. After a grant, a request should occur between 15 to 20 t.u"*.

Table 1. Performance analysis.

φ_s		φ_{re}		φ_{cs}	
|tr|	t_Update (sec)	|tr|	t_Update (sec)	|tr|	t_Update (sec)
10,000	9.895	10,000	16.354	100	3.402
20,000	20.323	20,000	32.323	200	13.583
30,000	29.722	30,000	48.902	300	29.846
40,000	40.007	40,000	65.908	400	53.192
50,000	49.869	50,000	83.545	500	82.342
60,000	59.713	60,000	99.088	600	120.931
70,000	72.494	70,000	117.852	700	169.233

Results and Analysis. Results of the performance analysis for φ_s, φ_{cs}, and φ_{re} are reported in Table 1. Entry \|tr\| (resp. t_Update) indicates the length of the considered traces (resp. the total execution time of functio n Update).

As expected, for the safety property (φ_s), we can observe that t_Update increases linearly with the length of the input trace. Moreover, the time taken per call to Update (which is $t\_Update/|tr|$) does not depend on the length of the trace. This behavior is as expected for a safety property: function Update is always called with only one event which is read as input (the internal buffer σ_{mc} remains empty). Consequently, the state of the TA is updated after each event, and after receiving a new event, the possible transitions leading to a good state from the current state are explored.

For the co-safety property (φ_{cs}), the considered input traces are generated in such a way that they can be corrected only upon the last event. Notice that t_Update is now quadratic. For the considered input traces, this behavior is as expected for a co-safety property because for an input sequence of length \|tr\|, function Update is invoked \|tr\| times, starting with a sequence of length 1 that is incremented by 1 in each iteration.

For the regular property (φ_{re}), the considered input traces are generated in such a way that it can be corrected every two events. Consequently, function Update is invoked with either one or two events. For the considered input traces, t_Update is linear in \|tr\|, and thus the time taken per call to Update (which is $t\_Update/|tr|$) does not depend on the length of the trace. For input traces of same length, the value of t_Update is higher for φ_{re} than the value of t_Update for φ_s. This stems from the fact that, for a safety property, function Update is invoked only with one event.

Implementation of Simplified Algorithms for Safety Properties. As explained in [1], for safety properties, the internal memory is never used, since the decision of whether to output an event or not has to be taken when receiving it. Thus, the functional definition can be simplified, and consequently the enforcement monitors and algorithm can be also simplified. The simplified algorithm is also implemented in TiPEX, and experiments were conduced using several safety properties (see [1] for details and evaluation results). From the results in [1], we can notice that for safety properties, using the simplified algorithm gives better performance. The time taken per call to Update reduces by around 0.2 ms using the simplified algorithm.

Remark 1. More experimental results used to assess the influence of the size, class, and pattern of a property on the monitoring metrics are available in [1, 7].

4   Summary and Discussion

TiPEX implements and assesses the enforcement monitoring algorithms for timed properties in [1]. It demonstrates the practical feasibility of our theoretical results.

TiPEX consists of 3 modules. Module EMTA consists of functionalities to synthesize enforcement monitors from a TA, and module EME is a test harness for monitors. Module TAG consists of features to automatically generate TAs from some input data such as the actions, pattern, and time constraint constant. To the best of our knowledge, there is no available tool to help formalizing real-time requirements. As shown in the examples, the input data required by TAG can be easily inferred from the informal description of a requirement. Moreover, TAG composes TAs using Boolean operations, and identifies the class of a given TA.

Assessing the performance of runtime enforcement monitors is crucial in a timed context as the time when an action happens influences satisfaction of the property. We also evaluated the performance of enforcement monitors for several properties, and considering very long input executions. As our experiments in Sect. 3 show, the computation time of the monitor upon the reception of an event is relatively low. For example, for safety properties, one can see that, on the used experimental setup, the computation time of function Update is below 1ms. Moreover, given some average computation time per event and a property, one can determine easily whether the computation time is negligible or not for an application domain in consideration. By taking guards with constraints using integers above 0.1s, one can see that the computation time can be negligible in some sense as the impact on the guard is below 1 %, and makes the overhead of enforcement monitoring acceptable.

For co-safety and regular properties, the computation time of function Update depends on the property and the input trace. For example, for a co-safety property with a loop in a non-accepting location, the execution time of Update depends on the length of the minimal prefix of the input sequence allowing to reach an accepting state.

Finally, note that while the monitoring algorithm implemented in EME is used with traces, it is an online algorithm. To use TiPEX within a system for online runtime enforcement, one needs to define the implementation of the delaying of an action in the monitored system by, for instance, suspending the thread performing the delayed action.

Acknowledgments. This work has been partly done in the context of the ICT COST Action IC1402 Runtime Verification beyond Monitoring (ARVI).

A   Demonstration of TiPEX

We illustrate the features of TiPEX discussed in the paper via some examples. All the source files with examples, prerequisites, and some documentation are available at:

http://srinivaspinisetty.github.io/Timed-Enforcement-Tools/

A.1   Modules EMTA and EME

In the following subsections, we describe how to test the input-output behavior of an enforcement monitor, and how to collect performance data for a property.

Testing the Behavior of an Enforcement Monitor. We present how the input-output behavior of enforcement monitors for some properties is tested. We consider three example properties (used in Sect. 3). We also provide the TAs defining these properties in UPPAAL format (.xml files) inside the source folder.

- **Example_Safety.xml** defines a safety property expressing that *"There should be a delay of at least 5 t.u. between any two request actions"*.
- **Example_CoSafety.xml** defines a co-safety property expressing that *"A request should be immediately followed by a grant, and there should be a delay of at least 7 t.u. between them"*.
- **Example_Response.xml** defines a regular property, and expresses that *"Resource grant and release should alternate. After a grant, a request should occur between 15 to 20 t.u."*. Note that this property is neither a safety nor a co-safety property.

To test the functionality, with these properties for some input traces, simply run the test script `testFunctionality.py` (available inside the source folder). For each property, the input trace provided and the output of the EM is printed on the console. On the console, we can observe that for each property, for the provided input, the output satisfies the property (soundness) and the other constraints (transparency, optimality).

Collecting Performance Data. We explain via an example how the main test method is invoked via Python command line to collect performance data for a property (see Fig. 5). The steps are the following:

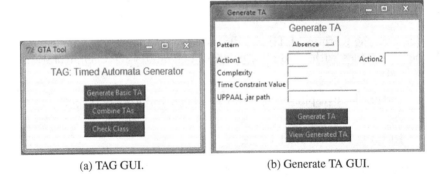

(a) TAG GUI.   (b) Generate TA GUI.

Fig. 5. Collecting performance data.

- Import the MainTest module.
- Specify the property by indicating its path. "Example_Safety.xml" is the property in this example, which is a UPPAAL model stored as ".xml".
- Specify the accepting locations in the input TA. For instance, by typing "accLoc=['S1, 'S2']", one specifies that the set of accepting locations in the input TA is {S1, S2}.
- Specify the possible actions. For instance by typing "actions = ['a,'r']" one specifies that the set of actions is {a, r}.
- Define the range of possible delays.
- Invoke method `testStoreProcess` in module MainTest, providing the following arguments in order: property, accepting locations, actions, delays, # traces incr.

"#traces" is the number of traces used for testing (3 in the example above), each trace varying in length, and "incr" is the increment in length per trace (1,000 in the example above). As shown in Fig. 5, a list of triples (trace length, total execution time of the Update function, average time per call of the Update function) is returned as the result.

A.2   Module TAG

Module TAG has a basic GUI. The following lines demonstrate how to launch the GUI via Python command line.

- Browse to the folder containing the source code.
- Execute the script `GUI_TAG_Tool.py` entering the following line in the command prompt `python GUI_TAG_Tool.py`.
- A GUI will be launched (shown in Fig. 6a), using which the user can select to generate a basic TA, or to combine TAs, or to check the class of a TA.

We demonstrate how to use each feature via an example.

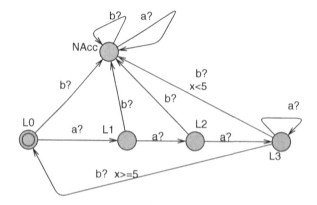

Fig. 6. GUI.

Generating Basic Timed Automata. We present some TAs generated using module *TA Generator*. Clicking "Generate Basic TA" launches the GUI shown in Fig. 6b. To generate a TA defining the requirement *"In any time interval of 10 t.u., there cannot be 3 or more a actions"*, the values of the input parameters provided the tool are:

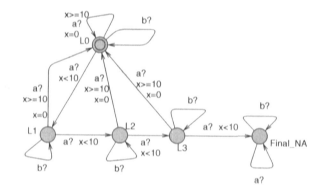

Fig. 7. Automaton belonging to the precedence pattern.

- *PATTERN* = absence,
- *COMPLEXITY_CONSTANT* = 3,
- *TIME_CONSTRAINT_CONSTANT* = 10,
- *ACTION1* = a, and *ACTION2* = b.

Figure 8 shows the representation in UPPAAL. In this TA, L0 is initial location, {L0, L1, L2, L3} is the set of accepting locations, and the only non-accepting location is Final_NA. In L0, upon action a, if the value of clock $x \geq 10$, then the clock x is reset and the TA remains in the same location. We can see that the

TA moves to a non-accepting (trap location) Final_NA upon 3 *a* actions within 10 time units. To generate a TA defining the requirement *"A sequence of 3 a actions enables action b after a delay of at least 5 t.u."*, the values of the input parameters provided to the tool are:

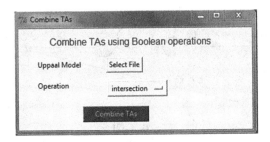

Fig. 8. Automaton belonging to the absence pattern.

- *PATTERN* = precedence,
- *COMPLEXITY_CONSTANT* = 3,
- *TIME_CONSTRAINT_CONSTANT* = 5,
- *ACTION1* = a, and *ACTION2* = b.

Figure 7 shows its representation in UPPAAL tool. In this TA, L0 is the initial location, {L0, L1, L2, L3} is the set of accepting locations, and the only non-accepting location is NAcc. We can see that from locations L0, L1, and L2, if a b action occurs then the TA moves to the trap state, since 3 preceding a actions are missing.

Composing Timed Automata. Clicking "Combine TAs" launches the GUI shown in Fig. 9. Clicking "Select File" button allows the user to select an input UPPAAL model. The input UPPAAL model (stored as .xml) selected by the user, should contain two input TAs (defined as two different templates). Note that in the input TAs, names of accepting locations should be prefixed by "Final". The user should select an operation. The resulting TA will be written as another template in the UPPAAL model file given as input by the user.

Let us now see an example of the resulting TA obtained after combining two TAs using the *Boolean Operations* functionality. The two input TAs are shown in Figs. 10a and b. Figure 10c shows the resulting TA after combining the two input TAs using Union operation.

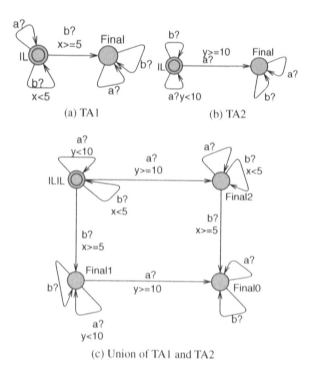

(a) TA1

(b) TA2

(c) Union of TA1 and TA2

Fig. 9. Combine TA GUI.

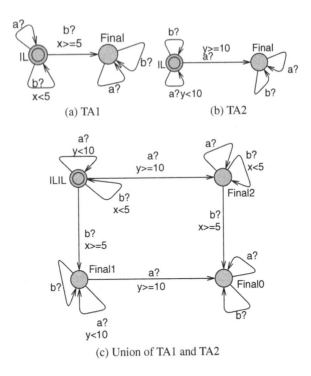

(a) TA1   (b) TA2

(c) Union of TA1 and TA2

Fig. 10. Example: Combining TAs using Boolean operations.

References

1. Pinisetty, S., Falcone, Y., Jéron, T., Marchand, H., Rollet, A., Timo, O.N.: Runtime enforcement of timed properties revisited. Formal Methods Syst. Des. **45**, 381–422 (2014)
2. Falcone, Y., Havelund, K., Reger, G.: A tutorial on runtime verification. In: Engineering Dependable Software Systems. vol. 34, pp. 141–175. IOS Press (2013)
3. Alur, R., Dill, D.L.: A theory of timed automata. Theor. Comput. Sci. **126**, 183–235 (1994)
4. Bengtsson, J.E., Yi, W.: Timed automata: semantics, algorithms and tools. In: Desel, J., Reisig, W., Rozenberg, G. (eds.) Lectures on Concurrency and Petri Nets. LNCS, vol. 3098, pp. 87–124. Springer, Heidelberg (2004)
5. Larsen, K.G., Pettersson, P., Yi, W.: UPPAAL in a nutshell. Int. J. Softw. Tools Technol. Transfer **1**, 134–152 (1997)
6. Gruhn, V., Laue, R.: Patterns for timed property specifications. Electron. Notes Theor. Comput. Sci. **153**, 117–133 (2006)
7. Pinisetty, S. et al.: TiPEX website (2015). http://srinivaspinisetty.github.io/Timed-Enforcement-Tools/

Tutorial Papers

Machine Learning Methods in Statistical Model Checking and System Design – Tutorial

Luca Bortolussi[1,2,3]($\boxtimes$), Dimitrios Milios[4], and Guido Sanguinetti[4,5]

[1] Modelling and Simulation Group, University of Saarland, Saarbrücken, Germany
[2] Department of Mathematics and Geosciences, University of Trieste, Trieste, Italy
[3] CNR/ISTI, Pisa, Italy
luca@dmi.units.it
[4] School of Informatics, University of Edinburgh, Edinburgh, UK
dmilios@staffmail.ed.ac.uk
[5] SynthSys, Centre for Synthetic and Systems Biology,
University of Edinburgh, Edinburgh, UK
gsanguin@inf.ed.ac.uk

Abstract. Recent research has seen an increasingly fertile convergence of ideas from machine learning and formal modelling. Here we review some recently introduced methodologies for model checking and system design/parameter synthesis for logical properties against stochastic dynamical models. The crucial insight is a regularity result which states that the satisfaction probability of a logical formula is a smooth function of the parameters of a CTMC. This enables us to select an appropriate class of *functional priors* for Bayesian model checking and system design. We give a tutorial introduction to the statistical concepts, as well as an illustrative case study which demonstrates the usage of a newly-released software tool, U-check, which implements these methodologies.

1 Introduction

Verification of temporal logic formulae via model checking is one of the major success stories of theoretical computer science [1]. An important development has been the introduction of probabilistic model checking [2–4], which aims to verify logical formulae on trajectories of stochastic processes such as Continuous Time Markov Chains (CTMCs): here, due to the intrinsic stochasticity of the system and the fact that formulae may evaluate differently on different trajectories of the same system, the purpose of probabilistic model checking is therefore to quantify the probability of a formula being true. From the theoretical point of view, probabilistic model checking has stimulated a remarkable cross-fertilisation between applied mathematics and computer science, resulting

D. Milios and G. Sanguinetti acknowledge support from the ERC under grant MLCS 306999. L.B. acknowledges partial support from EU-FET project QUANTICOL (nr. 600708), by FRA-UniTS, and by the German Research Council (DFG) as part of the Cluster of Excellence on Multimodal Computing and Interaction at Saarland University.

in a renaissance in algorithms for computing transient probabilities in Markovian processes [5]. From the practical point of view, the impact of probabilistic model checking has arguably been even greater, since ideas from verification and formal modelling could now be applied to a wide array of models from the physical sciences and engineering disciplines. Partly as a result of these developments, formal modelling is now a major player in applications as diverse as systems biology, ecology, performance modelling and smart cities.

While probabilistic model checking is undoubtedly a major player in all applications of formal modelling, it is not without its challenges. Despite many elegant algorithms for computing transient probabilities have been developed, exact probabilistic model checking is still computationally too demanding to be deployed on many realistic problems. *Statistical* model checking (SMC) algorithms are often employed in these circumstances [6–8] if the underlying system can be simulated efficiently, one can simply draw several independent trajectories from the system, evaluate the formula of interest on each trajectory and obtain in this way a Monte Carlo estimate of the desired probability. However, in many applications, a more fundamental difficulty is encountered, as models are often incompletely specified, relying on a parametrisation which can be highly uncertain. For example, in a systems biology application a parameter may represent a kinetic reaction rate which can only be measured with considerable approximation; in a smart-city application, a parameter may model how a group of transport users may behave in a hypothetical scenario, which cannot be accurately measured before the scenario is actually implemented. In many cases, therefore, it is of primary importance not only to quantify the probability that a trajectory of the system will satisfy a certain property, but also how this probability may depend on uncertain parameter, and how to select parameter values which will (robustly) yield consistent behaviour. While direct parameter exploration is in some cases possible [9,10], it is always computationally intensive.

Recently, we proposed a novel family of algorithms for statistical model checking and parameter synthesis on CTMC models with parametric uncertainty, which can achieve considerable computational savings over parameter exploration methods [11–15]. Our methods are theoretically grounded on a novel characterisation of the functional dependence of the satisfaction probability of a formula on the parameters. This regularity result enables us to use powerful methodologies from Bayesian machine learning, obtaining efficient algorithms with theoretical guarantees. Recently, some of these methods have been implemented in the open source U-check software suite [16], a flexible tool which can interface with some of the most widely used modelling languages.

In this paper, we provide a tutorial introduction to these novel algorithms and their use. We focus on providing an accessible introduction to the relevant statistical machine learning concepts, as well as demonstrating the use of the U-check tool on a non-trivial case study. The rest of the paper is organised as follows: we start by reviewing briefly basic concepts of temporal logics and (Bayesian) statistical model checking. We then introduce the notion of satisfaction function for models with parametric uncertainty, and introduce Gaussian processes, a suitable class of functional priors. GPs are at the heart of Smoothed model checking, a Bayesian statistical algorithm that directly performs model checking of the whole satisfaction function. We then discuss the parameter synthesis problem and introduce the GP-UCB algorithm, a provably globally convergent optimisation algorithm which is at the basis of the parameter synthesis routines in U-check. Finally, we illustrate the use of the U-check tool on an example, with the aim of facilitating the use of these novel tools in practical applications.

2 CTMCs, Temporal Logics and Statistical Model Checking

2.1 Continuous-Time Markov Chains

In this paper we will be mostly concerned with Continuous-Time Markov Chains (CTMC), which are memoryless stochastic processes on a countable state space evolving in continuous time [17]. CTMC are the most widespread class of stochastic models in many areas, including performance and systems biology. In these domains, they usually take the form of Population CTMC (PCTMC), describing how a population of agents evolves in time [18]. Typically, the state of a PCTMC $\mathcal{M}$ is represented as a vector of integer-valued variables $\boldsymbol{X} = (X_1, \ldots, X_n)$, while the dynamical evolution is represented by a set of transition classes. These specify events changing the state of some agents, and are easily represented in the biochemical reaction style as follows:

$$r_1 X_1 + \ldots + r_n X_n \xrightarrow{\alpha(\boldsymbol{X}, \theta)} s_1 X_1 + \ldots + s_n X_n.$$

Each such a rule specifies that r_1 agents in state X_1, r_2 in state X_2, and so on, interact and are replaced by s_1 copies of X_1 agents, s_2 of X_2 agents, and so on. Hence, the net change of agents is given by the update vector $\boldsymbol{v}$ defined by $v_i = s_i - r_i$. Each reaction happens with a rate or frequency given by the function $\alpha(\boldsymbol{X}, \theta)$, depending on the current state of of the system and on a vector of parameters θ.

Example. In order to illustrate the description of a PCTMC, we consider here a simple example from system biology, describing the (uncontrolled) transcription and translation of a gene into a protein. We need two variables, X_m and X_p, counting the amount of messenger RNA and of protein in the system. We further need four transition classes: transcription of DNA into mRNA ($\emptyset \xrightarrow{k_r} X_m$), degradation of mRNA ($X_m \xrightarrow{k_{dm} X_m} \emptyset$), translation of mRNA into the protein $X_m \xrightarrow{k_t X_m} X_p$, and degradation of the protein $X_p \xrightarrow{k_{dp} X_p} \emptyset$. In all cases, we assume a mass action rate, proportional to the amount of reactants involved. Note that the state space of this model is the countably infinite set $\mathbb{N}^2$.

Uncertain PCTMC. The dynamic behaviour of a PCTMC $\mathcal{M}$ can heavily depend on the parameters θ, a fact we make explicit in the notation $\mathcal{M}_\theta$. As discussed in the introduction, the values of θ are seldom known exactly, hence often we can only assume that they belong to a certain compact, connected subset $\mathcal{D}$ of $\mathbb{R}^d$, where d is the dimension of the parameter space. By varying $\theta \in \mathcal{D}$, we have a family of PCTMC models, which we will refer as an *uncertain CTMC*.

We conclude this section noting that we can consider different classes of stochastic models, including Stochastic Differential Equations and Stochastic Hybrid Systems. We refer the reader to [12,14,15] for a more detailed discussion in this sense.

2.2   Metric Interval Temporal Logic

In order to describe behavioural properties of biological and complex systems we will consider formal languages satisfying two main constraints:

- the language should capture properties of single executions of the system, as this is the only way we can experimentally observe such a system;
- properties should be time-bounded, as we can observe a real system only for a finite amount of time.

In this paper, we stick to the linear-time temporal-logic based formalism of Metric Interval Temporal Logic [19,20], which is defined by the following syntax:

$$\varphi := \mathtt{tt} \mid \mu \mid \neg\varphi \mid \varphi_1 \wedge \varphi_2 \mid \varphi_1 \mathbf{U}_{[a,b]} \varphi_2.$$

Atomic predicates $\mu = \mu(\boldsymbol{x}(t))$ are evaluated pointwise on time bounded trajectories $\boldsymbol{x} : [0, T] \to \mathbb{R}^n$, and are usually boolean inequalities of the form $f(\boldsymbol{x}(t)) \geq 0$. Boolean operators work as usual, while the time-bounded until $\varphi_1 \mathbf{U}_{[a,b]} \varphi_2$, with $a < b$, holds in a trajectory at time t_0 whenever the formula φ_1 is satisfied from t_0 to a time point $t \in [t_0 + a, t_0 + b]$, at which φ_2 must hold. The time-bounded eventually and always operators are definable as usual: $\mathbf{F}_{[a,b]}\varphi := \mathtt{tt}\mathbf{U}_{[a,b]}\varphi$ and $\mathbf{G}_{[a,b]}\varphi := \neg\mathbf{F}_{[a,b]}\neg\varphi$. MITL can be given a boolean semantics in a standard way, see [19,20] for details. Furthermore, it can be assigned a quantitative satisfaction score along the lines of [21,22]. This semantics is obtained by essentially using maxima (minima) and suprema (infima) in place of conjunction (disjunction) and universal (existential) quantification, respectively, and by replacing atomic predicates $\mu(\boldsymbol{x}(t)) := f(\boldsymbol{x}(t)) \geq 0$ with the real value $f(\boldsymbol{x}(t))$. It associates with a formula φ and a trajectory $\boldsymbol{x}$ a real number $\rho(\varphi, \boldsymbol{x})$ whose sign is associated with satisfiability of φ (true if and only if $\rho(\varphi, \boldsymbol{x})$ is positive), and whose absolute value measures how robustly the formula is satisfied by the trajectory. Both boolean and quantitative semantics can be efficiently checked on sample trajectories by monitor algorithms, see [20,22].

The boolean semantics of MITL can be extended to stochastic models by considering the probability $p(\varphi) = p(\varphi = \mathtt{tt})$ of the set of trajectories which satisfy a formula φ. For the quantitative semantics, instead, this extension produces a probability distribution over real numbers, see [13,15] for further details.

We remark here that the use of MITL is not mandatory: any linear-time, time bounded formalism will do, provided it is equipped with a monitoring routine.

2.3   Statistical Model Checking

The goal of probabilistic model checking is to compute the satisfaction probability of a MITL formula (in accordance with the boolean semantics) for a given stochastic (PCTMC) model. Numerical algorithms for this problem [23] are prohibitively costly, hence the standard approach is to rely on statistical methods. Basically, one combines a simulation algorithm for the stochastic process (e.g., Gillespie's algorithm [24] for PCTMC) with a monitor routine for the MITL formula φ, thus generating samples from a Bernoulli random variable with probability $p(\varphi)$. Then, standard stastistical tools can be used to obtain an estimate $\hat{p}$ of $p(\varphi)$, with a given error and confidence, or to test if $p(\varphi)$ is greater or smaller than a threshold q, see [6–8]. Of particular interest in the context of this paper are Bayesian methods [8], which assume a prior distribution over $p(\varphi)$, and compute the posterior distribution, given the observed Bernoulli samples. Typically, this prior is the Beta distribution, which is conjugate [25] with the Bernoulli distribution, meaning that the posterior is still a Beta and hence analytically computable [8].

When the quantitative semantics is concerned, pipelining a simulation algorithm for PCTMC with a monitor will produce samples of a real valued random variables, which can again be analysed with statistical means. In particular, in [13,15], the authors focus on the average quantitative score as a measure of robustness of the property in the stochastic model, which can be estimated by standard statistics.

3   Smoothness and Functional Priors

3.1   Satisfaction Functions

We now switch our attention to examine the behaviour of the truth probability of a formula as we change the model within a parametric family of models. The scenario we consider is the following: let φ being a proposition in a suitable temporal logic (e.g. MITL) which we wish to verify over the trajectories of a stochastic process. Let $\mathcal{M}_\theta$ be an *uncertain CTMC* whose transition rates depend on a set of parameters $\theta \in \mathcal{D}$ where $\mathcal{D}$ is a connected, compact domain in $\mathbb{R}^d$, as in Sect. 2.1. For a fixed value of the parameters θ, model checking the formula φ would return the probability $p_\theta(\varphi) = p(\varphi = \mathtt{tt} \mid \mathcal{M}_\theta)$ that the formula will be evaluated as true on a randomly sampled trajectory of the system. This procedure therefore defines a function from the parameters domain $\mathcal{D}$ to the interval $[0, 1]$. We can formalise this in the following definition.

Definition 1. *Let $\mathcal{M}_\theta$ be an uncertain CTMC indexed by the variable $\theta \in \mathcal{D}$, and let φ be a temporal logic formula. The satisfaction function $f_\varphi : \mathcal{D} \to [0, 1]$ associated with φ and $\mathcal{M}_\theta$ is*

$$f_\varphi(\theta) = p(\varphi = \mathtt{tt} \mid \mathcal{M}_\theta)$$

i.e., with each value θ in the space of parameters $\mathcal{D}$ it associates the satisfaction probability of φ for the model with that parameter value.

The following theorem characterises the dependence of the satisfaction function on its parameters, and was proved in [12].

Theorem 1. *Let φ be a formula in a suitable temporal logic and let $\mathcal{M}_\theta$ be an uncertain CTMC indexed by the variable $\theta \in \mathcal{D}$. Denote as $\alpha(X, \theta)$ the transition rates of the CTMC and assume that these depend smoothly on the parameters θ and polynomially on the state vector of the system X. Then, the satisfaction function of φ is a smooth function of the parameters, $f_\varphi \in \mathcal{C}^\infty(\mathcal{D})$.* □

3.2 Prior Distributions over Smooth Functions – Gaussian Processes

Our discussion in Sect. 3.1 highlights the fact that, for uncertain CTMCs, the concept of satisfaction probability must be replaced with a functional analogue, which takes into account the influence that model parameters may have on the satisfaction probability of the formula. From the statistical model checking perspective, this suggests that Monte Carlo estimation should be replaced by function approximation. We will retain a Bayesian perspective in this paper, and construct a statistical model checking method based on Bayesian functional approximation: this requires the definition of a suitable class of probability distribution over functions. Our theoretical analysis in Theorem 1 enabled us to conclude that the satisfaction function is a smooth function of its arguments, the model parameters: a natural choice of prior distribution over smooth functions is a *Gaussian Process* (GP [26]). Formally, the definition of a GP is as follows:

Definition 2. *A GP is a collection of random variables indexed by an input variable x such that every finite dimensional marginal distribution is a multivariate normal distribution.*

In practice, a sample from a GP is a random function; the random vector obtained by evaluating a sample function at a finite set of points $x_1, \ldots, x_N$ is a multivariate Gaussian random variable. A GP is uniquely defined by its *mean* and *covariance* functions, denoted by $\mu(x)$ and $k(x, x')$; the mean vector (covariance matrix) of the finite dimensional marginals are given by evaluating the mean (covariance) function on every (pair of) point in the finite sample. Naturally, by subtracting the mean function to any sample function, we can always reduce ourselves to the case of *zero mean* GPs; in the following, we will adopt this convention and ignore the mean function.

A popular choice for the covariance function, which we will also use, is the *squared exponential* covariance function

$$k(x, x') = \sigma^2 \exp\left[-\frac{(x - x')^2}{\lambda^2}\right] \tag{1}$$

with two hyper-parameters: the amplitude σ^2 and the characteristic length scale λ^2 [26].

The covariance function endows the space of samples from a GP with a metric: this is an example of a Reproducing Kernel Hilbert Space (RKHS). A complete characterisation of such spaces is non-trivial; for our purposes, however, it is sufficient to show that their expressivity is sufficient to approximate a satisfaction function by a sample from a GP. The following result is a simple corollary of the results in [27]:

Theorem 2. *Let f be a continuous function over a compact domain $D \in \mathbb{R}^p$. For every $\epsilon > 0$, there exists a sample ψ from a GP with squared exponential covariance such that*

$$\|f - \psi\|_2 \leq \epsilon$$

where $\| \cdot \|_2$ denotes the L_2 norm.

The results of Theorems 1 and 2 jointly imply that the satisfaction function of a formula can be approximated arbitrarily well by a sample from a GP, justifying the use of GPs as priors for the satisfaction function.

4   Smoothed Model Checking

To see how this fact enables a Bayesian statistical model checking approach *directly at the level of the satisfaction function*, we need to explain the basics of posterior computation in GP models. Let x denote the input value and let $\hat{\mathbf{f}} = \{\hat{f}_1, \ldots, \hat{f}_N\}$ denote observations of the values of the unknown function f at input points $x_1, \ldots, x_N$. We are interested in computing the distribution over f at a *new* input point x^* *given* the observed values $\hat{\mathbf{f}}$, $p(f(x^*)|\hat{\mathbf{f}})$. A priori, we know that the true function values at any finite collection of input points is Gaussian distributed, hence $p(f(x^*), f(x_1), \ldots, f(x_N)) = \mathcal{N}(\boldsymbol{\mu}, \Sigma)$, with $\boldsymbol{\mu}$ and Σ obtained from the mean and covariance function as explained before. This prior distribution can be combined with likelihood models for the observations, $p(\hat{f}|f)$ in a Bayesian fashion to yield a joint posterior

$$p\left(f(x^*), f(x_1), \ldots, f(x_N)|\hat{\mathbf{f}}\right) = \frac{1}{Z}p\left(f(x^*), f(x_1), \ldots, f(x_N)\right) \prod_i p(\hat{f}_i|f(x_i))$$

where Z is a normalisation constant. The desired posterior predictive distribution can then be obtained by integrating out (*marginalising*) the true function values $f(x_1), \ldots, f(x_N)$

$$p(f(x^*)|\hat{\mathbf{f}}) = \int \prod_{i=1}^{N} df(x_i)p\left(f(x^*), f(x_1), \ldots, f(x_N)|\hat{\mathbf{f}}\right). \tag{2}$$

Equation (2) plays a central role in non-parametric function estimation; the inference procedure outlined above goes under the name of *GP regression*. It is important to note that, in the case of Gaussian observation noise, the integral in Eq. (2) can be computed in closed form. For further details see e.g. [26].

Important Remark: GP regression provides an analytical expression for the predicted mean and variance of the unknown function at all input points.

In our case, observations of the satisfaction function are obtained through boolean evaluations of a formula over individual trajectories at isolated parameter values. The satisfaction of a formula φ over a trajectory generated from a specific parameter value θ is a Bernoulli random variable with success probability $f_\varphi(\theta)$. In order to map this probability to the real numbers, we introduce the *inverse probit* transformation

$$\psi(f) = g \Leftrightarrow f = \int_\infty^g \mathcal{N}(0,1) \quad \forall f \in [0,1], g \in \mathbb{R}$$

where $\mathcal{N}(0,1)$ is the standard Gaussian distribution with mean zero and variance 1. The function $g_\varphi(\theta) = \psi(f_\varphi(\theta))$ is by construction a smooth, real valued function of the model parameters, and can therefore be modelled as a draw from a GP.

We can summarise the algorithm as follows: we draw m binary evaluations of satisfaction at each of N parameter values $\theta_1, \ldots, \theta_N$; these are collected in a (binary) data matrix $\mathcal{D} = [\mathbf{d}_1, \ldots, \mathbf{d}_N]$ whose rows $\mathbf{d}_i$ are the boolean m-vectors of evaluations at θ_i. By construction, at each θ_i value the observations are independent draws from a $Binomial(m, f_\varphi(\theta))$. The inverse probit transform of the satisfaction function $g_\varphi(\theta) = \psi(f_\varphi(\theta))$ is a smooth function of the parameters and is assigned a GP prior. Denote as $(g^*, \mathbf{g})$ the vector containing the values of g_φ at a new parameter value θ^* and at the training parameter values $\theta_1, \ldots, \theta_N$. Using Bayes theorem and the marginalisation property (2) of GPs, the posterior estimate of $g_\varphi(\theta^*)$ at a new parameter value is given by

$$p\left(g_\varphi(\theta^*)|\mathcal{D}\right) \propto \int d\mathbf{g} \mathcal{N}\left((g^*, \mathbf{g})|\mathbf{0}, \Sigma\right) \prod_{i=1}^N (f_\varphi(\theta_i))^{\sum \mathbf{d}_i} (1 - f_\varphi(\theta_i))^{m - \sum \mathbf{d}_i}. \quad (3)$$

Computing this posterior distribution can be done accurately and efficiently using the Expectation-Propagation algorithm described in [12].

5   Learning and Designing Systems from Logical Constraints

Smoothed model checking provides an effective algorithm for approximating the satisfaction function of a formula, in other words, to examine the sensitivity of the formula's truth probability to the parameters of the uncertain CTMC. A related set of problems, which can also benefit from a machine learning approach, is concerned with reducing the uncertainty in the model, either by incorporating observations of the system, or by enforcing requirements in a system design scenario. Parameter synthesis from observations of the state of a stochastic process is a well studied problem in computational statistics and machine learning (see, e.g. [28,29]). Here we focus instead on the less studied problem where observations are truth values of a (set of) formula over individual realisations of the process (trajectories). The two questions we aim to address are the following:

1. **Learning Problem.** Given truth evaluations of a set of formulae over independent individual realisations of a stochastic process, how can we find the parameter set which optimises their probability (maximum likelihood)?
2. **Probabilistic Design Problem.** Given a desired target (joint) probability distribution for the truth of a (set of) formula, how can we find the parameter set for a system which will optimally meet these requirements?
3. **Robust Design Problem.** Given a behavioural requirement expressed as a MITL formula, how can we find the parameter set for a system which will satisfy this requirement as robustly as possible?

In this section, we review a GP-based approach to address these problems, which was first presented in [11, 14] for qualitative semantics (problems 1 and 2) and in [13, 15] for quantitative semantics (robustness of a formula, problem 3).

5.1   Observations, Constraints and Objective Functions

All of these problems can be effectively addressed as optimisation problems; the first step is therefore to define a suitable objective function. We focus our description on the Learning problem with qualitative semantics as it is the most direct in terms of exposition; similar general considerations apply in the other scenarios, although additional technical difficulties are encountered for quantitative semantics [13, 15].

The first step in setting up an optimisation procedure is to define an objective function. Let $\varphi_1, \ldots, \varphi_M$ be the formulae being monitored over system trajectories, and arrange in the $M \times N$ *design matrix* D the observed truth values of the M formulae over N independent trajectories. Assuming one could access the true joint satisfaction function of the formulae $p(\varphi_1, \ldots, \varphi_M | \theta)$ (an 2^M vector valued function of the parameters), a natural objective function would be the *log-likelihood* function

$$\mathcal{L}(D, \theta) = \sum_{j=1}^{N} \log[p(\varphi_1(T_j), \ldots, \varphi_M(T_j) | \theta)] \tag{4}$$

where $p(\varphi_1(T_j), \ldots, \varphi_M(T_j) | \theta)$ denotes the entry of the function $p(\varphi_1, \ldots, \varphi_M | \theta)$ corresponding to the actual truth values observed on trajectory j. If the joint satisfaction function is known analytically, one might be able to apply a variety of optimisation methods to identify the maximum likelihood parameter set. Unfortunately, the log-likelihood (4) is never analytically available, except in the simplest of cases.

In [11, 14] we proposed an alternative, statistical approach to optimise the uncomputable log-likelihood (4). This is based on obtaining noisy estimates of the function from a limited number of SMC runs, and then adopting a reinforcement learning approach to obtain a provably optimal solution. In the next subsection, we briefly detail the algorithm we use.

Th same optimisation approach can be used for problems 2 and 3. Probabilistic design can be rephrased as the minimisation of a suitable distance function (the Jansen-Shannon divergence) between the target joint probability and the joint distribution $p(\varphi_1, \ldots, \varphi_M | \theta)$ for a fixed θ, see [11,14] for details. Robust design, instead, has been modelled in [13,15] as the maximisation of the expected quantitative score for the formula φ expressing the desired requirement.

5.2 Optimising Un-Computable Functions – The GP-UCB Algorithm

We have seen in Sect. 4 that Smoothed Model Checking can provide an accurate reconstruction of the satisfaction function of a formula from a limited set of truth evaluations. A naive idea would be to plug the Smoothed Model Checking approximation in (4) and then directly optimise the resulting function. This however would be a suboptimal procedure: as we are often interested in joint probabilities, the computation of the training set for Smoothed Model Checking might become computationally intensive (intuitively, we have to estimate 2^M satisfaction functions). It is therefore advantageous to use an adaptive strategy to select the least possible number of parameter values where to evaluate the log-likelihood (4).

The key insight we adopt comes from reinforcement learning: there, one is tasked with devising an optimal strategy for an agent acting in an incompletely known environment. A central object of study in reinforcement learning is the trade-off between exploitation and exploration: the agent may settle for the best known policy so far (exploitation), or it may choose better policies potentially still unknown (exploration). Bayesian optimisation algorithms export this paradigm to the world of optimisation by constructing a statistical model of the unknown function which not only can predict the unknown function values, but also quantify the uncertainty in the unknown function values.

More specifically, suppose one has already acquired function evaluations $\hat{\mathbf{f}}$ at a number of initial training points $x_1, \ldots, x_N$. In order to choose a subsequent point, we first construct a GP model of the unknown function f by using GP regression. To achieve a trade-off between exploration and exploitation, one then optimises a *quantile* of the process (rather than the mean): in this way, rather than choosing a point where the expectation is maximal, one chooses a point where the function could be even greater. Formally, we introduce the concept of *acquisition function*, an auxiliary function constructed from the statistics of the GP model which is optimised to obtain the next evaluation point. Let the unknown function $f \sim \mathcal{GP}(\mu, k)$ and let μ_N and β_N be the posterior mean and variance after N observations. The acquisition function we will use is defined as

$$\alpha_N(x) = \mu_N(x) + \lambda_N \beta_N(x) \tag{5}$$

where λ_N is a constant factor (which depends on the number of points acquired only).

The algorithm we use, called GP Upper Confidence Bound (GP-UCB), iteratively selects novel points for approximate function evaluation by optimising the auxiliary function (5), which is known analytically due to the properties of GP regression. Importantly, Srinivas et al. [30] showed that the GP-UCB algorithm is globally convergent with high probability for a particular choice of the constants λ_N in (5) (which depends on the probability of globally converging). Our approach to learning from logical constraints therefore relies on applying the GP-UCB algorithm to Eq. (4) (or the analogous objective functions for system design/robustness optimisation, see [14,15]).

5.3   Related Work: Learning Formulae

Our previous description has focussed on the scenario where a fixed formula was evaluated over runs of an uncertain model. In reality, formulae may themselves come in parametric families, and there may be uncertainty over the parametrisation/structure of the formula. This is often the case for temporal logic formulae, when the temporal bounds of formulae that best characterise a behaviour may be subject to uncertainty (e.g. an oscillator of imprecisely known period in the case of Signal Temporal Logic). In the most general case, one may have uncertainty over both model *and* formulae parameters.

This general problem can also be addressed using ideas from machine learning and in particular GPs. In [31] a general strategy was proposed where, given observations of the state of a real system, one would learn a statistical model of the system, and then optimise formulae parameters using GP-UCB to obtain formulae that could optimally characterise a system (in the sense that they would be satisfied by the system with high probability). This approach was applied to the problem of discriminating cardiac arrhythmias from electro-cardiogram data: the authors fitted hidden Markov models (HMM) to annotated sequences to learn models of the different type of arrhythmias, and then applied the GP-UCB procedure to determine temporal logic formulae which could optimally discriminate different conditions.

6   The U-Check Software Suite

All the algorithms discussed above have been implemented in the open source tool U-check [16], available online[1]. U-check has been implemented in Java, it runs cross platform, and can be used as a Java library or as a standalone software, with a command line interface.

The simple interface of the tool takes as input an option file, which specifies the algorithm to run. The choice at the moment is between smoothed model checking (Sect. 4), parameter estimation from qualitative data and system design using the MITL quantitative semantics (Sect. 5). The option file has additional fields specifying additional properties of the algorithm, see [16] and the online

---

[1] http://homepages.inf.ed.ac.uk/dmilios/ucheck.

documentation for further details. Furthermore, one has to specify the link to a model file and to the properties file.

U-check supports models specified in several modelling languages, some of them of common use, such as PRISM guarded commands [2] and Bio-PEPA [32]. It also supports models in the SimHyA modelling language [33]. Properties, instead, can be specified only in MITL for the moment, though a spatio-temporal extension of MITL [34] will be supported soon.

In the following section, we will illustrate the methods discussed and the use of U-check through a simple example of a virus infection.

7   Case Study: A CTMC Model of Viral Infection

In this section, we show the statistical verification methods at work on a viral infection model appeared in [35]. This model, in particular, is stiff, which makes stochastic simulation very expensive. Therefore, any statistical method to explore the parameter space should minimise the number of simulation runs to keep the analysis efficient. In this scenario, the use of smoothed model checking and of active learning strategy for optimisation is of highest value.

The model has three counting variables keeping track of three species: the viral template T, the viral genome G, and the viral structural protein S. Its dynamics is given by the reactions of Table 1. It is assumed that nucleotides and amino acids are available at constant concentrations, and their contributions to the rate functions are encoded in the model parameters. In the initial state, we assume 1 molecule for T and zero for the rest of the species. In the experiments that follow, we vary c_n and c_a, which are coefficients that control the concentrations of nucleotides and amino acids correspondingly.

Table 1. Rate functions and default parameter values for the viral model.

Reaction	Rate function	Kinetic constant
Nucleotides $+ T \xrightarrow{k_1} G + T$	$k_1 X_T c_n$	$k_1 = 1, c_n = 1$
Nucleotides $+ G \xrightarrow{k_2} T$	$k_2 X_G c_n$	$k_2 = 0.025$
Nucleotides $+$ amino acids $+ T \xrightarrow{k_3} S + T$	$k_3 X_T c_n c_a$	$k_3 = 100, c_a = 1$
$T \xrightarrow{k_4} \emptyset$	$k_4 X_T$	$k_4 = 0.25$
$S \xrightarrow{k_5} \emptyset$	$k_5 X_S$	$k_5 = 0.2$
$G + S \xrightarrow{k_6} V$	$k_6 X_G X_S$	$k_6 = 7.5 \times 10^{-6}$

The trajectories of the model in question are characterised by irregular fluctuations around a fixed level. We formalise this concept by the following formula that captures fluctuations of a certain magnitude:

$$\varphi = \mathbf{F}_{[100,150]}(G > T_{hi} \ \wedge \ \mathbf{F}_{[1,20]}(G < T_{lo} \ \wedge \ \mathbf{F}_{[1,20]}G > T_{hi})) \qquad (6)$$

The property will be satisfied if at lest one fluctuation occurs for the genome population in the area specified by the threshold parameters T_{lo} and T_{hi}.

The PRISM specification of the viral model, the MITL properties considered, and the inputs for the experiments that follow, are distributed along with the source code of U-check.

7.1 Using the Command-Line Version of U-Check

The U-check executable has to be provided with a configuration file that specifies the properties of a certain experiment. The experiment options are in the form of assignments as follows:

```
OPTION = VALUE
```

where VALUE can be a number, a truth value, or a string, depending on the option. A comprehensive summary of the options available is given in [16], while a exhaustive description can be found in the user manual associated with the code release. We highlight the most important options required to execute the algorithms supported.

- modelFile: A file that contains the model specification.
- propertiesFile: A file that contains one or more MITL properties.
- observationsFile: A file that contains qualitative observations; it is required for parameter inference from qualitative data only.
- mode: It can be either inference, robust or smoothedmc.

The parameters to be explored have to be defined by a declaration of the form:

```
parameter NAME = [A, B]
```

which implies that NAME is assigned with the interval between A and B.

7.2 Smoothed Model Checking

We demonstrate the configuration required to perform smoothed model checking for the viral expression model. The code that follows dictates that the c_n parameter (k_nucleotides) is explored in the interval $[0.8, 2]$ and c_a (k_amino_acids) in $[0.5, 1]$. In the viral.mtl we have specified the fluctuation formula in (6) for $T_{lo} = 280$ and $T_{hi} = 320$.

```
modelFile = viral.sm
propertiesFile = viral.mtl
mode = smoothedmc
parameter k_nucleotides = [0.8, 2]
parameter k_amino_acids = [0.5, 1]
endTime = 200
runs = 10
initialObservtions = 100
numberOfTestPoints = 1600
```

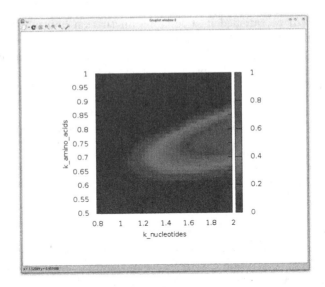

Fig. 1. U-check screenshot: smoothed model checking result presented via gnuplot

According to the `initialObservtions` option, the satisfaction probability will be evaluated on a grid of 100 regularly distributed parameters values. The `runs` and `endTime` options imply that for each parameter value 10 trajectories will be sampled up to time 200. The `numberOfTestPoints` option means that satisfaction function will be eventually estimated on a grid of 1600 points.

Eventually, U-check produces a csv file that contains the estimated satisfaction probabilities for the specified grid of points, as well as a matlab/octave script file that allows easy manipulation of the results. Automatic plotting for up to two dimensions is also possible via the gnuplot program. Figure 1 depicts a screenshot of the current smoothed model checking result.

7.3 Robust Parameter Synthesis

The configuration that follows is an example of robustness optimisation.

```
modelFile = viral.sm
propertiesFile = viral.mtl
mode = robust
parameter k_nucleotides = [0.001, 2]
parameter k_amino_acids = [0.001, 2]
endTime = 200
runs = 10
initialObservations = 40
numberOfTestPoints = 100
```

The `initialObservtions` option specifies the number of points that are required for the initialisation of the GP-UCB algorithm; these will serve as the initial training set for the GP that emulates formula robustness. The option `numberOfTestPoints` controls the size of the GP test set used in each iteration

Fig. 2. U-check screenshot: robust parameter synthesis terminal output

of the algorithm. Increasing this value will increase the possibility of discovering a new potential maximum, assuming there is one.

The program output that contains the solution obtained and its robustness value, as well as additional information regarding the progress of the optimisation process; a screenshot can be seen in in Fig. 2. The most robust values found for c_n and c_a have been 1.929 and 0.766 correspondingly, with robustness value 20.4. This implies that the system robustly fluctuates around in the area specified by $T_{lo} = 280$ and $T_{hi} = 320$.

7.4   Learning from Qualitative Observations

We shall demonstrate U-check capability of learning the model parameters from qualitative observations on some artificial data. We make use of three variations of (6), which capture fluctuations of different magnitude. The values used for (T_{lo}, T_{hi}) have been: $(290, 310)$, $(280, 320)$ and $(270, 370)$. Artificial observations have been generated by considering $c_n = 1.5$ and $c_a = 0.75$. We have sampled 100 independent trajectories from this fixed model and performed model checking, resulting in a $n \times m$ matrix of boolean observations, where $n = 100$ and $m = 3$; these are stored in the observations file `viral.dat`. Given that the formulae are specified in a file named `viral_inference.mtl`, the following configuration will perform parameter inference:

```
modelFile = viral.sm
propertiesFile = viral_inference.mtl
observationsFile = viral.dat
mode = inference
parameter k_nucleotides = [0.001, 2]
```

```
parameter k_amino_acids = [0.001, 2]
endTime = 200
runs = 10
```

The program output is depicted in Fig. 3. The optimal values for c_n and c_a have been 1.445 and 0.762 correspondingly. The solution obtained is a good approximation of the actual parameters that produced the data.

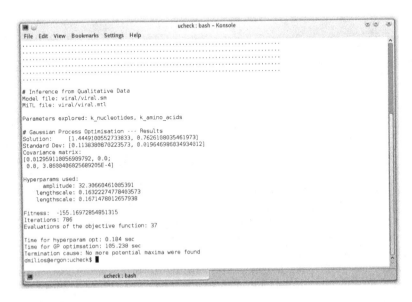

Fig. 3. U-check screenshot: terminal output for inference from qualitative observations

8   Discussion

In this paper we gave a simple introduction to recent development at the border between machine learning and formal methods, leading to statistically grounded methods for the analysis of uncertainty in stochastic models. We used a simple but representative case study of viral infection taken from system biology, to show how these analyses can be performed with the tool U-check. The reader interested in a more exhaustive discussion about performance and accuracy of these these methods is referred to [12,14,15]. Applications of these techniques are naturally found in domains as diverse as systems and synthetic biology, cyber-physical systems, smart cities and collective adaptive systems. We believe that the methods presented here, and related approaches, can provide effective tools to investigate and design the behaviour of such systems.

Related Work. The cross fertilisation between ideas from statistical machine learning and formal methods/verification is a novel area of research which is gaining momentum. The bulk of works of the authors discussed in this paper is part of this growing trend.

Parameter estimation using temporal logic and qualitative data has been discussed in [36], using heuristic methods based on evolutionary algorithms to explore the state space. This is in contrast with our approach [11, 14], in which we rely on more advanced optimisation techniques from active learning, providing guarantees on finding the maximum likelihood estimate.

The same optimisation approach has then been used in [13, 15] with the purpose of system design of stochastic models, using temporal logic specifications and leveraging its quantitative semantics.

Another problem which received considerable attention is the synthesis and parameter exploration problem, where one is interested in the satisfaction probability as a function of some parameters. Besides our statistical approach [12], there are some numerical methods based on exaustive exploration of the state space combined with error bounds [9, 10]. These methods, however, are much more affected by the curse of dimensionality and by scalability issues.

A complementary problem which has been tackled with similar methods is that of learning temporal logic formulae that best characterise model properties or that explain observed data. In this respect we recall works of some of the authors [31, 37], exploiting active learning, possibly combine with heuristic searches in the space of formulae. Other works dealing with learning of temporal logic specifications are, for instance, [38, 39].

Another area of formal methods in which machine learning methods have a large potential is that of abstraction, recasted in a statistical sense. At the moment, these ideas have been used to speed up simulation of systems with multiple time scales [40] and systems where only a small portion is simulated explicitly, while the rest of the system is abstracted by a Gaussian Process [41]. They have also been used for modular decomposition of systems in parameter estimation tasks [42].

Finally, the integration of machine learning and formal methods is happening also at the level of modelling languages. In [43], a novel process algebra is defined, with a semantics in terms of uncertain CTMC, and equipped with inference routines to reduce parametric uncertainty in presence of observations.

References

1. Baier, C., Katoen, J.-P.: Principles of Model Checking. MIT Press, Cambridge (2008)
2. Kwiatkowska, M., Norman, G., Parker, D.: PRISM 4.0: verification of probabilistic real-time systems. In: Gopalakrishnan, G., Qadeer, S. (eds.) CAV 2011. LNCS, vol. 6806, pp. 585–591. Springer, Heidelberg (2011)
3. Baier, C., Haverkort, B., Hermanns, H., Katoen, J.: Model checking continuous-time Markov chains by transient analysis. In: Proceedings of CAV, pp. 358–372 (2000)
4. Katoen, J.-P., Khattri, M., Zapreevt, I.S.: A markov reward model checker. In: Proceedings of QEST, pp. 243–244 (2005)

5. Mateescu, M., Wolf, V., Didier, F., Henzinger, T.: Fast adaptive uniformisation of the chemical master equation. IET Syst. Biol. **4**(6), 441–452 (2010)
6. Legay, A., Delahaye, B., Bensalem, S.: Statistical model checking: an overview. In: Proceeding of RV, pp. 122–135 (2010)
7. Younes, H.L., Simmons, R.G.: Statistical probabilistic model checking with a focus on time-bounded properties. Inf. Comput. **204**(9), 1368–1409 (2006)
8. Zuliani, P., Platzer, A., Clarke, E.M.: Bayesian statistical model checking with application to simulink/stateflow verification. In: Proceedings of HSCC, pp. 243–252 (2010)
9. Brim, L., Češka, M., Dražan, S., Šafránek, D.: Exploring parameter space of stochastic biochemical systems using quantitative model checking. In: Sharygina, N., Veith, H. (eds.) CAV 2013. LNCS, vol. 8044, pp. 107–123. Springer, Heidelberg (2013)
10. Češka, M., Dannenberg, F., Kwiatkowska, M., Paoletti, N.: Precise parameter synthesis for stochastic biochemical systems. In: Mendes, P., Dada, J.O., Smallbone, K. (eds.) CMSB 2014. LNCS, vol. 8859, pp. 86–98. Springer, Heidelberg (2014)
11. Bortolussi, L., Sanguinetti, G.: Learning and designing stochastic processes from logical constraints. In: Joshi, K., Siegle, M., Stoelinga, M., D'Argenio, P.R. (eds.) QEST 2013. LNCS, vol. 8054, pp. 89–105. Springer, Heidelberg (2013)
12. Bortolussi, L., Milios, D., Sanguinetti, G.: Smoothed model checking for uncertain continuous time Markov chains. CoRR arXiv:1402.1450
13. Bartocci, E., Bortolussi, L., Nenzi, L., Sanguinetti, G.: On the robustness of temporal properties for stochastic models. In: Proceedings of HSB, vol. 125. EPTCS, pp. 3–19 (2013)
14. Bortolussi, L., Sanguinetti, G.: Learning and designing stochastic processes from logical constraints. Logical Methods Comput. Sci. **11**(2:3), 1–24 (2015)
15. Bartocci, E., Bortolussi, L., Nenzi, L., Sanguinetti, G.: System design of stochastic models using robustness of temporal properties. Theoret. Comput. Sci. **587**, 3–25 (2015)
16. Bortolussi, L., Milios, D., Sanguinetti, G.: U-Check: model checking and parameter synthesis under uncertainty. In: Campos, J., Haverkort, B.R. (eds.) QEST 2015. LNCS, vol. 9259, pp. 89–104. Springer, Heidelberg (2015)
17. Durrett, R.: Essentials of Stochastic Processes. Springer, Berlin (2012)
18. Bortolussi, L., Hillston, J., Latella, D., Massink, M.: Continuous approximation of collective systems behaviour: a tutorial. Perform. Eval. **70**(5), 317–349 (2013)
19. Alur, R., Feder, T., Henzinger, T.A.: The benefits of relaxing punctuality. J. ACM **43**(1), 116–146 (1996)
20. Maler, O., Nickovic, D.: Monitoring temporal properties of continuous signals. In: Lakhnech, Y., Yovine, S. (eds.) FORMATS 2004 and FTRTFT 2004. LNCS, vol. 3253, pp. 152–166. Springer, Heidelberg (2004)
21. Donzé, A., Maler, O.: Robust satisfaction of temporal logic over real-valued signals. In: Chatterjee, K., Henzinger, T.A. (eds.) FORMATS 2010. LNCS, vol. 6246, pp. 92–106. Springer, Heidelberg (2010)
22. Donzé, A., Ferrère, T., Maler, O.: Efficient robust monitoring for STL. In: Sharygina, N., Veith, H. (eds.) CAV 2013. LNCS, vol. 8044, pp. 264–279. Springer, Heidelberg (2013)
23. Chen, T., Diciolla, M., Kwiatkowska, M., Mereacre, A.: Time-bounded verification of CTMCs against real-time specifications. In: Fahrenberg, U., Tripakis, S. (eds.) FORMATS 2011. LNCS, vol. 6919, pp. 26–42. Springer, Heidelberg (2011)
24. Gillespie, D.T.: Exact stochastic simulation of coupled chemical reactions. J. Phys. Chem. **81**(25), 2340–2361 (1977)

25. Bishop, C.M.: Pattern Recognition and Machine Learning. Springer, Berlin (2006)
26. Rasmussen, C.E., Williams, C.K.I.: Gaussian Processes for Machine Learning. MIT Press, Caambridge (2006)
27. Steinwart, I.: On the influence of the kernel on the consistency of support vector machines. J. Mach. Lear. Res. **2**, 67–93 (2002)
28. Andreychenko, A., Mikeev, L., Spieler, D., Wolf, V.: Approximate maximum likelihood estimation for stochastic chemical kinetics. EURASIP J. Bioinf. Syst. Biol. **1**, 1–14 (2012)
29. Opper, M., Sanguinetti, G.: Variational inference for Markov jump processes. In: Proceedings of NIPS, pp. 1105–1112 (2007)
30. Srinivas, N., Krause, A., Kakade, S., Seeger, M.: Information-theoretic regret bounds for Gaussian process optimisation in the bandit setting. IEEE Trans. Inf. Theory **58**(5), 3250–3265 (2012)
31. Bartocci, E., Bortolussi, L., Sanguinetti, G.: Data-driven statistical learning of temporal logic properties. In: Legay, A., Bozga, M. (eds.) FORMATS 2014. LNCS, vol. 8711, pp. 23–37. Springer, Heidelberg (2014)
32. Ciocchetta, F., Hillston, J.: Bio-PEPA: a framework for the modelling and analysis of biological systems. Theoret. Comput. Sci. **410**(33–34), 3065–3084 (2009)
33. Bortolussi, L., Galpin, V., Hillston, J.: Hybrid performance modelling of opportunistic networks. In: EPTCS, vol. 85, pp. 106–121 (2012)
34. Bortolussi, L., Nenzi, L.: Specifying and monitoring properties of stochastic spatio-temporal systems in signal temporal logic. In: Proceedings of VALUETOOLS (2014)
35. Haseltine, E.L., Rawlings, J.B.: Approximate simulation of coupled fast and slow reactions for stochastic chemical kinetics. J. Chem. Phys. **117**(15), 6959 (2002)
36. Donaldson, R., Gilbert, D.: A model checking approach to the parameter estimation of biochemical pathways. In: Heiner, M., Uhrmacher, A.M. (eds.) CMSB 2008. LNCS (LNBI), vol. 5307, pp. 269–287. Springer, Heidelberg (2008)
37. Bufo, S., Bartocci, E., Sanguinetti, G., Borelli, M., Lucangelo, U., Bortolussi, L.: Temporal logic based monitoring of assisted ventilation in intensive care patients. In: Margaria, T., Steffen, B. (eds.) ISoLA 2014, Part II. LNCS, vol. 8803, pp. 391–403. Springer, Heidelberg (2014)
38. Bartocci, E., Grosu, R., Katsaros, P., Ramakrishnan, C.R., Smolka, S.A.: Model repair for probabilistic systems. In: Abdulla, P.A., Leino, K.R.M. (eds.) TACAS 2011. LNCS, vol. 6605, pp. 326–340. Springer, Heidelberg (2011)
39. Kong, Z., Jones, A., Ayala, A.M., Gol, E.A., Belta, C.: Temporal logic inference for classification and prediction from data. Proc. HSCC **2014**, 273–282 (2014)
40. Bortolussi, L., Milios, D., Sanguinetti, G.: Efficient stochastic simulation of systems with multiple time scales via statistical abstraction. In: Proceedings of CMSB (2015)
41. Legay, A., Sedwards, S.: Statistical abstraction boosts design and test efficiency of evolving critical systems. In: Margaria, T., Steffen, B. (eds.) ISoLA 2014, Part I. LNCS, vol. 8802, pp. 4–25. Springer, Heidelberg (2014)
42. Georgoulas, A., Clark, A., Ocone, A., Gilmore, S., Sanguinetti, G.: A subsystems approach for parameter estimation of ode models of hybrid systems. In: Proceedings of HSB, vol. 92. EPTCS (2012)
43. Georgoulas, A., Hillston, J., Milios, D., Sanguinetti, G.: Probabilistic programming process algebra. In: Norman, G., Sanders, W. (eds.) QEST 2014. LNCS, vol. 8657, pp. 249–264. Springer, Heidelberg (2014)

RV-Android: Efficient Parametric Android Runtime Verification, a Brief Tutorial

Philip Daian[1], Yliès Falcone[4(✉)], Patrick Meredith[1],
Traian Florin Şerbănuţă[1], Shin'ichi Shiriashi[2], Akihito Iwai[3],
and Grigore Rosu[1,4]

[1] Runtime Verification Inc., Urbana, USA
support@runtimeverification.com
[2] Toyota InfoTechnology Center U.S.A., Mountain View, USA
sshiraishi@us.toyota-itc.com
[3] Denso International America Inc., San Jose, USA
akihito_iwai@denso-diam.com
[4] University of Illinois at Urbana-Champaign, Champaign, USA
{ylies,grosu}@illinois.edu

Abstract. RV-Android is a new freely available open source runtime library for monitoring formal safety properties on Android. RV-Android uses the commercial RV-Monitor technology as its core monitoring library generation technology, allowing for the verification of safety properties during execution and operating entirely in userspace with no kernel or operating system modifications required. RV-Android improves on previous Android monitoring work by replacing the JavaMOP framework with RV-Monitor, a more advanced monitoring library generation tool with core algorithmic improvements that greatly improve resource consumption, efficiency, and battery life considerations. We demonstrate the developer usage of RV-Android with the standard Android build process, using instrumentation mechanisms effective on both Android binaries and source code. Our method allows for both property development and advanced application testing through runtime verification. We showcase the user frontend of RV-Monitor, which is available for public demo use and requires no knowledge of RV concepts. We explore the extra expressiveness the MOP paradigm provides over simply writing properties as aspects through two sample security properties, and show an example of a real security violation mitigated by RV-Android on-device. Lastly, we propose RV as an extension to the next-generation Android permissions system debuting in Android M.

1 Introduction

With the rise in popularity of Android [1], a Linux-based consumer smartphone operating system, the need for effective techniques to improve the security and reliability of third-party applications running on end user devices is well established [2]. One solution explored by previous work in the field is the use of runtime verification and runtime enforcement to detect and recover from violations of formal safety properties during the execution of Android applications [2,3].

© Springer International Publishing Switzerland 2015
E. Bartocci and R. Majumdar (Eds.): RV 2015, LNCS 9333, pp. 342–357, 2015.
DOI: 10.1007/978-3-319-23820-3_24

Some previous work in this space has relied on using kernel modifications to the Linux base of Android to generate the runtime traces required to verify safety properties [3,4]. This solution is inflexible for several reasons: it requires root access to the device to install, requires reinstallation on each operating system upgrade, and provides few additional guarantees from a compromised kernel over a userspace monitoring solution.

Other RV-based Android work has used JavaMOP, an experimental monitor oriented programming framework, to generate Android monitoring libraries which are weaved into third-party userspace applications, providing monitoring functionality and guarantees without requiring kernel-level modifications [2].

This approach has been demonstrated using AspectJ [5] for weaving, and allows us to weave binary bytecode useful towards instrumenting off-the-shelf third party packaged applications (apk's) [2,4]. Our work focuses on improving these approaches with efficient and versatile runtime verification tools that benefit from the previous research endeavors related to JavaMOP, resulting in a unified and open framework for runtime verification and analysis of Android applications.

1.1 Contributions

RV-Monitor is a proprietary library generation technology, allowing for the runtime monitoring, verification, and enforcement of safety properties through the generation of generic monitoring libraries. RV-Monitor is provided free for non-commercial use, and represents the evolution of the prototype JavaMOP tools with improvements in the codebase and core algorithms. Like JavaMOP, RV-Monitor supports logic plugins, allowing for the specifications of properties in multiple formalisms including regular expressions, context-free grammars, automata, and past-time linear temporal logic.

We make the case for the future use of RV-Monitor and its related Android runtime library for use in runtime verification and runtime enforcement of Android applications. We compare monitor-oriented programming techniques to popular aspect-oriented techniques, acknowledging the usefulness of both and supporting both as property inputs to our tools. We analyze a real security violation on the Android platform with the potential to be stopped by monitor-oriented programming, including the relevant property with our tool's distribution. Lastly, we discuss the future of RV on the Android platform and lay out a roadmap for future industry-lead work in the space.

2 RV-Android Overview and Build Process

RV-Android consists of two components, a monitoring library generation tool and a runtime environment used in the generation of these libraries for dynamic on-device property monitoring and violation recovery. For the first of these RV-Monitor is used off-the-shelf, allowing for the specification of both formal properties over events and the instrumentation points for these events in a single monitor-oriented file. This monitor-oriented programming is achieved through a new version of JavaMOP, a lightweight compiler that generates RV-Monitor (monitoring library) and AspectJ (program instrumentation) output. Unlike versions of JavaMOP used in previous work, which were fully responsible for monitoring applications and did not leverage RV-Monitor, this next-generation JavaMOP stands to benefit from the significant core algorithmic improvements that form the basis of the RV-Monitor IP [6] while completely separating the generation of efficient monitoring libraries from application instrumentation.

In our work, we will separate the discussion on instrumentation from the discussion on event and property definitions. We do this to leave open the possibility of future instrumentation models. While we focus on instrumentation methods using AspectJ in this work, other instrumentation mechanisms for packaged Android binaries have already been effectively demonstrated and proved [2,4,7,8]. RV-Monitor is compatible with any Java instrumentation method, and the JavaMOP project can be extended to generate the required input for other instrumentation tools if necessary.

Our website, http://runtimeverification.com/android, provides downloads and full instructions for the use of RV-Android, as well as the examples we discuss in the remainder of the paper and a video demonstrating a few currently available capabilities of the tool.

2.1 Build Process

The RV-Android process (shown above in Fig. 1) forms the basis of all tools based on RV-Android. Taking either a binary packaged Android application or set of source files as input, RV-Android additionally optionally takes any (or all) of aspect files, RV-Monitor properties, and monitor-oriented programming (MOP) files compatible with the JavaMOP tool. This flexibility in input allows RV-Monitor to be used with a wide variety of property formats, including aspect-oriented AspectJ properties that do not require formalisms or the additional features provided by RV-Monitor or JavaMOP.

By being able to mix and bundle these diverse formats together into a single set of properties as input to a single tool, property developers and application developers have an easy way to develop, apply, and share dynamic properties of their choice without the need to constrain themselves to a single tool. Futhermore, property developers have the ultimate control over the instrumentation of their properties in the original application: they can choose to use AspectJ directly, use MOP, or use other techniques of manual instrumentation. In doing so, the goal is to create a platform in which all developers of runtime properties for the Android platform feel comfortable using their preferred technologies, encouraging third-party property development.

RV-Monitor also features a flexible plugin architecture that allows for the development of custom or third-party formalisms supported by the tool, allowing virtually unlimited expressiveness in the properties it defines. By combining this with instrumentation in a single monitor-oriented programming files,

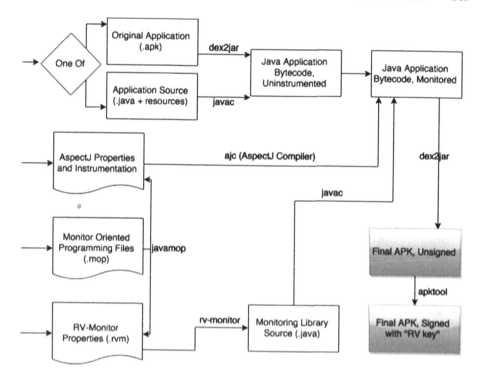

Fig. 1. RV-Android build process

advanced developers can write complex properties succinctly while defining simple properties not requiring dedicated formalisms in native Java directly through AspectJ.

RV-Android is also an open source project built around the closed source RV-Monitor project, but can be used without RV-Monitor as an aspect oriented programming platform, as well as extended to work with any number of tools supporting Java transformation and analysis. Because it is open source, RV-Android can also be extended by other tool developers who provide runtime analysis and verification of applications to integrate any technique into its workflow. We are already developing prototype extensions for taint analysis and other popular dynamic analysis techniques, extending the capabilities of RV-Android beyond the capabilities of any single tool.

Figure 1 shows the output of RV-Android as a signed, packaged Android application to be distributed to users. By signing all verified and monitored applications with an "RV" key from a source trusted by the user, the user's smartphone can then verify that the application has been correctly monitored and transformed to the specifications provided as input to the tool.

Excluded from the figure is the inclusion of the AspectJ and RV-Monitor runtimes in the monitored and instrumented application. These runtimes are needed for the instrumentation and monitoring of the application on-device, and are simply the binary runtimes as provided by each project.

2.2   RV-Android for Developers

In order to provide a full framework for runtime verification and enforcement on the Android platform, we must allow developers to complete their two primary tasks of interest with regards to runtime verification: developing new properties to check on their applications and third-party applications, and checking their own applications against existing property sets. To do this, we provide two versions of RV-Android for developers, targeted at two possible use cases. The first allows developers to integrate RV-Android into projects where they are using the standard Android build process and have access to the source code of the application, instrumenting source code directly. The second version is able to monitor properties of binary Android applications, or apks, and can be used on any application that runs on the Android platform.

Monitoring Source Code. To monitor source code, we provide a version of RV-Android called the "developer source" edition. Found in the "developer_src" subdirectory of the RV-Android distribution, this edition requires the developer to create two directories, "aspects" and "properties". By placing AspectJ files and RV-Monitor or MOP properties in the relevant directories and following the remainder of the setup instructions for the source edition, developers can integrate monitors and runtime verification in their build and testing process with no modification required to the source of the application itself.

This provides a convenient way for developers interested in obtaining the maximum assurance from their Android applications to leverage runtime verification. Additionally, developers using the default Android build process who wish to ship monitors integrated with their final application to end users (for assurance, security, or enforcement purposes) can use this version to monitor their source directly, requiring no binary transformations.

Monitoring Binary APKs. The second and more flexible distribution of RV-Android for developers focuses on monitoring arbitrary binary Android applications, and is referred to as the "command line" distribution. This distribution can also be used by advanced users who are comfortable using command-line tools. Similarly to the previous application, the tool takes both properties and aspects, and has a simple command-line interface with parameters as follows:

```
./rv_android [apk] [keystore] [keystore password]
[signing key alias] [monitors_directory] [aspects_directory]
```

Because of its simplicity and extensibility, this version of RV-Android can be integrated into any environment or build process. We recommend this version to all new developers interested in RV on Android.

2.3   RV-Android for End Users - GUI Frontend

For end-users who are not familiar with command-line applications and property development, but still wish to gain some additional assurance in or control over their applications, we provided a GUI version of RV-Android. The architecture of this system is shown in Fig. 2. RV-Android runs entirely on a remote server in the cloud, which runs the same CLI version of RV-Android with the workflow in Fig. 1. The program on the user's device is simply a shell allowing them to manage and select properties, and select an application on their device to instrument. This is similar to previous approaches applied to runtime verification on Android [9].

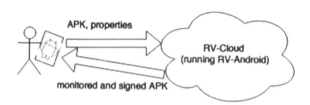

Fig. 2. RV-Android on-device architecture

Through this graphical user interface, we allow users that may be completely unfamiliar with RV or its concepts to apply generic "properties" to any of the applications currently on their device. We also allow them to download third-party sets of properties and read their descriptions.

Such an application aims to bring RV to the mainstream by providing simple, human-readable descriptions of what each property does or checks for and allowing any property to be used with any userspace application on any Android smartphone, without requiring root access. In the user frontend, there is no distinction made between properties written as aspects, monitors, or other formats, all of which are simply referred to as "properties".

We believe such a platform is an ideal introduction point to runtime verification for users and developers alike. With the increased importance of security on mobile devices, which often carry personal information and other sensitive data [10,11], and the ability to instrument any arbitrary binary Android application by virtue of the Java bytecode format used, we are able to show off the powerful and generic nature of runtime verification technology in an environment becoming increasingly important to end users.

Figure 3 shows two screenshots of the RV-Android frontend for end-users, currently in beta. Users select an application followed by a set of properties to apply to the application, with the remainder of the process being automated. These properties have extended descriptions that can be viewed by the user, and can be extended to include custom or user-defined properties. Applications can also be filtered by those requesting a set of permissions considered by the user to be particularly sensitive.

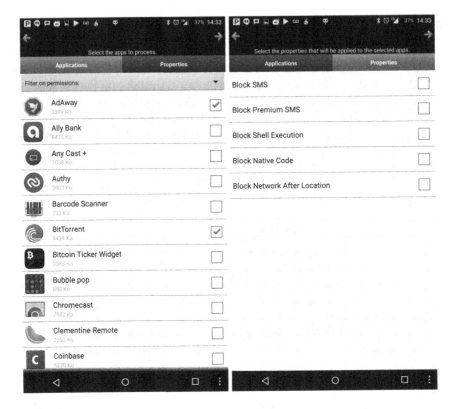

Fig. 3. RV-Android screenshots, application and property selection

3 Towards Practicality - RV-Android Case Studies

Having presented the overall architecture and currently available distributions of the RV-Android tool, the question of whether such techniques are practical and cost effective for use on real applications and devices arises naturally. The practicality of the tools presented hinges on the ability to develop a useful set of properties supported by the tool, which can then be shared, packaged, and distributed to end users for monitoring of arbitrary applications on-device or used by developers to test and evaluate their applications against the given set of API rules, coding best practices, and security properties.

To address the matter of usable properties, we will first consider the ideal language for expressing properties. Because RV-Monitor supports a variety of techniques for writing properties, including raw aspect-oriented properties and monitor-oriented properties that define both formal mathematical properties and their instrumentation, it is important to note the drawbacks and advantages of both techniques.

3.1   Two Properties in MOP and AspectJ

Blocking Device Location and Network Accesses. The first property is a security property intended to block malicious or questionably-sourced applications from accessing a user's location through the Android location API. The second property is not security oriented as the first one is. Instead, it merely logs and notifies the user when an application attempts to use an Android API call related to networking and connections to the Internet.

The Properties in AspectJ. We present how to implement monitors for the two properties in AspectJ. Note, the monitors make use of the following imports: import android.app.Activity; import android.content.Context; import android.content. ContextWrapper; import android.widget.Toast;

The monitor for blocking the device location is shown in full in aspect form in Listing 1.1. It prints a message to the user and log noting the attempted location access, and denies the access by returning null to the aspect around() join point rather than proceeding with the original call. It is clear from examining the property that there is a lot of code that can be automatically generated, including the code required to track the current activity in order to show the notification to the user.

The monitor for keeping track of network accesses is shown in full in aspect form in Listing 1.2. The monitor does not attempt to preserve any security properties (such as an unknown application cannot access user location). Instead, it merely logs and notifies the user when an application attempts to use an Android API call related to networking and connections to the Internet.

The monitors for these properties share a large amount of code, which is expected as both are fundamentally performing the same task (notifying the user of some event occurring on the device). This also suggests that there is a significant potential for automatically generating the monitor, and that both monitors could be expressed more concisely.

The Properties in MOP. While aspect-oriented programming is one approach to monitoring and analyzing applications on the Android platform [4], a newer paradigm familiar to the runtime verification community involves using the monitoring-oriented programming paradigm. Listing 1.3 shows the same property being enforced as in Listing 1.1 with a monitor defined with significantly less code. Using several keywords provided by RV-Monitor and RV-Android, particularly __TOAST and __SKIP, which in addition to __ACTIVITY form the basic keywords for user interaction currently supported by RV-Monitor, we automatically generate much of the code performing similar functions to the previous monitors in AspectJ.

Similarly, Listing 1.4 shows the same monitor as in Listing 1.2 using MOP format. Some clear advantages include shorter property that is easier to write, debug, and validate for developers and even advanced end-users.

Neither of these properties, however, leverage the primary feature of RV-Monitor, which is the ability to define logical properties over the event trace of an application in a variety of formalisms.

```
aspect BlockGetLocation extends Activity {

  private ContextWrapper contextWrapper;
  private Activity activity;
  private Object object;

  Object around(): call(* android.location..*(..))
    && !within(BlockGetLocation)
  {
    String method = thisJoinPoint.getSignature().getName();
    String classe = thisJoinPoint.getSignature().getDeclaringType().
      getName();
    /* Log information about method and class */;
    Object object = thisJoinPoint.getThis();
    Toast.makeText(
        ((android.content.ContextWrapper) object).
          getApplicationContext(),
        "Application accessing location information", Toast.
          LENGTH_LONG).show();
    return null;
  }

  // Advice to get the context application
  after(): execution(void Activity.onCreate(..))
    && !within(BlockGetLocation) {
  try {
    activity = new Activity();
    object = thisJoinPoint.getThis();
    System.out.println((object instanceof Activity));
    contextWrapper = new ContextWrapper(
        ((android.content.ContextWrapper) object)
        .getApplicationContext());
  } catch (Exception e) {
      System.err.println(e.toString());
    }
  }
}
```

Listing 1.1. Aspect-oriented property blocking location accesses

One example of using such formalisms is shown in Listing 1.5, which combines the previous two properties by denying all network-related API calls after the user's location is accessed. The access is otherwise permitted by the system.

The property is formally defined by a finite state machine in which the first state is safe, as the application has not accessed any location information. The application accessing any location information brings it to an unsafe state, after which any network access lead to a "denied" state. On entering the denied state, the monitor skips the function call to the network, returning null rather than executing that call. The distinction between the unsafe and deny states is that the unsafe state does not skip the call, allowing for further location accesses after the first access, but not for further.

Such a property is useful to users concerned about the leakage of their location data, though it is not in its current form comprehensive for all possible data exfiltration channels on Android devices.

In addition to allowing for the addition of logic to Android programming, RV-Monitor can extremely efficiently monitor parametric properties, or properties

```
 1  aspect WebAspect extends Activity {
 2      // Android Internet methods
 3      pointcut webCall() : call(* android.net..*(..)) || call(* android.
            webkit.WebView..*(..)) || call(* java.net.HttpURLConnection
            ..*(..)) && !within(WebAspect);
 4      pointcut onCreate(): execution(* onCreate(..)) && !within(
            WebAspect);
 5
 6      private ContextWrapper contextWrapper;
 7      private Activity activity;
 8      int count;
 9      after(): webCall() {
10      try{
11          if(count == 0){
12          if(contextWrapper != null && activity != null && count==0){
13              activity.runOnUiThread(new Runnable() {
14              public void run() {
15                  count++;
16                  // Toast message to inform
17                  Toast.makeText(contextWrapper.getApplicationContext(),
18                  "Application accessing to Internet", Toast.LENGTH_LONG).
                        show();
19              }
20              });
21          }
22          else { /* Log error about the missing context application */ }
23          }
24      } catch(Exception e){
25          /* Log exception using thisJoinPoint.getTarget().toString() */
26      }
27      }
28      // Advice to get the context application
29      after(): onCreate() {
30          try {
31              count=0;
32              activity = new Activity();
33              Object object = thisJoinPoint.getThis();
34              contextWrapper = new ContextWrapper(((android.content.
                    ContextWrapper) object).getApplicationContext());
35          } catch (Exception e) { /* Log error message */ }
36      }
37  }
```

Listing 1.2. Aspect-oriented property monitoring network accesses

of a specific Java object, class, or memory location and allowing for millions of monitors to be created with low runtime overhead [6]. This expressiveness and low overhead makes RV-Monitor ideal for a wide range of properties, from simple global properties like the above to complex parametric properties.

3.2   Preventing Security Violations - A Real Attack

While the above properties may be useful for users wishing to gain fine grained control over the privacy of their data when faced with potentially malicious applications, they are generally ineffective in protecting against real attacks. Listing 1.6 shows a MOP monitor in blocking a wide range of attacks. Similarly to the monitors in the previous subsection, this is a simple monitor designed to skip all calls to any exec method in the Runtime class. This method in the Android

```
 1  import java.lang.*;
 2
 3  Android_DenyLocation() {
 4
 5      // Deny all location package calls
 6      event location Object around(): call(* android.location..*(..))
        {
 7          __TOAST("Application accessing location information.");
 8          __SKIP;
 9      }
10  }
```

Listing 1.3. Monitor-oriented property blocking location accesses

```
 1  import java.lang.*;
 2
 3  Android_MonitorNetwork() {
 4
 5      // Display application toast on all network API calls
 6      event web_call after(): call(* android.net..*(..))
 7          || call(* android.webkit.WebView..*(..))
 8          || call(* java.net.HttpURLConnection..*(..)) {
 9          __TOAST("Application accessing the Internet,");
10      }
11
12  }
```

Listing 1.4. Monitor-oriented property monitoring network accesses

API allows developers to execute shell code directly through the currently running process, allowing for arbitrary commands interpreted by the Linux kernel underpinning Android [12].

One potential practical application of this property is the disabling of currently available Tor libraries, which are becoming widely used on Android in a malware context [13]. The Tor network allows malware, including spyware, adware, and ransomeware, to obfuscate its network connections to command and control servers, the location of which can be hidden from law enforcement and the public [14]. A 2014 survey of Android security by Google specifically mentions ransomware as an up-and-coming problem needing to be addressed by the Android security team, further suggesting the application of dynamic and static analysis techniques against spyware and other malicious applications which often use Tor to communicate with their operators [13,15].

The above property disbales Tor due to the code in Listing 1.7, which needs to install executable binary blobs of native code. Because there is no native file permission API on Android, the above aspect blocks all attempts to change file permissions and thus install native code from any third-party applications. In doing so, it blocks a wide range of potential attacks and privilege escalation exploits which rely on shell access, rendering it a powerful practical defense against violations of user privacy by malware that leverages the Tor network.

To test this property, it is sufficient to instrument the "Orbot" application in the Play store and attempt to run it on-device for the first time. We include detailed instructions and a sample of such monitored applications on

```
import java.lang.*;

Android_MonitorLocationNetwork() {

    event web_call Object around(): call(* android.net..*(..))
        || call(* android.webkit.WebView..*(..))
        || call(* java.net.HttpURLConnection..*(..)) {
        _TOAST("Application accessing the Internet,");
    }

    event location Object around(): call(* android.location..*(..))
        {
        _TOAST("Application accessing location information.");
    }

    fsm :
        start [
            location -> unsafe
            web_call -> start
        ]
        unsafe [
            web_call -> deny
            location -> unsafe
        ]
        deny [
            web_call -> deny
            location -> unsafe
        ]

        @deny {
            _SKIP;
        }

}
```

Listing 1.5. Monitor-oriented FSM property preventing network accesses after location

https://runtimeverification.com/android, one of which is a sample of real spyware disabled through the monitoring and enforcement of the above property.

4 Into the Future - Beyond Android Permissions

The future of the Android platform brings a substantial amount of change, with an ever increasing level of the platform's popularity and a significant number of potentially harmful applications still being deployed to user devices regularly [15].

4.1 Android M - A New Permissions Model

One of the most recently announced changes in the fundamental security model of the Android platform is the change in the permissions system being released with Android M. Rather than simply granting an application blanket permission to perform all operations in a given category, application permissions can be revoked at any time by the user [16]. One example of this is the revocation of

```
1  import java.lang.*;
2
3  Android_BlockShellExec() {
4
5      // Skip all shell execution calls
6      event shell_call Object around(): call(* Runtime+.exec(..)) {
7      __SKIP;
8      }
9  }
```

Listing 1.6. Monitor-oriented property blocking shell calls

```
1  public static void copyRawFile(Context ctx, int resid, File file,
       String mode, boolean isZipd) throws IOException,
       InterruptedException
2      {
3      ... // Copy file
4      // Change the permissions
5      Runtime.getRuntime().exec("chmod "+mode+" "+abspath).waitFor
           ();
6  }
```

Listing 1.7. Potentially malicious code installing the Tor network from orbot

location permissions from applications which may be leaking user data to third parties. This replaces many of the simpler security properties and aspects previously written targetting Android permissions, including the location property presented in this paper.

Despite this, as shown in Listing 1.5, RV-Android can provide much finer grained control over how permissions are used on device, revoking or granting permissions dynamically based on logical properties of the application state or current trace. In this way, context-sensitive permissions become possible for cases where a high level of control is desirable. One perfect example of this is the revocation of the Internet permission we discussed, which is now granted by default and without user confirmation to all applications being installed in Android M [17]. This change potentially removes some control from the user related to which applications have network access. However, because almost all applications rely on network access, context-sensitive permissions in which allowed hosts are whitelisted and certain services (like Tor or known ad networks) are blacklisted, and in which the level of action reacts to other system events may be more appropriate for informing the end user and providing them with ultimate control.

Using runtime verification and monitoring, one can control every category of permission and API access, specifically defining the access patterns and data allowed to the application. By defining such specific and tightly controlled executions, users can notice and prevent malicious or unexpected application behavior. Such control may be useful for employers with employees dealing with sensitive data on Android devices, and in all security-sensitive Android applications. The ability to run third-party applications on such devices introduces security vulnerabilities, a wide range of which can be detected and prevented with runtime verification.

4.2   Integrating with Other Approaches

In addition to preventing security violations as they occur, RV-Android can be used as a testing tool on a large number of applications to detect the presence of such violations in third party applications. In doing so, RV-Android can leverage a number of automated unit testing tools already available for Android designed to mimic and mock user behavior on the platform [18,19], checking a large number of properties automatically.

In addition to testing, RV-Android could potentially integrate with other dynamic analysis tools, including popular tools designed to ensure data security through taint analysis. Taint analysis is a popular technique that tracks sensitive information as it is handled by applications, preventing it from leaving through any unprivileged API calls or other "sinks" [20,21]. By integrating many such techniques, we aim to create the foremost security tool and platform for Android, with an ability to implement any future dynamic analysis techniques desirable to users and developers.

Lastly, runtime verification can integrate with static analysis to improve its efficiency and inform the automatic generation of properties checkable at runtime [22]. While there are no concrete plans to do so in RV-Android currently, this remains a future potential research direction.

4.3   Towards a Public Property Database

Undoubtedly the most important work in developing a framework for practical Android runtime verification is the development of properties that thoroughly encompass both known misuses of the Android and Java API's and violations of secure states by previously observed malware. To this end, we are developing a property database which provides annotated copies of both the Android and Java API's with RV-Monitor properties and AspectJ instrumentation built in. The current property database can be viewed and downloaded for free at https://github.com/runtimeverification/property-db/, and can be used by RV-Android with minimal modification. The property database currently contains around 180 safety properties of the Java API, which can be practically simultaneously monitored by our technology. These properties differ substantially from the security properties presented in this paper in that they monitor correct use of the API and thus functionality of the application rather than attempting to enforce the security of the device itself. This flexibility of RV-Android in capturing a wide range of potential properties on Android, together with this robust database of existing properties provides a good starting point for the development of a comprehensive dynamic analysis and runtime verification tool.

We further plan on providing additional privacy profiles focused on stronger security guarantees for the security conscious user, such as profiles useful in avoiding data exfiltration when using specific API's. While we will still allow users to define their own properties, the utility of future iterations of RV-Android will stem partially from the robustness of the default properties in our property database.

Acknowledgements. We would like to thank Patrick Meredith for developing the initial prototype of RV-Monitor applied to Android applications and continued feedback, as well as our partners at ITC and Denso for their continued support in the investigation of Android-related work for the automotive domain. We would also like to thank the miSecurity application team, for providing a basis for the graphical user frontend we describe.

References

1. Google Inc.: Android Developers (2014). http://developers.android.com
2. Falcone, Y., Currea, S., Jaber, M.: Runtime verification and enforcement for Android applications with RV-Droid. In: Qadeer, S., Tasiran, S. (eds.) RV 2012. LNCS, vol. 7687, pp. 88–95. Springer, Heidelberg (2013)
3. Bauer, A., Küster, J.-C., Vegliach, G.: Runtime verification meets Android security. In: Goodloe, A.E., Person, S. (eds.) NFM 2012. LNCS, vol. 7226, pp. 174–180. Springer, Heidelberg (2012)
4. Falcone, Y., Currea, S.: Weave Droid: aspect-oriented programming on Android devices: fully embedded or in the cloud. In: [23], pp. 350–353
5. Eclipse: The AspectJ project (2014). http://eclipse.org/aspectj
6. Luo, Q., Zhang, Y., Lee, C., Jin, D., Meredith, P.O.N., Şerbănuţă, T.F., Roşu, G.: RV-Monitor: efficient parametric runtime verification with simultaneous properties. In: Bonakdarpour, B., Smolka, S.A. (eds.) RV 2014. LNCS, vol. 8734, pp. 285–300. Springer, Heidelberg (2014)
7. Mulliner, C.: Dynamic binary instrumentation on Android (2012)
8. Bodden, E.: Instrumenting Android apps with Soot (2014). http://www.bodden.de/2013/01/08/soot-android-instrumentation/
9. Binns, P., Englehart, M., Jackson, M., Vestal, S.: Domain specific software architectures for guidance, navigation and control. J. Softw. Eng. Knowl. Eng. **6**(2), 201–227 (1996)
10. Enck, W., Ongtang, M., McDaniel, P.: Understanding Android security. IEEE Secur. Priv. **7**(1), 50–57 (2009)
11. Shabtai, A., Fledel, Y., Kanonov, U., Elovici, Y., Dolev, S., Glezer, C.: Google Android: a comprehensive security assessment. IEEE Secur. Priv. **8**(2), 35–44 (2010)
12. Google Inc.: Runtime—Android Developers (2015). http://developer.android.com/reference/java/lang/Runtime.html
13. TrendMicro Security Intelligence Blog: Android ransomware uses tor (2014). http://blog.trendmicro.com/trendlabs-security-intelligence/android-ransomware-uses-tor/
14. PCWorld: Cybercriminals are using the Tor network to control their botnets. (2013) http://www.pcworld.com/article/2045183/
15. Google Inc.: Google report Android security 2014 year in review (2014). https://static.googleusercontent.com/media/source.android.com/en/us/devices/tech/security/reports/Google_Android_Security_2014_Report_Final.pdf

16. BGR: This will be the most important (and possibly most overlooked) new android m feature (2015). http://bgr.com/2015/05/28/android-m-granular-permissions-controls/
17. Android Police: Android M will never ask users for permission to use the internet, and that's probably okay (2015) Published on the 06 June 2015 at www.androidpolice.com
18. Amalfitano, D., Fasolino, A.R., Tramontana, P., Carmine, S.D., Memon, A.M.: Using GUI ripping for automated testing of Android applications. In: [23], pp. 258–261. http://wpage.unina.it/ptramont/GUIRipperWiki.htm
19. Wontae Choi on Github: Swifthand (2015). https://github.com/wtchoi/swifthand
20. Arzt, S., Rasthofer, S., Fritz, C., Bodden, E., Bartel, A., Klein, J., Le Traon, Y., Octeau, D., McDaniel, P.: Flowdroid: precise context, flow, field, object-sensitive and lifecycle-aware taint analysis for Android apps. ACM SIGPLAN Not. **49**, 259–269 (2014). ACM
21. Fritz, C., Arzt, S., Rasthofer, S., Bodden, E., Bartel, A., Klein, J., Le Traon, Y., Octeau, D., McDaniel, P.: Highly precise taint analysis for Android applications. EC SPRIDE, TU Darmstadt, Technical report (2013)
22. Bodden, E., Hendren, L., Lam, P., Lhoták, O., Naeem, N.A.: Collaborative runtime verification with tracematches. In: Sokolsky, O., Taşıran, S. (eds.) RV 2007. LNCS, vol. 4839, pp. 22–37. Springer, Heidelberg (2007)
23. Goedicke, M., Menzies, T., Saeki, M. (eds.): IEEE/ACM International Conference on Automated Software Engineering, ASE 2012, Essen, Germany, 3–7 September. ACM (2012)

LearnLib Tutorial

An Open-Source Java Library for Active Automata Learning

Malte Isberner[1]([✉]), Bernhard Steffen[1], and Falk Howar[2]

[1] TU Dortmund University, Chair for Programming Systems,
44227 Dortmund, Germany
{malte.isberner,steffen}@cs.tu-dortmund.de
[2] IPSSE/TU Clausthal, 38678 Clausthal-zellerfeld, Germany
falk.howar@tu-clausthal.de

Abstract. Active automata learning is a promising technique to generate formal behavioral models of systems by experimentation. The practical applicability of active learning, however, is often hampered by the impossibility of realizing so-called *equivalence queries*, which are vital for ensuring progress during learning and finally resulting in correct models. This paper discusses the proposed approach of using *monitoring* as a means of generating counterexamples, explains in detail why virtually all existing learning algorithms are not suited for this approach, and gives an intuitive account of TTT, an algorithm designed to cope with counterexamples of extreme length. The essential steps and the impact of TTT are illustrated via experimentation with *LearnLib*, a free, open source Java library for active automata learning.

1 Introduction

Most systems in use today lack adequate specification or make use of under-specified or even unspecified components. In fact, the much propagated component-based software design style typically leads to under-specified systems, as most libraries only provide partial specifications of their components. Moreover, typically, revisions and last minute changes hardly enter the system specification. This hampers the application of any kind of formal validation techniques like model based testing or model checking. Active automata learning [2] has been proposed as a technique to apply model-based techniques in scenarios where models are unavailable, possibly incomplete, or erroneous [8,24].

Characteristic for active automata learning is its iterative alternation between a "testing" phase for completing the transitions relation of the model aggregated from the observed behavior, and an equivalence checking phase, which either signals success or provides a counterexample, i.e., a behavior that distinguishes the currently learned model from the system to be learned.

While implementing the testing phase is quite straightforward, the necessity of an equivalence checking phase poses a major hurdle for practical applications

© Springer International Publishing Switzerland 2015
E. Bartocci and R. Majumdar (Eds.): RV 2015, LNCS 9333, pp. 358–377, 2015.
DOI: 10.1007/978-3-319-23820-3_25

of active automata learning. Under certain assumptions, model-based conformance testing techniques may provide definite answers, or at least statistical guarantees. However, in the general case, every model inferred by a learning algorithm should always be treated as preliminary, that is, as a hypothesis which might turn out to be (partially) incorrect.

Thus, a truly robust learning-based solution must continuously validate the inferred models, and be able to detect errors and adapt to them by adequately refining the models to accommodate the observed diverging behavior. This particularly includes monitoring the regular operation of the system to be learned over extended periods of time. If, at some point, the behavior of the system is found to diverge from what was predicted by the model, the recorded trace up to that point constitutes a counterexample.

Compared to counterexamples generated through model-based conformance testing, counterexamples obtained through the above mechanism typically are several orders of magnitude longer. This poses a challenge for learning algorithms, as the length of counterexamples directly influences the overall complexity. The TTT algorithm [15] is the first algorithm to overcome this through its ability to extract the *essence* of a counterexample, i.e., analyzing it in such a way that the resulting impact on the internal data structures is the same as if an optimal (shortest) counterexample were processed.

In this tutorial we present the state of the art of practice-oriented, active automata learning by using *LearnLib* [16],[1] a free, open-source Java library for active automata learning, as a means to infer models of software systems. The open-source version of *LearnLib* is the result of 10 years of research and development: It is the result of a redesign and re-implementation of the closed source *LearnLib* [21,26], which has originally been designed to systematically build finite state machine models of unknown real world systems (telecommunication systems [8], web applications [25], communication protocols [1] etc.).

A decade of experience in the field led to the construction of a platform for experimentation with different learning algorithms as well as for statistically analyzing their characteristics in terms of learning effort, run time and memory consumption. More importantly, *LearnLib* provides a lot of infrastructure, enabling easy application in the domain of software systems.

For the sketched application scenario of generating counterexamples through monitoring, *LearnLib* is used to illustrate the practical impact of the way classical learning algorithms handle long counterexamples, as well as how the TTT algorithm's counterexample handling behaves differently. In the hands-on part of the tutorial, users can experiment with *LearnLib* to explore these effects, and will be instructed on how to use *LearnLib* in custom settings.[2]

Outline. Section 2 sketches the basics of active automata learning, before Sect. 3 discusses various realizations along a concrete example. Then, Sect. 4 describes

---

[1] http://www.learnlib.de.

[2] Supporting material for the hands-on session can be found at http://learnlib.de/rv2015.

the envisioned approach of *life-long learning*, where learning and monitoring are combined, and discusses why the presented learning algorithms are not suited for this scenario. Subsequently, Sect. 5, presents the TTT algorithm, which is particularly designed to overcome the previously identified deficiencies of other algorithms. The paper closes with a demonstration of how *LearnLib* can be used to explore the impact of long counterexamples on the data structures of the various algorithms in Sect. 6, and some conclusions and perspectives in Sect. 7.

Note: This paper is partially based on the supporting paper [12] for the *LearnLib* tutorial held at the ISoLA 2014 conference in Corfu, Greece, with an added emphasis on the application in a Runtime Verification context.

2   An Introduction to Active Automata Learning

We will start by introducing some basic notation and then give a rough sketch of active learning. Let Σ be a finite set of *input symbols* $a_1, \ldots, a_k$. Sequences of input symbols are called *words*. The empty word (of length zero) is denoted by ε. Words can be concatenated in the obvious way: we write uv (or sometimes also $u \cdot v$) when concatenating two words u and v. Finally, a *language* $\mathcal{L} \subseteq \Sigma^*$ is a set of words.

Definition 1 (Deterministic finite automaton). *A deterministic finite automaton (DFA) is a tuple* $\langle Q, q_0, \Sigma, \delta, F \rangle$, *where*

- *Q is the finite set of states,*
- $q_0 \in Q$ *is the dedicated initial state,*
- Σ *is the finite input alphabet,*
- $\delta : Q \times \Sigma \to Q$ *is the transition function, and*
- $F \subseteq Q$ *is the set of final states.*

We write $q \xrightarrow{a} q'$ *for* $\delta(q, a) = q'$ *and* $q \xRightarrow{w} q'$ *if for* $w = a_1 \cdots a_n$ *there is a sequence* $q = q^0, q^1, \ldots, q^n = q'$ *of states such that* $q^{i-1} \xrightarrow{a_i} q^i$ *for* $1 \leq i \leq n$.   □

A DFA $\mathcal{A}$ accepts the regular language $\mathcal{L}_\mathcal{A}$ of words that lead to final states on $\mathcal{A}$, i.e., $\mathcal{L}_\mathcal{A} = \left\{ w \in \Sigma^* \mid q_0 \xRightarrow{w} q, \text{ with } q \in F \right\}$.

For words over Σ, we can define their *residual (language)* wrt. $\mathcal{L}$, which is closely related to the well-known Nerode relation [22]: for a language $\mathcal{L}$ let the residual language of a word $u \in \Sigma^*$ wrt. $\mathcal{L}$, denoted by $u^{-1}\mathcal{L}$, be the set $\{v \in \Sigma^* \mid uv \in \mathcal{L}\}$.

Definition 2 (Nerode equivalence). *Two words* w, w' *from* Σ^* *are equivalent wrt.* $\mathcal{L}$, *denoted by* $w \equiv_\mathcal{L} w'$, *iff* $w^{-1}\mathcal{L} = w'^{-1}\mathcal{L}$.   □

By $[w]$ we denote the equivalence class of w in $\equiv_\mathcal{L}$. For regular languages (where $\equiv_\mathcal{L}$ has finite index), a DFA $\mathcal{A}_\mathcal{L}$ for $\mathcal{L}$ can be constructed from $\equiv_\mathcal{L}$ (cf. [10]): For each equivalence class $[w]$ of $\equiv_\mathcal{L}$, there is exactly one state $q_{[w]}$, with $q_{[\varepsilon]}$ being the initial one. Transitions are formed by one-letter extensions, i.e. $q_{[u]} \xrightarrow{a} q_{[ua]}$.

Finally, a state is accepting if $[u] \subseteq \mathcal{L}$ (if not, then $[u] \cap \mathcal{L} = \emptyset$, as either ε is in the residual or not). No DFA recognizing $\mathcal{L}$ can have less states than $\mathcal{A}_\mathcal{L}$, and since it is unique up to isomorphism, it is called the *canonical* DFA for $\mathcal{L}$. This construction and the Nerode relation are the conceptual backbone of active learning algorithms.

Active learning aims at inferring (unknown) regular languages. Many active learning algorithms are formulated in the MAT-learning model introduced by Angluin [2], which assumes the existence of a *Minimally Adequate Teacher* (MAT) answering two kinds of queries.

Membership queries test whether a word $w \in \Sigma^*$ is in the unknown language $\mathcal{L}$. These queries are employed for building hypothesis automata.

Equivalence queries test whether an intermediate hypothesis language $\mathcal{L}_\mathcal{H}$ equals $\mathcal{L}$. If so, an equivalence query signals success. Otherwise, it will return a *counterexample*, i.e., a word $w \in \Sigma^*$ from the symmetric difference of $\mathcal{L}_\mathcal{H}$ and $\mathcal{L}$.

The key idea of active learning algorithms, the most prominent example being Angluin's L* algorithm, is to approximate the Nerode congruence $\equiv_\mathcal{L}$ by some equivalence relation $\equiv_\mathcal{H}$ such that $\equiv_\mathcal{L}$ (not strictly) refines $\equiv_\mathcal{H}$. This approximation is achieved by identifying *prefixes* u, which serve as representatives of the classes of $\equiv_\mathcal{H}$, and *suffixes* v, which are used to prove inequalities of the respective residuals, separating classes. Throughout the course of the learning process, the sets of both prefixes and suffixes grow monotonically, allowing for an increasingly fine identification of representative prefixes.

Having identified (some) classes of $\equiv_\mathcal{L}$, a hypothesis $\mathcal{H}$ is constructed in a fashion resembling the construction of the canonical DFA (cf. [14] for a detailed account). Of course, some further constraints must be met in order to ensure a well-defined construction. For a more detailed description, also comprising the technical details of organizing prefixes, suffixes and the information gathered from membership queries, we refer the reader to [2] and [29].

As sketched above, $\mathcal{H}$ is subjected to an equivalence query, which either signals success (in which case learning terminates) or yields a counterexample. This counterexample serves as a witness that the approximation of $\equiv_\mathcal{L}$ is too coarse, triggering a refinement of $\equiv_\mathcal{H}$ (and thus $\mathcal{H}$). This alternation of *hypothesis construction* and *hypothesis validation* is repeated until an equivalence query finally signals success. Convergence is guaranteed as $\equiv_\mathcal{H}$ is refined with each equivalence query, but always remains a (non-strict) coarsening of $\equiv_\mathcal{L}$.

Practical Aspects of Active Automata Learning. In the above description, we followed Angluin's description of learning a regular language, represented by a DFA. For the practical case of learning reactive systems, however, Mealy machines [20] are a much better suited machine model, as they allow to directly model which outputs are produced by the system in reaction to inputs, instead of requiring to describe the I/O behavior of the system in the somewhat awkward terms of a (regular) language.

Luckily, translating the ideas of active DFA learning to the learning of Mealy machines is relatively straightforward (cf. [23, 28]), as the differences are mostly of merely technical nature. These technical differences, however, prolong and complicate the description of how learning algorithms work, which is why we will stick to the scenario of learning DFAs in the scope of this paper. An elaborate description on how the respective concepts can be transferred to the Mealy setting, and also on other aspects of the practical application of active automata learning, can be found in [29].

3   Realization: The L* Algorithm and Its Variants

In this section, we will briefly (and partially) discuss the ideas behind the seminal L* algorithm for active automata learning, as well as a number of suggested improvements to this algorithm that lead to better performance and thus an increased practicality.

3.1   Running Example

Figure 1 shows the smallest deterministic automaton for our running example: a language of all words over the alphabet $\{a, b\}$ with at least two a's and an odd number of b's.

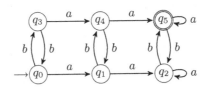

Fig. 1. Minimal acceptor for our running example.

3.2   Initial Approach: Observation Table à la Angluin

In her 1987 paper describing the L* algorithm, Angluin [2] introduced the *observation table* data structure as a means to realize the Nerode approximation as described in Sect. 2. Essentially, an observation table is a two dimensional array partitioned in an upper and a lower part, where the upper part is intended to model the states of a minimal acceptor, and the lower part models the transitions. Rows are labeled with reaching words (also called *access sequences* or *short prefixes*), and columns with distinguishing futures, i.e., words that are used to prove that the residual languages of two reaching words are different, or equivalently, that these reaching words cannot lead to the same state. The cell corresponding to a row labeled with $u \in \Sigma^*$ and a column labeled with $v \in \Sigma^*$ contains the outcome of the membership query for the word uv.

The contents of a row serve to identify the state reached by the corresponding prefix. The L* algorithm will organize the observation table in such a fashion that all states of a hypothesis are contained in the upper part of the table, i.e., the content vectors of the rows in the lower part must also occur in the upper part. This property is referred to as *closedness*. It is furthermore possible that several rows in the upper part of the table correspond to the same state, i.e., have the same contents. In this case, it is required that, for every input symbol $a \in \Sigma$, the rows for the corresponding transitions are equal as well, a property called *consistency*.

Counterexamples in the L* algorithm are handled by simply adding all prefixes of a counterexample $w \in \Sigma^*$ to the upper part of the table. This violates consistency, which then can be restored by adding an additional column with a new distinguishing future to the table. This is done in such a fashion that the set of distinguishing suffixes is always *suffix-closed*, while the set of all prefixes in the upper part of the table remains *prefix-closed*.

Two of the observation tables obtained when learning the running example (Fig. 1) using L* are shown in Fig. 2. The first one (Fig. 2, middle) is the initial one, whereas the second one (Fig. 2, right) is the final one, where the word *bbabbab* was used as the first and only counterexample.

The main weakness of this data structure is that it applies the distinguishing power of a certain distinguishing future similarly to all reaching words, without consideration of the structure of the system. First, however, we will discuss issues with the treatment of counterexamples described in the original L* algorithm, as well as ways to overcome them.

3.3   Improvement 1: Rivest and Schapire's Counterexample Analysis

The observation table depicted in the right of Fig. 2 contains a lot of redundancy: several rows in the upper part are completely identical. As a consequence, some of the states in the final hypothesis (Fig. 1) correspond to multiple prefixes. For example, the state q_0 is identified by both ε and bb. Each of these identifying prefixes requires k rows in the lower part of the table. The cells in all these rows at some point need to be filled by performing membership queries, resulting in an unnecessarily large number of queries.

The redundancy induced by having several rows corresponding to a single state can be eliminated by a change in the way how counterexamples are handled. Rivest and Schapire [27] presented a method that, instead of directly adding prefixes to the table and thus violating uniqueness of representatives (which leads to an inconsistency and in turn to a new column), directly adds a single *suffix* (i.e., column) to the observation table. As a result, the table is guaranteed to no longer be closed. Restoring the closedness property comprises moving rows from the lower to the upper part of the table, thus augmenting the set of states.

The suffix to be added can be found efficiently, using only $O(\log m)$ membership queries for a counterexample of length m. The original algorithm used a binary search for this task (cf. also [29]); however, other search strategies

	ε	a	ba	b	aa
ε	0	0	0	0	0
bb	0	0	0	0	0
bba	0	0	1	0	0
$bbab$	0	1	0	0	1
$bbabb$	0	0	1	0	0
$bbabba$	0	0	1	1	0
$bbabbab$	1	1	0	0	1
b	0	0	0	0	1
a	0	0	1	0	0
ba	0	1	0	0	1
bbb	0	0	0	0	1
$bbaa$	0	0	1	1	0
$bbaba$	1	1	0	0	1
$bbabbb$	0	1	0	0	1
$bbabbaa$	0	0	1	1	0
$bbabbaba$	1	1	0	0	1
$bbabbabb$	0	0	1	1	0

Fig. 2. Initial 1-state hypothesis, corresponding observation table, and observation table for final hypothesis after processing counterexample $w = bbabbab$.

might perform significantly better on long counterexamples, while maintaining the worst-case complexity [17].

Using this strategy, rows are only ever moved to the upper part of the table because they represent a previously undiscovered state: otherwise, they would not cause an unclosedness. This in turn means that all upper rows refer to distinct states in the hypothesis, i.e., identifying prefixes are unique!

An important observation is that the prefix-closedness property of the short prefix set is maintained. Along with the aforementioned uniqueness property, the short prefixes now induce a *spanning tree* on the hypothesis. The corresponding "tree" transitions are shown in bold in Fig. 3 (right). The remaining, "non-tree" transitions correspond to the long prefixes.

A Side-Effect: Instable Hypotheses. While the set of short prefixes remains prefix-closed, the suffix-closedness of the set of distinguishing futures is no longer preserved. This does not hurt the correctness of the algorithm, as suffix-closedness of the discriminator set is not mandatory for realizing the Nerode approximation described in Sect. 2. However, there is a curious side effect: in spite of a closed observation table, the hypothesis might no longer be consistent with the observations stored in this table. In fact, it might not even be canonical, as the example of a closed observation table and non-canonical hypothesis displayed in Fig. 4 shows. There, the second hypothesis still accepts the empty language $\emptyset$, which is also the language accepted by the first hypothesis (cf. Fig. 2).

	ε	bbab	bab	b	aba
ε	0	0	0	0	1
a	0	1	0	0	1
ab	0	0	1	0	0
aba	1	0	1	0	0
aa	0	1	0	1	1
b	0	0	0	0	0
aab	1	0	1	0	0
$abab$	0	1	0	1	1
abb	0	1	0	1	1
$abaa$	1	0	1	0	0
aaa	0	1	0	1	1
ba	0	0	1	0	0
bb	0	0	0	0	1

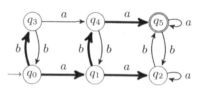

Fig. 3. Observation table obtained using Rivest & Schapire's counterexample analysis method.

Luckily, there is a simple remedy: for each cell in the observation table, we check if its contents match the output predicted by the hypothesis. If this is not the case, we have another counterexample which can be treated in the same fashion as above. Concerns have been voiced that this might lead to an infinite loop, as in some cases neither the counterexample nor the language accepted by the hypothesis changes. However, this is not the case: the counterexample analysis is based on transforming prefixes of the counterexample to access sequences in the hypothesis. Progress is then ensured by the growth of the state and thus access sequence set.

Following [14], we refer to hypotheses that do not predict the observation table contents correctly as *instable* hypotheses. This is due to the fact that they themselves form a source of counterexamples (in conjunction with the underlying data structure), triggering their own refinement without the need for an "external" equivalence query.

3.4   Improvement 2: Discrimination Trees

Rivest&Schapire's counterexample analysis method ensures that the number of both rows and columns is bounded by kn and n, respectively. As every cell in the observation table is filled by performing a membership query, in total $O(kn^2)$ queries are required for constructing the table (which is asymptotically optimal [3]), plus another $O(n \log m)$ for counterexample analysis (m being the length of the longest counterexample). This constitutes a major improvement over the original L* algorithm, where the number of rows can be as large as knm, resulting in a query complexity of $O(kmn^2)$.

We can also conclude that the *minimum* number of columns is $\lceil \log_2 n \rceil$, as c columns allow distinguishing 2^c states. However, this is a rather hypothetical

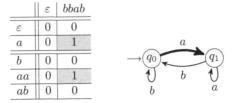

	ε	$bbab$
ε	0	0
a	0	1
b	0	0
aa	0	1
ab	0	0

Fig. 4. Intermediate (closed) observation table and corresponding non-canonical hypothesis during Rivest&Schapire's algorithm. The highlighted cells induce the counterexamples $a \cdot bbab$ and $aa \cdot bbab$ wrt. to the hypothesis, which accepts the empty language $\emptyset$.

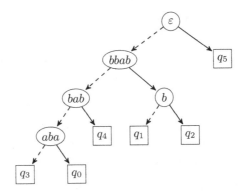

Fig. 5. Discrimination tree for final hypothesis, obtained using the Observation Pack algorithm.

case: the obtained suffixes will usually not be that "informative". In the example above (cf. Fig. 3), in fact 5 suffixes are required to distinguish 6 states, even though theoretically, 3 could suffice ($2^3 = 8 \geq 6$).

How does this affect the learning process? To answer this question, let us take a closer look of what happens when we add new rows to the observation table after moving a row from the lower to the upper part of the table (i.e., after fixing an unclosedness). The process of filling these new rows with data values through membership queries has the goal of determining the target state of the respective transition.

The contents of row $abaa$ can be represented as the 5-dimensional bit vector $1, 0, 1, 0, 0$. However, the first value alone is enough to rule out any other existing state except for q_5! Determining the values for all cells in this row thus is not necessary to accomplish our stated goal of finding the successor state.

The data structure of a *discrimination tree*, introduced into the context of active automata learning by Kearns&Vazirani [19], allows for a more fine-grained classification scheme for distinguishing between states. An example for such a discrimination tree is shown in Fig. 5. Leaves in this tree are labeled with states of the hypothesis, while inner nodes are labeled with discriminators. Each inner node has two children, the 0-child (dashed line) and the 1-child (solid line). The semantics of a discrimination tree is best explained in terms of the "sifting" operation: given a prefix $u \in \Sigma^*$, at each inner node labeled with a discriminator v a membership query for $u \cdot v$ is posed. Depending on the outcome of this query (0 or 1), we move on to the respective child of the inner node. This process is repeated until a leaf is reached, which forms the result of the sifting operation. Each state labels the leaf in the discrimination tree which is the outcome of sifting its access sequence into the tree.

For each distinct pair of states, there is exactly one *lowest common ancestor* (LCA) in the discrimination tree. The label of the LCA is sufficient evidence for separating the two states, as it proves them to be Nerode-inequivalent. Discrimination trees are thus redundancy-free in the sense that *exactly one* such separator is maintained for every distinct pair of states. In an observation table, in contrast, the number of discriminators to distinguish any pair of two states is always fixed, regardless of "how different" the states are: state q_5, for example, is very different from the other states due to its being accepting. This is the reason why only a single discriminator is enough to distinguish it from any other state.

The discrimination tree in Fig. 5 was obtained through the Observation Pack [11] algorithm, which builds upon Rivest&Schapire's algorithm, but replaces the observation table with a discrimination tree. As such, it is not surprising that the overall set of discriminators is the same as that in Fig. 3 (left). Also, the short prefixes (access sequences), along with the spanning tree structure (Fig. 3, right), remains the same.

4   Life-Long Learning

In the previous sections, we have described how the L* and other active learning algorithms construct hypotheses by means of membership queries, and how these hypotheses are refined using counterexamples. The question of how such counterexamples are obtained was deliberately left open. In fact, the problem of generating counterexamples poses a major hurdle for the practical application of automata learning. The so-called *equivalence query* was an abstraction introduced by Angluin with the purpose of allowing a complete and correct algorithm to solve the problem of identifying a regular language to be formulated. Clearly, however, determining whether an inferred DFA recognizes the exact target language requires precise knowledge of the target language itself, the lack of which is the very reason that learning is employed in the first place.

It has commonly been suggested (e.g., in [4]) to resort to model-based conformance testing techniques (such as the W-method [7]), some of which may guarantee that a counterexample is always found if some assumptions about the target system (e.g., about its state count) hold. In other cases, random sampling [2,6] may provide stochastic guarantees about the correctness of the inferred model.

In any case, there can never be absolute certainty that a model inferred by a learning algorithm is final. Instead, it should always be treated as a preliminary hypotheses, which at some (possibly much later) point may be proven to inadequately describe some aspects of the system's behavior. Thus, a truly robust application of automata learning should continuously monitor the system's execution and validate the model against these observations.

4.1   Learning and Monitoring in the Connect Project

The aim of the CONNECT project[3] [18] was to automatically synthesize mediators between networked systems, to enable interoperability in environments consisting of heterogeneous components, that, for instance, rely on incompatible communication protocols. Among other things, connector synthesis requires formal models of the systems to be connected.

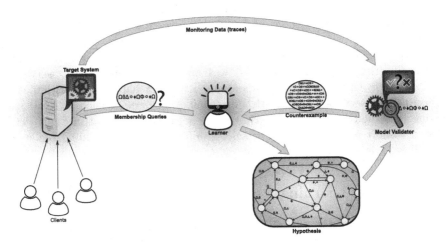

Fig. 6. A setup with continuous learning and monitoring [15]

In the CONNECT architecture, *LearnLib* is used to infer these models of the networked systems. The fact that learned models may be incorrect is addressed by the integration of a monitoring subsystem, which monitors the execution of the synthesized connectors and is thus able to detect divergences between the actual behavior of a networked system and its inferred model. The idea of this *continuous validation*, or *life-long learning* approach, which has been proposed in [5], is sketched in Fig. 6: a *Learner* infers a model of a *Target System* using membership queries. The system is instrumented to report its execution traces during actual deployment to a *Model Validator*, which checks the observed traces for compliance with the inferred model, i.e., the most recent *Hypothesis*. If diverging behavior is observed, a *Counterexample* is reported to the *Learner*, which in a refinement step poses further membership queries to the *Target System*,

---

[3] http://www.connect-forever.eu.

resulting in an updated *Hypothesis*. This next *Hypothesis* is then used by the *Model Validator* for checking future traces, resulting in a feedback loop between the learning and monitoring subsystems.

4.2 The Problem of Long Counterexamples

Compared to counterexamples generated through model-based or random testing, execution traces recorded by a monitor might be several orders of magnitudes longer. This poses a major problem for active learning algorithms, due to the way in which counterexamples are handled (cf. Sect. 3).

In the L* algorithm, all prefixes of a counterexample are added to the upper part of the table. Thus, if m is the length of a counterexample, this results in km additional rows being added to the table. In the Observation Pack algorithm, which replaces the observation table with a discrimination tree, the size of the discrimination tree always remains linear. However, the length of the suffixes that label the inner nodes of the tree, may become as long as $m - 1$. Since the time required for performing a membership query can be assumed to be linear in its length,[4] long counterexamples may still render learning infeasible. This is further aggravated by the fact that the internal data structures in both cases grow monotonically, i.e., once an excessively long prefix or suffix (or a large number of them) has been added, it will linger and may cause severe performance degradation in *every* future refinement step.

It should be noted that this paper does not give a comprehensive overview about all counterexample handling strategies for active learning algorithms that have been suggested. Some heuristics, like SUFFIX1BY1 [13], may often perform well in practice. However, it is always possible to construct cases where effects similar to the ones described above manifest themselves. The aim should thus be to come up with a robust approach that works decently in all cases.

5 The TTT Algorithm

Looking at the discrimination tree in Fig. 5, one notices that even in this case the discriminators are rather long: while no distinguishing suffix in the observation table in Fig. 2 has a length greater than 2, the longest discriminator in the discrimination tree has length 4. As noted above, discriminators are derived as suffixes of former counterexamples, thus their length is bounded by $m - 1$. Moreover, as the introduction of new transitions in the hypothesis requires sifting through the whole tree, this means that an unfavorably long counterexample

---

[4] Classically, the performance of learning algorithms is measured in terms of the number of queries they pose. This is justified as long as most queries are of rather uniform length, especially since the *reset* that must occur between two queries often takes a significant amount of time. However, especially when learning systems such as web-services, executing every single symbol of a query takes considerable time (due to latency), which is why a realistic performance must take into account the overall number of *symbols* as well.

obtained in one hypothesis validation round can affect the lengths of membership queries in *all* subsequent hypothesis construction phases. The result is the above-mentioned performance degradation due to the fact that membership queries keep getting longer.

5.1   The Big Picture

The TTT algorithm [15] addresses this problem by ensuring that the length of every discriminator in the tree is bounded by n. It does so by re-establishing the suffix-closedness property of the discriminator set. This enables a very compact representation of this set, which can then be stored as a *trie*: a root-directed tree in which each node corresponds to a word, which can be obtained by con-catenating the symbols on the path to the root.

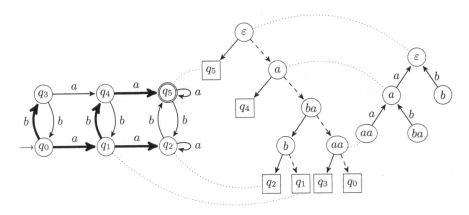

Fig. 7. The three tree-based data structures of TTT: the spanning tree-based hypoth-esis, the discrimination tree, and the suffix trie. A subset of the connection between the data structures is represented using dotted lines.

An instance of such a trie can be seen in the right of Fig. 7, corresponding to the discriminator set $\{\varepsilon, a, ba, b, aa\}$. Note that this discriminator set is the same as that of the classic L* algorithm (cf. Fig. 2).

Figure 7 moreover shows an exemplary view on TTT's data structures, which also explain its name: on the left is the transition graph of the hypothesis, which is constructed around the *spanning tree* (highlighted transitions). Each state in this graph corresponds to a leaf in the *discrimination tree* (middle). The discriminators labeling inner nodes in this tree are then stored in the mentioned *suffix trie*, such that each inner node of the discrimination tree corresponds to a node in the suffix trie.

The redundancy-freeness of this setup is underlined by the fact that the overall space requirement is asymptotically the same as that of the transition graph alone, $O(kn)$. The short-prefix set Sp can be obtained from the spanning tree, and the discriminators can be obtained from the suffix trie. Moreover, the number of nodes in each of the trees is bounded by $2n$.

5.2   Background: Discriminator Finalization

The TTT algorithm is very similar to the Observation Pack algorithm [11], but extends it by one key step: *discriminator finalization*. This step ensures that every discriminator occurring at an inner node is a suffix of another discriminator, which allows it to be stored in the suffix trie.

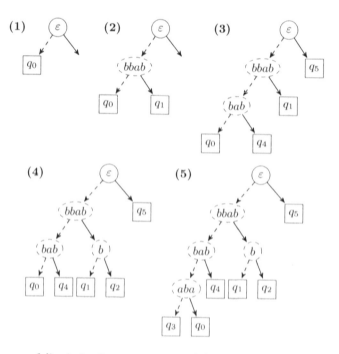

Fig. 8. Sequence of discrimination trees generated during hypothesis stabilization. The dashed inner nodes are temporary, and will be finalized in a later step.

The process of obtaining such discriminators by prepending a single symbol to existing discriminators is closely related to the process of *minimization* (cf. [9]). For the technical details, we refer the reader to [15] and focus on the "visible" effect on the internal data structures.

As remarked in Sect. 3, intermediate (instable) hypotheses might be non-canonical. In these cases, there are pairs of state for which no discriminator can be obtained from the hypothesis, as they might be equivalent. This calls for fully stabilizing the hypothesis first, before discriminators can be finalized. During stabilization, the discrimination tree grows (cf. Fig. 8), but the newly inserted inner nodes are marked as *temporary* (dashed outline). These temporary

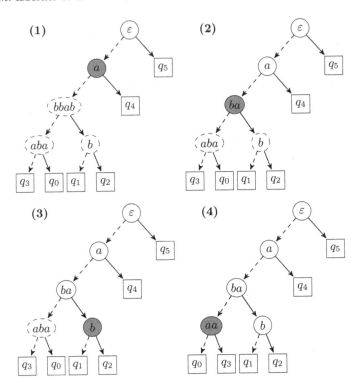

Fig. 9. Sequence of discrimination trees generated during discriminator finalization. The gray node is the inner node with the most recently finalized discriminator.

discriminators are then *finalized* in a second step, which is illustrated in Fig. 9. In each of the finalization steps, a temporary discriminator is replaced by a new, final one, which is backed by the hypothesis.

Considering the last discrimination tree shown in Fig. 8(5), only the root (which is always ε) is final. Hence, any new final discriminator has to consist of a single symbol (prepended to the empty word). The leaves in the left ("false") subtree are q_0 through q_4. Looking at the hypothesis (Fig. 3, right), this set of nodes can be partitioned by the discriminators a or b, of which the former is chosen (Fig. 9(1)). Note that the new, final discriminator is always placed above *all* temporary discriminators, ensuring that all descendant inner nodes of a temporary inner node are also temporary. Also note that the structure of the discrimination tree can change, as is the case here, causing the maximum depth to increase by one. However, experiments have shown that the step of discriminator finalization often *decreases* the average tree depth, leading to not only shorter but also *fewer* membership queries [15].

The remainder of Fig. 8 shows the discrimination trees that occur in the course of complete finalization, and terminates with a discrimination tree where all discriminators are final (and the set of all discriminators is suffix closed).

Note that in this example, the topology (i.e., the structure) of the tree remains unchanged. This, however, is not generally the case, as final discriminators may partition the set of states in different ways than the temporary discriminators they replace.

6   Experimentation with *LearnLib*

As the name suggests, *LearnLib* [16] is primarily a library that can be used programmatically via its API. The use of this API to learn custom systems will be the subject of the hands-on part of the tutorial. Additionally, *Learn-Lib* also provides visualization capabilities that facilitate the understanding of learning algorithms. This section demonstrates how the *LearnVIZ* tool shipped with *LearnLib* can be used to directly and intuitively visualize the impact of long counterexamples, and thus foster an improved understanding of the role of counterexample analysis, and the differences between algorithms such as L* and TTT.

6.1   The L* Algorithm

In a first step, the L* algorithm (cf. Sect. 3) is applied to the target system introduced as the running example (Fig. 1). *LearnVIZ* is run in interactive mode, which means that the user manually needs to supply counterexamples (there is also a non-interactive mode, where counterexamples are automatically generated). Automata are rendered using the *GraphVIZ* dot tool[5] and displayed in a browser, which enables the user to easily jump back to previous intermediate steps.

The L* algorithm starts with an initial one-state hypothesis (Fig. 10a), constructed from an observation table. The user is prompted to enter a counterexample, which in the illustrated case is *bbabbab*. This results in several new rows being added to the observation table. The updated observation table, as well as the new intermediate hypothesis (which is not yet the final one) are then displayed, along with the new queries that have been asked in the completed round (Fig. 10b).

6.2   The TTT Algorithm

The TTT algorithm (cf. Sect. 5) was designed to mitigate the effects of excessively long counterexamples. In particular, it ensures that at the end of each intermediate steps, the length of all suffixes is linearly bounded. Furthermore, it replaces the observation table data structure with a binary decision tree (called discrimination tree).

The TTT algorithm analyzes counterexamples (here, we use the same counterexample as before, namely $w = bbabbab$) by applying prefix transformations

---

[5] http://www.graphviz.org/.

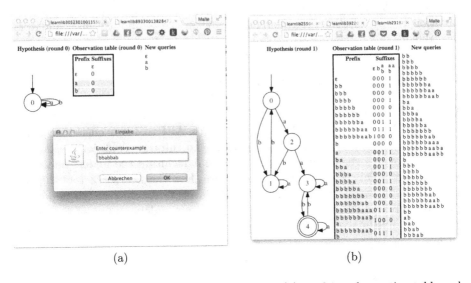

Fig. 10. (a) Prompt for entering a counterexample; (b) resulting observation table and hypothesis

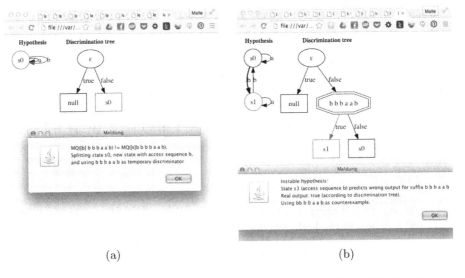

Fig. 11. (a) First counterexample analysis in the TTT algorithm; (b) detection of instable hypothesis

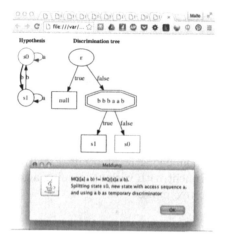

Fig. 12. Counterexample analysis step resulting from an instable hypothesis

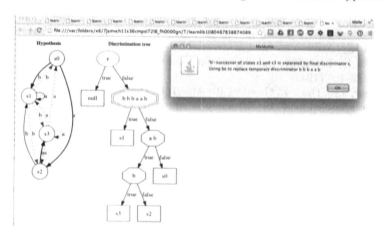

Fig. 13. Finalization step in the TTT algorithm

(Fig. 11a). The hypothesis resulting from the first step, however, contradicts the observations stored in the discrimination tree (Fig. 11b). This situation is referred to as an *instable hypothesis*. Furthermore, while the discrimination tree contains long suffixes (*bbbaab* in this case), these are marked as temporary (octagon shape) and will be replaced later.

An instable hypothesis gives rise to a new counterexample, which TTT handles in the ordinary fashion (Fig. 12). After a few more iterations of counterexample analysis and hypothesis stabilization, the (long) suffix *bbbaab* can be *finalized* (Fig. 13), replacing it with a shorter suffix (*b*). Message boxes inform the user about the progress in detail, and colored nodes in the data structure draw the attention to the important and changing parts.

7 Conclusions

In this paper and the accompanying tutorial we reviewed active automata learning and its combination with monitoring. After providing the theoretic foundations, we discussed how the length of counterexamples affects the behavior and performance of classical learning algorithm. We then analyzed how the TTT algorithm handles counterexamples, and how it remedies the problems we identified in the other algorithms. The optimization of its internal data structures qualifies TTT, above all other algorithms, to be employed in a setting where counterexamples of astronomic length can occur. Finally, we showed how *Learn-Lib* can be used to experiment with various learning algorithms, and to explore the impact of long counterexamples.

References

1. Aarts, F., Jonsson, B., Uijen, J.: Generating models of infinite-state communication protocols using regular inference with abstraction. In: Petrenko, A., Simão, A., Maldonado, J.C. (eds.) ICTSS 2010. LNCS, vol. 6435, pp. 188–204. Springer, Heidelberg (2010)
2. Angluin, D.: Learning regular sets from queries and counterexamples. Inf. Comput. **75**(2), 87–106 (1987)
3. Balcázar, J.L., Díaz, J., Gavaldà, R.: Algorithms for learning finite automata from queries: a unified view. In: Advances in Algorithms, Languages, and Complexity, pp. 53–72 (1997)
4. Berg, T., Grinchtein, O., Jonsson, B., Leucker, M., Raffelt, H., Steffen, B.: On the correspondence between conformance testing and regular inference. In: Cerioli, M. (ed.) FASE 2005. LNCS, vol. 3442, pp. 175–189. Springer, Heidelberg (2005)
5. Bertolino, A., Calabrò, A., Merten, M., Steffen, B.: Never-stop learning: continuous validation of learned models for evolving systems through monitoring. ERCIM News 2012(88) (2012)
6. Cho, C.Y., Babić, D., Shin, R., Song, D.: Inference and analysis of formal models of botnet command and control protocols. In: Proceedings of the CCS 2010, pp. 426–440. ACM, Chicago (2010)
7. Chow, T.S.: Testing software design modeled by finite-state machines. IEEE Trans. Softw. Eng. **4**(3), 178–187 (1978)
8. Hagerer, A., Hungar, H.: Model generation by moderated regular extrapolation. In: Kutsche, R.-D., Weber, H. (eds.) FASE 2002. LNCS, vol. 2306, pp. 80–95. Springer, Heidelberg (2002)
9. Hopcroft, J.E.: An $n \log n$ algorithm for minimizing states in a finite automaton. Technical report, Stanford, CA, USA (1971)
10. Hopcroft, J.E., Motwani, R., Ullman, J.D.: Introduction to Automata Theory, Languages, and Computation. Addison-Wesley series in computer science, 2nd edn. Addison-Wesley-Longman, Reading (2001)
11. Howar, F.: Active learning of interface programs. Ph.D. thesis, TU Dortmund University (2012). http://dx.doi.org/2003/29486
12. Howar, F., Isberner, M., Steffen, B.: Tutorial: automata learning in practice. In: Margaria, T., Steffen, B. (eds.) ISoLA 2014, Part I. LNCS, vol. 8802, pp. 499–513. Springer, Heidelberg (2014)

13. Irfan, M.N.: Analysis and optimization of software model inference algorithms. Ph.D. thesis, Université de Grenoble, Grenoble, France, September 2012
14. Isberner, M., Howar, F., Steffen, B.: Learning register automata: from languages to program structures. Mach. Learn. **96**(1–2), 65–98 (2014). http://dx.doi.org/10.1007/s10994-013-5419-7
15. Isberner, M., Howar, F., Steffen, B.: The TTT algorithm: a redundancy-free approach to active automata learning. In: Bonakdarpour, B., Smolka, S.A. (eds.) RV 2014. LNCS, vol. 8734, pp. 307–322. Springer, Heidelberg (2014)
16. Isberner, M., Howar, F., Steffen, B.: The open-source LearnLib. In: Kroening, D., Păsăreanu, C.S. (eds.) CAV 2015. LNCS, vol. 9206, pp. 487–495. Springer, Heidelberg (2015)
17. Isberner, M., Steffen, B.: An abstract framework for counterexample analysis in active automata learning. In: Clark, A., Kanazawa, M., Yoshinaka, R. (eds.) Proceedings of the ICGI 2014. JMLR W&CP, vol. 34, pp. 79–93 (2014)
18. Issarny, V., Steffen, B., Jonsson, B., Blair, G.S., Grace, P., Kwiatkowska, M.Z., Calinescu, R., Inverardi, P., Tivoli, M., Bertolino, A., Sabetta, A.: CONNECT challenges: towards emergent connectors for eternal networked systems. In: ICECCS, pp. 154–161 (2009)
19. Kearns, M.J., Vazirani, U.V.: An Introduction to Computational Learning Theory. MIT Press, Cambridge (1994)
20. Mealy, G.H.: A method for synthesizing sequential circuits. Bell Syst. Tech. J. **34**(5), 1045–1079 (1955)
21. Merten, M., Steffen, B., Howar, F., Margaria, T.: Next generation LearnLib. In: Abdulla, P.A., Leino, K.R.M. (eds.) TACAS 2011. LNCS, vol. 6605, pp. 220–223. Springer, Heidelberg (2011)
22. Nerode, A.: Linear automaton transformations. Proc. Am. Math. Soc. **9**(4), 541–544 (1958)
23. Niese, O.: An integrated approach to testing complex systems. Ph.D. thesis, University of Dortmund, Germany (2003)
24. Peled, D., Vardi, M.Y., Yannakakis, M.: Black box checking. In: Wu, J., Chanson, S.T., Gao, Q. (eds.) Proceedings of the FORTE 1999, pp. 225–240. Kluwer Academic (1999)
25. Raffelt, H., Merten, M., Steffen, B., Margaria, T.: Dynamic testing via automata learning. Int. J. Softw. Tools Technol. Transf. **11**(4), 307–324 (2009)
26. Raffelt, H., Steffen, B., Berg, T., Margaria, T.: LearnLib: a framework for extrapolating behavioral models. Int. J. Softw. Tools Technol. Transf. **11**(5), 393–407 (2009)
27. Rivest, R.L., Schapire, R.E.: Inference of finite futomata using homing sequences. Inf. Comput. **103**(2), 299–347 (1993)
28. Shahbaz, M., Groz, R.: Inferring mealy machines. In: Cavalcanti, A., Dams, D.R. (eds.) FM 2009. LNCS, vol. 5850, pp. 207–222. Springer, Heidelberg (2009)
29. Steffen, B., Howar, F., Merten, M.: Introduction to active automata learning from a practical perspective. In: Bernardo, M., Issarny, V. (eds.) SFM 2011. LNCS, vol. 6659, pp. 256–296. Springer, Heidelberg (2011)

Monitoring and Measuring Hybrid Behaviors
A Tutorial

Dejan Ničković[✉]

AIT Austrian Institute of Technology GmbH, Vienna, Austria
dejan.nickovic@ait.ac.at

Abstract. Continuous and hybrid behaviors naturally arise from many dynamical systems. In this tutorial, we present state-of-the-art techniques for qualitative and quantitative reasoning about such behaviors. We introduce Signal Temporal Logic and Timed Regular Expressions as specification languages that we use to describe properties of hybrid systems. We then provide an overview of methods for (1) checking whether a hybrid behavior is correct and robust with respect to its specification; and (2) measuring of quantitative characteristics of a hybrid system by property-driven extraction of relevant data from its behaviors. We present the tools that support such analysis and discuss their application in several application domains.

1 Introduction

Complex systems evolve in time and generate behaviors which are progressions of state observations. For continuous and hybrid systems, such observations are typically real-valued quantities that evolve in real time. We typically evaluate the system's correctness, efficiency and robustness according to the properties of these behaviors. We can, for example, require or forbid sequences of events that follow a certain pattern. We can also measure some quantitative properties of the behavior such as temporal distance between events, or the sum of the values of some state variable in a temporal window.

We use the term monitoring technology for the collection of techniques for specifying what we want to detect and measure and how to extract the information from the behaviors. Monitoring can be applied to real systems during their execution, for example, monitoring a chemical or a nuclear process, where the behaviors are constructed from sensor readings. In this case the monitoring procedure can give real time alerts about a potential deviation of the system from normal behaviors and even take some corrective action. Monitoring can also be applied during the (model-based) design process of the systems where behaviors correspond to simulation traces. In this context, monitoring can be viewed as part of the verification and validation process, a lightweight form of formal verification which gives up the complete coverage associated with verification, but still uses a clean declarative specification language to classify behaviors. Monitoring as verification has been practiced in the development of digital circuits (assertion checking, dynamics verification) and software (testing, runtime

© Springer International Publishing Switzerland 2015
E. Bartocci and R. Majumdar (Eds.): RV 2015, LNCS 9333, pp. 378–402, 2015.
DOI: 10.1007/978-3-319-23820-3_26

verification). This tutorial explains how these techniques are adapted to timed, continuous and hybrid behaviors.

Major classes of complex systems that produce continuous and hybrid behaviors are control systems such as in avionics, automotive or military applications, analog and mixed signal (AMS) circuits, but also biological and medical processes. The first two examples correspond to engineered systems, their design is heavily supported by simulation tools and there are traditional and sub-domain-specific ways to evaluate behavior. Property-based monitoring of continuous and hybrid behaviors has been subject to vivid research in the recent years, and we provide a survey of the latest results in this tutorial. In particular, we focus on the following specification formalisms:

1. Signal Temporal Logic (STL) which extends the established specification language Llinear-time Temporal Logic (LTL) used in discrete verification, towards dense time and continuous values. We show how monitoring real-valued signals against STL specification works;
2. Timed Regular Expressions (TRE) which allows one to express properties of Boolean signals and sequences of time-stamped events. We describe a recent algorithm for (two-sided) pattern matching for these expression;
3. Finally, we describe a new declarative measurement language where a special class of regular expressions is used to define temporal intervals where measures are to be taken.

We present the tools that support monitoring of such specifications and provide an overview of some applications from several domains in which these techniques were used. We show several extensions of the formalisms presented in the tutorial and discuss which features we believe are still missing in order to have a wider industrial adoption of this technology.

2 Specification Languages for Hybrid Behaviors

In this section, we study the desired features for specification languages that target description of common hybrid systems properties. We mainly focus on the system-level view where properties of interest are temporal patterns occurring in the transient behavior of the system. Consequently, specification languages for this class of continuous and hybrid behavior requirements shall have the following properties:

1. Allow reference to real-valued variables, for instance via numerical predicates;
2. Provide operators for describing events as real-valued patterns with shapes and durations; and
3. Facilitate expressing timing constraints between such events.

The choice of the right specification language for hybrid systems also depends on the type of analysis we want to make:

1. Checking the correctness and/or robustness of continuous and hybrid behaviors with respect to their specification; or

2. Measuring the quantitative properties of hybrid systems by extracting and processing relevant data from their executions.

Finally, the facility of specifying properties by experts from a specific application domain that are not trained in formal methods is another aspect that is crucial in successful exportation of formal methods to real applications. It is important that the end user of the technology adopts the specification language and is able to use it without excessive training - in the failing case the impact of the underlying technology remains limited to the small community of formal methods research.

Example 1. We illustrate some common system-level hybrid requirements on the Distributed Systems Interface (DSI3) example from the automotive application domain. DSI3 is a flexible and powerful bus standard [29] developed by the automotive industry. It is designed to interconnect multiple remote sensor and actuator devices to a digital controller and allow them to communicate according to a well-defined protocol. The controller interacts with the sensor devices through the *voltage* and *current lines*.

DSI3 protocol consists of multiple modes that are activated sequentially. We focus on its initialization phase that is called *discovery mode*. In the discovery mode, prior to any interaction the power is turned on, resulting in a voltage ramp from 0V to V_{high}. The communication is initiated by the controller that probes the presence or absence of sensors by emitting analog pulses on the voltage line. Connected sensor devices respond in turn with another pulse sent over the current line. At the end of this interaction, a final short pulse is sent to the sensors interfaces, marking the end of the discovery mode. Figure 1 illustrates the behavior of a system with a single connected sensor device in the DSI3 discovery mode.

In this example, we focus on the requirements relating the expected time between consecutive discovery pulses. In order to characterize a discovery pulse, we first define three regions of interest – when the voltage v is (1) below V_{low}; (2) between V_{low} and V_{high}; and (3) above V_{high}. We denote these regions of interest by v_l, v_b and v_h, respectively. Next, we describe the shape of a discovery pulse. Such a pulse starts at the moment when the signal v moves from v_h to v_b. The signal then must go into v_l, v_b and finally come back to v_h. In addition to its

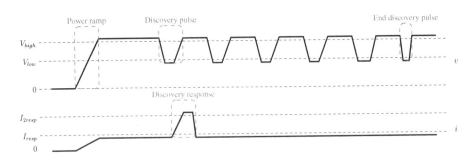

Fig. 1. DSI3 discovery mode overview.

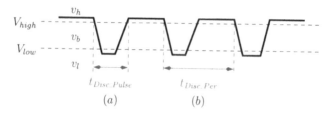

V_{high}
v_h
v_b
V_{low}
v_l
t_{Disc_Pulse}
t_{Disc_Per}
(a)   (b)

Fig. 2. DSI3 discovery mode: (a) discovery pulse; and (b) timing between two consecutive pulses.

shape, the DSI3 specification requires the discovery pulse to have a duration of t_{Disc_Pulse} μs (see Fig. 2 (a)). This timing requirement allows distinguishing a discovery pulse from other pulses, such as the end-of-discovery pulse which has the same shape but a shorter duration. Finally, the DSI3 standard bus states that the distance between two consecutive discovery pulses shall be t_{Disc_per} μs (see Table 6-2 in [29] and Fig. 2 (b)).

We now formulate several questions regarding the features of the specification languages that we want to have:

Q1: Can we precisely describe the discovery pulse pattern?
Q2: Can we precisely express the property regarding the timing of consecutive discovery pulses?
Q3: Can we measure quantitative aspects of the property such as the average distance between consecutive pulses?
Q4: How difficult is it to express the above properties?

3 Signal Temporal Logic and Timed Regular Expressions

We present in this section two specification languages for hybrid systems: Signal Temporal Logic [33,34] and Timed Regular Expressions (TRE) [4,5] and we study for them the questions raised in Sect. 2. We first introduce STL with qualitative semantics, and then show how the language is extended with the quantitative semantics in order to reason about robustness properties. We then introduce a variant of TRE and finally present a simple measurement specification language built on top of TRE that allows to reason about quantitative properties of the system. This section focuses on specifying behaviors of hybrid systems - we defer our discussion on how to effectively monitor and measure such behaviors to Sect. 4.

3.1 Signal Temporal Logic with Qualitative Semantics

Signal Temporal Logic is a formal language for specifying real-time properties of continuous and hybrid behaviors. It is interpreted over continuous (dense) time and extends Metric Temporal Logic (MTL) [31] with numerical predicates over real-valued variables. This specification language enables expressing complex timing relations between digital and real-valued events in hybrid behaviors.

Similarly to other temporal logic, the semantics of STL is defined in terms of a satisfaction relation which determines whether a behavior satisfies a formula at any given point in time. The logic is closed under all boolean operations.

These properties of the language make STL a suitable candidate for specifications aimed at monitoring hybrid behaviors. Firstly, the satisfaction relation of the language provides the information about the satisfaction (and violation) of the property (but also all of its sub-formulas) at any point in time. In addition, the presence of the negation enables combining existential and universal quantification over time. It follows that in STL one can easily express the requirement that something must *always* hold as well as that it must happen *at least once*. We now formally define the syntax of STL and its qualitative (correctness) semantics.

Let X and P be sets of *real* and *propositional* variables and $w : \mathbb{T} \to \mathbb{R}^m \times \mathbb{B}^n$ a multi-dimensional signal (behavior), where $\mathbb{T} = [0, d)$ for some strictly positive d, $m = |X|$ and $n = |B|$. For a variable $v \in X \cup P$ we denote by $\pi_v(w)$ the projection of w on its component v.

We consider the variant of STL that has both *past* and *future* temporal operators. The syntax of a STL formula φ over $P \cup X$ is defined by the grammar

$$\varphi := p \mid x \sim u \mid \neg\varphi \mid \varphi_1 \vee \varphi_2 \mid \varphi_1 \mathcal{U}_I \varphi_2 \mid \varphi_1 \mathcal{S}_I \varphi_2$$

where $p \in P$, $x \in X$, $\sim \in \{<, \leq\}$, $u \in \mathbb{Q}$, and I is an interval that is a subset of $\mathbb{R}^+$. The semantics of a STL formula with respect to a signal w is described via the satisfiability relation $(w, t) \models \varphi$, indicating that the signal w satisfies φ at the time point t, according to the following definition.

$$
\begin{aligned}
(w, t) &\models p &&\leftrightarrow \pi_p(w)[t] = \top \\
(w, t) &\models x \sim u &&\leftrightarrow \pi_x(w)[t] \sim u \\
(w, t) &\models \neg\varphi &&\leftrightarrow (w, t) \not\models \varphi \\
(w, t) &\models \varphi_1 \vee \varphi_2 &&\leftrightarrow (w, t) \models \varphi_1 \text{ or } (w, t) \models \varphi_2 \\
(w, t) &\models \varphi_1 \mathcal{U}_I \varphi_2 &&\leftrightarrow \exists t' \in (t + I) \cap \mathbb{T} : (w, t') \models \varphi_2 \text{ and } \forall t < t'' < t', (w, t'') \models \varphi_1 \\
(w, t) &\models \varphi_1 \mathcal{S}_I \varphi_2 &&\leftrightarrow \exists t' \in (t - I) \cap \mathbb{T} : (w, t') \models \varphi_2 \text{ and } \forall t' < t'' < t, (w, t'') \models \varphi_1
\end{aligned}
$$

We say that a signal w *satisfies* a STL formula φ, denoted by $w \models \varphi$, if $(w, 0) \models \varphi$. We define a *satisfaction signal* w_φ for a formula φ such that $w_\varphi[t] = \top$ iff $(w, t) \models \varphi$. From the basic definition of STL, we can derive other standard operators as follows: $\top = p \vee \neg p$, $\bot = \neg\top$, $\varphi_1 \wedge \varphi_2 = \neg(\neg\varphi_1 \vee \neg\varphi_2)$, $\Diamond_I \varphi = \top \mathcal{U}_I \varphi$, $\Box_I \varphi = \neg \Diamond_I \neg\varphi$, $\Diamonddown_I \varphi = \top \mathcal{S}_I \varphi$ and $\boxdown_I \varphi = \neg \Diamonddown_I \neg\varphi$.

Strict Semantics of STL. In contrast to LTL [38], the semantics of the temporal $\mathcal{U}_I$ and $\mathcal{S}_I$ operators in STL are *strict* in both arguments, as originally proposed in [2]. We shortly discuss why this strictness is needed in the continuous time setting. Let us denote by $\bar{\mathcal{U}}$ the classical non-strict LTL until operator[1], and by $\mathcal{U}$ its strict counterpart. We note that in LTL, due to its discrete-time

---

[1] To simplify the discussion about strictness of temporal operators, we restrict ourselves to the future fragment of the logics. The same argument applies for their past fragments.

interpretation and in contrast to STL, the logic also has the *next* $\bigcirc$ operator. In fact, in discrete time, the logic is $\bar{\mathcal{U}}$ and $\bigcirc$ can be shown to be equivalent to the logic with $\mathcal{U}$ only. In particular, we have the following equivalences.

$$\varphi_1 \mathcal{U} \varphi_2 \equiv \bigcirc(\varphi_1 \bar{\mathcal{U}} \varphi_2)$$
$$\bigcirc \varphi \equiv \bot \mathcal{U} \varphi$$
$$\varphi_1 \bar{\mathcal{U}} \varphi_2 \equiv \varphi_2 \vee (\varphi_1 \wedge (\varphi_1 \mathcal{U} \varphi_2))$$

Due to its dense-time interpretation, STL does not have the next operator. In fact, the logic with the strict semantics of its temporal operators is strictly more expressive than its non-strict counterpart[2]. In particular, the major practical consequence of the strict semantics for $\mathcal{U}_I$ and $\mathcal{S}_I$ operators is that it enables defining instantaneous *events* as syntactic sugar.

Events in STL. Instantaneous events take place in singular intervals of zero duration and represent rising and falling edges in boolean signals. Due to the dense-time semantics in STL, we allow signals that do not change their value at some specific time point but in the neighborhood of that point. The *rise* ↑ and *fall* ↓ operators are defined as STL syntactic sugar as follows.

$$\uparrow \varphi \equiv (\varphi \wedge (\neg\varphi \, \mathcal{S} \top)) \vee (\neg\varphi \wedge (\varphi \, \mathcal{U} \top))$$
$$\downarrow \varphi \equiv (\neg\varphi \wedge (\varphi \, \mathcal{S} \top)) \vee (\varphi \wedge (\neg\varphi \, \mathcal{U} \top))$$

Example 2. We now respond to the questions from Example 1 regarding the specification of DSI3 requirements in STL. We start with Question Q1 and show that with some effort we can capture the discovery pulse in STL. We first need to define three predicates: when the voltage v is (1) below V_{low}; (2) between V_{low} and V_{high}; and (3) above V_{high}.

$$v_l \equiv v \leq V_{low}$$
$$v_b \equiv V_{low} \leq v \leq V_{high}$$
$$v_h \equiv v \geq V_{high}$$

Next, we describe with φ_{shape} the shape of a discovery pulse. Such a pulse starts at the moment when the signal v moves from v_h to v_b. The signal then must go into v_l, v_b and finally come back to v_h. In addition to its shape, the DSI3 specification requires the discovery pulse to have a duration of t_{Disc_Pulse}. We note that in hybrid behaviors, it is very unlikely that a precise timing constraint is met, hence we relax the constraint by adding a small tolerance τ and accordingly define the interval $I_{Disc\_Pulse} = [t_{Disc\_Pulse} - \tau, t_{Disc\_Pulse} + \tau]$ instead. We formalize the timing requirement of the pulse as the property φ_{dur}. Finally, the discovery pulse φ_{pulse} is the conjunction of φ_{shape} and φ_{dur}.

$$\varphi_{shape} \equiv \downarrow v_h \wedge (v_b \, \mathcal{U} v_l \, \mathcal{U} v_b \, \mathcal{U} v_h)$$
$$\varphi_{dur} \equiv \downarrow v_h \wedge (\neg v_h \, \mathcal{U}_{I_{Disc\_Pulse}} \uparrow v_h)$$
$$\varphi_{pulse} \equiv \varphi_{shape} \wedge \varphi_{dur}$$

---

[2] The strictness of its temporal operators "forces" the time to advance.

Given the characterization φ_{pulse} of the discovery pulse, it is possible to express that two consecutive pulses must have a distance of t_{Disc_per} between them. It follows that Question Q2 is answered positively for STL. Similarly to the previous property, we allow a small tolerance for the timing constraint, and define the interval $I_{Disc\_per} = [t_{Disc\_per} - \tau, t_{Disc\_per} + \tau]$, where τ is a small tolerance constant. We also observe that the property shall say that after the last pulse, no more discovery pulses will be encountered until the end of the trace. We formalize the property as follows:

$$\square(\varphi_{pulse} \to ((\neg\varphi_{pulse}\,\mathcal{U}\,_{I_{Disc\_per}}\varphi_{pulse}) \vee \square(\neg\varphi_{pulse})))$$

Using STL with qualitative semantics does not provide any means for reasoning about quantitative properties of behaviors, hence Question Q3 is answered negatively. The answer to Question Q4 is not straightforward. On one hand, we have seen that formalizing the discovery pulse in STL requires some effort. In fact, STL may not be a natural candidate for defining such sequential patterns. On the other hand, describing the global timing property between consecutive pulses is easy and natural.

3.2   Signal Temporal Logic with Quantitative Semantics

Signal Temporal Logic with qualitative semantics, presented in Sect. 3.1, allows to reason about *correctness* of continuous and hybrid behaviors with respect to specifications and provides a purely boolean (yes/no) answer to the problem. In many real-life applications involving continuous and hybrid dynamics with real-valued quantities, such qualitative reasoning may not be sufficient. Continuous dynamical systems typically have a certain degree of sensitivity with respect to initial conditions and system parameters. In addition, the precision of the sensors may affect the accuracy to the measured behaviors. As a result, a small perturbation in the behavior, the parameter of the system or a measurement error can influence the correctness verdict.

Example 3. Consider the DSI3 discovery pulse introduced in Example 1 and the behaviors depicted in Fig. 3. The imperfections in the behavior, possibly due to random noise or measurement inaccuracies, may result in short but unexpected crossings of the V_{min} and V_{max} thresholds (see Fig. 3 (b)) . It follows that the

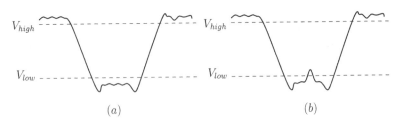

Fig. 3. Two DSI3 discovery pulses with small perturbations - the second one violates the qualitative specification of a pulse.

φ_{pulse} property could be violated when we expect it to be satisfied and hence the discovery pulse may not be recognized by the formula.

In order to address this problem, Fages and Rizk [40] and Fainekos and Pappas [23] proposed to augment LTL over real-valued sequences and STL, respectively, with *quantitative* information about the satisfaction of a formula. Consider the numerical predicate $x < c$ which splits the domain $\mathbb{R}$ into two partitions: (1) the set of all real values strictly smaller than c; and (2) the set of all values greater or equal than c. When we choose a number x in $\mathbb{R}$, the answer to the qualitative satisfaction question just tells us whether the number is below or above c, but not its relative position with respect to it. The quantitative *robustness degree* gives a richer feedback on how far is the value of x from satisfying/violating the property $x < c$.

Augmenting STL with quantitative semantics does not affect the syntax of the logic, except that it does not allow propositional variables, hence we use the slightly adapted grammar from Sect. 3.1 to specify properties. In order to adapt the STL semantics to the quantitative setting, we adopt the notation proposed in [19]. Given a STL formula φ, a signal w, and time $t \in \mathbb{T}$, the quantitative semantics $\rho(\varphi, w, t)$ is defined by induction as follows:

$$\rho(\top, w, t) \quad\quad = \top$$
$$\rho(x \sim u, w, t) \quad = u - \pi_x(w)[t]$$
$$\rho(\neg\varphi, w, t) \quad\quad = -\rho(\varphi, w, t)$$
$$\rho(\varphi_1 \vee \varphi_2, w, t) = \max\{\rho(\varphi_1, w, t), \rho(\varphi_2, w, t)\}$$
$$\rho(\varphi_1 \mathcal{U}_I \varphi_2, w, t) = \sup_{t' \in (t+I) \cap \mathbb{T}} \min\{\rho(\varphi_2, w, t'), \inf_{t'' \in (t,t')} \rho(\varphi_1, w, t'')\}$$
$$\rho(\varphi_1 \mathcal{S}_I \varphi_2, w, t) = \sup_{t' \in (t-I) \cap \mathbb{T}} \min\{\rho(\varphi_2, w, t'), \inf_{t'' \in (t',t)} \rho(\varphi_1, w, t'')\}$$

We illustrate the difference between qualitative and quantitative semantics for STL in Fig. 4. The quantitative semantics of STL has two fundamental properties that relate it to the qualitative satisfaction semantics. Whenever $\rho(\varphi, w, t) \neq 0$, its sign indicates the satisfaction/violation verdict of the formula. Moreover, if w satisfies φ at time t, any other signal w' whose pointwise distance from w is smaller than $\rho(\varphi, w, t)$ also satisfies φ at time t.

The above quantitative semantics of STL enable measuring *spatial* robustness degree of hybrid behaviors, however it does not address the *time* robustness of STL. Quantitative semantics for STL that combine *both* space and time robustness were proposed in [20]. More recently, an extension of STL with *averaged* temporal operators that also combine space and time robustness was proposed in [1].

The addition of the quantitative semantics to STL has allowed to measure both the space and time robustness of continuous behaviors with respect to specifications. This extension of the logic successfully addresses some of the issues related to the perturbations in the system, its parameters or the measurements. However, STL with quantitative semantics does not provide a fully satisfactory solution to the above-mentioned problem. Due to the min/max aggregation of values when computing robustness degree of operators, glitches of small duration but high amplitude may still considerably affect the robustness degree of the formula. This problem has been recently addressed by proposing the Skorokhod

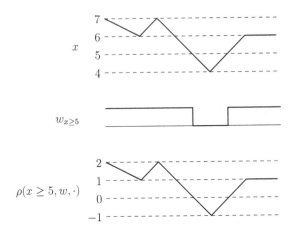

Fig. 4. Comparison of evaluating $x \geq 5$ with qualitative and quantitative semantics.

metric for measuring distances between continuous behaviors and devising an algorithm for effectively computing the distance [14,32]. The advantage of the Skorokhod metric is that it allows mismatches in both space and time and quantifies temporal and spacial variation of hybrid behaviors.

3.3 Timed Regular Expressions

Timed regular expressions extend regular expressions with real-time constraints and thus enable matching patterns over continuous time behaviors. We consider the variant of TRE from [25,43] that also allows numerical predicates over real-valued variables. In contrast to STL, the semantics of TRE is not defined relative to single time point, but rather a pair of points (t, t') which determine a segment of the behavior that matches the expression. This property of TRE makes the formalism useful for identifying and capturing segments in a trace that match a given regular expression. Similarly to standard regular expressions, TREs existentially quantify over time - the matching semantics looks for the existence of a behavior segment that matches an expression. Finally, the negation is not allowed in TRE except at the level of propositional variables and numerical predicates.

The signals in TRE are defined in the same way as in STL, see Sect. 3.1 for details. A *proposition* θ is taken to be either a propositional variable p, a predicate $x \sim u$ over some real variable x, or their negation $\neg p$ and $\neg(x \sim u)$, respectively. We denote by Θ the set of propositions derived from real and propositional variables. We now define the syntax of *timed regular expressions* according to the following grammar:

$$\alpha := \epsilon \mid \theta \mid \alpha_1 \cdot \alpha_2 \mid \alpha_1 \cup \alpha_2 \mid \alpha_1 \cap \alpha_2 \mid \alpha^* \mid \langle \alpha \rangle_I$$

where θ is a proposition of Θ, and I is an interval of $\mathbb{R}_+$.

The semantics of a timed regular expression α with respect to a signal w and times $t \le t'$ in $[0, d]$ is given in terms of a satisfaction relation $(w, t, t') \models \alpha$ inductively defined as follows:

$$
\begin{aligned}
(w, t, t') &\models \epsilon & &\leftrightarrow t = t' \\
(w, t, t') &\models \theta & &\leftrightarrow t < t' \text{ and } \forall t < t'' < t', \pi_\theta(w)[t''] = 1 \\
(w, t, t') &\models \alpha_1 \cdot \alpha_2 & &\leftrightarrow \exists t \le t'' \le t', (w, t, t'') \models \alpha_1 \text{ and } (w, t'', t') \models \alpha_2 \\
(w, t, t') &\models \alpha_1 \cup \alpha_2 & &\leftrightarrow (w, t, t') \models \alpha_1 \text{ or } (w, t, t') \models \alpha_2 \\
(w, t, t') &\models \alpha_1 \cap \alpha_2 & &\leftrightarrow (w, t, t') \models \alpha_1 \text{ and } (w, t, t') \models \alpha_2 \\
(w, t, t') &\models \alpha^* & &\leftrightarrow \exists k \ge 0, (w, t, t') \models \alpha^k \\
(w, t, t') &\models \langle \alpha \rangle_I & &\leftrightarrow t' - t \in I \text{ and } (w, t, t') \models \alpha
\end{aligned}
$$

We characterize the set of segments in w that match the expression α by their *match set*. The match set $\mathcal{M}(\alpha, w) = \{(t, t') \in \mathbb{R}^2 \mid (w, t, t') \models \alpha\}$ of expression α over w is the set of all pairs (t, t') such that the segment of w between t and t' matches α.

Conditional TRE. The matching semantics of TRE identify trace segments that satisfy the entire expression. In many cases, it is necessary to further condition the matching to a sub-expression only when its pre- and post-conditions are satisfied. *Conditional timed regular expressions* (CTRE) is an extension of TRE proposed in [25] that enables to condition the match of a TRE to a prefix or a suffix. Two new binary operators are introduced in the syntax of CTRE, "?" for pre-conditions, and "!" for post-conditions. Given expressions α_1 and α_2, a signal w matches the expression $\alpha_1 ? \alpha_2$ at (t, t') if it matches α_2 and there is an interval ending at t where w matches α_1. Symmetrically, w matches the expression $\alpha_1 ! \alpha_2$ at (t, t') if it matches α_1 and there is an interval beginning at t' where w matches α_2. The difference between the precondition and post-condition operators on one hand, and the concatenation on the other hand is in the definition of their semantics (and consequently their match set), which is defined for the two former operators as follows:

$$
\begin{aligned}
(w, t, t') &\models \alpha_1 ? \alpha_2 & &\leftrightarrow (w, t, t') \models \alpha_2 \text{ and } \exists t'' \le t, (w, t'', t) \models \alpha_1 \\
(w, t, t') &\models \alpha_1 ! \alpha_2 & &\leftrightarrow (w, t, t') \models \alpha_1 \text{ and } \exists t'' \ge t', (w, t', t'') \models \alpha_2
\end{aligned}
$$

Events in TRE. Another important aspect of CTRE is that they enable defining *rise* and *fall events* of zero duration associated to propositional terms. The rise edge $\uparrow \theta$ associated to the propositional term θ is obtained by syntactic sugar as $\uparrow \theta := \neg \theta ? \epsilon ! \theta$, while the fall edge $\downarrow \theta$ corresponds to $\downarrow \theta := \uparrow \neg \theta$. We note that the rise and fall operators in TRE are slightly less powerful than their STL counterparts, in that they cannot recognize zero-duration pulses in signals.

Example 4. We study the questions from the Example 1 regarding the specification of DSI3 requirements in TRE. We borrow from Example 2 the definition of predicates and of the timing intervals. The specification of the discovery pulse is done in TRE using concatenation and time constraint operator, and results in the following expression, thus positively answering Question Q1.

$$
\alpha_{pulse} = \downarrow (v_h) \cdot \langle v_b \cdot v_l \cdot v_b \rangle_{I_{Disc\_Pulse}} \cdot \uparrow (v_h)
$$

As we can see, the formalization of an individual DSI3 discovery pulse in TRE is easy. In a similar manner, we can also capture all the segments that match two consecutive pulses in the signal. However, checking whether their distance is *always* bounded by t_{Disc_per} is not possible without additional machinery. In order to express such a property, we would need either to universally quantify over all the consecutive DSI3 discovery pulses or to allow negating TRE sub-expressions, and neither is possible in TRE. This motivates the introduction of a simple measurement specification language on top of TRE that we present in the next section.

3.4   Measurement Specification Language

In this section, we present a simple specification language [25] built on top of conditional TRE that enables describing declarative measurement properties of continuous and hybrid behaviors. We first recall that the match set of a TRE defines all the trace segments that match the expression. The number of such segments can be infinite. An *event-bounded* TRE (E-TRE) is an expression of the form

$$\psi := \uparrow p \mid \psi_1 \cdot \alpha \cdot \psi_2 \mid \psi_1 \cup \psi_2 \mid \psi_1 \cap \alpha$$

with p a proposition, and ψ_1, ψ_2 event-bounded TRE. Such expressions have the following important property - given an arbitrary finitely variable signal w, an E-TRE can be matched in w only a finite number of times.

In this approach, we will use *measure patterns* based on timed regular expressions to specify signal segments of interest. More precisely, a measure pattern consists of three parts: (1) the *main* pattern; (2) the *precondition*; and (3) the *postcondition*. The main pattern is an E-TRE that specifies the portion of the signal over which the measure is taken. Using E-TRE to express main patterns ensures the finiteness of signal segments, while pre- and post- conditions expressed as general TRE allow to define additional constraints. A measure pattern α is a CTRE of the form $\alpha_1 ? \psi ! \alpha_2$, where α_1 and α_2 are TRE, while ψ is an E-TRE. Preconditions and postconditions are optional - we have $\epsilon ? \alpha \equiv \alpha$ and $\alpha ! \epsilon \equiv \alpha$. Hence, we use the simpler formula ψ to express the measure pattern $\epsilon ? \psi ! \epsilon$.

Powerful declarative and pattern-driven performance evaluation of hybrid and continuous systems is built on top of the match set for measure patterns. Given a measure pattern α and a signal w, we describe a two stage analysis of w. In the first step, we compute a scalar value for each segment of w that matches α, either from absolute times of that match, or from the values of a real signal x in w during that match. A measure is then written with the syntax $\text{op}(\alpha)$ with $\text{op} \in \{\text{time}, \text{value}_x, \text{duration}, \inf_x, \sup_x, \text{integral}_x, \text{average}_x\}$ being some sampling or aggregating operator. The semantics $[\![\,]\!]_w$ of these operators is given in Table 1; it associates to a measure $\text{op}(\alpha)$ and behavior w a multiset containing the scalar values computed over each matched interval.[3]

---

[3] We use *multiset* semantics as several patterns may have exactly the same measured value, in which case *set* semantics would not record its number of occurrences.

Table 1. Standard measure operators.

$$\llbracket \mathrm{time}(\uparrow p) \rrbracket_w = \{t \; : \; (t,t) \in \mathcal{M}(\uparrow p, w)\}$$
$$\llbracket \mathrm{value}_x(\uparrow p) \rrbracket_w = \{\pi_x(w)[t] \; : \; (t,t) \in \mathcal{M}(\uparrow p, w)\}$$
$$\llbracket \mathrm{duration}(\alpha) \rrbracket_w = \{t' - t \; : \; (t,t') \in \mathcal{M}(\alpha, w)\}$$
$$\llbracket \mathrm{inf}_x(\alpha) \rrbracket_w = \{\min_{t \le \tau \le t'} \pi_x(w)(\tau) \; : \; (t,t') \in \mathcal{M}(\alpha, w)\}$$
$$\llbracket \mathrm{sup}_x(\alpha) \rrbracket_w = \{\max_{t \le \tau \le t'} \pi_x(w)(\tau) \; : \; (t,t') \in \mathcal{M}(\alpha, w)\}$$
$$\llbracket \mathrm{integral}_x(\alpha) \rrbracket_w = \{\int_t^{t'} \pi_x(w)(\tau) d\tau \; : \; (t,t') \in \mathcal{M}(\alpha, w)\}$$
$$\llbracket \mathrm{average}_x(\alpha) \rrbracket_w = \{\tfrac{1}{t'-t} \int_t^{t'} \pi_x(w)(\tau) d\tau \; : \; (t,t') \in \mathcal{M}(\alpha, w)\}$$

In the second step, we reduce the multiset of scalar values computed over the signal matched intervals in $\mathcal{M}(\alpha, w)$ to a single scalar. Typically, given the multiset $A = \llbracket \mathrm{op}(\alpha) \rrbracket_w$ of scalar values associated with these signal segments, this phase consists in computing standard statistical indicators over A, such as the average, maximum, minimum or standard deviation. This final step is optional as the set of basic measurements sometimes provides sufficient information.

Example 5. We have defined in Example 4 the TRE pattern α_{pulse} that characterizes the DSI3 discovery pulse. We now formalize the pattern that matches all consecutive discovery and show how to express the quantitative property of measuring the average time between two consecutive discovery pulses. We first characterize the signal segments that we want to measure. The pattern starts at the beginning of a discovery pulse and end at the beginning of the next one, as depicted by the ψ region in Fig. 5. It consists of a discovery pulse α_{pulse}, followed by the voltage signal being in the v_h region, and terminating when the voltage leaves v_h. This description is not sufficient – we also need to ensure that this segment is effectively followed by another discovery pulse. Hence we add a postcondition that specifies this additional constraint. The measure pattern $\alpha \equiv \alpha_1 \, ? \, \psi \, ! \, \alpha_2$ is formalized as follows.

$$\alpha_1 \equiv \epsilon$$
$$\psi \equiv \alpha_{pulse} \cdot v_h \cdot \downarrow (v_h)$$
$$\alpha_2 \equiv \alpha_{pulse}$$

Finally, we evaluate the measure expression $\mathcal{D} = \mathrm{duration}(\alpha)$ which represents the set of durations between all consecutive discovery pulses matched in w. Their average value is simply obtained by the following computation

$$\frac{\Sigma_{\delta \in \mathcal{D}} \, \delta}{|\mathcal{D}|}$$

We note that the measuring patterns can also be used to answer whether all the consecutive pulses are separated by a duration in I_{Disc_per} with the following predicate

$$\max\{\delta \mid \delta \in \mathcal{D}\} \in I_{Disc\_per}$$

It follows that we can use the TRE with measure operators to positively answer both Questions Q2 and Q3. We now answer the Question Q4. We have seen

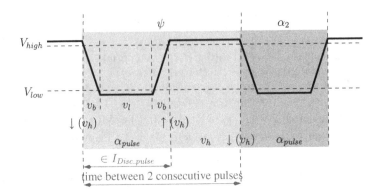

Fig. 5. DSI3 discovery mode - timing between two consecutive pulses.

the TRE allow to easily capture continuous signal patterns and analog events. Combined with measure operators, TRE enable taking quantitative measures from signals in a natural way. On the other hand, timed regular expressions do not facilitate specification of complex temporal properties that combine existential with universal quantifications over time. We needed additional measure operators in order to enable specification of such temporal relations in the signal.

4   Monitoring and Measuring Hybrid Systems Properties

The analysis of behaviors generated by some system can take different forms, depending on the nature of the system-under-test (SUT) and the mechanism used to connect it to the tool that analyzes its behaviors. The system generates behaviors by computing observable states sequentially.

Real-time monitoring: The generator creates behaviors in real-time and the monitor cannot influence the frequency at which the system operates. In this setting, the monitor must be able to read and process new data in real time, hence it shall run at lease as fast as the system in order to guarantee that no important data is missed. This situation typically occurs when monitoring physical systems and systems such as nuclear plants, semi-conductor devices and embedded systems. In safety critical applications, there may be a feedback loop between the system and the monitor which allows taking corrective action and putting the system in the safe mode upon detection of violation.

Online monitoring: Similarly to their real-time counterparts, online monitors run in parallel with the system generating the behaviors. The main difference is that in this case, the behavior generator is typically a *simulator* that creates new data on-the-fly, but not in real time. It follows that the monitor is allowed to introduce some computational overhead and even slow down the simulation. The benefit of connecting online monitors to simulators generating behaviors is that an early detection of property violation allows stopping behavior generation and thus saving precious simulation time.

Offline monitoring: In this setting, the behaviors are completely generated by the system before the monitoring procedure starts. Typically, offline monitoring algorithms are the simplest to implement, since the behaviors, saved on a disk drive, can be read and analyzed in both directions. The main benefit of the offline monitoring approach is that the monitor can read arbitrary behaviors - it can remain agnostic to the provenience of the behaviors and is thus applicable to both traces generated from simulators as well as physical devices.

In the remainder of this section, we first discuss some issues that are specific to the analysis of continuous and hybrid behaviors. We also provide an overview of different methods for monitoring STL with qualitative and quantitative semantics and matching timed regular expression patterns. We focus on giving some intuition behind the described procedures and do not aim to be complete. We point the reader to the relevant literature for technical details and full description of the algorithms.

4.1 Handling Numerical Predicates

In order to implement monitoring and measuring procedures for STL and TRE, we need to address the problem of the computer representation of continuous and hybrid behaviors. Both STL and TRE have a dense-time interpretation of continuous behaviors which are assumed to be ideal mathematical objects. This is in contrast with the actual behaviors obtained from simulators or measurement devices and which are represented as a finite collection of $(w(t), t)$ value-timestamp pairs. The values of w at two consecutive sample points t_1 and t_2 do not precisely determine the values of w inside the interval (t_1, t_2). We need to handle this issue pragmatically, by using the *interpolation* to "fill in" the missing values between consecutive samples. Some commonly used interpolations to interpreted sampled data are *step* and *linear* interpolation. We note that monitoring procedures are sensitive to the interpolation used, as shown in Fig. 6.

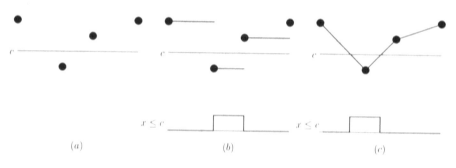

Fig. 6. Signal x - (a) samples; (b) step interpolation; and (c) linear interpolation.

4.2 Monitoring STL with Qualitative and Quantitative Semantics

In this section, we informally present monitoring techniques for STL properties with qualitative and quantitative semantics. We start with an *offline* procedure for qualitative STL monitoring - unlike automata-based monitoring algorithms, it directly works on the input and STL satisfaction signals. The procedure is recursive on the structure (parse-tree) of the formula - it propagates the truth values upwards from input signals via super-formulas up to the main formula. For every subformula ϕ of φ, it computes the satisfaction signal w_ϕ. Most of the work in the algorithm is done by the method that computes the satisfaction signal for a given STL operator. For some operators, this computation is easy - for instance, computing the satisfaction signal w_φ for the negation $\varphi = \neg\phi$ is done by taking the signal w_ϕ and switching its truth value. The more difficult computations are related to the tempooral operators. We give an intuition on the computation of w_φ where $\varphi = \Diamond_I \phi$ and refer the reader to [34] for the technical description of the algorithm for the full STL. The procedure is based on the following observation - whenever ϕ holds throughout an interval J, φ must hold throughout $(J \ominus I) \cap \mathbb{T}$, where $J \ominus I = \{t - t' \mid t \in J \text{ and } t' \in I\}$ is the Minkowski difference. Hence, the essence of the procedure is to back-shift (Minkowski difference saturated by $\mathbb{T}$) all the positive intervals in w_ϕ and thus obtain the set where $\Diamond_I \phi$ holds. This method is illustrated in Fig. 7.

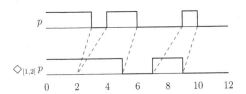

Fig. 7. Example of offline marking for $\Diamond_{[1,2]} p$.

We now sketch an *incremental* procedure for monitoring STL that combines the simplicity of the offline method with the advantages of online monitoring - possibility of detecting early an error and typically smaller memory footprint. The incremental procedure works as follows. After observing a prefix of the input signal over some interval $[0, t)$, we apply the offline procedure. If the satisfaction signal w_φ of the top formula φ is determined at time 0, the satisfaction/violation of the formula is known and we are done. Otherwise, we wait to observe the new segment of w over the interval $[t, t')$, and repeat the offline procedure. We note that whenever the satisfaction of a formula φ is determined in some interval $[0, t)$, we only need to keep the information about the satisfaction of its sub-formulas after t and discard the rest. This observation allows a memory-efficient implementation of the algorithm. For the complete presentation of the incremental procedure, see [34].

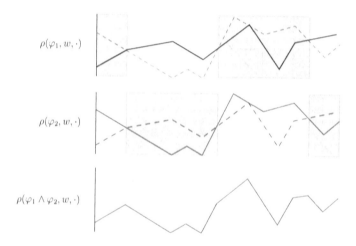

$\rho(\varphi_1, w, \cdot)$

$\rho(\varphi_2, w, \cdot)$

$\rho(\varphi_1 \wedge \varphi_2, w, \cdot)$

Fig. 8. Example of computing space robustness for $\varphi_1 \wedge \varphi_2$.

The procedure for offline monitoring of STL with qualitative semantics can be adapted to compute the quantitative semantics. We illustrate the idea of the extension for the case of space robustness. Similarly to the qualitative setting, the procedure for computing the state robustness $\rho(\varphi, w, t)$ is inductive in the structure of the formula. Instead of computing the satisfaction (true/false) value of an STL operator, the algorithm computes its real-valued robustness degree defined by the quantitative semantics. For example, consider the formula $\varphi = \varphi_1 \wedge \varphi_2$. In the qualitative setting, computing the satisfaction signal w_φ at time t consists in intersecting pointwise the values of satisfaction signals w_{φ_1} and w_{φ_2}. In the quantitative setting, computing $\rho(\varphi, w, t)$ consists instead of taking the minimum value between $\rho(\varphi_1, w, t)$ and $\rho(\varphi_2, w, t)$ in time t, where robustness degrees for φ_1 and φ_2 at time t are also real-valued quantities. This scenario is illustrated in Fig. 8.

There are several algorithms available in the literature for computing robustness degree of STL formulas. The algorithm for computing the space robustness of a continuous behaviour with respect to a STL specification was originally proposed in [23]. In [19], the authors develop a more efficient algorithm for measuring space robustness by using an optimal streaming algorithm to compute the min and the max of a numeric sequence over a sliding window and by rewriting the timed until as a conjunction of simpler timed and untimed operators. The procedure that combines monitoring of both space and time robustness is presented in [20]. Finally, the only algorithm for computing space robustness online that we are aware of is given in [16].

4.3   Pattern Matching TRE

We sketch the algorithm proposed in [43] for computing *offline* the set of all matches of a timed regular expression in a continuous or hybrid signal. The procedure relies on the observation that any match set can always be represented

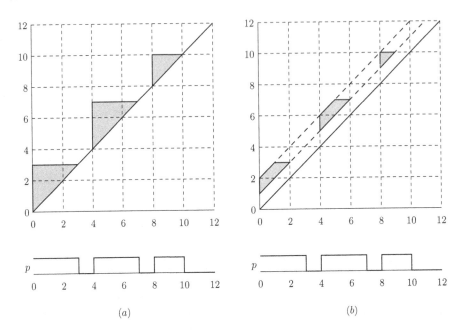

Fig. 9. Example of a match set - (a) p; and (b) $\langle p \rangle_{[1,2]}$.

as a finite union of two-dimensional *zones*. We recal that in $\mathbb{R}^n$, zones are special class of convex polytopes definable by intersection of inequalities of the form $x_i \geq a_i$, $x_i \leq b_i$ and $x_i - x_j \leq c_{i,j}$ or corresponding strict inequalities. For instance, the match set $\mathcal{M}(\epsilon, w)$ for the empty word ϵ is the diagonal zone $\{(t, t') \in \mathbb{T} \times \mathbb{T} \mid t = t'\}$, while the match for a literal p or $\neg p$ is a disjoint union of triangles touching the diagonal whose number depends on the number of switching points in $\pi_p(w)$. The match set of the time restriction operator is obtained by intersecting the match set with the corresponding diagonal band, hence $\mathcal{M}(\langle \alpha \rangle_I, w) = \mathcal{M}(\alpha) \cap \{(t, t') \mid t' - t \in I\}$. The match sets for p and $\langle p \rangle_{[1,2]}$ are depicted in Fig. 9. For the computation of the math sets for the other TRE operators, we point the reader to [43].

5   Beyond STL and TRE

In the past years, the specification languages STL and TRE have inspired a number of extensions that we describe in this tutorial and give references to the relevant literature.

Combined Time and Frequency Specifications. Combining time and frequency properties was first reported in [13] in which the authors describe predicates over the Fourier coefficients in the context of hybrid systems verification. Time-Frequency Logic (TFL) was introduced in [21] as a specification language for capturing both time-domain and frequency-domain properties of signals. This logic essentially extends STL interpreted over discrete time with time-frequency predicates that provide a tighter coupling of time and frequency domains. In order to define time-frequency predicates, TFL enables taking a Short-Time Fourier Transform (STFT)[4] around a given frequency f and time t, which yields a spectral signal which tracks the evolution of the STFT coefficient at f over time.

STL *with freeze quantifiers.* Motivated by oscillatory dynamics encountered in biological applications, the temporal logic STL* is proposed in [10,15] as an extension of STL augmented with a freezing operator that allows to record the signal values during the evaluation of a sub-property, and to reuse it for comparison in the other parts of the formula. This operator increases the expressive power of STL and for instance enables to express and capture various dynamic aspects of oscillations. The quantitative semantics of STL* is proposed and studied in [11].

Learning and Synthesis of STL *formulas and parameters from behaviors.* Behavioral specifications of complex systems are often unknown or only partially known. In engineered systems such as analog and mixed-signal designs, the top-down design paradigm starts with an abstract behavioral model, which is then iteratively designed. While some structural properties of the system may be known in advance, many parameters are decided only during different stepwise refinements of the design. In non-engineered applications, such as biology or medicine, even structural specification of the system may be unknown - the system already exists and by observing its behavior, one attempts to learn its structural and quantitative properties.

Parametric identification of STL properties is proposed and studied in [6]. The problem is stated as follows - given an STL formula with timing and magnitude parameters and a behavior of a system, find the range of parameters that makes the formula satisfied with respect to the behavior. The paper proposes two procedures for identifying such parameters using quantifier elimination and approximating Pareto fronts by adaptive sampling of the parameter space.

In a recent work [9,12], the authors solve a more ambitious problem of learning STL formulas from behaviors. This problem is motivated by the medical application of assisted ventilation in intensive care patients. The proposed procedure first builds statistical models of expected and faulty behaviors, and then finds an STL formula that optimally discriminates good from bad traces. In this work, both the space of formula structures and their space of parameters is explored using an evolutionary algorithm combined with Bayesian optimization.

Spatio-Temporal Extensions of STL. Spatial-Temporal Logic (SpaTeL) [27] was recently proposed as a unification of STL and Tree Spatial Superposition Logic (TSSL) [26]. This specification formalism is motivated by the applications from distributed and networked dynamic systems, ranging from robotic teams to collections of genetically engineered living cells. In particular, SpaTeL enables

---

[4] Computing STFT of a signal requires choosing a window function - TFL leaves the possibility of choosing different window functions.

expressing spatial patterns that evolve over time. The logic is equipped with quantitative semantics and statistical model checking is used to analyze the simulated behavior of networked dynamic systems.

6   Tools

In this section, we present four tools that implement monitoring algorithms for STL. Some of them are prototypes, some consider STL with qualitative and others STL with quantitative semantics. There are still no publicly available tools for TRE pattern matching and measuring, despite a prototype implementation [25, 43] used to evaluate the approach.

AMT. Analog Monitoring Tool (AMT) [37] is a standalone tool for monitoring STL properties interpreted with the qualitative semantics. The tool implements both an offline and an incremental monitoring algorithm, and supports several common input formats from the semi-conductor industry, such as Value Change Dump (VCD) and the Nanosim output format.

Breach. Breach [18] is a Matlab toolbox for simulation-based analysis of deterministic hybrid dynamical systems. The tool allows to approximate the reachable set of a hybrid system with a finite number of simulations by applying sensitivity analysis. Declarative properties of the hybrid system can be expressed in STL interpreted with the quantitative semantics from [23]. The tool implements efficient algorithms for monitoring both boolean and quantitative (robust) satisfaction of STL formulas.

CPSGrader. CPSGrader [30] is a tool for automatic grading of student lab assignments in the field of embedded and cyber-physical systems. The tools is used in the following flow: (1) the student develods a dynamical model as part of the assignment in the virtual lab; (2) the correctness property, used as the reference for grading the assignment, is expressed in STL; (3) the simulation test benches for exploring the model combine manual environment setup and simulation-based falsification, (4) if the correctness property is satisfied, the assignment is considered to be correct; (5) otherwise the model traces are compared to known faulty properties in an attempt to provide feedback to the student explaining the reasons of the model fault.

S-TaLiRo. S-TaLiRo [3] is a Matlab toolbox for temporal logic falsification. The tool searches for counterexamples to STL properties interpreted with quantitative semantics for non-linear hybrid systems through global minimization of the robust satisfaction of the specification. In order to achieve this, S-TaLiRo combines robust satisfaction monitoring with stochastic simulation. The output of the tool is the simulation trace with the smallest robustness value with respect to the associated STL formula that is found during the model simulation. The traces with negative robustness values indicate the (boolean) violation of the formula.

7   Applications

In this section, we provide an overview of several application domains in which analysis methods based on STL and TRE specifications have been used.

Automotive Applications. Both STL and TRE have been recently used to specify, monitor and measure hybrid properties of the DSI3 standard [25,36]. A counterexample-guided inductive synthesis approach to controller synthesis for cyber-physical systems subject to STL specifications, operating in potentially adversarial nondeterministic environment was applied to a case study in autonomous driving in [39]. An approach for automated directed test generation that uses STL specification as one of the ingredients to guide the search has been applied to an automotive powertrain control system in [22]. S-TaLiRo has been applied to two automotive examples [24], an automatic transmission model and a powertrain system, to check quantitative STL properties. The online robustness STL monitoring procedure has been used to compute the robustness degree of the Port Fuel Injected spark ignition model in [16].

Biological Applications. STL has been used to define qualitative properties of the behavior of several cellular mechanisms and to characterize the parameter that yield satisfying behaviors. This methodology has been applied to angiogenesis, the onset of new blood vessel sprouting [17], to programmed cell deat (apoptosis) [42] and the study of the effect of iron metabolism on blood cell specialization [35]. The logical characterization of an oscillator of the circadian clock in Ostreococcus Tauri, a simple unicellular alga, was done in [9] by learning TFL properties from a parameterized statistical model of the organism. Synthetic biology is an emerging field the consists in designing artificial living systems with a predictable behavior. A novel approach of compositionally designing synthetic biologic circuits from modules specified in STL with quantitative semantics was proposed in [7]. In [8], the authors investigated the notion of robust semantics of STL for stochastic models on three biological systems: the Schlögl system, which is a simple set of biochemical reactions exhibiting a bistable behavior, the Incoherent type 1 Feed-forward loops, which is a frequent motif in gene regulatory systems, and the Repressilator, a synthetic biological clock implemented as a gene regulatory network.

Medical Applications. Temporal logic specifications have played a role in several medical application. The problem of insulin pump usage parameter synthesis was studied in [41]. Insulin pumps are medical devices that are typically used by patients having diabetes type-1 to control their blood glucose level. The authors propose a model-based approach to find ideal parameters for regulating the insulin glucose. In this approach, the authors assume the availability of a mathematical model with parameters fitted to a particular patient, and formulate a function that rewards prescribed ranges of glucose levels, while penalizing hypoglycemia and hyperglycemia. The desired properties of the insulin infusion process were formalized in STL interpreted with the quantitative semantics and the pump usage is calibrated by optimizing the trace robustness. An approach to automatically detect ineffective breathing efforts in patients in intensive care subject to assisted ventilation, based on synthesis of STL formulas that discriminate between normal and ineffective breaths was proposed in [12]. Learning STL formulas from electro-cardiogram data in the context of discriminating different types of cardiac malfunctions was studied in [9].

Musical Applications. The applicability of temporal specifications in formalizing and recognizing melodies was studied and demonstrated in [21]. The specification language TFL combines both time and frequency features of the logic to characterize notes and specify melodies. In particular, the framework was used in an experiment where a Blues melody played on a guitar was checked against its TFL specification.

8   Discussion and Future Perspectives

Specification-based monitoring of continuous and hybrid behaviors has drawn considerable attention in the past decade and has found its application in versatile domains. We observe that one of the main obstacles for making this technology more mainstream is the nature of the specification languages. On one hand, formalisms based on temporal logics and regular expressions have a mathematical flavor that enable rigorous analysis of behaviors. On the other hand, such specification languages do not always appeal to the end user from application areas that are not related to formal methods. We believe that a real effort needs to be done to adapt formal specification formalisms to the notations that are familiar in a specific domain.

For instance, analog designers are used to requirements that are given in the form of timing diagrams, where expected behaviors and the associated timing constraints are specified in a combination of graphical and tabular form - see Fig. 10 as an example taken from the DSI3 Bus Standard. Providing higher level graphical and domain specific specification languages that could be mapped to STL and/or TRE would tremendously help their wider adoption. Recently, a graphical formalism for writing and visualizing STL specifications was developed and presented in [28]. This is the first attempt that we are aware of in bringing STL closer to the non-expert user.

We also observe that little effort has been invested in making specifications reusable, by allowing property templates and libraries. While not being a scientific topic, reusability of specifications is essential in the industrial context. We illustrate the advantages of reusable specifications on the DSI3 Bus Standard. For example, the standard is expected to be used in the entire automotive industry - specifications that formalize the protocol remain the same regardless of the car manufacturer. Such specifications could also be used to communicate the requirements along different actors in the value chain. Since DSI3 is intended to be a generic automotive protocol, it can be used for different products developed in the same company. Finally, specifications could be reused along different

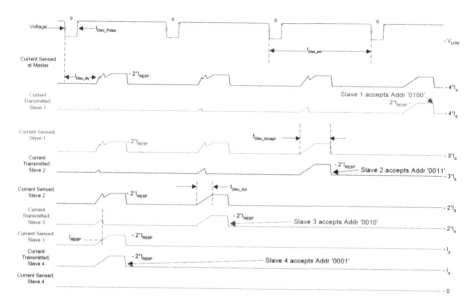

Fig. 10. Discovery mode example for a 4 device bus segment [29].

phases of the design - during the pre-silicon simulation, design emulation and post-silicon validation. In order to achieve the reusability of specifications, we need to provide syntactic constructs that allow developing property templates and creating libraries of specifications.

Acknowledgements. This work was supported by the MISTRAL project A-1341-RT-GP coordinated by the European Defence Agency (EDA) and funded by 8 contributing Members (France, Germany, Italy, Poland, Austria, Sweden, Netherland and Luxembourg) in the framework of the Joint Investment Programme on Second Innovative Concepts and Emerging Technologies (JIP-ICET 2) and the IKT der Zukunft of Austrian FFG project HARMONIA (nr. 845631).

We are grateful to Oded Maler for his comments on the earlier drafts of this tutorial.

References

1. Akazaki, T., Hasuo, I.: Time robustness in MTL and expressivity in hybrid system falsification. In: Kroening, D., Păsăreanu, C.S. (eds.) CAV 2015. LNCS, vol. 9207, pp. 356–374. Springer, Heidelberg (2015)

2. Alur, R., Feder, T., Henzinger, T.A.: The benefits of relaxing punctuality. J. ACM **43**(1), 116–146 (1996)

3. Annpureddy, Y., Liu, C., Fainekos, G., Sankaranarayanan, S.: S-TaLiRo: a tool for temporal logic falsification for hybrid systems. In: Abdulla, P.A., Leino, K.R.M. (eds.) TACAS 2011. LNCS, vol. 6605, pp. 254–257. Springer, Heidelberg (2011)

4. Asarin, E., Caspi, P., Maler, O.: A Kleene theorem for timed automata. In: Logic in Computer Science (LICS), pp. 160–171 (1997)

5. Asarin, E., Caspi, P., Maler, O.: Timed regular expressions. J. ACM **49**(2), 172–206 (2002)
6. Eugene Asarin, Alexandre Donzé, Oded Maler, and Dejan Nickovic. Parametric identification of temporal properties. In Runtime Verification - Second International Conference, RV 2011, San Francisco, CA, USA, September 27–30, 2011, Revised Selected Papers, pages 147–160 (2011)
7. Bartocci, E., Bortolussi, L., Nenzi, L.: A temporal logic approach to modular design of synthetic biological circuits. In: Gupta, A., Henzinger, T.A. (eds.) CMSB 2013. LNCS, vol. 8130, pp. 164–177. Springer, Heidelberg (2013)
8. Bartocci, E., Bortolussi, L., Nenzi, L., Sanguinetti, G.: System design of stochastic models using robustness of temporal properties. Theor. Comput. Sci. **587**, 3–25 (2015)
9. Bartocci, E., Bortolussi, L., Sanguinetti, G.: Data-driven statistical learning of temporal logic properties. In: Legay, A., Bozga, M. (eds.) FORMATS 2014. LNCS, vol. 8711, pp. 23–37. Springer, Heidelberg (2014)
10. Brim, L., Dluhos, P., Safránek, D., Vejpustek, T.: STL*: extending signal temporal logic with signal-value freezing operator. Inf. Comput. **236**, 52–67 (2014)
11. Brim, L., Vejpustek, T., Safránek, D., Fabriková, J.: Robustness analysis for value-freezing signal temporal logic. In: Proceedings Second International Workshop on Hybrid Systems and Biology, HSB 2013, Taormina, Italy, 2nd September 2013, pp. 20–36 (2013)
12. Bufo, S., Bartocci, E., Sanguinetti, G., Borelli, M., Lucangelo, U., Bortolussi, L.: Temporal logic based monitoring of assisted ventilation in intensive care patients. In: Margaria, T., Steffen, B. (eds.) ISoLA 2014, Part II. LNCS, vol. 8803, pp. 391–403. Springer, Heidelberg (2014)
13. Chakarov, A., Sankaranarayanan, S., Fainekos, G.E.: Combining time and frequency domain specifications for periodic signals. In: Runtime Verification - Second International Conference, RV 2011, San Francisco, CA, USA, September 27–30, 2011, Revised Selected Papers, pp. 294–309 (2011)
14. Deshmukh, J.V., Majumdar, R., Prabhu, V.S.: Quantifying conformance using the skorokhod metric. In: Kroening, D., Păsăreanu, C.S. (eds.) CAV 2015. LNCS, vol. 9207, pp. 234–250. Springer, Heidelberg (2015)
15. Dluhos, P., Brim, L., Safránek, D.: On expressing and monitoring oscillatory dynamics. In: Proceedings First International Workshop on Hybrid Systems and Biology, HSB 2012, Newcastle Upon Tyne, UK, 3rd September 2012, pp. 73–87 (2012)
16. Dokhanchi, A., Hoxha, B., Fainekos, G.: On-line monitoring for temporal logic robustness. In: Bonakdarpour, B., Smolka, S.A. (eds.) RV 2014. LNCS, vol. 8734, pp. 231–246. Springer, Heidelberg (2014)
17. Donzé, A., Fanchon, E., Gattepaille, L.M., Maler, O., Tracqui, P.: Robustness analysis and behavior discrimination in enzymatic reaction networks. PLoS ONE **6**(9), e24246 (2011)
18. Donzé, A.: Breach, a toolbox for verification and parameter synthesis of hybrid systems. In: Touili, T., Cook, B., Jackson, P. (eds.) CAV 2010. LNCS, vol. 6174, pp. 167–170. Springer, Heidelberg (2010)
19. Donzé, A., Ferrère, T., Maler, O.: Efficient robust monitoring for STL. In: Sharygina, N., Veith, H. (eds.) CAV 2013. LNCS, vol. 8044, pp. 264–279. Springer, Heidelberg (2013)
20. Donzé, A., Maler, O.: Robust satisfaction of temporal logic over real-valued signals. In: Chatterjee, K., Henzinger, T.A. (eds.) FORMATS 2010. LNCS, vol. 6246, pp. 92–106. Springer, Heidelberg (2010)

21. Donzé, A., Maler, O., Bartocci, E., Nickovic, D., Grosu, R., Smolka, S.: On temporal logic and signal processing. In: Chakraborty, S., Mukund, M. (eds.) ATVA 2012. LNCS, vol. 7561, pp. 92–106. Springer, Heidelberg (2012)
22. Dreossi, T., Dang, T., Donzé, A., Kapinski, J., Jin, X., Deshmukh, J.V.: Efficient guiding strategies for testing of temporal properties of hybrid systems. In: Havelund, K., Holzmann, G., Joshi, R. (eds.) NFM 2015. LNCS, vol. 9058, pp. 127–142. Springer, Heidelberg (2015)
23. Fainekos, G.E., Pappas, G.J.: Robustness of temporal logic specifications for continuous-time signals. Theor. Comput. Sci. 410(42), 4262–4291 (2009)
24. Fainekos, G.E., Sankaranarayanan, S., Ueda, K., Yazarel, H.: Verification of automotive control applications using S-TaLiRo. In American Control Conference, ACC 2012, Montreal, QC, Canada, June 27–29, 2012, pp. 3567–3572 (2012)
25. Ferrère, T., Maler, O., Ničković, D., Ulus, D.: Measuring with timed patterns. In: Kroening, D., Pǎsǎreanu, C.S. (eds.) CAV 2015. LNCS, vol. 9207, pp. 322–337. Springer, Heidelberg (2015)
26. Gol, E.A., Bartocci, E., Belta, C.: A formal methods approach to pattern synthesis in reaction diffusion systems. In: 53rd IEEE Conference on Decision and Control, CDC 2014, Los Angeles, CA, USA, December 15–17, pp. 108–113 (2014)
27. Haghighi, I., Jones, A., Kong, Z., Bartocci, E., Grosu, R., Belta, C.: SpaTeL: a novel spatial-temporal logic and its applications to networked systems. In: Proceedings of the 18th International Conference on Hybrid Systems: Computation and Control, HSCC 2015, Seattle, WA, USA, April 14–16, pp. 189–198 (2015)
28. Hoxha, B., Bach, H., Abbas, H., Dokhanci, A., Kobayashi, Y., Fainekos, G.: Towards formal specification visualization for testing and monitoring of cyber-physical systems. In: International Workshop on Design and Implementation of Formal Tools and Systems, DIFTS 2014 (2014)
29. Distributed System Interface. DSI3 Bus Standard. DSI Consortium
30. Juniwal, G., Donzé, A., Jensen, J.C., Seshia, S.A.: CPSGrader: Synthesizing temporal logic testers for auto-grading an embedded systems laboratory. In: 2014 International Conference on Embedded Software, EMSOFT 2014, New Delhi, India, October 12–17, 2014, pp. 24:1–24:10 (2014)
31. Koymans, R.: Specifying real-time properties with metric temporal logic. Real-Time Syst. 2(4), 255–299 (1990)
32. Majumdar, R., Prabhu, V.S.: Computing the Skorokhod distance between polygonal traces. In: Proceedings of the 18th International Conference on Hybrid Systems: Computation and Control, HSCC 2015, Seattle, WA, USA, April 14–16, 2015, pp. 199–208 (2015)
33. Maler, O., Nickovic, D.: Monitoring temporal properties of continuous signals. In: Lakhnech, Y., Yovine, S. (eds.) FORMATS 2004 and FTRTFT 2004. LNCS, vol. 3253, pp. 152–166. Springer, Heidelberg (2004)
34. Maler, O., Nickovic, D.: Monitoring properties of analog and mixed-signal circuits. STTT 15(3), 247–268 (2013)
35. Mobilia, N., Donzé, A., Moulis, J.M., Fanchon, E.: Producing a set of models for the iron homeostasis network. In: Proceedings Second International Workshop on Hybrid Systems and Biology, HSB 2013, Taormina, Italy, 2nd September 2013, pp. 92–98 (2013)
36. Nguyen, T., Ničković, D.: Assertion-based monitoring in practice – checking correctness of an automotive sensor interface. In: Lang, F., Flammini, F. (eds.) FMICS 2014. LNCS, vol. 8718, pp. 16–32. Springer, Heidelberg (2014)

37. Nickovic, D., Maler, O.: AMT: a property-based monitoring tool for analog systems. In: Proceedings of the Formal Modeling and Analysis of Timed Systems, 5th International Conference, FORMATS 2007, Salzburg, Austria, October 3–5, 2007, pp. 304–319 (2007)

38. Pnueli, A.: The temporal logic of programs. In: 18th Annual Symposium on Foundations of Computer Science, Providence, Rhode Island, USA, 31 October - 1 November 1977, pp. 46–57 (1977)

39. Raman, V., Donzé, A., Sadigh, D., Murray, R.M., Seshia, S.A.: Reactive synthesis from signal temporal logic specifications. In: Proceedings of the 18th International Conference on Hybrid Systems: Computation and Control, HSCC 2015, Seattle, WA, USA, April 14–16, 2015, pp. 239–248 (2015)

40. Rizk, A., Batt, G., Fages, F., Soliman, S.: On a continuous degree of satisfaction of temporal logic formulae with applications to systems biology. In: Heiner, M., Uhrmacher, A.M. (eds.) CMSB 2008. LNCS (LNBI), vol. 5307, pp. 251–268. Springer, Heidelberg (2008)

41. Sankaranarayanan, S., Miller, C., Raghunathan, R., Ravanbakhsh, H., Fainekos, G.E.: A model-based approach to synthesizing insulin infusion pump usage parameters for diabetic patients. In: 2012 50th Annual Allerton Conference on Communication, Control, and Computing, Allerton Park & Retreat Center, Monticello, IL, USA, October 1–5, 2012, pp. 1610–1617 (2012)

42. Stoma, S., Donzé, A., Bertaux, F., Maler, O., Batt, G.: STL-based analysis of TRAIL-induced apoptosis challenges the notion of type I/type II cell line classification. PLoS Comput. Bio. 9(5), e1003056 (2013)

43. Ulus, D., Ferrère, T., Asarin, E., Maler, O.: Timed pattern matching. In: Legay, A., Bozga, M. (eds.) FORMATS 2014. LNCS, vol. 8711, pp. 222–236. Springer, Heidelberg (2014)

Software Competitions

Second International Competition
on Runtime Verification
CRV 2015

Yliès Falcone[1]($\boxtimes$), Dejan Ničković[2], Giles Reger[3]($\boxtimes$), and Daniel Thoma[4]

[1] Univ. Grenoble Alpes, Inria, LIG, F-38000 Grenoble, France
ylies.falcone@imag.fr
[2] AIT Austrian Institute of Technology GmbH, Graz, Austria
Dejan.Nickovic@ait.ac.at
[3] University of Manchester, Manchester, UK
giles.reger@manchester.ac.uk
[4] University of Lübeck, Lübeck, Germany
thoma@isp.uni-luebeck.de

Abstract. We report on the Second International Competition on Runtime Verification (CRV-2015). The competition was held as a satellite event of the 15th International Conference on Runtime Verification (RV'15). The competition consisted of three tracks: offline monitoring, online monitoring of C programs, and online monitoring of Java programs. This report describes the format of the competition, the participating teams and submitted benchmarks. We give an example illustrating the two main inputs expected from the participating teams, namely a benchmark (i.e. a program and a property on this program) and a monitor for this benchmark. We also propose some reflection based on the lessons learned.

1 Introduction

Runtime Verification (RV) [8,14] is a lightweight yet powerful formal specification-based technique for offline analysis (e.g., for testing) as well as runtime monitoring of system. RV is based on extracting information from a running system and checking if the observed behavior satisfies or violates the properties of interest. During the last decade, many important tools and techniques have been developed and successfully employed. However, it has been observed that there is a general lack of standard benchmark suites and evaluation methods for comparing different aspects of existing tools and techniques. For this reason, and inspired by the success of similar events in other areas of computer-aided verification (e.g., SV-COMP, SAT, SMT), the First Internal Competition on Software for Runtime Verification (CSRV-2014) was established [2]. This is the second edition of the competition and the general aims remain the same:

– To stimulate the development of new efficient and practical runtime verification tools and the maintenance of the already developed ones.

© Springer International Publishing Switzerland 2015
E. Bartocci and R. Majumdar (Eds.): RV 2015, LNCS 9333, pp. 405–422, 2015.
DOI: 10.1007/978-3-319-23820-3_27

- To produce benchmark suites for runtime verification tools, by sharing case studies and programs that researchers and developers can use in the future to test and to validate their prototypes.
- To discuss the metrics employed for comparing the tools.
- To compare different aspects of the tools running with different benchmarks and evaluating them using different criteria.
- To enhance the visibility of presented tools among different communities (verification, software engineering, distributed computing and cyber security) involved in monitoring.

CRV-2015 was held between January and August 2015 with the results presented in September 2015 in Vienna, Austria, as a satellite event of the 15th International Conference on Runtime Verification (RV'15). This report was produced in June 2015, prior to the evaluation stage of the competition described later. Therefore, results of the competition have not been included and will be available on the competition website.[1]

This report will begin (Sect. 2) by looking at the changes to the competition between this and the previous edition. There is then a discussion of the format of the competition (Sect. 3) where the three tracks (Offline, Java, and C) and the three stages (Benchmark Submission, Monitor Submission, and Evaluation) are discussed. To illustrate this process, we provide an example using data from the competition (Sect. 4). We then present and briefly describe the participants to each track (Sect. 5), followed by an overview of the benchmarks submitted in each track (Sect. 6). Finally, we reflect on the challenges faced and give recommendations to future editions of the competition (Sect. 7) before making some concluding remarks (Sect. 8).

2   Changes from CSRV 2014

In this section, we highlight and discuss the changes from the first edition of the competition - CSRV 2014.[2]

2.1   Towards Standardisation

One of the major difficulties faced when organising a competition is designing it so that tools can compete on the same benchmarks. For this to work it is convenient to conform to certain common standards. Prior to the previous competition there was very little focus on standardisation in the Runtime Verification community and it is still an area requiring much work.

The previous competition introduced a standard format for traces used in Offline Monitoring and these have been updated this year, as described in

---

[1] See http://rv2015.conf.tuwien.ac.at - CRV-2015 Competition.

[2] The steering committee of the competition decided to change the name of the competition from CSRV (Competition on Software for Runtime Verification) to CRV (Competition on Runtime Verification) to reflect the intended broader scope of the competition.

Sect. 3.2. The formats have been changed to conform with general formats for CSV, JSON and XML files (see Sect. 3.2).

Currently, there are two important aspects of the runtime verification process that have not yet been standardised. Firstly, there are no standard specification languages for Runtime Verification, and most tools use their own language. Secondly, there is no standard instrumentation format for Online Monitoring, although for Java programs AspectJ is becoming a de-facto standard, although there are also other instrumentation techniques often used. There exists a working group[3] looking at these issues and it is hoped that standards in this area will be available for the future editions of the competition.

2.2 Providing a Resource for the Community

As discussed previously, there is a lack of benchmarks for comparing Runtime Verification techniques. To make the submitted benchmarks accessible and usable, the organizers have used a Wiki[4] to host the benchmarks and submissions this year.

Each benchmark has its own page containing three main sections:

– **Benchmark Data.** Describing the property to be monitored (formally and informally) and the artefact to be monitored i.e. trace or program.
– **Clarification Requests.** A space for benchmark clarifications (see below).
– **Submitted Specifications.** The specification used to capture the monitored property from each team participating on the benchmark.

As well as providing benchmarks for evaluation, this information can provide an insight into how different specification languages can be used to express the same property. For further information, see the details about the format of the competition in Sect. 3.

2.3 Transparency and Communication

One of the observations made after the previous competition was that communication often occurred in emails between the chairs and participants without all participants necessarily being involved. This had two disadvantages:

1. Clarifications and instructions can be spread across many email threads with the most recent version being difficult to find.
2. Information relevant to all participants is not necessarily received by all participants, or participants may receive information at different times.

For CRV 15, there has been an effort to ensure that all communication between chairs and participants, and between participants themselves, was conducted via the Wiki in either a separate *Rules* page or the *Clarification Request* section of a benchmark.

---

[3] https://www.cost-arvi.eu/.
[4] https://forge.imag.fr/plugins/mediawiki/wiki/crv15/index.php/Main_Page.

3   Format of the Competition

In this section we describe in detail all the phases of the competition.

3.1   Declaration of Intent

The competition was announced in relevant mailing lists starting from November 2014. Potential participants were requested to declare their intent to participate to CRV 15 via email[5]. The deadline was January 30, 2015. The information requested from the participants included: institute(s), contact person and email, alternate contact persons and emails, tool home page, references to the tool, programming language of the tool, specification language(s), features of the specification languages handled by the tool (logical/dense time, propositional/-parametric, etc.), and a reference to the specification language. This information was purposed to let the chairs and participants having early information about the competing tools and to get familiar with the tools and their supported specifications languages. Participants had to also indicate the track(s) in which they intended to participate in. Identification numbers (ids) were assigned to participants. As indicated in Sect. 2, a Wiki was created for the competition and participants had to register to it. For each of the three tracks (Offline, C and Java), the teams participating in the competition are listed in alphabetical order in Tables 1, 2, and 3, respectively. See Sect. 5 for further details on participants.

3.2   Submission of Benchmarks and Specifications

In this phase, participants were asked to prepare benchmark/specification sets. The deadline was March 15, 2015. The benchmarks and specifications were collected in a shared repository[6]. The repository was made accessible through SFTP and SSH protocols to facilitate the upload of benchmarks by allowing easy transfer and Unix commands to participants. The benchmarks were collected and classified into a hierarchy of directories. The hierarchy of directories has been arranged according to tracks and teams, following their ids. The hierarchy was the following:

```
falcone@lig-crv15:/work$ ls *
    C_track:
1_MarQ 2_E-ACSL 3_RiTHM 4_RV-Monitor 5_TimeSquareTrace 6_RTC
    Java_track:
1_MarQ 2_TJT 3_Java-MOP 4_Mufin
    Offline_track:
1_MarQ 2_RiTHM 3_OCLR-Check 4_RV-Monitor 5_OptySim 6_AgMon
    7_Breach 8_LogFire
```

Each of these directories had 5 sub-directories:

---

[5] crv15.chairs@imag.fr.

[6] crv15.imag.fr.

`Benchmark1 Benchmark2 Benchmark3 Benchmark4 Benchmark5`.

Each track directory contained a directory per participating team. Each team directory contained a directory per benchmark. Files had to be placed in the directory relevant to the track, team, and benchmark.

In this hierarchy, participants had reading rights to all directories and writing rights in their directories only.

Online Monitoring of Java and C Programs Tracks. In the case of Java and C tracks, each benchmark contribution was required to be structured as follows:

– *Program package* containing the program source code, a script to compile it, a script to run the executable, and an English description of the functionality of the program.
– *Specification package* containing the associated property, the instrumentation setup, and some explanations. The property description had to contain a formal description of it in the team's specification language, informal explanations, 6 short traces demonstrating valid and invalid behaviors (3 of each), and the expected verdict (the evaluation of the property on the program).

Each specification consisted of a list of properties, with instrumentation information, and explanations. The instrumentation information mapped the events referred to in the properties to concrete program events. A property consisted of a formalization (automata, formula, etc.), an informal description, and the expected verdict (indicating whether the program satisfies the property or not). Instrumentation was a mapping from concrete events (in the program) to abstract events (in the specification). For instance, considering the classical HasNext property on iterators, the mapping should have indicated that the has-Next() event in the property refers to a call to the hasNext() method on an Iterator object. Several concrete events could be associated to one abstract event.

Remark 1. The following additional guidelines were conveyed to participants:

– Too comprehensive properties should have been avoided, in order not to refrain other participants from competing on such properties.
– Programs exhibiting non-deterministic behaviors were prohibited in order to avoid interference with verdict detection.
– Benchmarks were requested to be standalone, not depending on any third-party program.

Offline Monitoring Track. In the case of offline track, each benchmark contribution was required to be structured as follows:

– a *trace* in either XML, CSV, or JSON format, with, for each event appearing in the trace, its number of occurrences;
– a *specification package* containing the formal representation of the property, informal explanation and the expected verdict (the evaluation of the property on the program), and informal explanations; *instrumentation information* indicating the mapping from concrete events (in the trace) to abstract events (in the specification).

At an abstract level, we defined traces as sequences of named records of the form:

```
NAME{
  field1 : value1,
  ...
  fieldn : valuen
}
```

We defined an event as an entity that has a name and arguments each of which has a name and a value.

Below, we present some example traces illustrating the three formats accepted for traces, where an_event_name ranges over the set of possible event names, a_field_name ranges over the set of possible field names, a_value ranges over the set of possible runtime values.

– In XML format:

```
<log>
  <event>
    <name>an_event_name</name>
    <field>
      <name>a_field_name</name>
      <value>a_value</value>
    </field>
    <field>
      <name>a_field_name</name>
      <value>a_value</value>
    </field>
  </event>
</log>
```

– In CSV format (following the standard http://www.ietf.org/rfc/rfc4180.txt), where the spaces are intended and required. Note the required header:

```
event, a_field_name, a_field_name, a_field_name
an_event_name, a_field_value, a_field_value, a_field_value
```

– In JSON format (following the standard https://tools.ietf.org/html/rfc7159):

```
an_event_name: {
a_field_name: a_value,
a_field_name: a_value
}
```

A tool was also provided to translate traces between the different formats.

3.3   Sanity-Check Phase

After the benchmark and specification phase ended on March 15, 2015, the organizers performed a sanity check over the submitted benchmarks and specifications. The purposes of the sanity check were to ensure that (i) the benchmarks and specifications were complete and followed the required formats, (ii) sufficient and unambiguous explanations of the specifications were provided. The sanity check resulted in clarification requests made to participants using the Wiki. Clarification requests were made on the benchmark page of the participants and were publicly available, for communication and transparency purposes. The sanity check phase ended on March 30, 2015.

3.4   Training Phase and Monitor Collection Phase

The training phase started on March 30, 2015. During this phase, all participants were supposed to train their tools with all the available benchmarks in the repository. This phase was scheduled to be completed by June 10, 2015, when the participants would submit the monitored versions of benchmarks.

In this phase, competitors provided monitors for benchmarks. Participants decide to compete on a benchmark described by a pair (team_id, benchmark_number) where the team_id is the id of the team who has provided the benchmark and benchmark_number is the number of the benchmark provided by the team. That is, a contribution is related to a benchmark and contains monitors for the properties of this benchmark. Each monitor is related to one property.

More precisely, a contribution takes one of the two forms below depending on whether a program or a trace is monitored.

Java and C Tracks. In the Java and C tracks, each contribution should contain the following elements:

1. The monitor given by two scripts to build and run the monitored program.
2. The property from which the monitor has been synthesized, where the property is described by:
   (a) a formal definition of the property in a well-defined specification language;
   (b) a reference to the specification language;
   (c) an informal explanation of the property.
3. The source code for instrumentation (e.g., AspectJ file for the Java track).
4. The source code of the monitoring code.

A monitor consists of two scripts, one for building the monitored version of the program, one for running it. The actions performed by the script should be documented. The description of the property should contain a formal definition of the property in the specification language chosen by the participants. References to the specification language should be given. An informal description of the property should be provided to help understanding the formalization. If the property that was used to synthesize the monitor has been expressed in a different specification language than the one used to define the benchmark, explanations should be given as of why the submitted specification indeed corresponds to the one in the benchmark. A contribution also contains the source of the code for monitoring.

Offline Track. Similarly, for the offline track, each contribution should take the following form:

1. The monitor given by two scripts to build and run the monitor over the trace.
2. The property from which the monitor has been synthesized, where the property is described by:
    (a) a formal definition of the property in a well-defined specification language;
    (b) a reference to the specification language;
    (c) an informal explanation of the property.
3. The code that is used to build concrete events out of the log entries.

The above elements are supposed to follow the same constraints as in the Java and C tracks.

3.5   Benchmark-Evaluation Phase

The competition experiments for evaluation are performed on DataMill (http:// datamill.uwaterloo.ca), a distributed infrastructure for computer performance experimentation targeted at scientists that are interested in performance evaluation. DataMill aims to allow the user to easily produce robust and reproducible results at low cost. DataMill executes experiments on real hardware and incorporates results from existing research on how to setup experiments and hidden factors.

Each participant had the possibility to setup and try directly their tool using DataMill or by using the virtual machine provided by DataMill. The final evaluation will be performed by the competition organizers.

Computing Scores. For CSRV 2014, the organizers designed an algorithm to calculate the final score for each tool. We do not want to reiterate the description of the algorithm but give an overview of the algorithm below and refer to [2] for more details.

Essentially, the final score of each team is obtained by summing the score obtained by this team on each available pair of benchmark and property on which the team has competed. The score of a team on a benchmark consists of three subscores: the first one for correctness, the second one for time overhead, and the third one for memory overhead. The correctness score assesses whether the tool produces the expected verdict for the property on the benchmark. A penalty is applied in case of an incorrect verdict reported or in case if the tool crashes. The scores for time and memory overheads assess how better is the overhead obtained by the tool compared to the other tools. The score of each team is influenced not only by the overhead of the team but also by the factor by which it is better or worse than the average overhead obtained by the teams competing on this benchmark.

4   Illustrative Example

We use a concrete benchmark submitted to the Java track to illustrate how a benchmark is submitted by a team and how a specification and monitor are submitted for that benchmark by a different team.

4.1   Benchmark Submission

As an example benchmark we consider the first benchmark submitted by team 3 in the Java track i.e. MUFIN (see Sect. 5). The following description of the specification to be monitored was uploaded to the Wiki.

It should be verified that no iterator object is used (by invoking the method `Iterator.next()`) after the corresponding collection has changed (by an invocation of `Collection.add()`). The property could be stated, for example, in Linear Temporal Logic enriched with predicates and quantification over object identities (cf. [4]) as

$$\forall c \forall i : G(\texttt{create}(c, i) \rightarrow G(\texttt{modify}(c) \rightarrow G \neg \texttt{next}(i)))$$

where $\texttt{create}(c, i)$ holds iff the method Collection.iterator() is invoked on some collection c instantiating an iterator i. The predicate $\texttt{modify}(c)$ holds at those positions in the program execution trace where `Collection.add()` is invoked on some collection c and $\texttt{next}(i)$ is true whenever `Iterator.next()` is called on an iterator i. The resulting symbolic monitor is the following:

- State space $Q = \{1, 2, 3, 4\}$
- Quantification: $\forall c, \forall i$
- Transition function δ
  - $\delta(1, \neg\texttt{create}(c, i)) = 1, \delta(1, \texttt{create}(c, i)) = 2$
  - $\delta(2, \neg\texttt{modify}(c)) = 2, \delta(2, \texttt{modify}(c)) = 3$
  - $\delta(3, \neg\texttt{next}(i)) = 3, \delta(3, \texttt{next}(i)) = 4$
  - $\delta(4, true) = 4$
- Accepting states (with output) $F = \{1, 2, 3\}$

Importantly, this description contained an informal description of the property being monitored and a formal specification in a well-defined specification language [4]. The program to be monitored in this benchmark was uploaded to the repository and described on the Wiki, including metadata such as the number of each kind of event. In this case there are 2,000,001 `create` events, 10 `modify` events and 1 `next` event. It is indicated that the program is expected to violate the property. Additionally, team 3 provided AspectJ pointcuts to connect the specification and monitored program. For example, the `create` event is associated with the following pointcut and advice:

```
public pointcut iteratorCreate(List l) :
    call(Iterator List.iterator(..)) && target(l);
after(List l) returning(Iterator i): iteratorCreate(l) { ... }
```

Finally, a number of short traces are given to illustrate valid and invalid behaviour. For example the trace

$$\texttt{create}(1,2).\texttt{create}(3,4).\texttt{next}(2).\texttt{modify}(1).\texttt{next}(4)$$

is given as a valid behaviour and the trace

$$\texttt{create}(1,2).\texttt{next}(2).\texttt{modify}(1)\texttt{next}(2)$$

is given as invalid behaviour.

4.2   Clarifications

After the benchmark has been submitted there is a time for sanity checking where clarification requests can be made. In the case of this benchmark only a few requests were made with respect to presentation.

4.3   Specification/Monitor Submission

We now consider how team 1 in the Java track (i.e. MARQ, see Sect. 5) submitted a specification and monitor for this benchmark. The first step involved placing a specification of the property on the Wiki as follows.

> The property can be captured in the QEA language of MARQ as follows:
> ```
> qea(unsafeIter){
>   Forall(c,i)
>   accept skip(start){  create(c,i) -> created }
>   accept skip(created){  modify(m) -> modified }
>   accept skip(modified){ next(i) -> failure }
> }
> ```
> This QEA quantifies universally over c and i. Note that the domain of quantification for QEA is defined by matching symbolic events in the specification against concrete events from the trace. The event automaton uses four states and three transitions to capture the path to a failure. The skip annotation on states indicates that events that do not match a transition are implicitly skipped.

The next step involved uploading the two relevant scripts to the FTP. The first script must compile the monitored program. For this team 1 submitted an AspectJ file and a script to weave this into the provided source code. The AspectJ code uses an API to construct the QEA given above and a monitor from that specification.

```
public void init(){
    QEABuilder b = new QEABuilder(''unsafeIter'');
    //Quantified Variables
    int c = -1; int i = -2;
    b.addQuantification(FORALL,c,i);
    //Transitions
```

```
b.addTransition(1,CREATE,c,i,2);
b.addTransition(2,MODIFY,c,3);
b.addTransition(3,NEXT,i,4);
//Sate modifiers
b.setAllSkipStates();
b.addFinalStates(1,2,3);
//Create monitor
monitor = MonitorFactory.create(b.make(),GarbageMode.LAZY);
}
```

The pointcuts provided by team 3 are then used to submit events to the monitor and check that the verdict is safe - reporting an error if not. An example of advice submitting an event to the monitor is given below.

```
after(List l) returning(Iterator i): iteratorCreate(l) {
  synchronized(LOCK){
    check(monitor.step(CREATE,l,i));
  }
}
```

As the MARQ tool relies on a number of libraries (such as `aspectjrt.jar`) the installation script also downloads these before weaving the source code using the command:

```
java -cp "lib/*" org.aspectj.tools.ajc.Main -source 1.7 -d bin -sourceroots src
```

The running script then runs the instrumented program using the command:

```
java -cp "lib/*:bin"
de.uni_luebeck.isp.rvwithunionfind.benchmarks.benchmark1.MainBad
```

5   Participating Teams

In this section, for each track, we report on the teams and tools that participated in CRV'15. Table 3 (resp. 2, 1) gives a summary of the teams participating in the Offline (resp. Java, C) track. In the following of this section, we provide a short overview of the tools involved in the competition.

MARQ. MARQ [18] (Monitoring at runtime with QEA) monitors specifications written as Quantified Event Automata [1] (QEA). QEA is based on the notion of trace-slicing, extended the existential quantification and free variables. The MARQ tool is written in Java.

OCLR-CHECK. OCLR-Check [7] is a toolset to perform offline checking of OCLR properties on system execution traces. OCLR is a temporal extension of OCL (Object Constraint Language) which allows users to express temporal properties using property specification patterns.

RV-MONITOR. RV-Monitor [15] is a runtime verification tool developed by Runtime Verification Inc. (http://runtimeverification.com), capable of online and

Table 1. Tools participating in online monitoring of C programs track.

Tool	Ref.	Contact person	Affiliation
E-ACSL	[5]	J. Signoles	CEA LIST, France
MARQ	[18]	G. Reger	University of Manchester, UK
RITHM-v2.0	[16]	Y. Joshi	McMaster Univ. and U. Waterloo, Canada
RV-MONITOR	[15]	P. Daian	Runtime Verification Inc., Urbana, IL
RTC		R. Milewicz	University of Alabama at Birmingham, USA
TIMESQUARE	[3]	F. Mallet	Univ. Nice Sophia Antipolis

Table 2. Tools participating in online monitoring of Java programs track.

Tool	Ref.	Contact person	Affiliation
JAVAMOP	[11]	Y. Zhang	U. of Illinois at Urbana Champaign, USA
MARQ	[18]	G. Reger	University of Manchester, UK
MUFIN		D. Thoma	University of Lübeck, Germany

Table 3. Tools participating in the offline monitoring track.

Tool	Ref.	Contact person	Affiliation
AGMON	[13]	A. Kane	Carnegie Mellon University, USA
BREACH	[12]	A. Donzé	University of California, Berkeley, USA
LOGFIRE	[10]	K. Havelund	NASA JPL, USA
MARQ	[18]	G. Reger	University of Manchester, UK
OCLR-CHECK	[7]	W. Dou	University of Luxembourg, Luxembourg
OPTYSIM	[6]	A. Salmerón	University of Mlaga, Spain
RITHM-v2.0	[16]	Y. Joshi	University of Waterloo, Canada
RV-MONITOR	[15]	H. Xiao	University of Illinois at Urbana Champaign, USA

offline monitoring of properties written in a variety of formalisms ("logic plug-ins"). RV-Monitor separates instrumentation and library generation.

RITHM-v2.0. RITHM-v2.0 [16] takes a C program under inspection and a set of First Order Linear Temporal Logic properties as input and generates an instrumented C program that is verified at run time by a time-triggered monitor. RITHM-v2.0 provides two techniques based on static analysis and control theory to minimize instrumentation of the input C program and monitoring intervention.

OPTYSIM. OPTYSIM [6] is a tool for the analysis and optimization of heterogeneous systems whose behaviour can be observed as execution traces. OPTYSIM is based on the Spin model checker and analyzes systems observed as execution traces. OPTYSIM supports Linear Temporal Logic specifications.

AGMON. AGMON is a monitoring framework and tool for the offline monitoring of temporal formulae expressed in a bounded variant of MTL. The monitoring strategy is based on sampling, i.e. the events in the trace are time-triggered. AGMON takes traces expressed in the CSV format as input.

BREACH. BREACH [12] is a Matlab toolbox supporting quantitative monitoring of Signal Temporal Logic (STL) properties. BREACH provides a set of simulation-based techniques aimed at the analysis of deterministic models of hybrid dynamical systems.

LOGFIRE. LOGFIRE is a rule-based runtime verification tool. It is based on the RETE [9] algorithm, and is built as an API in the Scala programming language. A monitor is an instance of a monitor class. Specifically a monitor is a user-defined Scala class that extends a pre-defined Monitor class defined in the LOGFIRE API.

JAVAMOP. Monitoring-Oriented Programming (MOP), is a software development and analysis framework which aims to reduce the gap between formal specification and implementation by allowing them together to form a system. In MOP, monitors are automatically synthesized from specified properties and integrated with the original system to check its dynamic behaviors during execution. JavaMOP [11] is an instance of MOP for Java.

MUFIN. MUFIN (Monitoring with Union-Find) is a framework for monitoring Java programs. (Finite or infinite) monitors are defined using a simple API that allows to manage multiple instances of monitors. Internally MUFIN uses hash-tables and union-find-structures as well as additional fields injected into application classes to lookup these monitor instances efficiently. The main aim of MUFIN is to monitor properties involving large numbers of objects efficiently.

E-ACSL. E-ACSL [5] is both a formal specification language and a Frama-C plug-in. The formal specification language is a behavioral first-order typed specification language which supports in particular function contracts, assertions and built-in predicates (like \valid(p) which indicates that the pointer p points to a memory location that the program can write and read).

TIMESQUARE. TimeSquare [3] is an MDK (Model Development Kit) provided as a set of Eclipse plugins that can be downloaded or installed over an existing Eclipse. TimeSquare is based on the formal Clock Constraint Specification Language (CCSL), which allows the manipulation of logical time. Logical time is a relaxed form of time where any events can be taken as a reference for counting (e.g. do something every 30 openings of the door). It can be used for specifying classical and multiform real-time requirements as well as formally specifying constraints on the behavior of a model (either a UML-based or a DSL model).

RTC. RTC (Run-Time error check for C programs) is a runtime monitoring tool that instruments unsafe code and monitors the program execution. RTC is built on top of the ROSE compiler infrastructure [17]. The tool finds memory bugs and arithmetic overflows and underflows, and run-time type violations. Most of the instrumentation code is directly added to the source code and only requires a minimal runtime system.

6   Benchmarks

We give a brief overview of the benchmarks submitted to each track.

6.1   Offline Track

There were 30 benchmarks submitted to the offline track by 6 teams - MARQ, RITHM-v2.0, OCLR-CHECK, RV-MONITOR, BREACH and LOGFIRE. Generally each team submitted benchmarks from a particular domain:

- 4 benchmarks on Java API properties from RV-MONITOR
- 5 benchmarks on resource management from LOGFIRE
- 5 abstract benchmarks using letters from OCLR-CHECK and 1 from RV-MONITOR
- 5 concurrency benchmarks from RITHM-v2.0
- From MARQ 1 benchmark on security, 1 on programming and 3 on abstractions of online systems

The benchmarks varied in complexity of specification and length of log file. Some log files consisted of a few hundred events whilst others contained tens of millions of events. Most events were relatively simple, consisting of a small number (one or two) of parameters and a small number (two to four) of different event names. The specification languages had a wide range of features leading to a distinctive collection of specifications. Some of these features (e.g. the second-order numeric constraints on quantifiers used by RITHM-v2.0 and scoping modifiers used by OCLR-CHECK) led to the modification of specification languages used by other tools.

6.2   Java Track

There were 13 benchmarks submitted to the Java track by 3 teams - MARQ, JAVA-MOP and MUFIN. All three teams used ASPECTJ as an instrumentation tool, allowing for easy reuse of instrumentation code.

Specifications in this domain from the literature have tended to focus on properties of Java API. However, this year saw a wide range of domains covered by submitted benchmarks. Five benchmarks are concerned with properties of data structures. The rest were from the following varied domains:

- A protocol property about communicating nodes
- A property about the lifetime of channels in multiplexer usage
- A property about a modal device and the correct usage of actions in modes
- A property about resource usage
- A property capturing an abstract notion of SQL injection

– A marking policy property for an abstract exam system

Whilst there were a variety of domains represented in the properties being monitored, most programs had been written for the competition as short programs that captured the desired behaviour (or not). This raises the question as to whether the results are reflective of monitor usage in the real world.

Finally, one submitted property aimed at exposing the different ways monitors for Java programs treated equality i.e. either semantically via `equals` or referentially by `==`. Benchmarks that test the expressiveness and usability of tools in this way are helpful in a competition and should be encouraged.

6.3 C Track

There were 18 benchmarks submitted to the C track by 4 teams - E-ACSL, RiTHM-v2.0, RV-Monitor and RTC. Thirteen of the benchmarks are concerned with C-specific properties such as:

– Out of bounds array access
– Signed overflow
– Memory safety i.e. invalid memory deallocation or reallocation
– Heap-based buffer overflow
– Correct calling of functions such as `strcat`, `strcopy`, `memcpy`

Some of these also incorporate semantic properties such as sortedness of arrays. Many of the benchmarks were modified versions of those used in static analysis and two of the tools have this background (E-ACSL and RTC).

The five benchmarks from RiTHMv-2.0 are semantic properties related to the usage of sockets and threads (and are the online version of the offline concurrency benchmarks).

7   Reflection

As would be expected in an endeavour of this kind, we have encountered considerable challenges. Here we reflect on these challenges and suggest how they could be tackled in future iterations of the competition.

7.1   Participant Engagement

The benefit of the competition relies on engagement from participants so that it can be presented as a reflection of the current status in the field. Therefore it is necessary to consider how best to encourage participant engagement.

There are two factors that influence a participant's likeliness to engage with the competition: a *low cost* to entry and a *benefit* to entry.

Low Cost of Entry. This has been a considerable challenge in both years the competition has run. The burden on participants is relatively high, especially when compared to competitions such as SAT, SMT and CASC. The effort required is more similar to that required in SV-COMP. Below we discuss why this level of effort is required in a competition of this maturity i.e. lack of standardisation.

One key issue is that entering the competition requires the participant to carry out more tasks than just submitting a monitoring tool. Due to a lack of standard specification languages, it also involves understanding and translating specifications written in another language to the participant's own specification language. Additionally, due to a lack of standard notions of how monitoring tools should be executed, it is necessary for participants to write and submit scripts allowing their tools to be run. In the case of online monitoring requiring instrumentation, it may be necessary to write such a script for each benchmark. Addressing these issues of standardisation is key to the future of the competition.

Finally, the organizers of the competition have been attempting to move towards more automated methods of evaluation. Continuing this automation is necessary to lift the burden on both the participants and organizers.

Benefit of Entry. Whilst it may be obvious that this competition is important for the runtime verification community in general, it is also important to ensure that participants receive some benefit from entering. Only one tool can claim to be a winner in each track, and in some cases tools may be confident that they will not win before entry. Therefore, a benefit beyond the chance of winning is required.

One suggestion is that the future editions of the competition invite participants to submit 2-page *system description* papers that are included in the proceedings of the conference. This is a practice taken by some other competitions and acts as an obvious benefit to entry.

7.2 Engaging with Static Analysis Based Tools

In recent years, the runtime verification community has made a special effort to engage with the static analysis community and this effort has been successful. It is an exciting result that we are seeing tools with roots in static analysis adopting runtime verification techniques and participating in the competition. However, it is therefore necessary to consider how this difference in viewpoint effects the design of the competition.

One point that was raised during the competition was that tools that perform static analysis do not typically deal with a concepts of *events* and *traces* and extensions to dynamic analysis typically involve introducing runtime assertions and additional code to track data values, rather than extracting events.

7.3 The C Track

Whilst the areas of runtime verification for log file analysis and monitoring Java programs have received a reasonable amount of attention in the literature, there has not been as much focus on monitoring C programs. Additionally, C programs are more likely to be targeted by tools coming from the domain of static analysis, as mentioned above. Consequently, there continues to be issues surrounding the definition of benchmarks and monitors in the C track.

8   Concluding Remarks

This report was written during the training phase. Once this phase is complete, the organizers will evaluate all the submitted monitors using the scoring mechanism introduced in [2] and outlined in Sect. 3.5. The results of the competition are expected to be announced during the RV 2015 conference in Vienna, Austria. This report is published to assist future organizers of CRV to build on the efforts made to organize CSRV 2014 and CRV 2015.

Acknowledgment. The organizers would like to thank Christian Seguy from the IT team of Laboratoire d'Informatique de Grenoble for his help on setting up the the the repository hosting the benchmarks. The organizers are also grateful to Yuguang Zhang from the DataMill team for setting up a convenient and powerful evaluation infrastructure on DataMill. This work has been partly done in the context of the ICT COST Action IC1402 Runtime Verification beyond Monitoring (ARVI).

References

1. Barringer, H., Falcone, Y., Havelund, K., Reger, G., Rydeheard, D.: Quantified event automata: towards expressive and efficient runtime monitors. In: Giannakopoulou, D., Méry, D. (eds.) FM 2012. LNCS, vol. 7436, pp. 68–84. Springer, Heidelberg (2012)
2. Bartocci, E., Bonakdarpour, B., Falcone, Y.: First international competition on software for runtime verification. In: Bonakdarpour, B., Smolka, S.A. (eds.) RV 2014. LNCS, vol. 8734, pp. 1–9. Springer, Heidelberg (2014)
3. DeAntoni, J., Mallet, F.: Timesquare: treat your models with logical time. In: Furia, C.A., Nanz, S. (eds.) TOOLS 2012. LNCS, vol. 7304, pp. 34–41. Springer, Heidelberg (2012). https://hal.inria.fr/hal-00688590
4. Decker, N., Leucker, M., Thoma, D.: Monitoring modulo theories. In: Ábrahám, E., Havelund, K. (eds.) TACAS 2014 (ETAPS). LNCS, vol. 8413, pp. 341–356. Springer, Heidelberg (2014)
5. Delahaye, M., Kosmatov, N., Signoles, J.: Common specification language for static and dynamic analysis of c programs. In: Proceedings of SAC 2013: the 28th Annual ACM Symposium on Applied Computing, pp. 1230–1235. ACM (2013)
6. Díaz, A., Merino, P., Salmeron, A.: Obtaining models for realistic mobile network simulations using real traces. IEEE Commun. Lett. **15**(7), 782–784 (2011)
7. Dou, W., Bianculli, D., Briand, L.: A model-driven approach to offline trace checking of temporal properties with ocl. Technical report. SnT-TR-2014-5, Interdisciplinary Centre for Security, Reliability and Trust (2014). http://hdl.handle.net/10993/16112
8. Falcone, Y., Havelund, K., Reger, G.: A tutorial on runtime verification. In: Broy, M., Peled, D., Kalus, G., (eds.) Summer School Marktoberdorf 2012 - Engineering Dependable Software Systems, vol. 34, pp. 141–175. IOS Press (2013)

9. Forgy, C.: Rete: a fast algorithm for the many patterns/many objects match problem. Artif. Intell. **19**(1), 17–37 (1982)
10. Havelund, K.: Rule-based runtime verification revisited. Int. J. Softw. Tools Technol Transfer (STTT) **17**, 143–170 (2014)
11. Jin, D., Meredith, P.O., Lee, C., Roşu, G.: JavaMOP: efficient parametric runtime monitoring framework. In: Proceedings of ICSE 2012: The 34th International Conference on Software Engineering, Zurich, Switzerland, June 2–9, pp. 1427–1430. IEEE Press (2012)
12. Juniwal, G., Donzé, A., Jensen, J.C., Seshia, S.A.: Cpsgrader: synthesizing temporal logic testers for auto-grading an embedded systems laboratory. In: Mitra, T., Reineke, J. (eds.) 2014 International Conference on Embedded Software, EMSOFT 2014, New Delhi, India, October 12–17, 2014, pp. 24:1–24:10. ACM (2014)
13. Kane, A., Fuhrman, T.E., Koopman, P.: Monitor based oracles for cyber-physical system testing: practical experience report. In: 44th Annual IEEE/IFIP International Conference on Dependable Systems and Networks, DSN 2014, Atlanta, GA, USA, June 23–26, 2014, pp. 148–155. IEEE (2014)
14. Leucker, M., Schallhart, C.: A brief account of runtime verification. J. Logic Algebraic Program. **78**(5), 293–303 (2008). http://dx.doi.org/10.1016/j.jlap.2008.08.004
15. Luo, Q., Zhang, Y., Lee, C., Jin, D., Meredith, P.O., Serbanuta, T., Rosu, G.: Rvmonitor: efficient parametric runtime verification with simultaneous properties. In: Proceedings of Runtime Verification - 5th International Conference, RV 2014, Toronto, ON, Canada, September 22–25, 2014, pp. 285–300 (2014)
16. Navabpour, S., Joshi, Y., Wu, C.W.W., Berkovich, S., Medhat, R., Bonakdarpour, B., Fischmeister, S.: RiTHM: a tool for enabling time-triggered runtime verification for c programs. In: ACM Symposium on the Foundations of Software Engineering (FSE), pp. 603–606 (2013)
17. Quinlan, D.J., Schordan, M., Miller, B., Kowarschik, M.: Parallel object-oriented framework optimization. Concurr. Comput.: Pract. Exp. **16**(2–3), 293–302 (2004)
18. Reger, G., Cruz, H.C., Rydeheard, D.: MarQ: monitoring at runtime with QEA. In: Baier, C., Tinelli, C. (eds.) TACAS 2015. LNCS, vol. 9035, pp. 596–610. Springer, Heidelberg (2015). http://dx.doi.org/10.1007/978-3-662-46681-0

Rigorous Examination of Reactive Systems:
The RERS Challenge 2015

Maren Geske[✉], Malte Isberner, and Bernhard Steffen

Chair for Programming Systems, TU Dortmund University,
44227 Dortmund, Germany
{maren.geske,malte.isberner,steffen}@cs.tu-dortmund.de

Abstract. In this paper we present the RERS challenge 2015, a free-style program analysis challenge on reactive systems to evaluate the effectiveness of different validation and verification techniques. It brings together researchers from different areas including static analysis, model checking, theorem proving, symbolic execution, and testing. The challenge characteristics and set-up are discussed, while special attention is given to the Runtime Verification track that was newly introduced.

1 Introduction

As the name RERS[1] – being an acronym for *Rigorous Examination of Reactive Systems* – suggests, the focus of this challenge lies on reactive systems. These were chosen due to their being omnipresent in industry and research, manifesting themselves as, e.g., web services, decision-support systems, or logical controllers. Validation techniques for reactive systems are as diverse as their appearance and structure. The used techniques comprise various forms of program analysis [16], symbolic execution [13], software model checking [3,6,10], statistical model checking [14], model-based testing [5], inference of invariants [4,8], automata learning [18], run-time verification [15], and monitoring [9], often tailored to rather special assumptions about the respective environments. Thus, it is almost impossible to compare these techniques in a common setting, let alone to establish clear application profiles as a means for recommendation. The RERS challenge aims at overcoming this situation by providing a forum for experimental profile evaluation based on specifically designed verification tasks. The benchmarks are automatically synthesized from chosen properties and tailored to exhibit selected language features which allows us to generate various grades of difficulty. A characteristic of the RERS challenge is that no restrictions are placed with respect to computational means, in terms of both hardware and software, and that the tools are not required to be fully automated, allowing participants to interact with them during the challenge phase. This creates a set-up that makes it difficult to define a global ranking. For this reason, we have

---

[1] RERS originally was an acronym for *Regular Extrapolation of Reactive Systems*. Although the acronym remained, the challenge itself has evolved towards a broader focus, which lead to a change of the name and scope.

© Springer International Publishing Switzerland 2015
E. Bartocci and R. Majumdar (Eds.): RV 2015, LNCS 9333, pp. 423–429, 2015.
DOI: 10.1007/978-3-319-23820-3_28

several rankings for different purposes: for example, some are purely numerical, simply based on a "multiple choice" test which may be solved in a "free-style" fashion, whereas others consider the approach taken, the underlying ideas, and the concrete realization. In the remainder of this paper we will describe the challenge's characteristics (Sect. 2) and the benchmarks generated (Sect. 3). In Sect. 4, we will take a closer look at the Runtime Verification-style challenge, and describe what had to be adapted to meet the communities needs.

2   Challenge Set-Up

At first sight, real world applications would be the most attractive challenge problems. However, they pose two intrinsic problems: it is hardly possible to have a guaranteed property profile, and it is very difficult to tailor the degree of difficulty. Moreover, we experienced that companies are very hesitant to provide their code.

In order to avoid these drawbacks, RERS challenge problems are artificially constructed to satisfy a pre-selected set of properties: our corresponding benchmark generator automatically synthesizes challenge problems directly from the considered set of properties, while it at the same time obeys structural restrictions for tailoring the degree of difficulty [19].

In the following, we sketch the programs and the properties we use in the verification tasks. Further details and the actual challenge problems can be found on the RERS website [1].

2.1   Properties

For each challenge problem, there exists a set of 200 properties that need to be analyzed. Points are awarded for correctly analyzed properties, with mistakes resulting in negative points. No answer given for a certain property leaves the score unchanged. The overall set of properties is divided into two categories, each of which containing 100 properties.

Reachability Properties. The properties are implicitly defined by 100 error codes (exceptions or failed assertions, with identifying messages or labels) distributed across the source code. Some value assignments to internal state variables correspond to error states, which cause the system to trigger the respective error condition. Not all of those error states are reachable, and the goal is to check which of these error states can in fact be reached (it is not expected to provide an access sequence). Those errors come in the form of either an IllegalStateException (Java) or a specific error label with a failed assertion (C). The label error23 in Fig. 1a is an example for this class of properties.

LTL Properties. An execution trace of a reactive system consists of a sequence of inputs and outputs, each from a finite alphabet. For each of the systems, a file is provided, containing a set of 100 LTL properties for which the contestants have to check whether they are satisfied by all traces, or if there are traces that violate them (it is not expected to also provide these traces as witness). The properties are given both as an LTL formula and as a textual description. To allow an intuitive mapping from LTL expressions to textual descriptions, the properties to be checked are closely adhering to the patterns in property specifications from the literature [7].

The LTL formulae are given in a standard syntax, and make use of the following temporal operators:

- $\mathbf{X}\,\phi$ (next): ϕ has to hold after the next step,
- $\mathbf{F}\,\phi$ (eventually): ϕ has to hold at some point in the future (or now),
- $\mathbf{G}\,\phi$ (globally): ϕ has to hold always (including now),
- $\phi\,\mathbf{U}\,\psi$ (until): ϕ has to hold until ψ holds (which eventually occurs),
- $\phi\,\mathbf{WU}\,\psi$ (weak until): ϕ has to hold until ψ holds (which does not necessarily occur), and
- $\phi\,\mathbf{R}\,\psi$ (release): ϕ has to hold until ψ held in the previous step.

The atomic propositions correspond to input and output symbols, where the prefix i is used for input and o is used for output symbols, to allow a clear distinction. For example, G (! oU) means that output U never occurs. In other words, the expression states that it is not possible – by any sequence of input events – to make the system produce the output action U.

3   White-Box Problems

White-box problems have a long tradition in the RERS challenge. The problem instances are scaled in several dimensions: size of the internal state space, number of inputs, number of abstract program states, used data types and language constructs (from mere assignments to pointer arithmetics). All problems are generated in C and Java. Labels in the code are used to encode reachability properties, more complex properties are written as LTL formulae over inputs and outputs (cf. Sect. 2.1). The challenge task is to answers properties according to best knowledge, without restriction to a specific tool or technique.

The problems are programs consisting of a main method with a while(true) loop (cf. Fig. 1b), in which an input is read and passed to a method that calculates the updates on internal states and generates an output. In the most basic form, the data types occurring in the programs are restricted to integers. The problems are designed in reminiscence of controller software (e.g., for PLCs [2]), which also typically consists of a loop that is executed in each cycle, and in which the internal state is modified and outputs are produced according to inputs such as sensor readings.

Figure 1a shows a source code snipped of the C version of a white-box problem. The program logic is contained in a method called calculate_output, which is a sequence of (nested) if-else blocks. The state of the system is represented by a set of variables. At the bottom of this function, a sequence of if statements checks whether the system is in an invalid state. If this is the case, an error is raised through a failed assertion. To identify the specific error in the source code, the assertion is labeled with the error ID.

```
int x1 = 1;                          int main() {
int x2 = 2;                            while (1) { // main i/o-loop
  ...                                    int input, output;
                                         scanf("%d", &input);
int calc_output(int input) {             output = calculate_output(input);
  if(input == 3 &&                       if (output == -2) {
    (x7 != 0 && x0 == 9)) {               fprintf(stderr, "Invalid: %d\n");
    x9 = 4;                             } else if (output != -1) {
    return 24;                           printf("%d\n", output);
  }                                      }
  if((x23 == 0 && x3 != 0)) {         }
    error23: assert(0);             }
  }
  ...
}
```

(a) Variables and logic in C   (b) Main method with infinite loop

Fig. 1. White-box problem example in C

From 2014 to 2015. In the 2014 version of the RERS challenge, we observed that a large number of inserted errors were found at the same level and in close proximity of only a few system states. The problems were also considered as being too large, forcing the participants to guess a large share of the properties, as they could not be properly computed in full. Therefore, in 2015, the code size was drastically reduced by decreasing the number of state variables. The problem of unevenly distributed errors was solved by inserting some of them with the help of counter variables instead of explicitly coded transitions. This measure increases the effective state space, without increasing the size of the source code itself.

4   Runtime Verification-Style Track

Generally speaking, the RERS white-box problems could be used to conduct runtime verification without further changes. The problem with this is that monitoring the execution of a problem can only detect property violations in the exhibited behavior, but cannot prove the absence of such violations in all possible executions. Instead, a test suite that steers the program execution in such a fashion that the behavior it exhibits is sufficient to decide whether properties are validated is required. This test suite can only be provided by the challenge organizers, and will be made available only 2 days before the challenge deadline. To complicate this track for white-box analyzers and testers, who benefit extremely from an analysis time of 2 months, the problems had to be adapted.

To ensure that the effective analysis time for those participants is reduced, while at the same time allowing RV-style participants sufficient time to instrument the code for monitoring, we decided to withhold a part of the program's logic to be released only 2 days before the challenge deadline. The idea behind

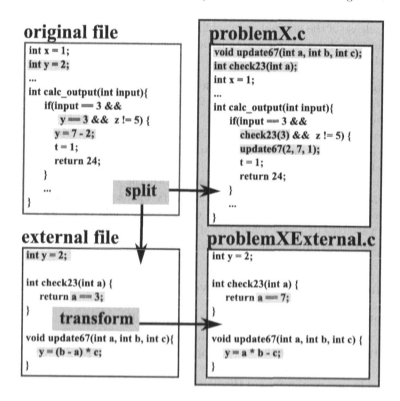

Fig. 2. Monitoring program example in C

this is that the monitoring code can be inserted into the main body of the problem and only the internal logic of some external methods is going to be replaced. To explain this idea in detail, let us take a look at the code extraction from the challenge problems in Fig. 2. The original problem, which is basically a white-box problem as described in Sect. 3, is split into two files (`problemX` and `problemXExternal`) by moving some of the internal logic in form of state variables to another file and replacing variable accesses and assertions with external method calls. All changed code parts are marked in grey. After the external file is created, the internal logic is altered, so that the program is still executable but exhibits different behavior, thus no longer adhering to the specification. This can be seen in the lower part of Fig. 2.

The challenge task for monitoring track can be summarized as follows:

1. Instrument the `problemX` file of the problem with monitors for all LTL properties in the corresponding property file.
2. Build a runtime environment suitable for their monitoring needs, that allows to feed input sequences in form of strings to the program. To test the construction, it is suggested to feed random input sequences generated from the input alphabet.

3. Upon release of the original external file: run your monitors with the provided set of input sequences and generate the solutions according to the instructions from the RERS website [1].

At this point, it is important to acknowledge that the reachability properties are not part of the Runtime Verification challenge part, as these can be decided by merely executing the sequences. Another important fact is that the provided set of input sequences is guaranteed to exhibit all finitely provable violations of the provided LTL properties. Violations that require witnesses of infinite length are not considered for the score.

We are looking forward to a discussion with the community to make the RERS challenge more attractive for participants with a background in Runtime Verification. A perspective for this kind of challenge would be to ask for certain values of variables or the reachability of arbitrary labels, which ranges beyond the analysis of the input/output behavior alone.

5   Conclusion and Perspectives

The RERS challenge 2015 was the fourth successfully conducted iteration in a series of challenges. Each time, the challenge scenario was adapted and refined after fruitful discussions with the participants. This lead to productive enhancements of the generation framework, which in turn enabled better assessment of the strengths and weaknesses of the participants' tools.

While the benchmarks of the first challenge, held in 2012 [11], contained only simple programming language features and guarded if-else statements, the 2013 challenge [12] featured more complex control structures and additional features in multiple languages. It had tracks for black-box, white-box and grey-box (a mixture of the former two, with partially unknown code passages) problems. The 2014 challenge focused mainly on small fundamental changes, like larger input alphabets and overall denser but smaller program code.

With the 2015 challenge, we attempted to attract people from the Runtime Verification community by creating problems that can be solved using monitoring. For future challenges, we hope to integrate more interesting language features and a greater variety of supported programming languages, as well as a track for concurrent benchmarks based on the generation process developed in [17].

Acknowledgment. We would like to thank Ylis Falcone, Jaco van de Pol, and Markus Schordan for their feedback regarding the challenge problems, and for serving as members of the RERS 2015 Committee.

References

1. RERS challenge website. http://www.rers-challenge.org/
2. Almeida, E.E., Luntz, J.E., Tilbury, D.M.: Event-condition-action systems for reconfigurable logic control. IEEE Trans. Autom. Sci. Eng. 4(2), 167–181 (2007)

3. Beyer, D.: Status report on software verification. In: Ábrahám, E., Havelund, K. (eds.) TACAS 2014 (ETAPS). LNCS, vol. 8413, pp. 373–388. Springer, Heidelberg (2014)

4. Beyer, D., Henzinger, T.A., Majumdar, R., Rybalchenko, A.: Path invariants. In: Proceeding PLDI, pp. 300–309. ACM (2007)

5. Broy, M., Jonsson, B., Katoen, J.-P., Leucker, M., Pretschner, A. (eds.): Model-Based Testing of Reactive Systems. LNCS, vol. 3472. Springer, Heidelberg (2005)

6. Clarke, E.M., Grumberg, O., Peled, D.: Model Checking. MIT Press (2001)

7. Dwyer, M.B., Avrunin, G.S., Corbett, J.C.: Patterns in property specifications for finite-state verification. In: Proceeding ICSE, pp. 411–420. ACM (1999)

8. Ernst, M.D., Cockrell, J., Griswold, W.G., Notkin, D.: Dynamically discovering likely program invariants to support program evolution. IEEE Trans. Softw. Eng. 27(2), 99–123 (2001)

9. Havelund, K., Roşu, G.: Monitoring Java programs with Java PathExplorer. ENTCS 55(2), 200–217 (2001)

10. Holzmann, G.J., Smith, M.H.: Software model checking: extracting verification models from source code. Softw. Test. Verification Reliab. 11(2), 65–79 (2001)

11. Howar, F., Isberner, M., Merten, M., Steffen, B., Beyer, D.: The RERS Grey-Box Challenge 2012: analysis of event-condition-action systems. In: Margaria, T., Steffen, B. (eds.) ISoLA 2012, Part I. LNCS, vol. 7609, pp. 608–614. Springer, Heidelberg (2012)

12. Howar, F., Isberner, M., Merten, M., Steffen, B., Beyer, D., Păsăreanu, C.: Rigorous Examination of Reactive Systems. The RERS Challenges 2012 and 2013. Softw. Tools Technol. Transfer 16(5), 457–464 (2014)

13. King, J.C.: Symbolic execution and program testing. Commun. ACM 19(7), 385–394 (1976)

14. Legay, A., Delahaye, B., Bensalem, S.: Statistical model checking: an overview. In: Barringer, H., Falcone, Y., Finkbeiner, B., Havelund, K., Lee, I., Pace, G., Rou, G., Sokolsky, O., Tillmann, N. (eds.) Runtime Verification. Lecture Notes in Computer Science, vol. 6418, pp. 122–135. Springer, Berlin Heidelberg (2010)

15. Leucker, M., Schallhart, C.: A brief account of runtime verification. J. Logic Algebraic Program. 78(5), 293–303 (2009)

16. Nielson, F., Nielson, H.R., Hankin, C.: Principles of Program Analysis. Springer, Heidelberg (1999)

17. Steffen, B., Howar, F., Isberner, M., Naujokat, S., Margaria, T.: Tailored generation of concurrent benchmarks. Int. J. Softw. Tools Technol. Transf. 16(5), 543–558 (2014)

18. Steffen, B., Howar, F., Merten, M.: Introduction to active automata learning from a practical perspective. In: Bernardo, M., Issarny, V. (eds.) SFM 2011. LNCS, vol. 6659, pp. 256–296. Springer, Heidelberg (2011)

19. Steffen, B., Isberner, M., Naujokat, S., Margaria, T., Geske, M.: Property-driven benchmark generation: synthesizing programs of realistic structure. Softw. Tools Technol. Transfer 16(5), 465–479 (2014)

Author Index

Printed in the United States
By Bookmasters